# Crime, Cultural Conflict, and Justice in Rural Russia, 1856-1914

# STUDIES ON THE HISTORY OF SOCIETY AND CULTURE
*Victoria E. Bonnell and Lynn Hunt, Editors*

# Crime, Cultural Conflict, and Justice in Rural Russia, 1856-1914

Stephen P. Frank

UNIVERSITY OF CALIFORNIA PRESS
Berkeley   Los Angeles   London

University of California Press
Berkeley and Los Angeles, California
University of California Press, Ltd.
London, England
© 1999 by
The Regents of the University of California

Library of Congress Cataloging-in-Publication Data
Frank, Stephen P., 1955–
    Crime, cultural conflict, and justice in rural Russia,
1856–1914 / Stephen P. Frank.
        p.   cm. — (Studies on the history of society and
culture : 31)
    Includes bibliographical references and index.
    ISBN 0-520-21341-6 (alk. paper)
        1. Criminal justice, Administration of—Russia—
History—19th century.   2. Criminal justice, Administration
of—Russia—History—20th century.   3. Rural crimes—
Russia.   4. Peasantry—Russia—History—19th century.
5. Peasantry—Russia—History—20th century.   6. Serfs—
Emancipation—Russia.   7. Russia—Rural conditions.
8. Russia—Social conditions—1801-1917.   I. Title.
II. Series.
HV9960.R9F7   1999
364.947′09034—dc21                                    98-41218
                                                              CIP
Printed in the United States of America

9  8  7  6  5  4  3  2  1

This book is dedicated
to my mother
and to the memory of
Eric Charles

# CONTENTS

# LIST OF FIGURES AND TABLES

# GLOSSARY

| | |
|---|---|
| circuit court | *okruzhnyi sud* |
| clerk (village or township) | *pisar'* |
| communal court | *mirskii sud* |
| criminal court (pre-emancipation) | *ugolovnyi sud* |
| district | *uezd* |
| district assembly | *uezdnyi s"ezd* |
| district board for peasant affairs | *uezdnoe po krest'ianskim delam prisutstvie* |
| district court (pre-emancipation) | *uezdnyi sud* |
| hamlet, village | *derevnia* |
| hundreder (village policeman) | *sotskii* |
| judicial chamber | *sudebnaia palata* |
| judicial investigator | *sudebnyi sledovatel'* |
| justice of the peace court | *mirovoi sud* |
| land captain | *zemskii nachal'nik* |
| lord | *barin* |
| municipal court | *gorodskoi sud* |
| peace mediator | *mirovoi posrednik* |
| police captain | *stanovoi pristav* |
| police commandant | *ispravnik* |
| police guard | *strazhnik* |
| precinct | *uchastok* |
| precinct constable | *uriadnik* |
| province | *guberniia* |
| provincial board for peasant affairs | *gubernskoe po krest'ianskim delam prisutstvie* |
| tenner (village policeman) | *desiatskii* |
| township | *volost'* |
| township assembly | *volostnoi skhod* |
| township court | *volostnoi sud* |
| township elder | *starshina* |

| | |
|---|---|
| village or hamlet | *derevnia* |
| village (with a church) | *selo* |
| village assembly | *sel'skii skhod* |
| village court (pre-emancipation) | *sel'skaia rasprava* |
| village elder | *starosta* |

Note: Russian provinces were subdivided into administrative units called districts (*uezdy*), which contained subdivisions known as townships (*volosti,* sometimes translated as "canton"). The latter were the lowest level of state administration in the countryside.

# ABBREVIATIONS AND FOOTNOTING

Standard abbreviations are used in footnoting archival sources: f. = *fond* [collection], st. = *stol* [desk]; ot. = *otdelenie* [section or division]; op. = *opis'* [list]; sv. = *sviazka* [bundle]; d. = *delo* [file] (plural: dd.); l. = *list* [sheet or page] (plural: ll.); ob. = *oborotnaia storona* [*verso*].

Frequently cited archives, journals, newspapers, and other works have been abbreviated as follows:

| AHR | *American Historical Review* |
| EtnogO | *Etnograficheskoe obozrenie* |
| GARF | *Gosudarstvennyi Arkhiv Rossiskoi Federatsii* |
| GARO | *Gosudarstvennyi Arkhiv Riazanskoi Oblasti* |
| IaGV | *Iaroslavskie gubernskie vedomosti* |
| IAOiRS | *Izvestiia Arkhangel'skogo Obshchestva izucheniia Russkogo Severa* |
| ISSSR | *Istoriia SSSR* |
| IuV | *Iuridicheskii vestnik* |
| IuZh | *Iuridicheskii zhurnal* |
| IV | *Istoricheskii vestnik* |
| JGO | *Jahrbücher für Geschichte Osteuropas* |
| JIH | *Journal of Interdisciplinary History* |
| JMH | *Journal of Modern History* |
| JSH | *Journal of Social History* |
| LSR | *Law and Society Review* |
| KD | *Krest'ianskoe dvizhenie* |
| MosVed | *Moskovskie vedomosti* |

| | |
|---|---|
| MVD | *Ministerstvo Vnutrennykh Del* (Ministry of Internal Affairs) |
| NizhL | *Nizhegorodskii listok* |
| Otchety | *Otchet Ministerstva Iustitsii* |
| OrlV | *Orlovskii vestnik* |
| PSZ | *Polnoe sobranie zakonov* |
| PV | *Povolzhskii vestnik* |
| RB | *Russkoe bogatstvo* |
| RGIA | *Rossiiskii Gosudarstvennyi Istoricheskii Arkhiv* |
| RIAMZ | *Riazanskii Istoriko-Arkhitekturnyi Muzei-Zapovednik* |
| RiazEV | *Riazanskie eparkhial'nye vedomosti* |
| RiazGV | *Riazanskie gubernskie vedomosti* |
| RiazV | *Riazanskii vestnik* |
| RiazZh | *Riazanskaia zhizn'* |
| RR | *The Russian Review* |
| RSP | *Rukovodstvo dlia sel'skikh pastyrei* |
| RusM | *Russkaia mysl'* |
| RusRech' | *Russkaia rech'* |
| RusVed | *Russkie vedomosti* |
| SAA | *Soviet Anthropology and Archeology* |
| SarGV | *Saratovskie gubernskie vedomosti* |
| SbNIuO | *Sbornik narodnykh iuridicheskikh obychaev* |
| SbSiBKNR | *Sbornik svedenii dlia izucheniia byta krest'ianskogo naseleniia Rossii* |
| SbSSMIu | *Sbornik statisticheskikh svedenii Ministerstva Iustitsii* |
| SbSSMPPS | *Sbornik sochinenii po sudebnoi meditsine, sudebnoi psikhiatrii, meditsinskoi politsii, obshchestvennoi gigiene, epidemiologii, meditsinskoi geografii i meditsinskoi statistike* |
| SE | *Sovetskaia etnografiia* |
| SEER | *Slavonic and East European Review* |
| SevK | *Severnyi krai* |
| SevV | *Severnyi vestnik* |
| SimbGV | *Simbirskie gubernskie vedomosti* |
| SPb | St. Petersburg |
| SPbVed | *Sankt-Peterburgskie vedomosti* |
| SR | *Slavic Review* |
| SudG | *Sudebnaia gazeta* |
| SudO | *Sudebnoe obozrenie* |
| SudZh | *Sudebnyi zhurnal* |

| | |
|---|---|
| SV | *Sel'skii vestnik* |
| Svody | *Svod Statisticheskikh svedenii po delam ugolovnym* |
| SZU | *Svod zakonov ugolovnykh* |
| TambGV | *Tambovskie gubernskie vedomosti* |
| TiurV | *Tiuremnyi vestnik* |
| TsGIAgM | *Tsentral'nyi Gosudarstvennyi Istoricheskii Arkhiv goroda Moskvy* |
| Trudy | *Trudy komissii po preobrazovaniiu volostnykh sudov* |
| TrudyIVEO | *Trudy Imperatorskogo vol'nogo ekonomicheskogo obshchestva* |
| Trudy MKNSP | *Trudy mestnykh komitetov o nuzhdakh sel'skokhoziaistvennoi promyshlen-nosti* |
| VE | *Vestnik Evropy* |
| VestP | *Vestnik prava* |
| VOGSP | *Vestnik obshchestvennoi gigieny, sudebnoi i prakticheskoi meditsiny* |
| VolzhV | *Volzhskii vestnik* |
| ZhGUP | *Zhurnal grazhdanskogo i ugolovnogo prava* |
| ZhivRus | *Zhivopisnaia Rossiia* |
| ZhivSt | *Zhivaia starina* |
| ZhMIu | *Zhurnal Ministerstva Iustitsii* |
| ZhUPP | *Zhurnal ugolovnogo prava i protsessa* |

# ACKNOWLEDGMENTS

This study was made possible with the generous support of numerous agencies and institutions. For financial assistance that funded the initial research from which this work eventually emerged, I thank the State University of New York at Plattsburg and Brown University. Grants from the following sources made possible several additional research trips to Russia, which in turn allowed for the transformation of a doctoral dissertation into the present book: the International Research and Exchanges Board, the National Endowment for the Humanities, the Social Science Research Council, the Kennan Institute for Advanced Russian Studies, and the Academic Senates of the University of California at Riverside and Los Angeles.

Equally invaluable has been the assistance of the many staff members at libraries and archives in the United States, the Soviet Union, and Russia, without whose kindness and expertise this study certainly could never have been completed. I am therefore very pleased, at last, to offer my warmest thanks to the staffs of the Rockefeller Library of Brown University, Harvard University's Widener Library, the New York Public Library, the Library of Congress, the former State Lenin Library in Moscow, the Library of the Academy of Sciences (BAN) and the Saltykov-Shchedrin Public Library in Leningrad/St. Petersburg, and to the interlibrary loan offices at Boston University's Mugar Library and Rivera Library at the University of California, Riverside. Although perpetually puzzled if amused at how we Americans could possibly be interested in such peculiar topics ("Are you a jurist?" I was repeatedly asked), assistants at the Central State Historical Archive (now the Russian State Historical Archive) in Leningrad/St. Petersburg, the Central State Historical Archive of the city of Moscow, the State Archive of the Russian Federation (formerly TsGAOR) in Moscow, and above all the State Archive of Riazan' *Oblast'* and the Riazan' Historico-Architectural

Museum, nevertheless proved cheerful and energetic as they lugged endless piles of musty documents from sometimes crumbling, unlighted, or flooded holding facilities. I am especially grateful to Andrei Nikolaevich Mel'nik, deputy director of the Riazan' *oblast'* archive, for his assistance and cooperation and for generously sharing his knowledge of this province's history.

Many friends and colleagues have provided equally crucial assistance and support during the years of research and writing. In addition to directing the dissertation from which this study began and patiently encouraging its lengthy transformation, Abbott Gleason has remained an unflagging friend and supporter as well as a meticulous reader of its many drafts. At various times throughout its preparation, Victoria Bonnell, John Bushnell, Robert Edelman, Ben Eklof, Daniel Field, Victor Frank, Gregory Freeze, Carlo Ginzburg, Leopold Haimson, Patricia Herlihy, Daniel Kaiser, Gail Lenhoff, Timothy Mixter, David Sabean, Mark Steinberg, Lynne Viola, Allan Wildman, and Christine Worobec read all or parts of the manuscript and offered invaluable criticisms and suggestions. I would like to single out Hans Rogger, in particular, for his generosity and friendship, and for his painstaking reading at a late stage, which forced me to clarify prose and sharpen my arguments while preventing numerous errors.

A portion of chapter 7 appeared in *Jahrbücher für Geschichte Osteuropas* 45, no. 3 (1997), and an earlier version of chapter 8 previously appeared in *The Russian Review* 46, no. 3 (1987). I thank both publishers for permission to reprint these now much revised works.

Russian terms used in this study have been transliterated following the Library of Congress system, with the exception of the names of monarchs and such commonly accepted spellings as Witte (rather than Vitte). Adjectival endings have been dropped from province, district, and township names. Pre-1917 spelling has been updated to conform to modern Russian. All dates are given according to the Julian calendar then in use.

# Introduction

*To say that law's violence is legitimate is, in the modern age, to juxtapose the alleged rationality of legal coercion and the irrationality of a violence that knows no law. It is to claim that law's violence is controlled through the legal articulation of values, norms, procedures, and purposes external to violence itself. It is to claim that the force of law serves common purposes and advances common aims in contrast to the anomic or sectarian savagery beyond law's boundaries.*

AUSTIN SARAT AND THOMAS KEARNS, *LAW'S VIOLENCE*, 1992

At the end of July 1901 the governor of Riazan' province received a petition from two agricultural laborers requesting his "gracious" assistance in their search for justice. The women had been recruited that winter in Kaluga province for work on a Riazan' district estate, and a legal contract was drawn up specifying the duration, nature, and conditions of their employment. Once at the estate, the plaintiffs explained, they and other workers were ill-used by the owner, who fed them meager meals of bread and water and rarely gave them hot food. "He worked us very hard in the field, driving us out to start [chores] at three in the morning and finishing at nine-thirty in the evening without rest." Although their contract expressly stated that no work would be done on holidays, the owner nevertheless forced them to labor on these occasions and also demanded that the women guard his horses at night despite their exhaustion. When one petitioner's husband came to the estate and saw the conditions under which his wife was toiling, he declared that they were going home and that she should settle up with the owner. But the latter refused to pay her the ten rubles she was owed or to return her passport, saying that she could not break the hiring contract. Hoping to resolve this matter through appeal to the law, her husband trekked to the precinct land captain and requested his aid, and when this official failed to take action, he journeyed on to Riazan' itself and petitioned the district police commandant, who grudgingly issued a command that the passports be returned. Although the order was obeyed, no wages were paid. When at last the woman and her husband set out to leave the estate without her earnings, she continued, the steward "rushed after me and tore from my hands [a purse containing] three rubles and my coat and pushed me so hard that I fell to the ground." Two other women who attempted to leave at the same time found themselves chased down by the owner and a constable and forced to return to the estate. In light of these "criminal" events, the petitioners humbly begged His Excellency, the governor, to investigate the owner's actions, which were "illegal in all respects," to force him to pay their wages and return the stolen purse and coat, and stated that "we will await the legal satisfaction of our petition."[1]

Several aspects of this far from untypical complaint bear comment, for they lead directly to the subject of this book. Clearly knowledgeable about rural Russia's often confusing mixture of judicial and administrative instances, these women had correctly brought their grievance before the land captain, an official with jurisdiction over hiring contracts and other disputes between peasants and their employers. When denied justice through his failure to hear the case, they moved on to the police commandant and, finally, the provincial governor, who was the tsar's direct representative in the countryside—a step not unlike that practiced by peasants for centuries when asking for the monarch's intervention to correct injustices.[2] Their task was made no easier by the fact that, being illiterate, they had to pay someone to compose the petitions. Yet one is struck by the conviction with which they stressed the illegality of the estate owner's denial of wages and the steward's violence and by their determination to press charges despite the odds being so obviously stacked against them. Equally evident is the owner's belief that these women had broken a legal contract obliging them to work for a stipulated period of time. From his perspective, he had done no wrong. Given his friendly relations with the district police (its captain had served as his hiring agent that winter), he also knew that his position and connections with the authorities protected him should questions arise about his actions. Both law and administration appeared to be on his side, as did the knowledge that, having to find work elsewhere, the plaintiffs would likely fade quickly from sight and not be heard from again. In fact, with the conclusion of this case in a five-page report and its relegation to the governor's archive among hundreds of others, the laborers and estate owner alike vanish from their fleeting appearance in the historical record. For that brief moment, however, far more than an everyday labor dispute was visible in this seemingly petty altercation. Both the petitioners' pained, angry words and the owner's self-righteous, even cruel treatment lay bare alternative definitions

1. GARO, f. 5, st. 1, op. 2, d. 2336, ll. 1–2. This case concluded without result. The governor did request his land captain to try the case, and the latter dutifully, if perhaps deviously, sent letters to the women telling them that their original petition had been improperly written and filed and would therefore have to be resubmitted. Having no current address, he forwarded his comments to the women's native village and reported back to the governor in November that they could not be located. Ibid., ll. 3–50b.

2. Among many studies see, e.g., P. K. Alefirenko, *Krest'ianskoe dvizhenie i krest'ianskii vopros v Rossii v 30–50-kh godakh XVIII veka* (Moscow, 1958), 270 ff.

of legality, justice, and the very constitution of a criminal act—distinctly conflicting opinions by no means limited to a singular incident but diffused throughout imperial Russian society.

This study of rural crime and justice in the postemancipation countryside takes as its primary focus these critical social junctures and cultural intersections at which law brought together competing definitions of criminality and claims of justice. Such points of contact were numerous and varied—far more so than previously recognized in the historical literature. Yet a fuller understanding of the linkages between different sociocultural fields and the fundamental conflicts and contradictions they reveal requires a deliberately shifting perspective from realities to representations and back again. We must move within and between village life and the administrative agencies that claimed to govern it, for instance, examining the intricate webs that bound them together as well as the way these connecting strands influenced each individual sphere and its relation to the other. We must negotiate the cultural maze within which crime was understood, experienced, perpetrated, and fought by peasants, without losing sight of rural crime's culturally embedded representations among members of educated society or its official definition in state law. The variance between the reality of criminal activity and how it was explained by nonpeasants provides a particularly useful framework for situating and analyzing broader cultural conflicts, for these important differences—which might better be termed arguments—serve as a constant reminder that "crime" in imperial Russia, like appeals to "justice" or "the law," stood as a contested metaphor about social order. We need to examine not only the uses that peasants made of courts and law but how they appropriated and reworked elite representations of themselves and their culture, interpreted and reinterpreted the law to their own advantage, or openly rejected basic principles of tsarist legislation.[3] At the root of these complex processes, of course, lay more fundamental issues of power and resistance. But as Edward Thompson has pointed out, we must not overlook the fact that even as villagers constructed their own culturally grounded vision of justice, their illegal actions repeatedly echoed official and elite discourses of the law by persistent references to justice and injustice.[4] Far greater consideration also has to be given to the shortcomings

3. For examples of this approach, see Jean Comaroff, *Body of Power, Spirit of Resistance: The Culture and History of a South African People* (Chicago, 1985); Steven Feierman, *Peasant Intellectuals: Anthropology and History in Tanzania* (Madison, Wisc., 1990).

4. E. P. Thompson, "The Crime of Anonymity," in Douglas Hay, Peter Linebaugh, John G. Rule, E. P. Thompson, and Cal Winslow, *Albion's Fatal Tree: Crime and Society in Eighteenth-Century England* (New York, 1975), 255–308. See also Antonio Gramsci, "Notes on Italian History," in *Selections from the Prison Notebooks,* ed. by Quintin Hoare and G. N. Smith (New York, 1971), 44–120; Florencia E. Mallon, "The Promise and Dilemma of Subaltern Studies: Perspectives from Latin American History," *AHR* 5, no. 99 (1994), 1491–1515

of official institutions and law enforcement agencies, and especially to the ways in which villagers adapted to these deficiencies by seeking out or creating alternative methods of control within the community setting.

This shifting of focus complicates our task, but it is the only means by which we may begin to draw a more complete picture of rural crime and justice. In particular, such an approach seems by far the most fruitful method for examining a range of long-standing questions about peasant society and the nature of law, justice, and crime within an agrarian, autocratic state. This book thus contains several related themes that cannot be adequately treated independently of one another. They reflect at once the methodological approach mentioned above and the necessity of addressing in depth the virtual nonexistence of scholarship on crime and justice in a historical literature nevertheless rich with discussions of conflict, lawlessness, and the legal position of Russian citizens under the old regime.[5] My basic aim, therefore, is to provide a broad view of crime and justice in late imperial Russia that does not simply stress the scope and nature of criminal activity and its treatment both within and outside the judicial system but reveals the extent to which crime was an intrapeasant phenomenon. Here I part ways in important respects with earlier literature, which has focused predominantly on noble-peasant hostilities, not to contradict an outstanding body of scholarly work but to begin the process of enlarging a very partial picture of rural social conflict. Peasants were not only perpetrators of offenses like poaching, theft of wood, land seizures, and assaults on noble estates; they were, at the same time, the primary victims of petty and serious crimes alike—including theft, arson, assault, and murder. My treatment of rural justice likewise seeks to correct a number of contemporary myths that have survived in the historiography, coloring the way that Russian peasant soci-

5. The only monograph that attempts to deal with crime rather than its representations is S. S. Ostroumov, *Prestupnost' i ee prichiny v dorevoliutsionnoi Rossii* (Moscow, 1960, 1980). This work, however, relies entirely on secondary summations of criminal statistics and employs the constricting analytic framework within which Soviet scholars were compelled to write. See also B. G. Litvak, "Zabytyi istochnik po istorii krest'ianskogo dvizheniia v Rossii vtoroi poloviny XIX–nachala XX veka (Svod statisticheskikh svedenii o delakh ugolovnykh, 1872–1914 gg.)," *Ezhegodnik po agrarnoi istorii vostochnoi Evropy 1970 g.* (Riga, 1977). Among the still small number of Western studies, see Stephen P. Frank, "Popular Justice, Community and Culture among the Russian Peasantry, 1870–1900," *RR* 46, no. 3 (1987), 239–65; Frank, "Narratives within Numbers: Women and Crime in the Russian Judicial Statistics, 1834–1913," *RR* 55, no. 4 (1996), 546–51; Timothy Mixter, *Revolution in the Bear's Corner: Villagers and Authority in Saratov Province, 1890–1908* (forthcoming); Joan Neuberger, *Hooliganism: Crime, Culture, and Power in St. Petersburg, 1900–1914* (Berkeley, 1993); Neil B. Weissman, "Rural Crime in Tsarist Russia: The Question of Hooliganism, 1905–1914," *SR* 37, no. 2 (1978), 228–40; Christine D. Worobec, "Horsethieves and Peasant Justice in Post-Emancipation Russia," *JSH* 21, no. 2 (1987), 281–93.

ety is presented and understood. Within this broader framework, I explore the gap between peasant and elite attitudes about crime, justice, and law, which entails analysis of the representations produced by educated society and officialdom. Comparison of popular thinking with these government and middle- or upper-class understandings of peasant thought and action is used as a key for revealing both the nature and depth of cultural conflict within the social formation that was late imperial Russia. It also uncovers an array of alternative and competing beliefs about law and justice so widespread in rural society that they raise questions about our use of terms like "dominant" and "subordinate" in the cultural realm. Social and cultural conflict are also woven into my discussions of the institutional structures through which the autocracy sought to rule the postemancipation countryside, and in my analysis of the deficiencies of these structures. The state's insistence on exercising tutelage from above and on relying upon its administrative apparatus rather than a judicial system that it did not trust, as well as its approach to governing the peasantry and its attitudes toward the rural population, all played extremely important roles in determining that some of the most basic conflicts in Russian society would remain unresolved or be further exacerbated during the postemancipation era. Moreover, such attitudes and methods of rule would not disappear with the monarchy's demise in 1917 but persisted into the Soviet period as well.

Crime proved at once a simple yet immensely complex matter in late imperial Russia. On an individual level, it was readily knowable for rich, middling, and poor victims alike, or for members of "respectable society" whose anxiety over public order rose steadily along with the growing quantity of lurid stories and news accounts that had become commonplace reading by the 1870s. Likewise, the tsarist government, which defined illegality through its compilations of punishable offenses that constituted Russia's criminal code, certainly knew what it meant by "crime," although in practice it was judges (or, after 1864, juries), not a given article of imperial law, that ultimately determined the definition of crime through the verdicts and sentences they handed down.[6] The question of crime, then—particularly its boundaries and how it should be understood—remained a contested one throughout this era of dynamic transformation and upheaval. From the reign of Emperor Nicholas I to the era of the Great Reforms, the counterreforms of the 1880s, revolution and beyond, state and society found little

6. On the defining of crime and criminality by juries and judges, see Carolyn A. Conley, *The Unwritten Law: Criminal Justice in Victorian Kent* (New York, 1991), 4 and *passim*. William G. Wagner likewise stresses the importance of Russia's reformed civil courts in the making of law. *Marriage, Property and Law in Late Imperial Russia* (Oxford, 1994), esp. 11–12, 206–23, 337–77.

agreement on this dilemma apart from the elementary fact that crime could be and often was of concern to everyone. Nor did consensus prove more easily attainable within the arenas of justice or law—themselves also contested terrains. In broad terms, of course, peasants, agricultural and migrant laborers, factory workers, shopkeepers, bourgeois professionals, government officials, and nobles all fretted over crime, complained about poor policing, litigated before courts, and stood subject to elements of the empire's criminal code. Yet even after 1861, when one would have expected—and, indeed, many Russians did expect—the emancipation to have narrowed the distance between former serfs and the rest of society, the state's insistence on retaining a hierarchical division of legally enshrined social estates (sing.: *soslovie*), each with specific privileges and obligations, and its continued assertion of the principle that personal, patriarchal authority could not be limited by law signified that each component of this segmented society would understand criminality quite differently while experiencing justice in ways unique to itself.[7]

Rural society in Russia after serfdom's abolition reflects these issues with particular clarity. The statutes on emancipation freed serfs from personal bondage but left them a juridically isolated estate denied full civil rights and freedom of movement and with limited access to the reformed legal system, while their local institutions functioned as the lowest rungs within the state's administrative apparatus. Even in the sphere of justice, peasant class courts fell under the supervision of the Ministry of Internal Affairs (MVD) rather than the Ministry of Justice, which oversaw what contemporaries tellingly termed the "regular" court system. Although the judicial reforms of 1864 have been widely lauded for creating independent courts ostensibly free from monarchical or administrative interference, introducing trial by jury, adopting a range of Western judicial procedures, engendering a legal profession, and propounding that all Russian citizens were equal before the law, these reforms had a direct impact on only a small fraction of the Rus-

7. Recent years have witnessed a revival of interest in the tension, long emphasized by Soviet and Western historians, between administrative authority and the judicial independence created by the judicial reform of 1864. See Richard S. Wortman, *The Development of a Russian Legal Consciousness* (Chicago, 1976); H. McCoubrey, "The Reform of the Russian Legal System under Alexander II," *Renaissance and Modern Studies* 24 (1980), 115–30; Laura Engelstein, *The Keys to Happiness: Sex and the Search for Modernity in Fin-de-Siècle Russia* (Ithaca, 1992); N. E. Kholiavitskaia, "Byl li sud nezavisim posle reformy 1864 goda?" *Vestnik Moskovskogo universiteta,* series 8: *Istoriia,* no. 4 (1993), 24–34; Wagner, *Marriage, Property and Law;* Reginald E. Zelnik, *Law and Disorder on the Narova River: The Kreenholm Strike of 1872* (Berkeley, 1995). For an analysis of *soslovie,* see Gregory Freeze, "The Estate (*Soslovie*) Paradigm and Russian Social History," *AHR* 91, no. 1 (1986), 11–36.

sian population—primarily urban dwellers.[8] In the lives of peasant villagers during the decades following their liberation, administrative authority and estate-based institutions would play a far more significant and intrusive role than the general courts and laws of the empire. This was due not only to their peculiar legal status but to the fact that, from 1861 onward, peasant society concerned the state in two basic if limited ways: It served as the government's chief financial resource (mainly through taxes and redemption payments) while presenting a potential and often real source of social disorder. Whether formulated in terms of administrative reform, agricultural improvement, or civil rights, the major governmental debates involving peasant policy that continued, both publicly and within ministerial chambers, from emancipation to the outbreak of World War I centered squarely on these issues without ever resolving them.[9] In effect, this meant that the official and narrowly conceived definition of rural crime would remain closely bound up with the state's fiscal needs and its fears of disorder—a definition clearly reflected in the criminal statistics.

In various ways, the postemancipation Russian countryside bore much more than a superficial resemblance to colonial settings.[10] Woefully under-

8. On the judicial reforms, see V. A. Shuvalova, "O sushchnosti sudebnoi reformy 1864 g. v Rossii," *Sovetskoe gosudarstvo i pravo* 10 (1964), 121–27; B. V. Vilenskii, *Sudebnaia reforma i kontrreforma v Rossii* (Saratov, 1969); John W. Atwell, Jr., "The Jury System and Its Role in Russia's Legal, Social, and Political Development from 1857 to 1914" (Ph.D. diss., Princeton University, 1970); Friedhelm B. Kaiser, *Die russische Justizreform von 1864: Zur Geschichte der russischen Justiz von Katherina II bis 1917* (Leiden, 1972); M. G. Korotkikh, *Sudebnaia reforma 1864 goda v Rossii* (Voronezh, 1994); Wortman, *Development of a Russian Legal Consciousness;* Brian Levin-Stankevich, "Cassation, Judicial Interpretation and the Development of Civil and Criminal Law in Russia, 1864–1914: The Institutional Consequences of the 1864 Court Reform in Russia" (Ph.D. diss., SUNY, Buffalo, 1984); William G. Wagner, "Tsarist Legal Policies at the End of the Nineteenth Century: A Study in Inconsistencies," *SEER* 54 (1976), 378–85; Wagner, *Marriage, Property and Law.* Classic prerevolutionary treatments are I. V. Gessen, *Sudebnaia reforma* (SPb, 1905), and N. V. Davydov and N. N. Polianskii, eds., *Sudebnaia reforma,* 2 vols. (Moscow, 1915).

9. These opinions and problems have been treated in a number of works, including George L. Yaney, *The Systematization of Russian Government: Social Evolution in the Domestic Administration of Imperial Russia, 1711–1905* (Urbana, 1973); Yaney, *The Urge to Mobilize: Agrarian Reform in Russia, 1861–1930* (Urbana, 1982); James I. Mandel, "Paternalistic Authority in the Russian Countryside, 1856–1906" (Ph.D. diss., Columbia University, 1978); Neil B. Weissman, *Reform in Tsarist Russia: The State Bureaucracy and Local Government, 1900–1914* (New Brunswick, N. J., 1981); David A. J. Macey, *Government and Peasant in Russia, 1861–1906: The Prehistory of the Stolypin Reforms* (DeKalb, Ill., 1986); Thomas S. Pearson, *Russian Officialdom in Crisis: Autocracy and Local Self-Government, 1861–1900* (Cambridge, 1989); Francis William Wcislo, *Reforming Rural Russia: State, Local Society, and National Politics, 1855–1914* (Princeton, 1990).

10. To my knowledge, the only formulation of this perspective with relation to imperial Russia is Hans Rogger, "Reforming Jews—Reforming Russians," in Herbert A. Strauss, ed., *Hostages of Modernization: Studies on Modern Antisemitism 1870–1933/39. Austria-Hungary-Poland-Russia* (Berlin and New York, 1993), 1208–29. For a different usage, see Alvin W. Gouldner, "Stalin-

governed, it was administered primarily by capital-appointed, noble officials who knew little about their village wards, and its subaltern peasant population remained subject to a separate body of law and a unique structure
of justice and provided the state with the essential resources it required to
rule. An internal passport system regulated peasant movement, ensuring
that they paid state taxes and rendered a host of other obligations such as
road repair and firefighting.[11] As had been true under serfdom, elected
peasant officials found themselves in the uncomfortable, often impossible
position of working to defend community interests while also fulfilling the
demands of intrusive provincial or district administrators under threat of
punishment. The nonpeasant officials that villagers most commonly encountered were the rural police, whose primary duties with regard to the
peasantry entailed traveling from hamlet to hamlet in their precincts collecting state taxes, supervising the seizure and public auction of property
belonging to those in arrears, enforcing a seemingly endless number of government regulations, and performing similar tasks that did little to endear
them to the population.[12] Because the state proved unable or unwilling to
commit resources necessary for reforming and enlarging this police force,
military detachments functioned as the major means of suppressing popular disorder, and communities were largely left to regulate themselves when
it came to everyday law enforcement.

Ruling the countryside like local satraps or colonial administrators,
landed provincial nobles acting in official positions of marshals of the nobility or district police commandants (*ispravniki*), among others, also exhibited an overriding concern with order. Even before the ink had dried on
the 1861 legislation that deprived them of unfree labor, noble landowners
and officials were already complaining loudly about the growing criminality of liberated peasants and demanding greater protection of their persons
and property. Government commissions formed to study problems of peasant administration or agriculture (particularly from the 1880s to 1904) received voluminous reports from the provincial nobility bemoaning the continuous depredations upon their property by what they saw as a peasantry
sunk in ignorance and utterly devoid of anything but the most primitive un-

---

ism: A Study of Internal Colonialism," *Telos*, no. 34 (Winter 1977–78), 5–48. Most recently,
Geoffrey Hosking, *Russia, People and Empire* (Cambridge, Mass., 1997), frames Russia's imperial
past in much the same context.

11. Villagers could, for example, be prosecuted for not rendering assistance to fight fires
in their neighborhood—including those that occurred on state property or a landed estate.
See, e.g., GARO, f. 5, st. 3, op. 4, dd. 4731, 4733, 4735–39, 4741, 4743, 4994–5013.

12. GARO, f. 5, st. 1, op. 2, d. 1652 (1879), ll. 1–2.

derstanding of law.[13] As agricultural crisis and economic necessity during the 1880s and 1890s drew many nobles back to the land, where they sought to administer their estates more profitably, they confronted at close range the unresolved conflicts with village communities that had existed since emancipation. Only now they found peasants less deferential and more threatening, still conducting their centuries-old guerrilla warfare against landed proprietors—both noble and nonnoble—but doing so, it seemed, brazenly. Unlike those who had known serfdom at first hand, one nobleman argued in 1902, "this generation of peasants has grown up without character, wild, lazy, thievish, obstinate, afraid to be alone, impudent and frenzied, like a beast in a crowd. . . . The Russian peasant does not wish to understand that another's property is sacred, and that infringement upon it is termed theft."[14] By the 1890s, middle-class professionals would join this chorus of frightened concern over a seemingly lawless countryside (and over the influx of uncultured peasant migrants into urban centers), bringing crime ever more frequently before public attention. The late 1880s and 1890s also witnessed the beginning of a gradual rise in criminal conviction rates that would continue until 1912—a correspondence with elite attitudes that was far from coincidental.

Elite complaints, however, are themselves less important than the way in which they were voiced and how explanations of rural criminality were formulated, for here, too, the colonial analogy comes readily to mind. Members of all groups within educated society (as upper- and middle-class Russia designated itself) drew upon a rich language and imagery of their cultural distinction from the peasantry. Some relied on the same tried and tested paternalistic formulations used under serfdom to explain and excoriate peasant lawbreaking. Others, more attracted by the scientific advances of this age of progress, utilized a Western evolutionary or anthropological perspective to formulate nearly identical arguments. But all worked from the same starting point, combining pre-existing stereotypes of peasant culture with pessimistic analyses that bemoaned the collapse of "traditional" village life under the disruptive forces of late nineteenth-century economic

13. For examples of such opinions, see Ministerstvo Finansov, *Trudy MKNSP,* 58 vols. (SPb, 1903–1905); S. I. Shidlovskii, *Zemel'nye zakhvaty i mezhevoe delo* (SPb, 1904); K. K. Arsen'ev, V. M. Gessen, I. V. Gessen, M. I. Ippolitov, et al., *Nuzhdy derevni po rabotam komitetov o nuzhdakh sel'skokhoziaistvennoi promyshlennosti,* 2 vols. (SPb, 1904).

14. M. I. Ippolitov, "Spetsial'nye pravonarusheniia v usloviiakh sel'skogo byta," in Arsen'ev et al., eds., *Nuzhdy derevni,* 216. The "return to the land" is treated in Leopold H. Haimson, ed., *The Politics of Rural Russia, 1905–1914* (Bloomington, 1979), 1–29, 262–63; Roberta T. Manning, *The Crisis of the Old Order in Russia: Gentry and Government* (Princeton, 1982), chs. 1–2.

and social change.[15] Through its own cultural spectrum, educated society constructed a broad, explanatory rubric for understanding rural crime that outlasted the old regime and the Soviet state. By no means limited to discussions of criminal conduct, this view, which looked upon former serfs and state peasants as culturally underdeveloped, backward, ignorant, immoral, and even degenerate, granted its many proponents reassurance from the more threatening implications of offenses against noble property or crimes that reflected a rejection of state law. It allowed these acts to be "understood" and perhaps even pardoned on cultural grounds and fed the circular reasoning behind arguments—such as that proffered by Chief Procurator of the Holy Synod Konstantin Pobedonostsev—about the backward "dark masses" of peasants requiring state protection and supervision.[16]

At the center of government concerns over order and elite representations of "peasant criminality" stood the individuals, families, and relationships that constituted village communities. They form the core actors of this book, while their interactions and conflicts with one another, with outsiders, and with state officials and institutions are the scenarios for analyzing and understanding both the realities of rural crime and law enforcement as well as peasant thinking about crime and justice. These conflicts also enable us to delve beyond what James C. Scott has termed the "public transcript" of official discourse and to examine the various meanings and functions of that transcript.[17] Until quite recently, nearly all historical studies treating rural conflict did so mainly through a focus on the widespread resentments fostered among peasants by emancipation and its land settlement. Critical as those conflicts are to understanding the problems and issues that characterized the postreform countryside's economic, social, and political landscape, and important as they remain to this study, they are only the most visible and dramatic manifestations of competing visions of justice or divergent explanations of crime and law.[18] Historians have commonly neglected

15. It should come as no surprise that young agricultural and migrant laborers, a segment of rural society viewed by educated Russians as most corrupted and, therefore, most dangerous to "settled" peasants, would be heavily represented within the criminal statistics.

16. Rogger, "Russian Ministers and the Jewish Question, 1881–1917," in Rogger, *Jewish Policies and Right-Wing Politics in Imperial Russia* (Berkeley, 1985), 67. The contemporary literature is replete with similar opinions. See below, Chapter 1.

17. James C. Scott, *Domination and the Arts of Resistance: Hidden Transcripts* (New Haven, 1985).

18. Among a substantial literature that centers on gentry-peasant disputes and other conflicts stemming from the emancipation settlement, see the still unsurpassed, multivolume *Krest'ianskoe dvizhenie v Rossii v XIX–nachale XX veka* (Moscow-Leningrad, various years), ed. by N. M. Druzhinin, and B. G. Litvak's historiographical survey *Krest'ianskoe dvizhenie v Rossii v 1775–1904* (Moscow, 1989). Recent scholarship that has moved away from this specific focus includes Ben Eklof, *Russian Peasant Schools: Officialdom, Village Culture, and Popular Pedagogy, 1861–1914* (Berkeley, 1986); Roger Bartlett, ed., *Land Commune and Peasant Community in Rus-*

the fact that for every peasant assault upon a gentry estate, for every act of mass cutting in state-owned forests, for each clash with district surveyors on disputed land, hundreds of smaller if no less significant conflicts were played out in rural life. It has been long overlooked, for instance, that lengthy efforts at resolution in other forums frequently preceded such conflicts. Peasants flooded courts and administrative bodies alike with petitions and suits asking, in effect, for official support of their vision of justice. Violent assaults upon landed property or state forests likewise took place against a backdrop of incessant, petty incursions that tested the resolve of villagers' opponents while feeling out the parameters of the law's repressive will.[19] If we are to reach a deeper understanding about how peasants experienced and understood law and justice, or why they perpetrated deeds that this law had criminalized and how such actions reflected broader strategies of resistance, we need to focus closely on these everyday conflicts as they transpired both within the established legal system and beyond its porous boundaries.

Equally important, and a major theme of this book, is the simple fact that most rural crimes did not occur in the context of disputes between villagers and landed proprietors. To a great extent, crime remained an intrapeasant phenomenon reflecting the disparate conflicts endemic to rural communities: insults inflicted during the heat of the moment or those spoken with malice; pilfering from a neighbor's barn or field; drunken brawls on the village street; familial animosities; struggles over inheritance and land divisions; feuding between political factions seeking dominance in the village assembly and greater control over the distribution of local resources; arguments over land use; jealousies aroused in any number of situations ranging from infidelity within marriage to hostility toward a well-to-do fellow villager.[20] These and many other scenarios lay bare a crucial aspect of rural life commonly masked by the collective front of solidarity presented by peasants in the face of threats from without and reveal a more complete picture of village society than that which has existed until now. A survey of "ordinary" rural crime also exposes the very serious dangers that communities faced from outside assaults upon their property and, at times, their persons as well, and that created widespread insecurity as the century wore on. The

*sia: Communal Forms in Imperial and Early Soviet Society* (London, 1990); Christine D. Worobec, *Peasant Russia: Family and Community in the Post-Emancipation Period* (Princeton, 1991); Esther Kingston-Mann and Timothy Mixter, eds., *Peasant Economy, Culture, and Politics of European Russia, 1800–1921* (Princeton, 1991); Jeffrey Burds, *Peasant Dreams and Market Politics: Labor Migration and the Russian Village, 1861–1905* (Pittsburgh, 1998).

19. On this point, see also Mixter, *Revolution in the Bear's Corner.*

20. For a similar view, see Martin Chanock, *Law, Custom, and Social Order: The Colonial Experience in Malawi and Zambia* (New York, 1985), 12–13.

networks of organized horsethieves who mercilessly preyed upon peasantry, clergy, and nobility alike are by far the best example here, although robbers, bandits, arsonists, escapees from prison or exile, swindlers, confidence men and women, and vagrants made up sizable portions of rural Russia's little-known criminal underworld.

Crimes committed by villagers against one another provide a unique avenue into areas of peasant culture that demonstrate the depth of cultural conflict during this period as it was expressed and played out through the multifaceted interactions between culture and law. How villagers dealt with witchcraft accusations when courts would no longer hear their cases, how they appropriated and utilized the symbols of official Orthodoxy in efforts to protect themselves and their communities from the supernatural, and how they resisted or accommodated religious persecution of their sectarian faiths all reveal far more than a small realm of criminalized activities. These examples also speak of popular determination and assertion of beliefs in the face of criminalization and demonstrate the varied ways that peasants perceived and treated the inadequacies of law. Resistance at many levels of the cultural sphere thus surfaces in both the mundane as well as the more spectacular disagreements over the meaning of crime. A narrow, selective reading of such acts, of course, helped to reinforce the representations of rural life that pervaded educated society and to maintain the gap in understanding that separated these two cultures.

Given the nature of rural administration after emancipation, crime and its control proved particularly problematic for peasant communities during the decades leading up to World War I. So, too, did their search for justice. The emancipation settlement created, from the outset, a broad new realm of criminalized behaviors that saw villagers subject to punishment by courts or administrative officials for efforts to right what they believed to be the injustices of this legislation. The government's heightened state of insecurity and fear over liberation, for example, allowed severe floggings for the act of "incorrectly" or "improperly" interpreting the Imperial Manifesto on Emancipation.[21] As one district marshal of the nobility put it in an 1861 report to the governor of Riazan' province, disputes between peasants and landowners had arisen the moment that emancipation was announced. "But things could not be any other way. On many estates the peasants, who wrongly understand freedom and are being carried away by false rumors about their new position, are refusing to fulfill their obligations to the owner and are demanding that the new relationships be introduced at once."[22] Conflict thus ensued immediately as peasants disputed, sabotaged,

21. See e.g., GARO, f. 5, st. 3, op. 4, d. 620 (1861), ll. 61–61ob.
22. Ibid., Kasimov district, l. 31.

or openly rejected criminalization of their "legitimate" actions, giving rise to one of the most crucial disagreements of the late imperial era and one that centered directly upon the definition of crime. As for ordinary crimes, glaring deficiencies of state administration and law enforcement together with equally serious shortcomings of the reformed court system determined that communities were left on their own to manage as best they could. These two problems would play a critical role in shaping peasant attitudes toward imperial law and justice, but only by examining them in conjunction can the full implications and impact of such attitudes be revealed.

Long before emancipation, of course, serfs, crown and state peasants alike, had found numerous avenues for expressing grievances over injustice and by various means sought redress through something they envisioned as justice. Although Western historians have proved reluctant to acknowledge it, during the centuries of serfdom, villagers learned the law, interpreted and reinterpreted it, and attempted to utilize it to their advantage in unequal struggles against owners and the state. Following emancipation, similar practices continued. Still ensconced in familiar, multiple layers of asymmetrical power relations with local and higher officialdom, peasants would perpetuate time-worn tactics of everyday resistance while also seeking to bend the law and the judicial system if not into a more equitable form then at least into one from which they, too, could derive advantage or redress.

Yet, in their new position of freedom, peasants also expected more from the legal and judicial system. To a very great extent, those expectations would be disappointed. The decades following emancipation—particularly from the 1880s on—witnessed a substantial increase of serious crimes that threatened local communities but that villagers were increasingly unable to prevent or solve. Arson, horsetheft, and robbery, peasants complained, were on the rise, bringing fear and instability to their localities. Protection by the regular rural police and prosecution through the courts, however, proved sporadic at best, creating broad dissatisfaction among those victimized by or fearful of crime and leading communities to turn more frequently to extrajudicial measures, including vigilante violence and banishment. In other words, peasants sought out alternative avenues of justice to meet the needs generated by the deficiencies of state agencies. Resentment spread further in the face of the fact that those agencies—police, courts, and administrative officials—proved far more effective when it came to protecting gentry property against peasant incursions or defending state interests.

That this situation encouraged peasant rejection of critical elements of postemancipation law while simultaneously fostering a lack of faith in official justice cannot be doubted. More ominously, these problems and peasant responses to them speak to a widening of the gap of understanding that separated village culture and society from educated Russia and the state alike. As villagers in ever greater numbers complained of their victimization by criminals and pleaded with administrative agents to protect their communities, the state's responses came in peculiar if perhaps understandable forms, given its firm beliefs on law and administration as well as its limited resources. Convinced that the primary cause of rural disorder was the absence of enlightened, paternal supervision, for example, the monarchy introduced land captains in 1889 to oversee peasant administration and justice, thus relying again on an appointed colonial administrator to serve as an arbiter between the subaltern and the landowning elite while solving the vast array of problems that beset village communities by means of tutelage from above, cajoling, strict supervision, and, when necessary, punishment. This colonial solution, with its tutelary officials and stereotypes about the rural population, persisted until the end of the old regime and would be taken up by the Bolshevik successors to tsarism. As recent scholarship has shown, the peasantry's lack of trust in formal justice and official law also carried over into the Soviet period, bringing with it many of the same conflicts and patterns of resistance that had defined the countryside since at least the time of emancipation.[23]

The primary geographic locus of this study is central Russia, and particularly the Central Industrial and Central Agricultural Regions. Within that broad territory, the province of Riazan' forms a core focus and source base, although substantial materials are drawn from Moscow, Iaroslavl', Nizhnii Novgorod, Orel, Smolensk, and Vladimir provinces. For additional comparison I have culled information from other surrounding provinces, venturing farther afield into the north and south. I have relied most heavily, however, on the rich, previously closed Riazan' provincial archive, which has allowed me to construct a multilevel analysis that moves between the telling detail of a local study to broader, regional comparison and generalizations.

Although this book draws from a wide range of contemporary sources, both archival and published, virtually all of them "implicate in one way or another those people who to some extent exercise domination over the peasant," as historian David Sabean has put it and as has been widely discussed in the literature of peasant studies.[24] The truncated crime reports of overburdened police officers, peasant court records consciously composed with the knowledge that they might be read by higher officials, criminal

23. See Sheila Fitzpatrick, *Stalin's Peasants: Resistence and Survival in the Russian Village After Collectivization* (New York, 1994); Lynne Viola, *Peasant Rebels Under Stalin: Collectivization and the Culture of Peasant Resistance* (New York, 1996).

24. David Warren Sabean: *Power in the Blood: Popular Culture and Village Discourse in Early Modern Germany* (Cambridge, 1984), 2.

court documents flush with formalisms but sparse in detail about the offenses and offenders being tried, village petitions directed to state institutions or administrators, the massive body of published criminal statistics,
newspaper crime columns, ethnographic descriptions, and other contemporary commentary—all have their own complex stories to tell and must be
considered with this fact prominently in mind.

An equally intriguing story exists in the very manner whereby decisions
have been made whether to preserve or discard archival documents. Since
the 1950s, several archival commissions determined that millions of prerevolutionary documents in regional holding facilities should be destroyed.
We know nothing, of course, about how or why a given body of material was
purged apart from the fact that it was. Yet certain questions do come to
mind about the persistence of attitudes and patterns of thought discussed
in this book. Why, to take but one example, do postemancipation criminal
court holdings contain almost no cases involving witchcraft, although they
have been somewhat better preserved for the pre-1861 period? We know
from press reports and other sources that numerous trials did take place in
which peasants stood charged with the torture or murder of a suspected sorcerer, yet the court documents no longer exist. Did the decision to jettison
such records reflect a continued embarrassment over peasant "benightedness," whereas the retention of cases involving gentry-peasant conflict or resistance to state officials reveals a conscious choice to reconstruct history to
reflect ideological correctness? There is certainly an important tale to tell
here and one that contains overtones of continued colonial thought by
those entrusted to preserve their country's past.

# PART I

# Representations, Institutions, and the Problem of Order

*The inner life of our peasantry is so distant from us that any observations about it by persons of the privileged classes will, for the most part, amount to nothing. . . . If personal observations are to have any meaning, a great many extremely important conditions are required. First of all, the observer should be completely impartial, forgetting all his convictions, the life of his civilized circle, schooling, and our legislation. . . . He should know that he has arrived in a terra incognita, where all is dark, unknown and utterly different. He should study this unknown with the same interest with which . . . Livingston studied Africa. He will be bitterly mistaken if he is satisfied with questioning peasants themselves about their law. Peasants never think about their law and, therefore, cannot communicate anything.*

I. VERIGIN, "THE PRINCIPLES OF POPULAR LAW AND
LEGAL PROCEDURE," *RUSSIAN SPEECH,* 1879

*There can be no doubt that* volost' *court decisions are based on local custom [because] the peasant, like any uncultured person, is not capable of abstract judgment, and hence is not able . . . to deduce general, guiding juridical principles.*

P. S. TIMOFEEV, "IN DEFENSE OF THE *VOLOST'* COURT AND
CUSTOMARY LAW," *ST. PETERSBURG GAZETTE,* 1902

*Whatever laws might be published, whatever measures established for the improvement of agriculture, they will not achieve their goals if the culture of the peasantry does not reach that level at which each individual will recognize not only his rights, but also his duties. Before introducing improvements in farming, it is necessary to educate the peasantry, to imbue them with a strict and precise fulfillment of their obligations and a consciousness of their own worth; it is necessary to develop within them a love of property, a love of order and purity, both moral and physical. Without these elementary requirements, no measures will succeed in their aims.*

N. V. DMITRIEV, REPORT TO THE ARDATOVSK DISTRICT (NIZHNII NOVGOROD
PROVINCE) COMMITTEE ON THE NEEDS OF AGRICULTURE, 1903

# CHAPTER 1

# Colonial Perspectives

## Representations and Realities
## of Rural Crime and Justice

*The collapse of the peasants' economic life began the moment they received the ability to be completely and freely in charge of both their persons and their property, when outside supervision was removed from them, and above all when they were granted broad self-government. As the supervisory authority in the villages weakens, so their impoverishment is more and more noticeable. . . . The twenty-five-year life of the peasants [since emancipation] . . . testifies sufficiently to the fact that the population cannot improve its material situation without the help of far-sighted, intelligent, and concerned local authorities who can constantly guide them . . .*
GOVERNOR'S ANNUAL REPORT, RIAZAN' PROVINCE, 1886

## EMANCIPATION AND THE FIRST CRIME WAVE

In the summer of 1864, barely three years after the start of Russia's serf emancipation, the Ministry of Internal Affairs (MVD) instructed the governor of Nizhnii Novgorod province to investigate an alarming rise in rural crime. Felony statistics, the ministry claimed, had registered remarkable increases between 1854 and 1863. Cases of murder in this province grew by 54 percent over these ten years, arson by 61, theft by 179, and robbery by a frightening 274 percent.[1] As the chief agency for maintaining security and order in the countryside, it is little wonder that such figures proved unsettling to the MVD. When combined with growing press coverage of crime and lawlessness among the newly freed peasant population, however, concerns over public order spread far beyond the walls of a single government ministry. They also bolstered worries within important segments of educated

---

1. A. S. Gatsiskii, "Materialy dlia ugolovnoi statistiki Nizhegorodskoi gubernii," *Nizhegorodskii sbornik* 1, part 1 (1867), 121–25. The source for these figures was not given, although published statistics show a 33.9 percent increase in total crimes for the years in question. *Otchet Ministerstva Iustitsii* [hereafter: *Otchety*], vols. 23–31 (SPb, 1858–66). See also Gatsiskii, "Opyt ugolovnoi statistiki Nizhegorodskoi gubernii," *Pamiatnaia knizhka Nizhegorodskoi gubernii na 1865 g.* (Nizhnii Novgorod, 1864), 94–111. Governors of some central provinces, such as Riazan', however, reported insignificant increases or even drops in the number of crimes during these years. See, e.g., GARO, f. 5, st. 1, op. 2, d. 1028 (1861), ll. 390b–40.

society—particularly local administrative and police officials—that emancipation may have come at a serious cost to social tranquillity, justifying preexisting fears over the destabilizing consequences of unsupervised peasant freedom.

By 1865, Nizhnii Novgorod provincial councilor A. P. Smirnov had compiled a survey of opinions on the causes of rural crime from district court judges, prosecutors, police commandants, peace mediators, marshals of the nobility, parish priests, and others.[2] A few respondents questioned the MVD's data and suppositions with good reason, pointing out that the statistical increase did not stem from a crime wave but resulted largely from the fact that seigneurial peasants, who had been tried by their masters for most infractions prior to emancipation, were now coming before state courts and swelling the judicial record, creating the impression of a vast upsurge in the number of offenses committed.[3] Yet if they were aware of this fact, most who answered the survey ignored it, expressing instead a dual anxiety about the moral state of emancipated peasants and the apparent inability of either police or judicial agencies to exercise control over them. These opinions offer significant insight into the attitudes of provincial officialdom toward rural criminality and the peasantry in general—an important starting point, for the beliefs they expressed changed little during the remaining decades of the old regime.

The primarily noble respondents voiced general agreement with a peace mediator's claim that the increase in crime was a direct result of emancipation, "because [peasants] lost the careful supervision over them which is required due to the coarseness of their morals." Hearkening back to prereform times, some greatly exaggerated the efficiency of estate regimes. As one official wrote:

> During the era of serfdom, landowners or their stewards . . . insured that farmers worked and fulfilled all labor obligations. They also curtailed drunkenness. This served as a basis for mutual benefit and common satisfaction. Un-

2. Gatsiskii, "Materialy," 125–26. Created in 1861 and empowered with police and judicial functions, peace mediators served as local agents to oversee the emancipation and resolve disputes between peasants and their owners during the redemption process. K. A. Sofronenko, comp., *Krest'ianskaia reforma v Rossii 1861 goda: sbornik zakonodatel'nykh aktov* (Moscow, 1954), 141–42; Jerman Walter Rose, "The Russian Peasant Emancipation and the Problem of Rural Administration: The Institution of the Mirovoi Posrednik" (Ph.D. diss., University of Kansas, 1976), 69–70.

3. "The growth in the number of theft cases does not at all attest to the actual number of crimes," one peace mediator argued. "With the abolition of serfdom, a large number of thefts that previously remained unknown and were punished by the serfowner now became public and subject to [official] investigation." Another mediator made much the same point, noting that after emancipation "the influence of the serfowner's court and punishment came to an end, and all cases now come before the regular judicial administration." Gatsiskii, "Materialy," 139–40.

der serfdom, estate police existed in each settlement, so that not a single peasant had the right to absent himself without the knowledge of estate officials; hence serfs remained under constant and vigilant supervision and, as a result, were kept from committing crimes. Above all, they were restrained from criminal activity by the fear that, even if they did not receive punishment from a court, the landowner could send them off to military service, subject them to corporal punishment or exile them to Siberia.[4]

Others said much the same. "One of the chief reasons for the increase in crime is the rapid transition of peasants from serfdom to complete freedom," declared a marshal of the nobility. "In earlier times, estate owners supervised their peasants' morality and therefore . . . legal order was maintained."[5] But owing to this freedom that they did not yet understand, one police commandant added, "our peasants—or at least 99 percent of them—are not aware that a person is obliged to be honest and to recognize his duty to obey government orders and lead a patriarchal family life." Instead, wrote a peace mediator, once liberated from the strict supervision of his owner, "the former serf completely surrendered himself to his unbridled passions."[6]

Nearly all respondents found morality to be in a woeful state of decline after emancipation, as shown by the spread of taverns, drunkenness, smoking, and other vices. Claimed one noble administrator, "Crimes are committed by peasants primarily under the influence of that savage and crude moral condition in which they exist."[7] Sounding a theme commonly heard from clerical and other observers long before emancipation (and one that would be echoed again with particular vehemence toward the century's end), respondents worried especially about a marked weakening of deference toward elders. "So soon after emancipation," a police commandant warned, "they are complaining in the villages about young people not obeying or submitting to parental authority." The great increase in rural alcohol consumption that many believed accompanied serfdom's abolition only worsened this problem, for "the drunkard does not understand gray hair, and here is the basis of disrespect toward elders, fathers, mothers, and officials."[8] More than any other single factor, drinking was blamed for the

---

4. Ibid., 130. Elite commentaries about crime in other postemancipation settings were quite similar to those expressed in Russia, raising the spectre of the increasingly disorderly, criminal, and uncivilized masses. See, e.g., Martha K. Huggins, *From Slavery to Vagrancy in Brazil: Crime and Social Control in the Third World* (New Brunswick, N.J., 1985); David V. Trotman, *Crime in Trinidad: Conflict and Control in a Plantation Society, 1838–1900* (Knoxville, Tenn., 1986), esp. ch. 4; Edward L. Ayers, *Vengeance and Justice: Crime and Punishment in the Nineteenth-Century American South* (New York, 1984).

5. Gatsiskii, "Materialy," 142.

6. Ibid., 127, 131.

7. Ibid., 137.

8. Ibid., 127.

peasants' dreadful moral state and the rise of rural criminality. "The growth of this vice is the chief cause of increased thefts and fires," said one official, and another explained that alcohol abuse developed gradually, beginning with the loss of outside supervision, which allowed the peasant "to give himself over to the weakness of excessive drinking." Cheap liquor made the peasant a poor farmer who first neglected his work and family and then, in order to satisfy a growing desire for alcohol, "turns to easy means of acquiring money and begins to steal, first trifles from his neighbors, then finally committing [felonies]." In short, "the rising number of petty offenses—fights, rowdiness, swindling, family discord, carelessness with fire, and so on—is occurring because of the proliferation of drinking establishments and the excessive cheapness of vodka."[9]

Ignorance and lack of education, respondents argued, also contributed to the crime wave because peasants did not understand the freedom and self-administration granted to them. In a telling testimony to prereform justice, one district marshal remarked that "simple folk" continued to believe they could commit crimes and avoid punishment by means of bribery, as had been done in the past.[10] Others stressed that allowing peasants to elect their own policemen (a practice that actually dated to the eighteenth century) had unwittingly contributed to the growth of crime because villagers choose for these positions people who best suited their needs—those of bad moral character who were submissive, discreet, did not interfere in the peasants' merrymaking and disorders, and did nothing to prevent or investigate offenses.[11] Some went further and blamed the reformed legal order itself for encouraging crime because it did not allow for immediate punishment, as under serfdom, but required lengthy investigation and court proceedings. "Before emancipation, punishment did not necessitate the superfluous evidence that is needed today and as a result of which criminals get off with no punishment at all . . . The homespun police measures of preemancipation times kept the immorality of the rabble [*chern'*] in bounds, whereas the new order of things has led to its increase."[12]

9. Ibid., 131–32, 133. For various estimates on the extent to which rural drinking establishments were increasing after emancipation, see GARO, f. 5, st. 1, op. 2, d. 953, l. 53; Boris Mironov, "The Russian Peasant Commune after the Reforms of the 1860s," *SR* 44, no. 3 (1985), 461; *Trudy MKNSP,* vol. 24: *Nizhegorodskaia guberniia* (SPb, 1903), 45; vol. 25: *Novgorodskaia guberniia* (SPb, 1903), 202; and others.

10. Gatsiskii, "Materialy," 137. For a similar opinion, see Bogoslovskii, "Obshchii ocherk obraza zhizni i kharaktera zhitelei Novgorodskoi gubernii," *Novgorodskii sbornik,* no. 1 (1865), part 1, 7–8. On bribery both prior to 1861 and after, see N. Davydov, *Ugolovnyi sud v Rossii* (Moscow, 1918), 182–84; A. A. Fet [A. A. Shenshin], *Moi vospominaniia, 1848–1889,* 2 vols. (Moscow, 1890), 2:227.

11. Gatsiskii, "Materialy," 128.

12. Ibid., 144–45.

Nobles also implicated rural poverty and an unfathomable yet growing peasant desire for material improvement that drove them to commit crimes in order to fulfill their new materialistic cravings. A rapid expansion of Russia's seasonal and migrant labor market similarly fed the supposed crime wave, for along previously sleepy Volga river towns it swelled the population with thousands of laborers who could easily be tempted once outside the constraints imposed by their families and native villages. Indeed, the free movement of lower-class people throughout the countryside greatly disturbed local officials. Outsiders posed a constant threat to defenseless communities, it was noted, and villagers had to tolerate criminals in their midst because they could not afford the expense incurred by banishing offenders. As one respondent put it, these incorrigible criminals acted as a "moral disease" upon everyone around them.[13]

Nizhnii Novgorod's parish clergy echoed many of these opinions, stressing the abolition of serfdom and of corporal punishment by state courts as responsible for the spread of crime in their parishes. Drunkenness stood out among the chief factors clerics cited when accounting for rural criminality, as did the presence of "harmful and dangerous people" in villages. Some priests added to this list villagers' declining respect for Church and clergy, the schism, lack of belief in an afterlife and its punishments, the election of village officials "through an appeal to vodka rather than the blessing of God," and the ever greater mobility of their flock, which exposed peasants to the corrupting influences of factory and city through outwork or travel to regional markets. Unlike other respondents, however, individual priests pointed to a lack of moral influence from nonpeasant officials, their unjust and arbitrary conduct, poor harvests, a decline of handicraft industries, begging, inflation, population growth with its resultant land shortage, and the widespread news about crime, which contributed to the perception of its increase.[14] At least one provincial lawyer would restate this last point twelve years later: "Not long ago," he wrote, "they were shouting about the

13. Ibid., 133. Peasant communities were required to pay for an offender's imprisonment prior to exile, as well as for transportation and clothing; see Chapter 7. In other national settings, too, "outsiders" were commonly blamed for bringing crime to otherwise peaceful rural communities. David J. V. Jones, *Rebecca's Children: A Study of Rural Society, Crime, and Protest* (Oxford, 1989), 162; Carolyn A. Conley, *The Unwritten Law: Criminal Justice in Victorian Kent* (Oxford, 1991), 166.

14. Gatsiskii, "Materialy," 149. Unfortunately, the editor chose not to print opinions provided by local clerics, possibly because many were overly critical of the provincial administration and police. Gatsiskii himself, however (150–53), also questioned several assertions made by officials, including their linkage of drinking and crime. For additional commentary on declining faith in the Church and clergy, see "Odna iz prichin nedoveriia i nedruzheliubnogo otnosheniia prikhozhan k svoemu pastyriu," *RSP,* no. 3 (1886), 53–61; no. 49, 404–13; N. O. Osipov, *O prichinakh upadka vliianiia dukhovenstva na narod* (SPb, 1900).

constantly growing number of crimes in Russia dating from the time of [emancipation], but subsequently it turned out that it was not the number of crimes that had increased, but only the means for spreading news about crime throughout society—i.e., the press."[15]

## CRIME AS CULTURAL IMPOVERISHMENT

Opinions in the 1864 survey represented no significant shift in attitudes toward the rural population from those of earlier times, and they remained familiar refrains until the fall of the old regime and beyond. A similar sense of uncertainty and crisis at the beginning of the twentieth century took much the same form. What distinguished the atmosphere of 1864 was emancipation itself, which intensified older feelings of fear and hostility toward the peasantry. In 1847, for example, a district marshal of the nobility from Smolensk province had argued that "the ignorance of the peasants, their superstitions, incorrigibility, and irreversible attachment to the old ways, make them incapable of accepting legal statutes and assimilating the consciousness of civil dependency."[16] Serfowners and administrators of state peasants voiced endless concern over what they, too, saw as an ever growing incidence of crime, disorder, immorality, drunkenness, and lack of respect for private property. According to an 1826 report from one estate steward in the Skopin district of Riazan' province, peasants of Vysokoe village not only persistently shirked labor duties and disobeyed the authorities; they also deliberately damaged the lord's grain and meadows and surreptitiously cut wood in his forest "both night and day."[17] Such complaints are legion in archival and published records, as is evidence about how justice was meted out to peasants who broke local law or estate regulations. On Prince Gagarin's Petrovskoe estate in Tambov province, 424 out of 1,626 serfs (26 percent) were annually subjected to some form of punishment or fine, with the most common offenses being theft of the lord's property, poor work, and pasturing communal livestock on the estate's winter crops.[18]

15. V. S. Krotkov, *Volch'e stado. Zapiski provintsial'nogo advokata. Tseny i kartiny sel'skogo suda* (Moscow, 1876), 10.

16. Francis W. Wcislo, *Reforming Rural Russia: State, Local Society, and National Politics, 1855–1914* (Princeton, 1990), 15.

17. M. A. Rakhmatullin, *Krest'ianskoe dvizhenie v velikorusskikh guberniiakh v 1826–1857 gg.* (Moscow, 1990), 62. See also Rodney Bohac, "Everyday Forms of Resistance: Serf Opposition to Gentry Exactions, 1800–1861," in Esther Kingston-Mann and Timothy Mixter, eds., *Peasant Economy, Culture, and Politics of European Russia, 1800–1921* (Princeton, 1991), 236–60; and, for a broader discussion, James C. Scott, *Weapons of the Weak: Everyday Forms of Peasant Resistance* (New Haven, 1985).

18. I. D. Koval'chenko, *Krest'iane i krepostnoe khoziaistvo Riazanskoi i Tambovskoi gubernii v pervoi polovine XIX v.* (Moscow, 1959), 168, 241. Judicial statistics for the pre-emancipation years

Drawing from his observations around Arkhangel'sk province during the early 1860s, ethnographer Petr S. Efimenko wrote that "respect toward property is being lost little by little, and there are even habitual thieves in some villages." The result, he claimed, was a sizable increase in the number of thefts.[19]

Officials and members of educated society had long argued that ignorance, immorality, and vice lay at the root of most crimes perpetrated by peasants. As an inspector (*revizor*) of state peasant settlements noted in the late 1830s, villagers of both sexes were quite simply being ruined by liquor. "In the bootlegging establishments people . . . gather, drink together, entertain one another . . . and often forget their children, who are left at home without a crust of bread. They drink at all times and everywhere. . . . On holidays these taverns around the villages and along the roads are completely filled."[20] Year after year and from one decade to the next, nonpeasant reporters claimed that village drinking and immorality were on the rise. "Drunkenness has, without a doubt, increased among the peasantry," a 1869 study stated. "They drink openly; both rich and poor, village elder and police go to the tavern at any time and drink, as they say, 'out of grief or out of joy.'"[21]

Most historical studies treating educated Russia's attitudes toward peasants have tended to focus on the idealization of a simple country folk who embodied whatever positive characteristics or hopes a given author or group projected onto them; however, such positive views accounted for only a small if influential portion of those in circulation. Even a cursory examination of contemporary writings provides ample evidence that the "simple folk" imagined in intelligentsia mythology from the 1840s on looked quite different to officialdom at all levels, to many clerics, and influential members of educated society. To them, rural life appeared bru-

1832–1861 show that offenses against state and private property (particularly wood theft) proved the most numerous of all crimes for which peasants came to trial. See *Otchet Ministerstva Iustitsii*, vols. 1–35, and Chapter 2.

19. P. S. Efimenko, *Sbornik narodnykh iuridicheskikh obychaev Arkhangel'skoi gubernii* (Arkhangel'sk, 1869), 225. For a range of complaints by former serfowners, see GARO, f. 694, op. 1, sv. 10, d. 194 (1861), ll. 1–245.

20. N. M. Druzhinin, *Gosudarstvennye krest'iane i reforma P. D. Kiseleva*, 2 vols. (Moscow-Leningrad, 1946, 1958), 1:374. Identical complaints would be voiced by temperance advocates and other social reformers during the late nineteenth and early twentieth centuries, as well as by those seeking the causes of "hooliganism." See Stephen P. Frank, "Confronting the Domestic Other: Rural Popular Culture and Its Enemies in *Fin-de-Siècle* Russia," in Stephen P. Frank and Mark D. Steinberg, eds., *Cultures in Flux: Lower-Class Values, Practices, and Resistance in Late Imperial Russia* (Princeton, 1994), 80–85. Compare Gregor Dallas, *The Imperfect Peasant Economy: The Loire Country, 1800–1914* (Cambridge, 1982), 248.

21. Efimenko, *Sbornik*, 227–28. See also E. Ozenbriuggen, "O sredstvakh k umen'sheniiu prestuplenii," *Zhurnal Ministerstva Narodnogo Prosveshcheniia* 54 (1847), part 2, 1–27.

tal, coarse, and growing worse, a point emphasized at length in 1869 by populist V. V. Bervi-Flerovskii in his now largely forgotten *The Condition of the Working Class in Russia.*[22] Many Orthodox priests, before and after emancipation, wrote highly negative appraisals of their rural parishioners, dwelling on the corrupting and ruinous vices, the terrible brutality of family life—what they sometimes termed the bestial relations between men and women—and the immorality, ignorance, and deep-rooted superstition so prevalent in peasant communities. Local officials and literate members of provincial society proved no less negative in their assessments.[23]

One widely shared perception of rural life in 1864 and afterward was that of moral decay and disorder, of growing disrespect for the law, of a population in dire need of renewed supervision as well as education and general enlightenment. This was particularly the viewpoint of officials and administrators who dealt most directly with the peasantry, although they were by no means the sole propagators of that perspective. Nonofficial conservative and traditionalist publicists also called for renewed deference toward the authorities and spoke of the necessity to buttress and protect village society by reimposing strong, paternal authority that peasants would fear and obey. It is not surprising that those who recently lost their nearly absolute power over the rural population should view the postemancipation countryside in such a negative light. Yet similar opinions could be heard not only from former serfowners, rural police, and government ministers but also from the press and the broader sphere of educated society, where news of emancipation had initially been greeted enthusiastically. Liberals and reformers believed the problem to be the emancipation settlement itself. It had freed the peasants but cut them off from the rest of society, governed by a separate body of law and restrictions that perpetuated their underdevelopment by limiting their rights and preventing their integration into society as full citizens.[24] Commentaries on the condition of the countryside between the 1860s and 1890s found much the same causes of rural crime and disorder as had been

22. V. V. Bervi-Flerovskii, *Polozhenie rabochego klassa v Rossii* (SPb, 1869).

23. For a selection of views, see A. V. Selivanov, "O merakh protiv narodnoi bednosti," GARO, f. 869, op. 1, d. 777 (1872), ll. 24–28; V. N. Nazar'ev, "Sovremennaia glush'. Iz vospominanii mirovogo sud'i," *VE*, no. 2 (1872), 604–36; no. 3, 131–81; "Pechal'nye iavleniia v domashnem krest'ianskom bytu i otnosheniia k nim prikhodskikh sviashchennikov," *RSP,* no. 13 (1879), 342–48; N. M. Astyrev, "S sil'nym ne boris'! Iz pamiatnoi knizhki byvshego volostnogo pisaria," *VE,* no. 2 (1886), 508–52; L. Bezrodnyi, *Ob upadke chuvstva zakonnosti v narode* (SPb, 1892); P. I. Novgorodtsev, *Krizis sovremennogo pravosoznaniia* (Moscow, 1909).

24. For example, V. P. Meshcherskii, *Ocherki nyneshnei obshchestvennoi zhizni v Rossii,* vol. 1: *Pis'ma iz Srednikh Veliko-Rossiiskikh gubernii za 1867 god* (SPb, 1868); N. Selivanov, "Brodiagi, prazdnoshataiushchiesia i nishchie," *VestP,* no. 3 (1884), 73–90; no. 4, 77–90; V. D. Kuz'min-Karavaev, "Pravovye nuzhdy derevni," *Pravo,* no. 15 (1903), 1073–83; no. 16, 1154–61; no. 17, 1209–16; S. N. Prokopovich, *Mestnye liudi o nuzhdakh Rossii* (SPb, 1904); N. M. Druzhinin, *Russkaia derevnia na perelome 1861–1880 gg.* (Moscow, 1978), 25–28.

noted in 1864 and even earlier, and these were reinforced by a number of government commissions that gathered information on the workings or deficiencies of peasant institutions and the conditions of village life.[25]

Writers of all political leanings retreated time and again to the ready explanation of cultural deficiency when pronouncing upon the negative aspects of rural life. The anonymous author of *Sketches of Peasant Life* (1880) declared that "there is more immorality than honesty in the countryside, the causes of which, of course, are underdevelopment, illiteracy, bad examples, bad companionship, disrespect toward the priest, and laziness toward the divine liturgy."[26] In 1888 the ethnographer and jurist A. A. Titov likewise saw the primary reasons for a peasant's turn to crime as poor upbringing, bad examples set by parents, poverty, idiocy, and "an unfortunate encounter with passion." Into this causal hodgepodge he also tossed the by-then popular factor of heredity, bringing the harsh, unforgiving gaze of social Darwinism to bear on his subjects. Some families in the village examined by Titov "are known for their criminal inclination that stretches back to their grandfather or great-grandfather—that is, the venom of criminality is passed on imperceptibly by inheritance."[27]

This notion of cultural impoverishment served a wide range of purposes, which helps to explain its popularity among persons whose views on most burning issues of their day were often diametrically opposed. For the intelligentsia it proved a useful tool with which to bludgeon the autocracy or a specific branch of government deemed responsible for the peasantry's continued plight. Conservatives used peasant backwardness to promote their argument that villagers had no understanding or respect for the law and were as yet unable to govern themselves. Therefore they required direct tutelage from above as well as stricter measures of law enforcement and punishment by police or judicial authorities.

Others, among them many leading jurists and educators, felt that in addition to schools, the newly reformed court system could, over time, educate villagers about the law by drawing them into the judicial process

25. George L. Yaney, *The Systematization of Russian Government: Social Evolution in the Domestic Administration of Imperial Russia 1711–1905* (Urbana, Ill.,1973); Yaney, *The Urge to Mobilize: Agrarian Reform in Russia, 1861–1930* (Urbana, Ill., 1982); James I. Mandel, "Paternalistic Authority in the Russian Countryside, 1856–1906" (Ph.D. diss., Columbia University, 1978); Wcislo, *Reforming Rural Russia*. Materials assembled on *volost'* court practice in the early 1870s by the Liuboshchinskii Commission, or those gathered a decade later by the Kakhanov Commission concerning peasant administration, for example, provided rich facts for radicals, liberals, and conservatives alike to support their differing analyses of peasant society and administration.

26. *Ocherki krest'ianskoi zhizni* (Moscow, 1880), 25.

27. A. A. Titov, *Iuridicheskie obychai sela Nikola-Perevoz, Suslovskoi volosti, Rostovskogo uezda* (Iaroslavl', 1888), 94.

through litigation or by serving as jurors in the new circuit courts. Rural justices of the peace were, in fact, instructed to teach peasants the law, although they should also acquaint themselves with local customs in order to win the villagers' trust and respect.[28] The court, according to one writer, "is not only a place where each finds satisfaction of his criminal or civil claims; it is also a school for adults where peasants learn about the law and justice, and hear opinions and decisions *about which they themselves would never think.*" City folk had many means to expand their horizons, but "peasants have none: they have the tavern, where people only drink and become disorderly; they have the school, though not everywhere . . . and they have the court." Indeed, at least some of the framers of the 1864 judicial reforms had conceived of courts as educational bodies that would serve to enlighten the lower classes, and supporters of this view propagated it long thereafter.[29]

Although the tsarist government did not disagree that popular education and enlightenment, properly regulated, should be supported as a means of fostering respect for the law, its overriding concern was maintaining public order in village communities and ensuring an uninterrupted flow of tax revenues from the countryside. The state's underdeveloped administrative structure outside major towns and cities, however, made this task difficult at best. Lacking a coherent district-level administration and a real or trustworthy government presence at the township or village levels, the MVD relied primarily upon its provincial governors and their local police to enforce the law, supervise tax collection, and perform a host of other duties.[30]

Furthermore, as William Wagner has recently stressed, the autocracy refused to permit the judicial reforms to place limits on its absolute power and remained committed to a traditional vision of legal paternalism exercised through personalized authority.[31] What did this mean for law and order as reports flowed from the provinces with worrisome news of growing crime and peasant hostility to the state's local agents? Suspicious of its own newly

28. I. M. Tiutriumov, "Ob usloviiakh primeneniia mirovymi sud'iami mestnykh obychaev pri razreshenii grazhdanskikh del," *RusRech'*, no. 3 (1881), 58–74. Also published in *ZhGUP*, no. 4 (1881), 70–85.

29. Ivan Sokolovskii, "Sudebnaia pravda dlia krest'ian," *RusM*, no. 7 (1899), 218. Italics are mine. On the educational value of courts, see M. Kh. Petrulan, *Sel'skaia zhizn' v proshlom i nastoiashem, v iuridicheskom i obshchestvenno-kul'turnom otnoshenii* (Vil'no, 1894), 9–10; M. Plotnikov, "Obshchestvenno-vospitatel'noe znachenie suda," *Obrazovanie*, no. 12 (1896), 20–32; A. A. Leont'ev, *Krest'ianskoe pravo. Sistematicheskoe izlozhenie osobennostei zakonodatel'stva o krest'ianakh* (SPb, 1909), 115–16.

30. Richard G. Robbins, Jr., *The Tsar's Viceroys: Russian Provincial Governors in the Last Years of the Empire* (Ithaca, 1987), 183–99.

31. William G. Wagner, *Marriage, Property and Law in Late Imperial Russia* (Oxford, 1994), 379–81.

created judicial institutions, the state sought to meet these challenges much as it had in the past, by relying on already overburdened provincial officials and police. Yet without a substantial augmentation of their resources, traditional rural authorities simply could not keep up with the increased demands placed upon them. Instead, they focused their limited energies on criminal activities deemed most dangerous and disruptive. This would be particularly true after 1900, when there was a very real breakdown of order throughout the country. Rarely daring to take the initiative, however, local authorities usually waited for new directives from the MVD that would shift their attention from one sphere of concern to another. The results were, at times, peculiar indeed. In 1916, for instance, with Russia's armies being bled white by their third year of warfare and with discontent and disorders mounting on the home front, provincial governors received an urgent MVD circular concerning the spread of gambling among peasants and the ruinous losses and abuses accompanying such a pastime. Reminding governors that the police should strictly observe that illegal games of chance not take place and that gatherings for such purposes should be dispersed, the MVD turned police attention from its previous crisis over rural hooliganism to the task of seeking out and closing down card games.[32]

There was, however, one important aspect of "cultural underdevelopment" that made it a useful construct for both state and peasantry in negotiating the hostilities that so often lay just below the surface of their interactions. If peasants perpetrated crimes out of ignorance and superstition or because they had been tempted into vice and immorality, they could be excused from full culpability before a paternal criminal law that allowed for mitigation of punishment in such circumstances. This fact the peasants knew well and, as their testimony before police, judicial investigators, and courts shows, they took advantage of the law's patriarchal forgiveness of their "backwardness." Dissimulation had functioned as an effective defense from state law and retribution in the past, and for many rural criminal defendants it did so after emancipation as well. The autocracy's continued practice of granting clemency through periodic imperial manifestos also helped to preserve the functional value of backwardness, while stressing the paternal magnanimity of an understanding tsar.[33] "Ignorance," in short, was

32. GARO, f. 695, op. 26, sv. 277, d. 32, ll. 1–1050b. From a more practical perspective, of course, losing money at cards could lead one into tax arrears.

33. The impact of imperial clemency varied greatly from year to year. In 1841, for example, 27.8 percent of all criminal defendants received pardons. Five years later only 1.7 percent were pardoned, and in 1866, 2.8 percent benefited from an imperial manifesto. *Otchety*, vols. 10, 15, 35. Such data were not included in publications on reformed courts, but the continued use of pardons can be seen from court documents and published discussions. See *SZU*, part 1: *Ulozhenie o nakazaniiakh ugolovnykh i ispravitel'nykh* (SPb, 1885), 34, art. 167.

an historically tested weapon of the weak commonly deployed in the other-wise unequal contests between peasant and state authority—a winking game of sorts that could be used to the mutual advantage of each side.

For the state, the presumed ignorance of its subjects was a protective device from what it would otherwise have been forced to interpret as open disobedience, resistance, or outright rejection of its laws. Cultural under-development thus functioned as a safety valve, much as did the peasant and state-supported myth of "naive monarchism" and the "benevolent tsar."[34] It allowed authorities to mitigate punishments under such coded terms as the peasants' "lack of understanding," "ignorance of the law," "terrible super-stition," and, as formulated in hundreds of judicial decisions, "the accused's extreme backwardness." Viewed in this light, assaults on noble estates, ille-gal cutting in state forests, and resistance to police agents during their tax-collecting rounds could all be reworked into far less threatening acts. The palliative of ignorance also performed the highly practical function of al-lowing a wide range of crimes committed within village communities to be classified as petty misdemeanors and tried before *volost'* rather than state courts. Property offenses are an excellent example, for the public transcript of educated society and officialdom alike posited that peasants had little or no understanding of the concept of private property. Therefore they looked upon theft leniently, this text read, and to bring such offenses before higher courts for harsh punishment would be unfair to a population sunk in igno-rance. On the practical side, such thinking allowed the government to keep its courts from being swamped by tens of thousands of theft cases each year. As we shall see, even with this system in place, higher courts would never-theless find it difficult to cope with their growing case loads by the 1890s. Lastly, if peasants did not look upon property crime as a serious offense, then rural police could focus on matters of greater concern to the state while village communities policed petty infractions committed by their members. Given the inadequate police forces at the government's disposal and their essential role as state fiscal agents, any lessening of the law enforcement bur-den served in the short term to relieve an otherwise serious need for aug-menting these forces of order with an expenditure of scarce resources.

## FORCES OF ORDER? LAW ENFORCEMENT AND THE POLICE

By far the greatest stumbling block to the maintenance of rural law and order was the state's lack of an effective police force. Like most of Europe, Russia only created its first regular rural police in the second quarter of the nineteenth century, and at the start of the 1900s that force remained rudi-

34. Daniel Field, *Rebels in the Name of the Tsar* (Boston, 1976).

mentary at best. Understaffed, underpaid, and for the most part untrained, it proved incapable of adequately policing the countryside throughout the postemancipation era.[35] This predicament is particularly important given a rising crescendo of complaints from villagers across the empire who felt, for the most part, unprotected and at the mercy of criminals because of police inefficiency, corruption, or simple neglect. But many in educated society and in government also believed that the growth of crime would only continue unless the rural police was reformed and enlarged.

To indicate the problem's scope, in 1857 the MVD employed 244 policemen to oversee a population of over 950,000 in the central industrial province of Iaroslavl', 194 (80 percent) of whom were stationed in towns and cities. In rural areas, each district commandant (*ispravnik*) had only two captains (sing.: *stanovoi pristav*) and one or two other officers to assist him.[36] By 1900, the Department of Police counted 47,866 officers for an empire of nearly 127 million, including the force of constables (*uriadniki*) introduced in 1878 to assist police captains. In effect, as historian Neil Weissman has argued, primary responsibility for regular law enforcement "remained where it had been placed at the time of emancipation some four decades earlier, in the hands of the peasantry."[37] Finally, the creation in 1903 of a new force of 40,000 mounted rural guards (*strazhniki*) marked "the first serious attempt by the tsarist state to establish a direct presence in the village." Yet shortly after its formation, this force was deployed to suppress peasant uprisings during the 1905–1907 agrarian revolution and therefore performed few regular policing functions.[38]

35. There is still no study available on the regular police in tsarist Russia, even though historians have paid inordinate attention to the political police. For background, see I. T. Tarasov, "Istoriia russkoi politsii i otnosheniia ee k iustitsii," *IuV,* no. 2 (1884), 177–212; no. 3, 383–411; no. 4, 551–74; no. 11, 412–45. On Europe, see David H. Bayley, "The Police and Political Development in Europe," in Charles Tilly, ed., *The Formation of National States in Western Europe* (Princeton, 1975), 328–79.

36. Robert J. Abbott, "Police Reform in the Russian Province of Iaroslavl, 1856–1876," *SR* 32, 2 (1973), 293.

37. Neil B. Weissman, *Reform in Tsarist Russia: The State Bureaucracy and Local Government, 1900–1914* (New Brunswick, N.J., 1981), 11, 23–24; Weissman, "Regular Police in Tsarist Russia, 1900–1914," *RR* 44, no. 1 (1985), 47, 49–50. See also V. K. Antsiferov, "Uriadnik i institut sel'skoi politsii," *ZhGUP,* no. 1 (1881), 45–66; I. T. Tarasov, "Reformy i politsiia," *IuV,* no. 3 (1885), 473–84; Tarasov, "Reforma russkoi politsii," *IuV,* no. 6–7 (1885), 222–40; no. 8, 612–57; no. 9, 22–60; no. 11, 394–409. On the authority and duties of constables, see N. I. Aref, comp., *Instruktsiia politseiskim uriadnikam* (SPb, 1894); A. P. Romanovskii, comp., *Sistematicheskoe rukovodstvo dlia politseiskikh uriadnikov,* 2nd ed. (Kishinev, 1895); V. P. Urusov, comp., *Politseiskii uriadnik: sbornik svedenii, neobkhodimykh dlia nizshikh chinov uezdnoi politsii,* 2nd ed. (Moscow, 1895); GARO, f. 1298, op. 1, sv. 3, dd. 64–66 (1863).

38. Weissman, "Regular Police," 50, 51; *Sprævka o chislennom sostavie politsii otdel'nykh mestnostei 50-ti gubernii imperii* (N.p., 1913); L. Dashkevich, "Sel'skaia politseiskaia strazha," *VE,* no. 1 (1904), 373–77.

A closer look at Riazan' province reveals these shortcomings even more sharply. In 1888 Riazan' district counted four captains and eleven constables to police a territory of 3,719 square kilometers and a population of 174,790, or an average of one constable per 15,890 inhabitants. This distribution proved even less favorable in more rural parts of the province like Kasimov district, where 4,743 square kilometers and 150,908 inhabitants were policed by three captains and ten constables. In seven out of twelve districts for which data remain, sixteen captains and sixty constables were responsible for law enforcement among a population of 965,765 dispersed throughout 139 townships—a ratio of 1 : 16,096 for constables, or 1 : 12,707 if captains are included.[39] When the governor queried his district commandants that year concerning the state of their forces, all replied that their greatest need was for additional officers and a reduction in the size of precincts (*uchastki*). Ranenburg's district commandant pointed out that each constable required between three and five days to patrol his precinct. Under such conditions, police could rarely apprehend criminals simply because it took them so long to arrive at the scene and conduct an investigation. The growth of railroads had placed even greater burdens on this district's small force, since its duties included patrolling train stations as well as major roads. Worse, the introduction of a state liquor monopoly in 1894 opened a vast new area of criminal activity in the form of bootlegging, which officers were powerless to control because of their small number.[40] Some numerical improvements were made during the next twenty years. In 1913, Riazan''s rural police force counted 58 captains and 251 constables, but this increase was largely negated by population growth, which had swelled the number of rural inhabitants to over 2 million.[41]

The government exacerbated the difficulties of policing by demanding that its officers perform a host of administrative functions—particularly tax collection—which left little time for their regular duties. In 1872, law enforcement accounted for roughly half of all police duties in Iaroslavl' province; 12.5 percent of officers' time was spent at tax collection and another 30 percent carrying out services for government ministries and commissions.[42] Thirty years later the empire's police force remained similarly burdened. Weissman notes that in 1908 alone it brought in over 22 million

39. GARO, f. 5, st. 3, op. 4, d. 2539, ll. 93–99. See also A. N. B—skii, "K voprosu o reforme sel'skoi politsii," *VestP,* no. 2 (1901), 78. Concerning the composition of constables and rapid turnover in their ranks, see GARO, f. 4, op. 876, sv. 1, dd. 1–6, 14, 17–18, 23.

40. GARO, f. 5, st. 3, op. 4, d. 2539, ll. 16–190b. On the seriousness of the bootlegging problem, see GARO, f 5, st. 1, op. 2, d. 2794 (1907), ll. 1–103.

41. *Spravka o chislennom sostavie politsii.*

42. Abbott, "Police Reform," 298. See also "Reforma uriadnikov," *Nedelia,* no. 39 (1887), 1237–38.

rubles in tax arrears, a fact that underscores the continued underdevelopment of state administration. Such service tasks proved particularly distractive "at a time when tsarist police were encountering increasing challenges in fulfilling their primary function of controlling deviance," and they did little to alter the population's view that police were nothing more than intrusive, often brutal government agents concerned primarily if not exclusively with extracting taxes from poor peasants.[43]

Peasants themselves filled the lowest ranks of rural law enforcement. Each year, villagers elected local policemen known as "tenners" (*desiatskie*) and "hundreders" (*sotskie*), whose primary charge consisted of overseeing and maintaining order in their communities, protecting state, community, and private property, and carrying out all orders of village and *volost'* officials as well as the regular police. Hundreders, who at least by law commanded the more numerous tenners, owed direct responsibility to the police captain for whom they served as messengers or errand runners.[44] Apart from their numerous administrative assignments, which by most reports they performed grudgingly and poorly, tenners and hundreders were instructed to watch out for criminals. "The moment it becomes known that thieves, military deserters, escapees from exile, and similar persons have appeared in their locality," the law stipulated, they were to report within one day to higher authorities. In particular, they should seize criminals and ensure that they did not flee and "take care that the inhabitants do not commit mob beatings [*samosud*] of the suspect."[45] In 1888 the 4,633 rural communities of Riazan' province counted 4,414 tenners and 960 hundreders, who were expected to perform all of these duties and more while earning for the year, on average, 3.35 and 32.66 rubles, respectively.[46] Although perhaps capable of assisting village elders to maintain general order within their own village, accompany prisoners to the *volost'* jail, and deliver messages, these elected policemen could do little about serious crime like arson, robbery, and horsetheft, often fearing for their safety or even their lives if they actu-

43. Weissman, "Regular Police," 57; N. P. Eroshkin, *Istoriia gosudarstvennykh uchrezhdenii dorevoliutsionnoi Rossii* (Moscow, 1983), 293; Mandel, "Paternalistic Authority," 99.

44. GARF, f. 586, op. 1, d. 118 (Riazan' province), l. 25; d. 120 (Smolensk province), l. 18; V. Vinogradov, comp., *Volostnoe pravlenie, Volostnoe Sud i ikh deloproizvodstvo* (SPb, 1904), 208–32; N. N. Blinov, comp., *Sel'skaia obshchestvennaia sluzhba* (SPb, 1882), 113–26; Blinov, *Tolkovaia knizhka o sel'skom upravlenii*, no. 5 (Moscow, 1888); N. K. Brzhevskii, *Natural'nye povinnosti krest'ian i mirskie sbory* (SPb, 1906), 69–70. Among their duties, tenners and hundreders were to be present at all public gatherings, markets, and bazaars, ensure that no merchants cheated customers or sold illegal goods, check weights and measures, protect against fires, and regularly inspect stoves and chimneys in peasant homes.

45. Blinov, *Sel'skaia sluzhba*, 118.

46. GARO, f. 5, st. 3, op. 4, d. 2503, l. 3. See also "Sel'skaia politsiia na gorodskoi lad," *Nedelia*, no. 20 (1871), 658–59.

ally dared to arrest a suspect. At best tenners performed routine village duties and carried out the elder's orders. At worst they disobeyed their superiors, cooperated with criminal gangs, and committed crimes themselves.[47]

In practice virtually all initiative for everyday law enforcement rested with the village, since routine patrolling on the part of regular police was impossible. Police captains, for instance, only took action after receiving a written report from a peasant hundreder or a formal complaint from a crime victim. Such information might sit for some time because captains were frequently away from their place of residence, and given the cost of having a formal complaint composed, many peasants simply did not report crimes. Instead, when significant offenses like horsetheft occurred, victims more often than not tried to solve and punish the crime themselves, or to gather evidence that might be passed on to the judicial investigator rather than the police.[48] Concerned above all with protecting their own communities and property but receiving little if any help from police officials, peasants proved, reasonably enough, uncooperative when captains or constables demanded assistance in matters of greater importance to authorities. As one historian has noted, "Peasants were much more eager to hunt down and punish those who had injured them, particularly arsonists and horsethieves, rather than those who had damaged state or [noble] interests by . . . cutting down trees in state-owned forests, squatting on privately owned land, or selling liquor without a license."[49]

If Russians of all classes agreed upon anything concerning law and order, it was that the police were not up to their tasks. This proved especially true from the 1890s on, when crime of all sorts appeared to be on the rise throughout the countryside. Nowhere did that opinion find stronger expression than among peasants. When questioned by ethnographers during the late 1890s, usually restrained village respondents sometimes spoke with open contempt of the police. Peasant complaints about criminality and their lack of protection from theft, robbery, arson, and other dangers also

47. See, e.g., GARO, f. 640, op. 54, sv. 31, d. 80; ibid., f. 5, st. 3, op. 4, dd. 3207, 4774; GARF, f. 586, op. 1, d. 118, l. 27.

48. K. A., "Nabliudeniia i zametki ob usloviiakh sledstvennoi deiatel'nosti v provintsii," *SudZh*, no. 5 (1873), 19. As this discussion makes clear, the 1860 introduction of independent judicial investigators led directly to conflict with police commandants, who considered themselves (and, in practice, were) the highest local organ of administrative authority, and who previously had served investigative functions for the criminal courts. Hence the new investigators' demands for information, assistance, and cooperation frequently met with inaction on the part of district police. See also D. Antsiferov, "Nabliudeniia nad ugolovnoi praktikoi nashei provintsial'noi mirovoi iustitsii," *IuV*, no. 1 (1883), 126; A. F. Koni, "Sudebnye sledovateli," in *Sobranie sochinenii*, vol. 1 (Moscow, 1966), 110–38; M. G. Korotkikh, *Sudebnaia reforma 1864 goda v Rossii (sushchnost' i sotsial'no-pravovoi mekhanizm formirovaniia)* (Voronezh, 1994) 92–105; *Razvitie russkogo prava vo vtoroi polovine XIX–nachale XX veka* (Moscow, 1997), 112-14.

49. Mandel, "Paternalistic Authority," 120.

contain veiled or forthright criticism of police inaction. Commandants and captains almost never traveled to villages under their jurisdictions, and on those occasions when they did appear, they came only to oversee tax collections or recruit musters. Villagers regularly spoke of police corruption (which could extend to outright extortion), rudeness, abuse of authority, and brutality. They had least respect for or trust in the rural constables, who, as an 1898 report from Smolensk province noted, accepted all bribes offered to them and pandered to criminals.[50] More often than not complaints against police wrongdoing came to naught. A woman from the Riazan' village of Sarai lodged a protest with the governor in 1907 when 100 rubles went missing after a search of her home by a police captain and members of the newly established rural guards. Despite an investigation of her charges (conducted by the precinct commandant), the case was dismissed because of lack of evidence and the plaintiff's "bad reputation."[51]

Or consider another incident that same year in Troitsa village—one that would later lead to an assault by villagers against police officers and thereby enter the chronicles of the 1905–1907 revolution. On February 15, the captain of the second precinct, together with one of his constables, the steward, and the distiller of a local landowner, came to the home of one peasant, where they began drinking. When they were already inebriated, the peasant's wife sent for several young women to dance for "the officials." A wild party ensued, during which the women's husbands showed up demanding that their wives stop this shameful activity and return home. In response, the constable ordered them to leave and threatened them with his pistol if they did not obey. From that moment on, young village men sought an opportune moment to take revenge upon the officers involved and did so during Carnival, when this constable appeared alone at the local market. There a crowd surrounded him and started singing a song (obviously composed with this occasion in mind) in which the police captain "threatens us with prison and steals our wives." After extricating himself from the crowd, the frightened and insulted officer reported to his captain that peasant youths at the bazaar had been singing "revolutionary songs." The captain arrived several days later with a detachment of police guards to arrest the culprits.[52]

50. GARF, f. 586, op. 1, d. 120, l. 86.

51. GARO, f. 5, st. 3, op. 4, d. 4777, ll. 1–10. Compare similar attitudes toward police in rural settings such as Missouri during the 1860s and 1870s, or nineteenth-century England and Wales. David Thelen, *Paths of Resistance: Tradition and Dignity in Industrializing Missouri* (New York, 1986), 106–8; Douglas Hay, "Crime and Justice in Eighteenth- and Nineteenth-Century England," in Norval Morris and Michael Tonry, eds., *Crime and Justice: An Annual Review of Research* (Chicago, 1980), esp. 58–64; David Jones, "Rural Crime and Protest in the Victorian Era," in G. E. Mingay, ed., *The Unquiet Countryside* (London, 1989), 112–13; Jones, *Rebecca's Children: A Study of Rural Society, Crime, and Protest* (Oxford, 1989), 153–54.

52. GARO, f. 5, st. 3, op. 4, d. 4517, ll. 3–11.

The rural police thus served as a force of order mainly in extreme circumstances such as assaults upon noble or state property, local revolts, or rebellion. Otherwise, at least from the village perspective, they appeared among the rural population primarily as tax collectors who could have a devastating impact on individuals and even entire communities by ordering peasant property auctioned off to pay arrears. Despite numerous government directives that essential property such as farming equipment should never be sold for taxes, the practice did not end until tax policy itself was changed early in the twentieth century.[53] The hostility of the lower classes to the police in much of nineteenth-century Europe was even greater among Russian peasants not only because police were inattentive to ordinary crimes but also because of the intrusive and often punitive nature of their fiscal duties.

## RURAL JUSTICE AND THE NEW LEGAL ORDER

Perhaps the most important of rural Russia's postreform institutions was the court system, which marked the peasantry's legal separateness from other classes and which, in all of its peculiarity, closely mirrored prevailing elite opinions about peasant life. Both past and recent assessments have misunderstood or misrepresented the origins, complexity, organization, functions, and limitations of this judicial structure, the competence and often confused jurisdictions of its administrative organs and courts, and even the bodies of law under which the latter operated. The great majority of Russians who wrote about local justice spoke as though the rural population prior to emancipation had no experience with either courts or laws. With rare exceptions, historians, too, have overlooked the important predecessors of postreform rural courts. Instead they have treated the class courts created for peasants in 1861 as something entirely new and unique to the countryside, ignoring the highly litigious nature of village society under serfdom and the numerous judicial institutions—both official and unofficial—to which peasants had recourse.[54] Indeed, one could easily assume from such studies that neither seigneurial serfs nor state peasants ever litigated before courts and, as numerous contemporaries argued throughout the imperial period, had no knowledge of the law. Historians also accept

53. Ibid., st. 1, op. 2, d. 1652 (1879), ll. 1–2. For examples of this policy in practice, see ibid., f. 697, op. 1, sv. 6, d. 242; sv. 7, d. 275; f. 709, op. 1, sv. 2, d. 63; f. 721, op. 14, sv. 18, dd. 37, 55; f. 1298, op. 1, sv. 3, dd. 64–66; S. Khrulev, "Mysli provintsiala o provintsii," *ZhGUP,* no. 1 (1889), 66–70.

54. The litigious character of pre-emancipation villagers has been well documented by Soviet historians, although it still awaits its own study. C. A. Frierson, "Rural Justice in Public Opinion: The Volost' Court Debate, 1861–1912," *SEER* 64, no. 4 (1986), 526–45, treats the debates that swirled around rural judicial institutions.

that local justice was based upon and operated according to certain norms of customary law, although this notion has never been defined in any writings to date.[55]

The 1864 judicial reform statutes separated administration from justice, created a bar, introduced a simplified court system and trial by jury, and appointed judges who could only be removed from office for misconduct. Yet in contrast to the principles of judicial independence that underlay the reforms of 1864, rural justice remained linked to administration and police throughout our period. The 1861 emancipation legislation had already established *volost'* courts (corresponding to the lowest unit of rural administration over which the state maintained some form of supervision) to try petty offenses and hear civil suits between peasants registered within the same township. They were to serve as the lowest level of justice in the countryside. As class courts limited before 1889 to the peasant population and administered through the MVD rather than the Ministry of Justice, they stood apart from the reformed judicial system to which all other classes turned.[56]

Peasants, however—and especially state peasants—found little new in these courts apart from organizational changes and unsuccessful efforts to insulate them from local influences and corruption by placing them outside and above the village administration at the township level. Officially sanctioned judicial institutions, together with various local moots, had for centuries served as arenas of peasant litigation and dispute settlement. The legal scholar A. Kistiakovskii noted that as early as the reigns of Ivan III (1462–1505) and Ivan IV (1533–1584), the village commune served as the primary organ of local justice with broad jurisdiction and the right to impose penalties up to and including sentences of death, without participation by outside officials. Villagers selected judges (*sudnye muzhi*) from

55. For examples of such views, see Peter Czap, Jr., "Peasant Class Courts and Peasant Customary Justice in Russia, 1861–1912," *JSH* 1, no. 2 (1967), 149–78; Moshe Lewin, "Customary Law and Russian Rural Society in the Post Reform Era," *RR* 44, no. 1 (1985), 1–19; Michael Confino, "Russian Customary Law and the Study of Peasant Mentalites," *RR* 44, no. 1 (1985), 35–43; Laura Engelstein, *The Keys to Happiness: Sex and the Search for Modernity in Fin-de-Siècle Russia* (Ithaca, 1992), 25, 114–27; Jane Burbank, "A Question of Dignity: Peasant Legal Culture in Late Imperial Russia," *Continuity and Change* 10, no. 3 (1995), 391–404; Cathy A. Frierson, "'I Must Always Answer to the Law . . .' Rules and Responses in the Reformed *Volost'* Court," *SEER* 75, no. 2 (1997), 308–34.

56. Sofronenko, *Krest'ianskaia reforma*, 60–63. The contemporary literature on *volost'* courts is vast. An outstanding compilation of sources is E. I. Iakushkin, comp., *Obychnoe pravo. Materialy dlia bibliografii obychnogo prava*, 4 vols. (Iaroslavl', 1875–1909). For more recent treatments, see T. A. Tarabanova, "Volostnoi sud v Rossii v pervoe poreformennoe desiatiletie" (Ph.D. diss., Moscow State University, 1993); Corinne Gaudin, "Governing the Village: Peasant Culture and the Problem of Social Transformation in Russia, 1906–1914" (Ph.D. diss., University of Michigan, 1993), ch. 6.

among elders and other "good people."[57] In the second half of the eighteenth century, the government took measures to regularize rural courts and control widespread peasant efforts to litigate before higher state courts. Legislation from the Catherinian era (1762–1796) reflected this concern over the number of petty cases being tried by regular courts and spoke of putting a stop to such litigation by peasants "because of the ruin that this often causes them."[58] Therefore, between 1764 and 1797 a series of laws allowed nonseigneurial peasants to be judged by their own elected officials in each village. The *volost'* court traced its earliest predecessor to a 1797 reform dividing state settlements into townships, or *volosti,* each with an administration and chief who also served as judge and administered punishments in cases of petty disputes.[59] Among seigneurial serfs, most criminal offenders as well as civil litigants came before a communal court (*mirskii sud*) consisting of elected officials and elders, or the communal assembly (*skhod*)—decisions of which could be overruled by the estate steward.[60]

During Nicholas I's reign (1825–1855), Minister of State Domains P. D. Kiselev introduced a series of reforms between 1837 and 1841 that gave state peasants (roughly 45 percent of Russia's peasant population) new judicial institutions. Village courts (*sel'skie raspravy*) were created as courts of first instance for minor infractions and civil suits, while *volost'* courts (*volostnye raspravy*) served primarily as a second or appellate instance for cases heard at the village level. *Volost'* courts were staffed by elected judges and chaired by the *volost'* chief. Similarly, a village court consisted of two judges (*dobrosovestnye*) and the village elder, who was empowered to remove the other judges or even arrest them if necessary. Kiselev's legislation explained

57. A. Kistiakovskii, "Volostnye sudy, ikh istoriia, nastoiashchaia ikh praktika i nastoiashchee ikh polozhenie," in P. P. Chubinskii, ed., *Trudy etnografichesko-statisticheskoi ekspeditsii v zapadno-russkii krai* vol. 6 (SPb, 1872), 3–5.

58. Ibid., 7; E. Kartsev, "Sel'skoe pravosudie. Iz zhizni russkoi derevni," *VE,* no. 1 (1882), 319–21. The laws can be found in *PSZ,* vol. 16, no. 12075, March 5, 1764; vol. 19, no. 14133, March 5, 1774.

59. St. Cherniavskii, *Narodnyi sud* (Kamenets-Podol'sk, 1901), 10; M. I. Zarudnyi, *Zakony i zhizn'. Itogi issledovaniia krest'ianskikh sudov* (SPb, 1874), 48; Druzhinin, *Gosudarstvennye krest'iane,* 1:546–53; Kistiakovskii, "Volostnye sudy," 8–9. See also N. V. Kalachov, "O volostnykh i sel'skikh sudakh v drevnei i nyneshnei Rossii," *Sbornik gosudarstvennykh znanii,* no. 8 (1880), 128–48; D. Meichik, "Krest'ianskie sudy v starinu," *IV,* no. 3 (1880), 796–802; N. M. Kolmakov, "Staryi sud," *Russkaia starina,* no. 12 (1886), 511–14; K. Tur, "Narodnyi sud," *Nedelia,* no. 38 (1898), 1215–19.

60. L. S. Prokof'eva, *Krest'ianskaia obshchina v Rossii vo vtoroi polovine XVIII–pervoi polovine XIX v. (na materialakh votchin Sheremetevykh)* (Leningrad, 1981), 157–62; M. M. Bogoslovskii, *Zemskoe samoupravlenie na russkom severe v XVII v.,* vol. 1 (Moscow, 1909), 220. See also Edgar Melton, "Enlightened Seigneurialism and Its Dilemmas in Serf Russia, 1750–1830," *JMH* 62, no. 4 (1990), 675–708.

that participation by the elder was necessary "because of the still insufficient education of our peasants."[61] In a more practical sense, because *volost'* and village elders could be held accountable to higher authorities, their pres- ence on the courts gave at least a pretense of more effective local state con- trol. A rural judicial code (*Sel'skii Sudebnyi Ustav*) published in 1839 defined punishments to be imposed by the new courts, and with some modifications it would remain in use until 1917.[62] Although village courts were structured and regulated by the Ministry of State Domains, they differed little in prac- tice from the local moots that had long existed among seigneurial and state peasants.

For nearly a century prior to emancipation, then, peasants had recourse to officially sanctioned courts and institutions like the village assembly, which had always served judicial functions. Soviet historians and ethnogra- phers have convincingly demonstrated that state peasants and seigneurial serfs both made ready and regular use of the law to defend their interests.[63] Nor should we forget that, throughout the first half of the nineteenth cen- tury and earlier, higher criminal courts tried tens of thousands of villagers charged with serious offenses. The peasant of 1861, in short, was quite fa- miliar with courts and official law, a fact that should put to rest the often repeated and ahistorical suppositions that only after emancipation did peas- ants begin to engage in litigation or initiate interaction with the law. One of the unfortunate spinoffs from sociological theories of modernization, as Gareth Stedman Jones noted some time ago, is the historians' temptation to begin with something called "traditional society." They know a great deal about one period, Jones wrote, "which blurs into a relative ignorance of what came before and what came afterwards."[64] Whether we have, in fact, a "traditional" baseline against which to analyze Russia's postemancipation rural judicial structure (and other matters as well) and how that baseline is to be defined, understood, and temporally demarcated are questions that are commonly glossed over in historical writings about "change" during the nineteenth century. Rather, given the inordinate influence among Russian historians of binary categories drawn, whether consciously or not, from modernization theories, many have simply contented themselves with an

---

61. Druzhinin, *Gosudarstvennye krest'iane*, 1:555–72. In English, see Olga Crisp, "The State Peasants under Nicholas I," in Crisp, *Studies in the Russian Economy before 1914* (London, 1976), 73–95.

62. Druzhinin, *Gosudarstvennye krest'iane*, 1:575; Vinogradov, *Volostnoe pravlenie*, 233–48; E. Tikhonov, *Volostnoi sud i mirovoi sud'ia v krest'ianskikh seleniiakh* (Kovno, 1872).

63. On this point, see chapter 3.

64. Gareth Stedman Jones, "Class Expression versus Social Control? A Critique of Recent Trends in the Social History of 'Leisure,'" in Stanley Cohen and Andrew Scull, eds., *Social Con- trol in History and Sociology* (New York, 1983), 46.

idealized starting point upon which forces of change and transformation suddenly began to work sometime after the Great Reforms.[65]

Among its numerous complexities, Russia's 1861 emancipation entailed the replacement of serfowners' judicial authority with institutions presumed capable of administering local justice while assuring the state that rural order would not collapse. In a compromise reached by the legislation's framers, a class court was introduced at the *volost'* level consisting of four to twelve elected peasant judges empowered to try petty disputes between villagers. Judges were assisted by a hired clerk (*pisar'*) (frequently a nonpeasant, especially before the 1880s) whose duties included recording court decisions and explaining the law to illiterate judges and litigants.[66] Throughout the court's fifty-eight-year existence, various nonpeasant officials and local administrative organs supervised its activities with broad powers to order that cases be retried, appeals heard, and court decisions reversed; after 1889 land captains selected candidates for judgeships, approved elections of peasant judges, and could remove these judges from office. This system of "self-administration" governed the vast majority of the Russian population through procedures and laws separate from those applied to other classes. It also ensured that, unless peasants committed serious infractions or engaged in suits against nonpeasants, they were largely denied access to the regular system of justice.[67] All villagers, of course, still remained subject to state law as exercised by officials with both administrative and judicial powers. The *volost'* court thus represented a simple con-

65. On this problem, see Martin Chanock, *Law, Custom, and Social Order: The Colonial Experience in Malawi and Zambia* (New York, 1985),10; Sally Falk Moore, *Social Facts and Fabrications: "Customary" Law on Kilimanjaro, 1880–1980* (New York, 1986), 320–22. See also note 54.

66. Among many descriptions, analyses, and debates surrounding this court "of the people, for the people," see A. Pestrzhetskii, "O sude krest'ian, vyshedshikh iz krepostnoi zavisimosti," *ZhMIu,* no. 7 (1861), 3–30; F. Voroponov, "Poleznost' volostnogo suda," *Nedelia,* no. 23–24 (1872), 712–17; D. "Po voprosu o volostnykh sudakh (Zametki mirovogo posrednika)," *SudZh,* no. 3 (1873), 1–26; D. Mordovtsev, "Ne podozhdat'-li otnimat? (Po povodu predpolozhenii o preobrazovanii volostnykh sudov)," *Delo,* no. 11 (1875), 323–60; no. 12, 353–74; Vasilii Ivanov, "Krest'ianskii sud i formal'noe pravosudie," *RB,* no. 12 (1880), 39–52; Kartsev, "Sel'skoe pravosudie," no. 1 (1882), 305–35, no. 2, 755–73; A. A. Leont'ev, *Volostnoi sud i iuridicheskie obychai krest'ian* (SPb, 1895); M. Stival, "Narodnyi sud i narodnoe pravo," *SevV,* no. 12 (1896), 99–113.

67. A wave of public debate followed the introduction of land captains and reform of *volost'* courts in 1889. See, e.g., "Novyi volostnoi sud," *Nedelia,* no. 36 (1889), 1139–40; V. Baftalovskii, "Obzor mestnogo upravleniia i suda," *Russkoe obozrenie,* no. 5 (1895), 375–91; Leont'ev, *Volostnoi sud,* 67–87; N. S. Illarionov, "Sudebno-krest'ianskaia reforma Imperatora Aleksandra III-go i sviazannye s nei novye zadachi iuridicheskoi nauki i praktiki," *SudG,* no. 34 (1897), 3–4; N. Druzhinin, "Krest'ianskii sud v ego poslednem fazise," *Nabliudatel',* no. 2 (1892), 213–31; no. 3, 238–57; no. 4, 269–79; no. 5, 252–62; Druzhinin, "Preobrazovannyi volostnoi sud," in Druzhinin, *Iuridicheskoe polozhenie krest'ian* (SPb, 1897), 298–370; "Nedostatki volostnykh sudov," *Vestnik Iaroslavskogo zemstvo,* no. 27 (1906), 3–5; no. 30, 7–8.

cession to reality, as Francis Wcislo has rightly noted, "that would relieve overburdened local officials and imperial courts of adjudicating civil and criminal misdemeanors," but this did not mean that the state simply washed its hands of local justice.[68] Rather, its insistence on regulating the reformed *volost'* courts through officials beholden to the MVD, however haphazardly or poorly this task was actually performed, demonstrates that order and control remained uppermost among state concerns.

Cases before *volost'* courts could be tried either on the basis of law or "existing customs," although important and long ignored qualifications must be recognized here. To begin, custom's jurisdiction reached only into the sphere of civil law; as with justices of the peace, no criminal offenses could be legally decided by peasant judges on the basis of custom. Moreover, there are only two brief references to "custom" in the regulations on emancipation, and the term "customary law" never appears in this legislation. The complete article 38 stipulates that "in carrying out inheritance of property, peasants *are permitted* to be guided by their local customs," a right already belonging to village assemblies long before 1861.[69] Article 107, which has been most widely misinterpreted, issued the following instructions to peasant judges: "During the examination of suits within the *volost'* court itself, the judges, having heard out the litigants, will strive to reconcile them. . . . If the sides cannot reach a peaceful agreement, then the court decides the case either on the basis of transactions and obligations certified in the *volost'* administration office, if these were concluded between the disputants, or, in the absence of such transactions, on the basis of local customs and rules that are accepted in peasant life."[70]

68. Wcislo, *Reforming Rural Russia,* 30.

69. Sofronenko, *Krest'ianskaia reforma,* 47. To my knowledge, Olga Crisp ("Peasant Land Tenure and Civil Rights Implications before 1906," in Olga Crisp and Linda Edmondson, eds., *Civil Rights in Imperial Russia* [New York, 1989], 40) is the only historian who has recognized how narrow was the sphere to which the emancipation edicts limited custom. Indeed, she writes, "the very terms used [concerning custom], *dozvoliaetsia* ('it is permitted'), *ne vospreshchaetsia* ('it is not forbidden'), indicate that it was intended that the use of customary law be concessionary rather than obligatory."

70. Sofronenko, *Krest'ianskaia reforma,* 62; N. S. Illarionov, *Znachenie obychnogo prava v narodnom sude* (Khar'kov, 1893), 9–10. On discussions within the editorial commissions concerning customary law, see N. P. Semenov, *Osvobozhdenie krest'ian v tsarstvovanie Imperatora Aleksandra II,* vol. 1 (SPb, 1889), 345; vol. 3 (SPb, 1892), part 1, 338–39. For later views, see G., "Ob obychnom prave," *ZhMIu,* no. 8 (1866), 189–206; no. 10, 3–26; I. Orshanskii, "Narodnyi sud i narodnoe pravo (Po povodu voprosa o preobrazovanii volostnykh sudov)," *VestP,* no. 4 (1875), 140–223; no. 5, 60–142; A. I. Efimenko, "Odna iz nashikh narodnykh osobennostei," *Nedelia,* no. 3–5 (1876), 116–22; Efimenko, *Issledovaniia narodnoi zhizni,* part 1: *Obychnoe pravo* (Moscow, 1884); L., "Chto schitaet pravom nash narod," *RB,* no. 8 (1884), 260–72; A. V. Filippov, "Sovremennye zapisi obychnogo prava i ikh kharakternye osobennosti," *SevV,* no. 7 (1887), 45–63; A. Pakharnaev, *Zakon, obychai i volostnoi sud* (Perm, 1894); Leon'tev, *Volostnoi*

However imprecise this latter wording, the emancipation framers left no doubt as to the subordinate position that custom occupied, for no custom could be applied that contravened existing laws.[71] Custom was restricted to civil disputes of local interest, such as inheritance, domestic relations, and farming and land division practices, that is, to areas about which the state knew little and over which it had even less control. These remained areas of fundamental importance to the village community, of course, determining access to land and regulating kinship relations, but even such broad realms were allowed only provisional status that left them by no means off limits to administrative and legislative interference. Although unevenly and inconsistently applied, state law and administrative regulation stood as dominant forces in peasant life. This official, unequal relationship established between a largely unknown custom and a more tangible body of state law in 1861, like the larger structures of law and justice created during the reform era, bore a more than passing resemblance to modern colonial legal systems not merely in form but in content, context, and practice. As Sally Falk Moore has succinctly described the colonial vision of law and courts in twentieth-century British Tanganyika, "Local courts were to be run by Africans and would apply African 'customary law' but were to do so in a manner consistent with basic British legal principles and the objectives of colonial administration." The text, in other words, "says repeatedly that Africans are best qualified to know and handle their own business and should do it according to their own rules. The subtext says that the colonial government knows best, and must reserve the power to intervene when Africans fail to deliver 'justice.' The voice that gives legitimacy to African ways speaks again and takes back that recognition by giving it only conditionally."[72] By legislating a restricted place for local customs that emphasized their asymmetri-

---

*sud,* ch. 5; N., "Narodnye iuridicheskie obychai po ukazaniiam sudebnoi praktiki," in S. V. Pakhman, ed., *SbNIuO,* vol. 2 (SPb, 1900), 301–37; A. A. Bashmakov, "Otnoshenie suda k obychaiu po novomu proektu ustava grazhdanskogo sudoproizvodstva," *VestP,* no. 2 (1901), 1–26; Bashmakov, *Ocherki prava rodovogo, nasledstvennogo, i obychnogo* (SPb, 1911); P. N. Obninskii, "Oproshchennoe sudogovorenie," in Obninskii, *Sbornik statei* (SPb, 1914), 113–41.

71. This would be confirmed by rulings of the Governing Senate's Cassational Department in 1869 (no. 175) and 1870 (no. 380). Pakharnaev, *Zakon, obychai i volostnoi sud,* 30; I. P. Kupchinov, *Krest'ianskoe samoupravlenie: ocherk zakonov, blizkikh k krest'ianskoi zhizni,* 2nd ed. (Moscow, 1905), 94–95.

72. Sally Falk Moore, "Treating Law as Knowledge: Telling Colonial Officers What to Say to Africans about Running 'Their Own' Native Courts," *LSR* 26, no. 1 (1992), 12, 24. See also Moore, *Law as Process: An Anthropological Perspective* (London, 1978), 13–22; J. A. Barnes, "The Politics of Law," in Mary Douglas and Phyllis M. Kaberry, eds., *Man in Africa* (London, 1969), 99–118; Sandra B. Burman and Barbara E. Harrell-Bond, eds., *The Imposition of Law* (New York, 1979); Clifford Geertz, *Local Knowledge: Further Essays in Interpretive Anthropology* (New York, 1983), 167–234.

cal relationship to law, the Russian government (whether wittingly or not) also stressed the archaism of custom, folklorizing it and placing it at the distant end of an evolutionary scale while increasing the gap "between official government conceptions and the realities of local affairs."[73]

As for contemporary champions of "customary law" who believed that it formed a model of society through which they could come to know the peasantry, their very notion of customary law as representing what anthropologists would more properly term "indigenous law" remains problematic, as some critics at the time rightly noted. Customary law is most commonly defined as the outcome of historical struggles between village elites and their superiors or owners. Far from being a survival of some misty traditional past, custom is "continually renegotiated as conditions change"; hence the very content of customary rules "reflects political and economic circumstances in which they are negotiated."[74] This negotiation process and its outcomes in the Russian case remain largely unknown as we await detailed local studies; however, the historical collusion between village elders and estate regimes or government agents to control labor and maintain the authority of household heads should suffice as a reminder that custom itself did not mean the same thing to all. That this latter group continued to define, change, and recreate local customs after emancipation is clear enough from the complaints of those who did not benefit from "tradition" to the extent that ruling elders did. Disgruntled villagers often spoke disparagingly of custom: "Custom—that's vodka or the will of the elders [*bol'shaki*]." Elders and the wealthy, peasants noted, had direct access to the sources of custom and justice through their participation in the village assembly and relations with judges, priests, and other figures of authority. They not only could offer more substantial bribes, if necessary, but gained even greater influence through their social networks and connections.[75]

73. Moore, *Social Facts,* 319.

74. June Starr and Jane F. Collier, eds., *History and Power in the Study of Law: New Directions in Legal Anthropology* (Ithaca, 1989), 8–9. See also V. A. Aleksandrov, *Obychnoe pravo krepostnoi derevni Rossii XVIII–nachala XIX v.* (Moscow, 1984), 234–49; Richard A. O'Connor, "Law as Indigenous Social Theory: A Siamese Thai Case," *American Ethnologist* 8, no. 2 (1981), 223–37. There is a wealth of material available for the study of village custom, although to date historians have yet to begin the necessary work of local analysis. Among many source collections, see L. I. Kuchumova, comp., *Dokumenty po istorii krest'ianskoi obshchiny 1861–1880 gg.,* 2 vols. (Moscow, 1983–84).

75. V. Shchochkin, "O primenenii obychnogo prava," *SudG,* no. 35 (1892), 3. See also A. A. Charushin, "Volostnye sudy v bytovom ikh osveshchenii," *IAOiRS* 4, no. 21 (1912), 986; A. Redkin, "Zametka o volostnykh sudakh," *Nedelia,* no. 19 (1881), 647–49; and the instructive commentary by a former *volost'* elder in S. Matveev, "V volostnykh starshinakh," *RB,* no. 5 (1912), 181. Of the very few local studies available in English, see Steven Hoch, *Serfdom and Social Control in Russia* (Chicago, 1986); Edgar Melton, "Household Economies and Commu-

Because they determined local rules through the assembly, elders could readily claim that a given decision was based on custom (whether such custom existed or not), using their knowledge of "tradition" as a tool for control—demanding submission, obedience, and respect from young migrant laborers, for instance, or upholding patriarchal authority over women through these same claims to tradition or custom. Moore has also stressed the extent to which abiding by tradition is often the privilege of those who can afford it:

> Social reproduction . . . is a luxury. Meeting cultural conventions . . . is something not all can afford. Failure to maintain tradition . . . is also something with which the well-off can belabor the poor. The well to do can be at once more modern and more traditional than their less fortunate relatives. The provision for sons, the payment of generous amounts of bridewealth, the holding of large celebrations for baptisms [and] weddings, . . . the provision of tubs of beer, all these involve substantial economic investments which are less and less possible for poor families. The poor know the techniques of production of all the necessary items of ritual exchange, but they lack the means. The poor cannot afford to be properly traditional and they certainly cannot afford to be modern. How ill conceived are the usual remarks about the nonprogressiveness of peasants.[76]

An overview of rural justice in Russia from 1861 to 1914 should serve to clarify the peculiar nature of these institutional arrangements (see figures 1.1 and 1.2). Between 1861 and 1868, the emancipation and supplementary legislation established *volost'* courts for all categories of peasants, modeled after Kiselev's *volostnaia rasprava,* while taking into account some of the latter's deficiencies. By the legislation's simple omission of previously existing juridical bodies (such as village courts of state peasants), all lower courts were effectively abolished—relegated to "discovery" by ethnographers and others who would, especially during the 1860s and 1870s, find these "traditional" or "customary" courts still functioning throughout much of the Great Russian countryside. In this process state peasants—that is, one-half of the peasant population—lost their two-tier court system and, with it, the right of appeal. The only exception was the village assembly, whose judicial authority now contracted to consideration of cases involving inheritance, family division, and similar civil matters; in criminal affairs

---

nal Conflicts on a Russian Serf Estate, 1800–1817," *JSH* 26, no. 3 (1993), 559–86; Rodney D. Bohac, "Family, Property, and Socioeconomic Mobility: Russian Peasants on Manuilovskoe Estate, 1810–1861" (Ph.D. diss., University of Illinois, 1982).

76. Moore, *Social Facts,* 300. On employing claims of tradition in the exercise of power, see Terence Ranger, "The Invention of Tradition in Colonial Africa," in Eric Hobsbawm and Terence Ranger, eds., *The Invention of Tradition* (Cambridge, 1983), esp. 254–62.

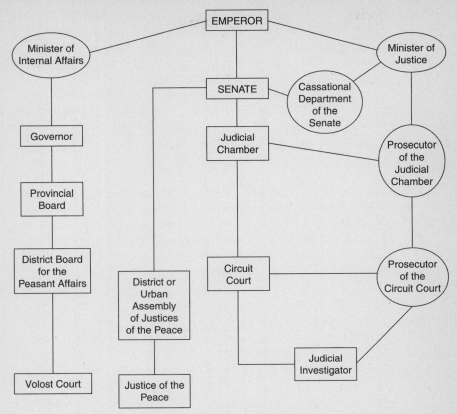

Figure 1.1. Russia's Judicial-Prosecutorial System under the 1864 Judicial Code

it retained the right to banish community members by administrative process.[77]

*Volost'* court decisions were initially considered final, but new regulations in 1866 permitted cassational hearings of their rulings by the district assembly of peace mediators, which might overturn the sentence, change it, or return the case for retrial. Appeals could not involve the essence of a

77. Sofronenko, *Krest'ianskaia reforma*, 49–50, art. 51; Cherniavskii, *Narodnyi sud*, 15; N. M. Druzhinin, "Obshchestvennoe ustroistvo gosudarstvennykh krest'ian po zakonam 1838–1839 gg., sravnitel'no s ustroistvom krest'ian pomeshchich'ikh po polozheniiam 19 fevralia 1861 g," in Druzhinin, *Ocherki krest'ianskoi obshchestvennoi zhizni* (SPb, 1905), 236–37; A. A. Kornilov, "Krest'ianskoe samoupravlenie po Polozheniiu 19 fevralia," in *Velikaia reforma*, vol. 6 (Moscow, 1911), 150.

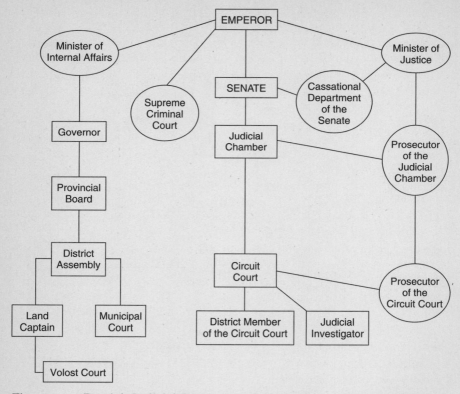

Figure 1.2. Russia's Judicial-Prosecutorial System after the Law of July 12, 1889

decision but only procedural errors such as when a court exceeded its jurisdiction, imposed punishments beyond those specified in article 102 of the emancipation regulations, or tried a case without summoning all involved parties to the hearing.[78] With the abolition of peace mediators in 1874, cassational authority passed to a district board for peasant affairs (*uezdnoe po krest'ianskim delam prisutstvie*), whose chairman and permanent member often consisted of a former mediator. Decisions of district boards

78. Cherniavskii, *Narodnyi sud,* 22; Igor Tiutriumov, "Krest'ianskii sud i nachala narodno-obychnogo prava," *RB,* no. 9 (1883), 214–21; Druzhinin, *Iuridicheskoe polozhenie krest'ian,* ch. 11; N. Koliupanov, "Uezdnye krest'ianskie prisutstviia," *RusM,* no. 12 (1880), 141–70; Evgenii Markov, "Uezdnoe upravlenie," *RusRech',* no. 9 (1881), 266–315. In practice, *volost'* courts regularly did all of these things. See, e.g., GARO, f. 695, op. 6 (1895), sv. 88, d. 474; ibid., f. 697, op. 1, sv. 1, d. 27 (1876); sv. 11, d. 449; ibid., f. 717, op. 40 (1890), sv. 80, d. 21.

could, in turn, be appealed to the provincial board for peasant affairs (*gubernskoe po krest'ianskim delam prisutstvie*).

This structure would be revised yet again in 1889 with the creation of a new office of land captain (*zemskii nachal'nik*),whose primary duties involved direct supervision of peasant administration and courts, thereby combining both administrative and judicial authority in one position.[79] These MVD-appointed officials not only approved elections of *volost'* judges, with the right to remove them and other peasant officials from office, but by replacing rural justices of the peace also represented a new court instance that tried a range of criminal offenses perpetrated by peasants—particularly disputes that arose between villagers and the landowning nobility. Themselves often noble landowners, these powerful new officials could punish villagers with a fine or jail sentence for disobeying their orders and, like the former peace mediators, could bring peasants before the *volost'* court for prosecution—which meant possible corporal punishment, given their influence over judges. Whereas the majority of former peace court cases passed to *volost'* courts in 1889 (thereby bringing nonpeasant rural inhabitants under this court's jurisdiction as well), land captains would now try serious offenses punishable by up to one year in prison and those crimes of greatest concern to landowners—trespass, illegal wood cutting, and breaking or violating labor contracts by hired agricultural workers.[80] In short, through the creation of land captains and abolition of most justices of the peace, the government unburdened its judicial system of the largest portion of "petty" cases and, except for felonious offenses, made the legal isolation of the countryside virtually complete.

A new body called the district assembly (*uezdnyi s"ezd*), divided into administrative and judicial sections, would now serve as the appellate instance for *volost'* court and land captain cases alike, as well as offenses tried in new municipal courts. Chaired by the district marshal of the nobility, the assembly's judicial section consisted of one circuit court representative, land captains, and honorary justices of the peace (where they still existed). Decisions of the district assembly could still be appealed to the provincial board,

79. There is a substantial historical literature on the land captains. See, e.g., P. A. Zaionchkovskii, *Rossiiskoe samoderzhavie v kontse XIX stoletiia* (Moscow, 1970); Mandel, "Paternalistic Authority," chs. 4–5; Yaney, *Urge to Mobilize*, chs. 3–4; Wcislo, *Reforming Rural Russia*, ch. 3; Corinne Gaudin, "Les zemskie nachal'niki au village. Coutumes administratives et culture paysanne en Russie 1889–1914," *Cahiers du Monde russe* 36, no. 3 (1995), 249–72.

80. See GARO, f. 70, op. 1 (1898), d. 1; ibid., f. 74, op. 25, dd. 4, 9; ibid., f. 81, op. 30 (1902), d. 3; K. Ia. Kozhukhar, "Zemskie nachal'niki," *VestP,* no. 5 (1905), 93–98; Zaionchkovskii, *Rossiiskoe samoderzhavie,* 198; Mandel, "Paternalistic Authority," 196–98; Wcislo, "The Land Captain Reform of 1889 and the Reassertion of Unrestricted Autocratic Authority," *Russian History* 15, no. 2–4 (1988), 285–326.

also reorganized into administrative and judicial departments and chaired by noble officials without legal training.[81]

Three aspects of this system exemplify the official definition of authority, its exercise in rural settlements, and the unequal relationship between custom and law, while demonstrating the contradictions that underlay local justice. First, a vast realm of administrative authority continued to influence peasant life in very significant ways. Such power rested not only in the hands of land captains or district and provincial boards, however. Provincial governors, rural police officials, tax inspectors, and *volost'* and village elders also exercised various levels of semijudicial and police authority, which gave them the right to punish without turning to the courts, or allowed them to demand that *volost'* courts sentence accused wrongdoers.[82] Alongside and often above regular justice, then, stood what on the surface appeared to be a far more powerful administrative apparatus designed to safeguard state interests, but one whose limited resources could not ensure its effective operation in practice.

Second, although *volost'* courts could base civil decisions on local custom within a restricted sphere, the institutions established to hear appeals of these decisions usually had little knowledge of custom. Some of the more diligent members of district boards and district assemblies occasionally sought to establish whether a given custom did, in fact, exist; however, the procedure for doing so simply involved sending a police official or land captain to pose this question to the village assembly, where the most influential members, already knowing the circumstances of the case, answered as their interests dictated. For the most part, however, cassational boards and assemblies paid little heed to custom and based their rulings instead on the law.[83]

---

81. Kozhukhar, "Zemskie nachal'niki," no. 5, 109–10; S. A. Mikhailovskii, "Sudebno-administrativnye uchrezhdeniia Tverskoi gubernii za piatiletie 1892–1897 godov," *Sbornik pravovedeniia i obshchestvennykh znanii*, vol. 8 (Moscow, 1898), 156–57; D. L., "Neskol'ko slov o gubernskikh po sudebnym delam prisutstviiakh," *ZhGUP*, no. 10 (1893), ch. 10, 55–67. Concerning higher appeals, see "O raz"iasnenie gubernskim po krest'ianskim delam prisutstviiam, chtoby ne predstavliali v pravitel'stvuiushchii senat zhalob po delam, reshennym volostnymi sudami," *Vestnik Iaroslavskogo zemstva*, no. 1–2 (1881), 4–5.

82. This authority is discussed further in Chapter 7. See Sofronenko, *Krest'ianskaia reforma, passim;* V. A. Beer, *Administrativnyi ustav o nakazaniiakh, nalagaemykh sel'skim starostoi i volostnym starshinoi* (SPb, 1899); Khrulev, "Mysli provintsiala o provintsii," 57. On police authority, see I. T. Tarasov, *Lichnoe zaderzhanie kak politseiskaia mera bezopasnosti*, part 2: *Politseiskii arest v Rossii* (Kiev, 1886).

83. Ivanov, "Krest'ianskii sud i formal'noe pravosudie," 48–49; "K voprosu o iurisdiktsii volostnogo suda," *SudG*, no. 34 (1892), 1–2; Illarionov, *Znachenie obychnogo prava*, 10–11; Illarionov, "Sudebno-krest'ianskaia reforma," 4; Leon'tev, "V poiskakh za obychnym pravom," *RB*, no. 11 (1894), 168–79; A. Grekov, "Obychnoe pravo v delakh volostnykh sudov," *SPbVed*, no. 264 (1900), 1; Z., "Neustroistvo v krest'ianskikh pravovykh otnosheniiakh," *SPbVed*, no. 81 (1902), 2; I. M. Tiutriumov, comp., *Praktika Pravitel'stvuiushchego Senata po krest'ianskim delam* (SPb, 1914), 926–48.

Given that these bodies met irregularly and most often with few of their members actually present, large numbers of appeals were decided quickly with no discussion of custom. Between 1892 and 1897 in Tver province, for instance, the provincial board met once per month on average, and during the course of a five-to-seven-hour session decided upwards of 130 appellate cases. With far larger caseloads than the provincial board, district assemblies held an average of twenty-seven sittings per year and resolved as many as 300 appeals in a single session.[84] A paradox was thus created between the stated purpose of local justice and the government's ability to undermine peasant institutions by abrogating their decisions or, in appellate instances, by ignoring the use of custom that it had granted.

Certainly the most significant contradiction within the everyday operation of rural justice can be found in the numerous ways that peasants found to circumvent or subvert state regulations on *volost'* court procedure. Here, too, we see compelling analogies with colonial administrations under which "the local court escapes its designers in a thousand ways."[85] Although judicial sessions were conducted orally, Russian law required that township clerks record these proceedings and court decisions in special books to create a written record that would be subject to official inspection. The extent to which such records reflected reality, however, could only be decided by the clerk and other local officials, who, through "irregularities" and record-keeping "failures," constructed their own version of each case history and thereby determined how information would be presented to higher authorities. Given that they were often the only literate figures within township administrations (especially before the 1890s), *volost'* clerks exercised substantial authority, and even after literacy rates began to improve among peasant judges and elders, clerks still controlled knowledge of procedure and law and retained great influence over court hearings and decisions.[86] Contemporary discussion, however, usually concerned the clerk's real or exaggerated corruption of peasant self-government rather than the ways in which recordkeeping itself was appropriated and used to serve local interests.

State regulations, for example, did not call for the recording of disputes concluded through reconciliation (which some early estimates calculated at

84. Mikhailovskii, "Sudebno-administrativnye uchrezhdeniia," 156–57; D. L., "Neskol'ko slov," 56–67.

85. Moore, "Treating Law as Knowledge," 38.

86. On the influence of *volost'* clerks, see, e.g., GARF, f. 586, op. 1, d. 117 (Pskov province), ll. 33–34; d. 114 (Orel province), l. 22; d. 120, ll. 54, 61, 89; F. Marichev, "Volostnoi pisar' i volost': po lichnym vospominaniiam i nabliudeniiam," *VE*, no. 5 (1902), 240–72; Ivan Kupchinov, *Iz dnevnika volostnogo pisaria* (Moscow, 1910); N. M. Astyrev, *V volostnykh pisariakh. Ocherki krest'ianskogo samoupravleniia,* 3rd ed. (Moscow, 1904); Petr Skorobogatyi, "Vliianie starshin i pisarei na otpravlenie volostnoi iustitsii," *IuV*, no. 12 (1881), 607–23; N., "Nashi volostnye pisaria," *Nedelia,* no. 40 (1876), 1297–1301; N. Dmitriev, "Pisaria i krest'iane," *SV*, no. 191 (1913), 2–3.

50 to 75 percent of all cases coming before *volost'* courts). The extent to which this fact played a role in village dispute resolution is a question that surely needs to be considered, given that reconciliation ensured that one's conflict and name would not become part of an official record. It also meant that local authorities like village or *volost'* elders, who encouraged reconciliation, maintained greater control by not allowing disputes (and information) to move into the arena of official knowledge.[87] Township record books therefore contain only the most serious conflicts or cases in which judges had been unable to reconcile litigants. Even then, clerks generally wrote down only the bare essentials of disputes, while filling up pages with legally required formalities. Little can be gleaned about the relationships between litigants, background and details of disputes, evidence, testimony, and similarly critical information, and those "facts" that were entered into the record can only be understood in the framework of a conscious decision as to which information would be excluded.[88] Therefore, although recorded cases are certainly of value for asking a limited set of questions, they lend themselves neither to generalization nor to in-depth case studies of village dispute resolution precisely because those who controlled record-keeping frustrated official surveillance through a "carelessness" that outsiders would misinterpret as ignorance or as the peasants' dislike of formalism. The state's inability to exercise strict oversight of rural justice thus allowed communities to retain an important degree of power over their members. More significantly, through its very demand for written records the government provided ordinary peasants and village elites with the means to hinder authorities by taking advantage of the impossibility of "knowing"—a weapon available to villagers in the past and readily adapted to changing postemancipation conditions.

87. Skorobogatyi, "Mirovye sdelki v volostnom sude," *IuV,* no. 7 (1881), 422–23; Kozhukhar, "Zemskie nachal'niki," no. 11, 63; I. N. Aristov, comp., *Volostnoi sud po zakonu 12-go iiulia 1889 goda* (Kazan', 1893), 15. Reconciliation is discussed in Chapter 3.

88. When recording court decisions, a *volost'* clerk was required to include the date, the judges' names and those of the litigants or the accused and victim, a short description of the case, and the court's final decision. Aristov, *Volostnoi sud,* 15; MVD, *Sbornik uzakonenii, opredeliaiushchikh prava i obiazannosti volostnykh starshin i pisarei* (SPb, 1904), 59–62. See also "Narodnoe pravosudie," *Nedelia,* no. 23 (1888), 728; and the many examples in TsGIAgM, ff. 749, 1943, 1443, and others.

# CHAPTER 2

# A Portraiture of Numbers

## *Rural Crime and Peasant Felons*
## *in the Judicial Statistics*

"Nothing serves as such a true indicator of a people's cultural state as do criminal statistics," declared an 1897 article in the periodical *The Week*. "The incidence of crime is the real barometer of a nation's morality, enlightenment, and progress."[1] This was a common belief throughout Europe during the late nineteenth century, and as the twentieth century dawned the drive to understand criminality took on ever greater urgency. As Vladimir Kopiatkevich wrote in his 1913 examination of judicial statistics from Olonets province, "At present, when Russia is living through a major crisis which has seized the economic life that lies at the foundation of human relations as well as the very psyche of the masses, the study of crime takes on the highest degree of importance and necessity."[2]

Judicial statistics, of course, were but one of numerous filters through which officials and other educated Russians viewed crime. An increasingly literate public found even more accessible information on crime and courts in literature, newspapers, and scholarly or popular journals of every sort, from Dostoevskii, Kuprin, and Tolstoi to the bandit tales avidly consumed by lower-class readers. By the 1880s, popularized criminological theories from Europe and the United States were being disseminated widely and played an important role in forming public representations of crime.[3] Yet

1. "Prestupnost' v Rossii," *Nedelia*, no. 4 (1897), 102.

2. Vladimir Kopiatkevich, "Prestupnost' v Olonetskoi gubernii za piatnadtsatiletie 1897–1911 g.g.," *Izvestiia Obshchestva izucheniia Olonetskoi gubernii*, no. 5–6 (1913), 97.

3. For various treatments of this subject in historical literature, see Jeffrey Brooks, *When Russia Learned to Read: Literacy and Popular Literature, 1861–1917* (Princeton, 1985); Joan Neuberger, *Hooliganism: Crime, Culture, and Power in St. Petersburg, 1900–1914* (Berkeley, 1993); Daniel R. Brower, "The Penny Press and Its Readers," in Stephen P. Frank and Mark D.

the nineteenth-century faith in the new science of statistics found fertile ground within Russia's reading public and, especially, among those directly involved in administration, law enforcement, and justice. To be sure, the occasional critic could be found, but by the second half of the century this faith in judicial statistics had become firmly entrenched. Like middle-class creators of statistical science in the West, Russian criminologists "had no doubt that there was such a thing as the 'facts of crime.'"[4]

This chapter examines the statistical representation of rural crime and its convergence with elite and especially state views of the peasantry after 1861. It demonstrates how the peculiarities of Russia's postemancipation judicial structure created a highly distorted quantitative depiction of what was termed peasant criminality—a depiction that gained broad acceptance precisely because it neatly matched prevailing opinions of village culture as well as explanations for the types of crimes perpetrated by the rural population. It thus bears emphasizing that the quantitative sources utilized by government officials or analyzed and discussed by criminologists do not offer an especially revealing or accurate picture of crime. Such sources, as shown by pioneers in the history of crime, are filtered "through the prejudices, assumptions, and administrative capacities of those who hold power in society: of those . . . who define crime and who bring those whom they identify as criminals to justice." Put differently, criminal statistics "index public and official attitudes at least as much as delinquent behavior, and reflect the interests of the public order system."[5]

In the Russian case, too, patterns of prosecution recorded in judicial compilations provide insights into questions concerning imperial law enforcement. What effect, for example, did the 1903 introduction of a new rural police guard some 40,000 strong have on the movement of recorded

---

Steinberg, eds., *Cultures in Flux: Lower Class Values, Practices, and Resistance in Late Imperial Russia* (Princeton, 1994), 147–67.

4. Michelle Perrot, "Delinquency and the Penitentiary System in Nineteenth-Century France," in Robert Forster and Orest Ranum, eds., *Deviants and the Abandoned in French Society* (Baltimore, 1978), 219.

5. V. A. C. Gatrell, Bruce Lenman, and Geoffrey Parker, eds., *Crime and the Law: The Social History of Crime in Western Europe since 1500* (London, 1980), 2–3; Ted Robert Gurr, *Rogues, Rebels and Reformers* (Beverley Hills, 1976), 20. In *The Politics of Crime and Conflict: A Comparative History of Four Cities* (Beverly Hills, 1977), Gurr contended that shifts in crime rates represented above all changes in perceptions on the part of the political elite, whose interests shaped legal definitions of crime. For more nuanced analyses, see Douglas Hay, "Property, Authority, and the Criminal Law," in Hay, Peter Linebaugh, John G. Rule, E. P. Thompson, and Cal Winslow, *Albion's Fatal Tree: Crime and Society in Eighteenth-Century England* (New York, 1975); E. P. Thompson, *Whigs and Hunters: The Origins of the Black Act* (London, 1975), 17–63; John C. Weaver, *Crimes, Constables, and Courts: Order and Transgression in a Canadian City, 1816–1970* (Montreal, 1995), ch. 5.

crimes—and, in particular, on the growth of administrative offenses? Similarly, are we to interpret rising numbers of prosecutions in categories like "resistance to authorities" as a significant upsurge of lawbreaking or as the attempt of a beleaguered government that lacked an adequate law enforcement arm to concentrate its resources on tasks deemed most necessary to maintaining state authority? The sources, in short, are rich in interpretive potential but must be approached cautiously and with a broad perspective that considers such critical factors as elite attitudes, state concerns, the problems of policing, and the functioning of judicial institutions.

Yet the statistics do provide a basis for understanding widespread peasant complaints about crime and about the poor performance of the reformed justice system itself. Villagers' growing lack of trust in the criminal courts and the subsequent decline of their legitimacy in many peasants' eyes stemmed, in great part, from the inability of prosecutors and courts to investigate and prosecute an ever larger number of cases. Furthermore, if peasants believed that rural police officials could do little to solve crimes and that courts were ever less capable of ensuring that serious offenders would be convicted and punished, an increase in cases of popular retribution against criminals becomes more readily comprehensible. Indeed, peasant attitudes toward higher courts, like their conviction that the law often fostered injustice, contributed to rural conflict after 1861, and the judicial statistics show that those attitudes had a solid basis in fact.

## SOURCES AND THEIR SHORTCOMINGS

Like most European states, during the first half of the nineteenth century imperial Russia's Ministry of Justice began publishing criminal statistics that provided a rich base of data for most of the empire. Starting in 1832 annual accounts [*otchety*] made available information on convictions by type of crime, province of commission, and social estate of the perpetrator. Data for the servile population were enumerated within the familiar legal categories of state or crown peasants, seigneurial, household, or factory serfs, and others.[6] The *Otchety* continued until 1868 and were largely superseded in 1872 by the more ambitious *Collection of Statistical Information on Criminal Affairs*, an annual compilation of cases tried by the reformed courts (both circuit courts and justices of the peace) and published for the period 1872–1913.

---

6. *Otchet Ministerstva Iustitsii*, 34 vols. (SPb, 1835–71) (hereafter: *Otchety*). To my knowledge the only contemporary studies that made use of this source are *Materialy dlia statistiki Rossii sobiraemye po vedomostvu Ministerstva Gosudarstvennykh Imushchestv*, part 6: *Ugolovnaia statistika gosudarstvennykh krest'ian. Po dannym za desiatiletie 1847–56* (SPb, 1871); E. N. Anuchin, *Issledovanie o protsente soslannykh v Sibir' v period 1827–1846 gg. Materialy dlia ugolovnoi statistiki Rossii* (SPb, 1873).

They contain a wealth of detailed material on the number of cases arising annually, convictions and acquittals, sentences imposed, and information on the convicts themselves (e.g., profession, social estate, marital status, age, education, nationality, and religion). The data are organized both geographically by court circuit (or by province, in the case of peace courts) and by type of crime, with figures provided in each category on such matters as seasonality of offenses, place of perpetration, and recidivism.[7]

Despite their obvious value, Russian statistics suffer many of the same problems that beset similar compilations from other countries and are even more problematic because of shortcomings unique to the empire's judicial system. To begin with, the Ministry of Justice gave detailed information only for felony convictions, which accounted on average for less than one-fourth of all felony charges examined by prosecutors. These publications also included no more than 8 to 10 percent of the total misdemeanor cases tried by peace courts—91 percent of which were property offenses. Although the number of offenses known to the police offers the most precise index of crimes committed, available data cover at best a mere fraction of criminal infractions.[8] Because of its small size, rudimentary training, inefficiency, and corruption, the country's police force was simply incapable of enforcing the law adequately among a rapidly growing population. After 1890, prosecutors also were burdened by rising caseloads and therefore proved unable to investigate or try substantial numbers of those crimes that police did manage to solve. Arrests and prosecutions, in other words, were but dim reflections of offenses committed.

Other difficulties further hinder an analysis of the country's criminal statistics. The 1864 judicial reform did not and could not transform the country's legal institutions overnight, but spread gradually throughout the empire until its completion just a few years before the monarchy crumbled in 1917. Ministry of Justice statistics, however, included only the activities of reformed courts, which, by 1873, formed six judicial chambers, or *sudebnye palaty* (St. Petersburg, Moscow, Khar'kov, Odessa, Kazan', and Saratov), containing forty-one circuit courts. Over the next forty years, these numbers rose steadily as the reforms came to other parts of the empire. In 1874,

---

7. *Svod statisticheskikh svedenii po delam ugolovnym,* 42 vols. (SPb, 1873–1914) (hereafter: *Svody*). Supplemental data can be found in *SbSSMIu,* 31 vols. (SPb, 1887–1914); *Dopolnenie k Sbornike statisticheskikh svedenii: obzor deiatel'nosti sudebno-mirovykh ustanovlenii,* 31 vols. (SPb, 1887–1915). Unless otherwise indicated, all data in this study are drawn from the *Svody* and the *Otchety.*

8. Thorsten Sellin, "The Significance of the Records of Crime," *Law Quarterly Review* 65 (1951), 489–504; V. A. C. Gatrell and T. B. Hadden, "Criminal Statistics and Their Interpretation," in E. A. Wrigley, ed., *Nineteenth-Century Society: Essays in the Use of Quantitative Methods for the Study of Social Data* (Cambridge, 1972), 351.

ten more courts were created. By 1884, the judicial establishment had grown to sixty-one circuit courts dispersed among eight chambers (with the addition of the Kiev and Vil'no chambers). Expansion was even more rapid between 1894 and 1899, with three new judicial chambers (Irkutsk, Omsk, and Tashkent) and twenty-eight circuits established. The reforms continued up to the eve of war, and by 1913 the country had ninety-eight circuit courts organized within thirteen judicial chambers (Novocherkassk and Tiflis were added in 1904 and 1907, respectively).[9] This constant increase in the number of courts and consequent shift in the data base significantly distorted felony statistics. To calculate the actual movement of recorded felonies or convictions, therefore, it is necessary either to limit our analysis to a control group of the original circuits existing in 1874 (which, at the time, counted fifty-one court circuits that included nearly all of Great Russia and about 70 percent of the empire's population), or determine growth within each individual circuit; both methods have been followed in this chapter.

Certainly the greatest deficiency of Russian statistics is the omission of the vast majority of misdemeanors. In courts under the Ministry of Justice, responsibility for misdemeanors rested with justices of the peace, who tried, on average, 88 percent of all criminal cases heard by circuit and peace courts combined. But Russia's criminal statistics enumerated only those peace court convictions punishable by imprisonment—that is, about 8 percent of the total. During the period 1901–1905, for example, 314,681 persons were sentenced to prison by peace courts, but convictions for all offenses totaled 4,320,171—nearly fourteen times the number of prison sentences.[10] Also omitted from official statistics are cases in which justices of the peace or, after 1889, their land captain successors, reconciled the sides—a common practice if litigants wished to avoid trial, and one recommended by the state. One contemporary estimated that 20 percent of all peace court cases were settled in this manner.[11] Hence only a small portion of misdemeanors tried by Russia's official courts appears in the judicial statistics—a particularly serious deficiency since the most rapid increase of

9. Regarding implementation of the judicial reform, see N. N. Efremova, *Ministerstvo Iustitsii Rossiskoi Imperii 1802–1917 gg.* (Moscow, 1983), 87–109; I. V. Gessen, *Sudebnaia reforma* (SPb, 1905), 122–29; B. G. Litvak, *Perevorot 1861 goda v Rossii: pochemu ne realizovalas' reformatorskaia al'ternativa* (Moscow, 1991), 214–28; B. V. Vilenskii, *Sudebnaia reforma i kontrreforma v Rossii* (Saratov, 1969), 199–219.

10. *SbSSMIu*, vols. 18–22; E. N. Tarnovskii, "Dvizhenie prestupnosti v Rossiiskoi imperii za 1899–1908 gg.," *ZhMIu*, no. 9 (1909), 53–54.

11. N. Kholev, "Desiatiletie mirovoi iustitsii Kerchenskogo okruga," *ZhGUP* 11, no. 4 (1881), section 8, 2–3; see also "Desiatiletie sudebno mirovykh uchrezhdenii Temnikovskogo okruga, Tambovskoi gubernii," *ZhGUP* 10, no. 4 (1880), section 10, 59–75.

TABLE 2.1   Criminal Cases in Rural Jurisdictions of Riazan' Province

| Year | Circuit Courts | District Assemblies | Land Captains | Volost' Courts |
|---|---|---|---|---|
| 1892 | 395 | nd | 6,270 | 13,905 |
| 1898 | 347 | nd | 6,653 | 14,331 |
| 1900 | 324 | 2,802 | 5,763 | 14,379 |
| 1901 | 356 | 3,411 | 6,716 | 15,867 |
| 1902 | 342 | nd | 6,461 | 16,446 |
| 1903 | 323 | 3,301 | 6,824 | 18,147 |
| 1908 | 438 | 2,028 | 8,542 | 20,048 |

SOURCE: *Svody,* part 2, table 2; GARO, f. 695, op. 6, sv. 75, d. 12; op. 10, sv. 134, d. 5; op. 12, sv. 162, dd. 5–7; op. 13, sv. 169, d. 1.

recorded crimes after 1874 occurred among offenses that came before justices of the peace.[12]

The unknown figure in Russian criminal statistics takes on especially great significance because peasants were largely excluded from the reformed courts' jurisdiction unless they perpetrated a felony, committed a crime against nonpeasants, or repeated the same type of misdemeanor three times. Instead, *volost'* courts adjudicated minor infractions committed by the peasant population, and the number of criminal cases these rural tribunals heard usually surpassed the combined total for circuit and peace courts. Whereas individual *volost'* courts might try as few as 50 crimes or less each year, in 1890 those in Moscow province handled a total of 11,211 criminal cases; circuit courts, justices of the peace, and land captains together tried just over 10,000 offenses.[13] Information from Riazan' province (table 2.1) presents a similar picture. By 1911, this province's *volost'* courts handled 100,931 cases, of which approximately 30,600 were criminal; by contrast, only 447 rural crimes brought convictions by the Riazan' circuit court that year.[14]

Data from other provinces confirm that the majority of crimes tried by administrative and judicial authorities were not included in Ministry of Justice compilations. The *volost'* courts of Saratov province decided nearly three times as many criminal cases as did land captains between 1891 and

12. E. N. Tarnovskii, "Dvizhenie prestupnosti v evropeiskoi Rossii za 1874–94 gg.," *ZhMIu,* no. 3 (1899), 129; Stephen P. Frank, "Narratives within Numbers: Women, Crime, and Judicial Statistics in Imperial Russia, 1834–1913," *RR* 55, no. 4 (1996), 551.

13. RGIA, f. 1284, op. 223, d. 169–1891 g., ll. 118, 122–23. For additional years, see d. 152, ll. 100, 105–6; d. 177, l. 95; and d. 68-B, l. 94; *Svody,* part 2, table 1.

14. GARO, f. 695, op. 21, sv. 232, d. 9, ll. 1–263; *Svody,* part 2, table 2.

1903, and as many as thirty times the number tried in the circuit court.[15] Published data for 1896 show that *volost'* courts of sixteen provinces heard as few as 12,436 (Nizhnii Novgorod) and as many as 58,978 (Perm) criminal cases annually, with an average of 25,761 per province. A 1900 MVD survey of *volost'* courts in sixteen districts of eight provinces found that the average load per district was 2,496 criminal cases, far surpassing the totals for circuit courts, peace courts, or land captains in these same localities.[16] Even during the revolutionary year of 1905, when many offenses normally tried in townships were dealt with administratively or by courts martial, 1,121,191 crimes still passed through the rural courts of forty-three provinces in European Russia.[17]

Although these figures attest to the substantial volume of offenses tried in *volost'* courts, the MVD's failure to publish systematic data makes impossible the comprehensive analysis of misdemeanors. The fact that in many townships during the 1870s an estimated three-quarters of all village disputes were resolved unofficially or reconciled by peasant judges and not recorded swells the unknown figure of Russian crime to enormous dimensions. Equally important to our purposes, within most European court records this dark figure "was not only much larger than for police records, but also for property crimes such as theft it increased drastically during the course of the [nineteenth] century due, at least in part, to the inability of law-enforcement agencies to keep up with rises in population and crime levels."[18] Hence, increases in theft rates have usually been significantly underestimated; in Russia this problem was greatly exacerbated by the nature of court jurisdictions and the continued mingling of judicial and administrative authority.

15. K. Ia. Kozhukhar, "Zemskie nachal'niki," *VestP,* no. 11 (1905), 66.

16. D. N. Zhbankov and V. I. Iakovenko, *Telesnye nakazaniia v Rossii v nastoiashchee vremia* (Moscow, 1899), 47–76; M. A. Mikhailovskii, "Sudebno-administrativnye uchrezhdeniia Tverskoi gubernii za piatiletie 1892–1897 godov," in *Sbornik pravovedeniia i obshchestvennykh znanii,* vol. 8 (1898), 160–61; MVD, *Trudy redaktsionnoi kommisii po peresmotru zakonopolozhenii o krest'ianakh,* vol. 3 (SPb., 1904), 470–75.

17. Tarnovskii, "Dvizhenie prestupnosti za 1899–1908," 59–60. This author estimated the actual number of criminal cases during normal times as being closer to 2 million. See also Tarnovskii, "Prestupnost'," in V. I. Kovalevskii, ed., *Rossiia v kontse XIX veka* (SPb, 1900), 934; S. A—v., "Ugolovnoe zakonodatel'stvo Rossii za 1906–1910 gg.," *Drug provintsii,* no. 3 (1911), 1.

18. Howard Zehr, *Crime and the Development of Modern Society: Patterns of Criminality in Nineteenth-Century Germany and France* (London, 1976), 119. By contrast, V. A. C. Gatrell has argued that theft as well as violent crime witnessed overall declines in nineteenth-century England. "The Decline of Theft and Violence in Victorian and Edwardian England," in Gatrell, Lenman, and Parker, eds., *Crime and the Law,* 238–370. See also Weaver, *Crimes, Constables, and Courts,* 198–204.

## STATISTICAL PICTURES: THE VIOLENT PEASANT

Because government compilations did not include most lower court prosecutions, virtually all contemporary analyses of the criminal statistics found quite uniform patterns when comparing urban and rural felonies. Violent crime, they noted, was endemic to the countryside, whereas property offenses tended toward a more even distribution between town and village. Among total murders for which circuit courts handed down convictions from 1874 to 1913, an average of 84.5 percent occurred in rural localities. This figure reached 87.4 percent for the murder of a spouse or relative, 88.4 percent for infanticide, and 91.6 percent for concealing a newborn's corpse. The countryside also accounted for 88.9 percent of all persons convicted for inflicting mortal injury, 85.1 percent of assaults, 90 percent of uprisings or resistance to authorities, and 91.7 percent of arsons. By contrast, only 67.2 percent of recorded robberies took place outside urban areas. As for burglary, theft, and dealing in stolen goods, their rural proportions in the statistics averaged 69.4, 59.2, and 51.8 percent, respectively.[19]

These findings fit well with contemporary notions about rural and urban crime, for the by then dominant Western assumption that industrialization and urbanization brought a significant increase and change in the nature of crime proved popular not only among Russian criminologists but among people of all professions and political persuasions. Indeed, once given firmer theoretical grounding by the founders of modern sociology and criminology (such as Émile Durkheim and Ferdinand Tönnies) at the turn of century, and later buttressed by modernization and structural theorists, this "nearly canonized" view remains a powerful and widely accepted myth.[20] Its proponents posited a predominance of criminality in towns and cities and argued that property offenses in particular were most common there due to greater concentrations of wealth and poverty. Crimes committed by country dwellers, on the other hand, were said to be proportionately fewer in number and tended to involve violence against persons rather than depredations

19. *Svody,* vols. 3–42, part 2, table 19.

20. Critiques of this myth may be found in Eric H. Monkkonen, *The Dangerous Class: Crime and Poverty in Columbus, Ohio, 1860–1885* (Cambridge, Mass., 1975); Vincent E. McHale and Eric A. Johnson, "Urbanization, Industrialization, and Crime in Imperial Germany," *Social Science History* 1, no. 1 (1976), 45–78; 1, no. 2 (1977), 210–47; David Cohen and Eric A. Johnson, "French Criminality: Urban-Rural Differences in the Nineteenth Century," *JIH* 12, no. 3 (1982), 477–501; Eric A. Johnson, *Urbanization and Crime: Germany 1871–1914* (Cambridge, 1995), esp. 158–71; Eric A. Johnson and Eric H. Monkkonen, eds., *The Civilization of Crime: Violence in Town and Country since the Middle Ages* (Urbana, Ill., 1996). See also Francis G. Snyder, "Law and Development in the Light of Dependency Theory," *LSR* 14, no. 3 (1980), 723–804.

upon property, which farmers and rural wage laborers possessed in scarce quantity.[21]

According to an 1893 commentary published by the Russian journal *The Northern Herald*, "Criminal statistics attest that crime is greater in cities than in villages. The peasant . . . is morally led astray under conditions of urban life. It is easier to perpetrate crimes in towns than in villages, and bad examples have a stronger influence in towns."[22] Few Russians knowledgeable about their country's judicial statistics would have disagreed with this claim. "Everywhere," wrote A. N. Trainin in 1909, "we find that with the flowering of urban civilization comes an increase in urban crime."[23] In large part social structure itself seemed to explain why cities gave rise to crime, or why criminality was less pervasive in rural areas. As Trainin noted, the general instability of material security in towns made life difficult to endure for the laboring classes, who could "quickly and unexpectedly slip from relative security to a complete lack of work." In the "impoverished countryside," by contrast, the peasant psyche and the very character of life proved in some sense an advantage. "From father to children," he argued, "the peasant's long-standing and even startling ability to be satisfied with little is passed along. The deterioration of the peasant's economic well-being occurs very gradually. First of all, a peasant will sell off his household equipment, after which he sells his work animal, further reducing the area under crops . . . The road from rye to "famine bread" is strewn with unnoticed transitions that deaden the peasant's sense of protest and teach him to wait patiently."[24] Most important, claimed Trainin, was the basic fact that villagers possessed little worth stealing apart from their horses—which they defended "with the cruelty of primitive people." Many peasants deprived of "social equilibrium" had little possibility to manifest their "antisocial mood" in the countryside; in order to perpetrate a crime "the peasant often finds himself forced to set out to the city, just as he would go there to buy salt or liquor."[25] Unlike the 1893 commentary cited above, Trainin believed that "preformed"

21. For examples and discussions of such views, see, e.g., Bruce Smith, *Rural Crime Control* (New York, 1933), ch. 1; Abdul Q. Lodhi and Charles Tilly, "Urbanization, Crime, and Collective Violence in 19th-Century France," *American Sociological Review* 79 (1973), 296–318; Zehr, *Crime;* Robert Tombs, "Crime and the Security of the State: The 'Dangerous Classes' and Insurrection in Nineteenth-Century Paris," in Gatrell, Lenman, and Parker, eds., *Crime and the Law,* 214–37; Louise Shelly, *Crime and Modernization: The Impact of Industrialization and Urbanization on Crime* (Carbondale, Ill., 1981).

22. "Provintsial'naia pechat'," *SevV,* no. 3 (1893), part 2, 34.

23. A. N. Trainin, "Prestupnost' goroda i derevni v Rossii," *RusM,* no. 7 (1909), 8. For similar commentary citing the works of such well-known figures as Henry Joly and Gabriel Tarde, see Trainin, "Prestupnost' stolits i gorodov," *Pravo,* no. 13 (1908), 729.

24. Trainin, "Prestupnost' goroda i derevni," 11–12.

25. Ibid., 12.

rural criminals were swept into cities by the ongoing wave of migration that constituted the primary source of late nineteenth-century Russia's urban growth.

If the statistics appeared to demonstrate a relationship between cities and crime, they also suggested to their interpreters a sharp distinction between the nature of urban and rural criminality. According to one jurist who ventured his opinions on this matter in 1913, crime tended "to soften" as it moved from countryside to towns and cities; the movement, that is, was from crimes against persons to offenses against property.[26] In other words, violence best characterized peasant crimes. Evgenii N. Tarnovskii, one of the most prolific of Russia's criminal statisticians, simply followed the lead of Cesare Lombroso and other adherents of the anthropological school when he argued in 1887 that an inverse relationship existed between population density and the crime of murder, for civilization, with its higher concentration of population and wealth, brought with it a lower incidence of homicides. By contrast, in sparsely settled societies like "the bloodthirsty tribes of Turkmen, Kurds, Malays, and Ashante," murder was a very common, "almost legal" affair. By analogy Tarnovskii extended the "social disorganization" of savage society to the Russian countryside. Whereas homicide rates were low in provinces blessed by the widespread development of personal gentry landownership (forthrightly equated by Tarnovskii to civilization) and a concentration of property in land and capital, murder raged throughout "peasant" provinces like Viatka and Orenburg, where property remained fragmented (that is, disorganized) in smallholdings. Tarnovskii concluded that "the concentration of wealth, corresponding to the development of civilization, leads to a lessening of crimes against life."[27] Whether familiar with the judicial statistics or not, many observers of village society readily agreed with these assessments. Nearly forty years after his service as a peace mediator in Tambov province during the early 1870s, N. V. Davydov claimed that peasant transgressions reflected the severity and crudeness

26. M. F. Zamengof, "Gorod i derevnia v prestupnosti," *ZhUPP,* no. 1 (1913), 79–80. This perspective was also widely used to distinguish the types of crimes committed by rural and urban women. See M. N. Gernet, *Obshchestvennye prichiny prestupnosti* (Moscow, 1906); Frank, "Narratives within Numbers."

27. E. N. Tarnovskii, "Prestupleniia protiv zhizni i usloviia obshchestvennogo byta," *IuV* 25, no. 8 (1887), 481, 487. Compare Cesare Lombroso, *Crime: Its Causes and Remedies* (Boston, 1918), 58–75. See also Tarnovskii, "Ocherk razvitiia prestuplenii protiv zhizni v sviazi s formami obshchestvennykh otnoshenii," *RusM,* no. 4 (1887), part 2, 1–13; M. N. Gernet, "Statistika gorodskoi i sel'skoi prestupnosti," *Problemy prestupnosti,* no. 2 (1927), 15–24. Similar analogies between lower-class criminality and "savage" or "primitive" society can be found during the Soviet and post-Soviet eras. See, e.g., D. S. Likhachev, "Cherty pervobytnogo primitivizma vorovskoi rechi," *Iazyk i myshlenie,* no.3–4 (1935), 47–100; Lev Samoilov (pseud.), "Ethnography of the Camp," *Anthropology and Archeology of Eurasia* 32, no. 3 (1993–94), 32–58.

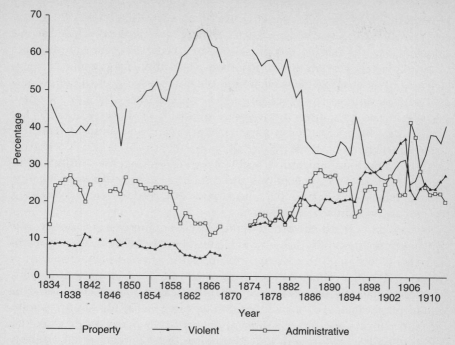

Figure 2.1. Categories of Offenses as Percent of All Felonies Tried, 1834–1913

of their morals. "In general," he asserted, "crimes in the northern districts are almost exclusively . . . murder during fights, torture, inflicting wounds, attacks on [gentry] estates, and other expressions of violence, savagery, and willfulness."[28]

How one views this rural-urban distinction depends, of course, on the data used. Contemporaries relied solely upon circuit court statistics in their quantitative examinations of rural crime, and with few exceptions what they read into these numbers confirmed the anecdotal evidence and musings that had long supported beliefs about peasant life. Property offenses accounted for 61.1 percent of all rural felony convictions in 1874, crimes of violence 13.6 percent, and crimes against the administrative order 13.9 percent (figure 2.1). But over the next forty years these proportions changed dramatically. Ten years later property crime had fallen to just 50.5 percent of felony convictions, whereas violent crimes grew to 21.4 percent and administrative offenses to 19.3 percent. In 1894 these figures stood at 32.8, 21.2, and 25.2 percent, respectively, and by 1906 we find property offenses

28. N. V. Davydov, *Iz proshlogo,* 2nd ed. (Moscow, 1914), 169.

constituting only 25.1 percent of convictions, with violent and administrative crimes having reached 23.8 and 42 percent.[29] Only after the revolutionary years 1905–1907 did property crime begin to regain ground, accounting for 30 percent of convictions in 1908 and 41.2 percent in 1913.

Property offenses lagged well behind the much faster growth rates of violent and administrative crimes. During the period 1874–1913, the average growth in property crime convictions stood at 3.6 percent, but crimes against persons rose at an average of 6.4 percent and administrative offenses at 8.8 percent. Even if we exclude the years 1905–1907, when prosecution of both administrative and violent crimes increased dramatically, the range in growth rates among these three categories does not change substantially, averaging 2.3, 6.4, and 5.5 percent, respectively, for property, violent, and administrative offenses.

For peasants, in other words, circuit courts were increasingly used mainly for the prosecution of serious crimes against persons or against the government order, although this tells us little about the actual distribution of rural offenses. Property crimes fell as a proportion of felonies not because of any dramatic decline in burglaries or thefts but because an ever larger proportion of property infractions was handed to lower courts for summary adjudication.[30] By far the most significant of such shifts occurred in 1882 and 1883, when the government moved upwards of 50 percent of all property offenses to justices of the peace. Upon the abolition of most peace courts in 1889, their caseloads went either to land captains or to the expanded jurisdiction of *volost'* judges, thereby removing still more property crimes from the statistical portrait as the peasantry's juridical isolation deepened.[31]

Prereform data demonstrate clearly that without these jurisdictional changes property offenses would have reflected a slow upward movement throughout the century and that the overall picture of rural crime would look substantially different as well. During the period 1834–60, theft of wood and illegal tree cutting in state forests accounted for 14.4 percent of

29. Violent crimes or crimes against persons peaked in 1905 at 37.4 percent of total rural felony convictions. The three categories used here include the following offenses: (1) property crimes: theft, burglary, robbery, sacrilege (theft from churches), dealing in stolen goods, and wood theft; (2) violent crimes: murder, mortal injury, assault, infanticide, and rape; (3) crimes against the administrative order: violations of customs, liquor, and tobacco regulations, violations of passport regulations, abuse of office, insulting or resisting officials, and uprisings.

30. This shunting of property crimes into summary jurisdictions occurred in a number of countries during the nineteenth century, with similar anomalies resulting in the statistical representations of property offenses. See, e.g., Clive Emsley, *Crime and Society in England, 1750–1900* (London, 1987), 25; Perrot, "Delinquency," 220–21.

31. S. Budzinskii, *Zakon 18 maia 1882 g. o krazhe* (Warsaw, 1886); E. Frantsesson, "Po povodu zakona 18-go maia 1882 goda 'o nakazaniiakh za krazhu so vzlomom,'" *SudG*, no. 12 (1884), 12–15; Aristov, *Volostnoi sud*, 56–60; "Zakon 18 dekabria 1883 g., o rasshirenii podsudnosti sudebno-mirovykh uchrezhdenii," *ZhGUP* 16, no. 2 (1886), 160–72.

all crimes tried by criminal courts. That proportion grew even larger between 1861 and 1868 among cases coming before nonreformed courts, averaging 26.9 percent. Wood theft accounted for between one-fourth and just under one-half of total property crimes recorded in the second quarter of the nineteenth century (with an average of nearly 20,000 cases tried each year). It increased both numerically and proportionately over this period and grew with particular speed from 1860 on—a point that should be emphasized in conjunction with the struggle over forest land that accompanied emancipation. By 1861, 60.2 percent of all enumerated crimes fell into the category of property offenses (figure 2.1). Crimes against persons, by contrast, made up just 5.6 percent of the total and never reached higher than 11 percent of all offenses, averaging 8.4 percent from 1834 to 1860 and declining gradually over this twenty-four-year span. As for administrative offenses, they fluctuated at about one-quarter of recorded crimes until 1858, then averaged roughly 14 percent through the first eight years of the 1860s—proportions that did not differ dramatically from those found in reformed court statistics after 1874.[32]

The most critical distinctions between pre- and postemancipation judicial statistics would thus appear to be the absence in the latter period of data on theft of wood and the increasing proportion of thefts and burglaries omitted from these compilations because they were prosecuted by lower courts. Sample caseloads from both *volost'* courts and land captains of two central provinces make clear where such cases were being tried after emancipation. In 1891, for example, three *volost'* courts in Moscow province examined 113 criminal cases, of which wood theft constituted 28.3 percent. All property infractions combined accounted for 60.2 percent of total offenses. Crimes against persons (insults to honor, threats, and violence) made up 15.9 percent of the caseload, and administrative infractions (mostly passport violations, breaking of fire regulations, and bootlegging) claimed 16.8 percent.[33] During 1905, the five land captains of one Riazan' district heard 629 criminal cases, of which 369 (58.7 percent) were property offenses. Nearly half of this number (172 cases, or 27.3 percent of all crimes) involved theft of wood from forests. Infractions of fire safety regulations accounted for another 8.6 percent (54 cases) of total cases heard, with disobeying the orders of authorities making up only 1.1 percent (7 cases). Similar patterns can be found in land captain cases from other districts.[34]

32. *Otchety,* vols. 1–34.

33. TsGIAgM, f. 28, op. 1, d. 19, l. 20b. (Dmitrovsk district). See also GARO, f. 71, op. 10 (1899), d. 23; op. 17 (1913), d. 35; f. 72, op. 10 (1900), d. 3; f. 76, op. 4 (1893), d. 9; op. 5 (1894), d. 6; op. 7 (1896), d. 12; op. 9, d. 5.

34. GARO, f. 721, op. 1, sv. 3, d. 167, ll. 420b., 45 (Spassk district). For additional districts, see, e.g., f. 74, op. 25 (1890), d. 5; op. 26 (1891), d. 15; op. 28 (1896), dd. 38, 39, 47; f. 75,

Using these percentages to gauge the quantity of property offenses tried in lower judicial or administrative instances can provide at least a rough sense of how large the "dark figure" was in Russian crime. Riazan' province is a good test case here, for its overall known crime rates remained moderate throughout the last decades of the old regime. If we estimate conservatively (based on a sample of annual reports) that after 1889 some 40 percent of all crimes tried by this province's land captains and *volost'* courts fell into the category of property infractions, then in 1892 there was a combined total of over 7,000 such offenses, and more than 10,000 in 1903.[35] Justices of the peace in Riazan' and other provinces also tried several thousand rural property offenses each year until their 1889 abolition. As for the number of thefts or burglaries that never reached either lower or circuit courts, a 1904 government commission admitted that the police investigated as few as ten out of every hundred thefts, as a result of which "the vast majority of victims of theft do not even bother to report the crimes."[36]

Courts constituted only one of several arenas in which rural crimes might be punished, however; various officials could also try and sentence peasants without recourse to any judicial body. Empowered with both administrative and judicial authority, land captains represented one such alternative. Much closer to daily life, village and township elders handled unknown but by all accounts sizable numbers of criminal offenses, settling them through reconciliation or by fines and short jail sentences. At the other end of the administrative hierarchy, a law of July 13, 1876, gave provincial governors additional police authority by empowering them to issue "binding regulations" (*ob"iazatel'nye postanovleniia*) concerning public order and crime. Yet as Richard Robbins has written, the power accorded governors by this statute "paled when compared to the potential for control created by the infamous decree [of August 14, 1881] on 'measures to preserve state order and public tranquillity.'"[37] Often called the "extraordinary measures," a form of martial law introduced throughout most of the empire in the wake of Emperor Alexander II's assassination, this law significantly broadened

---

op. 23 (1890), dd. 7, 17, 31, 47–49, 51–52; op. 24 (1891), dd. 25, 38, 65; op. 26 (1893), dd. 6–11, 16, 18, 23, 28; f. 1256, op. 1, d. 12.

35. These figures are derived from data in GARO, f. 695, op. 6, sv. 75, d. 12; op. 10, sv. 134, d. 5; op. 12, sv. 162, dd. 5–7; op. 13, sv. 169, d. 1. In many localities, *volost'* offices recorded property offenses separately when filing reports with land captains. As a result their general reports reflect very small proportions of thefts—sometimes as low as 10–15 percent of all offenses. See, e.g., GARO, f. 71, op. 18 (1914), sv. 11, d. 82, ll. 1–13; f. 72, op. 10 (1900), d. 3, ll. 1–139.

36. D. S. Fleksor, comp., *Okhrana sel'skokhoziaistvennoi sobstvennosti* (SPb, 1904), 53–54.

37. Richard G. Robbins, *The Tsar's Viceroys: Russian Provincial Governors in the Last Years of the Empire* (Ithaca, 1987). 180–81. See also Vilenskii, *Sudebnaia reforma,* 305–34; N. A. Troitskii, *Tsarizm pod sudom progressivnoi obshchestvennosti, 1866–1895* (Moscow, 1979), 46–76.

governors' police power by allowing them to suspend civil rights and, through their district police commandants, to arrest and punish accused criminals using administrative rather than judicial process. Not widely employed until the 1905 Revolution, various "binding regulations" and the "extraordinary measures" resulted in hundreds of peasants being punished annually during the years thereafter, most charged with mass cutting of trees, assaults on landed estates, robbery and banditry, or hooliganism. Historians estimate that by 1912 some form of martial law governed the lives of all but 5 million Russians.[38]

In sum, published judicial statistics provide a tidy yet woefully inaccurate depiction of rural crime. As early as the 1860s, the overwhelming majority of known property offenses were tried before lower court instances and not enumerated in official sources. By the 1880s, substantial numbers of crimes fell under the purview of administrative authorities. These figures grew larger throughout the 1890s and especially after 1905. Still more crimes either went unreported because of the peasants' lack of faith in the police or remained unsolved due to inadequate rural policing. It is clear, however, that the largest known category of prosecuted property offenses in the post-emancipation countryside was theft of wood and illegal cutting on state or private forest lots, much as had been the case before 1861. The same held true across much of rural Europe at mid-century, after which time some governments either decriminalized the offense or shifted it to a lesser jurisdiction.[39] When Russian authorities transferred first wood theft and later an estimated half or more of property crimes to lower courts, these offenses simply vanished from the statistics, thereby dramatically raising the proportions of crimes against persons or the administrative order.

Despite their familiarity with evidence disproving it, many criminologists and jurists continued to promote the notion of a countryside characterized by "bloody crimes." That they did so testifies to the tight intertwining of long established attitudes about rural society with the "facts" of crime as represented in official publications. The data served to substantiate already formed opinions. Poor, ignorant, superstitious, increasingly immoral, and

38. Robbins, *The Tsar's Viceroys*, 181; Robert Thurston, "Police and People in Moscow, 1906–1914," *RR* 39, no. 3 (1980), 321–22; Peter Waldron, "States of Emergency: Autocracy and Extraordinary Legislation, 1881–1917," *Revolutionary Russia* 8, no. 1 (1995), 1–25. For examples of these measures in practice, see GARO, f. 5, st. 3, op. 4, dd. 4945–4948 (1909), 5395–5396 (1911), and Chapter 9.

39. See Perrot, "Delinquency," 220–21; Joseph Mooser, "Property and Wood Theft: Agrarian Capitalism and Social Conflict in Rural Society, 1800–50: A Westphalian Case Study," in R. E. Moeller, ed., *Peasants and Lords in Modern Germany* (Boston, 1986), 52–80. In the Palatinate of southwestern Germany during the 1840s, one inhabitant out of every three was convicted for wood theft each year. Jonathan Sperber, *The European Revolutions, 1848–1851* (Cambridge, 1994), 41.

prone to violence in their everyday relations, it was argued, villagers had little worth stealing from each other and tended to resolve conflicts by force, employing the "law of the fist" as they had learned to do under serfdom. Furthermore, this view continued, because peasants were still largely untouched by the civilizing influence of education and lacked the paternalistic supervision believed necessary for instilling morality and order, they persisted in committing crimes precisely because of their ignorance, immorality, and uncontrolled passion.[40]

## PEASANT FELONS: A PECULIAR PROFILE

One issue little discussed by contemporaries was the concrete identity of rural offenders about whom conclusions of this sort were made. Particularly before 1905, most commentators had the classic peasant farmer firmly in mind when speaking of "peasant" criminality, but the data reveal a rather different picture. The legal category of "peasants" or serfs grew steadily as a percentage of persons convicted from 1834 to 1861, as figure 2.2 shows, then fell to early nineteenth-century levels between the mid-1860s and 1870s. This drop simply reflects the confusion that arose with the introduction of reformed courts into primarily urban settings, before new jurisdictional boundaries had been clarified in the countryside. By the late 1880s peasants' proportional representation among felons again equaled its prereform level and continued to increase thereafter, reaching as high as 80.9 percent in 1907, when government forces, having defeated the urban revolution, were still engaged in punitive pacification campaigns in the countryside.

But the juridical designation "peasant" masked the occupation at which a member of the peasant estate was engaged. We can tell this from two different data sets, starting with convicts' stated sources of primary income—published from 1872 until 1896. During that period, an average of 46.1 percent depended chiefly upon farming for support. By contrast, 20 percent of all convicts claimed their major means of support to be income derived from handicraft production, and another 14 percent made a living by outwork and day labor.[41] Equally revealing is information concerning the

40. This view proved even more common in countries to the west with stronger middle-class societies and can still be found among modern criminologists and historians of crime. See, e.g., Alain Corbin, *The Village of Cannibals: Rage and Murder in France*, 1870 (Cambridge, 1992); Peter Gay, *The Cultivation of Hatred* (New York, 1993), 130–31; Regina Schulte, *The Village in Court: Arson, Infanticide, and Poaching in the Court Records of Upper Bavaria, 1848–1910* (Cambridge, 1994), 58–75, 184–87; Ted Robert Gurr, "Historical Trends in Violent Crime: A Critical Review of the Evidence," in Norval Morris and Michael Tonry, eds., *Crime and Justice: An Annual Review of Research* (Chicago, 1981), 295–353.

41. *Svody*, vols. 3–42, part 2, "Religiia, sredstva k zhizni i zakonnost' rozhdeniia osuzhdennykh."

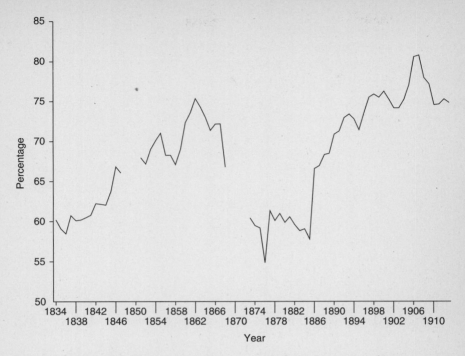

Figure 2.2. Juridical Peasants as Percent of Felony Convicts, 1834–1913

occupations of felony convicts (figure 2.3). Among all persons found guilty
by circuit courts for the years 1874–1913, an average of 53.9 percent were
employed in agriculture. Only 35.2 percent of these were farming peasants
(*khlebopashtsy*), whereas 15.9 percent worked as hired farm laborers (*sel'skie
rabochie po naimu*). Because many rural workers regularly entered the statistics under the broad heading of "day laborer" (*podenshchiki* or *cherno-
rabochie*), adjusted figures that take account of this anomaly bring the
proportion of rural laborers to approximately 22 percent. If the entire occupational group listed under "agriculture" is broken down, we find the
proportion of hired laborers rising steadily throughout our period, from
22.9 percent of all convicts engaged in agriculture for the five-year period
1874–78, to 37.2 percent for the years 1909–13. During these same two
periods, farmers fell from 70.5 percent to only 59.6 percent of convicts
making their living on the land.

These findings are among the most important to emerge from our analysis because they demonstrate for the first time the relatively small proportion of farming peasants among the felony convict population. Property
offenses by farmers would most often be adjudicated in *volost'* courts or dealt
with by village and township elders. The same can be said for a range of
other crimes. Generally hostile to the police and mistrustful of intervention

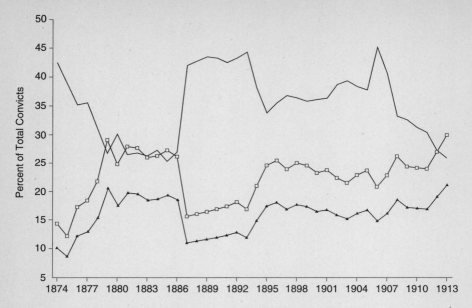

Figure 2.3. Primary Occupation of Peasant Felony Convicts, 1874–1913

by nonpeasant authorities, peasant communities also frequently concealed criminal offenses from outsiders in order to protect fellow villagers, or simply to ensure that prying investigators would not meddle in a local matter.[42] Persons of other classes and occupations (including rural wage laborers working away from their native townships), in short, were more likely to stand trial before circuit courts for property crimes and other offenses frequently dealt with differently in villages.

42. For examples, see V. V. Tenishev, *Administrativnoe polozhenie russkogo krest'ianina* (SPb, 1908), 47–9; K. A., "Nabliudeniia i zametki ob usloviiakh sledstvennoi deiatel'nosti v provintsii," *SudZh*, no. 5 (1873), 1–32; Kolmogorov, "O proizvodstve sledstvii v sel'skikh obshchestvakh (U gosudarstvennykh krest'ian bez upravleniia ot gosud. imushchestv)," *IuZh*, no. 4 (1860), part 3, 278–92; "Vzgliad krest'ian na prisiagu," *Sovremennaia letopis'*, no. 2 (1863), 16. Avoiding contact with police and other officials extended to hiding evidence about crimes that one had not even committed for the simple fact that any investigation would entail questioning and possibly detention of the person who reported the crime. For authorities this was a particular problem in case of corpses found in rural areas—a common occurrence throughout our period. As one legal journal described the problem in 1861, "It often happens that peasants, upon finding a dead body on their land, remove it to the land of a neighbor; he, in turn, moves it to another neighbor, and in this way the corpse crosses one boundary after another until traces of the crime completely disappear." "Delo o krest'ianine Il'mukhe Il'-mulline s tovarishchami, obviniaemykh v prezhdevremennom pogrebenii mertvogo tela soldatskoi docheri Kniarziani Izmailovoi," *ZhMIu*, no. 11 (1861), 327.

Such distinctions are especially evident when we compare felony conviction patterns among farming peasants and rural wage laborers (table 2.2). The data show that that the most significant differences are to be found not among violent crimes but with property and administrative offenses. Levels of crimes against persons remained similar between the two groups during the years 1874–1913, except for the period 1899–1903, when farmers' assault convictions swelled to nearly 23 percent of their total felonies, in contrast to 13 percent for hired laborers. Peasant farmers, in fact, had roughly twice the level of convictions on charges of revolt or resisting authorities that laborers did, which accounts for one substantial difference between their respective felony patterns. Whether these figures accurately depict the reality of participation in protests or assaults on officials, however, is questionable. The average villager arrested for revolt and resistance came before a circuit court; on the other hand, because their collective actions frequently took the form of strikes, rural laborers would more often be tried by special courts assigned to handle such cases, or else punished through administrative process.[43] Trials of peasant farmers therefore entered the judicial statistics, whereas those of laborers did so less frequently.

Property offenses reflect by far the sharpest measurable difference between convictions of peasant farmers and laborers and one that must also be attributed, in large part, to court jurisdictions. Theft, burglary, and robbery consistently made up a greater proportion of rural laborers' felonies than was the case for farming peasants. Here again, however, the latter came most often before *volost'* courts when charged with theft, whereas many hired agricultural workers ended up standing trial in higher courts because they were arrested outside of their townships or districts of legal registration. Under the circumstances of their work, the likelihood that laborers would perpetrate theft against nonpeasants was greater than for farmers, and before 1889 such cases were not tried by *volost'* courts. Economic hardship and the insecurities of the labor market likewise played an important role in determining that many laborers turned to theft for survival or to supplement incomes, especially during periods of unemployment or a decline in agricultural wages. Peasants, too, stole from need, of course, but if caught their deeds were less likely to enter the statistical record. Indeed, peasants could only come before circuit courts for theft if they had been convicted by *volost'* courts twice before on these same charges.

Upon closer examination, then, this rural population of felony convicts around which so much contemporary discussion turned does not easily match the popular profile of culturally underdeveloped peasant farmers given to crimes of violence far more than members of other social classes or

43. Among many examples, see GARO, f. 5, st. 3, op. 4, dd. 4703–15, 4721–24 (1907); ibid., f. 640, st. 3, op. 52, sv. 225, dd. 472–76.

TABLE 2.2　Felonies of Peasant Farmers and Hired Agricultural Laborers, 1874–1913 (As percent of total convicts in each group)

| Crimes | 1874–1878 | | 1879–1883 | | 1884–1888 | | 1889–1893 | |
|---|---|---|---|---|---|---|---|---|
| | Farmers | Laborers | Farmers | Laborers | Farmers | Laborers | Farmers | Laborers |
| Religious crimes | 0.8 | 0.3 | 0.6 | 0.4 | 1.2 | 1.2 | 2.3 | 0.9 |
| Sacrilege | 0.5 | 0.7 | 0.3 | 0.7 | 0.5 | 0.5 | 0.3 | 0.5 |
| Perjury and false evidence | 0.4 | 0.9 | 0.7 | 0.4 | 1.3 | 0.8 | 1.4 | 1.2 |
| State crimes | | | | | | | | |
| Uprisings and resistance to authorities | 0.9 | 0.3 | 1.5 | 1.0 | 4.7 | 2.7 | 5.1 | 1.9 |
| Insulting and disobeying authorities | 7.0 | 2.9 | 7.8 | 4.1 | 9.9 | 5.5 | 8.2 | 3.7 |
| Passport violations | 2.0 | 1.0 | 2.2 | 1.0 | 3.2 | 2.9 | 3.1 | 3.7 |
| Forgery | 0.9 | 0.5 | 1.1 | 0.7 | 1.5 | 0.9 | 1.1 | 0.5 |
| Beating and torture by officials | 1.1 | 0.3 | 1.5 | 0.5 | 2.0 | 0.2 | 2.4 | 0.2 |
| Abuse of public office | 5.6 | 2.3 | 6.1 | 3.0 | 7.8 | 2.9 | 10.6 | 1.6 |
| Liquor and customs violations | 0.4 | 0.2 | 0.4 | 0.2 | 1.5 | 2.5 | 0.6 | 0.8 |
| Against forest regulations | 2.9 | 0.8 | 3.8 | 1.5 | 3.6 | 0.9 | 1.6 | 0.6 |
| Against peace and safety | 0.6 | 0.7 | 0.5 | 0.4 | 0.4 | 0.8 | 0.7 | 1.2 |
| Fornication | 0.3 | 0.5 | 0.4 | 1.6 | 1.6 | 4.5 | 3.5 | 6.5 |
| Murder of spouse and relatives | 0.5 | 0.5 | 0.5 | 0.9 | 0.6 | 0.7 | 0.5 | 0.4 |
| Infanticide | 0.1 | 1.2 | 0.0 | 2.0 | 0.1 | 2.7 | 0.2 | 3.9 |
| Poisoning | 0.1 | 0.1 | 0.1 | 0.3 | 0.1 | 0.3 | 0.1 | 0.1 |
| All other murder | 5.4 | 5.0 | 5.8 | 5.8 | 7.2 | 7.1 | 6.0 | 5.3 |
| Endangerment and concealing corpse of newborn | 0.5 | 1.6 | 0.3 | 2.3 | 0.9 | 4.2 | 2.1 | 4.7 |
| Mortal injury | 2.6 | 2.1 | 3.7 | 2.7 | 4.0 | 3.8 | 3.6 | 2.6 |
| Assault | 6.1 | 4.2 | 7.4 | 6.7 | 9.7 | 7.7 | 10.7 | 7.4 |
| Rape | 0.4 | 0.9 | 0.5 | 1.2 | 0.6 | 1.8 | 0.6 | 0.8 |
| Insult | 0.2 | 0.3 | 0.3 | 0.2 | 0.3 | 0.2 | 0.5 | 0.2 |
| Adultery | 0.1 | 0.1 | 0.0 | 0.1 | 0.1 | 0.2 | 0.2 | 0.2 |
| Incest | 0.3 | 0.3 | 0.4 | 0.3 | 0.4 | 0.3 | 0.5 | 0.3 |
| Arson | 1.9 | 3.1 | 2.2 | 2.9 | 2.8 | 3.9 | 2.1 | 3.5 |

TABLE 2.2    (*continued*)

| 1894–1898 | | 1899–1903 | | 1904–1908 | | 1909–1913 | | 1874–1913 | |
|---|---|---|---|---|---|---|---|---|---|
| Farmers | Laborers | Farmers | Laborers | Farmers | Laborers | Farmers | Laborers | Farmers | Laborers |
| 1.9 | 1.1 | 1.4 | 0.7 | 0.8 | 0.5 | 1.8 | 1.1 | 1.4 | 0.8 |
| 0.4 | 0.4 | 0.3 | 0.5 | 0.2 | 0.6 | 0.3 | 0.5 | 0.4 | 0.5 |
| | | | | | | | | | |
| 1.1 | 0.9 | 1.5 | 1.0 | 0.6 | 0.3 | 1.4 | 0.6 | 1.0 | 0.8 |
| | | | | 1.8 | 2.7 | 2.1 | 1.6 | | |
| | | | | | | | | | |
| 4.7 | 1.6 | 6.1 | 3.5 | 2.3 | 10.8 | 9.5 | 3.6 | 7.0 | 3.2 |
| | | | | | | | | | |
| 5.7 | 2.1 | 8.3 | 3.4 | 6.4 | 2.7 | 5.1 | 1.6 | 7.3 | 3.3 |
| 1.5 | 1.9 | 1.2 | 2.2 | 0.7 | 1.2 | 0.8 | 1.0 | 1.8 | 1.9 |
| 1.4 | 0.9 | 0.9 | 0.9 | 0.5 | 0.5 | 1.0 | 0.7 | 1.1 | 0.7 |
| | | | | | | | | | |
| 1.7 | 0.2 | 2.8 | 0.2 | 1.3 | 0.2 | 1.0 | 0.2 | 1.7 | 0.2 |
| | | | | | | | | | |
| 7.8 | 1.2 | 7.2 | 1.6 | 3.7 | 1.3 | 3.5 | 0.9 | 6.5 | 1.9 |
| | | | | | | | | | |
| 0.5 | 0.9 | 1.3 | 3.5 | 1.6 | 4.1 | 2.3 | 4.0 | 1.1 | 2.0 |
| | | | | | | | | | |
| 1.2 | 0.3 | 1.2 | 0.3 | 1.2 | 0.4 | 1.6 | 0.3 | 2.1 | 0.7 |
| | | | | | | | | | |
| 0.6 | 0.5 | 1.1 | 2.1 | 0.7 | 1.7 | 0.5 | 0.6 | 0.6 | 1.0 |
| 6.6 | 8.2 | 4.5 | 5.7 | 0.0 | 0.0 | 0.9 | 0.3 | 2.2 | 3.4 |
| | | | | | | | | | |
| 0.6 | 0.4 | 0.5 | 0.6 | 0.5 | 0.5 | 0.7 | 0.5 | 0.6 | 0.6 |
| 0.3 | 5.0 | 0.1 | 1.7 | 0.1 | 1.8 | 0.1 | 2.5 | 0.1 | 2.6 |
| 0.2 | 0.0 | 0.1 | 0.1 | 0.0 | 0.0 | 0.1 | 0.0 | 0.1 | 0.1 |
| 5.6 | 5.0 | 5.9 | 5.2 | 6.3 | 6.8 | 9.7 | 9.3 | 6.5 | 6.2 |
| | | | | | | | | | |
| 2.1 | 3.2 | 2.2 | 3.6 | 1.4 | 2.4 | 1.0 | 1.9 | 1.3 | 3.0 |
| 4.8 | 3.0 | 4.7 | 3.3 | 6.3 | 5.3 | 8.0 | 7.4 | 4.7 | 3.8 |
| 15.5 | 9.1 | 22.6 | 13.2 | 16.6 | 11.8 | 8.8 | 8.4 | 12.2 | 8.6 |
| 0.6 | 1.2 | 0.4 | 1.1 | 0.5 | 0.7 | 0.8 | 1.3 | 0.6 | 1.1 |
| 0.5 | 0.2 | 0.6 | 0.3 | 0.5 | 0.2 | 0.7 | 0.2 | 0.5 | 0.2 |
| 0.4 | 0.4 | 0.3 | 0.4 | 0.1 | 0.2 | 0.1 | 0.1 | 0.2 | 0.2 |
| 0.5 | 0.2 | 0.3 | 0.2 | 0.1 | 0.1 | 0.2 | 0.1 | 0.3 | 0.2 |
| 1.8 | 2.6 | 1.2 | 2.2 | 1.4 | 1.6 | 1.8 | 1.8 | 1.9 | 2.7 |

(*continued*)

TABLE 2.2    (*continued*)

|  | 1874–1878 | | 1879–1883 | | 1884–1888 | | 1889–1893 | |
| --- | --- | --- | --- | --- | --- | --- | --- | --- |
| Crimes | Farmers | Laborers | Farmers | Laborers | Farmers | Laborers | Farmers | Laborers |
| Robbery | 6.5 | 7.0 | 5.9 | 6.2 | 5.3 | 6.2 | 3.1 | 4.6 |
| Burglary | 31.2 | 38.1 | 23.4 | 27.8 | 7.0 | 9.4 | 8.0 | 8.0 |
| Dealing in stolen goods | 0.7 | 1.3 | 0.8 | 0.5 | 0.4 | 0.3 | 0.4 | 0.4 |
| All other theft | 16.0 | 22.2 | 18.6 | 24.1 | 18.0 | 22.4 | 16.4 | 33.5 |
| Total theft | 54.4 | 68.7 | 48.6 | 58.7 | 30.6 | 38.3 | 27.9 | 46.4 |
| Property crimes | 55.0 | 69.4 | 49.0 | 59.3 | 31.1 | 38.8 | 28.2 | 46.9 |
| Violent crimes | 17.0 | 16.2 | 20.1 | 22.6 | 25.7 | 28.7 | 26.7 | 25.6 |
| Administrative crimes | 16.4 | 7.4 | 18.4 | 9.7 | 27.5 | 17.2 | 28.4 | 12.9 |

SOURCE: *Svody*, part 2, "Zaniatiia osuzhdennykh."

juridical estates.[44] Rather, its composition was to a very great extent deter-mined by which courts tried perpetrators engaged in different agricultural occupations. Because *volost'* courts held jurisdiction over most property offenses committed by peasant farmers—a sphere that expanded further after 1889—this group's proportional representation among circuit and peace court convicts remained far lower than what it would have been had a peasant estate court not been retained at the time of emancipation. As a consequence, the population of rural felons contained disproportionate numbers of agricultural wage workers and day laborers with high levels of property offenses, whereas the percentage of farming peasants among all convicts shrank steadily in direct correlation to the growing exclusion of rural property crimes from overburdened higher courts. The statistical sources used to support a highly inaccurate picture of peasant criminality could substantiate such a perspective only to those who possessed little un-derstanding of the administrative-judicial structure into which a majority of the Russian population had been placed at the time of emancipation.

## CRIME AND THE INTERESTS OF STATE

The same problems that skewed other aspects of the statistical representa-tion also make it difficult to calculate growth in rural felony convictions. Per

44. One of the only exceptions was Tarnovskii, who noted that peasant convicts could not be compared to those from other classes or occupations because most peasant offenders were tried in *volost'* courts. Still, even he argued that no other social or occupational group showed

TABLE 2.2    (*continued*)

| 1894–1898 | | 1899–1903 | | 1904–1908 | | 1909–1913 | | 1874–1913 | |
|---|---|---|---|---|---|---|---|---|---|
| Farmers | Laborers | Farmers | Laborers | Farmers | Laborers | Farmers | Laborers | Farmers | Laborers |
| 3.1 | 3.9 | 2.2 | 3.9 | 3.4 | 6.7 | 3.7 | 7.6 | 4.1 | 5.8 |
| 8.4 | 9.2 | 5.0 | 8.6 | 5.0 | 10.7 | 4.8 | 9.2 | 11.6 | 15.1 |
| | | | | | | | | | |
| 0.3 | 0.1 | 0.3 | 0.3 | 0.2 | 0.2 | 0.5 | 0.3 | 0.5 | 0.4 |
| 17.4 | 38.2 | 11.9 | 29.2 | 11.7 | 23.9 | 22.8 | 31.9 | 16.6 | 28.2 |
| 29.1 | 51.3 | 19.4 | 42.0 | 20.3 | 41.5 | 31.7 | 48.9 | 32.8 | 49.5 |
| 29.5 | 51.7 | 19.6 | 42.5 | 20.5 | 42.1 | 32.0 | 49.4 | 33.1 | 50.0 |
| 31.8 | 27.3 | 40.0 | 29.3 | 33.4 | 29.8 | 30.8 | 31.7 | 28.2 | 26.4 |
| | | | | | | | | | |
| 20.6 | 8.2 | 25.1 | 16.5 | 38.1 | 24.5 | 23.7 | 13.4 | 24.3 | 13.3 |

capita crime rates can only be analyzed at the provincial level, for example, without distinguishing rural from urban populations. This leaves a far less satisfactory measure based on simple numerical growth in rural and urban regions of each province. Yet here, too, caution is required above all because of the 1905 Revolution and its impact on the number of arrests and convictions. Without controlling for revolution or the new force of police guards, average growth among all court circuits enumerated in the judicial statistics between 1874 and 1913 shows a slightly higher annual increase for rural than for urban felonies (2.8 percent and 2.1 percent). If the revolutionary years 1905–1907 are excluded, however, these averaged rates fall to 0.9 and 0.8 percent. Yet because comparable data are lacking for property offenses in the countryside, even these figures are only vague indicators suggestive of more rapid rural growth rates, but by no means do they approach an accurate measurement.

Rates of growth for individual felonies prove somewhat more fruitful in shedding light on what the judicial statistics say about crimes tried by circuit courts. Table 2.3 presents crude average growth of selected rural felony convictions between 1874 and 1913. It demonstrates that offenses with the highest rates of increase included misuse of public office, insurrection or revolt, smuggling and bootlegging, and violation of passport regulations. Convictions for homicide and assault showed comparatively moderate growth, whereas arson, robbery, and other forms of theft, not surprisingly,

---

such high proportions of violent crime as did peasant farmers. "Raspredelenie prestupnosti po professiiam," *ZhMIu*, no. 8 (1907), 72, 74–75.

TABLE 2.3   Average Growth Rates for Rural Felonies, 1874–1913

| Offense | Men | Women | Total |
|---|---|---|---|
| Abuse of public office | 29.6 | | 29.6 |
| Uprising and resistance to authorities | 28.7 | 23.4 | 27.1 |
| Beatings and torture by officials | 15.8 | | 15.8 |
| Liquor and customs violations | 12.4 | 29.8 | 13.7 |
| Adultery | 16.0 | 17.4 | 12.0 |
| Rape | 11.8 | | 11.8 |
| Religious crimes | 11.2 | 21.0 | 10.9 |
| Dealing in stolen goods | 12.0 | 18.9 | 10.6 |
| Passport violations | 9.5 | 67.7 | 9.7 |
| Infanticide | | 8.4 | 8.4 |
| Mortal injury | 8.2 | 17.7 | 8.2 |
| Assault | 8.0 | 9.7 | 8.0 |
| Concealing corpse of newborn | | 7.8 | 7.6 |
| Defloration of minors | 7.5 | | 7.5 |
| Murder of spouse | 7.5 | 6.7 | 6.6 |
| Theft from churches (sacrilege) | 5.3 | 66.2 | 6.2 |
| Theft | 6.4 | 4.9 | 6.2 |
| Insulting or disobeying authorities | 6.1 | 5.8 | 5.9 |
| Murder (all) | 6.0 | 3.0 | 5.7 |
| Incest | 5.3 | 6.9 | 5.2 |
| Arson | 4.2 | 4.1 | 3.8 |
| Robbery | 3.9 | 9.1 | 3.8 |
| Burglary | 1.5 | 1.5 | 1.5 |

SOURCE: *Svody*, part 2, "Vremia i mesto soversheniia prestuplenii."

had the lowest increases. It was the category of administrative offenses that rose most rapidly during our period, but the agrarian revolution of 1905–1907 also played a significant role in this process. During the course of 1905, for example only 1,951 people in rural areas were convicted on charges of uprising. The following year, this number exploded to 12,683 (an increase of 487.8 percent) and reached 14,186 in 1907. Still, revolution cannot fully explain such high rates, since even when the years of upheaval are excluded, average growth for this crime stood at 16.5 percent.

Concerns of central government administrators within the MVD and the Ministry of Finance over disorder and revenue losses to state coffers stand at the forefront of factors shaping both patterns of convictions and growth rates among recorded felonies. That local authorities focused increasing and selective attention on particular offenses cannot be doubted. Loss of revenues to the flourishing illegal liquor trade, for instance, produced endless calls from the Ministry of Finance and the MVD for greater efforts at apprehension and prosecution on the part of provincial officials, as well as for stiffer penalties. As a direct result of these demands, in August 1910 the Riazan' Governor's Office ordered land captains to begin trying all cases of bootlegging out of turn and to increase the punishments meted out to offenders.[45] Fear of revolution and an enlarged rural police force also combined to influence significantly certain categories within the criminal statistics. This same focus could be found in the law enforcement activities of officials, like governors, whose police authority and broad powers of administrative punishment were directed above all at the prevention or suppression of localized peasant revolts before they could spread. Indeed, if such administrative cases were added to the general felony statistics, they would create a portrait of "crime" even more grossly weighted toward offenses such as revolt or disobedience to authorities.[46]

One additional set of factors that reflects upon the role of state concerns in shaping the empire's criminal statistics is that of nationality and religion. During the period 1874–1913 Russians accounted for an average of 74.3 percent of all felony convicts, with Poles occupying a distant second place at 7.2 percent. From 1874 to 1878, however, Russians had made up 86.1 percent of the convict population. This proportion declined consistently thereafter, reaching a low of only 63.7 percent for the years 1894–98, and 67.3 percent between 1909 and 1913. The shrinking Russian proportion among felony convicts is almost entirely attributable to increased repression against ethnic, national, and religious minorities within the multinational empire. When the Ministry of Justice began to include data for the Warsaw judicial circuit (which included all of tsarist Poland) in its annual compilations on crime, the number of Poles convicted suddenly exploded, reaching 16 percent of the empire's total convicts by 1894 and falling only slightly thereafter. Data on religious affiliation show equally striking trends. Orthodox

45. GARO, f. 5, st. 1, op. 2, d. 2794, ll. 8–80b. Regarding the rapid growth of this offense, one official wrote that "infractions of the liquor regulations, which were established exclusively to protect the financial interests of the state, . . . should now be treated as a threat to public safety. Punishment should be increased for the illegal sale of liquor because such sales are beginning to spread and take on the form of an industry." "Zapiska ob usilenii repressii za narushenie piteinykh pravil," *RiazZh*, no. 22 (1916), 4. See also "Pochemu osobenno vredny bezpatentnye shinki," *SV*, no. 38 (1883), 390–92.

46. For a selection of reports from 1906 that demonstrate which offenses were given greatest attention by Riazan' police officials, land captains, and governor alike, see GARO, f. 5, st. 3, op. 4, dd. 4204–13, which detail events in ten of twelve districts.

convicts fell from 91.6 percent of the total in 1874 to a low of 64.2 percent in 1894, after which time their proportion rose slowly to the high 60 percent range—especially during the 1905–1907 Revolution. Catholics, primarily Poles, made up fully 20 percent of total convicts in 1896 and 14.4 percent for the years 1904–1908. Muslims, whose representation among convicted felons averaged about 3 percent throughout most of our period, increased rapidly beginning in 1909 and reached 8.4 percent in 1912. Patterns for Jews differed from other groups, ranging slightly above their proportion of the empire's population through the 1870s and early 1880s, then peaking at a disproportionate 8.6 percent in 1888.[47]

It would be ludicrous to suggest that 15–20 percent of all crimes in the Russian empire were committed by Catholic Poles, or that from 1909 to 1913 Muslims suddenly began perpetrating criminal offenses in vastly greater numbers than before. Imperial policy toward certain of its minority populations, however, and especially government insecurities over western border territories like partitioned Poland, makes more comprehensible such disproportionate representations of particular nationalities or religious groups among the criminal population. Poland's eastern borderland, for example, served as a major area of smuggling activity—an offense seriously detrimental to state revenues. It is therefore not unexpected to discover that large percentages of Polish convicts had been charged with this crime; among Polish women found guilty by circuit courts, up to 80 percent ran afoul of the authorities for smuggling. Likewise, local revolts or resistance to authorities in such territories met with severe repression as the state sought to ensure that disorders did not become more generalized. Through these and other government actions taken among minority populations, then, criminal statistics were distorted even further.

Considering the limited size of the imperial government's rural law enforcement arm, which placed a heavy reliance upon administrative and military authorities to maintain order, and taking into account the growing social and political instability in the country by the 1890s, it is entirely understandable that the judicial statistics reflected selective patterns of enforcement and prosecution. For a government facing ever greater demands upon its institutional resources and a growing challenge to its authority and legitimacy, such focused deployment of law enforcement and repression was one of the sole avenues of control available given the state's stubborn refusal to allow any weakening of its authority. Still it must be emphasized again that although selective policing or prosecution speaks directly to state

47. *Svody*, part 2, "Religiia, sredstva k zhizni i zakonnost' rozhdeniia osuzhdennykh;" and "Narodnost', osobye primety i soznanie na sud." For discussion of nationality and religion within the judicial statistics, see Tarnovskii, *Itogo russkoi ugolovnoi statistiki za 20 let (1874–1894 gg.)* (SPb, 1899).

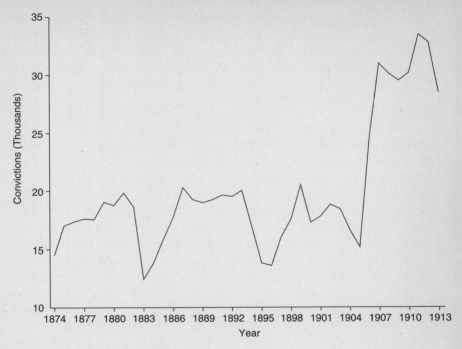

2.4. Rural Felony Convictions, 1874–1913

priorities, little is revealed about the nature of crime itself. In a very important sense, this was the dilemma faced by peasants seeking to deal with what
they believed to be a real increase of criminal activity in the countryside
(figure 2.4).

## VILLAGE PERCEPTIONS AND THE CRISIS OF LAW ENFORCEMENT

The fact that crimes against public order grew most rapidly in the statistical
compilations offers insight into the chief concerns of the state. For country
dwellers, however, the truly worrisome crimes were those that threatened
them most directly: arson, horsetheft, robbery, and a rash of other depredations against their property. Peasants saw such offenses as especially
heinous because they impoverished families, seriously compromised their
ability to farm, and threatened the very foundations of village society. Although Ministry of Justice statistics showed only moderate increases in most
of these crime categories (at least by comparison with growth rates of other
offenses), they were among the crimes most likely not to be investigated by
the rural police and to remain unsolved more often than felonies like assault or murder. From at least the 1880s on, villagers, their elected officials,
and many nonpeasant commentators felt that crime was on the rise and that

little was being done to put a stop to it. It is little wonder that peasants themselves dealt most harshly with captured arsonists, horsethieves, and robbers. Yet here, too, the judicial statistics provide concrete support to peasant claims that courts did not deal adequately with serious criminals. Charges that the police were more concerned with tax collection and public order than with crime detection, or that courts all too often released known criminals or else meted out lenient punishments, can in part be substantiated by the government's own published data. For our purposes, in fact, the most important aspect of Russia's reformed justice system that emerges from the criminal statistics concerns a remarkable plunge in the percentage of offenses prosecuted—a development, oddly enough, noted briefly by only one contemporary who wrote on crime in this period.[48]

Conviction rates by circuit courts declined modestly during our period, falling by just 5.3 percent (from 65.7 percent in 1874–78 to 62.2 percent in 1909–1913), but the rate of prosecution dropped much more sharply. Between 1874 and 1905, the number of reported offenses sent on by public prosecutors (sing.: *prokuror*) for trial fell 11.5 percent. But these figures do not tell the entire story, because prosecution rates had always been quite low in Russia. In 1874, only 30.2 percent of all cases investigated by judicial investigators and prosecutors ever came to trial. Improvement occurred during the 1880s, when caseloads for both investigators and prosecutors were reduced due to the large shift of property offenses to lower courts. In the period 1884–88, nearly 44 percent of investigated cases went on to be tried, with a peak of 48.7 percent reached in 1888. After that date conditions deteriorated rapidly. Total crimes investigated rose from 123,885 in 1889 to 195,208 in 1897—an increase of 25.9 percent. By 1905 this figure had reached 363,916, growing 86.4 percent in just eight years and causing investigators' caseloads to explode. The results were readily apparent. In 1897 only 27.4 percent of total cases were being sent to trial (a decline of 39.1 percent over 1888). Prosecution rates reached a record low of 21 percent in 1905, representing a 30 percent fall from the percentage of cases tried back in 1874, and a 56.9 percent plunge from the high point achieved in 1888.[49] Indeed, so serious and likely embarrassing was the problem that beginning in 1906 the Ministry of Justice no longer included such information in its annual compilations of crime data. Given the rapid growth of

48. Tarnovskii, "Dvizhenie prestupnosti po okruzhnym sudam evropeiskoi Rossii," *ZhMIu*, no. 8 (1905), 1–27. See also the data in P. Zepalov, "Prestupnost' piati severno-vostochnykh uezdov Vologodskoi gubernii za poslednie gody (1912–1915)," *Izvestiia Vologodskogo Obshchestva izucheniia severnogo kraia*, no. 4 (1917), 36–47; and, on conviction rates, Tarnovskii, "Opravdatel'nye prigovory v Rossii," *IuV*, no. 3 (1891), 425–41; no. 4, 607–20; Tarnovskii, "Repressiia suda prisiazhnykh po dannym za 1875–1900 gg.," *ZhMIu*, no. 1 (1904), 27–76.

49. *Svody*, part 1, tables 2–3.

cases tried between 1905 and 1913, though, we can deduce with some degree of certainty that the situation worsened still more in those years.[50]

No one seemed more aware of this deterioration than country dwellers concerned not only about crime but also about the apparent inability of prosecutors and courts to bring indictments, let alone convictions, against perpetrators. The great number of angry or desperate complaints from local communities to provincial governors, which we shall discuss in following chapters, provides vivid testimony of peasants' anger toward the criminal justice system. Adding to their frustration was a decline in convictions among those offenses which most worried them—property crimes. Whereas 52.9 percent of all arson cases tried between 1874 and 1878 resulted in convictions, by the period 1909–13 this figure had fallen to only 39.7 percent (a 25 percent decline). Conviction rates in robbery cases dropped from 62.5 percent to 46.2 percent between these two periods. Burglary convictions held up somewhat better, declining by only 10.8 percent (from a rate of 70 to 62.4 percent), whereas those for simple theft went from 70.2 to 61.9 percent (an 11.8 percent decline) and, for horsetheft, from 93.4 to 76.1 percent (a drop of 18.5 percent). By contrast, conviction rates improved substantially among offenses deemed most threatening to order, ideology, or state revenues. Whereas from 1874 to 1878 only 36.9 percent of cases involving insurrection or resistance to authorities ended in conviction, in the period 1909–13 courts convicted 61.2 percent of all persons thus accused (an improvement of 65.8 percent). Between these same five-year periods, rates for insulting authorities rose from 74.2 percent to 82.8 percent; infractions of passport regulations from 41.5 percent to 86.6 percent; offenses against tobacco and customs regulations from 51.9 percent to 77.1 percent; and religious crimes from 71.8 percent to 76 percent.[51]

With state courts overburdened, jail space at a premium, and the exile system in chaos, provincial administrations attempted to fill the most serious gaps in Russian law enforcement, but these efforts also led to criticism and protest from peasants. One increasingly common practice dating to pre-emancipation times was to leave accused criminals "under suspicion" due to lack of sufficient evidence and to place them under police observation.

50. Local archival data on growing caseloads, investigations, and prosecution rates in each court circuit may be culled from holdings for the district member of the circuit court (*uezdnyi chlen okruzhnogo suda*), the judicial investigator (*sudebnyi sledovatel'*), and the deputy prosecutor (*tovarishch-prokuror*). Information was usually compiled from the districts and held in the prosecutor's *fond*. See GARO, f. 641; TsGIAgM, f. 68 and 131 (annually). Civil caseloads grew even more rapidly, with similar results for the overburdened courts. *SbSSMIu*, vols. 1–31, part 1. This problem is discussed in William G. Wagner, *Marriage, Property, and Law in Late Imperial Russia* (Oxford, 1994), 48–58. On prosecutors, see A. G. Zviagintsev and Iu. G. Orlov, *Pod sen'iu russkogo orla. Rossiiskie prokurory. Vtoraia polovina XIX–nachalo XX v.* (Moscow, 1996).

51. *Svody*, part 2, table 1.

Already saddled with many more duties than they could possibly perform, the police spent little time checking up on such persons and often had no idea of their whereabouts. As a result, thousands of suspects were allowed to return to their communities—and often to their previous activities—where villagers fearful of revenge hesitated to bring charges against the returnees.[52] Other criminals sentenced by administrative order were simply banished to neighboring provinces and assigned to a given village for residence, creating the equally chaotic and often absurd situation of governors continuously exchanging local criminals for others who had no roots or kin in their new localities and who, in many instances, again turned to crime.[53]

From the perspective of villagers living in fear of acquitted criminals, those released without prosecution, placed "under police supervision," or set down in their midst by administrative sentence, law enforcement and justice were failing in the most basic sense. Since the data leave us with no means of knowing the full extent of this problem, we must rely on a range of different evidence and, to some extent, conjecture. Yet parallel patterns within the sources point to a similar conclusion. Throughout the postemancipation period, and particularly beginning in the 1890s, police reports contain progressively greater numbers of crimes reported to them by village and *volost'* authorities. Peasant complaints about local criminals left unpunished or about the growing problems of arson, horsetheft, and robbery besetting their communities similarly increased. Finally, as figure 2.4 shows, the judicial statistics demonstrate a significant rise in the number of criminal cases and convictions from the late 1880s on, and a veritable explosion during the years 1903–13. They also confirm that the complaints and fears of country dwellers had a solid basis in fact, for prosecution rates declined dramatically at the same time that conviction rates were falling. The countryside, then, faced a three-pronged crisis of increased crime, general insecurity, and an ever greater lack of faith in the judicial system.

We have moved some distance from the violent peasant depicted in contemporary statistics as well as in anecdotal accounts and literature. Yet the former have yielded several significant findings about postemancipation law enforcement and justice, beginning with the fact that the greatest pro-

---

52. For examples of this practice, see GARO, f. 5, st. 3, op. 4, dd. 1065 (1870), 2338–41 (1885), and others. Peasant complaints about such persons are equally plentiful. See, e.g., GARO, f. 5, st. 3, op. 4, d. 5186, ll. 3–40b.

53. See, for instance, Department of Police circular no. 356 (January 13, 1903), to provincial governors. GARO, f. 5, st. 3, op. 4, d. 3497, ll. 6–60b. See also GARO, f. 4, 1 otd., op. 100, sv. 436, d. 9693 (1865), ll. 36–37, placing restrictions on the types of villages to which such persons could be sent for resettlement.

portion of offenses perpetrated by ordinary farming peasants never appeared in Ministry of Justice compilations. Because the majority of these acts were property infractions relegated to adjudication by *volost'* courts, justices of the peace, or land captains, the profile of peasant criminality that emerges from statistical sources shows a preponderance of crimes against persons—a profile that conforms to one of the most widespread opinions concerning the nature of rural crime and its origins in the supposed brutality and lack of culture that characterized village life. The sources demonstrate that state law enforcement and prosecutorial resources were increasingly directed toward the maintenance of public order in the face of growing numbers of rural disturbances and revolts, the elimination of perceived or real threats by national minorities, and the punishment of smugglers, bootleggers, and others whose crimes deprived the government of sorely needed revenue. Most important, until the ministry ceased publishing data on prosecutors' activities, its statistics showed a steady deterioration of this critical arm of the judicial system, as evidenced in the steep decline of cases forwarded for prosecution after 1888. Conviction rates also fell among crimes that most directly threatened the peasant population.

At a point roughly corresponding to the opening salvo of Emperor Alexander III's counterreforms (1889), which included abolition of rural justices of the peace and the introduction of land captains to oversee peasant affairs, a number of interconnected developments directly influenced law enforcement and the administration of justice. Judging from the criminal statistics, nearly all felonious offenses began a sharp rise at about this time that continued largely unabated until the outbreak of war in 1914.[54] The police, increasingly directed to put down disorders, to conduct searches for illegal revolutionary literature, and to confirm the "political reliability" of new military recruits, in addition to its regular duties, had even less time than previously to pursue arsonists, horsethieves, and robbers. Hence its already low esteem sank further still, as could be seen from peasant opinions gathered at the end of the century by the Tenishev ethnographic survey.[55] Both developments, in turn, led to the judicial system's growing inability to try crimes brought before prosecutors. The state's

54. The first two years of war saw a significant decline in the number of criminal convictions. Some, like assistant Minister of Justice A. N. Verevkin ("Umen'shenie chisla sudebnykh del," *RiazZh*, no. 22 [1916], 4) attributed this drop to the introduction of prohibition, although even he was forced to admit that the siphoning off of vast numbers of men for military service likely played the most significant role. For an earlier comment stressing that war and the growth of patriotic sentiment serve to reduce crime, see "Tiflis, 2 oktiabria 1885 goda," *Iuridicheskoe obozrenie*, no. 236 (1885), 1165–70. On crime during the war, see M. N. Gernet, *Prestupnost' i samoubiistva vo vremia voiny i posle nee* (Moscow, 1927).

55. GARF, f. 586, op. 1, d. 114 (Orel province), ll. 4, 11–12; d. 118 (Riazan' province), ll. 26–7.

reaction to this multifaceted crisis was to focus the efforts of its administrative and judicial agencies on threats deemed most serious and immediate: disturbances in the countryside or among minorities, the loss of revenues to bootlegging and smuggling, and a wave of robberies of rural administrative offices containing tax receipts. In nearly all respects, these problems led to neglect of ordinary crime in rural areas, leaving peasants to fend for themselves as their government sought to stave off the weakening of its foundations.

# PART II

# Crime, Justice, and
# the Law in Village Life

## *Views from Below*

*Our Russian peasant (muzhichek) loves to be at law. If Fedot unexpectedly punches Ignat in his mug—off to the volost' court; someone curses Marena with bad words—again to court; if Fedor by mistake takes a wheel from Karp's shed—directly to court. The average number of such cases in each volost' during the course of a year is between 200 and 800. Although this is a round figure, the volost' courts very freely and quickly deal with such cases: some are reconciled, some they refuse to hear, and others . . . conclude with five to seven days in the 'cooler,' and there the case ends. Nearly every literate peasant can write a complaint to the volost' court.*

RIAZAN' LIFE, NO. 36, 1913

*Don't fight with the strong, and don't litigate with the rich.*

PEASANT SAYING

# CHAPTER 3

# Understandings of the Law

## *Property, Crime, and Justice through Peasant Eyes*

*Where there is law, there will be crime.*
PEASANT SAYING

In 1896 a noblewoman from the Porchesk district of Smolensk province filed suit with the precinct land captain charging that peasants of Sheptukha village were illegally tilling 189 acres on her estate. They had previously rented this area but gave up their lease that year to rent land elsewhere. Yet they continued to work the disputed property, now claiming it was theirs. The landowner disagreed and demanded its full restoration to her estate. Both the land captain and, on appeal, the district assembly ruled in her favor, and on June 2, 1897, the police captain was sent to enforce these decisions. Upon arrival in Sheptukha, he read out to a village assembly the legal ruling that had found in the landowner's favor, restored the land to her estate, and ordered that peasants cease any further illegal use of her property. Having listened politely and carefully, the villagers asked the captain to explain exactly which land they were not allowed to use. He retorted that he was "not their surveyor" and not obliged to allot land. The estate steward also declined to specify precisely which land the ruling concerned. Therefore, after the officer's departure villagers discussed the matter and decided that his orders surely referred to another part of the estate on which they formerly drove cattle. Still maintaining that the disputed land was their property, they now began to drive their cattle through a portion of it while continuing to farm the remainder. In effect, they used to their advantage the ruling's vagueness as well as their knowledge that lack of precise boundaries was the weakest link in property disputes, creating what they felt to be a compromise resolution.

For their blatant disobedience, the land captain who had first tried this case sentenced all peasants involved to seven days in jail, but upon release they resumed exploiting the land. A new complaint to the district assembly brought them thirty days' incarceration, with the same result. Since they had repeated this offense three times, the perpetrators came to trial before the Smolensk Circuit Court, were found guilty and handed one-year prison sentences, "but then, returning from prison to Sheptukha, they continued to exploit the land." Once more they came before the circuit court, charged with refusing to obey the law and ignoring a ruling of the district assembly. Taking into account the peasants' recidivism and their stubborn, even arrogant disavowal of guilt, the court now sentenced each of the accused to prison terms of sixteen months. The villagers appealed this decision to the Moscow Judicial Chamber, where the prosecutor argued that their low level of culture [*nekul'turnost'*], lack of legal consciousness, and complete disrespect for others' property demanded a guilty verdict and severe punishment that would teach the culprits a lesson. In spite of this staunch defense of property rights and bitter condemnation of peasant ignorance, the court dismissed all criminal charges against the villagers, basing its decision on a legal technicality that the defense attorney successfully employed to his clients' advantage. Yet the property dispute itself remained unresolved, and though the record of this case ceases with the peasants' appellate victory, one suspects that they resumed working the land that they felt to be theirs.[1]

This is but one of thousands of property disputes that clogged Russian courts in the years following emancipation and that frequently resulted in violence, resistance, or open attacks on landed estates by villagers. It testifies with some clarity to the nature of conflicts that arose over gentry maneuvers to take away some of the best peasant farmland while shifting many former serfs onto allotments with poorer soil. Entire villages suffered when landowners cut off customary access to water, forests, and common fields, thereby forcing peasants into rental agreements. Resentment over this process lasted for decades, and villagers passed stories of injustices from one generation to the next. When 600 peasant women from the village of Slotvina occupied a large, disputed plot in 1896, they insisted to the police that they had enjoyed the right to pasture livestock on this property "from time immemorial," that their grandfathers and great grandfathers had used the land, "and we won't give it up."[2]

Problems of imprecise boundaries and poor or questionable surveying further increased the potential for clashes and infringements against noble-

1. *Pravo*, no. 5 (1903), 310–11. For similar cases, see "Vyezdnaia sessiia Samarskogo okruzhnogo suda," *Pravo*, no. 13 (1900), 685–95; no. 14, 728–42; no. 15, 778–81; no. 16, 833–37; "Pogrom v imenii zemskogo nachal'nika Fediukina," *RiazV*, no. 59 (1909), 4; no. 60, 4.

2. "Zhitomir. (Babii bunt)," *NizhL*, no. 20 (1897), 3. See also "Soprotivlenie vlastiam," *Pravo*, no. 16 (1903), 1180–88; "Ranenburg. (Agrarnoe delo)," *RiazV*, no. 63 (1910), 3. On land settlements, see B. G. Litvak, *Russkaia derevnia v reforme 1861 goda: Chernozemnyi tsentr 1861–1895 gg.* (Moscow, 1972), 152–70; Alan K. Wildman, "The Defining Moment: Land Charters and the Post-Emancipation Agrarian Settlement in Russia, 1861–1863," *The Carl Beck Papers in Russian and East European Studies*, no. 1205 (1996).

owned property, creating a juridical situation characterized by contemporaries and historians alike as approaching "complete chaos."[3] That chaos stemmed fundamentally from the peculiar, dual nature of land tenure left in the wake of emancipation, which saw the simultaneous strengthening of property rights for private landowners and reinforcing of collective ownership among newly liberated peasants. Although opposition to communal land tenure already existed within Russian society and government and laws supporting household property rights had appeared well before emancipation, retention of joint ownership for peasant communities continued to guide state policy until the Stolypin reforms of 1906–1907.[4]

Land confrontations also reinforced an opinion widely shared within government circles and educated society that peasants had no understanding of the law and no respect for the concept or reality of private property. After a justice of the peace from Kursk province sentenced twenty-two villagers to jail for refusing to give up disputed land that they claimed had been illegally taken from them by a local noble, Kursk governor I. A. Zvegintsev wrote to the MVD that "in such cases severe, energetic measures are highly necessary to teach peasants to respect and fear the law, and to strengthen among them a sense of legality and respect for others' rights."[5] The belief that Russia's peasantry neither respected nor understood the law was by no means limited to the realm of property relations. It extended into the broader arena of crime and justice and was expressed in arguments that villagers were unprepared to participate in the regular judicial system and that, due to their ignorance, they commonly perpetrated crimes without even knowing the illegality of their actions.

Yet this discourse was by no means one-sided. Peasants often found that infringements of local rules and regulations were not treated as punishable offenses by official law. During the holiday of the Kazan' Mother of God, on July 8, 1894, a peasant in Tver province decided to take advantage of good weather by raking his hay despite a recent village assembly resolution forbidding work on holidays. When villagers learned what he was up to, they decided to punish him for breaking local law. They first brought out the fire hose and soaked his carefully spread hay, then tied him up when he cursed

3. David A. J. Macey, "The Peasant Commune and the Stolypin Reforms: Peasant Attitudes, 1906–14," in Roger Bartlett, ed., *Land Commune and Peasant Community in Russia* (London, 1990), 220; See also A. A. Leont'ev, "Agrarnye prestupleniia kak sledstvie neopredelennosti pozemel'nykh pravootnoshenii," *VestP* 35, no. 6 (1905), 60–73; Andrew Verner, "Discursive Strategies in the 1905 Revolution: Peasant Petitions from Vladimir Province," *RR* 54, no. 1 (1995), 65–90.

4. On the question of private versus collective land tenure, see Olga Crisp, "Peasant Land Tenure and Civil Rights Implications before 1906," in Olga Crisp and Linda Edmondson, eds., *Civil Rights in Imperial Russia* (New York, 1989), 33–64.

5. A. S. Nifontov and B. V. Zlatoustovskii, eds., *KD v 1881–1889 gg.* (Moscow, 1960), 62–63.

and ordered them to stop this "prank." Finally, they beat the culprit so severely that, in his words, "I was laid up until *Uspenie* [Feast of the Dormition]—through the most important part of the farming season." When he lodged a complaint against his assailants at the *volost'* court, one judge admonished him for resisting the other peasants and suggested that he "get drunk with them at holidays" instead. As it turned out, the village assembly's resolution was illegal. In a reply to the victim's letter concerning his ordeal, editors of *The Village Herald* noted that "neither a village nor a *volost'* assembly, nor a village or *volost'* elder, has the right to forbid peasants from working on a holiday. The resolution to this effect was completely illegal, and a complaint may be lodged with the land captain, who can abrogate it."[6]

That communal rules could be so easily overturned on orders from a state-appointed, nonpeasant administrator was viewed by peasants as an imposition of arbitrary authority. Indeed, from their vantage point state law unjustly oppressed them on two sides. It demanded that peasants respect ownership rights to property that they claimed had been illegally taken from them and held out the threat of punishment for perpetrating "crimes" against these newly defined or renegotiated rights. One immediate result of emancipation, therefore, was the creation of a range of new property offenses that did not exist (or existed in a more limited form) when peasants themselves had been the property of state, church, or private landowners. At the same time the state jealously retained the power to annul summarily any decisions taken by rural assemblies, to declare village laws illegal, and to impose sanctions if they remained in effect. This situation is similar to that witnessed earlier in a social setting as different as England, where, as historian Douglas Hay writes, "in their attitudes to property and popular custom, and hence to crime, the aristocracy, gentry, and prosperous middle class were exceptional minorities." Through the enclosure of ancient common lands by parliamentary act, they destroyed "a whole corpus of local customary law . . . [and] violated old and widely held community values. In the eyes of many Englishmen it was their rulers—landowners, entrepreneurs, magistrates, and judges—who were deviant. And it was inevitable, therefore, that legal definitions of crime did not correspond closely to the norms of a large part, perhaps the majority, of the population."[7]

6. *SV,* no. 18 (1895), 180. For further discussion, see I. P. Kupchinov, *Krest'ianskoe samoupravlenie,* 2$^{nd}$ ed. (Moscow, 1905), 136–38; GARF, f. 586, op. 1, d. 112, ll. 7–8; d. 118, l. 28; d. 120, l. 7.

7. Douglas Hay, "Crime and Justice in Eighteenth- and Nineteenth-Century England," in Norval Morris and Michael Tonry, eds., *Crime and Justice,* vol. 2 (Chicago, 1980), 46–47. See also J. M. Neeson, *Commoners: Common Right, Enclosure and Social Change in England, 1700–1820* (Cambridge, 1993). In the United States, too, the postemancipation redefinition of property rights led to criminalization of long-tolerated practices on the part of former slaves. See Eric Foner, *Nothing but Freedom: Emancipation and Its Legacy* (Baton Rouge, 1983); Edward L. Ayers,

In postemancipation Russia, many types of officially defined crimes stemmed from peasants' claims over rights, custom, and their own sense of justice. How they viewed crime, justice, and law in daily life and in the context of their interactions with landowners and government authorities, therefore, requires careful examination, for the two contexts were quite different. Consideration must be given to the way that peasant thinking shaped elite criticism of rural "legal consciousness," which often seemed to diverge sharply from the precepts of state law, and to the uses villagers made of educated Russians' beliefs, practices that simultaneously reinforced and exploited dominant stereotypes about their knowledge of the law. Put differently, it is necessary to examine both the practical benefits of "ignorance" and peasant understanding of and protest against the special legal status imposed upon them by emancipation.

## IGNORANCE AND UNDERSTANDING: A DIFFERENT VIEW

One of the most widely shared and influential nonpeasant opinions concerning justice in the Russian countryside held that villagers possessed little understanding of state law because of centuries of bondage, oppression, lack of education, and cultural backwardness. As we have seen, this perspective was used to justify retaining a separate corpus of law and a system of class courts among the peasantry, though liberal critics of the postreform judicial arrangement argued that villagers must be educated and brought into the regular system of justice as full citizens, viewing this apartheid in law as a temporary measure. The negative opinion can, of course, be traced far back into the era of serfdom. In his *Memoir on Ancient and Modern Russia* (1810–11), Nicholas Karamzin argued against emancipation because "[peasants] today have the habits of slaves," but freedom demanded "preparation through moral improvement." Once they were no longer subject to seigneurial justice, peasants would "take to fighting each other and litigating in the city—what ruin!" In 1847 a Smolensk district marshal of the nobility asserted even more forcefully that serfs "did not recognize the legal rights and mutual dependency of members of civil society."[8]

From the position of private landowners, these opinions are understandable. Whether opposed to emancipation or not, nobles rightly feared that freedom for their serfs would result in widespread offenses against their property, if not against their very persons. Certainly this fear had a direct impact on the final shape of Russia's 1864 judicial reform. That the elite pic-

---

*Vengeance and Justice: Crime and Punishment in the Nineteenth-Century American South* (New York, 1984).

8. Richard Pipes, *Karamzin's Memoir on Ancient and Modern Russia* (Cambridge, 1959), 165–66; Francis W. Wcislo, *Reforming Rural Russia* (Princeton, 1990), 12.

ture of peasant ignorance continued to dominate for decades after emancipation, however, was in large part a result of the way government and outsiders interpreted villagers' responses to the legislation. Whether through dissimulation, subterfuge, or open expressions of anger over emancipation's perceived and real inequities, peasants displayed an often intractable unwillingness to recognize the new notions of private property that the law sought to impose, at least when the issue involved demands for nonpeasant land, a distinction too often overlooked by contemporaries and historians.[9] For the state as well as those most directly affected, in turn, the safest response to official law's rejection by the majority of the population was to accept explanations like "ignorance" of the law, which, as Olga Crisp has noted, placed much of the blame for peasant shortcomings upon serfdom itself. This perspective worked to the benefit of all. Among the peasantry, defiance to the law had long been cloaked in dissimulation as a means of avoiding punishment. But through what James Scott has termed "tacit ideological complicity," the state, too, could take comfort in its self-deception, claiming that peasants did not maliciously reject its laws but simply did not understand them.[10] This standard explanation of peasant behavior worked to disguise, in the public arena, the dangerous tensions that underlay village disputes with nobles or the state over such matters as land cutoffs (*otrezki*), boundaries, and taxation.

Each in their own way, officials, liberal defenders of the rule of law, populists, socialists, and revolutionaries perpetuated a myth of rural ignorance. Writings on crime and rural justice throughout the postemancipation period are replete with commentary attesting to the myth's continued vitality. According to jurist M. N. Dukhovskoi in his lengthy study of property infractions tried by *volost'* courts during the early 1870s, "entire generations [of peasants] have lived without knowing that there are written laws."[11] Reports to a massive 1898 ethnographic survey suggested that little had changed by the century's end. A correspondent from Riazan's Skopinsk district stated that "peasants barely know the laws at all, and if they know some, then usually in an incorrect way." Another claimed that peasants in Orel province "are not only unfamiliar with the general civil and criminal laws, but are not even acquainted with the most elementary laws with which they

9. In his analysis of peasant petitions from Vladimir province, Andrew Verner shows how villagers "embraced the notion of private property . . . when it suited their own purposes." "Discursive Strategies," 88. See also Esther Kingston-Mann, "Peasant Communes and Economic Innovation: A Preliminary Inquiry," in Esther Kingston-Mann and Timothy Mixter, eds., *Peasant Economy, Culture, and Politics* (Princeton, 1991), 23–51.

10. Crisp, "Peasant Land Tenure," 46. This theme is explored at length in Daniel Field, *Rebels in the Name of the Tsar* (Boston, 1976).

11. M. N. Dukhovskoi, *Imushchestvennye prostupki po resheniiam volostnykh sudov* (Moscow, 1891), 23.

constantly come into contact. In many cases the only laws are those established by the commune—and these are sometimes entirely illegal."[12] Although openly hostile to the peasantry's legal inequality, the 1904 findings of Finance Minister Sergei Witte's Committee on the Needs of Agriculture embodied similar views. Many property infractions were said to arise "not as a result of a perpetrator's evil will, but from the extreme ignorance of the masses, from their elementary understanding of property, law, and order." Not only did villagers lack "the necessary legal consciousness and respect toward property," but "the present position of the peasantry in the realm of property relations is a direct result of its extremely low level of a sense of legality [*zakonnost'*]."[13]

How peasants actually conceived "the law" remains a perplexing question, and one that requires balancing both word and deed from sometimes peculiar sources. Though printed to entertain its mostly urban readership, a short article in a February 1892 issue of the newspaper *The Volga Herald* offers a possible way into this problem. It appears that in one district of Kazan' province, peasant children invented a new game that might be called (for they gave it no name) "the trial of the chairman of the district assembly." As this game was described to readers,

> one of the participants plays the unlucky chairman, another acts as a constable, others play the role of witnesses, and still another serves as the judge. First they catch and arrest the chairman for selling bad flour, and then he is tried and sent to the "cooler." This game is now widespread among children throughout the district, and rumors about it soon reached the chairman. . . . He ordered that rural schoolteachers not allow the game to be played among their pupils. This, of course, does not prevent them from playing it after school.[14]

Although turn-of-the-century schoolchildren certainly knew many games, the fact that this twist on "cops and robbers" attracted the attention of provincial officials and newspapers is, in itself, of interest and significance. The position of district assembly chair was usually held by the marshal of the nobility, a figure who, as chairman, wielded both administrative and judicial power over the local population, while his noble status spoke to relationships of deference and subordination still very much prevalent throughout the countryside. But as peasants knew well, neither noble status nor power prevented corruption, arbitrariness, or criminal conduct. The

12. GARF, f. 586, op. 1, d. 118, l. 28; d. 114, l. 103. See also Berendeev, "Derevenskie pis'ma. Krest'ianskie prestupleniia," *SevV,* no. 1 (1889), part 2, 41; V. V. Tenishev, *Administrativnoe polozhenie russkogo krest'ianina* (SPb, 1908), 1.

13. D. S. Fleksor, *Okhrana sel'skokhoziaistvennoi sobstvennosti* (SPb, 1904), 6–7, 13. See also I. Orshanskii, "Narodnyi sud i narodnoe pravo," *VestP,* no. 4 (1875), 213.

14. "Voskresnye nabroski," *VolzhV,* no. 38 (1892), 2.

fact that 1892 was a year of famine in the Volga region, and that in this game the chairman was being tried for selling bad flour (i.e., swindling to turn a profit), should not be overlooked. Many commoners saw corruption as synonymous with power and believed that the law often protected wrongdoers because of their social status. The children's game, then, created an imagined, equitable law that allowed for punishment irrespective of status or position, a perspective close to the stated intent of the 1864 judicial reform.

The figure of the assembly's chair is important because peasants most commonly encountered "the law" through personal contact with its nonpeasant representatives. The postemancipation countryside was awash with overlapping authorities designated to administer and explain laws and government regulations. In the daily life of most Russian peasants, the police, peace arbiters, land captains, district members of the circuit courts, and other figures *were* the law. Russian law thus remained highly personal from the peasants' perspective, and cases of arbitrariness or conflicts with officials served to provoke or confirm their suspicion of state law and resentment of their own subordinate status. Nor was arbitrary conduct difficult to find in a society where patriarchy and expectations of deference still reigned virtually supreme.

The long-running debate as to whether officials should address villagers using the informal "*ty*" (thou) as most did, rather than the formal and more respectful "*vy*" (you) is indicative of how deeply this clash between deference and respect was rooted in rural culture and Russian society more broadly. When peasants were asked their views of authorities during the late 1880s and early 1890s, many replied that they admired the judicial investigator far more than other officials because "his treatment of people is at the same time respectful and firm." In a district of Viatka province, villagers told one correspondent that most authorities simply shouted and terrified them. Before the investigator, however, "everyone is '*vy*'—yes, '*vy!*'" During questioning by this official "everything is asked, nothing's left out: how old are you, are you married, do you have lots of children, were you in the army, do you believe in God, are you a schismatic. This doesn't even happen before the priest at confession. Yes, the arrival of the investigator is a real event."[15]

Depending upon the official or institution involved, then, peasants encountered the law in a range of guises, either amicable, equitable, just, or paternal, arbitrary, even violent. Though justice often seemed to them a rare commodity in conflicts with social superiors, cases in which courts decided a legal suit in their favor held out the real possibility that a legal sys-

15. Tenishev, *Administrativnoe polozhenie*, 14. See also "Provintsial'naia khronika," *OrlV*, no. 12 (1898), 1; N. P. Druzhinin, "'Vy' i 'ty'. Po voprosu o tom, imeiut-li pravo zemskie nachal'niki govorit' podvedomstvennym im litsam 'ty' vmesto 'vy,'" *IuV*, no. 1 (1892), 119–25.

tem more supportive of their interests could be attained. This, after all, is the general understanding of equity in most societies and among most social groups. Yet the fact that police and district- or province-level authorities all too regularly took the side of landowners in their disputes with villagers certainly suggested to the latter that law and justice were anything but symmetrical, and that equity proved difficult indeed to achieve.

Peasants frequently reinterpreted law in the course of such conflicts, arguing that "fairness" (meaning "justice") was lacking when authorities rejected their claims and ordered them punished. This opinion found reinforcement through their everyday dealings with representatives of the administrative and legal systems. In 1891, for example, the peasant Timofei Shepel' argued with a local nobleman named Grigorii Pavlov and cursed him. Pavlov pressed charges before the precinct land captain claiming that Shepel' had also assaulted him. The land captain sentenced Shepel' to three months in prison (the maximum allowed) not for assault but because Pavlov, as a noble, was entitled to respect from a peasant.[16] Mistreatment by police authorities, the protection of landed interests by peace arbiters and land captains, or support for the requirements of social deference, convinced villagers that rejecting the law was their only option in certain situations. The law, in short, was often unjust, sanctioning and protecting inequality. Yet in peasant eyes, it should be a force for equity and "true" justice.

For this reason, peasants did not simply abandon the law but sought to employ it selectively for their own benefit. In the eighteenth and early nineteenth centuries, serfs had commonly used a knowledge of the law when resisting noble or state encroachments on their rights and put forward their own interpretation of particular laws, as several Soviet scholars have pointed out. When composing petitions (*chelobitnye*) or assembly resolutions, they drew directly from articles of the written law.[17] Historian D. I. Raskin has found that among 298 petitions written by monastery serfs during the early eighteenth century, 55 separate laws were mentioned, and A. V. Kamkin calculated that as many as 78 percent of all state peasant petitions made reference to specific legislative acts.[18] Ignorance of the law, then, cannot be said to have characterized the world view of Russia's serf population, and as later

16. "Iz praktiki uezdnogo suda," *SudG*, no. 34 (1891), 10.

17. A. V. Kamkin, "Krest'ianskoe pravosoznanie i pravotvorchestvo po materialam vtoroi poloviny XVIII veka," in *Sotsial'no-pravovoe polozhenie severnogo krest'ianstva* (Vologda, 1981), 40–54; Kamkin, "Pravosoznanie gosudarstvennykh krest'ian vtoroi poloviny XVIII veka," *ISSSR*, no. 2 (1987), 163–73; D. I. Raskin, "Ispol'zovanie zakonodatel'nykh aktov v krest'ianskikh chelobitnykh serediny XVIII v.," *ISSSR*, no. 4 (1979), 179–92; David Moon, *Russian Peasants and Tsarist Legislation on the Eve of Reform* (London, 1992).

18. Raskin, "Ispol'zovanie," 183–84; Kamkin, "Pravosoznanie," 167.

petitions would demonstrate, this was even more true during the post-emancipation era.[19]

The rare recorded instances when peasants spoke their mind about the legal system or law also offer insight into their views. In 1903, while the judges of one *volost'* court heard a complicated inheritance dispute, they asked their clerk how the law related to this particular case. The clerk replied that there was no applicable law and that the judges should decide the matter on the basis of local custom. "So there's no law written for us peasants?" one judge asked incredulously. "People are all the same, but we, you're saying, are without 'law.' What on earth do you mean?"[20] Rural opponents of Russia's class courts used a similar language of equity and justice, speaking as well of citizenship with its implicit legal equality for all. In 1910 a group of peasants wrote to the State Council concerning new legislation under consideration that preserved *volost'* courts for peasants. "But peasants are citizens of the empire, like persons of other estates, and therefore the existence of special peasant courts is not necessary." This class court, they declared, "has outlived its time, even if it is used only for petty cases."[21] During confrontations with landowners, peasants similarly argued that all should be accountable before the law. After not receiving their wages for harvesting on a Saratov estate in July 1896, rural laborers confronted the owner at a bazaar and demanded that he either pay them what they were owed or else accompany them to the police, where they intended to lodge a complaint. The estate owner instead drew a pistol and threatened the crowd, causing the assembled peasants to attempt to deal with him "in their own way." Later interrogated by the police captain while their case of "disorder" was being tried before the local land captain, one of the accused was asked why they attempted to bring the owner to his office. "And where else?" replied the defendant. "We were taking him to the authorities. When we are told to go there, we go, so that means one cannot refuse to go to the authorities. But he wouldn't go. Of course, we didn't want to act arbitrarily."[22]

Knowledge of the law and strong—if veiled—views concerning inequality did not, however, end the time-honored tactic of dissimulation when this served a protective purpose. In 1897, for example, peasants from a village

19. As one writer caustically noted of this perspective, "Characteristically, contemporary literature deals only with the legal consciousness of landowners, not with that of peasants, as if the peasant psyche was of a completely different nature." P. E. Mikhailov, *Obychnyi institut starozhil'stva i krepostnoe pravo* (SPb., 1912), 24.

20. "Volostnoi sud," *SudO,* no. 44 (1903), 828–29. See also "Iz Arkhangel'skoi gubernii. Volostnye sudy," *SevK,* no. 39 (1905), 2.

21. "Krest'iane protiv volostnykh sudov," *RiazV,* no. 318 (1910), 1.

22. "Sudebnaia khronika. Bezporiadki vo vremia bazara," *NizhL,* no. 245 (1896), 3.

of Orenburg province rejected a court ruling against them and resisted authorities in a dispute over ownership of a meadow. At his trial for confirming the communal resolution that sanctioned the illegal land usage, the village elder argued in his defense that he was illiterate and had affixed his seal to the resolution without knowing it was illegal.[23] *Volost'* judges used similar explanations when higher courts found their decisions contrary to law. When four peasant judges were tried by a circuit court in 1877 on charges of illegally abrogating a peace court decision and retrying the suit, all admitted having heard the case but denied guilt because, as they explained, the justice of the peace had decided the case unfairly and incorrectly. "Legal or not," one said, "we tried the case. What do we know? We peasants are ignorant, illiterate, and don't know the law." This ready use of accepted stereotypes worked to their advantage, for they were acquitted by the jury.[24] Within Russia's legal system, as so many peasants knew, ignorance could insure against conviction.

## JUSTICE AND THE "AMICABLE COMMUNITY"

In ways similar to legal systems of Western Europe, imperial Russia's postreform criminal law ostensibly centered on the idea of the public insult implicit in a given crime. Under this system, as Cynthia Herrup explains, "the state adopts the role of victim, and state courts become the sole sanctioned forum for conflict resolution. Because all crimes are anti-social rather than simply personal, uniformity is valued over flexibility. The public nature of crime under a system of state law precludes satisfaction by private compensation. The legal system functions not to recreate the victim's situation before the crime, but to reform criminals."[25] State law thus created punishments to fit the crime, not the criminal. In Russia, however, this was true primarily when nonpeasants came to trial. Much as did criminal courts before emancipation, circuit courts regularly reduced sentences or requested clemency because of a peasant's "backwardness" and "extreme ignorance." While conservatives spoke of the need to discipline the lower classes and liberals argued for equality before the law, higher courts and juries alike perpetuated the personal character of criminal law through consideration of defendants' class status and cultural level. This intriguing game of feigned

23. "Orenburgskii okruzhnyi sud. Soprotivlenie vlastiam," *NizhL*, no. 42 (1897), 3.
24. Mikhail Chentsov, "Krest'ianskie dela," *Otechestvennye zapiski*, no. 6 (1879), 245–46.
25. Cynthia Herrup, "Crime, Law and Society: A Review Essay," *Comparative Studies in Society and History* 27, no. 1 (1985), 160. On Russia, see M. N. Gernet, *Osnovnye poniatiia russkogo, gosudarstvennogo, grazhdanskogo i ugolovnogo prava* (Moscow, 1907); A. G. Zviagintsev and Iu. G. Orlov, *Pod sen'iu russkogo orla* (Moscow, 1996), 14–68.

or assumed benightedness within the judicial arena created a unique approach both in the way peasants dealt with higher courts and the manner in which these courts looked upon and treated the accused based on her or his social origin.[26]

By contrast, restitutive justice played a far more important role in Russian peasant communities than did punitive justice, and the most prevalent forms of restitution were reconciliation and compensation. Offenses like theft, for instance, were often settled among peasants by reconciling victim and criminal even though the law specifically limited reconciliation to civil suits.[27] An investigation of eighty-three *volost'* courts in Tambov province during the early 1870s found that a majority of peasant judges allowed reconciliation rather than employing punishment in a great many cases of theft. More than half of all cases arising in the Rostovsk district of Iaroslavl' province were regularly settled through reconciliation during the same period. Some rural courts concluded as many as four-fifths of all cases in this manner. In the most extreme examples uncovered by one government commission, courts "hardly ever pass sentence, because all cases end in reconciliation."[28] Nor did the use of reconciliation appear to decline significantly over time despite the growing complexity of legal suits. In 1900, 45 percent of cases coming before the *volost'* courts of Riazan's Mikhailov district were concluded through reconciliation. In four other districts this figure was 38, 37, 29, and 28 percent, respectively. *Volost'* authorities in this same province even allowed for reconciliation after sentence had been passed, including sentences of corporal punishment.[29]

The best examples of this informality are found in extrajudicial settlements arbitrated either at village moots, most of which had been officially abolished at the time of emancipation, or before respected members of the

26. GARO, f. 640, op. 51, sv. 121, d. 142 (1878), ll. 50–54 ("In view of the accused's extreme ignorance"); sv. 150, d. 527 (1892), ll. 46–47ob. ("Taking into account the accused's extreme underdevelopment and ignorance"); sv. 177, d. 897 (1907), ll. 86–87; op. 54, sv. 26, d. 15 (1911), ll. 49–51ob., for examples. By contrast, English judges considered class quite differently, using their courts as forums to discipline the working classes while protecting "respectable" society. See Carolyn A. Conley, *The Unwritten Law* (Oxford, 1991), 173–201.

27. Senate ruling of September 28, 1876, no. 7061. K. Abramovich, comp., *Krest'ianskoe pravo po resheniiam Pravitel'stvuiushchego Senata*, 2nd ed. (SPb, 1912), 36, no. 223.

28. Pavel Berezanskii, *Obychnoe ugolovnoe pravo krest'ian Tambovskoi gubernii* (Kiev, 1880), 199; M. I. Zarudnyi, *Zakony i zhizn'* (SPb, 1874), 108–9; Petr Skorobogatyi, "Mirovye sdelki v volostnom sude," *IuV*, no. 7 (1881), 422–23. See also I. L. Shrag, "Krest'ianskie sudy Vladimirskoi i Moskovskoi gubernii," *IuV*, no. 5–6, (1877), 62–63; Orshanskii, "Narodnyi sud," no. 4, 219–20; K. R. Kachorovskii, *Narodnoe pravo* (Moscow, 1906), 117–38.

29. GARO, f. 695, op. 11 (1900), sv. 161, d. 1, ll. 14–15, 30–31, 45ob.–46, 54–54ob., 71, 85ob.–86 (Egor'evsk, Zaraisk, Spassk, and Pronsk districts). See also TsGIAgM, f. 62, op. 4, d. 27, ll. 7–8, 16–17. For reconciliation after sentences of corporal punishment had been handed down, see GARO, f. 695, op. 1 (1890), sv. 18, d. 233, ll. 33, 35, 41–41ob., 49, 66–67.

community, the village elder, or some local power broker. Peasants continued for decades to utilize such methods in part because of their convenience, simplicity, and the public announcement of reconciliation that was standard procedure, a process usually helped along by liberal use of vodka. Thus, although *volost'* courts remained the only officially recognized judicial bodies at the local level after 1861, peasants often turned to these institutions when settlement could not otherwise be reached or if they strongly opposed an informal decision. As one investigator from Smolensk province put it in 1899, "Peasants look upon the court as a measure to which one turns only after all other means have been tried."[30]

Although informality characterized a substantial sphere of local justice, reconciliation was not a feature unique to peasant judicial practice. Official law sanctioned it, after all, and it had been an important feature of prereform justice as well. The emancipation regulations stipulated that peasant judges should strive to reconcile litigants before proceeding to a formal hearing. Justices of the peace, too, were encouraged to employ reconciliation, and some did so frequently. Even circuit courts occasionally dismissed cases after litigants had reconciled.[31] In the village context, however, caution is required before concluding that "amicable" settlements somehow imply that compromise was a key element of informal justice or, more broadly, of village life. As anthropologist Martin Chanock has noted, "Too much should not be made of the difference between courts which judge and family groups which mediate, because the threat of banishment was the implied threat in a mediated decision."[32]

Several qualifications should therefore be added to the contemporary picture of informal justice, for the most frequently mentioned "unofficial courts" had at one time held official status as judicial bodies. The village assembly, for instance, served for centuries as a court of first instance in criminal and civil matters, especially among privately owned serfs, and continued to do so during the postreform era when complaints from peasants were commonly heard that the commune "should be allowed to decide cases of greater importance than those that are now allowed by law."[33] Former state peasants often retained village courts created in the late 1830s or else, "in order not to bring a case to the *volost'* court, constituted a

---

30. GARF, f. 586, op. 1, d. 120, ll. 12, 61. See also d. 117, l. 33.

31. K A. Sofronenko, comp., *Krest'ianskaia reforma v Rossii 1861 goda* (Moscow, 1954), 62, art. 107; N. Kholev, "Desiatiletie mirovoi iustitsii Kerchenskogo okruga," *ZhGUP,* no. 4 (1881), 1–10; D. Antsiferov, "Nabliudeniia nad ugolovnoi praktikoi," 132; M. N. R. "Sud v derevne (Iz dnevnika byvshego mirovogo sud'i)," *Nabliudatel'*, no. 2, (1882), 95–96; "Prichinenie tiazhkogo uvech'ia," *RiazZh,* no. 15 (1913), 3. On the prereform period, see Richard S. Wortman, *The Development of a Russian Legal Consciousness* (Chicago, 1976), 20–21.

32. Martin Chanock, *Law, Custom, and Social Order* (New York, 1985), 7.

33. GARF, f. 586, op. 1, d. 120, l. 11.

temporary village court (sometimes called the "court of elders") to hear the dispute. The role of village and *volost'* elders as mediators also remained legally sanctioned in our period, for the state granted them police powers, authority to arbitrate disputes, to judge, and to punish for petty crimes.[34] In 1872, for example, officials from the Serenovsk township of Iaroslavl' province told investigators that "in all cases peasants turn first to the village elder, who tries to reconcile the litigants. If he fails, the case goes to the *volost'* elder, who also seeks to reconcile them," and only in the event that this effort was unsuccessful would the case be sent to the *volost'* court. Ethnographers at the turn of the century also found that this practice continued much as it had in the past. Writing about a village of Orel province, one correspondent noted that reconciliation of petty disputes remained among the elder's primary functions.[35]

Russian peasants retained informal village-level settlement for several reasons. For one, they did not place great faith in the reformed *volost'* court as a source of justice, although they litigated before it for lack of any other. Indeed, the *volost'* court bore the brunt of peasant grievances against local justice, since it was this body they had to deal with in the vast majority of cases. Court favoritism toward wealthy and powerful villagers, corruption, and bribery led many to conclude that "true" justice was impossible to find in the *volost'*, though they themselves proved by no means averse to engaging in bribery or other dealings if this would tip a case in their favor. A correspondent from Riazan' province noted in 1899 that peasants considered bribery to be "payment for one's services."[36] Still, the general view linking formal justice and corruption had long been sustained by a host of sayings,

34. Ibid. l. 61; Petr Skorobogatyi, "Ustroistvo krest'ianskikh sudov," *IuV,* no. 6 (1880), 309–46; Shrag, "Krest'ianskie sudy," no. 3–4, 37–40; V. V. Tenishev, *Pravosudie v russkom krest'ianskom bytu* (Briansk, 1907), 10–11; N. N. Blinov, *Sel'skaia obshchestvennaia sluzhba* (SPb, 1882), 1–18; V. V. Ptitsyn, *Obychnoe sudoproizvodstvo krest'ian Saratovskoi gubernii* (SPb, 1886), 39.

35. *Trudy Komissii po preobrazovaniiu volostnykh sudov,* 7 vols. (SPb., 1873–74), 3:74 (hereafter: *Trudy*); GARF, f. 586, op. 1, d. 114, l. 24. See also d. 118, ll. 7–8 (village of Beloomut, Zaraisk district). As Peter Czap has pointed out, the existence of these numerous instruments of mediation meant that *volost'* courts served not as the most proximate instance of justice but as a second or even third, with courts in certain townships hearing as few as one-tenth of all actual disputes arising within their boundaries. "Peasant Class Courts and Peasant Customary Justice in Russia, 1861–1912," *JSH* 1, no. 2 (1967), 158–59. For examples, see *Trudy,* 5:529; 6:162, 256, 300, 461; "Pravovye vozzreniia naroda, *Nedelia,* no. 26 (1880), 523–24. On informal settlement in other settings, see, e.g., Bruce Lenman and Geoffrey Parker, "The State, the Community and the Criminal Law in Early Modern Europe," in V. A. C. Gatrell et al., eds., *Crime and the Law* (London, 1980), 23–28; Chanock, *Law, Custom and Social Order,* 136–41; J. M. Conly and W. M. O'Barr, *Rules Versus Relationships: The Ethnography of Legal Discourse* (Chicago, 1990).

36. GARF, f. 586, op. 1, d. 118, l. 33 (Skopin district). See also d. 120, ll. 12, 14, 27, 62–64; d. 117, l. 36.

many dating back to the eighteenth century but still in use after emancipation, such as "Where there is a court, there is falsehood;" "One goes to court
but finds no justice;" "The court's pocket is like a priest's belly;" and "Pay the
judge so as not to end up in jail." It was best, in short, to avoid courts when
possible, relying instead on other means of face-to-face settlement. As one
villager put it in the early 1870s, "We hardly know the *volost'* court and have
no faith in it." Much the same opinions were found by surveys conducted
during the 1890s.[37]

Although complaints of this sort were often valid, they do not fully explain the aversion of otherwise litigious peasants to formal litigation, especially later in the century. To be sure, the predilection for amicable,
informal settlements stemmed partly from their age-old mistrust of official
law and their strong dislike for strict formality, but it was also deeply rooted
in community structures and village social relations. In Russia's rural settlements, where kinship ties formed one of the primary bases for social and
economic organization and most villagers knew one another, preservation
of peaceful relations was a fundamental purpose of dispute resolution. Local juridical structures were also personal and internal to social life, requiring that compromise or submission take precedence if order was to be
ensured. Writing about Aragonese peasants in a similar vein, anthropologist
Carmelo Lison-Tolosana noted:

> Justice or equity requires that kinship, with cordial relations and friendship,
> should have precedence over the law. Relatives and friends "come to an agree-
> ment," "have an understanding," make mutual concessions. Equity demands
> that they should be treated in a special . . . way, and neither convention nor
> the law should be allowed to intervene. Sociability and equity go hand in
> hand. A certain degree of intimacy is thus the generator of equity, and the less
> intimacy there is the further from equity and the closer to conventions.[38]

In her study of law in Tanganyika, Moore has pointed to the "tension between a centralized national system of courts with a standardized set of principles and rules, and the locally anchored, anti-centralized system of rural
communities. These communities try to control their own members and do
everything to maximize their internal autonomy, allowing their members
effective use of the courts only as they see advantage in doing so, bypassing
the courts and settling their own affairs internally as they choose."[39]

37. V. I. Dal', *Poslovitsy russkogo naroda*, vol. 1 (Moscow, 1984), 132–33; Tenishev, *Pravosudie*, 9–18; E. Kartsev, "Sel'skoe pravosudie," *VE*, no. 1 (1882), 756–57; GARF, f. 586, op. 1,
d. 120, l. 89.

38. Carmelo Lison-Tolosana, *Belmonte de los Caballeros: Anthropology and History in an
Aragonese Community* (Oxford, 1966), 256.

39. Sally Falk Moore, "Treating Law as Knowledge," *LSR* 26, no. 1 (1992), 12. See also Laura
Nader, *Harmony Ideology: Justice and Control in a Zapotec Mountain Village* (Stanford, 1990), 298.

Taking a petty criminal case to court could be the least effective means of insuring a quick and agreeable restoration of peace, and to do so might have just the opposite effect. As historians Bruce Lenman and Geoffrey Parker have noted of rural disputes in Western Europe: "Since the animosities aroused by a legal case, however trivial, could divide a village for generations, it was in the community's best interests—whatever the rights and wrongs of the matter—to engineer an early settlement."[40] Because serious grievances usually reached official courts only after attempts at extrajudicial settlement had failed, a decision to seek formal arbitration often represented the ultimate step in a quarrel. In order to conclude disputes quickly and obviate the danger of feuds that could engulf local society, peasants frequently relied on reconciliation instead of risking the potential escalation of hostilities that resort to the formal legal system oftentimes entailed. Informal reconciliation also remained popular because, with arbiters drawn from among the immediate community, village moots stood closest to peasant life and were best able to understand local problems and peculiarities, considering such subjective elements as the disputants' personal characters or their reputation and standing.[41] And given the physical distance of *volost'* courts from many settlements, unofficial bodies often proved the fastest, cheapest, and most accessible organs of justice. Yet even in villages close to a township seat, peasants preferred settling disputes and, when possible, punishing criminals outside the formal system, since enforcement of community norms and laws "was generally regarded as a village matter and not something that could be entrusted to strangers sitting on a *volost'* court."[42]

Social equilibrium and local solidarity certainly played an important role in the workings of local justice, but they should not blind us to the much neglected fact that every village contained competitive and antagonistic forces as well. There are superiors and inferiors in peasant communities, Moore reminds us: "There are more or less powerful persons [who] can mobilize more or fewer individuals in the local political arena. Individuals can not only be discredited, they can be expelled. What appears to be equilibrium from the outside is often a temporary moment of agreement in which a dominant segment of the group has prevailed and everyone recognizes that

40. Lenman and Parker, "State, Community," 22.

41. See, e.g., A. A. Charushin, "Otnoshenie naroda k koronnomu sudu," *IAOiRS,* 5, no. 2 (1913), 74; Skorobogatyi, "Ustroistvo," no. 6, 310; no. 7, 508; Orshanskii, "Narodnyi sud," no. 3, 73–75.

42. James I. Mandel, "Paternalistic Authority in the Russian Countryside, 1856–1906" (Ph.D. diss., Columbia University, 1978), 281–82; "Nabliudeniia mirovogo posrednika," *Osnova,* no. 2 (1862), 29; Ptitsyn, *Obychnoe sudoproizvodstvo,* 39–40; B. M. Firsov and I. G. Kiseleva, comps., *Byt velikorusskikh krest'ian-zemlepashtsev: opisanie materialov etnograficheskogo biuro kniazia V. N. Tenisheva (na primere Vladimirskoi gubernii)* (SPb, 1993), 58.

predominance and acquiesces in all public behavior. This is what often gives the appearance of unanimity to collective decisionmaking."[43] Within the rural social field there thus existed an "unofficial but efficacious structure of incentives and controls" to be manipulated by villagers themselves and, as Moore stresses, "It is not surprising that conformity to requirements that cannot be enforced in the formal legal system may be coerced or induced in the social arena of lineage and neighborhood."[44]

Turning to the village elder or another powerful person, after all, represented more than an effort simply to reach a quick resolution; it also involved disputants attempting to stack the odds against their opponent, mustering local resources, exploiting social ties, and calling in favors or dispensing bribes as a means of ensuring an auspicious outcome. Peasant manipulation of witnesses and evidence served much the same purpose not only in unofficial resolutions but also before formal courts. The long-standing practice whereby litigants paid their witnesses or treated them to vodka remained widespread at the century's end.[45] At the same time, the intervention of a powerful figure serving as arbiter often intimidated litigants to settle amicably, for they could hold out the threat of coercion or sanction in the face of obstinacy. Writing in 1881, Evgenii Markov claimed that township elders rarely allowed a case to reach the *volost'* court. "Because he is more accountable for his actions than are [*volost'* court judges], it is more important to the elder that complaints not go to the higher authorities." Therefore, when peasants expressed a preference to take their dispute before the court, the elder "shouts and threatens to throw them in jail" if they did not reconcile. "Then he sends them home."[46] Nor were *volost'* judges averse to using fear of punishment and disgrace to secure reconciliation, at least when they knew the litigants. In a *volost'* court of Penza province during a land dispute between two peasants in the 1890s, initial efforts at reconciliation had come to naught. At last the frustrated chief judge turned to the defendant and yelled: "You listen to me, Maksimka, you son-of-a-bitch, you've already been tried here before under article 142. If you keep

43. Moore, "Treating Law as Knowledge," 33.

44. Sally Falk Moore, *Social Facts and Fabrications* (New York, 1986), 302. See also Sally Humphreys, "Law as Discourse," *History and Anthropology* 1, no. 2 (1985), 243–45; Chanock, *Law, Custom, and Social Order*, 5–7.

45. See, for example, GARF, f. 586, op. 1, d. 114, l. 58; d. 118, l. 36; d. 120, ll. 26, 63, 64–65.

46. Evgenii Markov, "Sel'skoe pravosudie (K voprosu krest'ianskogo ustroistva)," *RusRech'*, no. 7 (1881), 220–21. For additional examples, see A. A. Charushin, "Narodnyi sud," *IAOiRS*, 5, no. 7 (1913), 312; N. Kostrov, *Iuridicheskie obychai krest'ian-starozhilov Tomskoi gubernii* (Tomsk, 1876), 108; Petr Skorobogatyi, "Primenenie nakazanii na volostnom sude," *IuV*, no. 8 (1882), 563–64.

coming to court everyone will turn against you and you'll end up in jail!" The cowed defendant quickly agreed to reconcile.[47]

Unlike state courts, then, peasant judicial institutions, including, to a certain extent, *volost'* courts, were not firmly bound by what outsiders recognized as strict legal formalities. Rather, alongside the requirements imposed by law, they embodied principles rooted in the cultural, economic, political, and social realities of rural life. Unofficial justice directed its energies toward ensuring that conflicts did not disrupt village social relations or draw outside officials and agencies into local matters; hence the overriding goal was to settle disputes "at home," within the cultural and social confines of the community itself, employing a range of forces that often escaped the notice and control of outsiders. Efforts at containing litigation thus helped to reproduce, simultaneously, long-standing patterns of unity, competition, and antagonism in peasant communities.

Although state and local judicial practice differed in significant respects, it cannot be said that the two systems evolved independently or existed in isolation from one another. Concepts of legal pluralism and dual legal orders are myths, as recent work in anthropology has made abundantly clear, that carry with them connotations of equality and "misrepresent the asymmetrical power relations that inhere in the coexistence of multiple legal orders." Various legal systems may, indeed, coexist, as they do in numerous colonial and postcolonial states, but they are by no means equal. "Legal ideas and processes maintained by subordinated groups are constrained in ways that the legal orders of dominant groups are not."[48] In rural Russia, official law and administrative authority regularly influenced and brought change to the practice of local justice through frequent interference at the village and *volost'* levels. There were many areas where peasants successfully rebuffed these efforts simply by ignoring government regulations, as they did with the 1886 law aimed at preventing or reining in an explosion of family divisions—in this case by continuing to subdivide households.[49] Yet

47. A. A. Charushin, "Volostnye sudy v bytovom ikh osveshchenii," *IAOiRS* 4, no. 21 (1912), 990.

48. June Starr and Jane F. Collier, eds., *History and Power in the Study of Law* (Ithaca, 1989), 9. See also A. L. Epstein, ed., *Contention and Dispute: Aspects of Law and Social Control in Melanesia* (Canberra, 1974); Manuela Carneiro da Cunha, "Silences of the Law: Customary Law and Positive Law on the Manumission of Slaves in 19th Century Brazil," *History and Anthropology* 1, no. 2 (1985), 427–43; George A. Collier, "The Impact of Second Republic Labor Reforms in Spain," in Starr and Collier, eds., *History and Power*, 201–2.

49. GARO, f. 71, op. 10 (1899), d. 23; TsGIAgM, f. 749, op. 1, dd. 16–17, 30–31; T. P. Prudnikova, "Krest'ianskii protest protiv soslovnoi neravnopravnosti v poreformennoi zapadnosibirskoi derevne (60–90-e gody XIX v.)," in *Krest'ianstvo Sibiri XVIII–nachala XX v.* (Novosibirsk, 1975), 157–58; P. B., "Krest'ianskii byt chrez dva desiatiletiia posle reformy," *Russkii vestnik,* no. 10 (1880), 454–56; "Ogranichenie semeinykh razdelov u krest'ian," *VolzhV,* no. 26

when villagers ignored or rejected state law (and even during unsuccessful efforts to do so), they devised strategies of avoidance that, by their very nature, acknowledged the asymmetry within Russia's legal system. Such strategies are most apparent in peasant thinking about property crime.

## LAND, OWNERSHIP, AND PROPERTY CRIME

Although nineteenth-century investigators agreed that peasant views about crime were far from coinciding with written law, it remains difficult to generalize about differences between village and state conceptions on the basis of contemporary studies. Most writers of the period examined peasant notions of specific crimes rather than general attitudes toward criminality, and such notions frequently differed from province to province or even from one village to another.[50] Investigators claimed to have had little choice when gathering this type of material, for nearly all ethnographic surveys conducted during our period asserted that villagers rarely expressed abstract ideas or philosophical attitudes on questions concerning crime or justice. Rather, as they often told interviewers, authority to judge and punish criminals "belongs to God and the law"—a practical perspective that, though more flexible, meshed comfortably with the empire's law.[51] The expectation (or lack thereof) that peasants should have thought about crime in terms familiar to educated Russians tells us much about the investigators themselves but reveals little about rural attitudes.

Contemporary sources did find, not unexpectedly, that peasants in nearly all regions of the empire formed their definition of crime from two elements: the infliction of material harm and the commission of sin. Threats of punishment by authorities or courts therefore presented only one restraint against committing a crime; perpetration of sin proved equally important, representing as it did an infringement against the religious commandments and Church law. As villagers in the Pronsk district of Riazan' province put it, "A crime is punished on earth by the court, while a sin is punished by God." Much the same was said in 1899 by peasants of Skopinsk district, who explained that if someone escaped punishment by the law, he would suffer divine torment in the form of disease among his livestock or the decline of his farm and household economy, or his children could be

---

(1899), 2; "Semeinye razdely krest'ian," *SevK*, no. 187 (1899), 1; N. K. Brzheskii, "Krest'ianskie semeinye razdely i zakon 18 marta 1886 goda," *Russkoe ekonomicheskoe obozrenie*, no. 4 (1900), 39–79; no. 5, 68–110; no. 6, 48–82.

50. E. T. Solov'ev, "Prestupleniia i nakazaniia po poniatiiam krest'ian Povolzh'ia," in S. V. Pakhman, ed., *Sbornik narodnykh iuridicheskikh obychaev*, vol. 2 (SPb, 1900), 278; Kartsev, "Sel'skoe pravosudie," 331.

51. GARF, f. 586, op. 1, d. 118, ll. 42–43; d. 120, l. 59.

born with physical defects.[52] Of course, peasants believed certain offenses like murder, arson, sacrilege, blasphemy, and armed robbery to be both sinful and criminal. Such mortal sins would bring not only retribution at the hands of official law but also eternal torment in hell. By contrast, God could forgive minor sins such as insult, deceit, petty theft, and fornication, even though courts might impose punishment.[53] These views reflect the tight interweaving of religious belief and law in the eyes of many Russian peasants, a linkage found among members of all classes in both town and countryside, but one that had largely, if not entirely, disappeared from the Criminal Code by the 1880s. They also indicate another way that certain infractions designated and prosecuted as criminal by official law could be explained by villagers as no more than minor sins: deeds, that is, for which one offered penance to God and received forgiveness, but which certainly should not be punishable under written law. Indeed, some acts of this sort were seen as neither sins nor crimes—an opinion that formed a major source of conflict with officials charged to enforce state law and that serves as one of the best examples of differences between peasant and official views of crime.

Of the numerous acts "not recognized" as crimes by the peasantry, unauthorized use of another's property proved by far the most common. "Our peasants," wrote a justice of the peace in 1872, "do not hesitate for a moment before taking the landowner's grain, hay, and straw, because the lord [*barin*] has lots of everything. None of these things are seen as criminal in the peasants' eyes."[54] This same justification continued in use at the end of the century, when such items as firewood and mushrooms belonging to noble landowners were seen as things "not needed by the lord because he has a lot, and therefore it is no sin to take it."[55] Villagers exhibited a similar attitude toward poaching or fishing on someone else's property, taking vegetables, fruit, berries, nuts, and mushrooms from gardens or private wood-

---

52. Ibid. d. 118, ll. 12, 14, 43. Identical explanations could be found throughout Great Russia. See, e.g., A. A. Charushin, "Vzgliad naroda na prestuplenie," *IAOiRS*, 4, no. 7 (1912), 316.

53. GARF, f. 586, op. 1, d. 118, l. 12; V. V. Tenishev, "Obshchie nachala ugolovnogo prava v ponimanii russkogo krest'ianina," *ZhMIu*, no. 7 (1909), 121–23; R. S. Lipets, "Izuchenie obychnogo prava v kontse XIX–nachale XX v.," in AN SSSR, *Trudy Instituta Etnografii*, vol. 24, no. 4 (Moscow, 1968), 91; A. A. Titov, *Iuridicheskie obychai sela Nikola-Perevoz, Sulostskogoi volosti, Rostovskogo uezda* (Iaroslavl', 1888), 93–94; M. V. Zagoskin, *Otvety na programmu Imperatorskogo Russkogo Geograficheskogo Obshchestva dlia sobiraniia narodnykh iuridicheskikh obychaev* (Irkutsk, 1891), 93.

54. V. N. Nazar'ev, "Sovremennaia glush'," *VE*, no. 3 (1872), 143–44. See also Stephen P. Frank, "Cultural Conflict and Criminality in Rural Russia, 1861–1900" (Ph.D. diss., Brown University, 1987), 224–27.

55. GARF, f. 586, op. 1, d. 118, l. 12.

lands, and grazing cattle on privately owned fields and meadows.[56] S. V. Maksimov, the prolific chronicler of late nineteenth-century rural life, directly attributed these views to a "labor principle" of property: "Anything to which labor has not been applied and which therefore is not acquired capital can be stolen without sin. Landowners' property, ever since private estates were legally sanctioned, has constituted a strong temptation, like peas and turnips growing by the roadside. . . . Anything that is the product of one's labor, care, or skill is protected, but anything belonging to priests or landlords is on the borderline, and beyond that the power to distinguish one's own property from other people's grows decidedly weaker."[57] More than thirty years later, one Tenishev correspondent wrote that because labor constituted the foundation of peasants' understanding of property,

> to mow another's grass or to pasture a horse along the road does not, in [their] opinion, constitute a crime, for "it is God's grass." Peasants hold the same view about hunting in another's forest, fishing in rivers and lakes, gathering berries or mushrooms . . . on another's property. "It is not the *barin* or merchant who seeded the beasts and birds in the forests," the peasants say. "God placed all creatures there for everyone's use. And how is it possible to say whose they are when they never stay in one place?" They say much the same about fish, which swim about from place to place. As for mushrooms, one must take them because "tomorrow they'll be eaten up by worms, and nobody will get any use out of them."[58]

56. Ibid. d. 114, l. 6; Tenishev, "Obshchie nachala," 128–29; Firsov and Kiseleva, *Byt velikorusskikh krest'ian*, 56–58; Chentsov, "Krest'ianskie dela," 242–55; "Odin den v volostnom sude," *SudO*, 2, no. 30 (1904), 606–7. On popular attitudes toward poaching in other national settings, see E. P. Thompson, *Whigs and Hunters* (New York, 1975); Regina Schulte, *The Village in Court*, trans. Barrie Selman, (Cambridge, 1994), part 3; John E. Archer, "Poachers Abroad," in G. E. Mingay, ed., *The Unquiet Countryside* (London, 1989), 52–64; Alun Howkins, "Economic Crime and Class Law: Poaching and the Game Laws, 1840–80," in S. B. Burman and B. E. Harrell-Bonds, eds., *The Imposition of Law* (London, 1979).

57. S. V. Maksimov, "Narodnye prestupleniia i neschastiia," *Otechestvennye zapiski*, 183 (1869), cited in Valerie Chalidze, *Ugolovnaia Rossiia* (New York, 1977), 6–7. That such views extended to Church as well as noble property is evident from the number of complaints lodged by priests against parishioners for theft or seizure of their property. See, e.g., GARO, f. 627, *stol* (st.) 1, op. 130, sv. 2054, d. 54, ll. 2–3, 7–10.

58. Charushin, "Vzgliad naroda," 316–17. Replying to a 1902 Imperial Geographic Society survey, I. V. Kostolovskii noted that in Iaroslavl' province the "labor principle" led peasants to argue that forests, water, and land belong to nobody but were God's and had been given to them by Him. "They do not recognize the forbidding of killing birds, for animals, birds, and bees should be used freely by any person without any prohibition from the authorities. In olden times, the peasants say, this is the way it was—if somebody needed something, he took it." Lipets, "Izuchenie obychnogo prava," 86. During this same period, Welsh commoners tried for poaching "refused to concede that rabbits, hares, and fowls . . . were anything but God's creatures." David Jones, *Rebecca's Children* (Oxford, 1989), 174.

With near unanimity, contemporaries bemoaned this costly plague of infractions against private and state property—especially forests—and most often pointed to peasant ignorance when seeking to explain it. "It is well known," said one justice of the peace, "that the rural population looks differently than does established law upon . . . felling trees in another's woodlot. The most honest peasant does not believe it is a sin to cut a cartload of wood in someone else's forest."[59] As with poaching and other property infractions, the attitude of villagers toward private property appeared to account for their readiness to break the law by trespass. "To fell trees in the forest, even without permission, is not a sin," claimed peasants in the El'ninsk district of Smolensk province. "The forest was grown by God, not by the lord. We have nowhere to get wood and the lord won't sell it." Reports gathered during the 1890s from nearly all provinces of central Russia quoted villagers as arguing that "cutting wood in the forest is not a sin because no one has planted the forest, only God, and it therefore belongs to all people because they are children of God."[60] According to another justice of the peace writing in 1886, peasants did not consider theft of wood to be at all shameful; on the contrary, since the forest was a gift from God and they lived near these forest lands, it would have been shameful to purchase wood.[61]

Peasants resorted to a tactful mixture of God's benevolence and the so-called labor principle to justify infractions against private ownership, persistently frustrating forest wardens deployed to guard against their illegal felling, police officers dispatched to apprehend malefactors, justices of the peace or land captains charged with trying thousands of these cases each year, as well as those educated Russians seeking to understand peasant juridical beliefs. "Our peasantry has conducted a war with the forest from time immemorial," lamented an 1875 commentary in *The Moscow Gazette*, cutting trees "without any need." Because of this relation with the forest, "the most confused understanding of the laws on forest property has been formed among our peasants." Similarly, one jurist claimed in 1882 that theft of wood simply verified that villagers lacked any "ethical inner attitudes toward crime." Peasant views concerning this infraction, as well as property crime in general, "attest to the most glaring manifestation of that

59. Orshanskii, "Narodnyi sud," no. 4, 213. See also P. P. Chubinskii, ed., *Trudy etnografichesko-statisticheskoi ekspeditsii v zapadno-russkii krai,* vol. 6 (SPb, 1872), 68.

60. S. V. Pakhman, "Ocherk narodnykh iuridicheskikh obychaev Smolenskoi gubernii," in Pakhman, ed., *SbNIuO,* 94; Nazar'ev, "Sovremennaia glush'," 145–46; Charushin, "Vzgliad naroda," 317; GARF, f. 586, op. 1, d. 118, l. 30. Compare Robert W. Bushaway, "From Custom to Crime: Wood-Gathering in Eighteenth- and Early Nineteenth-Century England," in John Rule, ed., *Outside the Law: Studies in Crime and Order 1650–1850* (Exeter, 1982), 65–101.

61. A. Zenchenko, "Derevnia i mirovoi sud," *VE,* no. 2 (1886), 639. See also I. M. Tiutriumov, "Krest'ianskaia sem'ia: ocherki obychnogo prava," *RusRech',* no. 4 (1879), 275–76.

terrible darkness of ignorance, that extremely low level of culture in which the majority of rural people live."[62]

At least a few writers, however, pointed out that the prevailing opinion of peasant leniency toward property offenses was not corroborated by *volost'* court decisions. "It is clear," wrote the jurist Il'ia Shrag in 1877, "that peasants treat wood theft no more leniently than they do other forms of theft and impose no less strict punishments for this infraction."[63] Villagers whose trees had been illegally felled brought charges either to the elder or the *volost'* court, demanding compensation for their loss and punishment of the thief. In most instances, the guilty party would be obliged to pay the value of the stolen trees. Rural courts also imposed fines in an amount previously determined by village resolutions designed to protect communal forests. When Matvei Nikolaev's sons were charged with illegal cutting in 1881, the Krestobogorodsk *volost'* court of Iaroslavl' province ordered Nikolaev himself to pay two rubles, basing its decision on an assembly resolution.[64] Localities with even stricter views sometimes used corporal punishment against those who broke communal forest regulations. In 1881 the Sarai *volost'* court of Riazan's Sapozhok district heard charges against Nikita Nikiforov Kanakov and his two children for illegal wood cutting in the communal forest. The court found them guilty, sentencing Kanakov to pay sixteen rubles for the wood and to serve seven days at the *volost'* jail; his sons each received twenty lashes of the birch. Many instances of corporal punishment also resulted when noble landowners lodged complaints with the *volost'* courts against peasant malefactors and used their influence to ensure that judges imposed the birch.[65]

The explanation for this quite different view toward theft committed against communal property or that of another villager can readily be located in a community's sharp differentiation between its own property and that of outsiders. "It must be noted," wrote V. V. Tenishev in 1909, that

62. *MosVed,* no. 259 (1875), 2; Kartsev, "Sel'skoe pravosudie," no. 1, 332. Similar comments are made in "Iz sela Pokcha, Cherdynskogo u., Permskoi gub.," *SV,* no. 21 (1888), 222.

63. Shrag, "Krest'ianskie sudy," no. 7–8, 62. See also GARF, f. 586, op. 1, d. 118, l. 30.

64. S. P. Nikonov and E. I. Iakushkin, *Grazhdanskoe pravo po resheniiam krestobogorodskogo volostnogo suda, Iaroslavskoi gubernii i uezda* (Iaroslavl', 1902), 151. For other cases, see *Trudy,* 1: 54, 138, 189; 2:499, 550; Dukhovskoi, *Imushchestvennye prostupki,* 270–78, 282–83; Konstantin Chepurnyi, "K voprosu o iuridicheskikh obychaiakh: ustroistvo i sostoianie volostnoi iustitsii v Tambovskoi gubernii," *Universitetskie izvestiia,* no. 10 (1874), part 2, section 2, ch. 4, 653.

65. GARO, f. 694, op. 21 (1881), sv. 392, d. 490, ll. 4–5. See also, f. 74, op. 27 (1893), d. 106, ll. 3–4; *Trudy,* 3:5, 40, 44, 46. For cases brought by landowners, see GARO, f. 694, op. 2 (1862), sv. 38, dd. 861, 866, 870; op. 21, sv. 392, d. 490; TsGIAgM, f. 1443, op. 1, d. 9 (1913); Dukhovskoi, *Imushchestvennye prostupki,* 272–73; Nikonov and Iakushkin, *Grazhdanskoe pravo,* 153–54.

villagers' indulgent attitude toward unauthorized use of property "ceases when the act is perpetrated against the peasants themselves."[66] *Volost'* court records are replete with complaints concerning trespass, theft from gardens or fields, and illegal wood cutting. The point is not that peasants displayed a reluctance to steal from one another or to trespass on another's property and allotment land; the great volume of incidents in which hay or straw was pilfered from peasant fields or sheds, grain stolen, trees cut down, or damage caused to crops, attests to the everyday nature of petty property offenses in which members of the same community played the roles of victim and perpetrator. All such acts were seen as crimes and could be punished within the community, by *volost'* courts, or by bringing the case before a justice of the peace.[67] So, too, with infractions against communal property. By contrast, to take from outsiders who possessed the most abundant or accessible tracts of woodland in a given locality did not represent an illegal act from the village perspective because the forest and its fruits, peasants could claim, belonged to all. This argument served to distinguish peasant property from that of persons who did not apply their own labor to it or who had gained possession through unjust appropriation. It sanctified as well the peasants' persistent guerrilla-like tactics of disobeying forest regulations by cutting wood on noble or state lands.[68]

These beliefs formed a code of resistance and opposition to laws that peasants perceived as protecting noble expropriation of land they believed to be theirs. Put differently, the emancipation settlement led to an increase of property crime by redefining peasant efforts to continue using land, forests, meadows, or waters that they had previously exploited. As Douglas Hay has written in another context, "immemorial custom had become trespass and theft."[69] Hence codes that spoke of a right of labor directly challenged the legitimacy of state law and, in the eyes of liberated villagers, justified their attempts to retake what had been lost or to expropriate landed estates altogether. The rights that peasants claimed, therefore, whether believed by all or not, served much the same purpose as did elite

66. Tenishev, "Obshchie nachala," 128–29; Tenishev, *Pravosudie,* 38.

67. GARO, f. 7, op. 1 (1884), d. 95, ll. 7ob., 120ob., 92; d. 535, 3ob., 22, 81; f. 70, op. 2 (1899), sv. 1, d. 3, ll. 33–34, 43–45; f. 76, op. 5 (1894), sv. 3, d. 6, ll. 23, 66; f. 811, op. 2 (1900), sv. 9, d. 15, ll. 5ob., 7, 390ob.; TsGIAgM, f. 703, op. 1, d. 48, ll. 10, 142; "Iz derevni Aksenovskoi, Zaraiskogo u., Riazanskoi gub," *SV,* no. 37 (1887), 366–67; "Mery k nasazhdeniiu i okhraneniiu lesov," *SV,* no. 7 (1888), 73.

68. See, e.g., L. T. Senchakova, "Krest'ianskie nakazy i prigovory 1905–1907 godov," in *Sud'by rossiiskogo krest'ianstva* (Moscow, 1996), 56–89. Compare Peter Sahlins, *Forest Rites: The War of the Demoiselles in Nineteenth-Century France* (Cambridge, 1994); Michael Taussig, *The Devil and Commodity Fetishism in South America* (Chapel Hill, 1980); David Blackbourn, *Marpingen: Apparitions of the Virgin Mary in a Nineteenth-Century German Village* (New York, 1993), 50–51.

69. Hay, "Crime and Justice," 71.

views that country folk simply did not understand the law. They provided a somewhat safer means of saying that which was illegal to say and of asserting demands that the state deemed criminal. "Commoners trespassing on what had been their communal property," argues Hay, "did not believe they were defying justice: their . . . landlords were."[70]

## THE STRUGGLE OVER FORESTS

Illegal felling of trees had plagued noble landowners and government throughout the century, as judicial statistics from the 1830s on show, but the struggle over woodlands and customary access rights intensified sharply after emancipation, in large part because of noble cutoffs and enclosures. As one commentator put it, "In former times peasants did not want for wood; they had what they needed from the landowner. But now they have received allotments without any forest land or with insufficient amounts. In many rural communities there is great shortage of wood. . . . Hence they go into the landowner's woodlot as they did in the past." The "forest question" thus served "to aggravate relations between the peasant population and the private landowning class."[71] Judging from the criminal statistics, need compelled most peasants to pilfer forest materials. The overwhelming majority of those convicted by circuit courts were over thirty years of age and had two or more children. By standards of the time, nearly 20 percent could be classified as elderly, that is, age fifty or older.[72] As forest areas shrank and restrictions on their use hardened, so, too, did shortage drive needy villagers to ignore and break the law.

Deforestation progressed unabated for centuries in European Russia, spurred on by an increase of timber exports during the eighteenth century and the demands of industry as well as population pressure in the nineteenth century. According to one estimate, the area under forest cover in most of Russia's central provinces had been reduced by half or more between 1696 and 1914, with the greatest portion of this loss occurring in the nineteenth century as a result of large-scale commercial cutting.[73] One result was

---

70. Ibid. 72. See also Robert W. Bushaway, "Rite, Legitimation and Community in Southern England 1700–1850: The Ideology of Custom," in Barry Stapleton, ed., *Conflict and Community in Southern England* (New York, 1992), 110–34; Bushaway, *By Rite: Custom, Ceremony and Community in England 1700–1880* (London, 1982), 167–279; Kenneth M. Stampp, *The Peculiar Institution: Slavery in the Ante-Bellum South* (New York, 1956), 126–27.

71. Zenchenko, "Derevnia i mirovoi sud," 644–45; A. Lukashevich, "K voprosu o peresmotre zakonodatel'stva o lesnykh porubkakh," *Iurist*, no. 7 (1905), 232.

72. *Svody*, part 2, "Vozrast osuzhdennykh."

73. R. A. French, "Russians and the Forest," in James H. Bater and R. A. French, eds., *Studies in Russian Historical Geography*, vol. 1 (London, 1983), 23–44. See also M. A. Tsvetkov, *Izmenenie lesistosti Evropeiskoi Rossii s kontsa XVII stoletiia po 1914 god* (Moscow, 1957).

a sharp rise in wood prices, making exploitation of the forest more lucrative. Many landowners carried out wholesale cutting for quick profit, themselves ignoring laws designed to preserve the country's woodlands. On a single estate in Perm province, for example, sales of timber provided Count Stroganov an annual income of 77,200 rubles in 1903, 160,700 in 1904, 139,800 in 1905, and 296,800 in 1906.[74] From the perspective of profit alone, then, owners of private forests viewed peasant depredations against their property with even greater intolerance than previously. But incursions by villagers became ever more necessary because the majority of Russia's remaining forest land belonged either to the state or private owners and existing supplies were insufficient for a rural population that nearly doubled over the second half of the century. This shortage "represents one of the sorest points of the peasant economy," while the need for forest materials "takes on a sharper character with every year."[75]

Local requirements went beyond the need for fuel and timber with which to build. Peasants had always relied on the forest for such things as grazing livestock (particularly during the winter months) and gathering products like berries and mushrooms. During the course of 1891 in Voronezh province, for instance, 34 percent of all persons convicted for infractions of forest regulations had illegally pastured their livestock on private or state woodlands. Another 64 percent were convicted for illegal cutting. Like private owners, peasants were also induced by rising prices to exploit their own and others' forests for profit, a fact that illuminates the sharpening conflict over woodlands. Cash-hungry or enterprising villagers could reap a substantial income from the sale of wood, and as they well knew, outsiders bought the product willingly, regardless of where it had been acquired. Nobles and priests alike could be good customers for illegally hewn trees; as one saying put it, "In the forest, even the priest is a thief" (*Na les i pop vor*).[76] Hence peasants viewed as unjust the state's constantly changing forest laws and the numerous regulations that appeared during the 1880s in an effort to preserve forest land by limiting cutting, particularly

74. A. M. Anfimov, "Chastnovladel'cheskoe lesnoe khoziaistvo v Rossii v kontse XIX–nachale XX v.," *IZ*, no. 68 (1958), 256.

75. Lukashevich, "K voprosu," 234. In the predominantly agricultural province of Voronezh near the century's end, peasants controlled only 44.9 percent of all forests; 50 percent was owned privately and 3.6 percent belonged to the state. *Pamiatnaia knizhka Voronezhskoi gubernii na 1893 god* (Voronezh, 1893), part 2, 90–91, 95.

76. *Pamiatnaia knizhka Voronezhskoi gubernii na 1893 god*, 95; Dal', *Poslovitsy*, 1:128; GARO, f. 627, st. 4, op. 236 sv. 28, d. 452; st. 5, op. 237, sv. 1, d. 8. On peasant economic exploitation of the forest, see "Spekuliatsiia krest'ianskim lesom (Pis'mo iz Viatskoi gubernii)," *SevV*, no. 12 (1886), 87–100; "Istreblenie lesov v Sibiri," *SV*, no. 31 (1884), 343; A. Kozhevnikov, "Prodazha krest'ianskikh lesov," *Pamiatnaia knizhka Olonetskoi gubernii na 1910* (Petrozavodsk, 1910), 214–15.

since they knew that private owners were actively engaged in commercial exploitation on a much greater scale.

Changes in the law, of course, could be turned to local advantage, particularly when villagers masked their deeds behind a pretense of ignorance and confusion over a regulation's precise meaning, a tactic of subversion not limited to illegal wood cutting. Such a scenario unfolded in 1892, when peasants of Bol'shie Ial'chiki, Kazan' province, were notified that because they were suffering from famine they would be allowed to use fallen trees and branches from a nearby state forest. This news quickly spread through the village, "and everyone with a horse and sledge immediately set out to gather fuel." The available windfall barely amounted to five or six sledge loads, however, leading several peasants to propose that they resort to cutting: "What are we to do if there is no windfall? We were given permission to gather fuel, and it's all the same whether it be trees or fallen wood." So the villagers set about cutting, felling a great quantity of wood until caught by the forest warden. At their subsequent trial, villagers claimed they were not guilty for they had found no fallen wood and only for this reason had they decided to cut trees. "How were we to know that we had to ask the guard where the windfall was?" they protested. "We didn't know this, but we even went searching for him."[77]

The common government practice of periodically granting clemency by imperial decree to large numbers of peasants found guilty for wood theft in state forests (and for other offenses as well) simply served to convince many that, even if caught and sentenced, they would probably be pardoned. In at least one instance, and likely in many more, peasants of Totemsk district, Vologda province, "understood" an imperial manifesto of May 15, 1883, to mean that the government had not only pardoned infractions against forest regulations committed prior to this date but also granted permission for continued cutting of wood without payment or punishment.[78]

It is little wonder, then, that illegal cutting not only continued unabated during the second half of the nineteenth century but seemed to be increasing at alarming rates. In some localities this struggle took on the deadly character of open warfare as landowners hired and armed guards to protect their property while villagers forcefully asserted their "right" to gather wood. In 1884, for example, one peasant from Egor'evsk district, Riazan' province, shot and killed the guard of a forest belonging to a local merchant.

77. "Delo o samovol'noi porubke kazennogo lesa," *VolzhV*, no. 215 (1892), 2. This practice of temporarily permitting free gathering of fallen wood, or even free cutting on a limited scale, was common during times of economic hardship. GARO, f. 5, st. 1, op. 2, d. 2151 (1898); st. 4, op. 5, d. 1944 (1892); d. 2186 (1897).

78. Nifontov and Zlatoustovskii, eds., *KD v 1881–1889 gg.*, 140–41. See also "Iunshumskomu volostnomu pravleniiu, Iaranskogo u., Viatskoi gub.," *SV*, no. 10 (1895), 110.

On the evening of June 4, 1898, a forest warden shot and seriously wounded the peasant Petr Ivanov Voronov of Orel province, suspecting that the latter had come to steal wood. It turned out that Voronov was only searching for his colt, which had wandered into the forest.[79] Police and press reports confirm the frequency of similar mistakes.

Yet most clashes presented clear cases of outright resistance to forest guards, themselves often brutal and corrupt, given to accepting bribes from organized gangs of thieves and allowing the latter to cut wood freely while preventing local peasants from pilfering in their domain.[80] When villagers from Sapozhok district were discovered cutting wood one night in February 1888, they attacked the warden with sticks and axes until the latter shot one of their comrades, causing the rest to flee. Also caught in the act of illegal cutting during the winter of 1898 was a peasant from Kazan' province, who resisted arrest and threatened the warden with an axe. The warden thereupon shot and killed him.[81]

Dramas involving individual peasants or small groups accounted for the greatest number of wood theft cases heard by justices of the peace and land captains throughout our period, with nearly 70,000 persons convicted in 1873 alone. Far more frightening to landowners and to rural order, however, were the large-scale assaults on private and state property that occurred when efforts at negotiation had failed. To give some sense of the scope such collective actions might take, in 1903 nearly 200 peasants from the Novo-Uspensk *volost'* stood trial for resistance to local authorities. In 1894 the peasants had filed a civil suit against the landowner Ia. A. Varshavskii, arguing that a forest lot of 1,350 acres belonged to them. Both the Kostroma Circuit Court and, on appeal, the Moscow Judicial Chamber found that only 140 acres could rightfully be considered theirs and that the remaining portion did, in fact, belong to Varshavskii. Disagreeing, the villagers continued pressing their claim to the land. Then, in December 1901, they appeared at Varshavskii's estate and declared that they would not allow workers to cart off timber and charcoal already prepared that summer. Some of the workers were beaten; all were driven from the disputed forest, together with the guards. When the district marshal of the nobility arrived, accompanied by the commandant, land captain, and other police and rural authorities, the peasants stood their ground, stating that they did not agree

79. GARO, f. 7, op. 1, d. 95, l. 34; "Sluchai," *OrlV,* no. 149 (1898), 1. On the increased use of armed forest guards, see *1905 god v Riazanskoi gubernii* (Riazan', 1925), 42–44; "Vnutrennie izvestiia," *RiazGV,* no. 26 (1896), 3.

80. For example, GARO, f. 640, op. 51, sv. 116 (1874), d. 89; sv. 117 (1876), d. 96; "Iz derevni Aksenovskoi, Zaraiskogo u., Riazanskoi gub.," *SV,* no. 37 (1887), 366–67.

81. GARO, f. 7, op. 1, d. 535, 100b.; "S. Chepchugi, Kazansk. gub. i u. (Krovavoe stolknovenie)," *VolzhV,* no. 13 (1899), 3; "Kadnikovskii uezd. (Vologod. g.)," *SevK,* no. 264 (1899), 1–2.

with the court ruling, that it was wrong, and that they would not allow workers and carters back into "their" forest. Only when authorities called in a sizable detachment of police could work be resumed.[82]

Like seizures of long-disputed cutoffs and other land that peasants deemed unjustly expropriated or belonging to them by customary use right, cutting of trees in private or state forests forms but one part of a much larger economic and social struggle waged for decades between villagers and their previous owners. The appearance after emancipation of a new, nonnoble landowning class did not change the situation; rather, from the peasants' perspective, it merely introduced new competitors into the equation of conflict. That some owners were aware of the precarious nature of their claims to land was even subtly conceded in official reports. Writing to the Riazan' governor in November 1906 about the mood among local peasants, for instance, the police commandant of Dankov district expressed fears that "now, because peasants look so lightly upon using others' property, the clandestine, nighttime cutting of forests might take the form of open robbery."[83] In other words, small-scale, covert wood theft by individuals, which had gone on for centuries, could be tolerated as long as claims to ownership were not challenged. The threat of massive cutting by entire villages was another matter entirely, for it entailed an open and direct rejection of ownership as well as laws protecting private property.

That the incidence of mass assaults on property continued on a large scale after 1905 suggests that despite the ferocity of government repression and the seeming calm forcibly restored to the countryside by 1907, a watershed had, nevertheless, been reached. For many peasants, the time for dissimulation and claims of ignorance had passed. During rural collective action villagers not only sought to rectify the injustices of landholding but also increasingly rejected what they viewed as symbolic of imposed law, refusing to "elect" *volost'* court judges and other officials who had been preselected by land captains and who did not sufficiently represent local interests. As a group of peasants from Tambov province put it in a petition composed early in 1905, "For the most part the *volost'* administration and court serve the needs of the government."[84] The state, in turn, responded

82. "Samoupravstvo," *Pravo,* no. 16 (1903), 1188–89. See also GARO, f. 5, st. 3, op. 4, tom 1, d. 2349 (1885); f. 640, op. 51, sv. 110, dd. 10–11; sv. 112, dd. 31–32.

83. U. L. Margulis, et al., comps., *KD v Riazanskoi gubernii v gody pervoi russkoi revoliutsii* (Riazan', 1960), 215.

84. "Zaiavlenie krest'ian Tambovskoi gub.," *Pravo,* no. 17 (1905), 1410. According to a 1905 report sent by one frightened township elder to the land captain of the third precinct of Moscow province's Mozhaisk district, not only were local peasants preventing tax collection, but they also forbade the implementation of any decisions handed down by the *volost'* court. TsGIAgM, f. 17, d. 4, tom 1, l. 150. See also L. T. Senchakova, *Prigovory i nakazy Rossiiskogo krest'ianstva 1905–1907 gg.,* vol. 1 (Moscow, 1994), 169–71.

with far less tolerance than it had previously, making use of military detachments and courts-martial, administrative exile, and even the death penalty as its regular police and courts proved incapable of dealing with these problems.

Contrary to assertions by supporters of the "rule of law" who believed that Russia was on a path toward civil equality for all, a position given momentary credence in 1906 when the tsarist government eliminated remaining estate distinctions and legal restrictions from the rural population, conflicting peasant-elite views of the law hardened after emancipation and grew further apart throughout this period. The bitter struggle over land made the stakes too high for compromise. Francis Wcislo has recently pointed out that, under Nicholas I, "an awareness of the fragility of the prereform social order . . . arose not from the threat of peasant retribution, but from the recognition that the state had failed to extend its own civil values into rural life."[85] That same failure stretched into the reform era, when it joined in a curiously complementary way with peasant dissatisfaction over their loss of land and customary rights, creating, over time, an increasingly volatile situation. Between 1905 and 1917, then, educated Russians who had earlier bemoaned villagers' "ignorance" of the law grew shrill and demanding in their calls for renewed efforts to transform rural culture, legal and otherwise. Indeed, when the government instituted the Stolypin agrarian reforms in 1906 with hopes of creating a new class of conservative, landowning peasants who would respect private property and, by extension, property law, it admitted to the realization that its law had been both subverted and openly rejected by a majority of the empire's population.

85. Wcislo, *Reforming Rural Russia*, 12. On the 1906 changes in peasant status, see L. M. Rogovin, *Ob otmene nekotorykh ogranichenii v pravakh sel'skikh obyvatelei i lits byvshikh podatnykh sostoianii. Vysochaishii Ukaz 5 oktiabria 1906 g.* (SPb, 1910).

CHAPTER 4

# The Hidden Realm of
# Rural Property Crime

*A: Last night forty people came to the orchard to steal; the guard fired off a shot and now someone is lying in the hospital. We have to call in a Cossack squadron—this is robbery by gangs.*
*V: It's only natural. Where there is food, peasants will find their way in. They are backwards. We don't go around stealing.*
*A: The problem is not the theft, but its character. These are gangs.*
ENTRY FROM AN UNPUBLISHED NOBLEMAN'S DIARY, TAMBOV PROVINCE, 1886

*The real rural calamity is . . . the increase of thefts committed by young people . . . Just recently an [independent farmer] returned from the city with a hefty sum of money after selling pigs. He came home, went to sleep, and during the night a gang of teenage street idlers crept up to his place and broke in to steal the money. . . . And yesterday a similar gang robbed another peasant of one hundred rubles. And two days ago they broke into a barn and stole thirty measures of rye . . . The countryside is groaning because of these street revelers—but it is not fighting the problem."*
TAMBOV PROVINCIAL GAZETTE, 1894

We have seen that in addition to unreported and unprosecuted offenses, Russian criminal statistics also failed to record the great majority of cases prosecuted by the empire's judicial-administrative institutions. Documents produced by these bodies tell a story that is very much different from that of the statistics, however, and one that brings us closer to a more balanced appraisal of rural crime. *Volost'* courts, justices of the peace, peace mediators, land captains, township elders, rural police commandants and their underlings, all shuffled vast quantities of paper through sluggish bureaucratic channels; most of it would simply be shelved without systematic compilation. At best, crime reports and trial outcomes made for brief mention in local newspaper columns. Yet whether as police logs, long ignored court records, cassational resolutions, or news accounts, these documents provide vivid testimony to the frequency of depredations against peasant and non-peasant property alike through petty theft, burglary, robbery, smuggling, arson, land seizure, and many other offenses.

This chapter surveys the main forms and targets of property crimes with a twofold purpose: to provide a sense of the variety and nature of offenses committed by peasants, and to serve as a counterweight to contemporary opinion and confusion over the extent of rural property infractions. If, as so many writers argued, country folk looked upon property in a way that placed them at odds with educated society and state law, it was easy to conclude that theft and pilfering among villagers did not merit serious attention from authorities. Views of this sort received substantiation in ethnographic and other writings on rural justice that appeared from the 1860s to the 1890s and that, however inaccurate or contradictory, suggested that peasants showed little concern about petty property offenses and committed them with hardly a thought. According to S. V. Pakhman's widely read *Customary Civil Law in Russia* (1877–79), "Peasants do not always recognize theft to be a crime in the proper sense of that term," and therefore "in a significant majority of cases it does not entail any punishment." He judged from published *volost'* court decisions that at least two-thirds of all thefts went unpunished.[1] Others offered a picture of villagers living with no moral codes at all when it came to property. Among the peasantry of Tomsk province, one author wrote in 1876, "it is considered a rule that, if something is lying around unwatched, it can be taken. Sons steal from fathers, and fathers from sons." Reports to the 1894 Tenishev ethnographic survey contained similar opinions. "Peasants steal not from need, but out of drunkenness and laziness," one respondent argued. "They steal from parents, fellow villagers, and even from the church." Every village had its thief, others claimed. Peasants who worked in factories, too, were quite adept at theft and "steal all sorts of things."[2]

Obviously, theft among fellow villagers certainly did not pose the kind of threat to the existing order that stealing from state and private owners did; instead it represented a constant nuisance that peasants had learned to tolerate. Only toward the end of the century would officials and nonpeasants begin to take somewhat more seriously complaints from villages about lawlessness in their midst, or show greater concern about the peasants' waning patience with official justice. Meanwhile, the jurisdiction of *volost'* courts, justices of the peace, and land captains over the vast majority of property infractions isolated these offenses from public attention and relegated them to the category of "petty" crime; it was assumed that villagers concurred with this designation. Violations of nonpeasant property rights, on

1. S. V. Pakhman, *Obychnoe grazhdanskoe pravo v Rossii*, vol. 1 (SPb, 1877), 341. Without explanation, this same author would argue twenty years later that, after murder, villagers considered theft to be the most serious of all crimes. "Ocherk narodnykh iuridicheskikh obychaev Smolenskoi gubernii," in Pakhman, ed., *SbNIuO*, vol. 2 (SPb, 1900), 92. See also K. Chepurnyi, "K voprosu o iuridicheskikh obychaiakh," *Universitetskie izvestiia*, no. 10 (1874), 652.

2. I. Kostrov, *Iuridicheskie obychai krest'ian-starozhilov Tomskoi gubernii* (Tomsk, 1876), 83; B. M. Firsov and I. G. Kiseleva, *Byt velikorusskikh krest'ian-zemlepashtsev* (SPb, 1993), 289.

the other hand, came most often before the public eye and were quantified in official judicial statistics.

The economic motivations that underlay a great many rural property offenses must also be considered, for however one assesses the economic state of the Russian countryside after 1861, it cannot be denied that vast segments of the peasant population lived precariously in an environment that provided little security against misfortune and hardship.[3] Of course, greed, envy, and class antagonism on the part of the poor cannot be ignored in any analysis of property depredations against the countryside's social and economic elite. Yet the very nature of rural property crime, dominated above all by small-scale pilferage of food, clothing, and other essentials, speaks to an undeniable relationship between need and a villager's risking punishment or even banishment by perpetrating a criminal act. The few sophisticated studies produced by Russian criminologists (mostly between 1908 and the 1920s) focused directly on this relationship as their authors endeavored, with some success, to identify correlations between crime and specific economic indicators such as grain prices and harvest size.[4]

## THEFT

On July 27, 1869, a woman charged with stealing another villager's coat valued at twenty-five rubles was tried before a *volost'* court of Moscow's Bogorodsk district. Two witnesses stated that they saw her wearing the stolen coat, and the village elder informed the court that she had previously been under suspicion for theft. Based on this evidence, the court sentenced her to three days in jail and a fine of twenty rubles to compensate the victim.[5] Another Moscow province *volost'* court heard the following argument during its April 25, 1871, session. A peasant had reported the theft of his daughter's boots some months earlier. Their whereabouts remained unknown until April 21, when, in church, the maiden saw them on another

3. For recent discussion of the peasant economy, see John Bushnell, "Peasant Economy and Peasant Revolution at the Turn of the Century: Neither Immiseration nor Autonomy," *RR* 47, no. 1 (1988), 75–88; Stephen G. Wheatcroft, "Crises and the Condition of the Peasantry in Late Imperial Russia," in Esther Kingston-Mann and Timothy Mixter, eds., *Peasant Economy, Culture, and Politics of European Russia, 1800–1921* (Princeton, 1991), 128–72; Steven L. Hoch, "On Good Numbers and Bad: Malthus, Population Trends and Peasant Standards of Living in Late Imperial Russia," *SR* 53, no. 1 (1994), 41–75.

4. A number of these studies were carried out in collaboration with or under the direction of criminologist Mikhail N. Gernet. See, e.g., *Seminarii po ugolovnomu pravu priv.-dots. M. N. Gernet,* part 1 (Moscow, 1908); V. G. Groman, ed., *Vliianie neurozhaev na narodnoe khoziaistvo Rossii,* part 2 (Moscow, 1927), 94–199; E. N. Tarnovskii, "Vliianie khlebnykh tsen i urozhaev na dvizhenie prestuplenii protiv sobstvennosti," *ZhMIu,* no. 8 (1898), 73–106.

5. *Trudy komissii po preobrazovaniiu volostnykh sudov,* 7 vols. (SPb, 1873–74), 2:157.

woman's feet and demanded their return, saying that her girlfriends could also identify them as hers. The accused claimed to have bought these boots in another village, a story supported by her husband. She also brought several witnesses to court who testified that they had seen her wearing these very boots the previous summer, that is, before the footwear in question had disappeared. Choosing the simplest method of resolving this case, the judges ordered both parties to try on the boots in their presence and, when it was clear that they fit the plaintiff far better, ruled in her favor and ordered the property returned. No additional punishment was meted out.[6]

Such were the everyday cases of theft brought before Russia's lowest courts during the first decade after emancipation, and over the years that followed the nature of these offenses changed but little. Thus in 1881 several sheaves of oats were taken from a field in Riazan' province's Sapozhok district and later discovered by the village elder in the culprits' barn. The Sarai *volost'* court imposed sentence of twenty rubles and fifteen lashes of the birch.[7] In November 1889 the Spas-Klepikovsk *volost'* court found a peasant guilty of filching a pair of boots, rejected his claim that he bought the disputed items from his accuser's wife, and sentenced him to fifteen lashes.[8] The brothers Fedor and Ivan Smetanin were handed similar sentences in December 1890 by another Riazan' township court for stealing rye from their older brother's barn. Although they appealed to the district assembly and the provincial board, and despite the fact that testimony appeared to favor their version of events, the court's decision was upheld. For losing this round in what appears to have been a long-simmering family feud over property division, Fedor got twenty lashes while Ivan spent seven days in the *volost'* jail.[9]

Many similar crimes were tried by justices of the peace and circuit courts, a fact that caused a confusion and blurring of jurisdictions between Russia's judicial instances that went largely unresolved under the old regime.[10] Among numerous cases he decided during 1889, a justice of the peace from Moscow's Bogorodsk district sentenced two peasants who had stolen an-

6. Ibid., 2:167–68.

7. GARO, f. 694, op. 21, sv. 392, d. 490, ll. 2–20b. See also op. 26, sv. 512, d. 582.

8. Ibid., f. 695, op. 1, sv. 17, d. 227, ll. 1–4.

9. Ibid., sv. 8, d. 230, ll. 2–8.

10. Confusion over peace and circuit court jurisdiction is discussed in E. Frantsesson, "Po povodu zakona 18-go maia 1882 goda 'o nakazaniiakh za krazhu so vzlomom,'" *SudG*, no. 12 (1884), 12–15. On the blurred jurisdictional boundaries between *volost'* and peace courts, see V. Likharev, "O podsudnosti ugolovnykh del mirovym sud'iam," *ZhMIu*, no. 4 (1868), 295–314; E. Tikhonov, *Volostnoi sud i mirovoi sud'ia v krest'ianskikh seleniiakh* (Kovno, 1872); "Volostnoi i mirovoi sud," *Nedelia*, no. 13 (1872), 404–9; I. Verigin, "Nachala narodnogo prava i sudoproizvodstva," *RusRech'*, no. 3 (1879), 129; A. E. Garnak, *Volostnoi sud. Zakony, rasporiazheniia pravitel'stva i tsirkuliary dlia krest'ian vsei Rossiiskoi Imperii,* 3rd ed. (Moscow, 1883).

other's pig to five months in prison. He also tried two villagers charged with
theft of cows and sentenced another to four months' incarceration for pilfering firewood.[11] As for trials in higher courts, we might randomly take that
of an indigent peasant who was brought before the Riazan' Circuit Court in
1889 on charges of stealing two hams worth six rubles from a neighbor's
loft, having gained entry by tearing through the straw roof. Owing to his
poverty, however, and regardless of his confession to the court (or possibly
because of it), the jury acquitted the thief.[12]

Whether we examine court decisions or bimonthly police reports, the
same monotonous profile of rural theft emerges year after year. By far the
most common property crimes reported to rural police officials of Riazan'
province, or tried in *volost'* and peace courts, were break-ins to steal grain,
seed, flour, and other agricultural produce, meat, farming tools, and clothing. Of peasants tried for property crimes by the Spas-Klepikovsk court over
the course of 1894, for example, one had stolen a silver watch worth 18
rubles; another took four sheaves from a rye field; a thirty-six year-old man
stole boots valued at 1.40 rubles; one villager made off with two of his neighbor's ducks; three were convicted for stealing hay.[13] A sample of 277 cases
drawn from police records for the years 1884, 1888, and 1891 shows that
21 percent involved theft of food or produce, while clothing accounted for
14 percent, cash for 15 percent, and horses for 20 percent. The objects of
the remaining 30 percent of these thefts were identified only as "property"
or "various property." Liquor shops presented another common target for
rural thieves (who made off with vodka far more frequently than money),
as did local stores and street stalls containing a variety of goods and equipment.[14] Given that villagers often did not bother to report large numbers of
petty thefts, we can also assume that these examples barely scratch the
quantitative surface of rural property offenses.

If "petty" theft accounted for most rural property crime, this is not to suggest that more valuable possessions did not fall prey to thieves. In 1888, for
instance, a woman from Spassk district had 1,500 rubles' worth of gold and
diamonds stolen from her home. A peasant woman of Nizhnii Novgorod

11. TsGIAgM, f. 703, op. 1, d. 48, ll. 400b., 93, 1170b., 1430b. See also f. 576, op. 1, d. 86
(1866), ll. 1–4; d. 137 (1882), ll. 1–25; f. 703, op. 1, d. 27 (1872).

12. GARO, f. 640, op. 51, sv. 144, d. 426, ll. 2–20b, 24–30. For similar circuit court cases,
see, e.g., sv. 112, d. 40 (1872); sv. 121, d. 144 (1878); sv. 134, dd. 307–8 (1884).

13. Ibid., f. 76, op. 5, sv. 3, d. 6, ll. 2–68. See also f. 70, op. 2, sv. 1 (1899), d. 3, ll. 9–45.

14. This sample is drawn from ibid., f. 7, op. 1, dd. 95, 535, 613. See also f. 5, op. 1, d. 4020
(1905), ll. 44, 53–530b. For comparisons with the objects of rural thefts perpetrated in other
village settings, see, e.g., David Warren Sabean, *Property, Production, and Family in Neckarhausen,
1700–1870* (Cambridge, 1990), 452–53; David Jones, "Rural Crime and Protest in the Victorian Era," in G. E. Mingay, Ed., *The Unquiet Countryside* (London, 1989), 117–18; Jones, *Rebecca's Children* (Oxford, 1989), 166–73.

province who had amassed 3,000 rubles in silver and gold coin was relieved of them in June 1896. In this case the victim was lucky, for shortly afterward several local peasants gave themselves away by foolishly converting the gold into paper currency.[15] One night in April 1898, a Simbirsk villager made off with 700 rubles as well as a variety of goods from a neighbor's storeroom. When apprehended, the thief returned all of the stolen property along with 21.65 rubles, claiming that he had taken no more than this. In February 1913 in the Riazan' village of Korovko, five peasant barns were robbed of property worth nearly 300 rubles.[16] Nor did thieves neglect possessions critical to peasant livelihood. Large quantities of grain or flax, tools, plows, barrows, and livestock were often taken, leaving victims in dire straits, especially in the case of horsetheft.

The local and regional markets dotting Russia's countryside provided peasants with a broad range of services and opportunities, from festivity and sociability that broke the monotony of their tedious labor and village life to marriage partners for their children and, of course, markets for selling goods and produce as well as buying an expanding range of consumer products. Throughout Europe the marketplace has always served as an ideal setting for theft, swindling, robbery, and a host of other disreputable activities. Russia was no exception. Its rural markets regularly attracted pickpockets and horsethieves who plied their trade or sold its fruits, not to mention smugglers, swindlers, forgers, and bootleggers. According to one former justice of the peace, "Our winter bazaars and summer markets are places where petty thieves find the greatest freedom. There they pick pockets and steal goods for domestic use for which they otherwise would have to spend money."[17] Larger markets served as sites where lucrative frauds might be attempted. At the start of 1916, for example, a Voronezh peasant showed up at Riazan''s central bazaar with thirty head of cattle, which he sold to several different meat traders, taking sizable advances from each and then disappearing with his livestock.[18] Given the prominent role of peasant women as buyers and traders, markets also provided female thieves with a ready source of goods. One report from the Riazan' village of Zadubrov'e, while noting that "women who practice theft as a trade are quite rare in rural life," described "the thieving tricks of Zadubrov'e women." They operated in gangs at the bazaars of surrounding villages, with a group of noisy "shop-

15. "Proisshestviia po Riazanskoi gubernii," *RiazGV,* no. 30 (1888), pt. 2, 4; *NizhL,* no. 172 (1896), 2. See also "Selo Bogoroditskie Riabinki, Bolkhovskogo uezda," *OrlV,* no. 3 (1898), 2.

16. "Der. Staraia Baeva, Ardatovskogo u. (Krazha)," *SimbGV,* no. 31 (1898), pt. 2, 3; "Krazha krest'ianskogo skarba," *RiazZh,* no. 47 (1913), 3. See also GARO, f. 640, op. 53, st. 4–5, sv. 11, d. 121 (1879); op. 55, sv. 49, d. 189 (1914); sv. 62, d. 422 (1913).

17. V. N. Nazar'ev, "Sovremennaia glush'," *VE,* no. 3 (1872), 149.

18. "Moshennichestvo," *RiazZh,* no. 5 (1916), 3. See also A. P. Mel'nikov, *Ocherki bytovoi istorii Nizhegorodskoi iarmarki (1817–1917),* 2nd ed. (Nizhnii Novgorod, 1993), ch. 5.

pers" distracting a merchant while several of the thieves made off with various goods that they would later sell. Some local women had been prosecuted and imprisoned, the report explained, but "this in no way has put a stop to the criminals' activities," which had recently expanded to markets in other districts. That this sort of crime flourished was "one of the shameful pages of village life."[19]

Although they received far greater publicity, assaults on landed property were by no means limited to conflicts between villagers and noble estate owners. Private peasant renters, small property owners, and entire settlements were ready targets for crop theft and land seizures. When in August 1884 twenty-five Sapozhok district peasants came to a nobleman's orchard to steal apples, they attacked and wounded the property's renter (another peasant).[20] Theft of crops from peasants' fields, boundary transgressions and illegal pasturing of livestock, cutting down trees on another's land, and even erecting buildings on someone else's property, as well as other crimes were a common feature of rural life, perpetrated against neighbors and fellow villagers. On occasion, unresolved property disputes led to large-scale, violent confrontations between village factions or even different villages. In southern Riazan' province, a long-simmering dispute concerning ownership of several sizable tracts of land by the villages of Koverdiako, on the Tambov side of the border, and Bakhmet'evskie Vyselki exploded into open conflict in 1890. On June 4, 500 of the Tambov peasants launched a mass assault on this property, during which they seized livestock and other goods valued at 5,956 rubles.[21]

Clearly, peasants constituted the primary victims of theft. Hence, in their search for a "peasant movement," compilers of published sources documenting villagers' assaults upon landed estates have painted an especially one-sided picture by ignoring intraclass criminality. This is obvious from police records that identify crime victims. Of 94 thefts reported around Riazan' province in 1884, peasants accounted for 70.2 percent of the victims, nobles for 7.4 percent, with priests close behind at 6.4 and merchants at 4.3 percent. During 1891, of 123 reports identifying crime victims, 80 percent were peasants, 9.7 percent noble landowners, 5.7 percent townspeople (*meshchanstvo*), and only 1.6 percent merchants.[22] With peasants providing the overwhelming majority of targets for property offenses, we

19. "Selo Zadubrov'e, Spasskogo uezda (Vorovskie prodelki krest'ianok)," *RiazV,* no. 280 (1910), 4.

20. GARO, f. 7, op. 1, d. 95, l. 63ob. See also "Krazha khleba s polei," *OrlV,* no. 229 (1898), 2; "Sedmiozernaia Pustyn', Kazanskoi gub. i u.," *VolzhV,* no. 85 (1899), 3; "Prichinenie tiazhkogo uvech'ia," *RiazZh,* no. 15 (1911), 3; "Dikaia rasprava," *RiazZh,* no. 239 (1913), 3–4.

21. GARO, f. 5, st. 3, op. 4, d. 2648.

22. Ibid., f. 7, op. 1, dd. 95, 613.

must question both the definition of such crimes as "petty" and their assignment to the lower jurisdictions of *volost'* courts, justices of the peace, or land captains. Criminal categories, jurisdictions, and punishments, after all, were decided by government ministries, not by the rural communities forced to deal on a daily basis with crime and with those judicial or administrative organs assigned to oversee the countryside after 1861. That peasants did not necessarily look upon all thefts as "petty" can be readily seen from their frequently treating perpetrators more harshly than permitted by law, by efforts to expel them from their midst and, on some occasions, even killing them. To a poor or middling peasant family dependent upon the harvest for a sizable portion of its annual income, pilfering sheaves of rye was not "petty theft" but a serious offense deserving of strict treatment. One commentator argued as early as 1881 that "petty theft will destroy the commune in the end" because perpetrators were rarely captured and fewer still came to trial due to insufficient evidence against them.[23] A growing number of rural voices criticizing both the courts and the lenient punishments meted out to thieves should thus caution against an uncritical acceptance of official definitions of property crimes.

## BOOTLEGGING

Although legally classified as a violation of liquor regulations and excise laws, bootlegging (*shinkarstvo*) was a serious infringement upon state control of a trade that provided the treasury with a large percentage of its revenue. Criminal statistics and a plethora of government reports all suggest that bootlegging (together with smuggling) became one of the country's fastest-growing crimes after the state established a liquor monopoly in the period 1893–94 and thereby created a large area of new offenses. Only a small fraction of prosecuted cases ever came before circuit courts, however; the great majority were assigned to lower courts or dealt with administratively through regulations established by excise authorities. An even greater number of cases never reached the courts because rural police found it nearly impossible to enforce the new law by apprehending those who evaded the monopoly.[24]

Bootlegging and illegal saloons (*shinki*) existed long before emancipation, but their numbers exploded with the government liquor monopoly. A

23. K. V. N., "Ssylka po prigovoram krest'ianskikh i meshchanskikh obshchestv," *RusRech'*, no. 3 (1881), 65.

24. See the comments on this problem from a police commandant in GARO, f. 5, st. 3, op. 4, d. 2539, ll. 16–190b. Criticism of police inactivity in the fight against bootlegging could be found throughout the empire. See, e.g., "Iz sela Gorkushinets, Mirgorodskogo u., Poltavskoi gub. (Ot mestnogo obyvatelia)," *SV*, no. 7 (1884), 81.

1914 survey conducted within Moscow district counted 630 such establishments in 110 settlements, or 5.7 per village. Indeed, despite the presence of state liquor shops and legal beer halls and taverns, this survey identified *shinki* in 69 percent of all villages.[25] In 1910 correspondents from neighboring Vladimir province had reported that "although there is but one state shop in [our] village, there are *shinki* in every home," and that *"shinki* sell more than state shops." A 1913 study estimated that bootlegging in Penza province accounted for at least 50 percent of all liquor sales in the countryside.[26] This business operated quite simply, with bootleggers often purchasing large quantities of vodka legally from state shops and reselling it at higher prices. Given the relatively small number of state liquor shops throughout the countryside, bootleggers thus filled a significant gap between rural supply and demand. On the eve of a holiday or any other time that the state stores closed, traders stocked up in advance and thus made substantial profits during the festivities.[27]

Rural women carved out a sometimes lucrative sphere of economic activity by exploiting the illegal liquor trade. Reports from many localities noted that bootlegging was the exclusive preserve of women. Replying to a 1910 survey on alcohol consumption in Vladimir province, one correspondent claimed, "There is no end to the *shinki*. On market days in our village, no less than thirty to forty women . . . with baskets on their backs rent out glasses and refill them as well." Another respondent similarly wrote, "During the bazaar, at every step stands a woman with vodka in her pocket, and this business provides support for their families." Young women of Zimenkovsk *volost'* engaged in bootlegging "to earn money for their dowries."[28] Among recorded rural crimes, women made up an above-average proportion of persons convicted for infractions against liquor regulations. Constituting only 9.7 percent of convicts within all felony categories during the period 1874–1913, they averaged 19.9 percent of persons convicted for bootlegging, reaching as high as 30 percent in some years and 26.7 percent between 1899 and 1903.[29] Following the August 1914 introduction of pro-

25. *Derevnia i zapreshchenie prodazhi pitei v Moskovskom uezde* (Moscow, 1915), 38–39.

26. V. A. Chernevskii, *K voprosu o p'ianstve vo Vladimirskoi gubernii i sposobakh bor'by s nim* (Vladimir na Kliaz'me, 1911), 24; D. N. Voronov, *Alkogolizm v gorode i derevne v sviazi s bytom naseleniia* (Penza, 1913), 35.

27. Voronov, *Alkogolizm,* 36. See also M. R., "Sud v derevne," *Nabliudatel',* no. 3 (1882), 47.

28. "S. Ashitkovo, bronnitskogo uezda. (Bor'ba s shinkami)," *RiazV,* no. 174 (1910), 3; Chernevskii, *K voprosu o p'ianstve,* 24.

29. *Svod statisticheskikh svedenii po delam ugolovnym,* 43 vols. (SPb, 1874–1916), part 2, table 1 (hereafter: *Svody*). For examples, see GARO, f. 79, op. 4 (1893), d. 29; f. 717, op. 45 (1895), d. 14; op. 55 (1905), d. 8. Such proportions continued after the 1917 Revolution as well. In 1922, women accounted for 34.2 percent of all persons convicted for illegally producing or selling liquor; in 1923, this percentage slipped to 30 percent, and to 29.6 per-

hibition, too, peasant women remained prominent players in both the illegal production and sale of moonshine (*samogon* or *khanzha*) as well as surrogates for vodka. In two townships of Ekaterinoslav district, for example, a 1915 study reported that "peasant women have appeared who prepare *khanzha* from horseradish roots."[30] With bootlegging, clearly, the state's creation of a large new category of crime brought peasants new opportunities for economic gain while providing law enforcement with additional woes.

## FROM ROBBERY TO ORGANIZED CRIME: GANGS, BANDITS, AND HORSETHIEVES

"Recently," noted columnist A. Petrishchev in a 1914 survey of the provincial press, "numerous gangs of robbers have appeared throughout Bessarabia. In Kursk province they cannot remember such an abundance of robbers and bloody goings-on. Residents of the Sukhumsk region . . . are selling their homes and moving away; many literally do not go out on the street, have placed strong iron bars on their doors and windows, and are afraid to open the doors at night." Of course, he added, the authorities had undertaken firm measures to end this rash of banditry. "The last months of 1913 witnessed a large number of trials: the Kushchi gang in Ekaterinoslavl', the 'Steppe Devils' in Ekaterinodar, the 'Turkestan Robbers' in Samarkand, the 'Forest Brotherhood' in Irkutsk, the 'Rural Robbers' in Pskov province, and so on. But with the capture of one gang, a new one appears, and over the closing months of 1913 bandit gangs were attacking trains, churches, estates, trading establishments, and many other places."[31]

By the mid-1890s judicial statistics showed a substantial increase in rural robberies of all forms. District police in Riazan' province found themselves overwhelmed and unable to deal with the crime reports flooding their

---

cent in 1924. M. N. Gernet, *Prestupnost' i samoubiistva vo vremia voiny i posle nee* (Moscow, 1927), 135.

30. P. K. Sokolov, ed., *Ekaterinoslavskaia derevnia posle zakrytiia vinotorgovli* (Ekaterinoslav, 1915), 46. On the use and sale of "surrogates" and home brew, see also *Derevnia i zapreshchenie prodazhi pitei v Moskovskom uezde*, 68–70; *God trezvosti v Kazanskoi gubernii* (Kazan', 1916), 68–74; D. N. Voronov, *Zhizn' derevni v dni trezvosti* (Petrograd, 1916), 46–53. Even earlier, as various chemical preparations began trickling into the country for use as intoxicants, women were also quick to see the profit in smuggling and selling. When anodine became popular in Russia during the early 1890s, peasant women played a major role as smugglers, accepting shipments from Prussia and distributing the drug in villages and towns alike. See "Vmesto vodki," *VolzhV*, no. 58 (1892), 3.

31. A. Petrishchev, "Khronika vnutrennei zhizni," *RB*, no. 1 (1914), 316. See also GARO, f. 5, st. 3, op. 4, dd. 4954, 4968, 4978 (1908); d. 5073 (1909); d. 5335 (1910); d. 5560 (1912); "Tiumen'," *NizhL*, no. 5 (1897), 3; "Sudebnaia khronika. Razboi," *NizhL*, no. 34 (1899), 4; "Delo i nuzhdy russkoi provintsii," *Vremennik zhivopisnoi Rossii*, no. 93 (1902), 323–24; Timothy Mixter, *Revolution in the Bear's Corner* (forthcoming).

offices.[32] In towns and villages alike robbers seemed to be growing more brazen and violent, particularly after the 1905–7 revolution had revealed more starkly than ever before the weakness of law enforcement. In March 1908, for instance, a peasant family traveling along the Oka River was attacked by five thieves armed with clubs and revolvers. The robbers shot and wounded the son, seriously beat the father, then made off with his fur coat and wallet containing over 100 rubles.[33] Four peasants riding through the village of Kasimovka late one night in early January 1910 also fell victim to robbers who beat them and stole their coats and hats.[34] Similar assaults on peasants occurred regularly throughout Riazan' and other provinces, especially from the 1890s on.

There were degrees of robbery in Russian law, ranging from *grabezh*—the forceful and direct seizure of property, which could involve anything from picking pockets to assault without resort to weapons—to armed robbery (*razboi*) by individuals or organized gangs employing threats, extortion, violence, bodily harm, and murder. As with theft and burglary, the property or sums of money taken by most rural robbers were small, particularly in the eyes of nonpeasant jurists and government officials.[35] Other cases of violence on the part of perpetrators proved more serious and certainly more frightening for victims. Ivan Isaev had such an experience one September morning in 1882 when, along a deserted road in Spassk district, he was robbed of the four rubles he had just been paid for work on a nearby farm. His assailant, a fellow farmhand, waylaid Isaev, knocked him to the ground, threw a jacket over his victim's head, and took his money. The crime was solved only because the culprit lost his belt during the attack, and Isaev recognized it as belonging to twenty-one-year-old Mikhail Terkhov, a fact corroborated by other villagers. Arrested and charged, Terkhov was found guilty by the Riazan' Circuit Court and sentenced to three years in a corrective penal division.[36]

32. For comparisons over time, see GARO, f. 5, st. 3, op. 4, dd. 673–85 (1863); d. 1265 (1873); dd. 2037–57 (1883); dd. 2774–85 (1893); d. 5073 (1909). Throughout the empire, the number of convictions for rural robberies remained relatively stable between 1874 and 1895 but increased significantly thereafter from 1,243 convictions in 1899 to 4,362 in 1908, then falling to just under 3,000 by 1913. *Svody*, part 2, "Vremia i mesto soversheniia prestuplenii."

33. GARO, f. 5, st. 3, op. 4, d. 4828, ll. 14–140b.

34. "Grabezh," *RiazV*, no. 10 (1910), 3. See also "Sessiia Riazanskogo Okruzhnogo suda v g. Ranenburge. Razboi," *RiazZh*, no. 50 (1912), 4; *IaGV*, no. 5 (1891), part 2, 2–3.

35. *SZU*, part 1: *Ulozhenie o nakazaniiakh ugolovnykh i ispravitel'nykh*, art. 1627–36 (*razboi*), 1637–43 (*grabezh*). See also S. S. Shaikevich, "Vooruzhennaia krazha," *SudZh*, no. 1 (1873), 1–22; P. Dashkevich, "'Grabezh', kak ugolovno-iuridicheskii termin obychnogo prava," *IuV*, no. 1 (1892), 168–71. Pickpockets who stole sums as small as one ruble, for example, could be tried for robbery rather than theft. GARO, f. 7, op. 1, d. 613, l. 20; d. 772, l. 2.

36. GARO, f. 640, op. 51, sv. 130, d. 265, ll. 5–50b., 26–32. See also sv. 154, d. 574, ll. 4–56.

"Petty" robberies of this sort certainly concerned government and law enforcement officials, but they did not threaten order directly and were mainly to be managed locally. Organized groups of robbers and bandits, however, presented far greater concern. Ever fearful of crowd activity, Russian law defined a "criminal gang" quite broadly, and a special section of the penal code (articles 922–931) criminalized belonging to a gang. Any group of people joining to perpetrate a single illegal deed could be considered such, as can be seen from an 1882 case.[37] On December 5, 1881, Ivan Fokin met Aver'ian Frantsuzov and Leonov Klevtsov at a tavern in Berezovo village, Spassk district, and was invited to go off with them. The three went first to Frantsuzov's house, where they picked up several rough-hewn clubs and then set out to the home of Andrei Ignatov, a forest warden, located in neighboring Sapozhok district. Upon arriving they pretended to be travelers and asked whether they could come in to warm themselves, to which request Ignatov acceded. Shortly thereafter the trio fell upon him and his wife, beat them both, and bound them with ropes. During this assault Frantsuzov also cut Ignatov with a knife. Finally, they took a trunk containing 130 rubles as well as other valuables and fled, leaving their victims bound. Within a few days the robbers' tracks were discovered and followed to Berezovo, where police began questioning local residents. They learned that on December 6 and 7 Fokin had changed a sizable quantity of five- and ten-ruble notes, spent money lavishly at the local tavern, and treated everybody there to vodka. He also tried to sell an expensive watch for 200 rubles. When interrogated, Fokin confessed to the crime and implicated his fellow conspirators, explaining that he had been an unwilling participant. He told the police that when Klevtsov and Frantsuzov began beating the Ignatovs he wanted to flee but they threatened to harm him. He had remained only out of fear for his own life. Taking the trunk into a nearby forest, the three broke the lock, divided up the contents, then returned to Berezovo, where

37. On the problem of defining gangs, see Eric J. Hobsbawm, *Bandits* (Harmondsworth, 1969); J. Sharpe, "Criminal Organization in Rural England 1550–1750," in G. Ortalli, ed., *Bande armate, banditi, banditismo* (Rome, 1986), 125–40; Paul Ginzborg, "After the Revolution: Bandits on the Plains of the Po, 1848–54," in John A. Davis and Paul Ginzborg, eds., *Society and Politics in the Age of the Risorgimento* (Cambridge, 1991), 128–51; R. Wells, "Popular Protest and Social Crime: The Evidence of Criminal Gangs in Rural Southern England, 1790–1860," in Barry Stapleton, ed., *Conflict and Community in Southern England* (New York, 1992), 170–72; Mixter, *Revolution*. Colonial administrations have historically proved especially fearful of collective crime. See, e.g., David Arnold, "Dacoity and Rural Crime in Madras, 1860–1940," *Journal of Peasant Studies* 6, no. 2 (1979), 140–67; Cheah Boon Kheng, "Social Banditry and Rural Crime in North Kedah, 1909–1929," *Journal of the Malaysian Branch of the Royal Asiatic Society* 54, no. 2 (1981), 98–130; Sandria B. Freitag, "Collective Crime and Authority in North India," in Anand A. Yang, ed., *Crime and Criminality in British India* (Tucson, 1985), 140–88; Donald Crummey, ed., *Banditry, Rebellion and Social Protest in Africa* (London, 1986), chs. 4–8.

they got soundly drunk. Tried by the Riazan' Circuit Court in April 1882 on charges of armed robbery, assault, and forming a criminal association, Fokin and Frantsuzov were deprived of all rights and received ten years each at penal servitude in Siberia. Klevtsov was sentenced to six years and eight months.[38]

Police were far more successful at apprehending "gangs" of this sort, of course, than at solving serious organized crimes; such efforts were all too often thwarted by ineptness, corruption, their pathetically small numbers, the difficulty of operating in rural areas, and also the shrewdness of their quarry. Cases in which police did manage to break up and arrest entire gangs, therefore, were given wide publicity, with officers receiving medals and commendations for their work.[39] In 1900, for example, a particularly vicious band of eight operating in Khar'kov province was not captured until it had committed a string of armed robberies of *volost'* offices, killing a total of seventeen people, including five guards and one policeman.[40] Another case involved a gang in Petersburg province consisting entirely of peasant women whose members lured their victims (usually merchants and traders) to places not far from the capital city itself and then murdered and robbed them. It took three years before the police succeeded in tracking them down and arresting them in 1909.[41] The boldness and all too frequent success of such undertakings hardly supports the image of tsarist Russia as a powerful, effective, and ubiquitous police state.

Although cases like these received extensive press coverage, horsetheft remained by far the most familiar and widely feared form of robbery perpetrated by highly organized gangs that operated primarily in the countryside. There is little doubt that horsetheft increased substantially following emancipation, as did the harm caused to farmers, breeders, carters, and cabbies, who depended upon horses for their livelihood. "A peasant who loses his horse is, as they say, without hands," stated a correspondent to *The Riazan' Herald* in 1909. "If he loses his horse, he either has to give up farming or hire himself out as a laborer [*batrak*]." As early as 1877, one commentator speculated that annual economic losses resulting from theft of

38. GARO, f. 640, op. 51, sv. 130, d. 266, ll. 5–70b., 66–76ob. In a less serious case (1869), a justice of the peace in Moscow province's Bogorodsk district tried a peasant named Goiachev on charges of having beaten his mother and for organizing a gang of thieves in his village. TsGIAgM, f. 702, op. 1, d. 14.

39. GARO, f. 5, st. 3, op. 4, d. 870, l. 15.

40. "Sudebnaia khronika. Delo o shaike grabiteli," *NizhL*, no. 3 (1901), 4. See also "Lesnye brat'ia," *SPbVed*, no. 233 (1911), 6; Mixter, *Revolution*, chs. 7–8.

41. "Arest zhenshchin-ubiits," *Golos* (Iaroslavl'), no. 42 (1909), 2. See also "Zhenshchina-razboinitsa," *RiazZh*, no. 73 (1912), 3, concerning the activities of one Matrena Lunina in the Odessa area.

horses probably exceeded the combined damage caused by fire, hail, "and all other misfortune."[42] Or as another writer stated twenty-five years later, "Periodic epidemics, crop failure, and other disasters cannot compare with the harm that horsethieves bring to the countryside. The horsethief holds peasants in perpetual, uninterrupted fear, terrorizes them, hinders agriculture, and undermines their well-being. Nowhere at present is this evil as great as in Russia."[43]

For reasons difficult to discern, the law only began catching up with this offense, albeit inadequately, during the late 1880s. At the time of emancipation most horsethefts fell within the jurisdiction of *volost'* courts—clear proof of the sharp differences already existing between state and peasant views regarding what constituted petty as opposed to serious property crime. Only after endless complaints from police and local authorities, landowners, horse breeders, and peasants was prosecution at last transferred to peace courts by a law of March 18, 1880. But here, too, both law enforcement authorities and the many peasants victimized by horsethieves felt that punishments remained far too mild, given that peace courts could impose a maximum one-year prison sentence.[44] Further tinkering with the penal code helped little. Under the 1880 law, horsethieves could be deprived of all rights and sentenced either to a corrective penal facility for a maximum of two and a half years or to Siberian exile for life if it could be proved that they practiced this crime as a profession. Needless to say, overburdened prosecutors found it nearly impossible to furnish sufficient evidence of thieves' "professional" activities and therefore could rarely apply the law. One critic declared it "a dead letter."[45]

42. "Bich derevni," *RiazV,* no. 143 (1909), 2; "Iazva konokradstva," *Nedelia,* no. 8 (1877), 251.

43. G. N. Breitman, *Prestupnyi mir: ocherki iz byta professional'nykh prestupnikov* (Kiev, 1901), 113. See also "O prichinakh krest'ianskikh ubytkov," *SarGV,* no. 89 (1895), part 2, 4; "Konokradstvo," *Volost' i derevnia,* no. 5 (1910), 14.

44. *Ustav o nakazaniiakh, nalagaemykh mirovymi sud'iami,* in *Sudebnye ustavy 20 noiabria 1864 goda,* 4th ed. (SPb and Moscow, 1870), 1; E. N. Barantsevich, *Konokradstvo i mery protivu nego v Rossii* (Moscow, 1898), 12; Avgust Levenstim, "Konokradstvo s iuridicheskoi i bytovoi storony," *VestP* 29, no. 2 (1899), 32; S. Gr—ii, "Bor'ba s konokradstvom," *NizhL,* no. 7 (1899), 2. At the end of the 1860s, the Fifth All-Russian Congress of Agriculturalists petitioned the government to hang horsethieves; during the next twenty years, calls were regularly voiced to replace imprisonment with penal servitude for life as punishment for this crime. Ivan Kashkarov, *Nuzhdy russkogo naroda* (SPb, 1880), 34–35; "O merakh protiv konokradstva," *SV,* no. 13 (1881), 123; "Mery protiv konokradstva," *VolzhV,* no. 166 (1899), 3. In 1912 the Duma did increase penalties, imposing penal servitude on a greater number of horsetheft cases. "Primenenie zakona o konokradakh," *RiazZh,* no. 116 (1912), 3.

45. GARO, f. 5, st. 3, op. 4, d. 1901, ll. 2–20b., 5–50b.; E. V., "O neudovletvoritel'nosti zakona o konokradstve v vide promysla," *SudG,* no. 19 (1884), 12–13. See also "Konokradstvo po remeslu i primenenie 1654¹ st. ulozh.," *SudG,* no. 15 (1894), 3–5; Gr—ii, "Bor'ba s konokradstvom," 2; Levenstim, "Konokradstvo," 32–33.

As early as 1848, the government had drawn up extraordinary regulations for a number of regions where horsetheft had long been widespread,
introducing special commissars to nine provinces. Yet if data from Riazan'
province are indicative of regional or national trends, they prove these efforts a dismal failure. In 1859 police commandants received reports of 257
cases of horsetheft with a loss of 385 animals; only 20 percent of these were
found and returned to their owners (though in many instances, owners
themselves found the horses, or the animals returned after escaping their
captors). Accounts from 1860 and 1861 showed only a slight improvement,
with roughly 30 percent of horses reported stolen returned. For the years
1864–66 that proportion averaged 34 percent.[46] Other provinces had far
lower success rates, particularly by the 1880s and 1890s. One author suggested that no more than 10 percent of all horsethefts were ever investigated, let alone prosecuted. Another found that in Khar'kov province between 1891 and 1899, only 639 (5.1 percent) out of 13,546 horses reported
stolen were recovered. The true figure of total cases, however, could easily
be doubled without fear of error, he stated, "because the victims . . . in most
cases never report their missing horses to the police." The fact that during
these same eight years Russia's circuit and peace courts together convicted
37,173 persons of horsetheft (an average of 4,130 per year) makes the true
dimensions of this crime as visible as the failings of police and prosecutors.[47]

Contemporary descriptions and government directives make it abundantly clear not only that horsethieves had established skilled and far-
reaching organizations long before emancipation but that police found it
virtually impossible to root them out. In the late 1850s and 1860s, the MVD
requested regular reports from governors as to the number of gangs discovered and brought to justice. By 1866 not one of Riazan' province's twelve
district police commandants could even claim to have discovered—let
alone broken up—a single gang of horsethieves.[48] In large part, their failure could be attributed to the level of organization achieved by rural gangs.
As noted in an 1886 commentary from Kursk province, horsethieves carried out their work so skillfully "that they almost always escape the police."
Most important, professional thieves formed extensive associations and networks with upwards of several hundred accomplices throughout the countryside, hiring wandering indigents as informants and scouts, paying off
police to ignore their activities, and in some cases even employing police

46. GARO, f. 5, st. 3, op. 4, d. 647, l. 59; d. 870 (1869), l. 111. As one justice of the peace
wrote in 1872, police almost never searched for stolen horses. Rather, the victims themselves
attempted to find the animals. Nazar'ev, "Sovremennaia glush'," no. 3, 153.

47. Levenstim, "Konokradstvo," 50; D. S. Fleksor, *Okhrana sel'skokhoziaistvennoi sobstvennosti*
(SPb, 1904), 194; *Svody*, vols. 18–26, part 2, table 1.

48. GARO, f. 5, st. 3, op. 4, d. 647, ll. 4, 59; d. 870, l. 111.

officials to operate way stations or perform other tasks. Village and township elders, too, could be found on the horsethieves' payroll.[49]

Some of these networks stretched across several provinces, with special "offices" located along designated routes at which stolen horses would be sorted, exchanged, and then moved on. As one writer explained about horsetheft in Saratov province, "Stolen horses are taken on a certain road to the Volga or the Sura rivers; in almost every settlement along that road there is a den of thieves who immediately transfer the horses to the next village. Thus in the event of suspicion or search, the first abductor can be sitting peacefully at home in an hour or two, as though nothing has taken place. . . . All stolen horses end up . . . beyond the province's borders, transferred either across the Sura into Penza and Simbirsk provinces, or across the Volga to Samara, while Saratov itself receives horses from these three provinces."[50] As a saying among horsethieves from Nizhnii Novgorod and parts of Moscow province put it, "Steal in Arat', sell in Iakosh', and cover your tracks in Murashkino."[51]

Numerous sources wrote of entire villages that specialized in horsetheft and where, according to an 1860 commentator, "If not everyone actually takes part in stealing, they conceal thieves and horses or help to transfer the latter." In 1901 a student of criminal life described these villages as "always more prosperous than those of honest peasants. . . . [V]ery often peasants envy the thieves, seeing how they live in complete satisfaction." Indeed, "A horsethief is usually considered a good match for a peasant girl."[52] Such was their power in some areas that thieves collected a special "tax" from peasant communities, promising in exchange not to steal their horses. Those that refused to cooperate received the ominous vow that they would spend the summer "plowing with roosters," for they would be left without any horses at all. Many knuckled under and paid off the thieves.[53] One 1885 description from a district of Kazan' province, where horsethieves held the entire population in fear, explained that "[the gang] has many agents who openly gather tribute from the villages. The 'elders' of this industry are escapees

49. "Vnutrennie izvestiia," *RusV,* no. 257 (1886), 3; Breitman, *Prestupnyi mir,* 119–22; L. Vesin, "Konokradstvo, ego organizatsiia i sposoby bor'by s nim naseleniia," *TrudyIVEO,* no. 3 (1885), 355–56; F. Shch—n, "Organizatsiia konokradov i skotokradov v Kubanskoi oblasti," *Nedelia,* no. 26 (1879), 779–85.

50. Vesin, "Konokradstvo," 356. See also "Konokradstvo i bezkormitsa," *MosVed,* no. 85 (1884), 3.

51. M—r., "O merakh preduprezhdeniia i presecheniia konokradstva v Rossii," *IuZh,* no. 3 (1860), part 3, 204. Locations in the saying are villages: the first in the Arzamassk district of Nizhnii Novgorod province, and the others in Kniagininsk district, Moscow province.

52. Ibid., 204; Breitman, *Prestupnyi mir,* 118.

53. Fleksor, *Okhrana,* 193. See also Vesin, "Konokradstvo," 350–51.

from Siberian exile . . . who go around collecting tribute, and woe to those who give less than expected."[54]

Regrettably, we know far too little about the perpetrators to offer more than generalizations concerning robbers, horsethieves, and members of organized gangs. Unlike theft and burglary, there is no easily identifiable correlation between robbery and standard economic indicators; on the other hand, it seems clear that the severe erosion of the state's already limited rural police authority during the decades prior to 1914 abetted an explosion of robberies throughout the countryside. Indeed, as early as 1889, there were claims that "the number of professional thieves is increasing every year."[55] The widespread perception by both peasants and nonpeasants that outsiders were often behind rural robberies also appears to be correct. Among all persons convicted on robbery charges by circuit courts between 1874 and 1913, farming peasants accounted for only 28.3 percent, a figure that declined steadily during our period, from 34.7 percent in the years 1874–78 to as low as 19.7 percent in the years 1909–13. Convicts identified as hired agricultural laborers or day laborers (a highly amorphous category) constituted 16.5 percent of this group from 1874 to 1913.[56] Although the judicial statistics do not indicate whether perpetrators were escapees from Siberian exile, scattered evidence does show that a sizable proportion of rural robbers and horsethieves came from the ranks of Russia's large, wandering population of escapees.[57]

Since peasants viewed organized robbery and horsetheft as two of the most serious crimes perpetrated against their communities, the inability of police to protect them from professional gangs and the growing percentage of cases dismissed by prosecutors only heightened villagers' already negative assessment of official justice, leading them to take matters into their own hands. Honest police officers, too, realized that even when courts

---

54. "Konokradstvo," *MosVed,* no. 214 (1885), 2. See also "Konokradstvo v Poles'i," *VolzhV,* no. 110 (1892), 3.

55. Berendeev, "Derevenskie pis'ma. Krest'ianskie prestupleniia," *SevV,* no. 1, part 2 (1889), 49.

56. *Svody,* part 2, "Zaniatiia osuzhdennykh."

57. The literature on Russia's exile system and the problem of escape is vast and, as yet, virtually unexplored by historians. See N. M. Iadrintsev, *V tiur'me i ssylke* (SPb, 1872); N. Selivanov, "Brodiagi, prazdnoshataiushchiesia i nishchie," *VestP,* no. 3 (1884), 73–90; "Brodiagi i brodiazhnichestvo," *TiurV,* no. 3 (1893), 96–106; *Ssylka v Sibir'. Ocherk ee istorii i sovremennogo polozheniia* (SPb, 1900), 259, 292–305; V. N. Gartvel'd, *Katorga i brodiagi v Sibiri* (Moscow, 1912); Iakov Kolalov, *Istoriia beglogo katorzhnika (napisannaia im samim)* (Piatigorsk, 1913); Alan Wood, "'General Cuckoo's Army': Siberian Brigands and *Brodyagi," Britain-USSR* 65 (1983); Wood, "Sex and Violence in Siberia: Aspects of the Tsarist Exile System," in J. M. Steward and Alan Wood, eds., *Siberia: Two Historical Perspectives* (London, 1984), 23–42.

convicted horsethieves, the punishments meted out remained inadequate. Sometimes police simply turned thieves over to villagers for retribution. In 1902, for instance, a constable and several hundreders arrested four peasants suspected of stealing horses from villagers in Stavropol' province. After the prisoners were severely beaten at the local jail, the constable came outside and asked a crowd of about 200 locals: "So, old men, will they be tried or will you 'teach them' yourselves?" Upon receiving a resounding cry of "Beat them," the constable invited peasants inside the jail "to warm yourselves." As a result, three of the suspects were beaten to death; the fourth remained barely alive.[58] The rising number of reports about rural communities brutally avenging thefts of their horses adds stark detail to the peasants' lack of faith in official justice.

## ARSON

One early November evening in 1897, the snow-covered village of Dmitrievka, situated in Riazan' province's Sapozhok district, was roused by a fire that ravaged the farm of Fedor Tiurin. Before they were extinguished, flames destroyed several outbuildings as well as livestock. As to the fire's origin, suspicion fell immediately upon Tiurin's neighbor, Karp Fionov, and with good reason. Fionov hated Tiurin because the latter, a newcomer to Dmitrievka, had received land transferred from Fionov's holdings. Furious over this transaction, Fionov refused to accept its outcome and took Tiurin to court in an effort to regain the property but lost his case. Even earlier, however, Fionov had threatened Tiurin on numerous occasions, both directly and through others, leading Tiurin to live in constant fear that he might be burned out or perhaps killed. With other villagers present, Fionov taunted and cursed Tiurin, called him by the name of a much despised *volost'* court judge, and threatened him with bodily harm. Finally, on the very day of the fire, the peasant Kolesov saw Fionov covering his straw roof with snow—a common means of protecting one's home from sparks and flying embers. At about 9:00 P.M., another villager happened by and noticed a still weak but spreading fire in Tiurin's yard, close to where it adjoined that of Fionov. As if he had not already attracted sufficient suspicion to himself through his actions, Fionov rushed from his home at that moment shouting, with exaggerated animation: "Good God, our neighbors are burning, and they didn't even tell us!" According to those present, Fionov's conduct during the fire was "abnormal." They also noted that the suspect had earlier removed all livestock from his yard and loaded a sledge with household belongings. On these grounds, Fionov was arrested several days

58. *Pravo,* no. 3 (1903), 173.

later. Though maintaining his innocence throughout the preliminary investigation, Fionov pleaded guilty before the Riazan' Circuit Court and was
sentenced to deprivation of all civil rights along with four years of exile at
hard labor.[59]

Luck was on the side of Dmitrievka that night for the blaze did not spread
to other homes, as happened too often in communities throughout the
Russian countryside. With wood and wattle the most common building materials and the use of thatch for roofing, flying embers could rapidly transform a localized fire into an inferno engulfing an entire village. Indeed, the
"red cock" (*krasnyi petukh*) visited peasant settlements with sickening regularity, and villagers found it extremely difficult to fight the dreaded "living
fire" as its flames leapt from one building to the next.[60] One 1884 incident of arson in Dankov district spread far beyond its intended victim to
consume 40 homes as well as numerous barns, outbuildings, and other
property, causing over 16,000 rubles in damages. Several days later, arson
destroyed 48 peasant homes together with outbuildings in a village of
Riazan' district; the cost of this crime was estimated at more than 14,000
rubles.[61] In 1906 two peasants from Kostroma province ignited another's
shed and the fire eventually engulfed 101 homes, 70 barns, 54 bathhouses,
and other property, resulting in losses valued at 144,080 rubles. In the wake
of this devastation "the peasants are now living all over: in still-intact sheds,
in bathhouses, with other villagers, some in Kostroma, and a large number
have gone to relatives in neighboring townships."[62]

The clandestine nature of arson and the extreme difficulty of determining a fire's origin made it impossible for authorities to calculate either the
extent of this crime or the precise losses that resulted. Yet even rough estimates from sample provinces provide some sense of its frequency, as table
4.1 indicates.

In 1908, out of 3,010 rural fires reported in Riazan' province, 913 (30 percent) resulted from "unknown causes," and 481 (23 percent) were caused by
arson. With 28,453 buildings burned that year and 12,757 homeowners suffering losses totaling 1,190,992 rubles, we can crudely calculate that arson
led to the destruction of at least 6,544 buildings with 2,934 victims and losses

59. GARO, f. 640, op. 51, sv. 158, d. 625, ll. 4–50b., 120, 128–29. Unfortunately, the documents do not tell us how recently Tiurin had moved to this village or the circumstances under which he did so. For a similar case, see "Kazanskii Okruzhnyi Sud. Sozhzhenie khleba u ku-
laka," *VolzhV,* no. 154 (1892), 2.

60. For descriptions, see N. V. Shchelgunov, *Ocherki russkoi zhizni* (SPb, 1895), 105–23;
"Ardatovskii uezd, Nizhegor. gub. (Zhivoi ogon)," *NizhL,* no. 150 (1896), 3; "Selo Kurakino,
Serdobskogo uezd. (Bol'shoi pozhar)," *NizhL,* no. 175 (1896), 3.

61. GARO, f. 7, op. 1, d. 95, ll. 49ob.–50.

62. "Selo Kunikovo, Kostromsk. u.," *PV,* no. 95 (1906), 3.

TABLE 4.1    Arson in Rural Russia, 1875–1894

| Province | Total Fires Reported | Known Arson Cases | Arson as Percent of Total |
|---|---|---|---|
| Iaroslavl' | 672 | 82 | 12.6 |
| Kaluga | 801 | 75 | 9.5 |
| Kostroma | 516 | 71 | 13.7 |
| Moscow | 834 | 115 | 13.9 |
| Nizhnii Novgorod | 1041 | 237 | 22.5 |
| Orel | 856 | 118 | 13.9 |
| Riazan' | 1281 | 152 | 12.7 |
| Saratov | 997 | 150 | 14.9 |
| Simbirsk | 994 | 226 | 22.6 |
| Tambov | 1614 | 230 | 15.2 |
| Tula | 997 | 152 | 15.5 |
| Voronezh | 1006 | 117 | 11.4 |

SOURCE: *Pozhary v Rossiiskoi imperii v 1875–1882 godakh* (Moscow, 1887), 142–59; *Pozhary v Rossiiskoi imperii v 1888–1894 godakh* (SPb, 1897), 66–76.

of 272,928 rubles.[63] These figures are surely low, however, since they count only proven cases of arson. One author claimed that at least 36 percent of all rural fires stemmed from arson.[64] Criminal statistics are useless here because so few suspects were ever apprehended, let alone prosecuted and convicted. Whereas the 1908 Riazan' report found arson to be at the root of 481 fires, this province's circuit court convicted only 23 arsonists that year out of a total of 597 persons sentenced in all categories of crime.[65]

As the foregoing cases suggest, and as studies from other countries confirm, revenge, enmity, and jealousy stood out as the most common factors motivating peasants to commit arson, a deed aimed at the very foundation of peasant life and livelihood and one that, by its nature, spoke to fractured interpersonal relations and to the perpetrator's rejection of social or even formal mediation in favor of "the magnificent announcement of immediate revenge," as one historian has aptly put it.[66] In 1897, for ex-

63. Data are from "'Krasnyi petukh' v Riazanskoi gubernii v 1908 g.," *RiazV*, no. 23 (1909), 2. See also "Krasnyi petukh," *RiazV*, no. 144 (1909), 2; and "'Krasnyi petukh' v Riazanskoi gub. v 1909 g.," *RiazV*, no. 14 (1910), 2–3. Russia's Central Statistical Committee calculated that during the period 1901–10, there were 720,000 fires in European Russia, causing over 1 billion rubles in damage. "Statistika pozhara," *Narodnyi zhurnal*, no. 23 (1913), 731–32.

64. *Sovremennyi sel'skii byt i ego nuzhdy* (SPb, 1893), 104.

65. "'Krasnyi petukh' v Riazanskoi gub. v 1908 g.," 2; *Svod statisticheskikh svedenii po delam ugolovnym...za 1908 god* (SPb, 1911), part 1, table 1. See also GARO, f. 7. op. 1, d. 535, ll. 580b–590b.

66. David Jones, *Crime, Protest, Community and Police in Nineteenth-Century Britain* (London, 1982), 61. Compare Regina Schulte, *The Village in Court, trans. Barrie Selman* (Cambridge,

ample, a peasant set fire to the house of a woman with whom she suspected her husband was having an affair; the flames quickly spread and destroyed seventeen homes. The Orel Circuit Court sentenced her to six years of penal servitude.[67] Revenge also lay at the root of a 1911 incident that occurred during a party (*vecherinka*) held at the home of a villager in Sapozhok district. A drunken guest started arguments with many of those present and a fight with the owner, her aunt. Thrown out into the street, she shouted that she would "bring the whole village here." A short time later the hostess' threshing barn began to burn, and the flames then moved to and consumed a neighbor's creamery. When later questioned, the rambunctious guest admitted that she had set the blaze as revenge for being driven from the party and was sentenced to a two-month prison term.[68]

If we exclude fires set during peasant uprisings, such as those that swept parts of the countryside from 1905 to 1907, disputes with landowners, merchants, and employers could nevertheless be found at the root of many rural arsons before and after emancipation.[69] Among all persons convicted of that crime by circuit courts between 1874 and 1913, 22.7 percent were hired agricultural workers, and farming peasants accounted for 43 percent. Although these figures cannot, of course, resolve the question of motive, they suggest that labor disputes lay behind a sizable proportion of intentional conflagrations.[70] During the night of September 16, 1892, for example, fire destroyed the stables at the Zybin estate in Sapozhok district. Several days before, the local peasant Maksim Semin had been fired from his job as a hired laborer for arguing with the estate steward. Having unsuccessfully tried three times to regain employment, he told the steward, "All right, I'm leaving, but I'll deal with you." Semin therefore became a suspect after the stable fire, and witnesses said they has seen him rushing into his nearby room not long after the blaze began. With no other evidence

---

1994), 24–57; John E. Archer, "Under Cover of Night: Arson and Animal Maiming," in Mingay, ed., *The Unquiet Countryside,* 65–79; André Abbiateci, "Arsonists in 18th-C. France: An Essay in the Typology of Crime," in Robert Forster and Orest Ranum, eds., *Deviants and the Abandoned in French Society* (Baltimore, 1978), 157–79; David Prochaska, "Fire on the Mountain: Resisting Colonialism in Algeria," in Crummey, ed., *Banditry, Rebellion and Social Protest,* 229–52.

67. "Iz-za revnosti," *OrlV,* no. 3 (1898), 2.

68. "Sessiia Riazanskogo okruzhnogo suda v g. Sapozhke. Skandal'naia gost'ia," *RiazZh,* no. 24 (1912), 4. For other examples, see "S. Zhmurovo, Mikhailovskogo uezda. (Podzhogi)," *RiazV,* no. 27 (1910), 2; "Sessiia okruzhnogo suda v g. Ranenburge. Podzhog," *RiazZh,* no. 20 (1911), 3.

69. On the quarter-century before emancipation in Riazan' province, see S. Slavutinskii, *Pozhary i podzhogi v provintsii* (Moscow, 1862).

70. *Svody,* part 2, "Zaniatiia osuzhdennykh." Regina Schulte (*Village in Court,* 26–34) found that farm servants and day laborers constituted the overwhelming majority of arsonists in upper Bavaria during this period.

against him other than references to his "bad character," Semin was found guilty before the circuit court and sentenced to settlement in Siberia.[71] A much longer and more dramatic conflict was played out between 1889 and 1893 in another district, where peasants lost the rental of a crown forest when the state transferred it to a landowner. In the end, the angry peasants "burned him out," in their words, for which twelve of them were sentenced to exile and penal servitude not only for arson but also for forming a criminal gang.[72]

An additional incentive for arson was the spread of zemstvo-sponsored fire insurance. In 1892, for example, the Sapozhok district home of Miladora Iurkova burned down. Several days earlier, when talking with neighbors about a conflagration that had recently destroyed several villagers' houses, Iurkova told them that she would gladly pay somebody to set fire to her house. Suspicion mounted further because on the very night Iurkova's house burned, she had gone to a neighbor's with her child and asked to spend the night, saying that someone had stolen the hinges from her front door and she feared that this was an act of sorcery. Following the fire, villagers told the police investigator that Iurkova had insured her home at more than twice its actual value. Charged with arson and tried by jury in early 1893, she was found innocent and acquitted.[73] An 1899 case tried before the Iaroslavl' Circuit Court saw the peasant woman Klavdiia Goricheva accused of setting a March 30 fire that consumed her home in the village of Vasil'evska, together with two neighboring houses. The indictment stated that on March 20 the accused had insured her home for 500 rubles, then carted all her belongings to the village of Ivanovsk, where she owned another property. Two neighbors testified that on the night of the fire they came outside and saw Gorcheva's house burning not from below but from above. "There's no question," they told the court, that Goricheva committed the arson." Still, as commonly happened with these cases, the accused was acquitted.[74] In the summer of 1891 a hungry peasant from the famine-stricken Sviiazhsk district of Kazan' province set fire to his home in order to collect insurance money, which, he later told the court, he desperately needed to keep from starving. "There was nothing to eat," he explained. "The horse, cow, hen, everything had already been eaten up. So I set fire to the house. I thought, 'It will burn down, I'll get the insurance from the zem-

---

71. GARO, f. 640, op. 51, sv. 151, d. 542, ll. 2, 26, 32, 34.

72. "Agrarnyi podzhog," *SudG*, no. 23 (1894), 11.

73. GARO, f. 640, op. 51, sv. 150, d. 522, ll. 2–3, 47–500b. On zemstvo insurance, see S. Frederick Starr, *Decentralization and Self-Government in Russia, 1830–70* (Princeton,1972), 302–4.

74. "Sud. Khronika. Podzhog." *SevK*, no. 320 (1899), 4. During the entire period 1874–1913, an average of only 33.6 percent of total arson cases tried by circuit courts resulted in convictions. The average conviction rate for all crimes was 57.6 percent.

stvo and buy food. . . .' Yes, I'm guilty." Unfortunately, as a result of strong winds this deed also destroyed forty other homes, for which the accused was subsequently convicted and sentenced to Siberian exile.[75]

## THE ECONOMICS OF PROPERTY CRIME

According to contemporary studies, a clear correlation existed between property offenses and such factors as harvest size and grain prices, especially the price of rye. E. N. Tarnovskii, who first attempted an examination of this type, argued in 1898 that the connection was easy to see. Comparing statistics on theft with grain prices and harvest conditions, he found that when prices rose sharply following a bad harvest in the 1880–1881 season, cases of property crime rose 20 percent above average. The famine of 1891 saw such offenses rise 10 percent above average—a significantly smaller increase, but it must be recalled that by this time upward of 50 percent of property crimes previously handled in circuit courts had been transferred to lower jurisdictions. By contrast, during years with below-average grain prices, property crimes, too, dropped below their average number.[76] Province-level analyses produced similar findings. After comparing harvest data, grain prices, and wages with property crimes tried by both the circuit and peace court administrations of Nizhnii Novgorod province in the years 1891–1904, S. Gurevich concluded that the dependence of property offenses on the population's economic situation could not be doubted. "With a natural regularity we observe an increase of crime after an economic downturn, whereas economic improvement witnesses a drop in crimes." Vladimir Moderov reached identical conclusions concerning property crime convictions from 1879 to 1907 in Kaluga province, where peasants spent 60 percent of their annual budget on grain. During this period, Moderov demonstrated, "The number of circuit court convictions for theft . . . is parallel with the price of grain and the population's corresponding shortfall in grain."[77]

More sophisticated studies appeared during the 1920s, though the results differed little from their predecessors'. Data on Ekaterinburg province analyzed by V. N. Kufaev for the years 1892 to 1913 showed that harvests and grain prices exerted a decisive impact on the perpetration of property

---

75. "Iz provintsial'noi pechati," *SevV*, no. 1 (1892), part 2, 49.

76. Tarnovskii, "Vliianie khlebnykh tsen," 81.

77. S. Gurevich, "Dvizhenie prestupnosti protiv sobstvennosti v Nizhegorodskoi gubernii v 1891–1904 gg. v sviazi s ekonomicheskim polozheniem gubernii," in *Seminarii po ugolovnomu pravu*, part 1, 29; Vladimir Moderov, "Sviaz' mezhdu prestupleniiami protiv imushchestva i ekonomicheskim polozheniem naseleniia Kaluzhskoi gubernii za period s 1876 po 1907 g.," in *Seminarii po ugolovnomu pravu priv. -dots. M. N. Gerneta* (Moscow, 1909), 28–29, 35.

offenses. "As a social phenomenon, the growth of criminality is dependent upon the harvest. Harvest failure sees members of society engaged in a struggle with the law (most often in the form of theft). During harvest failures, industry and production are reduced, unemployment rises, and people are thus forced to break laws concerning personal or state property." Even the composition of the criminal population changed as a result of low crop yield; years of poor harvest, for example, saw persons with families and children commit offenses more often than in normal times. Indeed, Kufaev argued, the poor harvest of 1906 (which fell to 74.3 percent of the norm) played perhaps as important a role as the 1905–1907 revolution in the sharp rise of criminal cases that year.[78] Other studies also demonstrated that despite industrialization, the expansion of outwork, and deep penetration of market relations into the countryside, harvests and grain prices continued to influence patterns of property offenses.[79]

My own analysis shows that, as with virtually all nineteenth-century European states, both burglary and ordinary theft in Russia remained closely linked to economic indicators like the price of staple grains (figures 4.1 and 4.2). Unfortunately, as contemporaries found, the far stronger correlation that existed until 1881 was greatly weakened as a result of changes in jurisdiction over theft and burglary. Near the end of the century an expanding market in both consumption and labor would further lessen the reliability of single-factor comparisons such as that of rye prices, since a more diverse economy requires consideration of a broader range of elements (wages and wheat prices, for example).

A voluminous body of nonstatistical evidence adds strength and nuance to the argument that hard times brought an increase in theft of all kinds, that is, those offenses that peasants and other lower-class Russians already committed more than any others. In Kazan' province during the terrible famine of 1891–92, for example, cases of theft by desperate and hungry villagers appeared daily in the local press. *The Volga Herald* reported that on Christmas eve peasants in a village of Sviiazhsk district heard a woman crying in the street and came running to learn what had happened. Impoverished by the famine and with her husband away at outwork, this woman had received a sack of oats from charity, but while she attended the evening

78. V. N. Kufaev, "Prestupnost' i urozhai v Ul'ianovskoi gubernii s 1892 po 1913 god," in Groman, ed., *Vliianie neurozhaev*, pt. 2, 133–34, 143.

79. D. P. Rodin, "Vliianie urozhainosti na prestupnost' po dannym Samarskoi gubernii," in Groman, ed., *Vliianie neurozhaev*, 156–99; M. N. Gernet, "Golod i prestupnost'," in Groman, ed., *Vliianie neurozhaev*, 94–132; Gernet, *Moral'naia statistika* (Moscow, 1922), 209–20. For one earlier, nonstatistical discussion, see D. A. Dril', "Bednost', kak prichina prestupleniia," *IuV,* no. 6 (1880), 347–70.

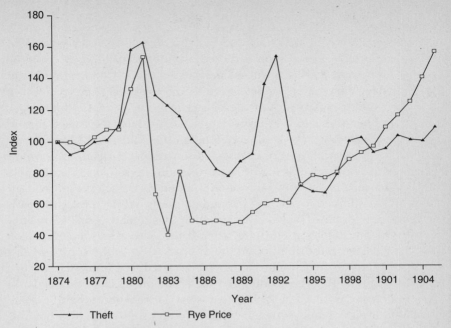

Figure 4.1.  Felony Theft Cases and the Price of Rye

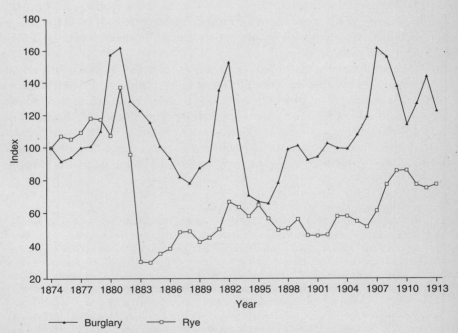

Figure 4.2.  Rural Burglary Convictions and the Price of Rye

church service a thief took advantage of her absence, tore a large hole through her straw roof, and stole the oats, leaving her exposed to the cold and snow as well. A crowd soon gathered, decided that the thief could be none other than a local Tatar whose family had already been without bread for many days, and thereupon set out to search for him. They soon found the culprit still struggling with the heavy sack of grain, so weak from hunger that he had been unable to carry it home. A court later sentenced him to six months in prison.[80] On February 18 in another village of this same district, two peasants without horses decided to steal a pair from their fellow villager Petrov. So late that night they broke into Petrov's barn and stable only to discover that he, too, had not only ended up horseless that year but had even been forced to sell his cows and chickens. While leaving the barn they chanced upon two sacks of wheat, which they took together with a few boards. On the following morning, after Petrov discovered and reported this crime, village authorities found the thieves' tracks in the snow and easily traced them to their home. Both were arrested and immediately confessed, explaining that they committed the crime out of extreme need and hunger. Petrov cursed them, saying he was no richer than they and that he also had a hungry family sitting at home. He had sold his bed to buy this wheat. "Well, if we only knew you had no horses, we wouldn't have come to your place," one of the culprits replied. "We also sold our beds. We've sold everything and eaten it all up. So we thought, 'Let's drive off a pair of horses and exchange them somewhere for two others.' But we only took the wheat incidentally." Charged with burglary, they received one year each in a corrective penal division.[81]

Whether perpetrating theft out of need or as a trade, Russia's substantial floating population of underemployed and unemployed, indigents, drifters, and escapees from prison or exile also fed the crime problem in countryside and town alike. As concern about "migratory criminals" mounted in the last decades of the century, Russians wrote voluminously on the problem of mendicancy with particular concern given to "professional" paupers who, though capable of work, shirked familial and social obligations for the

80. "Iz-za nuzhdy," *VolzhV,* no. 223 (1892), 2–3.

81. *VolzhV,* no. 223 (1892), 3. See also "Iz-za nuzhdy," *VolzhV,* no. 291 (1892), 2. Because the harvest failure created widespread unemployment in urban areas and factory towns throughout Kazan' province, it also brought with it a significant rise in thefts of peasant property from outside the village. By mid-August, one press account reported, the urban poor and unemployed were systematically stealing food from peasants in outlying suburbs and surrounding villages, forcing rural communities to hire guards in order to protect what little they possessed. "Votkinskii zavod, Sarapul. uezda," *VolzhV,* no. 27 (1892), 3; "Sistematicheskie krazhi kartofelia u krest'ian," *VolzhV,* no. 203 (1892), 3. See also "Golodnaia armiia," *OrlV,* no. 43 (1898), 2; D. P. Raskin, "Vliianie urozhainosti na prestupnost' po dannym Samarskoi gubernii," in Groman, ed., *Vliianie neurozhaev,* 190–91.

"easy" life of begging or pilfering.[82] According to the 1899 findings of one government commission, most provinces of central Russia, including Riazan', contained numerous villages whose residents collectively practiced begging as a trade. In the twelve Riazan' settlements subsisting primarily by mendicancy, for example, parents passed this profession on to their children. Yet most governors who reported to the commission stated that misfortune and poverty drove the majority of these peasants to their "trade."[83] It is clear from contemporary sources that mendicants (who commonly traveled in groups) often crossed the line between begging and outright expropriation, though the charge by some social reformers that they constituted "an army of thieves and robbers" was likely exaggerated. Still, for the elderly woman knocked down and relieved of her purse after refusing a request for alms, or the milkmaid chased down a deserted road by a beggar who made off with the full buckets she carried, mendicants presented yet another very real threat to peasant property and safety and one that stemmed in large part from poverty and need.[84]

Other compelling evidence of this relationship comes from discussions of seasonal fluctuations in the size of Russia's prison population. "In the perpetration of a crime that will result in prison incarceration," wrote I. Reva in 1885, "the overriding stimulus, the chief compelling reason is not the notorious 'evil will,' but insurmountable economic causes":

> A person deliberately goes to prison because he has no other choice. He instinctively protects his unfortunate life, saves himself from a hungry and cold death, and sells his "freedom" . . . for a ration of prison bread, for a warm corner, and for greasy prison soup [*pokhlebka*]. At the first sign of foul autumn weather, the first frost, the contingent of prison inmates immediately rises . . . because these people need the prison . . . as the sole sanctuary from winter. "Criminals" of this sort do not fit the usual standards. They not only do not conceal their criminal acts but advertise them before the very eyes of the

82. For examples, see D. A. Linev, "Prichiny russkogo nishchenstva i neobkhodimye protiv nikh mery," *TrudyIVEO*, no. 2 (1891), 175–218; A. F. Nedokhodovskii, "K kharakteristike sel'skogo nishchenstva," *Trudovaia pomoshch'*, no. 8 (August 1898), 177–81; Uchrezhdennaia pri Ministerstve Iustitsii kommisiia dlia razrabotki voprosa o merakh protiv professional'nogo nishchenstva i brodiazhestva, *Materialy*, vol. 1 (SPb, 1899); A. A. Levenstim, "Nishchenstvo v sovremennoi Rossii," *VestP*, no. 5 (1899), 120–37; Levenstim, "K voprosu o professional'nom nishchenstve," *VestP*, no. 8 (1899), 89–104; A. V. Lednitskii, "O bor'be s nishchenstvom," *Trudovaia pomoshch'*, no. 4 (1902), 510–30; no. 5, 621–39.

83. *Materialy*, 1:99–101, 103–7, 115; Levenstim, "Nishchenstvo," 130–31; "Nishchenstvo, kak promysel," *SV*, no. 4 (1885), 44; "Bor'ba s nishchenstvom," *Prikhodskaia zhizn'*, vol. 6 (1904), 312–15; "Zaboty o bednykh i bor'ba s nishchenstvom," *NizhL*, no. 85 (1899), 3. For further discussion, see L. Vesin, "Nishchenstvo na Rusi," *SevV*, no. 3 (1893), part 2, 28–33; "Semenovskii u. (Nishchenstvo)," *NizhL*, no. 29 (1901), 3.

84. Linev, "Prichina russkogo nishchenstva," 176; P. I. Astrov, "Osobyi vid nakazuemogo nishchenstva," *Trudovaia pomoshch'*, no. 3 (1901), 455.

police and almost compel the latter to arrest them. This seems improbable, but it is a fact.[85]

Numerous commentators made much the same observations, noting that during difficult times, some among the poor sought imprisonment "simply to get a piece of bread." A jail or prison sentence of several months handed down by a justice of the peace was seen as being placed "on state bread." Among the thousands of Russia's wandering vagabonds who had fled their places of exile, it was common practice to turn oneself over to authorities with the onset of winter, hoping for a warm prison cell until spring.[86] Judicial data demonstrate that property crimes were committed most frequently during the cold months, beginning in October and rising to a peak between December and February, after which they tapered off into the spring and summer. Statistics on incarceration gathered at the provincial level likewise show that Russia's general inmate population swelled most rapidly during the autumn and winter months.[87] More serious crimes, too, including arson, might be committed as a means of extricating oneself from a hopeless economic plight. In August 1891, for example, on a noble's estate in Smolensk province, Efim Ivanov set fire to a barn containing unthreshed grain. Ivanov openly confessed to authorities, explaining that he had perpetrated the crime because he wanted to be sent to Siberia or any other place, as long as the state would feed him. "At first I thought about burning a peasant building," he said, "but didn't do so because the peasant can't recover quickly [from fire]. But the lord can get over it quickly, and his neighbors will help."[88]

This close relationship between property offenses and the economic vagaries of everyday life is by no means unique to Russia, for criminologists and historians have found the same correlations in countries throughout the world. Nor is it limited to times of extreme deprivation, such as the 1891–92 famine, or to persons suffering abject poverty. Raw economic hardship alone, as Eric Johnson argues in his recent study of late nineteenth-century German crime, "explains a large amount of the ups and downs of economic crimes throughout the nineteenth and twentieth centuries. This can be demonstrated at the simplest level by observing that during the greatest periods of economic hardship the rates of personal crime took

85. I. Reva, "Russkaia tiur'ma i ee zhizni. (Nabliudeniia i zametki)," *IuV,* no. 5 (1885), 121.

86. *Ssylka v Sibir',* 271–73.

87. *Svody,* part 2, "Vremia i mesto soversheniia prestuplenii"; *Otchet po Glavnomu tiuremnomu upravleniiu,* 24 vols. (SPb, 1890–1913); GARO, f. 5, st. 1, op. 2, d. 1452, ll. 18–18ob.; d. 1659, ll. 259ob.–262; f. 5, st. 4, op. 5, d. 1452, l. 740b.; f. 857, op. 11, sv. 10, d. 5; op. 12, sv. 10, d. 2; op. 13, sv. 13, d. 7. Tarnovskii noted this same seasonal fluctuation. "Pomesiachnoe raspredelenie glavneishikh vidov prestupnosti," *ZhMIu,* no. 2 (1902), 111–12.

88. "Iz provintsial'noi pechati," 49, 50.

their greatest leaps forward, and that during more prosperous times they receded."[89] David Jones has written of rural England and Wales that "various surveys of the 1830s and 1840s revealed that riotous protest and arson were most common in districts and periods of poor employment and low wages, that theft fluctuated with the cost of living index, and that poaching and animal stealing increased noticeably once the harvest money had been spent." Writing on nineteenth-century France, Michelle Perrot argues that "the fact that so many children and vagrants were charged with 'pilfering food' affords a glimpse of the cramped horizon of a society of scarcity, and the existence of marginal but persistent hunger." Indeed, the poor "filled the prisons in such numbers that the prisons were conceived for them, in terms of their economic and cultural standards."[90]

Judging by peasant views of which crimes proved most common and harmful to their well-being, the contemporary statistical depictions of rural crime as a phenomenon dominated by interpersonal discord, violence, bloodshed, and low rates of property offenses had little basis in reality. Property crime looked dramatically different from the village perspective, and peasants believed it to be a far more serious problem than police, judicial officials, or legislators seemed to think. Indeed, a comparison of nonpeasant writings on rural crime with police registers and villagers' complaints gives the distinct if peculiar impression that two different societies are under discussion. Archival evidence shows that pilfering, burglary, robbery, horsetheft, and brigandage were far more prevalent in the Russian countryside than previously believed and that only a small (albeit important) portion of these offenses were perpetrated by villagers against noble and other private landowners.[91] A number of factors influenced the patterns of property crimes, with economic hardship standing well at the forefront. Of course

89. Eric A. Johnson, *Urbanization and Crime* (Cambridge, 1995), 137–38. See also Johnson, "The Crime Rate: Longitudinal and Periodic Trends in Nineteenth- and Twentieth-Century German Criminality, from Vormärz to Late Weimar," in Richard J. Evans, ed., *The German Underworld: Deviants and Outcasts in German History* (London, 1988), 181; Jones, "Rural Crime," 117.

90. Jones, "Rural Crime," 114–15; Perrot, "Delinquency," 224, 230. For the eighteenth century, see Douglas Hay, "War, Dearth and Theft in the Eighteenth Century: The Record of the English Courts," *Past and Present*, no. 95 (1982), 117–60.

91. The myth that rural regions demonstrated very low rates of property offenses—and of crime in general—has been challenged by a number of scholars in recent years. See, for example, Dirk Blasius, *Kriminalität und Alltag: Zur Konfliktgeschichte des Alltagslebens im 19. Jahrhundert* (Göttingen, 1978); David Cohen and Eric A. Johnson, "French Criminality," *JIH* 13, no. 3 (1982), 477–501; Robert J. Gordon and Mervyn J. Meggitt, *Law and Order in the New Guinea Highlands: Encounters with Enga* (Hanover, 1985), 5–7.

we should not simply assume that all incidents of burglary or theft stemmed from hunger and need, for the sources provide numerous cases in which rural laborers and peasant farmers sought profit and personal gain. Likewise, the countryside was home to a great many people who made their living by preying on peasant property. These included not only professional bandits, brigands, and horsethieves but also the untold legions of wandering, unregistered poor and escapees, many of whom also turned to pilfering or robbery to support themselves. However paltry the pickings may have been from an urban perspective, Russia's nineteenth-century countryside provided a vast and woefully undersupervised arena of opportunity for the impoverished peasant or laborer committing theft out of necessity, as well as for those intent on enriching themselves through horsetheft, robbery, swindling, and other shady endeavors.

Peasants saw their communities threatened both from within and without as property crime grew during the postemancipation era, yet their efforts to bring perpetrators to justice through the established police and judicial systems were increasingly frustrated. The state exacerbated this problem in a number of ways. Having classified the vast majority of these offenses as petty and turned them over for summary treatment to peace courts, land captains, or *volost'* courts, the government announced through its criminal law that the limited forces of order would be committed primarily to protecting the individual property of private owners. Though reformed and enlarged on several occasions, the country's rural police forces were never sufficient in size or competence to stem the tide of property infractions, especially since they showed greater concern for violent offenses and those that threatened order. Similarly, prosecutors were increasingly buried under a mountain of unindictable criminal cases as the century wore on, and their investigators proved too few to gather sufficient evidence for prosecution. This continued gap between state law and local reality was only too apparent to villagers victimized by arsonists, horsethieves, and others. In short, we have a countryside left largely to its own devices when dealing with depredations against village property and a peasantry ever less willing to forgive the shortcomings of their country's judicial system.

# CHAPTER 5

# From Insult to Homicide

*Honor, Violence, and*
*Crimes against Persons*

*What happens during rural holidays? [Peasants] drink themselves into an utter*
*frenzy, bite off one another's fingers, and often thrash each other to death.*
"ABOUT DRUNKENNESS," *THE ACTIVIST,* 1908

Judicial statistics seemed to confirm the views disseminated by Russia's burgeoning professional community and postreform press about the violence of rural life. Did the data not show that "bloody" crimes predominated in rural areas? According to the crudest and most common explanation of this "fact," peasant poverty determined a low rate of property offenses while lack of culture and ignorance accounted for the prevalence of crimes against persons as well as their savage character. Most important, until the 1890s, nonpeasant commentators blamed the closeness of village society itself—the tyranny of patriarchal relations and complexity of family and kin ties—for rural violence. As the century progressed they revised this perspective, arguing instead that the breakdown of these very factors that previously explained violent crime was now responsible for an upsurge of violence. Yet such a shift in viewpoint did not represent a radical turnabout. As we have seen, replies to the 1864 MVD survey showed that the same perspective that gained dominance toward the end of the century already prevailed among provincial officials, nobles, and many clerics at the time of emancipation. Throughout the postreform period, however, ignorance and cultural backwardness would provide the mainstays of any effort to understand or even to excuse violent crimes not only among peasants but throughout the lower classes.

This chapter looks at three of the main categories of crimes against persons committed in the countryside, beginning with seemingly mundane acts of personal insult and moving on to assault and homicide. To the extent that the sources allow, it seeks to burrow beneath cultural and statistical representations and examine less quantifiable but critical matters of motivation as well as the relationships, tensions, and disputes behind these crimes. The largely unexplored issue of honor within peasant communities,

(particularly officialdom), and even between serfs and masters during the prereform era, deference and honor among peasants have until recently been ignored in the historical literature.[6] Court records are especially fruitful sources here, for they reveal villagers defending their honor and community standing, seeking official exoneration for themselves and punishment for those who challenged or tarnished their reputation. The very fact that, both before and after emancipation, peasants brought so many cases to officials and courts rather than seeking reconciliation closer to home speaks to the importance of reputation throughout the postemancipation era and offers fresh insights into a fundamental sphere of village life. A sampling of cases shows how such situations and conflicts could arise.

At an 1871 session of a *volost'* court in Moscow province, peasant M. lodged a complaint against her fellow villager L. for cursing her with the most foul obscenities (*maternymi slovami*). Because of the shame this caused her, she requested that the court punish L. "in accordance with the law." Three female witnesses affirmed that L. had insulted M. so terribly that a woman could not even repeat the words he had used. For his part, L. claimed he had done nothing to M. "but to show her my ass." The court sentenced him to twenty lashes with the birch.[7] At an 1871 Stavrotinsk *volost'* court session in Iaroslavl' province, peasant E. charged that peasant M. had called him a "cunt-chaser" (*bliadun*) and shoved him in the presence of three witnesses. M. confessed to inflicting the insult on E., informing the judges that not only was E. a womanizer, but E.'s daughter was a "slut" (*bliad'*). In his own defense M. argued that he insulted E. so rudely because the latter had fornicated with M.'s wife and also called M. a thief. Ignoring these counter charges, which point to a deeper conflict between the litigants, the court found M. guilty of insult and ordered him to pay E. the equivalent of one year's tax assessment as well as a quarter of a year's tax assessment to E.'s daughter.[8] *Volost'* judges viewed some cases of insult to be

6. For exceptions, see M. M. Gromyko, *Traditsionnye normy povedeniia i formy obshcheniia russkikh krest'ian XIX v.* (Moscow, 1986); N. A. Minenko, *Zhivaia starina. Budni i prazdniki Sibirskoi derevni v XVIII–pervoi polivine XIX v.* (Novosibirsk, 1989); L. N. Pushkarev, *Dukhovnyi mir russkogo krest'ianina po poslovitsam XVII–XVIII vekov* (Moscow, 1994), ch. 3; Jeffrey Burds, *Peasant Dreams and Market Politics* (Pittsburgh, 1998). On the importance of honor and reputation in other national and social contexts, see, e.g., F. G. Bailey, *Gifts and Poison: The Politics of Reputation* (New York, 1969); Michael Herzfeld, "Honor and Shame: Problems in the Comparative Analysis of Moral Systems," *Man* 15 (1980), 339–51; Edward L. Ayers, *Vengeance and Justice* (New York, 1984); David D. Gilmore, *Aggression and Community: Paradoxes of Andalusian Culture* (New Haven, 1987).

7. *Trudy Komissii po preobrazovaniiu volostnykh sudov,* 7 vols. (SPb, 1873–74), 2:209 (hereafter: *Trudy*).

8. Ibid., 3:8.

so serious that they ignored the law and imposed penalties reminiscent of prereform court practice. When he used the term "slut" against a twelve-year-old village girl, one Tambov province peasant was sentenced to thirty lashes, ten more than the legal maximum.[9]

Insult could also take physical form, such as pushing, shoving, spitting, pulling of beard or hair, which Russian law termed "insult by deed." When insult by word and deed are considered together, as they were in compilations of the time, they account for one of the largest categories of offenses tried by township judges and peace courts alike during our period. As a rural attorney wrote in 1876 with some exaggeration, by far the greatest percentage of criminal cases encountered in *volost'* courts involved personal insult. A former justice of the peace noted in 1882 that the majority of crimes tried during his tenure in office fell into the category of insult.[10] These claims are at least partly confirmed by *volost'* and peace court records, which read like litanies of personal insults ranging from the most common verbal utterance to slander or even assault. Higher courts, too, tried many people on such charges both before and after emancipation. During 1860, 307 (or 11 percent) of 2,791 trials before the Riazan' Criminal Court involved insults to honor. From 1861 to 1869, cases of insult made up just under 10 percent of all criminal cases heard by Russia's higher courts before the government removed most such offenses to the competence of lower instances.[11] The proportion was much larger among misdemeanors. In 1890, for example, "insult to honor" accounted for 19.5 percent of all crimes tried by those peace courts still functioning in Kursk province. For municipal courts and land captains, the figure accounted for 21.5 percent of total crimes tried, and fully 40 percent of the criminal cases tried by *volost'* courts concerned insult to honor.[12] Among criminal trials recorded by township courts in the Dmitrovsk district of Moscow province that same year, 15.9 percent fell under the heading "insults to honor, threats, and violence." Records from *volost'* courts of Riazan' province show that, in some years, upwards of 50 percent of criminal offenses involved some type of insult,

9. Pavel Berezanskii, *Obychnoe ugolovnoe pravo krest'ian Tambovskoi gubernii* (Kiev, 1880), 208. After 1861, Russian law permitted a maximum of twenty lashes. See also N. A. Minenko, "The Living Past: Daily Life and Holidays of the Siberian Village in the Eighteenth and First Half of the Nineteenth Centuries," *SAA* 30, no. 1 (1991), 13.

10. V. S. Krotkov, *Volch'e stado* (Moscow, 1875), 17; M. N. R. "Sud v derevne," *Nabliudatel'*, no. 2 (1882), 115. Although taking note of its common nature, most contemporary sources paid only passing attention to this offense.

11. *Pamiatnaia knizhka Riazanskoi gubernii na 1860 g.* (Riazan', 1860), 163–64; V. A. Novakovskii, *Opyt podvedeniia itogov ugolovnoi statistiki s 1861 do 1871 goda* (SPb, 1891), 30–37.

12. *Pamiatnaia knizhka Kurskoi gubernii na 1892 god* (Kursk, 1892), part 2, 38–43.

though caution is required here for a large proportion of such cases involved fighting and assault.[13]

A number of particularly offensive terms demanded formal litigation if the insulted party's honor was to be redeemed. Among these, "thief," "swindler," "robber," and others suggestive of criminal behavior appear frequently in surviving records. One elderly peasant woman of Spassk district called the village and *volost'* elders "robbers and swindlers" when they came to collect a fine from her in 1878. Found guilty by the Riazan' Circuit Court of insulting officials, she received only seven days in jail because of her "extreme ignorance." In a similar case more than twenty years later, a Riazan' *volost'* court sentenced a peasant to ten days in jail for accusing his village elder of embezzlement and calling him a thief and swindler—charges that were probably deserved, judging from the records.[14] To be called a "witch," "sorcerer," devil," "bloodsucker," and other such names was also offensive, as one Tambov peasant learned in the early 1870s when the Viachkinsk *volost'* court handed him a sentence of twenty lashes for referring to a fellow villager as a "holy sorcerer." Another peasant received ten lashes for calling someone a sorcerer during a village assembly meeting.[15] In 1884 the Petrovsk *volost'* court heard a peasant charge his fellow villager with sorcery but found him guilty of insult because he could not prove his accusation and levied a one-ruble fine to compensate the victim and another ruble for community use.[16] *Volost'* courts treated charges of slander quite seriously for they could ruin a villager's reputation and standing. As the Petrovsk case shows, judges usually demanded that the accuser substantiate her or his claims, and if these proved unfounded, they might not only acquit the accused but sentence the accuser (i.e., the purported victim of slander) to punishment.[17]

Though seemingly petty in nature, personal insults carried deeper meanings that enhanced their significance. Thus, Russian villagers considered it a grave offense to knock off a man's hat or a woman's kerchief, especially if the

13. TsGIAgM, f. 28, op. 1, d. 19, l. 2; GARO, f. 721, op. 1, sv. 3, d. 167, ll. 1920b.–193. See also GARO, f. 1291, op. 31, d. 241, ll. 14–17; MVD, *Trudy redaktsionnoi komissii po peresmotru zakonopolozhenii o krest'ianakh*, vol. 3 (SPb, 1904), 470–73.

14. GARO, f. 640, op. 51, sv. 121, d. 142, ll. 3–30b., 46–54; f. 717, op. 51, sv. 85, d. 3, ll. 2–5, 9–10. See also f. 717, op. 42 (1892), sv. 81, d. 7; op. 43 (1893), sv. 81, d. 6; op. 44 (1894), sv. 82, dd. 20, 25, 28.

15. Berezanskii, *Obychnoe ugolovnoe pravo*, 207; S. Ponomarev, "Ocherki narodnogo prava. Osobennosti ego," *SevV*, no. 5 (1890), 100.

16. I. L. Shrag, "Krest'ianskie sudy Vladimirskoi i Moskovskoi gubernii," *IuV*, no. 7–8 (1877), 66. See also I. Kostrov, *Iuridicheskie obychai krest'ian-starozhilov Tomskoi gubernii*, (Tomsk, 1876), 81; Minenko, "Living Past," 12–13. Compare the facinating discussion of the linkage between accusations of theft and witchcraft in Suzette Heald, "Witches and Thieves: Deviant Motivations in Gisu Society," *Man*, n.s. 21, no. 1 (1986), 65–78.

17. Berezanskii, *Obychnoe ugolovnoe pravo*, 209.

deed occurred in public. One Iaroslavl' peasant received a two-day jail sentence in 1871 because he had knocked off another's hat during a quarrel.[18] Even more serious was the refusal to doff one's hat to an elder, official, priest, or any person whose status demanded deference and respect. A *volost'* judge from the Rostov region brought such a charge against three local youths in 1899, and the court sentenced each to fifteen blows with birch rods.[19] Among the most grievous insults inflicted by villagers was smearing tar or excrement on the gate of a peasant's home to call into question a woman's honor, chastity, or fidelity, for if left unchallenged, the insulted party faced local gossip, dishonor, humiliation, and stigma. In one case from Tambov province, a peasant was sentenced to ten lashes for tarring a woman's gate and ordered to pay the dishonored victim 35.76 silver rubles (one year's tax assessment).[20] In 1883 a woman complained before a peace court of Kursk province that two sisters had smeared tar on her gates in order to disgrace and shame her three unmarried daughters. After the accused were acquitted for lack of evidence, the plaintiff appealed the court's decision. Two maidens from Saratov province suffered similar shame in 1887, when tar was found on the gates of their homes one morning. Their parents immediately came before the village assembly and accused three suspected offenders—maidens who were competing with the victims for fiancés. The assembly first demanded vodka from the victims' parents, who supplied fifteen rubles' worth of drink, then ruled that the suspects would be punished by public shaming. A pot of tar was hung around each maiden's neck, and accompanied by a large crowd, they were taken to the defaced gates and forced to kiss them.[21]

Because reputation and honor played such important roles at all levels of rural society, these everyday cases of personal insult occupied a prominent

18. *Trudy*, 3:5, 45. For other examples, see V. V. Tenishev, "Obshchie nachala ugolovnogo prava v ponimanii russkogo krest'ianina," *ZhMIu*, no. 7 (1909), 127; A. A. Titov, *Iuridicheskie obychai sela Nikola-Perevoz, Sulostskoi volosti, Rostovskogo uezda* (Iaroslavl', 1888), 107.

19. "Iz zhizni v provintsii," *NizhL*, no. 149 (1899), 3.

20. K. Chepurnyi, "K voprosu o iuridicheskikh obychaiakh," *Universitetskie izvestiia*, no. 10 (1874), part 2, section 2, ch. 4, 650. Hanging a dead chicken covered with tar on a person's gate was one of several variations on this form of public denouncement. See Kostrov, *Iuridicheskie obychai*, 81. Such shaming practices were not limited to the peasant population. In the diary of a provincial nobleman, the author recalls having one of his rural domestic servants punished by cutting off her braid, a terrible humiliation for an unmarried maiden. GARO, f. 869, op. 1, d. 660, l. 80.

21. "Vymazyvanie degtem vorot dlia posramleniia zhivushchikh v dome zhenshchin," *Golos*, no. 41 (1883), 3; "Obrashchik krest'ianskogo suda," *MosVed*, no. 197 (1887), 4. See also "Derevenskii sud," *OrlV*, no. 229 (1898), 2; P. A. Dilaktorskii, "Sviatochnye shalosti v Pel'shemskoi volosti Kadnikovskogo uezda," *EtnogO*, no. 4 (1898), 134; S. S. Kriukova, *Russkaia krest'ianskaia sem'ia vo vtoroi polovine XIX v.* (Moscow, 1994), 106. Peasant migrants also brought this method of shaming to towns and cities. See, e.g., "U gorodskogo sud'i 2 uch. Vymazali degtem kryl'tso," *RiazZh*, no. 109 (1913), 3.

position among misdemeanors perpetrated by villagers. Insults not only called into question a peasant's honor but could imply a lack of honesty, industriousness, thrift, or virtue. An accusation that one was a thief or swindler could lose one the trust of fellow villagers, since theft or cheating within the community was seen as a particularly dishonorable act (although by no means an uncommon offense). Insults also created enmity between those who had to live in close proximity to one another and in an environment that stressed cooperation for the sake of the entire community. Thus the necessity of quickly redeeming one's honor and settling the conflict that had arisen because of what outsiders often deemed a petty insult. Villagers' use of shame as an instrument of social control also demonstrated the place occupied by public standing and the way that reputations could be quickly lost (or confirmed) if the community itself was offended by one of its member's actions.[22]

In a great many instances, village and township elders, judges, police officers, and parish priests were the insulted parties, though sometimes their charges proved tenuous at best and hid other motives like revenge. A Moscow province *volost'* court found one couple guilty in 1891 of falsely accusing their village elder of bribe taking when he allowed another peasant to build a house on their land, of indecently insulting him, and of knocking him down. Unable to prove their accusation of bribery, both husband and wife were sentenced to ten days in jail.[23] In Riazan' province, the Potapovo village elder brought charges against Ivan Belokurov for insulting him at a 1912 village assembly meeting. Before the Vereisk *volost'* court, the elder claimed that the accused had cursed him, using obscene and unseemly words, a charge confirmed by three witnesses. The court therefore levied a nineteen-ruble fine on Belokurov, who was not present, or ten days in jail if he could not pay. Belokurov appealed to the Riazan' District Assembly, arguing that he never received a notice from the elder to appear in court, that the elder harbored ill feelings against him because they were involved in a civil suit over a parcel of land, and that the three witnesses who testified against him had lied at the elder's urging. Five new witnesses stated that the elder and Belokurov had been drunk at the assembly meeting and that a loud discussion had indeed taken place between them but that Belokurov did not curse the elder. In light of this new evidence, the assembly overturned the *volost'* court decision.[24]

22. Gromyko, *Traditsionnye normy,* 105–17; Minenko, "Living Past," 6–15; Frank, "Popular Justice"; and Chapter 8.

23. TsGIAgM, f. 62, op. 3, d. 80, ll. 8–80b. The husband's term was later reduced on appeal. See also GARO, f. 717, op. 53, sv. 86, d. 1, ll. 9–10.

24. GARO, f. 717, op. 62, sv. 89, d. 12, ll. 17–170b. See also GARO, f. 693, op. 7 (1881), sv. 4, d. 5; op. 8 (1882), sv. 5, d. 26; f. 695, op. 44 (1906), dd. 31, 33; TsGIAgM, f. 576, op. 1, d. 80 (1866), d. 95 (1871); f. 1112, op. 1, d. 28 (1905), ll. 10–110b., 30–300b.

Like offenses against village or *volost'* officials, crimes of "resistance," "disobedience," and "insult" to police officers covered a gamut that stretched from mockery to assault. Cursing an arresting officer, showing brazen disrespect, or knocking off a policeman's hat, for example, could land the accused in jail for up to thirty days. Peasants hauled before a *volost'* court on such charges often countered by playing on the reputation of the rural police for dishonesty and corruption, claiming that it was the officer who had done the insulting or arguing, as one defendant did in 1912, that police testimony could not be trusted because "they are police officers and can say whatever they want."[25] But not only the police sought redress when insulted. All representatives of state and Church could request that peasants and other commoners be punished for disrespect and insult. When tried in 1910 before a Riazan' land captain in Kasimov district for peculation of cast iron from a factory owner, the peasant F. A. Astakhov declared to the land captain: "This is swindling. Thou [*ty*] cannot try me. I have [a legal suit] with you and besides, you're a friend of [the owner]. I should be tried by another land captain." Astakhov also called the owner's representative "Baldy." At his subsequent circuit court trial for insult, Astakhov explained that there was a conflict of interest because he was engaged in litigation with the land captain, that he had not insulted either party and had only used the term "Baldy" because he did not know the man's name. The accused received a one-month jail sentence, which he appealed to no avail.[26]

The most serious form of insult was to curse or speak rudely about the tsar or members of the imperial family. Thousands of these cases passed through Russia's courts and administrative offices before and after emancipation, increasing significantly in number from the 1870s on, and although scattered examples exist in which peasants rejoiced over an emperor's death or spoke of assassination, the majority involved contempt toward the monarch spoken during moments of heated discussion and often in a drunken state.[27] On December 9, 1905, for example, while discussing the Russo-Japanese war with other villagers at a teahouse in Riazan' province, the peasant Tit Motov said that Nicholas II was wrong to start the war in the first

25. GARO, f. 717, op. 62, sv. 89, d. 3, ll. 6–60b. See also f. 717, op. 52, sv. 85, d. 23; f. 74, op. 25 (1890), d. 19; f. 79, op. 1 (1890), d. 46; TsGIAgM, f. 62, op. 3, d. 438; f. 576, op. 1, dd. 83, 120, 124, 128; f. 577, op. 1, dd. 88, 98; f. 702, op. 1, dd. 19, 33, 39; I. Shcheglovitov, "Soprotivlenie i nepovinovenie vlastiam, kak osoboe prestuplenie," *IuV,* no. 2 (1886), 291–304; no. 3 (1886), 517–32.

26. "V sudebnoi palate. Oskorblenie zemskogo nachal'nika," *RiazZh,* no. 77 (1913), 3.

27. Judging by the numerical growth of cases over time, official concern about insulting the tsar rose steadily after emancipation. To date, one of the only works treating this crime is V. A. Vinogradov, "Antitsaristskie vyskazyvaniia krest'ian: forma ideinogo vyrazheniia klassovoi bor'by v poreformennoi derevne 60-e–nachalo 80-kh gg. XIX v.," in *Voprosy istoriografii i istorii krest'ianstva* (Kalinin, 1975), 50–68.

place because too many people had been killed, including Motov's son. In fact, he declared, if the tsar happened to be present at that moment then he, Motov, "would hit him in his mug" (*udaril by po morde*). The police arrested Motov upon learning of this incident and sent him on to the judicial investigator, who dropped charges because witnesses all claimed that they had been drunk and could remember nothing.[28] A similar scene was played out in 1906 at the Trifonov teahouse of Skopin district, where Vasilii Sipilov and Kuz'ma Orlov—both "very drunk," according to the indictment—argued loudly about religion, the existence of God, and the saints. At one point, Orlov explained to Sipilov that if there were two tsars, one in heaven and one on earth, then the latter was the emperor. To this Sipilov replied: "Yeah, and what a tsar we have! We'll kill him . . . and pick a tsar for ourselves whom we like." He then added several curses regarding Nicholas II. For such words, Sipilov was tried by the Riazan' Circuit Court, which took into account "the accused's ignorance" and sentenced him to ten days in jail.[29] A peasant from Dankov district received the same sentence for drunkenly shouting, in the presence of the land captain at a 1906 village assembly: "Nikola, the little tsar, is a son-of-a-bitch! He doesn't know how to rule, can't make decisions, and so we have no order. We don't need him!"[30]

Public insults and denunciations of the emperor worried authorities greatly for fear that they could spread sedition. Yet the methods of dealing with perpetrators offer an intriguing look at one important aspect of the law's silence during the imperial era. To insult the monarch or ruling family was punishable under article 246 of Russia's criminal code (1885 edition) by a maximum of six to eight years at penal servitude with loss of all civil rights. The penalty could be substantially lessened, however, if the guilty party perpetrated this crime "out of folly or ignorance, or in a state of drunkenness," in which case sentences ranged from imprisonment for two to eight months to a jail term for as little as seven days to three months.[31] This was the public transcript for use in the open forum of courts. At a different level, police and other officials under MVD command sought to prevent situations that could provoke insults to the imperial person. In 1880 the governor of Iaroslavl' province sent a special order to district commandants that their officers should in no case invoke the name of the emperor when speaking to drunkards or prisoners. More quietly and with obvious fear, Alexander III issued a secret instruction on June 10, 1881, that persons accused of insulting the tsar should not be brought before the courts

28. GARO, f. 640, op. 51, sv. 174, d. 838, l. 4.

29. GARO, f. 640, op. 51, sv. 179, d. 925, ll. 4, 29–30. For examples concerning the murder of Alexander II, see Vinogradov, "Antitsaristskie vyskazyvaniia," 59–61.

30. GARO, f. 640, op. 51, sv. 174, d. 843, ll. 4–40b.

31. *SZU*, part 1: *Ulozhenie o nakazaniiakh ugolovnykh i ispravitel'nykh*, 54.

but dealt with administratively through the MVD.[32] During the following decades, although some cases continued to come before circuit courts, the majority were, in fact, handled through the administrative system by provincial governors.

The different and legally stipulated punishments for insult reflected the estate character retained by the postemancipation judicial system. A peasant who insulted another peasant would be tried before a *volost'* court, which could sentence the accused to seven days in jail. For insulting someone of a different social estate, however, this same peasant would come before a peace or circuit court and possibly receive six or eight months in prison. The factor that tended to equalize punishments in practice was the alibi of ignorance. Handing out short jail sentences each year to hundreds if not thousands of "backward" peasants who had insulted the monarch while drunk or only "out of ignorance" was far safer than admitting the possibility that so many of his subjects did not fit the reigning public stereotype of peasant monarchists who cherished their little father (*batiushka*), the benevolent tsar. As in so many other instances, the peasantry's assumed ignorance served to insulate the state from open threats to its authority. Cases considered more serious and seditious would continue to be handled administratively, usually resulted in banishment to another province, and were thereby kept from public view.[33]

## ASSAULTS AND FIGHTS

As in all societies, physical assault in rural Russia played out through hundreds of varied scripts, with an equally diverse range of backdrops and settings that resist precise categorization. If we group this crime somewhat clumsily and broadly, however, we can say that it most commonly occurred in one of the following situations: verbal insults and disagreements that escalated to fights; acts of revenge often perpetrated with the assistance of others; attempted theft or robbery; drunken squabbles resulting in injury and sometimes death; organized brawls and turf battles between rival gangs or even entire villages; and sexual assaults perpetrated mainly upon girls and women.

We do not need to recount the tedious examples of everyday assaults, which differed little from rural to urban Russia. The press, not unexpectedly,

32. Vinogradov, "Antitsaristskie vyskazyvaniia," 54.

33. Many who received short jail sentences had often spent several months in preliminary detention, however. See, e.g., GARO, f. 5, st. 3, op. 4, d. 1929, ll. 1–273; f. 640, op. 51, sv. 173, d. 835, ll. 1–10b., 22, 26; A. Smirnov, "Predvaritel'nyi arest i zakliuchenie. Ocherk iz istorii russkogo ugolovnogo protsessual'nogo prava," *IuV,* no. 8 (1878), 57–83; no. 9, 236–83; no. 10, 411–61; M. N. R., "Sud v derevne," 96–97.

searched endlessly for tales of bloody fights that might feed the public's appetite for daily or weekly crime columns. The most dramatic stories served to cement and even strengthen grim perceptions of life among the peasantry. An 1899 fight between two drunken peasants in a backwoods district of Kazan' province, in the course of which one bit the other and tore a large piece of flesh from his arm, was titled "The Human Beast" (*chelovek zver'*). For another newspaper, it was nothing less than the "Power of Darkness," stemming from "ignorance and moral underdevelopment," that led a drunken peasant to argue with his son and stab him several times with a bread knife.[34] Still, as in cases of insult, the assumption that the peasantry's mental and moral state constituted extenuating circumstances brought reduced charges or even acquittals when villagers came to trial for battery. Often, as in a 1907 trial before the Riazan' Circuit Court, peasants found guilty of assault were given light sentences "because of their extreme ignorance." In this instance, the three drunken culprits had been beating a crossing guard when a fellow villager passed by and asked why they were doing this. For his interference they beat him unconscious, then attacked him again when he arrived home in their village. The assailants would receive two months in prison.[35]

After homicide, the type of rural violence for which the provincial press reserved its most sensational coverage was the ritual mass battle usually fought by males of different villages at holiday times (women sometimes joined in as well), though in large villages residents of separate wards organized physical competitions.[36] Ritual fighting had a long history in rural Russia, where it served not only as a common holiday pastime but also reinforced village solidarity, formed reputations, and earned respect for local "heroes." Fighting between competing groups of young males also proved common at evening parties, the primary form of youthful festivity during the autumn and winter. Yet rural fights only attracted widespread negative attention from provincial reporters toward the middle of the 1880s, when general criticism of peasant culture and "degeneracy" began to increase. By

34. *VolzhV,* no. 305 (1899), 3; "Karachevskaia khronika. Vlast' t'my," *OrlV,* no. 261 (1898), 3.
35. GARO, f. 640, op. 51, sv. 181, d. 952, ll. 45–46; part 2, ll. 6–8.
36. For examples, see G. K. Zavoiko, "Verovan'ia, obriady i obychai velikorossov Vladimirskoi gubernii," *EtnogO,* no. 3–4 (1914), 132; "Zhenshchiny v boiakh," *Kollektiv* (Riazan' province), no. 32 (1925), 2; T. D. Segalov, "P'ianye draki v gorode i derevne (Po materialam Mosgubsuda)," *Problemy prestupnosti,* no. 2 (1927), 88–99; E. P. Busygin, et al., *Obshchestvennyi i semeinyi byt russkogo sel'skogo naseleniia Srednego Povolzh'ia* (Kazan', 1973), 78–79; Gromyko, *Traditsionnye normy,* 241–42; T. A. Bernshtam, *Molodezh' v obriadovoi zhizni russkoi obshchiny* (Leningrad, 1988); Anne L. Bobroff, "Working Women, Bonding Patterns, and the Politics of Daily Life: Russia at the End of the Old Regime" (Ph.D. diss., University of Michigan, 1982), 237–39. Compare John C. Chasteen, "Violence for Show: Knife Dueling on a Nineteenth-Century Cattle Frontier," in Lyman L. Johnson, ed., *The Problem of Order in Changing Societies: Essays on Crime and Policing in Argentina and Uruguay, 1750–1940* (Albuquerque, 1990), 47–64; Blackbourn, *Marpingen,* 67–69.

the start of the twentieth century, holiday fights as well as those at evening parties had come to be viewed fearfully as both the breeding ground for hooliganism and a result of uncontrolled hooligan activity.[37]

An 1892 report from Orel province gives a good picture of how villagers organized and conducted such fights and suggests that battle lines were often drawn on the basis of economic and social distinctions or deep historical enmities between villages. Mass fistfights were especially common in Kromsk district and took place between the villages of Golubitsy and Shakhovo each year during the Christmas season and at carnival time. By tradition they were always held on Saturdays:

> On this day the peasants assemble in a field (spectators and combatants from both sides)—upwards of 1,000 to 1,500 people. There were about 1,500 on February 15. Men and lads came from both villages, partly to fight, partly to watch; women and maidens were there solely as spectators. From each side there were about 200 fighters. People fight without any order, and in a crowd. . . . They won't strike someone who has fallen, but if he is faking they stand him up and beat him severely. The residents of Golubitsy are state peasants, who are pretty well off with a lot of land. They are usually aided in these battles by peasants from Rassyl'noe (also state peasants), as well as from other villages [in the area]. Inhabitants of Shakhovo are former seigneurial peasants and are poorer and worse off. They receive help . . . from peasants of Khomytov, Orel district—also former serfs.[38]

Mass fights of this sort remained popular into the 1920s and much later in some parts of the country. Early twentieth-century press reports about traditional holiday battles in Riazan' province noted that all villagers participated, "from small children to the elderly." In Podvislovo, "there are two fistfights every year, one on Trinity Sunday and the other during the first three days of Christmas, where they beat one another to death, and even the local administration takes part."[39] For much of the Russian countryside,

37. S. V. Maksimov, *Sobranie sochinenii*, vol. 17: *Krestnaia sila* (SPb, 1909), 9; V. Postnikov, "Sviatki v derevne," *NizhL*, no. 1 (1900), 4; "Derevenskie nravy," *SudO*, no. 48 (1903), 928; "Dikie nravy," *SevK*, no. 59 (1905), 2; "G. Varnavin," *PV*, no. 40 (1906), 4; "Mologskii uezd. Dikost' nravov," *Golos* (Iaroslavl'), no. 18 (1910), 3–4; "Iz zaly suda," *SPbVed*, no. 220 (1911), 2–3; "Orel. Kulachnyi boi," *MosVed*, (February 20, 1913). Stephen P. Frank, "Confronting the Domestic Other," in Stephen P. Frank and Mark D. Steinberg, eds., *Cultures in Flux* (Princeton, 1994), discusses public concern over rural holidays.

38. "Ostatki stariny," *VolzhV*, no. 54, (1892), 3.

39. "Derevnia Derskovaia, Egor'evskogo uezda," *RiazV*, no. 132 (1907), 3; "Selo Petrovo, Riazhskogo uezda," *RiazV*, no. 55 (1911), 3; "Kulachnyi boi. S. Napol'noe, Sapozhkovsk. uezda," *RiazZh*, no. 42 (1914), 3; "Temnaia derevnia. S. Podvislovo, Riazhsk. u.," *RiazZh*, no. 21 (1913), 2. See also "Selo Letniki, Sapozhkovskogo uezda. Kulachnye boi," *RiazV*, no. 74 (1910), 3; "Selo Napol'noe, Sapozhkovskogo uezda," *RiazV*, no. 8 (1911), 3; "O kulachnykh boiakh. Pis'ma iz Zaraiskogo uezda," *Rabochii klich* (Riazan'), no. 25 (1923), 2; G. I. Fomin, *Kulachnye boi v Voronezhskoi gubernii* (Voronezh, 1925).

then, fighting remained closely associated with holiday festivity throughout our period and beyond. By the 1890s, however, this festive element receded before the "savage violence," bloodshed, and disorder of village fights in the eyes of educated society.

Punishable offenses certainly occurred during mass fights and at evening parties, particularly if a contingent of males from another village showed up to court maidens or otherwise challenge local turf. Beatings, stabbings, and the occasional murder were by no means uncommon in the battles that frequently ensued. Such was the scenario at an 1899 patronal festival in Kazan' province, where youths had gathered in a field to perform the traditional round dance (*khorovod*). When boys from a nearby community appeared, a fight broke out with local lads, one of whom was stabbed and seriously wounded.[40] Whether the number of such incidents rose substantially at the turn of the century, as claimed by the press, temperance advocates, and others, is difficult to determine. Felony statistics do show an increase of rural assault cases that averaged 10.4 percent between 1874 and 1913 (from 583 to 5,158 convictions), but most of this growth occurred prior to 1899. During the period 1899–1913, at the height of concern over rural violence and hooliganism, assaults grew by an average of only 1.5 percent. The number of convictions for murder committed during a fight also increased less rapidly than other categories of homicide, averaging 4.9 percent for the entire period 1874–1913 (from 378 convictions in 1874 to 2,002 in 1913), but 2.1 percent if the revolutionary years 1905–7 are excluded. Inflicting mortal injury, in fact, was the only violent felony that demonstrated a significant increase of prosecutions and convictions after 1900, although here, too, the 1905 Revolution sharply skewed the data.[41]

What does appear certain in the case of rural fights is that a group of peasant holiday behaviors and practices centered around physical competitions and confrontations was coming more frequently to the attention of middle- and upper-class Russians, who by the 1880s increasingly viewed them as symptomatic of the peasantry's cultural backwardness. Efforts by Church and state officials to ban evening parties, for example, paralleled their concern that customary rural festivals provided both the setting and

40. "Sedmiozernaia Pustyn', Kazanskoi gubernii i uezda," *VolzhV,* no. 301 (1899), 3. See also TsGIAgM, f. 62, op. 3, d. 57 (1891), ll. 1–4; f. 703, op. 1 (1888), d.48, l. 106; "Moskovskii okruzhnyi sud," *SudG,* no. 33 (1884), 7–8; "Sapozhok. Kulachnyi boi," *Riazanskii spravochnyi listok,* no. 144 (1904), 2; "Ubiistvo mal'chika," *RiazZh,* no. 239 (1913), 3. Such fights were more common to village males, but they were by no means unknown among women. At a 1875 evening party in the Odessa region, for example, an argument broke out among the maidens in attendance, owing to which eight girls fell upon another and began to thrash her, following which they raised her skirt and smeared tar over her entire body below the waist. E. I. Iakushkin, *Obychnoe pravo,* 4 vols. (Iaroslavl', 1875–1909), 2:70.

41. *Svody,* part 2, "Vremia i mesto soversheniia prestupleniia."

the incentive for violent crime. Although peasant communities themselves had long regulated these evening gatherings, the resistance that outside intervention encountered is indicative of how conflict within the cultural arena spilled over into the educated classes' growing worries and fears about rural degeneration, a breakdown of order and criminality.[42]

## SEXUAL ASSAULT

One other type of violence that educated Russians linked to a collapse of rural social order was sexual assault. Contemporaries agreed that violence against women pervaded Russian society and that the phenomenon nowhere reached such terrible proportions as in the countryside. Courts, police, and newspapers all document the regularity with which peasant women were beaten and tortured by husbands, relatives, fellow villagers, and strangers. Beatings of pregnant women resulted in hundreds of miscarriages each year.[43] Exceedingly few Russians wrote about the realities of sexual assault, however, and of those who turned their attention to rape, most focused on its treatment within the criminal law.[44] Although courts usually tried rape cases behind closed doors to protect the victim's reputation, especially if she was unmarried, judicial records nevertheless provide one of the few sources that allow us some insight into this crime.

Rural rapes occurred or were attempted in virtually all settings: along deserted roads, in forests, fields, sheds, barns, bathhouses, and peasant homes, and sometimes in the presence of others. On June 24, 1876, for example, Matvei Kobzev reported to the Sapozhok judicial investigator that his twelve-

42. Gromyko, *Traditsionnye normy,* 235–36; "Vrode domashnogo aresta," *Privolzhskii krai,* no. 170 (1906), 3; Bobroff, "Working Women," 294–95; Vera Shevzov, "Popular Orthodoxy in Late Imperial Russia" (Ph.D. diss., Yale University, 1994), ch. 3. On redefinitions of popular culture in Western Europe, see Robert D. Storch, "Persistence and Change in 19th-Century Popular Culture," in Storch, ed., *Popular Culture and Custom in 19th-Century England* (London, 1982), 1–14; J. M. Golby and A. W. Purdue, *The Civilization of the Crowd: Popular Culture in England, 1750–1900* (New York, 1984); Peter McPhee, *A Social History of France, 1780–1880* (London, 1992), ch. 12.

43. For examples, see GARO, f. 7, op. 1, d. 95 (1884), ll. 340b.–35; d. 535 (1888), ll. 80b., 250b.; d. 584 (1890), ll. 18, 29; See also Ia. Ludmer, "Bab'i stony (Iz zametok mirovogo sud'i)," *IuV,* no. 11 (1884), 446–67; no. 12, 658–79; Ludmer, "Bab'i dela na mirovom sude," *IuV,* no. 11 (1885), 522–31; "Ubiistva i uvech'ia, nanosimye zhenshchinam i detiam," *SevV,* no. 3 (1893), part 2, 34–42.

44. D. N. Zhbankov, "Polovaia prestupnost'," *Sovremennyi mir,* no. 7 (1909), 54–91, examines the statistical growth of rape during the years 1900–1904. For analysis of legal views, see Laura Engelstein, "Gender and the Juridical Subject: Prostitution and Rape in Nineteenth-Century Russian Criminal Codes," *JMH* 60 (1988), 458–95. See also Ardalion Popov, *Sud i nakazaniia za prestupleniia protiv very i nravstvennosti po russkomu pravu* (Kazan', 1902), 423–25; "Issledovanie devstvennosti," *SbSSMPPS,* vol.2 (1872), 79–128.

year-old daughter Praskov'ia had been assaulted one month earlier by a six-teen year old named Ivan Kopylov. Praskov'ia was strolling after lunch with her friend Matrena Iashina when Kopylov began chasing them, they later explained. He seized Praskov'ia, threw her to the ground, and "attempted to force her legs apart [and] commit a sin with her." Thanks to Matrena, who fought Kopylov, the latter failed in his efforts and both girls managed to get away and run home, terribly frightened, where they told Matvei Kob-zev what had happened. Kopylov at first denied the charges against him, claiming he had not even spoken with the girls and certainly did not chase after them. His nine-year-old brother corroborated this version of the story. On the basis of the girls' testimony and examination of Praskov'ia's torn un-dershirt, however, Kopylov was tried for attempted defloration of a minor (*rastlenie*), changed his plea to guilty but requested leniency, and received a two-week prison sentence.[45]

Elsewhere, Mikhail Malev attempted to rape Stepanida Titova (both six-teen years of age) in the woods some distance from their village in Iaroslavl' province. They had been walking from another village, and upon reaching the forest, Malev threw Titova to the ground, raised her dress, and when she began resisting and screaming, stuffed dirt in her mouth. "Only because of Titova's physical strength did he not succeed in perpetrating this terrible crime."[46] A woman walking to Riazan' in 1910 was assaulted by a fellow vil-lager who came riding along on his horse, struck her several times in the head, then raped her, after which he returned to their village. In Pronsk dis-trict that same year, one woman was attacked and sexually assaulted in a meadow by a house servant from a neighboring settlement.[47] Still another fell victim to an unknown peasant who offered to drive her to her village from the Riazhsk train station late in 1912. On February 6, 1912, at 4:00 P.M., E. S. Mikhina stepped into a Mikhailovka village shop only to find it empty except for a young man who resided in an adjoining apartment. The tenant confronted Mikhina, blocking her exit from the store, and when she sought to flee through the back entrance he gave chase, seized, and raped her there in the store.[48]

45. GARO, f. 640, op. 51, sv. 117, d. 102, ll. 2–15. Under the 1885 Penal Code, the maxi-mum punishment for defloration was loss of all civil rights and a sentence of penal servitude in Siberia for a period of four to ten years. *SZU*, part 9, ch. 6, section 1, art. 1524. In practice, however, courts frequently applied the law far more leniently.

46. "Listok proisshestvii," *SevK*, no. 225 (1899), 4. See also "Mestnaia khronika. Iznasilo-vanie," *NizhL*, no. 145 (1899), 2.

47. "Poliany, Riazanskogo uezda (Iznasilovanie)," *RiazV*, no. 181 (1910), 3; "Der. Ist'e, Pronskogo uezda," *RiazV*, no. 302 (1910), 3.

48. "V derevne," *RiazZh*, no. 23 (1913) 3; "Dnevnik proisshestvii. Iznasilovanie," *RiazZh*, no. 31 (1912), 3.

Though seldom mentioned in the press, court records reveal that sexual assault upon children was by no means a rarity in peasant communities. In 1904, for instance, a fifty-year-old man caught up with Aleksandra Andrianova, a girl of twelve, while she walked along a road in Iaroslavl' province, forced her into some nearby bushes, and raped her. The rapist was sentenced to nine-years at hard labor in Siberia for this crime.[49] During the Celebration of the Exaltation of the Cross on September 14, 1910, ten-year-old Pelageia Uvarova from the village of Sarai in Riazan' province was invited by a hired worker named Grigorii Khlobystov, with whom she and her mother shared neighboring living quarters, to hear him play the accordion in his room. After a short time Khlobystov set aside the accordion, lifted Pelageia onto his lap, raised her clothing, and attempted to penetrate her. Frightened by the girl's painful cries, however, he did not succeed. Rather, giving her two kopecks, he sent her off with a warning not to tell anyone what had happened. Tried in 1913, Khlobystov received a five-year sentence at a corrective penal division.[50] One Riazan' peasant got only two and a half years' incarceration when convicted in 1914 for the attempted rape of a four-year-old girl in Zaraisk district.[51]

Charges of defloration and incest were sometimes brought simultaneously, as in the case of Vasilii Aleksandrov from Zaraisk district, who was tried in 1877 for raping his fourteen-year-old daughter Nastas'ia and continuing to force himself upon her thereafter. Aleksandrov's wife Avdot'ia finally denounced him after she discovered her husband and daughter copulating in the shed. By this time, Nastas'ia was pregnant. When questioned by the judicial investigator, the girl explained that during the summer, while returning with her father from another village, he had ordered her to lie on the ground, threatening to kill her if she did not, then "took her innocence." Thereafter, the indictment reads, "her father continuously fornicated with her over the course of several months," until Nastas'ia finally confessed everything to her mother and begged her to lodge a complaint. Relatives had already noticed the peculiar relationship between father and daughter some time before, and as Avdot'ia would later testify, she, too, had seen that Aleksandrov "treated his daughter like a lover, laying with her on the same bedding, grabbing her breasts and . . . conducting himself much differently than a father should." In his own defense, Aleksandrov argued that both wife and daughter had falsely accused him in order to be rid of him "because he did not allow them to continue the depraved life they

49. "Sudebnaia Khronika," *SevK*, no. 78 (1905), 3.

50. GARO, f. 640, op. 51, sv. 193, d. 1187, ll. 4–5, 59–640b.

51. GARO, f. 640, op. 54, sv. 28, d. 38, ll. 5–6, 40–480b. See also f. 640, op. 51, sv. 190, d. 1126 (1910), ll. 4–5; op. 53, sv. 7, d. 75 (1875); op. 54, sv. 28, d. 38 (1914), ll. 5–6; f. 641, op. 3 (1868), d. 15; op. 4 (1869), sv. 9, d. 15; op. 36 (1901), sv. 103, d. 12a.

had led before his return from military service." Found guilty in December 1877, he was sentenced to loss of all rights and seven years' incarceration in a Siberian exile prison, followed by settlement for life in eastern Siberia.[52]

The sanctity of a marriage agreement could also shroud acts of rape, as the following 1897 incident from Nizhnii Novgorod province attests. A peasant in the village of Teliashevo found a potential bride for his son and negotiated the union with her parents "according to the old custom." The maiden was not asked her consent. In the peculiar formulation of the reporter recounting this incident, "whether because of the progressive movement of popular education, or because of the maiden's 'despair,' or for some other reason," once she learned how her fate had been decided the girl voiced strong protest. Still, plans went forward and the wedding day arrived, with the marriage conducted at the village church. When asked by the priest whether she was entering this marriage willingly (*okhotoi-li vykhodit za zhenikha?*), the young woman decisively answered no. Therefore, in accordance to Church stricture, the ceremony was halted. The events that followed remain rather veiled by the reporter's self-censorship, but the outcome is clear:

> The young woman was taken to the home of her fiancé where everyone gathered in the stable, laid out straw, brought in the fiancé and locked the door for the entire night. Then the relatives of both youths began to celebrate [*guliat'*]. In the seclusion of the long night, the particular mood, force on the part of the young man, all did their deed, and as a result there was rape. Now this case has been sent before the judicial investigator. How much more light is still needed in order to stop these bestial [*skotopodobnye*] unions![53]

Although jurists and others wrote at length and with great sympathy of the plight of peasant women victimized by violence and legal inequality, Russian law interpreted rape as a form of insult, situating it in a subsection of the criminal code's chapter on "Insults to Honor" and terming these acts "Crimes against the Honor and Chastity of Women."[54] Both before and after emancipation much the same attitude could be found in rural communities, where peasant judges and local officials viewed rape as an insult for which compensation should be made and reconciliation sought. Hence punishments differed little at all from those handed down in other cases of

---

52. GARO, f. 640, op. 53, sv. 10, d. 104, ll. 3–6, 44–550b. For incest cases treated without charges of rape, see f. 640, op. 51, sv. 151, d. 545 (1893); sv. 164, d. 700 (1900); f. 641, op. 36 (1901), sv. 102, d. 14.

53. "Lukoianovskii uezd," *OrlV,* no. 50, (1898), 3.

54. *SZU,* part 9, ch. 6, section 1, art. 1523–32. For earlier discussion, see O. A. Filippov, "Vzgliad na ugolovnoe pravo po predmetu oskorbleniia chesti zhenshchin," *IuV,* no. 2 (1862), 20–33.

insult—usually a fine paid to the victim "for her dishonor," though flogging was common if the accused already had a bad reputation. With most accusations of rape, however, "punishment is almost never imposed 'for lack of evidence.' "[55]

During the years 1874 to 1913, an average of only 641 rape and 133 defloration cases came to trial each year before Russia's circuit courts. Nevertheless, judicial statistics do provide several insights, beginning with social and judicial attitudes toward these offenses. Among all felonies for which men were tried, circuit courts proved least likely to convict on charges of rape, doing so in only 39.4 percent of cases throughout this period. For defloration of minors, on the other hand, courts convicted an average of 67.5 percent of those accused.[56] The question of how rapes were perpetrated is problematic, for published data offer several possible interpretations. Between 1874 and 1897, 50.9 percent of men convicted on charges of sexual assault had committed their offense with the participation of others. This figure changed only slightly throughout the postemancipation era, reaching a high of 55.4 percent in the period 1889–93 and a low of 45.6 percent over the next five years. By the period 1909–13, 51.2 percent of rape convicts had perpetrated their crime alone. Can we assume, based on these data, that a majority of sexual assaults against adult women were committed by groups? Were convictions simply easier to achieve when two or more persons took part in the crime, or, given the law's greater concern with offenses involving groups or gangs, was preference shown toward prosecuting gang rape? It is also possible that victims themselves proved more willing to report an assault in such instances. Unfortunately, none of these questions can be readily answered, for the quantitative sources provide no further clues. Oddly enough, the majority of published rape cases as well as those remaining in court archives involve single assailants rather than groups, though at least some contemporaries insisted that most rapes were perpetrated by more than one person.[57]

As regards the profile of offenders, table 5.1 provides the age and marital status for all peasants convicted in both categories of sexual assault. On

55. Kostrov, *Iuridicheskie obychai,* 74. See also S. P. Nikonov and E. I. Iakushkin, *Grazhdanskoe pravo po resheniiam Krestoborodskogo volostnogo suda, Iaroslavskoi gubernii i uezda* (Iaroslavl', 1902), 124–25. Not only peasant courts dropped charges for lack of evidence; so, too, did circuit court prosecutors. See, e.g., GARO, f. 641, op. 4 (1869), sv. 8, d. 15; and compare the attitudes discussed in Carolyn A. Conley, *The Unwritten Law* (Oxford, 1991), 81–95.

56. *Svody,* part 2, " Otnoshenie osuzhdennykh k poterpevshim ot prestupleniia i souchastie v prestuplenii."

57. Berendeev, "Derevenskie pis'ma. Krest'ianskie prestupleniia," *SevV,* no. 1, part 2 (1889), 50–55; B. Zmiev, "Prestupleniia v oblasti polovykh otnoshenii v gorode i v derevne," *Problemy prestupnosti,* no. 2 (1927), 41–50. Kostrov (*Iuridicheskie obychai,* 73) noted that of fifty rape cases tried in Tomsk province between 1836 and 1852, "most were gang rapes."

TABLE 5.1   Age and Marital Profile of Peasants Convicted for Rape and Defloration, 1874–1898

| Offense/Years | Total Convicts* | Age (%) | | | | | | Marital Status (%) | | |
|---|---|---|---|---|---|---|---|---|---|---|
| | | 12–17 | 17–21 | 21–30 | 30–40 | 40–50 | 50+ | Single | Married | Widowed |
| Rape | | | | | | | | | | |
| 1874–78 | 49 | 7.2 | 31.2 | 39.8 | 11.6 | 5.9 | 4.3 | 54.4 | 41.8 | 2.8 |
| 1879–83 | 80 | 4.6 | 34.3 | 36.2 | 16.0 | 6.2 | 2.6 | 53.5 | 44.8 | 1.5 |
| 1884–88 | 127 | 5.1 | 31.6 | 41.4 | 12.3 | 6.7 | 2.9 | 57.9 | 38.9 | 3.2 |
| 1889–93 | 123 | 6.2 | 31.4 | 38.8 | 15.5 | 6.6 | 1.4 | 58.4 | 39.2 | 2.2 |
| 1894–98 | 97 | 5.8 | 28.8 | 32.5 | 17.3 | 10.3 | 5.3 | 53.1 | 42.8 | 3.6 |
| "Defloration" of minors | | | | | | | | | | |
| 1874–78 | 25 | 20.5 | 32.0 | 22.0 | 11.1 | 8.7 | 5.7 | 64.6 | 33.2 | 1.5 |
| 1879–83 | 29 | 20.6 | 33.3 | 23.6 | 11.3 | 6.3 | 5.0 | 60.9 | 35.8 | 3.4 |
| 1884–88 | 36 | 23.8 | 25.0 | 25.6 | 13.3 | 7.5 | 4.9 | 66.0 | 29.5 | 4.5 |
| 1889–93 | 36 | 24.0 | 30.5 | 17.7 | 13.7 | 7.3 | 6.8 | 59.4 | 36.9 | 3.7 |
| 1894–98 | 27 | 24.6 | 29.8 | 20.0 | 13.9 | 5.9 | 5.8 | 69.2 | 28.6 | 2.1 |

SOURCE: *Svody*, part 2, "Otnoshenie k prestuplenii zaniatii osuzhdennykh v sviazi s usloviiami pola, vozrasta, semeinogo byta i obrazovaniia."
* Average annual number.

average in the period 1874–1898, 75.3 percent and 74.7 percent of offenders fell below thirty years old for rape and defloration, respectively. The larger proportion of unmarried males convicted on defloration charges (an average of 64 percent, compared with 55.4 percent for rape) is suggestive of several differences between this offense and that of rape perpetrated against adults. Consider that a much larger proportion of persons who committed defloration were related to their victims—12.3 percent for the entire period, reaching as high as 20 percent in 1882. The corresponding figure for rape was only 6.4 percent. Likewise, a substantially greater percentage of offenders fell below the age of seventeen in defloration cases—22.6 percent on average, with as much as 35.7 percent in 1888. In rape cases, 5.8 percent of convicts belonged to this cohort. Equally significant, and in sharp contrast to recorded rape cases, 84.2 percent of assaults upon children were committed by individuals acting alone. It seems clear from such data that we have uncovered the usually hidden act of sexual abuse of children often perpetrated by minor or unmarried kin, as well as by parents or other older relatives.[58]

How many cases of rape went unreported in the Russian countryside is impossible to know, of course, as is the number of sexual assaults settled informally through payment of compensation or punishment by village assemblies. Nor can we begin to guess about incidents hushed up to prevent scandal. Given the public condemnation, mockery, and ostracism—including *charivaris*—that met local maidens or women with reputations as sexual deviants, however, one can imagine the fear and constraint that kept rape victims from denouncing their assailants. An unmarried women also had to consider the likelihood that she would be unable to marry locally if the crime became public knowledge. In some instances, suspicion could easily fall upon the victim herself, particularly if her community standing already placed her in a vulnerable position that the accused might use to his own advantage before village elders. Moreover, as Carolyn Conley stresses in her study of crime in Victorian Kent, "a woman who brought a charge of sexual assault was making a public issue of her loss of virtue. Such brazenness was highly suspect." Hence victims of rape fell suspect on three separate counts: "they were female, they had been at least temporarily outside the supervision of male guardians . . . , and they were publicly announcing their loss of

58. *Svody*, part 2, "Otnoshenie osuzhdennykh k poterpevshim ot prestupleniia i souchastie v prestuplenii." Unfortunately, changes in the way these data were enumerated force my analysis to stop in 1898. Because the law defined *rastlenie* (lit.: the taking of one's virginity) as sexual intercourse, rupture of the hymen by means other than the penis were treated as inflicting a wound. See, e.g., "Issledovanie devstvennosti," 96–102; "Opredelenie Ostrogozhskogo Okruzhnogo Suda," *IuV*, no. 4 (1869), 59–61; "Rastlena li Mariia G., 10 let, i soversheno li rastlenie posredstvom polovogo sovokupleniia s nei?" and "Rastlena li 7-mi letniaia devochka Tat'iana T-va?" *VOGSP*, no. 2 (1897), part 3, 17–24.

TABLE 5.2    Rural Homicide Convictions, 1874–1913
(Annual average per five–year period)

| Period | Total Convictions | | | Murder of Parents | | | Murder of Spouse | | |
|---|---|---|---|---|---|---|---|---|---|
| | Men | Women | Total | Men | Women | Total | Men | Women | Total |
| 1874–78 | 832 | 145 | 977 | 10 | 1 | 11 | 45 | 45 | 90 |
| 1879–83 | 1,007 | 178 | 1,185 | 18 | 1 | 19 | 67 | 61 | 128 |
| 1884–88 | 1,444 | 233 | 1,677 | 20 | 1 | 21 | 82 | 61 | 143 |
| 1889–93 | 1,509 | 246 | 1,755 | 19 | 2 | 21 | 81 | 64 | 145 |
| 1894–98 | 1,512 | 237 | 1,749 | 21 | 3 | 24 | 94 | 73 | 167 |
| 1899–1903 | 2,372 | 221 | 2,593 | 19 | 1 | 20 | 112 | 67 | 179 |
| 1904–08 | 3,116 | 190 | 3,306 | 34 | 2 | 36 | 146 | 79 | 225 |
| 1909–13 | 5,758 | 283 | 6,041 | 68 | 2 | 70 | 271 | 100 | 371 |
| 1874–1913 (average) | 2,343 | 221 | 2,564 | 28 | 2 | 30 | 112 | 69 | 181 |

SOURCE: *Svody,* part 2, "Vremia i mesto soversheniia prestuplenii."

sexual innocence."[59] Given such powerful constraining factors, it is all the more remarkable that over the course of our period women appeared increasingly willing to take such risks and report rape. Numbers remained small, but the growth in prosecutions for this offense must be attributed primarily to a rise in reporting because arrest and prosecution came upon complaint of the victim, her parents, or husband.[60]

## HOMICIDE

Convictions for murders committed in the countryside from 1874 to 1913 rose at an average yearly rate of 5.7 percent (6.0 percent among men, and 3.1 percent for women). The 1905 Revolution significantly influenced these rates, however, which rose a remarkable 49 percent between 1904 and 1908, and they would have been even greater if data from summary courts martial were included. They were not because the state not only concealed certain violent offenses perpetrated against government officials as well as noble landowners or their estate managers but also hid its use of capital punishment.[61] Taking only published criminal statistics and excluding

59. Conley, *The Unwritten Law,* 95.
60. *SZU,* part 1, art. 1532; Zhbankov, "Polovaia prestupnost'," 56; E. N. Tarnovskii, "Dvizhenie prestupnosti v Rossiiskoi imperii za 1899–1908 gg.," *ZhMIu,* no. 2 (1902), 69–70.
61. In 1887, for instance, fourteen peasants from Penza province were sentenced to death by hanging after killing a steward during a confrontation over the grazing of village livestock on estate lands. An imperial pardon spared the lives of all but two, commuting their sentences

TABLE 5.2    (*continued*)

| Poisoning | | | Other Premeditated Murder | | | Other Unpremeditated Murder | | | Murder during Fights or Unintentionally | | | Infanticide |
|---|---|---|---|---|---|---|---|---|---|---|---|---|
| Men | Women | Total | Men | Women | Total | Men | Women | Total | Men | Women | Total | Women |
| 5 | 8 | 13 | 249 | 28 | 277 | 231 | 30 | 261 | 374 | 43 | 417 | 21 |
| 8 | 24 | 32 | 269 | 22 | 291 | 187 | 8 | 195 | 456 | 62 | 518 | 29 |
| 15 | 25 | 40 | 292 | 27 | 319 | 226 | 10 | 236 | 808 | 110 | 918 | 52 |
| 13 | 18 | 31 | 290 | 28 | 318 | 181 | 14 | 195 | 925 | 123 | 1,048 | 73 |
| 15 | 28 | 43 | 307 | 26 | 333 | 224 | 14 | 238 | 843 | 90 | 933 | 110 |
| 13 | 19 | 32 | 368 | 19 | 387 | 371 | 21 | 392 | 1,488 | 97 | 1,585 | 76 |
| 7 | 9 | 16 | 529 | 30 | 559 | 792 | 23 | 815 | 1,609 | 47 | 1,656 | 41 |
| 15 | 12 | 27 | 999 | 47 | 1,046 | 2,030 | 50 | 2,080 | 2,375 | 71 | 2,446 | 62 |
| 11 | 18 | 29 | 442 | 29 | 471 | 587 | 22 | 609 | 1,167 | 81 | 1,248 | 58 |

the revolutionary years 1905–7, the overall rate of increase in rural homicides falls to 3.3 percent, the lowest rate for any felony and one that gives cause for questioning contemporary claims of rampant violence and bloodshed among the rural population.

The judicial statistics divided homicide into several groups that provide a rough sense of this crime's character (table 5.2). By far the largest category of recorded rural murders between 1874 and 1913 (50.6 percent) was classified as "involuntary," due to carelessness or fights. Premeditated murder averaged 19.2 percent of the total, having declined from a high of 27.9 percent at the end of the 1870s, whereas intentional but unpremeditated murder accounted for 16.6 percent. Murder of a spouse or relative, which was enumerated separately, made up an average 8.3 percent of rural murders, though here a sharp difference between men and women must be noted. Among all female murderers, 32.1 percent were convicted for killing a spouse or relation, whereas only 5.5 percent of male murderers fell into this category—a fact that identifies one of the primary spheres of violent conflict for peasant women.[62]

---

to penal servitude for life; the remaining convicts were executed in Penza on November 10. "Pravosudie nad ubiitsami," *SV,* no. 47 (1887), 476. On death sentences by courts martial, see S. A—v., "Ugolovnoe zakonodatel'stvo Rossii za 1906–1910 gg.," *Drug provintsii,* no. 3 (1911), 2; G. Filat'ev, "Dorevoliutsionnye voennye sudy v tsifrakh," *Katorga i ssylka,* no. 7 (1930), 138–67.

62. *Svody,* part 2, "Vremia i mesto soversheniia prestupleniia." On spousal homicide, see Stephen P. Frank, "Cultural Conflict and Criminality in Rural Russia, 1861–1900" (Ph.D. diss.,

What these data cannot reveal are the circumstances under which rural homicide occurred, including motives, personal and social conflicts, and situations in which strangers were the perpetrators. We can begin our exploration by noting that murder frequently resulted from efforts by villagers to protect their homes and property. When, for instance, on a June night in 1891, a Riazan' peasant of Skopin district was awakened by his dog's howling, he quickly arose to discover three unknown persons robbing his larder. Two neighbors came running at Rudakov's shouts for help and a struggle ensued between them and the lone thief unfortunate enough not to have escaped in time. The badly beaten criminal was finally handed over to the village elder, only to die the following day while being conveyed by wagon to precinct police headquarters. Tried seven months later on charges of inflicting mortal injury, all three villagers were acquitted.[63] A Riazan' jury rendered the same verdict in early 1909 after considering murder charges against Grigorii Akimov Griaznov from the village of Konstantinovo. Griaznov had been awakened at about 2:00 A.M. one night in September 1907 by someone stealing from his cellar. Seizing a hunting rifle, Griaznov rushed out in pursuit of the culprit, chased him to the edge of the village, and fired a shot that inflicted a wound from which the thief died two days later.[64]

As was true of assault, and as criminal statistics show, insults, arguments, and fights provided the backdrop to numerous homicides. The peasant Kiril Nikiforov of Tula province went to town with a friend one day in 1870 hoping to find work. That evening they met three fellow villagers at a tavern, and all five eventually set out for home together. Along the way Nikiforov and one of his new companions got into a dispute during which Nikiforov called the latter a thief. He was promptly set upon by this trio, dragged from the cart, and beaten so severely that he died.[65] In 1911 Ivan Koshin came to buy oakum in a Sapozhok district village and stopped off at an acquaintance's

---

Brown University, 1987), ch. 3; Frank, "Narratives within Numbers," *RR* 55, no. 4 (1996), 554–55. For comparisons with other European states, see E. N. Tarnovskii, "Prestupleniia protiv zhizni po polam, vozrastam i semeinomu sostoianiiu," *IuV,* no. 10 (1886), 276–97.

63. GARO, f. 640, op. 51, sv. 140, d. 504, ll. 2–3, 47–500b.

64. "Sessiia okruzhnogo suda v Riazani," *RiazV,* no. 18 (1909), 3–4. Murder with weapons like knives and firearms grew more common in the postemancipation period, but most homicides were still perpetrated through physical force such as beating or strangulation. One study from Tula province for the years 1879 to 1884 found that 70.4 percent of all men and 42.9 percent of all women mudered had died from beatings. Among female victims, 21.4 percent had been strangled (11.1 percent for males). Another 28.6 percent of women died from firearms or knives, with 16.7 percent of men killed by such means. V. Smidovich, "O nasil'stvennykh i sluchainykh smertiakh v Tul'skoi gubernii za 1879–84 goda, sravnitel'no s drugimi guberniiami evropeiskoi Rossii," *Vestnik sudebnoi meditsiny i obshchestvennoi gigieny,* vol. 1 (1887), part 2, 20.

65. A. Liubavskii, *Ugolovnye dela iz praktiki Tul'skogo okruzhnogo suda* (Tula, 1874), 3–6.

home, where he began drinking vodka with Emel'ian Mamkin and Mikhail Upravitelev. For reasons left unexplained by both the indictment and witness testimony, Koshkin started a fight with Mamkin and called him out into the yard. Joined by Upravitelev, who broke Mamkin's nose before the latter wisely decided to flee, Koshkin gave chase. Mamkin ran to another peasant's yard, where he tried to hide, but upon hearing someone rushing from behind he seized a wooden post and struck Koshkin in the head as the latter ran into the yard, causing a mortal wound. When tried in June 1912, Mamkin received a reduced sentence of two months' imprisonment and church penance after the Riazan' Circuit Court took account of his "extreme ignorance and underdevelopment."[66]

The continued centrality of family and kinship in village life determined that a significant proportion of quarrels, civil litigation, and crime transpired within the domestic sphere or between feuding relatives. Many conflicts found their roots in economic disputes, as might be expected, and others arose from the disagreements and strife common to relations among siblings, parents and children, spouses, and more distant relatives. Certainly some of the most bitter disputes occurred over inheritance and family divisions. One such case from Sapozhok district involved the 1909 murder of Ol'ga Babkova by her son Petr and nephew Pavel. Babkova had previously divided the family land, giving some to Petr but leaving a sizable portion to support herself and her married daughter, with whom she lived. When she announced her intention to sell off a part of her property that Petr coveted for himself, the latter unsuccessfully sought to stop her by means of a court suit. On January 10 of that year, Petr and Pavel invited Ol'ga to come to their home in a neighboring village and discuss the dispute. Along the way Petr began cursing his mother, saying she had "deprived him of bread," then beat her to death. Petr would be sentenced to fifteen years at penal servitude for murder, but Pavel was acquitted of complicity.[67]

Mistreatment by relatives and in-laws, spousal abuse, and jealousies within the domestic sphere also served as reasons behind no small number of rural homicides. On Ascension Day (*Voznesenie*) in 1873, for instance, eighteen-year-old Marfa Aver'ianova took a knife and attempted to murder her father-in-law while he slept. As she would later explain to the judicial investigator, she had done so in desperation born of the man's stinginess

66. GARO, f. 640, op. 51, sv. 193, d. 1184, ll. 4–40b., 28–29. See also f. 5, st. 3, op. 4, d. 1256, ll. 62–620b.

67. "Sapozhok. (Drama iz-za zemli)," *RiazV*, no. 132 (1910), 3. See also "Kazanskii Okruzhnyi Sud. Ubiistvo iz-za nasledstva," *VolzhV*, no. 149 (1892), 2; "Bratoubiistvo," *RiazV*, no. 137 (1910), 3; "Ubiistvo iz-za zemli," *Krest'ianskoe delo*, no. 7 (1911), 146; "Krovavyi razdel," *RiazZh*, no. 164 (1912), 3. Violence resulting from land disputes was by no means limited to kin. See, e.g., "Iz-za zemli," *RiazZh*, no. 99 (1913), 3; "Egor'evsk. Ubiistvo," *RiazZh*, no. 154 (1914), 3.

because he either refused to feed her at all or only gave her moldy pieces of bread and oppressed her terribly at home. Tried by the Riazan' Circuit Court in early 1875, Aver'ianova pleaded guilty before a jury, which acquitted her.[68] In another part of this province Platon Inin returned home during a local, August 1912 holiday and discovered his father Konstantin "busying himself with his daughter-in-law"—that is, Platon's wife Mar'ia— "attempting to rape her." Platon seized a blunt instrument lying near at hand and struck his father in the head, inflicting a wound from which the fifty-eight-year-old peasant would die three days later. According to testimony supplied by the deceased's wife, from the first day of Platon's marriage Konstantin changed dramatically. In her words, "his love was transferred to the daughter-in-law, he beat me all the time—sometimes half to death— and our son stayed away from home in order to avoid arguments. Soon there were rumors that my old man was involved with the daughter-in-law, and the rumors were confirmed." Other villagers had also noticed "an abnormal relationship" between Konstantin and his daughter-in-law. As for the latter, the press account concerning this case suggested to its readers that she was "perhaps the main culprit of this nightmarish drama." A jury acquitted Platon of all charges at his trial in early 1913.[69]

Though few in number compared to other homicides, spousal murders occupied an inordinate amount of press and public attention during the latter half of the nineteenth century. For educated society, in fact, this crime proved the quintessential act of rural violence, embodying as it did all of the elements usually attributed to crimes against persons in the countryside— ignorance, savagery, the primitive level of interpersonal relations, and the extreme abuse to which peasant women were regularly subject. As one newspaper commentator put it, such homicides "result from those savage relations between husband and wife which are considered normal among the lower strata of the population."[70] The offense also helped to situate violent crime more directly within the peasant household. Writing about the growth of premeditated murder by women, E. N. Tarnovskii claimed in 1886 that "the criminal statistics provide irrefutable evidence of the number of bloody dramas enacted under conditions of contemporary Russian marriage." He pointed to the "unenviable situation of married women among the masses" when explaining these "bloody dramas." One year later, however, this author would argue that sexual passion led most women murderers to their crimes.[71]

68. GARO, f. 640, op. 53, sv. 6, d. 60, ll. 3–4, 22–240b.

69. "Sessiia okruzhnogo suda v g. Kasimove. Koshmarnoe delo," *RiazZh,* no. 35 (1913), 3.

70. "Smert ot strakha pred nagaikoi," *Kazanskii telegraf,* no. 2712 (1901), 2.

71. Tarnovskii, "Prestupleniia protiv zhizni po polam," 282; Tarnovskii, "Prestupleniia protiv zhizni i usloviia obshchestvennogo byta," *IuV,* no. 8 (1886), 506. Tarnovskii was by no means

Even a cursory look at contemporary sources makes clear that physical and mental abuse at the hands of a husband or in-laws was the chief reason for spousal homicide by women. In cases of men who murdered their wives, jealousy and adultery were frequently the cause, though deadly beatings inflicted in a drunken state appear even more common.[72] Thirty-two-year-old Anna Romanova from the Suzdal region had suffered beatings at the hands of her husband throughout their fourteen years of marriage. She fled several times but was always forced to return home because she had no passport. Following a severe beating inflicted by her husband and mother-in-law in 1868, Anna attempted to murder the latter with an ax, having decided that she was the instigator of her son's violence.[73] Forty-five years later, cases of this kind read much the same. When A. K. Zhirkova of Dankov district took her husband's life in July 1913, she, too, was responding to his merciless, drunken beatings. Trying to prevent him from entering their house and thereby protect herself from an inevitable beating, Zhirkova seized an ax and struck her husband several times in the head and back after he broke through the window. Following the murder, she went to confess before the priest and then reported her deed to the village elder.[74] Some women waited until abusive husbands slept before killing them; others did so during a beating; still others turned to poison (particularly arsenic) or went to a local diviner seeking advice on the best methods for ridding themselves of their spouse.[75]

By no means did all women charged with spouse murder appear as victims in court records or press accounts. Those who committed adultery and betrayed honest, hard-working husbands (as the latter were presented), for instance, were depicted as vicious criminals or, once Western criminology began to percolate through Russia's legal and medical professions, degenerates and psychopaths. In one case from 1902, the "biological aberrations" of a young peasant woman charged with spouse murder became the primary focus of an abbreviated account published after her trial. Noting the

---

alone in this later view. See, e.g., P. I. Kovalevskii, "Prestupleniia i revnost'," *ZhMIu*, no. 1 (1901), 56–91, and compare Ruth Harris, "Melodrama, Hysteria and Feminine Crimes of Passion in the Fin-de-Siècle," *History Workshop Journal*, no. 25 (1988), 31–63; Harris, *Murders and Madness: Medicine, Law, and Society in the Fin de Siècle* (Oxford, 1989).

72. Among numerous examples, see GARO, f. 7, op. 1, d. 95, ll. 390ob., 88ob.; d. 535, ll. 120ob., 210ob., 430ob., 66ob.; d. 613, l. 76ob.; f. 640, op. 53, sv. 1, d. 2 (1867).

73. "Sudebnoe zasedanie vo Vladimirskom Okruzhnom Sude po ugolovnomu otdeleniiu," *IuV*, no. 9 (1869), 63–77.

74. "Derevenskaia tragediia," *RiazZh*, no. 163 (1913), 3.

75. GARO, f. 640, op. 51, sv. 166, d. 735 (1902), ll. 2–40ob.; op. 53, sv. 12, d. 135 (1880), ll. 3–5; "Karachev," *OrlV*, no. 5 (1888), 2–3; "Otravlenie muzha," *VolzhV*, no. 65 (1892), 3; "Zadushenie muzha," *NizhL*, no. 63 (1897), 4; "Bezvremennaia zhertva svoenraviia muzha," *SevK*, no. 312 (1899), 4; "Muzheubiistvo," *Pravo*, no. 24 (1903), 1640; "Otravlenie muzha," *SudO*, no. 14 (1905), 306; "Ubiistvo muzha," *SPbVed*, no. 199 (1911), 3.

woman's genetic inheritance from an insane mother and alcoholic father, six psychiatric experts concluded that she suffered "a rare disorder in the mental sphere" and exhibited the physical signs of degeneration—clearly evidenced by her "irregular teeth and ears." Having concluded that she committed the crime in a pathological state "conditioned by the degeneracy of her crude heredity and the low level of her intellectual capabilities," the court ordered her incarcerated at a psychiatric hospital.[76] Although modern criminological-medical theory certainly changed the terms of turn-of-the-century discourses on the causation for crime, it nevertheless fit quite comfortably with the older and still dominant themes of cultural backwardness. It provided pseudo-scientific foundations for understanding backwardness and, more ominously, a rationale by which many whose views on the peasantry were already hardening might reject arguments that favored greater efforts at education and enlightenment among the "benighted" rural masses.

One last category of homicide requiring mention is murder committed during the perpetration of a robbery, for this offense linked violence to property crimes and was also commonly committed by strangers, including escapees from exile or prison. Four peasants from the Eletsk district of Orel province planned and perpetrated a robbery in 1897, for example, during which they bludgeoned to death a local miller and his sister and made off with a sizable sum of cash. Found guilty in 1898, the accused received sentences ranging from twelve to fifteen years at penal servitude.[77] Some who committed robbery-murders knew their victims, or at least knew that they possessed something worth stealing. One peasant tried by the St. Petersburg Circuit Court in 1891 murdered a village woman who, according to local rumor, kept a large amount of money hidden away in her home. A thief from Orel province broke into a neighboring woman's yard to steal flour in 1892, and when the owner came out and confronted him he murdered her with an ax. At the beginning of February 1899, an elderly woman and her granddaughter died at a neighbor's hands during a robbery in the village of Nizhnii Uslon, Kazan' province.[78]

Yet in a substantial and growing number of robbery-homicides, perpetrators did not know their victims; they encountered them by chance or, as already seen, through the commission of highway robbery and organized

76. "Muzheubiistvo," *SudG*, no. 23 (1902), 9–10. See also "Iunaia psikhopatka," *VolzhV*, no. 244 (1892), 3; A. Liubavskii, *Russkie ugolovnye protsessy*, vol. 3 (SPb, 1867), 272–332.

77. "Eletskia khronika," *OrlV*, no. 143 (1898), 2–4; no. 144, 2. See also "Nizhegorodskii okruzhnyi sud. Ubiistvo," *NizhL*, no. 9 (1899), 4; no. 10, 4; "Chetyre zhertvy ubiistva," *VolzhV*, no. 147 (1899), 3; "Ubiistvo trekh lits," *NizhL*, no. 38 (1901), 3.

78. "Ubiistvo s tsel'iu grabezha," *SudG*, no. 13 (1891), 9–10; "Nevol'nyi ubiitsa," *VolzhV*, no. 252 (1892), 3; "S. Nizhnii Uslon, Kaz. gub. Sviiazh. uezda," *VolzhV*, no. 35 (1899), 3.

assault. During the 1892 famine, Mukhamet Gaifullin was passing through one village of Kazan' province and stopped to beg hospitality from a local family, who offered him lodging for the night but refused him bread since they did not have enough even for themselves. Gaifullin arose during the night because of hunger, seized a hatchet, and murdered the entire family, then took food and other property and rode off on their horse.[79] In another case, two peasants who met by chance at a station of the Riazan'-Urals railroad in July 1895 went into a nearby woodlot to share two bottles of vodka and bread while waiting for a delayed train. On the following day, one of them was found murdered, having been killed by the other and robbed of wages he had just received.[80] As for those who practiced robbery, many were escaped Siberian exiles or belonged to organized gangs—themselves often led by escapees. In early 1912, a well-to-do flour trader was returning from business in Riazan''s Zaraisk district carrying no less than 1,000 rubles. Along the way he was attacked, robbed, and murdered by two repeat offenders, one of whom had escaped from the Iaroslavl' transit prison in 1910 while awaiting exile to Siberia.[81]

Representations of popular violence circulated widely throughout Russian society during the nineteenth and twentieth centuries and are readily available in the historical literature as well. These elite-generated images were not without foundation, for violence was a reality of daily life among peasants and workers alike and remained pervasive in a society where relations between superiors and subordinates so often rested upon violence or the threat of its application. The examples discussed in this chapter, and many more like them, attest to the role that aggression and confrontation played in rural communities that were characterized not only by solidarity against external and internal forces of disorder but by what anthropologist David Gilmore has termed "the unrelenting interpersonal combat of internecine rivalries and jealousies."[82] But such cases also demonstrate the distinct limits of informal community mechanisms of social control in channeling aggression or preventing confrontations from escalating to outright violence. External, formalized mechanisms, such as they were, usually fared

79. "Iz-za nuzhdy," *VolzhV,* no. 110, 1892, 3.

80. GARO, f. 640, op. 51, sv. 154, d. 575, ll. 4–7ob. See also "Kniagininskii uezd. (Ubiistvo)," *NizhL,* no. 42 (1901), 3.

81. Ibid., op. 55, sv. 42, d. 59, ll. 12–14, 97, 100–100ob., 204–5, 2300b.–233ob. See also "Arkhangel'sk. Ubiistvo," *SevK,* no. 68 (1899), 2–3. The sizable number of escapees later tried for perpetrating other crimes provides at least a rough sense of the quantitative dimension of this serious problem. See, e.g., GARO, f. 640, op. 52, sv. 111, d. 20 (1869); sv. 114, d. 70 (1873); sv. 120, dd. 124–127 (1877).

82. Gilmore, *Aggression and Community,* 27.

even worse, given the lack of a police presence at the village level, and state power in the form of law, higher judicial institutions, and district and provincial officials could do little to control, let alone prevent, localized or interpersonal violence.[83] From a local perspective, the state proved unable to manage effectively its prison and exile systems, which were ostensibly intended to remove sources of violence from society. Scarce resources and inefficient management allowed escapees by the thousands to wander the countryside, thereby contributing to some of the more frightening and worrisome violent crimes.

Apart from the salvos against official violence fired by educated opponents of the autocracy, however, the charge of violence came to rest squarely on the lower classes and to symbolize their cultural deficiencies. In the view of educated society, violence remained closely linked to what were seen as the terrible conditions of rural life. Sunk in ignorance and superstition, beset by poverty and degradation, peasants and workers alike, many argued, turned to alcohol, savage violence, and sexual depravity that merely reflected the decline of morality, the general collapse of the family and of patriarchal principles, and, increasingly, the degeneration to be found among lower-class Russians. In a very real sense, of course, these opinions simply fed upon themselves. As the many problems of peasant society came ever more frequently to public and government attention during the postemancipation decades, the "dark side" of village life looked ever darker until, for some, it seemed to dominate if not define the very character of "the peasant." Representations in the Russian press appeared to legitimize and reify such assumptions, and middle- and upper-class observers came to see violence as a natural if frightening feature of rural social relations. The lack of attention paid to honor among villagers, for example, determined that the many *volost'* court cases involving insult would be viewed in a much different context of malicious litigation over insignificant matters, a telling sign of the breakdown of the "traditional" peasant community. Ritual fighting, when shorn of its festive elements in brief news reports, offered a still sharper symbol of degeneration. Even violent assault and homicide fed representations of rural life in the very way they were reported. What was important to the press was not background detail or the complexity of relations between victim and assailant but, quite simply, the *fact* of brutal violence and bloodshed.

As with property offenses, in most crimes of violence committed against persons villagers were perpetrators and victims. Violent assaults upon mem-

---

83. The problem of social control in small communities has been widely studied by anthropologists. See, e.g., P. H. Gulliver, *Social Control in an African Society: A Study of the Arusha, Agrieultural Masai of Northern Tanganyika* (Boston, 1963); Gilmore, *Aggression and Community*, esp. 26–28; Laura Nader, *Harmony Ideology* (Stanford, 1990).

bers of privileged society or officialdom received far greater press coverage, however, as well as often severe treatment at the hands of the criminal courts and by administrative punishment or courts martial. In effect, a largely unwritten distinction in judicial and penal policy categorized violence according to its level of danger to the established order; less threatening cases could or had to be tolerated as a fact of village life. When perpetrated by peasants against other peasants, violence could be readily explained if not pardoned. Except for the most heinous crimes, thousands of incidents throughout our period show in no uncertain terms how courts mitigated sentences based on the "extreme ignorance" of the accused. Imperial manifestos served the same purpose. Since the state and many privileged Russians characterized peasant society by the mythical simplicity, ignorance, and embarrassing backwardness of its members, they could not be held fully accountable for the insult and violence they inflicted upon one another. Such a view thus rationalized intravillage violence, and at a subtler level it exonerated the state's inability or unwillingness to enter local society as a mediator of conflict rather than as a demanding and sometimes coercive collector of fiscal resources. This view also provides an important commentary on the lesser value that government and educated society placed upon life and person among the lower classes. Villagers therefore continued to deal with the consequences of uncontrolled (or uncontrollable) aggression much as they had in the past, utilizing public opinion or courts when this proved possible, but finding themselves increasingly forced to apply negative community sanctions at the most extreme level by meeting violence with violent reprisal.

# CHAPTER 6

# Questions of Belief

## *"Superstition," Crime, and the Law*

*Thou shall not permit a sorceress to live.*

EXODUS 22:18

As recounted by the well-known jurist and legal scholar P. N. Obninskii in *The Juridical Bulletin*, the following events took place during the early 1880s in a village "very close to one of [Russia's] cultural and industrial centers," with a population engaged for most of the year at factory work. The life of a peasant family of average means—husband and wife, both about forty years old, and the latter's mother, Mar'ia—went along peaceably and without discord, we are told, until a demon (*nechistaia sila*) disrupted their seeming harmony by possessing first the husband and then his wife. Though our source does not tell us how, the couple managed to rid themselves of the evil spirit but soon suspected that it had entered the old woman. Believing themselves now blessed with an ability to drive out the *nechistaia*, they exhorted Mar'ia to undergo an exorcism but she refused, fervently maintaining that no demon possessed her. The couple attributed such stubbornness to the spirit's malevolent power and resolved to use force and ritual to save the woman. For this purpose, relatives were summoned to a gathering at the family house. Then, with her mother sitting on a bench, the daughter held her hand firmly and repeated the incantation, "Begone, evil spirit, from Mar'ia, slave of God." Angrily, her mother pulled away, saying, "What are you doing casting spells on me? There's no demon inside me." But the daughter held her so tightly that she began to scream and turning to those in the room shouted, "And you just stand there, girls, while she's murdering me!" At this outburst her son-in-law jumped from his seat and struck Mar'ia in the head with a book for refusing to obey. While their relatives prayed fervently, Mar'ia was dragged into the street, where the "operation" continued in full view of a crowd of curious villagers. Struggling desperately to escape, the old woman begged her neighbors for help but was again struck in the head by her son-in-law and fell to the ground. The daughter quickly sat astride her mother and started choking her. "Strangle her," shouted one of the onlookers, as others cursed the evil spirit. Most stood silently by, crossing themselves. As she continued her "manipulations," the daughter repeated over and over, "Begone, evil spirit." Suddenly, a deathlike wheeze was heard, and when it ceased, Mar'ia was dead. After assuring one another that "the demon has been killed," the crowd dispersed.[1]

This incident can be read in various ways. For jurists and other educated Russians who learned of it through filtered accounts, Mar'ia's death was, indisputably, a homicide. Though some predictably referred to peasant ignorance and superstition and the low level of village morals, the facts, nevertheless, seemed irrefutable: A wife and her husband tortured, beat, and ceremonially murdered a helpless old woman in public, making no attempt to conceal their deed or to convince fellow villagers to remain silent about what had transpired. Therefore authorities took the couple into custody, subjected them to psychological examinations, and when they proved to be of sound minds, placed them on trial for murder.[2]

It is certainly possible that the daughter and son-in-law contrived this story of demonic possession as a convenient ploy to get rid of Mar'ia, who may have been a burden to them. Perhaps they hated her for unknown reasons and were determined to go to any lengths in order to be free of her. A dispute over family property and allotment land, their use or inheritance, too, may have been at the basis of these concealed tensions. Such background details often escaped police officials and judicial investigators and thus fail to appear in the court record. In view of what we know about popular religion and spirit possession among peasants in Russia and elsewhere, it is just as likely, however, that the couple firmly believed Mar'ia to be possessed and tried to save her through a combination of prayer and their understanding of how an exorcism should be performed. Orthodoxy and popular belief had, after all, blended quite comfortably within village culture over many centuries and continued to do so throughout our period, as shown by the villagers' use of prayer and their calling upon the powers of God. Equally important, the phenomenon of spirit possession remained widespread in postemancipation Russia, not only among the rural population but in towns and cities as well.[3]

1. P. N. Obninskii, "V oblasti sueverii i predrassudkov (Ocherk iz byta sovremennoi derevni)," *IuV*, no. 11 (1890), 360–62. For similar cases, see "Po Rossii," *OrlV*, no. 254 (1898), 3; "S. Vakino, Zaraiskogo uezda," *RiazV*, no. 262 (1909), 3.

2. Obninskii, "V oblasti sueverii i predrassudkov," 362.

3. On August 3, 1865, for example, the governor of Riazan' province received a letter from a thirty-year-old portrait painter who resided in the town of Ranenburg requesting that the governor use his influence and pressure Church authorities to drive out a demon that had possessed him. He explained that seven years earlier, while visiting the town of Tiumen in Tobol'sk province, this demon had entered through his breast while he was drinking tea. He had re-

Although these might all be plausible explanations, our source's silence prevents us from recovering the couple's true motivations. But we need not dwell over the question of whether, in this particular case, they actually believed in spirit possession or merely used the accusation for their own ends. Of greater importance is the fact that they justified their actions in a language drawn directly from village culture and experience (including the experience and understanding of Orthodoxy or its sectarian competitors), a language that not only reflected but also served to legitimate rural popular culture much as other cultural forms did within the urban milieu. It was a language often poorly understood by representatives of the state and by educated society, though villagers who witnessed the exorcism participated easily in the discourse unfolding before them and evidently accepted it, along with its deeper, symbolic implications. In accepting the language they endorsed the ideas that informed and shaped it, thereby bringing this cultural thread full circle. Together with similar cases tried before circuit and peace courts, then, Mar'ia's murder attests to the continued vitality of popular belief concerning sickness and the supernatural, as well as peasant understanding of the natural world and the forces by which it was governed.[4]

What is equally evident from this case is the way certain deep-rooted ideas held by peasants led to conflict with Church and state, both of which had long ago defined a large sphere of popular practices and beliefs as contrary to official Orthodoxy and law. Hence the real struggle should be viewed as a conflict between official and popular or what one historian has termed "alternative" beliefs, with the latter labeled superstitions not only by clerics and state officials but by other educated Russians as well.[5] Unlike

---

mained in Tiumen for four years "like a dead person," unable to work, then was brought back to Ranenburg by the police, but priests there would not agree to perform an exorcism. GARO, f. 5, st. 1, op. 2, d. 1200, ll. 1–4.

4. Among numerous sources discussing "unclean spirits," spirit possession, and magic, see RIAMZ, III/878, "Sueverie," no. 4 (Kasimov district, village of Telebukino); B. M. Firsov and I. G. Kiseleva, *Byt velikorusskikh krest'ian-zemlepashtsev* (SPb, 1993), 121–23; Stephen P. Frank, "Cultural Conflict and Criminality in Rural Russia, 1861–1900" (Ph.D. diss., Brown University, 1987), 102–13; Christine D. Worobec, "Witchcraft Beliefs and Practices in Prerevolutionary Russian and Ukrainian Villages," *RR* 54 (1995), 165–87. Compare Eugen Weber, *Peasants into Frenchmen* (Stanford, 1976), 23–29; Judith Devlin, *The Superstitious Mind: French Peasants and the Supernatural in the Nineteenth Century* (New Haven, 1987), 120–39; Jeanne Favret-Saada, *Deadly Words: Witchcraft in the Bocage* (Cambridge, 1980).

5. See Robert W. Bushaway, "'Tacit, Unsuspected, but Still Implicit Faith': Alternative Belief in Nineteenth-Century Rural England," in Tim Harris, ed., *Popular Culture in England, c. 1500–1850* (London, 1995), 189–215. As Roger Chartier has noted of the way clerics invented "popular religion" by the very act of defining it, "the religion of the masses, whether 'popular' or not, was determined by censorship that aimed to interiorize a system of perception created by the clergy." "Culture as Appropriation: Popular Cultural Uses in Early Modern Europe," in Steven L. Kaplan, ed., *Understanding Popular Culture* (New York, 1984), 229–31. See also Yves-Marie Hilaire, *Une chrétienté au XIXe siècle? La vie religieuse des populations du diocèse*

instances of collective community reprisal, however, those dealt with here did not necessarily entail villagers taking the law into their own hands to punish a criminal. Rather, peasants acted on faith and assumptions that what they were doing was necessary for ending a misfortune such as illness, drought, or crop failure or that it would bring them luck in life. Similar ideas might be employed to discover the perpetrator of a crime. But when popular belief led to actions that challenged the precepts of Church and state law, these not only became criminal deeds but, for government and educated society alike, proof of the peasantry's cultural deficiencies. Within the ambit of Russia's reformed courts, as in other arenas where peasant and official Russia met, two interconnected yet distinct cultures thus faced one another across a chasm of mutual suspicion and incomprehension.

According to critics like Obninskii, the new legal profession was itself chiefly responsible for this incomprehension, for its own preoccupations left it, at best, inadequately informed about what went on outside the major cities in district assemblies or in small towns and villages. What happens where "superstitious delusions" all too often intrude into judicial life, he complained, "we know about only in snatches and by chance."[6] Hence it was largely the press that disseminated images and interpretations of crimes committed as a result of "superstition" and thereby perpetuated the gloomy picture of peasant otherness. Some who interacted with peasants through the courts agreed fully with Obninskii and felt that significant aspects of rural juridical life were being ignored. As former justice of the peace P. A. Tulub wrote in 1901, "The question of superstition as a motive in the criminal infringement of the law is not an idle one, particularly for us in Russia, where many crimes occur precisely because of the superstitious ignorance of the Russian countryside. It is a pity, therefore, that nowadays almost nothing is written about the superstition of the masses, neither in general nor in specialized juridical literature." The jurist A. A. Levenstim also noted that, although journals in the 1860s had "paid much attention to superstition as a source of crime," it had recently "disappeared completely from juridical literature."[7]

The problem was certainly not that beliefs termed superstition had suddenly vanished among the rural—or urban—population. The Orthodox church, in particular, fretted about the dangers of popular superstitions

---

d'Arras (*1840–1914*), 2 vols. (Lille, 1977); John M. Ingham, *Mary, Michael, and Lucifer: Folk Catholicism in Central Mexico* (Austin, 1986).

6. Obninskii, "V oblasti sueverii," 359.

7. P. A. Tulub, "Sueverie i prestuplenie (Iz vospominanii mirovogo sud'i)," *IV* 83 (1901), 1082; A. A. Levenstim, "Sueverie v ego otnoshenie k ugolovnomu pravu," *ZhMIu*, no. 1 (1897), 157. Levenstim exaggerated here, for even in the 1860s only priests, folklorists, and amateur ethnographers wrote on this subject, usually in the provincial gazettes.

throughout our period and continued to be a primary force in defining the very parameters of "superstition" and of non-Orthodox or sectarian religious beliefs. Likewise, to a judge faced with the murder of a deformed child or a "possessed" old woman named Mar'ia, or a justice of the peace hearing pleas to try cases of witchcraft, rural Russia teemed with age-old, dangerous beliefs that were far from dying out. "Superstition is deeply imbedded within the dark masses of our peasants," declared Levenstim in 1897. "The masses to-day remain in an impenetrable darkness."[8] According to Tulub, superstition had settled firmly at the very depths of popular life, and to root it out was no easy matter for it provided "a quick and satisfactory answer to many questions which fill the mind of the simple person who stands face to face with nature, with its majestic and incomprehensible phenomena and with its misfortunes like bad harvests, drought, hail, sickness, and plague." Although Russia's progress could not be doubted, its main impact had been felt among the upper classes. The expansion of education and literacy was certainly a good thing, but these improvements "are like drops in a sea of popular darkness [*mrak*]."[9] In 1904 a member of Sergei Witte's Committee on the Needs of Agriculture claimed that "from childhood [the peasant] is used to finding everywhere in nature only evil beings: the wood goblin in the forest, a mermaid or sprite in the water, a house spirit [*domovoi*] around the home and yard, witches, etc., and therefore he fears all surrounding nature."[10] For his part, Obninskii argued that an understanding of crimes of superstition required "a certain evolution of juridical intellect and a broad erudition in anthropology, ethnography, and the history of epic popular beliefs."[11] Clearly, writers such as these believed that without concrete knowledge of popular life no insight could be gained into the complex link between crime and superstition.

There were several areas of peasant belief that led, in different ways, to contact and conflict with the state through crimes as defined under the empire's legal code. Although such acts accounted for only a small proportion of rural offenses recorded in Russia's judicial statistics, Church and government documents reveal that far more were not reported or not prosecuted for lack of evidence. Yet the fact that the press and reading public paid so much attention to these crimes tells us that they played a crucial role in forming elite representations of peasant criminality and culture, for few other acts, it was believed, spoke so directly to rural ignorance as did offenses committed as the result of peasant "superstition." The crimes them-

8. Levenstim, "Sueverie," no. 1, 160.

9. Tulub, "Sueverie," 1083.

10. N. L. Peterson, *Prosveshchenie. Svod trudov mestnykh komitetov po 49 guberniiam Evropeiskoi Rossii* (SPb, 1904), 10. See also RIAMZ, III/277, ll. 1–2.

11. Obninskii, "V oblasti sueverii," 362, 368–69.

selves, their interpretation by outsiders, and the beliefs from which they stemmed can serve as an important source for seeking out the attitudes of peasants and state law toward one another. At the same time, they help to explain why popular culture continued to be viewed with suspicion and hostility by Church and state, as well as why it came under increasingly bitter attack by members of Russia's new professions during the second half of the nineteenth century.

## FOUNDATIONS OF PERSECUTION: CRIMES AGAINST THE FAITH

The state and Church had sought for centuries to eradicate what they defined as the superstitious remnants of paganism that permeated popular culture. In the process, they displayed a staunch ideological intolerance toward unsanctioned faiths and beliefs deemed dangerous and created a body of criminal law for punishing deviants.[12] Throughout the nineteenth century the official church persisted in its struggle against rural superstition, but as was true in earlier times, its own symbols and rituals inadvertently provided guidance for many of the practices it condemned. As late as 1913, the Holy Synod wrote to the Ministry of Justice protesting a practice whereby judicial authorities in one court circuit requested local priests to make suspects swear their innocence or confess before a miracle-working icon. Priests were often forced to travel long distances for this purpose. In concurring with a complaint from diocesan officials, the Synod specifically protested the use of a holy icon as an instrument of crime detection and the participation of Church servants in that process.[13] No analogies were drawn, of course, between this apparently common ritual and those that Church and lay officials condemned as superstitious rural ignorance, despite their similarities in method and purpose. Indeed, the peasant practice of oath taking before a cross or icon was not an ancient, customary procedure

12. See, e.g., Daniel H. Kaiser, *The Growth of the Law in Medieval Russia* (Princeton, 1980); "Bor'ba pastyria Tserkvi s sueveriem," *RSP,* no. 8 (1889), 227–33; no. 10, 303–9; no. 11, 339–47; no. 14, 424–31; no. 18, 539–45; "Iz istorii bor'by pravoslavnogo dukhovenstva s sueveriiami," *RSP* 41, no. 19 (1900), 7–19; A. A. Levenstim, "Sueverie i ugolovnoe pravo. Issledovanie po istorii russkogo prava i kul'tury," *VestP,* no. 1 (1906), 291–343; no. 2, 181–251; N. N. Pokrovskii, "Dokumenty XVIII v. ob otnoshenii Sinoda k narodnym kalendarnym obriadam," *SE,* no. 5 (1981), 96–108.

13. "Ikony, kak orudie rozyska," *RiazV,* no. 163 (1913), 1. See also "Vrednoe nasledstvie odnogo narodnogo suevernogo obychaia," *Penzenskie eparkhial'nye vedomosti,* no. 3 (1869), 89–92; Sv. Evgenii Smirnov, "Po voprosu o bor'be sel'skikh pastyrei s znakhariami i vorozheiami," *RiazEV* 25, no. 5 (1890), 242–44; "O narodnykh sueveriiakh," *Saratovskie eparkhial'nye vedomosti,* no. 9 (1873), 218–34; "Bor'ba pastyria Tserkvi s sueveriem," *RiazEV* 25, no. 2 (1890), 100–102; N. F. Sumtsov, *O tom, kakie sel'skie pover'ia i obychai v osobennosti vredny* (Khar'kov, 1897).

followed in village courts but rather one that had been directly adopted from formal courts.[14]

The same can be said about villagers' employment of other religious symbols, such as the cross or holy water, in popular crime detection. In 1895 peasants from one Iaroslavl' village sought to determine who had cast a spell on a "hysterical" women by giving her holy water to drink. Shortly thereafter she was able to tell them the name of the culprit, who a crowd subsequently murdered.[15] Elsewhere, villagers would light a green candle before the church icon as a means of discovering who had perpetrated theft against them. Terrible torments stemming directly from heaven, it was believed, would force the thief to return the stolen goods. Saints, too, were commonly called upon to intervene in solving a crime.[16] The real issue in all such cases was not so much the *use* of religious objects outside the confines of the church; rather, it concerned the possession and misuse of holy objects by the laity. The power to employ religion within the broader realm of daily life lay at the heart of this long-running struggle.

The state usually supported Church efforts to control its symbols, combat superstition, and punish deviation from the faith, but authorities showed even greater concern about the possibility of sedition or disorder, which they believed were inherent to outlawed religious practices and movements. In 1864, for example, *The Moscow Herald* (*Moskovskie vedomosti*) reported that a Riazan' peasant had become renowned for his ability to perform miraculous cures and to drive demons from those possessed by evil spirits. This news so concerned Riazan''s governor that he ordered an investigation, and the resulting report provides several revealing hints as to what worried authorities most. One Vasilii Ermolaev from Dereviannoe village (Spassk district) was the peasant involved, and he had indeed attracted many people who asked him for prayers that would cure them of various illnesses. Ermo-

---

14. N. A. Minenko, "Traditional Forms of Investigation and Trial among the Russian Peasants of Western Siberia in the 18th and First Half of the 19th c." *SAA* 21, no. 3 (1982–83), 65. On oaths in peasant litigation, see GARF, f. 586, op. 1, d. 120, ll. 29, 113–16; d. 118, l. 19; A. A. Levenstim, "Prisiaga na sude po narodnym vozzreniiam," *VestP* 31, no. 6 (1901), 1–26; A. Pappe, "O dokazatel'stvakh na volostnom sude," in *Sbornik svedenii dlia izucheniia byta krest'ianskogo naseleniia Rossii (SbSiBKNR)*, M. N. Kharuzin, ed., part 1 (Moscow, 1889), 19–24.

15. *Nedelia*, no. 52 (1895), 1674–75.

16. E. I. Iakushkin, "Molitvy i zagovory v Poshekhonskom uezde," *Trudy Iaroslavskogo gubernskogo statisticheskogo komiteta*, no. 5 (Iaroslavl', 1868), 159–82; Iakushkin, "Zametki o vliianii religioznykh verovanii i predrazsudkov na narodnye iuridicheskie obychai i poniatiia," *EtnogO*, no. 2 (1891), 8–9; A. Fon-Kremer, "Obychai, pover'ia i predrassudki krest'ian sela Verkhotishanki," *Pamiatnaia knizhka Voronezhskoi gubernii na 1870–1871 god* (Voronezh, 1871), 279–81. Compare these practices with such rituals as *vmazyvanie* (discussed below), the purpose of which was identical.

laev satisfied their wishes by conducting prayer readings, some of which, the police report states, "even took place in public." No books contrary to the Christian religion could be found, however. Together with his daughter Anna, Ermolaev had also established a site for pilgrims in their village, and despite a direct order from the district commandant forbidding people from visiting it, large numbers continued to do so. As a result, "superstition grew among the peasants and rumors concerning unnatural prophesies quickly spread." With pilgrims flocking illegally to the Ermolaevs and strange rumors being disseminated (a perennial concern to the state), police arrested the faith healer and his daughter and turned them over for prosecution before the Spassk District Court (*uezdnyi sud*). Although authorities found that the Ermolaevs were guided solely by religious passion and had not engaged in any sort of deception or swindling for personal gain, their presence in Dereviannoe could not be tolerated because of possible disorder and the potential for sedition stemming from rumors.[17]

Certainly the best example of cooperation between Church and state in the definition and criminalization of popular belief can be found in their prosecution of religious offenses—crimes that remained felonies throughout our period. During the years 1834–60, nearly 5 percent of all peasants prosecuted before higher criminal courts stood charged with "crimes against the faith." For women, this figure reached as high as 18 percent in the 1850s and averaged about 12 percent during the second quarter of the nineteenth century.[18] Despite a sharp decline in prosecutions after emancipation, religious crimes could still bring some of the harshest punishments meted out under Russia's 1885 penal code. Blasphemy (*bogokhulenie*) in a church carried a twelve- to fifteen-year sentence of exile at hard labor and loss of all civil rights (art. 176), and speaking blasphemous words in a public place without intending to insult an object of worship, especially if this was done out of ignorance or when drunk, might bring a mitigated prison sentence of up to eighteen months (art. 180).[19] The Riazan' peasant Ignat Sedyi was thus charged at the beginning of 1913. When he returned home drunk one morning and began cursing his wife and brother, the latter told him to stop swearing because a church service was under way. Ignat re-

17. GARO, f. 5, st. 1, op. 2, d. 1166, ll. 1–30b.

18. *Otchet Ministerstva Iustitsii* (SPb, 1934–71), vols. 1–35 (hereafter: *Otchety*). See also E. N. Tarnovskii, "Religioznye prestupleniia v Rossii," *VestP,* no. 4 (1899), 1–27; Popov, *Sud i nakazaniia,* 201–370; A. M. Bobrishchev-Pushkin, *Sud i raskol'niki sektanty* (SPb, 1902); N. D. Sergeevich, "K ucheniiu o prestupleniiakh religioznykh," *ZhMIu,* no. 4 (1906), 13–49.

19. *SZU,* part 1, 37–38. See also "Iz Sbornika statei sudebnykh ustavov 20 Noiabria 1864 g., imeiushchikh otnoshenie k vedomstvu Pravoslavnogo Ispovedaniia," *Vladimirskie eparkhial'nye vedomosti,* no. 1 (1873), 18–24; *Razvitie russkogo prava v pervoi polovine XIX veka* (Moscow, 1994), 171–74.

sponded by uttering several particularly offensive curses, for which, after being denounced by his family, he was tried before a circuit court.[20]

The crime of faith deemed most dangerous by religious and secular authorities was adhering to what they labeled—in a revealing mystification— the "superstitious" and "fanatical" teachings of schismatic or heretical sects. Although legal prosecution of sectarians had subsided significantly after 1861, several heresies continued to be vigorously investigated and prosecuted. These were above all mystical sects like the *khlysty* (flagellants), *molokane* (milk drinkers), and *skoptsy* (castrators), whose teachings and practices not only challenged established Orthodoxy but seemed to scorn all accepted norms of marital and sexual relations.[21] Judging by church investigations and judicial prosecutions during the postemancipation era, the *skoptsy* presented the greatest threat to established moral authority. It is questionable, however, whether "heretical" religious beliefs and "superstition" constituted the true basis for persecution, or whether, as A. I. Klibanov suggests, efforts at suppression stemmed more from the rejection by *khlysty* or *skoptsy* of "the traditional basis of family as sanctified by the Church," expressed in an extreme asceticism that led some (both men and women) to practice castration or sexual mutilation. From this perspective, sectarians like the *skoptsy* represented sexual outlaws in the eyes of officialdom, and the body, sexuality, and procreation, rather than theology, formed the arena of contention.[22]

Whether their activities were real or imagined, *khlysty, molokane,* and *skoptsy* seemed to spring up throughout the Russian countryside, and police officials conducted innumerable investigations of their activities, usually at the behest of diocesan officials.[23] The sheer quantity of time dedicated to

20. GARO, f. 640, op. 51, sv. 196, d. 1243, l. 5. For additional examples, see, e.g., sv. 121, d. 161 (1878); sv. 138, d. 353 (1885); sv. 158, d. 619 (1897); sv. 182, d. 987 (1907). Insulting a priest or holy objects, or interrupting a church service, could bring one as much as fifteen years at hard labor in Siberia. Leaving the Orthodox faith also remained a punishable felony. *SZU*, part 1, 32–42, 44–46, arts. 184–95, 210–18.

21. These sects emerged during the 1760s out of the *Khristoverie* (the "faith of Christ"), which A. I. Klibanov argues was the initial form of religious sectarianism in Russia whose roots trace to the mid-seventeenth century in Vladimir and Kostroma provinces. *History of Religious Sectarianism in Russia (1860s–1917)* (Oxford, 1982), 44–56, and, on the *Molokane,* 151–225. See also Konstantin Kutepov, *Sekty khlystov i skoptsov* (Kazan', 1882); D. Chudovskii, *Sbornik tsirkuliarov i instruktsii Ministerstva Vnutrennikh Del za 1862, 1863 i 1864 gody* (SPb, 1873), 1–2.

22. Klibanov rightly cautions that missionary and Church literature reduced the religious practice of such sects almost wholly "to sexual orgies as an inevitable accompaniment of their ecstatic rites." This depiction, "intended to arouse public opinion against them and bring down on them the retribution of state authorities," carried over into the secular literature as well. *History,* 52–53. See also GARO, f. 640, op. 51, sv. 152 (1894), d. 563, ll. 1–48; N. Charov, "Chto takie 'skoptsy,'" *RiazZh,* no. 13 (1913), 3.

23. GARO, f. 627, st. 1, op. 139 (1880), sv. 2083, d. 41; op. 148 (1889), sv. 2102, d. 28; f. 641, op. 4 (1869), sv. 8, d. 10; f. 5, st. 3, op. 4, d. 1104 (1869); dd. 1214, 1216 (1872); d. 1522 (1875).

such inquiries is surprising in view of the slender police resources at each governor's disposal. Take, for example, the Skopin district of Riazan' province, where *skoptsy* fell subject to constant scrutiny and persecution both before and after emancipation. In this district's third *okrug,* Church and police officials spent nearly two years (1889–90) investigating a priest's denunciation of several of his parishioners who supposedly had become *skoptsy.*[24] In 1901, police arrested sixty peasants on charges of belonging to the *skoptsy* and conducted an extensive investigation. When they at last came to trial in 1904, most were found guilty and sentenced to exile (though appeals dragged on until 1910). At another mass trial of forty-seven in 1913, a jury acquitted the entire group.[25] That same year, the Riazan' Spiritual Consistory ordered a rural dean (*blagochinyi*) and police commandant to undertake an "exhaustive investigation" into the rumored "seduction" of a local peasant by members of the "fanatical sect" of *khlysty,* with particular attention to the sect's activities, its attempted castration of the peasant, and the mutilation of his sister.[26]

Unfortunately, Church and judicial records tell us little about those accused of heresy or castration and offer even fewer clues concerning their beliefs. Many, of course, simply denied the accusations against them, as did Stepan Vasil'ev Dorozhkin of Skopin district, who was tried by the Riazan' Circuit Court in 1916 for belonging to a sect, "one of whose chief dogmatisms is the fanatical teaching of the necessity of harming or removing the sexual organs in order to save one's soul," and for castrating himself. Dorozhkin had been denounced by a neighbor, Il'ia Pravikov, with whom his family was on bad terms. Pravikov claimed he had once seen Dorozhkin's mother washing men's linen "covered with blood" and that he overheard an argument between the accused and his father during which the latter called Stepan "*beziaichnyi*" ("without testicles"), to which Stepan replied, "Well, you did it to me." An official medical examination revealed that Dorozhkin's penis and testicles had been removed—sufficient evidence, that is, for trial to proceed. Dorozhkin pleaded innocent, stating that he did not belong to the *skopcheskii* heresy. Rather, as he explained, in 1907 he had gone to Riazan' and found employment as the helper of a priest's gardener named Kornei Leonov, working there for two years. One night, he said, Leonov came to his room, threw a scarf over his face and held it until he lost consciousness. "Around lunch time on the following day, I came to and saw that someone had cut off my sexual member and testicles. Because I was

---

24. GARO, f. 627, st. 1, op. 148, sv. 2103, d. 42, ll. 1–45. See also f. 5, st. 3, op. 4, dd. 18, 28–30 (1842); dd. 104, 112–13, 118–19 (1849).

25. GARO, f. 641, op. 36, sv. 104, d. 62, ll. 1–419; f. 5, st. 1, op. 2, d. 2465, ll. 1–19; "Skoptsy," *RiazZh,* no. 5 (1916), 3; no. 9, 3; no. 10, 3; no. 11, 3; no. 19, 3.

26. GARO, f. 627, st. 1, op. 171, sv. 2165, d. 8, ll. 1–17ob.

embarrassed by this I complained to nobody and did not go to a doctor. After this I left for home." Given the accused's denials and with no additional evidence other than a neighbor's suspicions, the jury acquitted Dorozhkin.[27]

By contrast, in December 1902, Fedora Ignat'evna Ivanova appeared before the Skopin judicial investigator after having been denounced and freely testified that in 1901, following her son's conviction for belonging to the *skoptsy* and castrating himself, she also decided upon "castration" in order to be incarcerated and reunited with her son in prison, for which she would receive the Kingdom of Heaven. On the holiday of the Kazan' Mother of God (October 22, 1901), she took a sharp knife and sliced off her nipples and labia. Nobody instructed her how to do this, Ivanova insisted when pressed to denounce complicitors; rather, although she could not recall precisely when, she explained that she had once heard someone reading from the Gospels: "Castrate yourself for Heaven." Based on her own testimony, together with that of a doctor, the parish priest, district missionary, and several neighbors, Ivanova was charged in July 1903 "for the error of religious fanaticism, observing the teachings of the *skopcheskii* heresy" and for willingly mutilating herself. When asked how she pleaded, she declared to the court: "God knows if I am guilty or not, but I castrated myself for the Kingdom [of Heaven]. I don't belong to the *skopcheskii* heresy—I am an Orthodox." Found guilty, Ivanova did not receive her wish to join her son; instead she was sentenced to loss of all rights and exile for settlement.[28]

As these cases attest, it was the act of self-mutilation more than "heresy" itself (the beliefs of which were never discussed either in the indictments or during trials) that brought sectarians before state courts. Yet the laws under which they stood charged stemmed directly from the Church's continued authority to define deviance, superstition, and some forms of criminal behavior. Within this realm of popular religious faith and deviation, Church and state power remained inseparable, albeit unequal and, at times, diverging in intention. That is the ideological and legal framework where persecution of popular belief after 1861 must be situated. Despite the many accounts of the Russian peasantry's supposed "dual faith" (*dvoeverie*) that have shaped historical understanding of rural religion, charges of "superstition" cannot be separated from villagers' Orthodox religious faith (as seen in Fedora Ivanova's declaration). Hence we need to view the interplay between popular belief and its treatment as crime from several vantage

27. GARO, f. 640, op. 54, sv. 29, d. 46, part 1, ll. 39–44; part 2, ll. 9–9ob., 18–18ob.

28. GARO, f. 640, op. 51, sv. 168, d. 766, ll. 4–5ob., 23–26, 36–37. Women accounted for an average of only 11.4 percent of all persons prosecuted by circuit courts between 1872 and 1913, but made up 43.5 percent of those accused of *skopchestvo* (a figure that reached as high as 69 percent in 1896, and 100 percent in other years). *Svod statisticheskikh svedenii po delam ugolovnym*, 43 vols. (SPb, 1874–1916), part 2, table 1 (hereafter: *Svody*).

points, examining, in particular, the role of such beliefs in daily life and the ways in which they fell outside of accepted Church-state ideology, thereby "becoming" criminal acts subject to much the same virulent denunciation and prosecution as were sectarians like the *skoptsy*.

## INVESTIGATING CRIME

As culturally and temporally relative concepts, evidence and proof differ from place to place, within and between societies, and from one period to another.[29] Russian peasants often put popular belief to practical use if a criminal's identity could not otherwise be determined, but when they did so they brought harsh criticism upon themselves from educated outsiders. As Levenstim wrote in 1899, judges who tried cases concerning the murder of horsethieves or sorcerers were often astounded not only by the peasants' cruelty "but by the complete lack of evidence regarding the murdered person's crime." Investigators simply could not understand "the obstinacy" of criminal accusations or the manner in which peasants commonly established facts "on the basis of beliefs, customs, and methods whose foundation is the crudest superstition." Such cases revealed the "abyss" that lay "between the views of the state court and the dark mass of the people about the force of evidence."[30] This was true enough from the author's perspective, but villagers did not believe that the evidence they possessed had no basis in fact. Experience taught that although their methods might not always prove effective, they had brought success on enough occasions to be retained as part of the peasants' crime-fighting arsenal; otherwise, they would surely have been abandoned. As Abner Cohen has argued, such "survivals from the past" continue in practice "not because of inertia or of conservatism, but because they play important roles within contemporary social settings."[31] That these methods were based on "the crudest superstition" was, doubtless, of little concern to peasants who employed them, for the term "superstition" as used by outsiders was rarely encountered in that distinct cultural language of the village except as adapted (or adopted) from teachings of priests and educators.[32]

29. Walter Goldschmidt, *Sebei Law* (Berkeley, 1967), 163–68, 225–44; Pierre Bourdieu, *Outline of a Theory of Practice* (Cambridge, 1977), 16–17; Clifford Geertz, *Local Knowledge: Further Essays in Interpretive Anthropology* (New York, 1983), 167–234.

30. A. A. Levenstim, *Sueverie i ugolovnoe pravo* (SPb, 1899), 59. See also GARF, f. 586, op. 1, d. 118, l. 18; I. Orshanskii, "Narodnyi sud i narodnoe pravo," *VestP*, no. 4, 208–11.

31. Abner Cohen, *Two Dimensional Man: An Essay on the Anthropology of Power and Symbolism in Complex Society* (London, 1974), 3. See also Favret-Saada, *Deadly Words*, 4–5.

32. Memoirs of peasant writers who had crossed cultural and class boundaries often display an embarrassed recollection of the "superstitions" that existed in their villages. See

One of the most common means for establishing guilt was to turn to a wiseperson (*znakhar'* or *znakharka*). Usually called upon for advice, to heal the sick, to cure disease among livestock, or to fight off a sorcerer's spells, they were also believed to possess the ability to see what others could not, and peasants came to them seeking assistance in finding lost objects, animals that had strayed, and stolen property. Since the powers of a *znakharka* and *znakhar'* were bestowed by God rather than the devil (from whom witches and sorcerers drew their strength), thieves could not hide from them. Belief in the divine origin of their knowledge helps to explain why peasants and, on occasion, even rural police, made such ready use of the wisewoman and her male counterpart, for these were powerful figures within the community. It is also an important reason why the evidence they offered was so readily accepted.[33]

As they did when healing, the *znakhar'* or *znakharka* combined prayer, incantations, and rituals to uncover the culprit in a creative appropriation and reworking of the symbols and spiritual power of official religion. Indeed, one reason the Church sought to root out this "superstition" was that practitioners appropriated and misused its rites and symbols.[34] In 1909, for example, a peasant woman in Iaroslavl' province turned to the wise women of her village for help in finding a thief. They told her to light a candle and place it before the royal gates of the church iconostasis, explaining that as the candle burned, the thief would suffer terrible convulsions and thereby

*RIAMZ*, no. 202: A. Algebranstov, "Ostatki iazychestva i predaniia moei rodiny;" no. 277: I. Sokolov, "Ostatki stariny sela Murmino, Riazanskogo uezda."

33. The role of a *znakhar'* was similar throughout the provinces of Russia and in much of rural Europe. See Firsov and Kiseleva, *Byt velikorusskikh krest'ian*, 129–30; M. Safonov, "Narodnoe znakharstvo," *SevV*, no. 5 (1894), pt. 2, 1–13; Evgenii Markov, "Derevenskii koldun," *IV* 28 (1887), 11–19; A. Kolchin, "Verovaniia krest'ian Tul'skoi gubernii," *EtnogO*, no. 3 (1899), 52–53; "S. Tuma, Kasimovskogo uezda," *RiazV*, no. 173 (1909), 3; Zavoiko, "Verovaniia, obriady i obychai," 114. On the divine origins of their powers, see RIAMZ, III/878, no. 292, "K materialam po Riazanskim sueveriiam," ll. 7–8; N. A. Minenko, *Zhivaia starina* (Novosibirsk, 1989), 113–26; M. M. Gromyko, *Traditsionnye normy povedeniia i formy obshcheniia russkikh krest'ian* (Moscow, 1986), 115–17. In *The People of the Sierra* (Chicago, 1971), 189–91, Julian A. Pitt-Rivers pointed to the powers of the wise woman in Spain as deriving from grace and noted that "the powers to whom her invocations are addressed are mainly [those] of the established religion." In Muscovite Russia, "*znakhar'*" referred to a witness for litigants in a trial. No reference is made to any special powers other than a good memory. Kaiser, *Growth of the Law*, 136–37.

34. *Materialy dlia geografii i statistiki Rossii, sobrannye ofitserami general'nogo shtaba. Riazanskaia guberniia* (SPb, 1860), 385–86; Smirnov, "Po voprosu o bor'be sel'skikh pastyrei," 242–43. For incantations, see E. N. Eleonskaia, *Skazka, zagovor i koldovstvo v Rossii* (Moscow, 1994; orig. 1917), 99–140; M. Zabylin, comp., *Russkii narod: ego obychai, obriady, predaniia, sueveriia i poeziia* (Moscow, 1989; orig. 1880), 320–34. On the appropriation of prayers used in incantations, see "O zaklinaniiakh," *RSP* 22, no. 48 (1881), 337–49. Prayer was a similarly essential element to folk healers in nineteenth-century rural France. Delvin, *Superstitious Mind*, 47–51.

be revealed.[35] The *znakhar'* might also employ a magical mirror that reflected a criminal's face after the Lord's name had been pronounced over it on three successive nights, or a cross that was passed over water to expose the thief. The *znakhar'* did not always provide a full description of the thief, however, but often told the victim only the guilty party's gender or hair and eye color. As a result, innocent people could be accused of crimes they did not commit. Beatings sometimes followed such accusations, and those charged with the crime "lose the trust and respect of the commune."[36]

Reading of cards by a fortuneteller or diviner (*gadal'shchik* or *gadalka*) was another tool employed to catch thieves. For example, in a small village near the town of Kherson, Marfa Artynova, a single, homeless woman, earned her keep by teaching peasant children to read and write, for which she received food and shelter. In 1884, while Artynova was teaching at the home of a local family, 100 rubles disappeared, and when a search turned up neither the money nor a suspect, the family consulted a fortuneteller. To everybody's surprise, this account reads, the cards implicated Artynova as the perpetrator. Since a fortuneteller's evidence was rarely questioned, Artynova's denials fell upon deaf ears. Her interrogators took her to the local cemetery, tied her to a cross, and whipped her until she was covered with welts, and when she persisted in denying any knowledge of the crime, they used pincers to pull the skin on her neck and tear her tongue, "until a stream of blood poured from her mouth." To her repeated entreaties for mercy villagers answered, "If you were innocent, then you would feel no pain." Finally Artynova was set free and managed to reach Kherson, where she lodged a formal complaint against her tormentors.[37]

Here is a good example of the type of incident against which Levenstim inveighed, and one that closely resembles cases of violent popular justice (*samosud*). Employing evidence based on their faith in divination, an informal gathering of peasants tried and punished Artynova for stealing. Perhaps

35. "S. Koz'modem'iansk, Posh. u," *Golos* [Iaroslavl'], no. 16 (1909), 3. This practice is also discussed in P. I. Astrov, "Ob uchastii sverkh"estestvennoi sily v narodnom sudoproizvodstve krest'ian Elatomskogo uezda Tambovskoi gubernii," Kharuzin, ed., *SbSiBKNR*, part 1, 56.

36. V. V. Tenishev, *Pravosudie* (Briansk, 1907), 152. See also Levenstim, *Sueverie i ugolovnoe pravo* (SPb, 1899), 64–66. In the 1920s peasants still turned to the *znakharka* to catch thieves. See, e.g., "'Znakharka.' Mishinskaia volost', Skopinskogo uezda," *Nasha derevnia* (Riazan'), no. 7 (1925), 3. Compare Robin Briggs, *Witches and Neighbors: The Social and Cultural Context of European Witchcraft* (New York, 1996), 171–87.

37. A. Kirpichnikov, "Ocherki po mifologii XIX veka," *EtnogO*, no. 4 (1894), 9–10. Divining was equally popular in towns and among educated Russians. I. P. Sakharov, *Skazaniia russkogo naroda* (SPb, 1885), 127; "Riazhsk. Gorod gadaet," *RiazZh*, no. 218 (1913), 3; "U gorodskikh sudei. Riazanskaia pifiia," *RiazZh*, no. 160 (1914), 3; V. Smirnov, "Narodnye gadan'ia Kostromskogo kraia," in *Chetvertyi etnograficheskii sbornik. Trudy Kostromskogo Nauchnogo Obshchestva po izucheniiu mestnogo kraia*, no. 41 (Kostroma, 1927), 17–91.

Marfa did steal the money and was willing to endure the villagers' wrath for a hundred rubles. Since the money could not be found, we have no way of knowing who took it. We do know, however, that in such cases the accused was often socially isolated within the community, having no family or property to provide protection and social standing. Artynova's social isolation and reliance on charity thus made her an ideal scapegoat. The only thing needed was evidence to support existing suspicions, and this the fortuneteller provided. It was, in fact, use of a fortuneteller that distinguished this case from other examples of *samosud,* as will be seen when we consider the role of the *znakhar'* and fortuneteller in establishing guilt.

Still another means of forcing a thief into the open was known, literally, as "cementing into the mouth of the stove" (*vmazyvanie v chelo*), a highly ritualized form of detection that appears to have been limited to northern provinces such as Novgorod and Vologda and to which peasants resorted when search, interrogation, and even divining had failed to solve a crime. As with most popular methods of detection, villagers conducted *vmazyvanie* publicly and usually with assistance from a *znakhar',* though a sorcerer might also be hired. During this ritual the victim took a piece of material similar to that which was stolen (such as sheepskin if the thief had made off with a coat, or fabric if linen had been taken) and glued it across the mouth of the stove while a *znakhar'* recited prayers designed specifically for this ceremony. When the stove was lit, the material smoldered and withered from the heat until finally consumed. As a result, it was believed, thieves would subsequently languish and grow sick or even die. If they did not confess, they would remain sickly and unable to work for the rest of their lives.[38] Describing such beliefs in Novgorod province, V. A. Antipov claimed that many peasants succumbed to the power of *vmazyvanie,* so convinced of this ritual's effectiveness that they confessed even before it began. In one village during the 1890s, a thief stole 500 rubles from a prosperous farmer, and while suspicion quickly fell on a young peasant who lived nearby, no incriminating evidence could be found. It was therefore decided "to cement the suspect in the stove," which was done with the use of a paper ruble and the aid of a sorcerer. The suspect, of course, was informed beforehand that the operation would soon take place. "From that time on," wrote Antipov, "he grew sickly. He had no particular illness but became weak and is now incapable of any type of work." Elsewhere in the same region, one woman stole some sackcloth from another. Knowing the thief's identity, the victim demanded that she return the cloth and, when she did not, threatened her with *vmazyvanie.* "On the following day, the thief began to have spasms in her arms and

38. V. A. Antipov, "Suevernye sredstva, upotrebliaemye krest'ianami dlia otkrytiia prestuplenii i prestupnikov," *ZhivSt* 15, no. 1, part 2 (1905), 552; N. Nadezhdin, "Nravy i obychai rodnogo severa," *ZhivRus* 2 (1902), 462; Iakushkin, "Molitvy i zagovory," 162.

legs, and she confessed to the crime and revealed where she had hidden the stolen fabric." Her affliction disappeared soon after.[39] Fear of *vmazyvanie* could even lead to an escalation of the crime, much as it did one day during 1894 in another village of Novgorod province where a suspected thief, fearful of the consequences of *vmazyvanie*, killed his accuser. Penal servitude, he calmly declared at his trial, was preferable. "At least I'll be healthy."[40]

Peasants in some localities possessed a unique method of compelling murder suspects to confess and sometimes solved the crime before investigating authorities arrived at the scene. To do so they gathered all villagers together and forced them to kiss the heel of the deceased. In parts of Novgorod province, for example, many believed that if a person was guilty, the corpse would give a sign, usually trembling or moving. Some claimed that it would leap up, seize the murderer, and strangle her or him. Such a possibility no doubt evoked sufficient fear to force a confession from any killer unwilling to tangle with the supernatural. When the night watchman was murdered during a local festival in a village of Ulomskaia township in 1894, several young men came under suspicion, but charges could not be brought for lack of witnesses. Still, wishing to clear their names, they demanded to kiss the corpse's heel and thereby prove their innocence. Perhaps they did not share the belief of their elders. Equally likely is that they did accept this belief and, knowing they had not committed murder, felt that kissing the corpse was the best way to end suspicion. The ritual was therefore arranged and each boy approached the corpse, crossed himself, then kissed its heel. After all of the suspects had performed this rite without eliciting any movement from the corpse, the remaining village boys were ordered to kiss its heel as well. When the turn of one quiet young man came, he stopped suddenly upon reaching the victim's body. As he later recounted, it seemed to him that the corpse began moving its brow and its fingers. The boy turned pale but he was seized and dragged forward. By this time he could no longer restrain himself, and in a quavering voice he shouted: "Stop, let me go! I killed him!" Several persons later testified that they had seen the corpse open its eyes and look directly at the murderer as he approached. The moment he confessed, the eyes closed.[41] Though conducted with less solemnity, variations on this practice were also noted among peasants of Riazan',

39. Antipov, "Suevernye sredstva," 552, 553.

40. Ibid., 533. Tenishev also notes a case of *vmazyvanie* that led to murder in the village of Parshino, Novgorod province. "Obshchie nachala," *ZhMIu*, no. 7 (1909), 119–58. See also V. Apellesov, "Strannyi sposob otyskivat' ukradennye veshchi," *Iaroslavskie eparkhial'nye vedomosti* (1871), 288.

41. Antipov, "Suevernye sredstva," 553–55. A similar case was recorded in this area as late as 1901.

Smolensk, and other central provinces at the end of the century. Here, however, a person suspected of homicide would simply be taken to view the corpse, "in the expectation that he will be unable to bear seeing the body and will therefore confess."[42]

Contrary to long-standing views of the Russian peasantry's "dual faith," popular religion posited a world in which the powers of God and those of the supernatural coexisted comfortably, with the line separating them often blurred or nonexistent. It was a religion well suited to the notions that God intervened in earthly matters to expose or punish a criminal and that people to whom particular skills had been granted could perform similar acts by calling upon God, the supernatural, or both.[43] Peasants treated such persons with a mixture of fear and respect and accepted evidence of guilt in criminal cases when it was presented by a *znakhar'* or diviner, for their faith provided a sound foundation of understanding on these matters. Belief, in turn, was the sole reason behind the success of rituals like *vmazyvanie,* which served also to maintain the reputation of a local sorcerer. In cases that involved divining, both the victim and other villagers had to believe in the powers of their *znakhar'.* During *vmazyvanie,* on the other hand, it became necessary to transform belief into terror, for otherwise the ritual would fail. Hence its public setting and the public announcement that it would be performed. Suspects were usually threatened beforehand, thereby allowing fear to take its toll. Belief in the ritual's effectiveness was strong enough to elicit confessions, as well as physical symptoms of illness or even murder committed by terrified thieves fearing for their lives.

Whether the diviner of signs and cards or the sorcerer at a *vmazyvanie* believed in their abilities is a different matter altogether. Judging by evidence from Russia, Western Europe, Africa, and Latin America, the primary role of "cunning folk" in village society was to provide their neighbors "with an explanation of and means for counteracting the hostile forces that assaulted them."[44] According to Keith Thomas, when detecting a thief, the cunning man "saw his main task as that of discovering the identity of the party whom the client himself most strongly suspected. Almost invariably, the client has a definite suspect in mind, but one for whose guilt conventional evidence is lacking. The diviner's task is to confirm those suspicions

42. GARF, f. 586, op. 1, d. 118, l. 36; d. 120, ll. 15, 19.

43. See ibid., d. 114, l. 6; d. 118, ll. 12, 14, 28; Zagoskin, *Otvety,* 93; Tenishev, "Obshchie nachala," 132–33; S. T. Semenev, *Dvadtsat' piat' let v derevne* (SPb, 1915), 42–43; Zavoiko, "Verovaniia," 115–19.

44. Clark Garrett, "Witches and Cunning Folk in the Old Regime," in Jacques Beauroy et al., eds., *The Wolf and the Lamb: Popular Culture in France from the Old Regime to the Twentieth Century* (Saratoga, CA, 1976), 56. See also Briggs, *Witches and Neighbors,* 122–26, 171–74; Robert M. Berndt, *Excess and Restraint: Social Control among a New Guinea Mountain People* (Chicago, 1962), 208–31; Devlin, *Superstitious Mind,* 109–11; Favret-Saada, *Deadly Words, passim.*

and thus enable the client to act upon a view he had already reached before the consultation began." Equally important, as Judith Devlin explains, "The utility of the diviner . . . lay in the fact that, while no one understood quite how his methods worked, certain procedures . . . were recognized by the community as appropriate and justifiable in view of the individual's suffering." Divination therefore served "to give social sanction to the individual's impulses and intuition."[45] When it was "proved" that Marfa Artynova (above) had stolen 100 rubles, for example, the diviner had little problem exposing the guilty party for there were few suspects to consider. If a client could suggest no possible culprits, the diviner or wise person offered more cautious evidence, such as "a man with brown hair and green eyes," thereby encouraging the community to mull over and decide who the culprit might be. Clearly divination served a particular need within a society like that of rural Russia, "which accepted the possibility of magic, operating both as a deterrent and a means of detection."[46]

## EXPLOITING POPULAR BELIEF

Professional swindlers, whose ranks included cunning folk, healers, and sorcerers, took full advantage of popular belief or religious faith and preyed upon the rural populace. Some cunning folk used their alleged medicinal knowledge as a means of extortion or to perpetrate thefts, as did sorcerers through their power to cast and undo harmful spells.[47] Indeed, it was a lucrative business. But it could also prove risky, for peasants often sought revenge if they felt they had been deceived. In 1896, for instance, a case of extortion led to a sorcerer's murder in one village of Penza province, where two brothers claimed the power to cast spells on people and animals and exploited their reputation for mercenary ends with one casting a harmful

45. Keith Thomas, *Religion and the Decline of Magic* (New York, 1971), 216–17; Delvin, *Superstitious Mind,* 109. On the use of such manipulation by diviners in the twentieth century, see Mary Douglas, ed., *Witchcraft Confessions and Accusations* (London, 1970); E. E. Evans-Pritchard, *Witchcraft, Oracles and Magic among the Azande* (Oxford, 1937); Bushaway, "Alternative Belief in Rural England," 202–4.

46. Thomas, *Religion,* 222. In 1894 one *znakhar'* in Podolia province was summoned to determine who had caused a family's cows to stop producing milk. After listening carefully to their complaint, the *znakhar'* announced that the animals had fallen prey to a witch's spell. "But to catch a witch is not easy," he explained cautiously. "A witch is not stupid. She won't turn herself in. You have to watch for her when she steals her way to the cows at night." In fact, it was only after the likely suspect (a neighbor) appeared at the scene and incriminated herself that the *znakhar'* was able to claim success in uncovering her identity. Tulub, "Sueverie i prestuplenie," 1087–90.

47. For example, Efimenko, *Sbornik,* 223; A. Khokhlovkin, "Znakharstvo i sharlatanstvo," *Mir Bozhii,* 13, no. 3 (1904), 107–21; "Krazhi i bor'by s nimi," *Izvestiia Kostromskogo gubernskogo zemstvo* (1916), 16.

spell and the other selling his services to remove it. This had been done with a peasant named Filatov, whose wife contracted a serious illness attributed to sorcery. Filatov paid the "good" brother or "unwitcher" to heal his wife, but she died nevertheless. When the unwitcher demanded further payment and threatened to cast a similar spell on Filatov, the latter killed him. He confessed to the murder at his trial, saying that he committed the crime out of fear of the sorcerer, and was sentenced to two years' imprisonment.[48] In another case from Samara province, the murderer of a sorcerer in Nikolaevsk district similarly confessed in court, stating, "I was right in killing him because he was a sorcerer and cast spells on people; he put a spell on my daughter, then allegedly cured her when I gave him vodka." As witnesses, two local priests proved especially convincing. One confirmed the victim's reputation as a sorcerer who had cast spells on many parishioners. "There was common agreement that he was an evil man who harmed people's health," Father Rassudov testified. "Everyone feared him—even I did. You would meet him and think to yourself, 'He should go to hell.' All the villagers were glad to be delivered from him." Likely of peasant origin himself, the priest shared the villagers' beliefs. On the basis of such testimony, a jury acquitted the murderer.[49]

Rural Russia teemed with swindlers of all sorts who exploited peasant religiosity. One common practice was to pose as a wandering pilgrim or holy person—figures usually treated with great respect in the countryside—and, making use of a feasible story, elicit money from villagers. Some did this regularly; others appeared briefly in a given locality and then moved on. A Moscow provincial peace court tried one peasant in 1873 for illegally collecting money, which, he claimed, would be used to build a church. Two others, arrested in 1891 near a Iaroslavl' village, possessed false passports as well as forged documents "authorizing" them to collect donations to be used for rebuilding a church that had burned down some time before.[50] "Maksim the preacher" turned up in a Nizhnii Novgorod village in 1896, gathered a sizable quantity of cash from villagers, and was not heard from again. In 1899 a woman arrived in the Armanikhinsk township of this

---

48. *Nedelia*, no. 43 (1896), 1388. See also *Nedelia*, no. 40 (1893), 1266. S. Ponomarev found cases of this sort common and noted that, as a result, "sorcerers often do not live out their lives and do not die from natural causes." "Ocherki narodnogo prava. Osobennosti ego," *SevV*, no. 5 (1890), 95.

49. *Nedelia*, 13, no. 8 (1880), 240–41. Peasant judges, too, acted upon their belief in sorcery, as happened during a case heard by one township court of Starobel'sk district, where a peasant brought suit against his neighbor, who was known to be a witch, for causing harm to his cattle. The judges summoned a *znakhar'* as an expert witness, and when he "recognized" that the accused was, indeed, a witch, the court sentenced her to pay damages. Iakushkin, *Obychnoe pravo*, 2:354. See also "Plody nevezhestva," *Nedelia* 19, no. 3 (1886), 1406.

50. TsGIAgM, f. 577, op. 1, d. 90; *IaGV*, no. 28 (1891), part 2, 3.

province claiming to be the mother superior of an unknown monastery charged with gathering alms. She so successfully convinced peasants that her appearance was a special manifestation of God's grace that they took her from village to village collecting donations.[51]

Although they were the primary victims of rural swindlers, villagers also sought to utilize popular beliefs for their own benefit. Numerous charms and rituals, for instance, could help secure a favorable outcome in court. According to responses received by the Tenishev ethnographic survey, most widespread was the conviction that a person should fast on the Friday before the day of Saints Kos'ma and Damien in order to win a case, or that one should carry a caul when going to court. Some people called upon the local *znakhar'* to assist them with upcoming litigation. In addition to their many other talents, cunning folk knew of certain incantations or charms which could ensure that a guilty person would not be punished. One report from Novgorod province told of a young man due to stand trial for arson. Before setting off to court he first stopped to see the local diviner and, for three rubles, bought a charm fashioned from special grasses and herbs, which he was told to hold close to his bosom throughout the hearing. When questioning started, the accuser trembled to such an extent and felt so poorly that he retracted the charges and himself began to vindicate the accused."[52] Particular plants might also mollify a judge, but most charms and incantations were directed against one's opponent in a trial. In parts of Orel province, it was believed that if one read the 90th and 108th psalms three times per day, or read the Gospels both morning and night, then one would win any court case.[53] Here again, peasants appropriated symbols of power and divine intervention from the Church for their own purposes. Some thieves did much the same thing to help them in their work, carrying prayers or incantations when they went off "on business."[54]

51. "Kozelets. (T'ma nevezhestva)," *NizhL*, no. 188 (1896), 3; "Nizhegorodskii uezd. (Na pochve legkomysliia)," *NizhL*, no. 61 (1899), 3. See also TsGIAgM, f. 700, op. 1, d. 12 (1876); A. V. Leonitskii, "O bor'be s nishchenstvom," *Trudovaia pomoshch'*, no. 4 (1902), 510–30. Similar uses of religious faith were common elsewhere as well. See, e.g., Weber, *Peasants into Frenchmen*, 24; Blackbourn, *Marpingen*, 181–88.

52. GARF, f. 586, op. 1, d. 120, ll. 12–13; Tenishev, *Pravosudie*, 22–23. See also Charushin, "Otnoshenie naroda k koronnomu sudu," 75.

53. GARF, f. 586, op. 1, d. 114, l. 6; Tenishev, *Pravosudie*, 26–32.

54. A horsethief apprehended in Kostroma province had the following prayer in his possession: "In the name of the Father and of the son and of the Holy Spirit, Amen. I, a servant of God, am setting forth on my dark path. The Lord Jesus Christ is approaching me from paradise, leaning on a golden crozier and on his golden cross. To my right is the Mother of God, the most holy virgin, with angels, archangels, seraphim and all of the celestial powers; on the left is the archangel Gabriel, and above me is Il'ia the Prophet, Slave of God, on his flaming chariot. He prepares my path and guards it with the holy and life-giving cross of God. The virgin is the lock and Peter and Paul are the key. Amen." Iakushkin, "Zametki o vliianii," 9–10.

Thieves took other practical measures to insure good luck. One of these was a form of ritual theft known as *zavorovyvanie,* the extent of which is unknown, though ritual theft for other purposes continued in practice among youth groups in the late nineteenth century.[55] According to this belief, those who stole something on the eve of the Feast of the Annunciation (or, less commonly, on the eve of Saints Boris and Gleb) without being caught would be guaranteed a successful and safe year regardless of how often they robbed. Such thefts were usually perpetrated against a neighbor and the stolen object returned the following day. Given the act's symbolic nature, skill and cunning mattered far more than the value of the item taken, since it was the former that provided a thief with insurance against capture and punishment. In Penza province, peasants reportedly believed that *zavorovyvanie* would protect them all year from being fined for illegally cutting wood.[56]

With the exception of outright swindling, it is doubtful that villagers viewed any of these acts to be criminal. I have found no evidence suggesting that ritual theft was vigorously prosecuted by *volost'* courts, for example. Likewise, a peasant may have protested another's use of sorcery in court not because it represented a crime but because it gave an opponent a decidedly unfair advantage against which one was helpless without similar access to magic or divine assistance. Apart from occasional false accusations when divination was employed to establish guilt, the practice likewise caused no real injury and actually seemed to function as a relatively effective means of criminal detection. These beliefs, in fact, constituted integral parts of the peasant world view; operating at the level of everyday life, they could be called upon to solve a difficult problem within the community (such as a crime), or to provide a sense of security at times of uncertainty (for an upcoming court case, or perhaps with regard to the coming year's criminal activities). Individual actions might be questioned at times, but the same cannot be said of the beliefs that gave such actions their form and meaning.

Official Russia, on the other hand, considered these practices illegal, though it remained virtually impossible to prosecute divination or the use of magic in peasant communities. Furthermore, by midcentury state courts

55. See Frank, "Confronting the Domestic Other," 86.

56. Iakushkin, *Obychnoe pravo,* 1:xxxiii–xxxiv; L. S. Belogrits-Kotliarevskii, "Mifologicheskii znachenie nekotorykh prestuplenii, sovershaemykh po sueveriiu," *IV* 33 (1888), 109–10; A. I. Ivanov, "Verovaniia krest'ian Orlovskoi gub." *EtnogO,* no. 4 (1901), 116; Levenstim, *Sueverie,* 114–15. Gerald Sider's intriguing study of ritual theft leads me to doubt that this was the sole function of *zavorovyvanie* in rural Russia. See "Family Fun in Starve Harbour: Custom, History, and Confrontation in Village Newfoundland," in Hans Medick and David Warren Sabean, eds., *Interest and Emotion: Essays on the Study of Family and Kinship* (Cambridge and Paris, 1984), 340–70.

had largely ceased hearing cases involving accusations of sorcery or witch-craft, thereby distancing official law from local practice.[57] With their perception of peasant culture as little more than a collection of superstitious, childish notions, officials and educated Russians appeared nearly unanimous in their hostility toward the villagers' mixture of popular belief and Orthodoxy with local justice. To change the cultural level of the countryside they deemed it necessary to eradicate superstition, for it impeded the progress of rural areas and hindered efforts to educate the dark masses. Yet such efforts would take time, and members of the judicial establishment in particular believed that stronger and more immediate measures were required. Of special concern to them were beliefs that led directly to the perpetration of crimes like theft or murder but that villagers generally did not recognize as criminal acts.

## FINE LINES: FROM SUPERSTITION TO CRIME

As the century waned, ethnographers found the commission of crimes based on popular beliefs to be gradually dying out in central Russia, particularly in more industrialized provinces like Vladimir and Moscow. Still, these offenses were by no means a rarity during our period.[58] As late as the 1890s, investigators reported that peasants in many localities believed a stolen object to be more valuable than one that had been acquired honestly. Villagers from a district of Iaroslavl' province sometimes stole flowers because they were thought to grow better than plants one had raised or received as a gift; theft of beehives had similar motives. In a Vologda district the belief existed that seeds pilfered from a neighbor who enjoyed good harvests would transmit abundance to the land of the thief.[59] An investigator in Petrushkovo village of Orel province learned from peasant maidens that flax grew much better when they stole flat cakes at Easter and ate them in the fields. Fishermen in Arkhangel'sk province found it easier to catch cod using stolen hooks. Levenstim even noted the widespread belief among cavalrymen that their horses became healthier and more beautiful when fed with stolen oats. The court of the St. Petersburg dragoon regiment tried such a case in the early 1870s, acquitting a soldier accused of

57. On tsarist legislation concerning sorcery, see Popov, *Sud i nakazaniia,* 370–82; and Chapter 8, below.

58. Vladimir respondents to the Tenishev ethnographic survey, for instance, reported that "crimes stemming from superstition do not exist nowadays." Firsov and Kiseleva, *Byt veliko-russkikh krest'ian,* 292. Similar responses can be found in GARF, f. 586, op. 1, d. 120, l. 7; Zagoskin, *Otvety,* 98–99.

59. Titov, *Iuridicheskie obychai,* 113; Tenishev, "Obshchie nachala," 124; Iakushkin, "Zametki o vliianii," 3–5.

stealing oats in view of the fact that he had acted under the influence of superstition.[60]

Belief in magic led to crimes far more serious than theft, however, including assault, torture, and murder. Nor did all attacks upon cunning folk and practitioners of magic take on a collective character. In particular, those suspected of sorcery continued to be subjected to various ordeals, usually with the aim of proving that they were indeed witches. The well-known ordeal by water, based on the belief that because of her relations with the devil a witch is lighter than other people and cannot sink, was still employed during the second half of the nineteenth century. In 1870, thirteen elderly women lodged a complaint against fellow villagers who had tied their hands together and plunged them into the water to see which of them was causing a drought.[61] Drought was also the reason why, in 1879, peasants from another village threw a women into the water, as a result of which she went mad. Elsewhere, a group of villagers asked the local gentry landowner in 1875 to allow them to swim several women in his pond, but he refused. Therefore they summoned a midwife and, with her assistance, examined the women to discover if any of them had a tail. A parish priest told of a similar incident in which a peasant woman "went to a doctor for a certificate to the effect that she was built like other women and did not have a tail."[62]

Despite fearing a sorcerer's power, peasants frequently acted individually to take revenge against a person whose magical or healing abilities had brought harm to their families. This was especially true "where the [village] assembly no longer pays attention to sorcery."[63] At the start of the 1880s in an Arkhangel'sk hamlet, for instance, the peasant Vashutin called on his fellow villager Nemtsova one evening and accused her of bewitching his daughter-in-law, bringing upon her a wasting disease. Vashutin knew that Nemtsova's husband was away at seasonal labor and had waited until then to level his accusation. When she denied the charges of sorcery, Vashutin seized the older woman and dragged her to his home, where he beat her, threw her to the floor, and began kicking her with his boots. Finally, he stopped and again ordered Nemtsova to remove the spell from his daughter-in-law. Since she was now in no condition to do so even had she been

60. GARF, f. 586, op. 1, d. 114, l. 6; Levenstim, *Sueverie,* 113.

61. *ZhivSt,* nos. 1–4 (1894), 122; Levenstim, *Sueverie,* 61. See also Russell Zguta, "The Ordeal by Water (Swimming of Witches) in the East Slavic World," *SR* 36, no. 2 (1977), 220–30.

62. Levenstim, *Sueverie,* 61; Bernard Pares, *Russia and Reform* (London, 1907), 116. The continued belief that witches had tails can be found in numerous sources from the end of the century and later. See, e.g., *RIAMZ,* III/878, no. 15, "Opisanie sela Kopanovo," l. 14; "Livenskii uezd. (Ubiistvo kolduna)," *OrlV,* no. 310 (1898), 3; Firsov and Kiseleva, *Byt velikorusskikh krest'ian,* 129. Compare Bushaway, "Alternative Belief," who discusses similar practices in late nineteenth-century Britain.

63. Ponomarev, "Ocherki narodnogo prava," 90.

capable of witchcraft, Vashutin tied her hands with a rope and dragged her to the river to drown her. Fortunately, the woman's desperate cries awakened the entire village, and neighbors came running to save her from probable death. After a month of recuperation Nemtsova lodged a complaint against her assailant before the local justice of the peace, who eventually resolved the case through reconciliation when Nemtsova agreed to make peace with Vashutin if he paid five rubles for the injury and shame he had inflicted.[64]

Nemtsova was lucky to survive Vashutin's assault. Many others were less fortunate. In 1884 Pavel Eliseev of Spassk district murdered a fellow villager for allegedly casting a spell on his wife. A local *znakhar'* of Mogilev province was similarly killed in 1889 by a peasant whose wife had not responded to the wise man's cures.[65] At least two cases of this sort were officially recorded in Riazan' province during 1890 alone. For practicing sorcery, a fifty-eight-year-old reserve soldier died at the hands of two peasants, and another villager received eight years at hard labor in Siberia for killing a sorcerer who he believed had caused both his daughter and daughter-in-law to become seriously ill. Even the threat of a harmful spell could lead to murder, as happened in 1902 near the village of Beloostrov, where the renowned healer and sorceress Anna Ille lost her life from a brutal beating after threatening to cast a spell on a peasant who badgered her for money to buy vodka.[66]

Russia's official courts also prosecuted persons for deaths resulting from exorcism or other forms of folk healing deemed dangerous. Yet information on such incidents is scarce because the use of a *znakhar'* and other healers was illegal under official law, making peasants understandably reluctant to discuss them with outsiders.[67] It is clear, however, that the growing number of health professionals played a significant if far from successful role in efforts to rid the countryside of medical superstitions, charlatans who preyed on peasants during times of illness, and folk healers, though their enthusiasm for enlightenment did not stem only from mere altruism. At

64. Ia. Ludmer, "Bab'i stony," *IuV,* no. 12 (1884), 658–59.

65. GARO, f. 7, op. 1, d. 95, l. 4; Levenstim, *Sueverie,* 43. See also "Ubiistvo zhenshchiny za koldovstvo," *Golos,* no. 127 (1880), 3; "Sud nad vorozheei," *VolzhV,* no. 214 (1892), 2.

66. GARO, f. 7, op. 1, d. 584, l. 20b.; L. Vesin, "Narodnyi samosud nad koldunami (K istorii narodnykh obychaev)," *SevV,* no. 9 (1892), 74; "Ubiistvo koldun'i," *SudO* 2, no. 3 (1904), 63. See also "Ubiistvo koldun'i v Sapozhkov. uezde, Riazan. gub.," *RusVed,* no. 75 (1883), 1; V. Lebedeva, "Klikushestvo i znakhari," *Krest'ianka,* no. 4 (1923), 23–24.

67. See Samuel Ramer, "Traditional Healers and Peasant Culture in Russia," in Esther Kingston-Mann and Timothy Mixter, eds., *Peasant Economy, Culture, and Politics of European Russia, 1800–1921* (Princeton, 1991), 207–32. Although cases of *znakharstvo* usually came before justices of the peace as misdemeanors, they might also be tried in a circuit court if the practitioner was accused of causing sickness or harm, possessing illegal medicines or poison, or similar infractions.

least some provincial doctors brought suits against unlicensed medical practitioners because the latter presented serious competition and peasants, seeing little difference between the abilities of their local healers and zemstvo doctors, often chose the former because they were close at hand and personally known to the patient. In 1872, for instance, two doctors in Moscow's Bogorodsk district lodged charges against a local *znakhar'* for illegally practicing medicine and possessing dangerous substances (silver nitrate and "Spanish fly"). This case was shunted back and forth between two jurisdictions for nearly two years until a justice of the peace finally dismissed it due to lack of evidence.[68] Guilty verdicts were more likely when a patient died as the result of folk medicine, though peasants rarely blamed the *znakhar'* in such cases. According to Samuel Ramer, they usually attributed the patient's death "to his own weakness" and to the fact that "he couldn't survive the medicine."[69]

One collective ritual performed by villagers to drive away cholera, though technically legal, was also attacked by the medical and legal professions, discussed repeatedly in the press, and included in most studies of crimes of superstition. Commonly known as *opakhivanie* or *zapakhivanie* ("the plowing"), the practice involved an icon procession conducted by peasant women during which they scraped a symbolic furrow into the earth around the entire village to keep or drive out the evil forces that had brought disease. Having gathered late at night near the edge of their settlement dressed simply in shirts and with hair unplaited, the women harnessed one of their number (either a virgin or someone who had not yet given birth) to the plow, and set out in procession.[70] This ritual survived into the twentieth century, even among peasants living close to major urban centers. It was practiced in a village only four kilometers from Nizhnii Novgorod, for example, where residents engaged primarily in carting and outwork. When a case of cholera created panic among villagers in 1892, they

68. The court did, however, confiscate this healer's remedies. TsGIAgM, f. 702, op. 1, d. 211, ll. 1–1010b. See also GARO, f. 717, op. 41 (1891), sv. 80, d. 19. Throughout the period under examination here (and beyond), medical and public health practitioners carried out a virulent campaign against nonprofessionals and folk healers like the *znakhar'* and *znakharka*. Although by no means hesitant to use the law and courts in this struggle, the primary vehicle in their campaign was the periodical press. See Nancy Mandelker Frieden, *Russian Physicians in an Era of Reform and Revolution, 1856–1905* (Princeton, 1981).

69. Ramer, "Traditional Healers," 21. For other cases heard by peace courts, see A. Zenchenko, "Derevnia i mirovoi sud," *VE*, no. 2 (1886), 653–55.

70. V. V. Selivanov, *God russkogo zemledel'tsa* (Vladimir, 1902), 92–93. For other descriptions, see Levenstim, *Sueverie*, 14–19; "Suevernyi obychai, trebuiushchii unichtozheniia," *RSP*, no. 43 (1865), 245–47; Belogrits-Kotliarevskii, "Mifologicheskoe znachenie," 106–9; M. Nikiforovskii, *Russkoe iazychestvo* (SPb, 1875), 32; "Obriad opakhivan'ia," *Chernigovskie eparkhial'nye izvestiia*, no. 18 (1876), 515–18; S. V. Maksimov, *Nechistaia sila. Nevedomaia sila. Sobranie sochinenii*, vol. 18 (SPb, 1896), 268–71.

turned to a remedy "that was practiced in olden times." At midnight, a crowd of women and maidens harnessed themselves to a plow and the procession began. "A young maiden went slowly in front . . . with an incense burner in her hands, muttering incantations and waving the incense before an old icon carried by two women walking ahead of her. . . . They circled the entire village with quiet, doleful singing and prayers."[71] Cholera outbreaks in 1910 saw peasants throughout much of central Russia turn to *opakhivanie* for protection. In one suburb of Dankov, a Riazan' provincial town, young men joined the women in a nocturnal procession and added a new element by marching in front firing rifles into the air to frighten away evil forces.[72]

## POWERS OF THE DEAD

As many villagers knew, the death of witches or sorcerers did not ensure safety against their malevolent power for they could cause drought, crop failure, and disease from the grave. Suicides, victims of poisoning or of sudden death, unbaptized infants, and schismatics were dangerous after death. Because these people had died without the benefit of Orthodox rites, they were unable to find peace in the afterlife. Some left their graves and harmed relatives or an entire community. Others became vampires, especially if they had been the first victims of an epidemic, and wandered the countryside at night terrorizing villagers, destroying livestock, and committing murder.[73]

A community had several means of protection from misfortunes wrought by the undead, nearly all of which entailed digging up the grave, a felony punishable under article 234 of the criminal code, which distinguished between committing this act with the aim of robbery or as a result of superstition.[74] Yet when a disaster like drought or epidemic threatened their

71. "Nizhegorodskii uezd (Iz narodnykh sueverii)," *VolzhV,* no. 206 (1892), 2. See also GARO, f. 5, st. 4, op. 5, d. 1979 (1892).

72. "Dankov. (Kholera i nevezhestvo obyvatelei)," *RiazV,* no. 196 (1910), 3–4. In this instance, town residents joined peasants to perform the ritual. See also *Trudy soveshchaniia g.g. vrachei i predstavitelei zemstva Riazanskoi gub. 10–12 fevralia 1911 goda po bor'be s kholeroi* (Riazan', 1911), 163–70; "Stanitsiia Aleksandro-Nevskaia," *RiazV,* no. 147 (1910), 3; "K voprosu ob opakhivanii," *EtnogO* 22, no. 3–4 (1910), 175–78; RIAMZ, III/878, no. 282 (Pronsk district, 1929), l. 3; no. 292 (Riazan' district, 1927), ll. 3, 10. For some observers, *opakhivanie* offered proof of the "ignorance of illiterate women" and "the inability of our primary schools to propagate enlightenment among the masses." *VolzhV,* no. 206 (1892), 2.

73. "Narodnye poveriia i obychai v g. Kasimove i ego uezde," *RiazEV (Pribavlenie),* no. 4 (1888), 109; Ivanov, "Verovaniia krest'ian," 95; Belogrits-Kotliarevskii, "Mifologicheskoe znachenie," 111–12; Levenstim, "Sueverie," no. 1, 212; V. N. Dobrovol'skii, "Narodnye skazaniia o samoubiitsakh," *ZhivSt,* no. 2, part 2 (1894), 204–14.

74. *SZU,* part 1, 51; *Razvitie russkogo prava,* 174. For robbing a grave, the guilty party was subject to a maximum punishment of loss of all rights and Siberian exile at hard labor for a pe-

community, peasants ignored the law. During droughts, villagers dug up the grave of a suicide, drunkard, or sorcerer and poured water over the corpse in order to bring rain. When epidemics raged, it was best to exhume a witch and drive an aspen stake into her heart, or to turn the body face down and pound the stake through its back. For ending the harm caused by suicides, an aspen stake would first be hammered into the corpse, then the body was removed from the cemetery and placed elsewhere.[75] Some parish clergy shared their parishioners' belief in a sorcerer's ability to project evil from beyond the grave. According to one investigator in the Urals, priests performed the rituals to nullify or drive off supernatural forces, placing salt beneath a dead sorcerer's face in the grave or performing the burial rites behind the grave rather than in front, as was normally done. In one district, the priest himself read prayers of damnation and hammered an aspen stake into a sorcerer's grave. In Shatsk district a priest accompanied villagers when they did so.[76]

Judicial investigator N. M. Timofeev recalled one particularly gruesome incident that occurred in his district in 1865. The son of a local peasant had died from smallpox, and three weeks after his death villagers discovered that his and five other bodies had been disinterred. But while the other corpses remained untouched, that of the young peasant was found horribly mutilated. "The head was severed from the torso and thrown into a ditch at the cemetery's edge," wrote Timofeev. "The eyes had been pierced and the nose and ears sliced off." In addition, the youth's coffin was smeared with tar and broken into pieces, his grave filled with rocks and straw, and three aspen stakes driven into the ground. The investigator also found a black cat in the grave, strangled with a cord. This incident caused great consternation among villagers, who knew that the devil often took the form of a cat. The village elder told Timofeev that someone had obviously disturbed the deceased and the latter had returned to walk the earth. "Everyone knows this," he declared when Timofeev laughed at him. "Ask any young child and they'll tell you that the dead walk." After a lengthy investigation Timofeev finally discovered that the boy's father committed the crime, convinced, along with other villagers, that his son was unhappy in the grave and would

riod of ten to twelve years. Committing this act out of superstitious belief, on the other hand, brought a more lenient sentence of settlement in Siberia and loss of civil rights. See also N. Treierov, "Prestupleniia protiv very i tserkvi po russkomu zakonodatel'stvu," *RSP,* no. 45 (1875), 313–24; Popov, *Sud i nakazaniia,* 392–93.

75. Ponomarev, "Ocherki," 99; M. N. Gernet, "Prestupnost' krest'ian v Rossii," *Vestnik prava i notariata,* no. 8 (1912), 240; Belogrits-Kotliarevskii, "Mifologicheskoe znachenie," 112; Levenstim, "Sueverie," no. 1, 213.

76. Ponomarev, "Ocherki," 98–99. This author notes that, in the past, serfowners "took an active part in the punishment of sorcerers," suggesting an historical legitimation of these practices by secular as well as clerical authorities.

return to claim the rest of his family. Village women began to shun his wife and daughter, saying that they would not live beyond the next harvest. The father therefore did what he believed was necessary to prevent further misfortune and salvage his family's reputation; he uncovered five additional bodies to draw attention from the actual crime.[77]

Peasants in Penza province perpetrated a similar offense at the Tashtamakov village cemetery in 1893, where they dug up the grave of a reputed sorceress, drove an aspen stake into her corpse so that she could not rise again, and then put the grave in proper order. Upon investigation, it was learned that the crime had been committed in accordance with a village assembly decision. "An epidemic was raging in the village and was attributed to the fact that each evening a fiery ball flew from the sorceress' grave and divided into smaller flames that carried the sickness to peasant homes. To rid themselves of this misfortune, villagers resolved to open the grave and drive an aspen stake into the old woman's back." The Kazan' Judicial Chamber later convicted twelve peasants for this deed, though "given the extreme backwardness of the accused and the fact that they acted only under the influence of superstition and for the sake of saving their families and themselves, the chamber resolved to petition His Highness [the emperor] for a reduction of punishment."[78] During the famine of 1891–92, cases of this sort increased greatly throughout the Volga region. Because of drought in Kazan' province, for instance, peasants of Bolgary village dug up the corpse of a drunkard with the intention of throwing it into the Volga River. Unfortunately, their plan was reported to the police before they could complete the task, but soon after exhuming the body the weather grew cooler and clouds appeared in the sky. These disappeared after a few days without giving rain, however, which villagers attributed to the fact that they had not succeeded in putting the body in the river.[79]

Drought was one of the major reasons for illegal gravedigging, together with epidemics, though villagers frequently turned to the Church before taking more extreme measures. Processions conducted by parish priests to beg God for rain were common throughout our period, providing peasants and nonpeasants alike with the faith that divine or supernatural intervention could bring an end to natural calamities.[80] Only if a procession failed

77. N. M. Timofeev, *Zapiski sledovatelia: sochinenie N. M. Timofeeva* (SPb, 1872), 291–323. See also "Delo o krest'ianakh Andree Kozakevich i drugikh, sudimykh za pokhoronenie zhivoi krest'ianki Man'kovoi," *ZhMIu*, no. 6 (1864), 707–13.

78. Levenstim, "Sueverie," no. 1, 215. For a nearly identical case from Kazan' province, see *Nedelia*, no. 11 (1893), 333–34. In both instances, peasants did not deny that they had dug up the graves but argued that they were not guilty of any crime.

79. "Spassk (Molebstviia o dozhde. Narodnoe sueverie)," *VolzhV*, no. 145 (1892), 2.

80. For example, Petr Malov, "Selo Podval'e v religiozno-nravstvennom otnoshenii," *RSP*, no. 41 (1863), 335–37; "Obraz soversheniia krestnykh khodov," *RSP*, no. 14 (1886), 438–42;

did peasants seek other remedies, usually tearing up a grave and throwing the corpse into a gully, lake, or river. The urgency of finding a solution, according to one writer, stemmed in part from the fact that peasants attributed lack of rain "to the influence of those who died without confession." Such people, like witches and vampires, "can milk the clouds and steal the dew from the ground of the village in whose cemetery they are buried."[81] For this reason a victim of poisoning was removed from a rural Saratov cemetery in 1889 and thrown into a nearby river. While net fishing in a river close to his estate during the summer of 1892, a Vladimir noble landowner hauled in a skeleton. The investigation that followed revealed that local peasants had attributed the previous year's drought to a suicide interred in their cemetery. They therefore dug up the corpse and reburied it in a ravine. But when the spring thaw washed it out of its new grave, the villagers weighted it down with rocks and tossed it into the river.[82] When drought struck Orenburg province in 1898, peasants of Pepel'nyi village were informed by their elder that God would only bring rain if they removed from the local cemetery the body of a man who had died of alcohol poisoning. Thirteen villagers carried out this deed, but news reached the authorities and they were brought to trial. To the prosecutor's sarcastic question: "Well, and when you had dug up and moved the body, did it rain?" they replied, "Yes, just a little." The village elder received three and a half years in jail for his crime; all other participants were sentenced to one and a half years each.[83] After a 1910 prayer vigil failed to bring rain in a village of Kiev district, local women went to the grave of a maiden who had committed suicide, burned a cross on her grave, then dug it up and "in turn, relieved themselves over the grave." Four women were later arrested on charges of desecration.[84]

During the 1891 drought and famine in a village of Samara province, local women determined that their misfortunes were caused by a sorceress buried in the cemetery. Led by the entire village administration, a group of fifty peasants dug up the sorceress's corpse and threw it in the river, weighted down with heavy stones. Ten villagers, including the elder, police officials, and tax collector, were finally brought to trial, and none denied the circumstances of their crime. The local priest testified that "an impenetrable darkness of ignorance" prevailed in his parish, giving "complete

*RiazEV,* no. 2 (1890), 101; "Molebstvie v gorode Riazani o dozhde," *RiazEV,* no. 11 (1892), 494–95.

81. Levenstim, "Sueverie," 216.

82. Sumtsov, *O tom, kakie sel'skie pover'ia,* 10–11.

83. "Na pochve vlasti t'my," *VolzhV,* no. 240 (1899), 3. See also Rodin, "Vliianie urozhainosti na prestupnost'," 158.

84. "Vlast' t'my," *RiazV,* no. 184 (1910), 4.

freedom to superstition, the belief in sorcerers and in mystical means for driving away misfortunes." In his own defense he noted that his strenuous efforts at enlightenment among the parishioners had proved fruitless. Reflecting a broader debate within educated Russian society, the defense attorney used this testimony to confirm the low level of development of the accused, claiming that their ignorance should be the main element considered when judging such actions. To be found guilty of ignorance, he concluded, was difficult, for their deed embodied no inherent evil. By contrast, the prosecution argued that ignorance could not justify an infraction of the law, especially since the accused had all confessed to committing the crime. The Saratov Judicial Chamber sided with its prosecutor and sentenced the accused to prison terms ranging from one to one and a half years, though the judges petitioned the emperor for a reduction of all sentences to one month in jail.[85]

Sometimes corpses were dug up to obtain talismans or medicinal remedies, though the crime appears to have been quite rare. Some thieves believed that the hand or finger of a corpse would allow them to carry out any deed without fear of being caught. Candles rendered from human fat served a similar purpose, for when thieves lit one in the house they intended to rob, the occupants would be unable to wake up. Although the great majority of reports appeared before the 1890s, corpses were exhumed throughout our period with the aim of obtaining magical items, and according to one writer, "There is reason to believe that not all instances of such [crimes] have been brought to light."[86] In April 1871, for example, in a village cemetery of Viatka district, the body of an infant was exhumed and cut open in order to remove the coagulated blood for use as a remedy. A large, commercial village of Khar'kov province witnessed another incident in 1891 when a widow discovered her husband's grave uncovered and the flesh stripped from the corpse's hand. Apprehended soon thereafter, the perpetrator of this crime confessed that he intended to make a candle. In 1866, a thief was seized in Sarapul'sk district by villagers who discovered "to their horror" that he carried with him a human hand as well as several teeth.[87] Some even murdered in order to acquire talismans, as occurred in 1869, 1881, and 1896 (Riazan', Penza, and Voronezh provinces, respectively), to cite only a few cases. A girl from Kursk province was killed in 1888 to obtain fat for a magical candle. Two teenage peasant apprentices from a village of Voronezh province abducted and murdered a twelve-year-old boy

85. *Nedelia,* no. 23 (1896), 717–18.

86. Iakushkin, "Zametki," 11. See also Belogrits-Kotliarevskii, "Mifologicheskoe znachenie," 110–11; Ivanov, "Verovaniia krest'ian," 115; Levenstim, *Sueverie,* 87–89.

87. Iakushkin, *Obychnoe pravo,* 1:xxxv; Levenstim, *Sueverie,* 82, 86–87; Sumtsov, *O tom, kakie sel'skie pover'ia,* 11–12.

in 1896, cutting open his stomach and removing the fat with the intention of making a "thieves' candle." Caught and convicted for their deed, the pair was sentenced to eight years at penal servitude.[88]

In conformity with Church teachings, peasants viewed the disturbing of graves as a serious sin. Yet they distinguished between grave robbery—a crime—and acts carried out to protect the community. Disturbing the dead could be justified in the face of some real threat like epidemic or drought. Otherwise, it was both criminal and sinful. Even attempts by authorities to disinter a body for official reasons could be met with staunch resistance. In an 1881 incident, nearly 1,500 villagers and their priest turned out to prevent a judicial investigator and medical assistant (*fel'dsher*) from exhuming a body in order to perform an autopsy. It was explained to the "officials" that once the burial service had been completed, a body could not be dug up. "It is illegal!" claimed the priest, while the crowd shouted, "Why dig him up? Why disturb him? It's not allowed, little father [*batiushka*]! We won't permit it!" The crowd was afraid of disturbing the dead, and their priest feared trouble from his parishioners.[89] Here is another illustration of the difficulties encountered in mediations between peasant and official views of morality and law. Peasants resisted disruptive incursions into their community and opposed what they saw as outside meddling in village affairs, particularly when such interference ran counter to their religious and moral beliefs. In this case, many obviously feared that exhumation and autopsy of a body could anger the deceased, with potentially bad consequences for the village and its inhabitants.

Like most crimes discussed in this chapter, digging up graves remained quite rare in the last decades of the old regime. Between 1874 and 1913, it accounted for an average of .06 percent of all offenses prosecuted by Russia's circuit courts, reaching a peak of .18 percent during the early 1890s, that is, during the 1891 famine that raged in a large swath of the country's central provinces. Before emancipation, from 1834 to 1861, this crime averaged only .02 percent of prosecuted felonies. Even at their highest points in 1868 and 1893, grave desecrations numbered only 190 and 103 cases, respectively, for the entire country.[90] Still, as with murder of sorcerers and witches, cases in which villagers exhumed corpses received dramatic press

88. "Vorovskaia svecha (Pis'mo iz Korotonka, Voronezhsk. gub.)," *Nedelia*, 29, 48 (1896), 1564–66; *NizhL*, no. 159 (1896), 3; "Chudovishchnoe prestuplenie," *RiazGV*, no. 58 (1869), 4.

89. M. F. Chulitskii, "Tolpa (Iz vospominanii byvshego sudebnogo deiatelia)," *IV* 110, no. 2 (1907), 914–19. See also V. Volzhin, "O prave politsii vskryvat' trupy," *SudG* 3, no. 28 (1884), 3–6.

90. *Svody*, vols. 3–43, part 2, table 1; and *Otchety*, vols. 1–28.

attention precisely because they addressed broader issues of peasant otherness, providing fodder for arguments that the countryside remained immersed in lawlessness and superstitious ignorance.[91]

Yet for many peasants, faith in the possibility of magic and the supernatural, which was often inseparable from faith in Orthodoxy or its various sects, helped to sustain their physical and mental worlds and had little bearing on their thinking about official law. Popular understandings of natural phenomena like drought, sickness, and epidemics remained closely bound up with a magical-religious concept of the universe in which both divine and supernatural forces acted alone or through human agents to cause and undo misfortune. These beliefs allowed villagers to serve as active agents for their own and the community's interests in what might otherwise have been a hopeless situation. Drought, for instance, could devastate an entire locality, forcing peasants to turn to begging and charity in order to survive; epidemics were equally harmful, carrying off healthy farmhands and leaving families bereft of sufficient labor power, or killing essential draft animals. If such a threat ended shortly after the exhumation of a suicide or a witch from the local cemetery, peasants could feel that their own actions had saved them, a feeling that reinforced and reproduced their faith. If, on the other hand, the drought or epidemic persisted, villagers had nevertheless done what was possible and the continued misfortune could be blamed on their limited skills, on the anger of God or demonic power, or on the intervention of outside authorities. Given the level of medical and scientific knowledge in the countryside, it is not surprising that peasant beliefs concerning the supernatural, together with the practices to which they gave rise, survived to the end of the century, many of them outlasting the old regime itself.

The great majority of urban commentators and the growing number of educated Russians working in rural areas, however, claimed to be unable to comprehend the depth or nature of popular belief. Whether the issue was "fanatical" sectarian practices, the employment of diviners to track down a thief, the use of magical charms and incantations in courts of law, the murder of a sorcerer, the desecration of graves, or even the use of traditional healers, educated Russians and higher clergy classified these phenomena as painful symbols of rural superstition and ignorance as well as crimes to be prosecuted. We see once again a confrontation between two dependent yet hostile cultures. One viewed itself as a moral and civilizing force, determined to extend its authority more completely over the rural population

91. For example, Belogrits-Kotliarevskii, "Mifologicheskoe znachenie," 110–11; Iakushkin, *Obychnoe pravo*, 1:xxxiv; Iakushkin, "Zametki," 11–12; Titov, *Iuridicheskie obychai*, 109; Levenstim, *Sueverie*, 80–98.

through enlightenment and law. The other, if far less consciously, retained those beliefs and practices that served to protect and preserve the village community. Though fully aware that, if caught, they would be punished under state law, villagers continued to ignore it until some other means was found to protect themselves from the ever present forces of the supernatural.

# CHAPTER 7

# Varieties of Punishment

### Between Court and
### Administrative Authority

*Don't beat a peasant with cudgels, beat him with rubles.*
POPULAR SAYING RECORDED IN 1822

The right of rural communities and courts to punish peasants generated heated debate among educated Russians from emancipation to the demise of the old regime. In large part this discussion grew directly from the historical fact of serfdom and the peculiarities of an emancipation settlement that retained a system of local justice limited exclusively to the newly free peasant population. The peasantry's juridical isolation, the absence of a legal code applicable to all classes, and the previous lack of an open, public exchange concerning law and justice combined to make the issue unique once the state permitted discussion within the bureaucracy and educated society.[1] Ultimately, the debate over punishment by *volost'* courts and village assemblies—in particular, corporal punishment—was part of a broader public argument about rural self-administration and its effectiveness, the peasants' juridical and civil status, and above all, their integration into "civilized society" under laws that governed the lives of other classes.

Among peasants the issue of punishment also led to questions of civil rights and equality with other classes, but they usually raised these matters in broader declarations about injustice and the arbitrary nature of local authority. Far more commonly than through words, however, the rural debate on punishments like imprisonment and flogging was situated within the everyday practice of justice. Although it could be risky to evade government regulations on proper procedure for determining judicial sanctions, peasant officials regularly adapted the law to suit local conditions. *Volost'* judges, for example, limited or even abolished corporal punishment simply

---

1. Richard S. Wortman, *The Development of a Russian Legal Consciousness* (Chicago, 1976); George L. Yaney, "Law, Society and the Domestic Regime in Russia in Historical Perspective," *American Political Science Review* 59, no. 2 (1965), 379–90.

by refusing to apply it. The generational differences that fostered familial and intravillage conflicts following emancipation added fuel to the dispute over punishment. Younger peasants in particular resented and opposed methods dating from the era of serfdom, especially when utilized by family heads to control their increasingly independent children, who also fought the monopoly of power that the older generation held over village economics and politics through its control of rural assemblies.[2]

Yet all of this occurred within the state's legal strictures. Penal codes applicable only to the peasantry still determined forms of punishment, and the government hindered or prevented a far-reaching reform of rural justice by retaining a body of administrative sanctions outside the regular judicial system that were exercised by functionaries with broad authority to punish peasants. Indeed, the retention of administrative punishment perpetuated models of arbitrariness and violence that local officials took as guides and that colored the way peasants viewed and understood "justice."[3] The 1864 judicial reforms did not disentangle justice and administration in the countryside, where both authorities remained tightly intertwined. This was certainly the case with village and township elders, who combined judicial and police authority as they had under serfdom. So too with powerful officials like peace mediators and land captains, who, though frequently neglectful of their duties, wielded great authority over peasant communities. Much has now been written on reforms of local administration as well as efforts to separate administrative and judicial authority and the state's ultimate unwillingness to do so.[4] Far less is known about the reality of punishment in everyday life, how it influenced the way peasants experienced legal retribution, or how justice and administration interacted, shaped, and deformed one another. A closer look at that experience requires a revision of several long-standing assumptions about punishment in the peasant's world.

## FOUNDATIONS OF PUNISHMENT IN RURAL COMMUNITIES

Like those established among state peasants during the years 1837–39, postemancipation *volost'* courts determined punishments on the basis of the 1839 Rural Judicial Code [articles 440–536]. These courts might—and fre-

2. For one important side of this conflict, see Jeffrey Burds, "The Social Control of Peasant Labor in Russia," in Esther Kingston-Mann and Timothy Mixter, eds., *Peasant Economy, Culture, and Politics of European Russia, 1800–1921* (Princeton, 1991), 52–100.

3. See the telling commentary in Bogoslovskii, "Obshchii ocherk obraza zhizni i kharaktera zhitelei Novgorodskoi gubernii," *Novgorodskii sbornik,* no. 1 (1865), part 1, 7–8.

4. George L. Yaney, *The Systematization of Russian Government* (Urbana, 1973); James I. Mandel, "Paternalistic Authority in the Russian Countryside, 1856–1906" (Ph.D. diss., Columbia University, 1978); Francis W. Wcislo, *Reforming Rural Russia* (Princeton, 1990). The standard work on administrative law is S. A. Korf, *Administrativnaia iustitsiia v Rossii,* 2 vols. (SPb, 1910).

quently did—simply issue a stern warning. They could also sentence peasants to public work for up to six days, a maximum fine of three rubles (which could be changed to a different punishment if the culprit could not pay), jail for up to seven days, or flogging with birch rods. The code set no limits on corporal punishment, and before 1863 rural courts ordered severe floggings (usually 30–40 lashes), much as did regular courts, where even harsher sentences of 70–100 lashes of the whip were common before the reign of Alexander II. For the new *volost'* courts, legislators set a maximum of 20 lashes of the birch.[5] Following the abolition of peace courts and introduction of land captains in 1889, *volost'* courts were governed by the Code of Punishments for Justices of the Peace, those sections of the Rural Judicial Code covering offenses punishable by flogging, and several articles of the regular Code of Punishments of the Russian Empire. Peasant courts could still issue warnings or sentence villagers to public work or corporal punishment. Maximum fines or jail sentences, however, increased; under the new laws courts could impose jail terms of up to one month (either simple or strict, the latter on bread and water only) and issue fines of up to thirty rubles. The codes changed once again when the government abolished corporal punishment in 1904, leaving fines and jail as the only legal sentences.[6] Peasant judges thus had several official sources at their disposal, none of which was what educated Russians persistently termed "customary" criminal law. Instead, guided by township clerks, judges turned to official codes or simply cited article 102 of the emancipation regulations, which defined the court's punitive authority. Indeed, villagers who sought to employ traditional methods of punishment or retribution frequently found themselves on trial before local and even higher courts for breaking the law.[7]

5. N. M. Druzhinin, *Gosudarstvennye krest'iane i reforma P. D. Kiseleva*, 2 vols. (Moscow-Leningrad, 1946, 1958), 1:565; K. A. Sofronenko, comp., *Krest'ianskaia reforma v Rossii 1861 goda* (Moscow, 1954), 60–63; MVD, *Sbornik uzakonenii, opredeliaiushchikh prava i obiazannosti volostnykh starshin i pisarei* (SPb, 1904), 77–91; A. Pestrzhetskii, "O sude krest'ian, vyshedshikh iz krepostnoi zavisimosti," *ZhMIu*, no. 7 (1861), 25–26. On corporal punishment in the eighteenth and early nineteenth centuries, see GARO, f. 5, st. 1, op. 2, d. 521 (1859); *Razvitie russkogo prava v pervoi polovine XIX veka* (Moscow, 1994), 161–71; John P. LeDonne, *Absolutism and Ruling Class: The Formation of the Russian Political Order, 1700–1825* (New York, 1991), ch. 11.

6. See, e.g., *Ustav o nakazaniiakh, nalagaemykh mirovymi sud'iami*, in *Sudebnye ustavy 20 noiabria 1864 goda*, 4th ed. (SPb, 1870); V. Vinogradov, comp., *Volostnoe pravlenie, volostnoi sud i ikh deloproizvodstvo* (SPb, 1904), 119–77; E. Tikhonov, *Volostnoi sud i mirovoi sud'ia v krest'ianskikh seleniiakh* (Kovno, 1872); MVD, *Trudy redaktsionnoi komissii po peresmotru zakonopolozhenii o krest'ianakh*, vol. 3 (SPb, 1904); I. M. Tiutriumov, comp., *Obshchee polozhenie o krest'ianakh*, 3rd ed. (Petrograd, 1915), 712ff.; V. Baftalovskii, "Obzor mestnogo upravleniia i suda," *Russkoe obozrenie*, no. 5 (1895), 375–91.

7. For examples, see GARF, f. 586, op. 1, d. 118, l. 28; K. Chepurnyi, "K voprosu o iuridicheskikh obychaiakh," *Universitetskie izvestiia*, no. 10 (1874), 650; "Obrashchik krest'ianskogo

But if the codes stipulated the sanctions to be applied to each crime, they usually did not prescribe the severity of punishments. Unfortunately, because of the brevity with which township scribes summarized criminal trials, court records offer little clue as to how such decisions were made. Still, two factors that appear repeatedly in the sources shed light upon this question. Most important, peasant judges considered the parties' reputation and standing in their communities, and much as did justices of the peace, they ruled "by conscience" (*po sovesti*). As in places as diverse as Scandinavian fishing settlements and Mexican and Ghanaian villages, what was done often was less important than who did it.[8] According to one observation from the mid-1870s, "judges know . . . which village women argue and why, which husbands beat their wives, which peasant is good and which is bad, who is a drunkard, lazy, a troublemaker, an informer, or a slanderer, which witnesses can be believed and those who cannot, who should be whipped and who can be fined or jailed without being ruined economically." More than thirty years later, another investigator found much the same. "Judges do not simply consider the immediate circumstances of a criminal case but examine all aspects of someone's life. If he is known for his good conduct and behavior, this will have an ameliorating affect and he may even be acquitted as a result."[9] *How* a crime was perpetrated also influenced judges' decisions, since deviant acts were themselves culturally defined according to social norms and codes of behavior that usually escaped the clerks' written records. Whether a crime had been committed at night, in a drunken state, or through breaking and entering, whether the accused had a prior record, was a suspect in other crimes, or simply had a bad reputation—all weighed against chances of acquittal or a light sentence.[10]

In addition to these individual considerations, both bribery and the intervention of influential villagers could play a significant role in swaying and shaping a *volost'* court's opinion. Its contemporary critics (and even some

suda," *MosVed,* no. 197 (1887), 5; "Rostov-na-Donu (Nakazanie)," *NizhL,* no. 105 (1899), 3; *Trudy,* 1:335; 6:189.

8. See, e.g., Barbara B. Yngvesson, "The Atlantic Fishermen," in Laura Nader and Harry F. Todd., Jr., eds., *The Disputing Process: Law in Ten Societies* (New York, 1978),59–85;*Yngvesson,* "Decision-Making and Dispute Settlement in a Swedish Fishing Village: An Ethnology of Law" (Ph.D. diss.,University of California, Berkeley, 1970).

9. I. Kostrov, *Iuridicheskie obychai krest'ian starozhilov Tomskoi gubernii* (Tomsk, 1876), 112; A. A. Charushin, "Volostnye sudy v bytovom ikh osveshchenii," *IAOiRS* 4, no. 21 (1912), 991. See also V. V. Ptitsyn, *Obychnoe sudoproizvodstvo krest'ian Saratovskoi gubernii* (SPb, 1886), 144. Petr Skorobogatyi, "Rol' krest'ianskikh sudei v protsesse," *IuV,* no. 6 (1881), 273–98, is the only study of *volost'* court judges.

10. Statistik, "O nakazaniiakh, nalagaemykh volostnymi sudami v Arkhangel'skoi gub.," *IAOiRS,* 5, 11 (1913), 506; GARF, f. 586, op. 1, d. 120, ll. 57–59; d. 118, ll. 13–14; Nader and Todd, eds., *Disputing Process,* 27. See also "Narodnoe pravosudie (Pis'mo iz provintsii)," *Nedelia,* no. 23, (1888), 729.

supporters) depicted rampant bribery and illegal interference in decision-making by township elders, clerks, and others. Such sources must be used with caution, yet there is no doubt that peasants regularly sought to influence the outcome of a case through the traditional method of "treating" their witnesses and elected magistrates. From districts throughout central Russia in the late 1890s, correspondents to the Tenishev ethnographic survey reported that paying witnesses continued as a widespread practice. "Not one trial takes place without the litigants treating their witnesses," wrote A. Kunitsyn from the Porkhovsk district of Pskov province in 1898, "and it often happens that they hire witnesses." In neighboring Smolensk province, "there are persons who, for a bottle of vodka, will serve a witnesses in any kind of [court] case. . . . Bribing witnesses or getting them drunk takes place everywhere, and [peasants] are so used to this that it is considered natural."[11] Paying *volost'* judges also remained prevalent at the end of the century, for as one saying succinctly put it, "What does the law matter to me if I know the judges?" Buying peasant magistrates vodka at the tavern, surreptitiously dropping off a half-bucket at their homes, and bringing them other gifts were common tactics in rural communities both prior to and long after emancipation.[12] Indeed, some judges demanded payment. One reporter from Smolensk province noted that the custom of taking fees in the form of vodka for hearing a court case "is considered a law." In 1875 the Riazan' Circuit Court tried a *volost'* judge on charges that he frequently demanded money from litigants to rule in their favor or to reduce sentences of those already convicted on criminal charges. He would usually send messengers from the local tavern, demanding that money be brought to him there. On other occasions he interrupted court sessions, took litigants into the shed at the *volost'* office, and there negotiated bribes.[13]

11. GARF, f. 586, op. 1, d. 117, l. 41; d. 120, l. 62. In Baklanova village of Riazan's Skopinsk district, peasants used a special term, *mogarych,* for the "treating" of witnesses, which took place upon the conclusion of a case. GARF, f. 586, op. 1, d. 118, l. 37.

12. The saying is from Charushin, "Volostnye sudy," 987. See also L. N. Pushkarev, *Dukhovnyi mir russkogo krest'ianina po poslovitsam XVII–XVIII vekov* (Moscow, 1984), 66–68; and, for examples, see GARF, f. 586, op. 1, d. 114, l. 58; "Sanktpeterburg. 16-go aprelia 1874," *Golos,* no. 105 (1874), 1–2; "Iz Epifani," *MosVed,* no. 142 (1876); D. F., "Iz praktiki volostnogo suda (Pis'mo iz Iranskogo uezda, Viatskoi gubernii)," *RusVed,* no. 254 (1885), 3; "Nashi volostnye sudy," *SudG* 23, no. 4 (1904), 7–8; K. Ia. Kozhukhar, "Zemskie nachal'niki," *VestP,* no. 11 (1905), 64–65. At least one defender of the *volost'* courts argued that bribe taking was an inevitable result of the fact that most township judges received either insignificant salaries or nothing at all for their work. "Vremennye uluchsheniia v organizatsii volostnogo suda," *Golos,* no. 237 (1872), 2. Figures on salaries for the early 1870s are available in *Trudy.* For later years, see GARO, f. 695, op. 21, sv. 232, d. 9 (1911), ll. 1–263.

13. GARF, f. 586, op. 1, d. 120, ll. 14, 30, 65; GARO, f. 640, op. 53, sv. 7, d. 74, ll. 2–30ob., 16–19. Writing in 1917, one land captain recalled discovering that a local beer hall had opened an account for the township judges, paid for by litigants. "Often the account was paid

Judges also experienced pressure from *volost'* elders, clerks, and other influential villagers and outsiders to decide cases in a particular manner, a type of interference that proved quite easy since, according to law, elders brought offenders before the court for trial, and there is no shortage of evidence showing how they stretched their legal authority by demanding that judges impose whatever sentence the elder deemed fit. Wrote one contemporary: "Even when a case is tried in the *volost'* court, peasants have no doubt that the elder ordered the judges to rule in a certain way and therefore lodge no complaints about the decision."[14] Township scribes, too, often told judges how to rule in judicial sessions. In 1898 a correspondent reported from Smolensk's Dorogobuzhsk district that the majority of *volost'* court cases were illegally decided under the direction of the clerk, which meant that decisions went in favor of those closest to this official. "Because of this the *volost'* court has no authority among the local population, and the peasants do not trust it."[15] Others simply took advantage of friendship or kinship ties with the judges, called in old favors or debts to influence a case, or used their personal power. Such was true of many noble landowners who maintained substantial power in their localities, including close ties with township elders, clerks, and even judges. As one correspondent was told about a particularly meddlesome landowner in the Viazemsk district of Smolensk province, "We can't litigate against him. He comes into the court at the *volost'* office and sits right down with the clerk and the judges, and you just stand there at the threshold with everybody looking at you. It's no good to litigate here, brother."[16]

It is impossible to know the full extent of these practices, but clearly they continued on a broad scale through the postemancipation decades. This is evident not only from turn-of-the-century ethnographic sources but also from the charges and complaints of abuse that came from all corners of the empire, leveled by outsiders as well as by exasperated peasants.[17] The very

---

twice—by both plaintif and accused." V. Polivanov, "Zapiski zemskogo nachal'nika," *RusM*, no. 9–10 (1917), 32.

14. Evgenii Markov, "Sel'skoe pravosudie," *RusRech'*, no. 7 (1881), 222. See also GARF, ibid., d. 120, l. 12; "Pravovye vozzreniia naroda," *Nedelia*, no. 26 (1880), 824; Petr Skorobogatyi, "Vliianie starshin i pisarei na otpravlenie volostnoi iustitsii," *IuV* 13, no. 12 (1881), 607–23; A. Redkin, "Zametka o volostnykh sudakh," *Nedelia*, no. 19 (1881), 648; "Vershilovskaia volost', Nizheg. gub.," *SevK*, no. 242 (1905), 3, for examples. Ptitsyn (*Obychnoe sudoproizvodstvo*, 81) estimated that at least one-fifth of all recorded *volost'* court cases were initiated by township or village elders.

15. GARF, f. 586, op. 1, d. 120, l. 12. See also d. 114, ll. 22, 122–24.

16. Ibid., d. 120, l. 12.

17. *Trudy Komissii po preobrazovaniiu volostnykh sudov*, 7 vols. (SPb, 1873–74), vol. 7, *passim* (hereafter: *Trudy*); V. S. Krotkov, *Volch'e stado* (Moscow, 1875), 127–50; A. A. Bashmakov, "Po puti k narodnomu pravosoznaniiu," *VestP* 31, no. 6 (1901), 34. Many claimed that the 1889 introduction of land captains curtailed abuse and corruption in the *volost'* courts, yet there is

methods of rural administration that carried over to the 1861 emancipation legislation abetted these abuses, for precisely because of their police powers to arrest and their judicial authority to punish, elders saw little wrong with their presence at court sessions to ensure that judges handed down a "proper" punishment. As the lowest level of rural police authority, elders behaved no differently from such of their superiors as the police captain and his underlings, the constables, who regularly ordered township courts to punish peasants or, as one *volost'* clerk recalled, forced the court to travel to villages where "legal" punishments would be meted out.[18]

Repeatedly condemned as a failure of rural self-administration, this ability to influence and appropriate local justice through bribes or other means proved one of the tried and tested avenues by which villagers could redress the asymmetrical power relationships that prevailed within rural society as well as in its relationship with state and law. Peasants were quite willing to protest if a situation grew too abusive, as often happened when powerful cliques or wealthy villagers exerted near total control over local justice and administration, or when a judge grew especially greedy.[19] But since they were limited to *volost'* courts for most civil suits and criminal trials, villagers participated, willingly or not, in the process of appropriating and reshaping the rural court system, retaining methods by which the wheels of local justice had long been greased and social control maintained through the incorporation of such factors as kinship, patron-client relations, and friendship into the judicial process.

## PUNISHMENT BY *VOLOST'* COURTS

Once judges decided a case, whether "by conscience," bribery, or pressure, they still had to accommodate state law when applying punishment. Despite the Rural Judicial Code, flexibility remained possible through the simple

---

little hard evidence either substantiating or contradicting this assertion. Although the 1861 laws forbade township elders from interfering or even being present at court sessions, it proved impossible to enforce this regulation. Perhaps conceding to local realities, the reforms of 1889 allowed district assemblies, if they felt it necessary, to appoint *volost'* elders as chief judge. Vinogradov, *Volostnoe pravlenie*, 119.

18. N. M. Astyrev, "V volostnykh pisariakh," *VE* 16, no. 7 (1885), 224.

19. Between 1885 and 1917, for example, the newspaper *Sel'skii vestnik* regularly published protests of this sort from peasants around the country. On the influence of local cliques prior to emancipation, see *Materialy dlia geografii i statistiki Rossii. Permskaia guberniia* (SPb, 1864), part 1, 552; N. A. Minenko, "Traditional Forms of Investigation and Trial among the Russian Peasants of Western Siberia in the Eighteenth and First Half of the Nineteenth Centuries," *SAA* 21, no. 3 (1982–83), esp. 60–63; Jerman W. Rose, "The Russian Peasant Emancipation and the Problem of Rural Administration" (Ph.D. diss., University of Kansas, 1976), 104; Edgar Melton, "Household Economies and Communal Conflicts on a Russian Serf Estate, 1800–1817," *JSH* 26, no. 3 (1993), 559–81.

mechanism of choosing one form of punishment over another. Although the law limited this choice by prescribing specific sanctions for certain crimes, the two most commonly employed punishments, fines and jail, were usually interchangeable and their application thus left to the judges' discretion. In other important areas, however, local opinion diverged sharply from the various regulations designed to guide peasant communities emerging from serfdom. Decades before the state did away with obligatory public labor in 1906, for instance, township courts had all but ceased using it as a punishment, and by the time of its abolition, flogging with birch rods was applied in only a small fraction of criminal cases. Hence if we are to judge only by the types of punishments handed down by *volost'* courts during the postemancipation era, in practice they functioned much the same as did justices of the peace, a large part of whose jurisdiction peasant courts inherited in 1889. The two bodies differed, however, in that administrative authority, both local and higher, greatly circumscribed the power of *volost'* courts, limiting the range of offenses with which they dealt while leaving violence and harsher punishments for administrative agencies.

*Public Work*

Both before and especially after emancipation, rural courts made little use of enforced public work, although various forms of this punishment had long existed under Russian law (and would be revived following the October Revolution). The majority of peasant officials questioned by the Liuboshchinskii Commission stated that their courts almost never handed down such sentences for the simple reason that villages had virtually no worthwhile tasks for guilty parties to perform.[20] Article 427 of the Rural Judicial Code prescribed that a person sentenced to public labor "should be sent to a model farm," which did not even exist in 1839 when the code was written, nor did *volost'* courts have access to those created after emancipation. More realistically, another article of the code suggested sweeping village streets and washing the floors of public buildings as possible tasks.[21] Still, courts were reluctant to impose public work since the community would have to hire a guard to make sure that the person sentenced actually performed the work. Many peasant officials simply felt that this punishment had no real benefit either for the guilty party or the community. A *volost'* official from Vladimir province called sweeping the street "a worthless punishment" in 1872, and an 1891 study of rural justice in the Irkutsk region

20. For example, *Trudy*, 2:112, 143; 3:301; Kostrov, *Iuridicheskie obychai*, 114.

21. M. V. Dukhovskoi, *Imushchestvennye prostupki po resheniiam volostnykh sudov* (Moscow, 1891), 41–42; Vinogradov, *Volostnoe pravlenie*, 239 (arts. 501–2). As late as 1902 one land captain was still calling for the establishment of colonies for juvenile offenders in each province. V. Ianovich, *Itogi shestiletiia (Zametki Zemskogo Nachal'nika)* (Perm', 1902), 125–26.

found that "public work is imposed very rarely because it is believed to be useless." The government, too, evidently doubted the efficacy of enforced community work since its rural code stipulated the sentence for very few infractions such as illegal family divisions, begging, and "for unmarried or widowed men and women found guilty of indecent conduct."[22]

In practice, then, *volost'* courts rarely imposed public labor—mainly on women and the elderly. As in earlier times, courts most commonly meted it out to those convicted for immoral behavior (*rasputstvo,* or debauchery), though it was employed on occasion in cases of theft, drunkenness, disorderly conduct, failure to appear in court, and disobedience to officials. Village and township elders, too, used the same penalty without turning to the court.[23] As for the tasks assigned, women sentenced to public work usually found themselves forced to wash the floor at the *volost'* office or—far more shameful—to sweep the village street. Offenders might also be ordered to clean roads and repair bridges, cut or split firewood, perform minor repairs to the township office, or do chores for the parish priest. In 1869 a *volost'* court of Iaroslavl' province tried a woman whose dog repeatedly bit passersby and sentenced her to work for three days mending the local bridge and to destroy the animal.[24]

It is quite likely that the sentence of public work functioned as a type of charivari in the past, given the emphasis on shaming the guilty party and the possible addition of public derision during the performance of such tasks. Several cases of charivari recorded after emancipation still incorporated elements of public labor combined with humiliation. Each incident saw peasants force offenders to sweep the streets while a crowd accompanied and mocked them. In 1883, a woman from the village of Karasusskoe was thus punished for showing disrespect to her father-in-law. After sentence had been passed, villagers gave her a broom and a crowd led her through the entire town, forcing her to sweep beneath the windows of each home as well as in front of the local school.[25] But by the second half of the nineteenth

22. *Trudy,* 2:60; M. V. Zagoskin, *Otvety na programmu Imperatorskogo russkogo Geograficheskogo Obshchestva, dlia sobiraniia narodnykh iuridicheskikh obychaev* (Irkutsk, 1891), 106–7; Vinogradov, *Volostnoe pravlenie,* 239 (arts. 167, 180–83, 499–502); Druzhinin, *Gosudarstvennye krest'iane,* 1:582.

23. *Trudy,* 2:41–42, 288; 3:2, 13, 91, 102; V. Kandinskii, "O nakazaniiakh po resheniiam volostnykh sudov Moskovskoi gub.," in M. N. Kharuzin, ed., *Sbornik svedenii dlia izucheniia byta krest'ianskogo naseleniia Rossii,* part 1 (Moscow, 1889), 17; I. I. Shrag, "Krest'ianskie sudy Vladimirskoi i Moskovskoi gubernii," *IuV,* no. 5–6 (1877), 87–88.

24. *Trudy,* 3:100, no. 40; 2:52. As stated by peasant officials in Vladimir province, they imposed punishments of this sort "as a warning" or to disgrace the accused. Skorobogatyi, "Primemenie nakazanii," 563.

25. "Publichnoe posramlenie zhenshchiny za nepochtenie k svekru," *RusVed,* no. 330 (1883), 2.

century, shaming punishments had for the most part devolved onto the community itself since the law no longer permitted their application by courts. As for public work as a legally sanctioned punishment, long after peasant courts had de facto done away with it the government formally abolished its use on October 5, 1906, because, according to an MVD circular, "It does not correspond to the contemporary principles of criminal law and is incompatible with the civil equality of rural inhabitants."[26]

### Fines

Most contemporary studies considered fines to be the most harmful of all punishments that *volost'* courts and other judicial or administrative agencies could impose. This was one reason, some argued, for the continued and widespread use of corporal punishment. During debates among members of the commission that produced Russia's emancipation legislation, supporters of the birch had claimed it must be retained because the peasantry did not have money to pay fines.[27] Later investigations appeared to confirm these views. In an 1880 study, for example, P. Berezanskii wrote that "a fine may bring financial hardship and prevent the guilty party from paying taxes which, under collective responsibility [*krugovaia poruka*], are the obligation of the entire commune."[28] Village and *volost'* officials from several localities told government investigators during the early 1870s that "even without fines the peasant already has nothing with which to pay taxes, and it is impossible to collect a fine from poor peasants without selling their property; this cannot be done, however, without ruining them." As a result, some townships imposed fines only on wealthier peasants, reserving harsher punishments for the poor. In Vsegodichesk *volost'*, Vladimir province, "only decent, respectable people are punished with fines, and the most worthless good-for-nothings who have no money to take are jailed or flogged."[29] Decisions about who would be fined thus had as much to do with status, reputation, and influence in the community as they did with ability to pay.

26. This circular is dated December 9, 1906. Statistik, "O nakazaniiakh," 494.

27. P. Bronovskii, "Pasynki russkogo zakonodatel'stva," *RusM*, no. 1 (1900), 131; G. Dzhanshiev, *Epokha velikikh reform* (Moscow, 1900), 219–33. If the person sentenced to a fine was unable to pay, however, the punishment could be changed to incarceration or public work. *Volost'* courts were instructed to calculate two rubles in value for each day of jail or public work. I. N. Aristov, comp., *Volostnoi sud po zakonu 12-go iiuliia 1889 goda*, (Kazan', 1893), 24; Tiutriumov, *Obshchee polozhenie*, 737.

28. Pavel Berezanskii, *Obychnoe ugolovnoe pravo krest'ian Tambovskoi gubernii* (Kiev, 1880), 165–68. See also Skorobogatyi, "Primenenie nakazanii," 569; *Trudy*, 1:358. For a contrary view, see Peter Czap, "Peasant Class Courts and Peasant Customary Justice in Russia, 1861–1912," *JSH* 1, no. 2 (1967), 170–71.

29. *Trudy*, 2:70; 3:13, 51; Shrag, "Krest'ianskie sudy," no. 5–6, 88–89.

Nearly all reports of this kind drew selectively from replies given early in the 1870s to members of the Liuboshchinskii Commission. We cannot know whether peasant officials exaggerated the frequency of strict punishments in order to emphasize the poverty of their community, since government officials were always believed to be seeking information that would help them collect more taxes. What we do know is that before emancipation, rural courts, village assemblies, serf owners, and other authorities regularly fined peasants for minor infractions, as had pre-emancipation village courts.[30] In other words, fines were widely used prior to the reform era, and even more so thereafter. An 1862 survey of Vitebsk province showed that they accounted for 32 percent of the punishments handed down by all peasant courts; for Tver province's 244 *volost'* courts, this figure was 37.5 percent in 1896.[31] Comparable information is available for individual townships such as Ol'gorsk, Moscow province, where fines were levied in 36 percent of all criminal cases tried during 1890. This is not to suggest that every community applied monetary punishments with equal frequency, for local economic conditions and personal and political considerations clearly played their part in determining the penalty judges chose. In a township bordering Ol'gorsk *volost'*, for instance, judges sentenced only four peasants—or 5 percent of the total—to fines in 1890.[32] Still, archival evidence in particular indicates that by the 1880s and 1890s (and probably much earlier), *volost'* courts were using fines and jail far more often than the birch. Indeed, whereas the emancipation regulations had allowed courts to substitute jail or flogging if peasants could not pay a fine, the 1889 reforms stipulated that fines could be used *in place of* a jail term.[33] This was much more useful, peasant judges told a correspondent in Iaroslavl' province's Poshekhonsk district in 1897, since the money collected benefited the entire community.[34]

Like justices of the peace prior to 1890, township courts and officials levied fines most frequently for disturbing the peace, drinking or celebrating when church services were being conducted, throwing garbage into the

30. GARO, f. 5, st. 1, op. 2, d. 1100, ll. 1–3; L. S. Prokof'eva, *Krest'ianskaia obshchina*, 159; A. Povalishin, *Riazanskie pomeshchiki i ikh krepostnye* (Riazan', 1903), 92; A. M. Traat, "Opyt i nekotorye rezul'taty statisticheskoi obrabotki dokumentatsii volostnykh sudov," in *Istochnikovedenie otechestvennoi istorii* (Moscow, 1986), 163–98.

31. "Volostnye sudy Vitebskoi gubernii," *SPbVed*, no. 187 (1865), 2; M. A. Mikhailovskii, "Sudebno-administrativnye uchrezhdeniia Tverskoi gubernii za piatiletie 1892–1897 godov," in *Sbornik pravovedeniia i obshchestvennykh znanii*, vol. 8 (1898), 161. See also *Trudy*, 1:813; 3:301; Zagoskin, *Otvety*, 105–6.

32. TsGIAgM, f. 28, op. 1, d. 19, 5–60b.

33. GARF, f. 586, op. 1, d. 123 (Iaroslavl' province), l. 14; d. 122 (Tula province), l. 20; d. 117, l. 43; Aristov, *Volostnoi sud*, 21; Tiutriumov, *Obshchee polozhenie*, 737.

34. GARF, f. 586, op. 1, d. 123, l. 14.

streets or polluting a local water source, selling spoiled food, riding reck-
lessly through a public place, and not appearing at a fire to render assistance.
Again stressing the importance of honor within village communities, the
Rural Judicial Code stipulated that any peasant who insulted another "by
word or by deed" should beg forgiveness or pay the victim "for this dishonor."[35] According to testimony gathered in the 1870s and 1890s, nearly
all *volost'* judges fined peasants for failure to appear in court or for not responding to a summons; given the frequency of this infraction, *volost'* coffers
certainly benefited from the funds collected. When, in 1890, rural courts began using the code of punishments formerly applied by justices of the peace,
income from monetary sentences increased significantly; not only had the
maximum level of fines risen tenfold, but even more infractions were now
punishable in this manner. Many rural courts certainly took to heart the old
saying, "Don't beat them with cudgels, beat them with rubles."[36]

It was not only the courts that forced peasant lawbreakers to dig into their
purses. Village and *volost'* elders as well as nonpeasant officials commonly
levied fines without formal trial or hearing. Elders could impose a fine of up
to one ruble for petty infractions, mostly regulations covering everything
from land use to housing construction, trade, the operation of taverns, and
a range of local norms.[37] Higher officials, too, had authority to fine and
arrest villagers on a broad array of charges, including failure to obey their
orders. Indeed, income derived from fines levied by land captains and
township elders contributed significantly to *volost'* coffers, sometimes greatly
exceeding the amount brought in by local courts. During 1893, *volost'* administrations in one precinct of Riazan' province collected 57.50 rubles in
fines, 75 percent of which was exacted by the land captain. In another
precinct, the land captain and *volost'* elders contributed 67 percent of all
fines collected; elsewhere, these figures ranged from 20 to 48 percent.[38]

35. Vinogradov, *Volostnoe pravlenie,* 240, art. 515; Compare the use of fines by peace courts,
such as that of the fourth precinct of Bogorodsk district, Moscow province. TsGIAgM, f. 703,
op. 1, d. 48, ll. 7ob., 110ob., 120ob., 20–200ob., 25, 32, 89, 93, 136. Before 1845, Russia's criminal code also imposed monetary compensation for insult and slander. *Razvitie russkogo prava,*
208–9.

36. Aristov, *Volostnoi sud,* 31–60; *Ustav o nakazaniiakh, nalagaemykh mirovymi sud'iami,* 29–
153; N. P. Druzhinin, "Krest'ianskii sud v ego poslednem fazise," *Nabliudatel'* 11, no. 3 (1893),
243–57; Druzhinin, "Preobrazovannyi volostnoi sud," in N. Druzhinin, *Iuridicheskoe polozhenie
krest'ian* (SPb, 1897), 332.

37. I. P. Pinkornelli, comp., *Rukovodstvo dlia sel'skikh starost* (Khorol', 1894), 20–21; A. A.
Kornilov, "Krest'ianskoe samoupravlenie po Polozheniiu 19 fevralia," in *Velikaia Reforma,* vol. 6
(Moscow, 1911), 148–49; Vinogradov, *Volostnoe pravlenie,* 11–12; MVD, *Sbornik uzakonenii,*
7–8.

38. GARO, f. 695, op. 5, sv. 62, d. 1, ll. 19–77 (Mikhailov and Spassk districts). On the authority of higher officials, see GARO, f. 5, st. 4, op. 5, d. 675 (1863); I. P. Kupchinov, *Krest'ianskoe samoupravlenie,* 2nd ed. (Moscow, 1905), 31–32; Pestrzhetskii, "O sude krest'ian," 20–21.

There were still other kinds of penalties or restitution imposed outside the courts either by village elders, by the assembly, or simply by peasants acting, as they saw it, in keeping with official law. When someone committed an infraction or caused damage requiring compensation, the perpetrator's property would be confiscated and sold, especially if those demanding payment were met with the culprit's refusal or inability to pay. This had long been official practice during the collection of tax arrears, and after emancipation it continued as a sanctioned administrative measure. Hence villagers adapted and extended state law to a broader range of infractions, pawning the property of guilty parties at the local tavern in exchange for vodka or selling it at auction. In effect, the accused "treated" the community to drinks, usually through the forced sale of clothing, agricultural tools, or even a wagon wheel.[39] Thus, when a Riazan' village woman stole a ham in 1867, the elder fined her one ruble. But when she claimed that she could not pay, he seized her sheepskin coat, pawned it, and bought vodka for himself and the victims of this crime. A more serious case from 1892 involved a township official in Viatka province who embezzled 2,000 rubles of public funds. At an assembly meeting called to discuss this matter, the *volost'* elder announced that "according to law" villagers had the right to sell off the culprit's possessions, "down to the last board," in order to make up the sum. So 400 angry township residents assaulted his property; livestock, trunks, grain, flour, furniture, wagons, carts, sledges, and even the doors from his house were taken and sold by the crowd. Forty-four people would later be charged with arbitrariness.[40]

## Incarceration

Regulations introduced for state peasants between 1837 and 1839 stipulated that jails be created for each village and *volost'* court. Laws published

---

MVD regulations stipulated that income from fines should be placed into a township's general fund or, by order of district boards for peasant affairs, be assigned for a specific purpose such as upkeep of public buildings or support of charitable institutions. Most *volost'* administrations used the bulk of this income to pay for repairs and maintenance to their own buildings and the local jail. GARO, f. 695, op. 5 (1894), sv. 62, d. 1, ll. 7–70b., 19, 29–300b., 33, 35, 58–59, 75–77.

39. A. A. Titov, *Iuridicheskie obychai sela Nikola-Perevoz, Sulostskoi volosti, Rostovskogo uezda* (Iaroslavl', 1888), 100; Skorobogatyi, "Primenenie nakazanii," 562, 563–64. On official uses of this punishment, including its frequent misuse by overzealous rural police, see GARO, f. 5, st. 1, op. 2, d. 1636 (1878); d. 1652 (1879), ll. 1–2; GARF, f. 586, op. 1, d. 123, ll. 3–11.

40. Iakushkin, *Obychnoe pravo*, 2:336, no. 2897; "Delo o samoupravstve krest'ianskogo obshchestva," *VolzhV*, no. 282 (1892), 3. For similar cases, see "V uezdnom s"ezde. 'Sborshchik podatei' i mir," *RiazV*, no. 142 (1910), 3; GARO, f. 697, op. 1 (1880), sv. 7, d. 275. V. Bez—ov., "Iz derevni (Pis'mo 4-e)," *Sovremennaia letopis'*, no. 31 (1863), 12, claims that this practice was on the rise after emancipation.

in 1868 ordered that a special cottage exist in every township seat to hold prisoners under jurisdiction of the peasant administration and that it be divided into sections for men and women; townships lacking a separate jail or the means to build one were permitted to use the administration building itself for this purpose.[41] Postreform *volost'* courts could, until 1889, impose sentences of up to seven days' incarceration; following the reforms of 1889, punishments ranged from fifteen to thirty days in this local lock-up or "cooler" (*kholodnitsa*), as it was commonly called. The law also allowed village and *volost'* elders to employ jail sentences for many administrative and criminal offenses.[42] By the 1880s—if not earlier in many parts of rural Russia—short-term imprisonment in local jails had become the most widespread form of punishment for petty crimes.

Despite government orders to create local jails, the postreform countryside suffered a serious shortage of proper facilities. Peasants sentenced by *volost'* courts and village or township elders most often served their time in a room at the *volost'* administration office, which might be without lighting, windows, or bars, unheated, and without a separation for men and women. In the early 1870s, some *volost'* offices did not even have a room for keeping prisoners, placing them instead in the building's shed (*seni*) or antechamber, and this remained common practice near the end of the century as well. The average *volost'* lock-up could hold from six to ten persons, and even when larger villages maintained separate huts as jails, the majority were cramped and often in terrible condition.[43] As one proponent of prison reform wrote in 1900, "[Rural] jails are of the most primitive sort: The walls are full of cracks and holes, the stove is nearly collapsing, soot covers everything and the floors are impossibly filthy." Such lock-ups averaged about seven cubic meters in size, but some were as small as two cubic meters. "And

41. *Svod zakonov Rossiiskoi imperii*, vol. 14: *Ustav o soderzhashchikhsia pod strazheiu*, unofficial ed. (Moscow, 1910),, art. 152; M. N. Gernet, *Istoriia tsarskoi tiur'my*, 3rd ed., vol. 2 (Moscow, 1961), 63; P. N. Zyrianov, "Sotsial'naia struktura mestnogo upravleniia kapitalisticheskoi Rossii (1861–1914 gg.)," *Istoricheskie zapiski*, no. 107 (1982), 249. On the small size of Russia's prison population before the 1830s, see Gernet, *Istoriia tsarskoi tiur'my*, vol. 1 (Moscow, 1951), 302–17.

42. *Svod zakonov*, vol. 14, art. 152; Vinogradov, *Volostnoe pravlenie*, 12–13, 119–26; Aristov, *Volostnoi sud*, 20; A. Gorodetskii, "Arestnye pomeshcheniia pri volostnykh pravleniiakh," *SudG*, no. 45 (1894), 6; S. Cherniavskii, *Narodnyi sud* (Kamenets-Podol'sk, 1901), 16. Peace courts could sentence to a maximum of three months in jail or up to one year in prison. *Ustav o nakazaniiakh, nalagaemykh mirovymi sud'iami*, art. 1.

43. *Trudy*, 2:28, 42, 52, 70; 3:2, 13, 20, 51, and *passim;* GARO, f. 695, op. 5, sv. 62, d. 1, ll. 19–20, 33, 59; GARF, f. 586, op. 1, d. 120, ll. 30, 65; d. 120, l. 15. See also Shrag, "Krest'ianskie sudy," no. 5–6, 91; Ptitsyn, *Obychnoe sudoproizvodstvo*, 155–57; Berezanskii, *Obychnoe ugolovnoe pravo*, 170–71; Titov, *Iuridicheskie obychai*, 97.

these bug-infested places are so packed with prisoners that one can neither sit nor lie down."[44]

For all that, incarceration in peasant communities was more relaxed and less dangerous than at overcrowded district or central prisons. *Volost'* courts accommodated the peasant work schedule as much as possible. Ignoring legal requirements that their decisions should be carried out within thirty days, peasant courts and officials commonly delayed sentences until the conclusion of fieldwork in autumn. Hence, jail populations tended to be small during spring and summer, swelling in autumn and winter as peasants appeared at the township office to serve their sentences.[45] At times, even the state allowed for such practices. In March 1911, for example, Riazan''s governor informed his district commandants that, due to the upcoming planting season, punishment of needy peasants arrested under the province's binding regulations (*obiazatel'nye postanovleniia*) could be postponed until the end of the work season.[46] Peasants could also ask the elder, whose duty it was to carry out court decisions, to delay implementation of their sentence, which was almost always allowed if the petitioner had a good reason. Many villagers staved off even short sentences for years by using the appellate process. In one typical case, a Riazan' villager was sentenced to fifteen days' incarceration in 1887, but because of appeals he did not actually serve his punishment until five years later.[47]

Conditions were not especially harsh for prisoners serving these jail stints unless they had been sentenced to strict incarceration on bread and water. Although the Rural Code required that prisoners be confined "under guard," peasants held at the *volost'* office were rarely supervised or forced to follow any scheduled regime. According to a 1912 report from Arkhangel'sk province, "Prisoners are strictly guarded only when the land captain pays a visit."[48] Family members usually brought food and drink; where

44. A. B., "Sel'skie arestantskie (Pis'mo iz Nikolaevskogo uezda, Samarskoi gub.)," *Nedelia*, no. 14 (1900), 496. Peasants also termed these jails "bug-infested" (*klopovnitsa*). GARF, f. 586, op. 1, d. 118, l. 37. On conditions in district prisons, see GARO, f. 5, st. 3, op. 4, d. 2376, ll. 1–5; f. 857, op. 25, sv. 30, d. 5; Ilinskii, "Tiur'my v g. Iur'eve, Vladimirskoi gubernii," *VOGSP*, vol. 1 (1872), 47–81; V. K—nev., "Zhizn' tiur'my v shestidesiatykh godakh," *VE*, no. 1 (1888), 151–206.

45. GARO, f. 70, op. 2, sv. 1, d. 3, ll. 1–43 (1899); f. 76, op. 5, sv. 3, d. 6, ll. 2–68 (1894); TsGIAgM, f. 1963, op. 1, d. 4.

46. GARO, f. 5, st. 3, op. 4, d. 5395, l. 1. These orders were quickly followed by the postponement of punishment for large numbers of peasants and the release of many others.

47. GARO, f. 72, op. 18, sv. 10a, d. 5, l. 2. Peace courts, too, made adjustments based on peasant requests for postponement of their sentence. See, e.g., TsGIAgM, f. 576, op. 1, d. 124, ll. 18–18ob., 20–21.

48. Charushin, "Volostnye sudy," 994.

this was not possible, township elders used public funds to feed prisoners. Provisions from the family commonly included alcoholic beverages and tobacco, and though officials complained about the practice, they did little to stop it. If the prisoners were locals they sometimes wandered about freely, even being released to attend mass or visit the tavern. "Jail has no benefit for the peasant and does not serve as punishment," griped *volost'* officials of Tambov province in 1872. "He sleeps all day in the cell and often gets drunk if the guard is not attentive." They looked upon incarceration as relaxation, a view shared by one village elder in Vladimir province: "Jail does nothing, and supervision at the lock-up is such that incarceration means the prisoners rest and get drunk." Numerous sources, in fact, spoke of prisoners drinking at the township jail or being released by the guard to drink tea or liquor at the tavern. One correspondent wrote from Smolensk province in 1898 that prisoners "almost never serve their sentences in the [lock-up]," but in the *volost'* office or "at complete liberty."[49]

This picture of rest and relaxation was probably exaggerated. Peasant prisoners frequently came before the court for rowdiness, causing disturbances in the lock-up, and attempted escape. Four Riazan' peasants sentenced to short jail terms in 1889 by their township elder caused a noisy row in the lock-up, during which they broke the stove and damaged the sleeping bench. The elder therefore brought his prisoners before the *volost'* court, requesting that they be punished "to the highest degree of the law" for causing damages while trying to escape. The court found all four prisoners guilty and sentenced one to twenty lashes, two to ten lashes, and one to three more days in the cooler.[50]

Physical assault and even torture of prisoners also proved common within the confines of the *volost'* administration building or its jail. Between 1872 and 1913, circuit courts annually tried an average of 936 officials on charges of assault or torture—a deceptively low figure since few villagers dared to bring charges given the likelihood of vengeance.[51] In November 1868, for example, Irina Karaseva came to a township seat in Riazan' province to lodge a complaint of insult against a fellow villager who had accused her of theft. Believing the charges against her, however, the village elder beat and flogged her with birch rods with the aim of forcing a confession.[52] In November 1914 a Mikhailov district village assembly resolved to

49. Berezanskii, *Obychnoe ugolovnoe pravo*, 168–70; *Trudy*, 2:54; B. M. Firsov and I. G. Kiseleva, comps., *Byt velikorusskikh krest'ian-zemlepashtsev* (SPb, 1993), 69; Ptitsyn, *Obychnoe sudoproizvodstvo*, 155–56; GARF, f. 586, op. 1, d. 120, l. 65. See also d. 123, l. 15; d. 117, l. 43.

50. GARO, f. 717, op. 1, sv. 1, d. 10, ll. 4–5.

51. *Svody*, part 2, table 1; GARO, f. 694, op. 2 (1862), sv. 39, dd. 843, 844, 853.

52. GARO, f. 641, op. 4, sv. 12, d. 14, ll. 3–3ob. See also GARF, f. 586, op. 1, d. 120, l. 13, noting that "interrogations under torture are frequent."

exile Grigorii and Vasilii Kutlev for "dangerous and depraved behavior." In an appeal of this sentence, Grigorii's wife claimed that her husband had been falsely implicated in a crime by Vasilii. She explained that two constables had arrested Vasilii on suspicion of burglary and, to force a confession, mercilessly beat him at the *volost'* office using a whip and a flail. It was only from terror and the beating that Vasilii confessed, the woman said, "hoping to save his life," and he also named her husband as an accomplice.[53] On occasion, police officers as well as village and *volost'* elders resorted to such extreme tortures (burning, whipping, and day-long beatings, to note but a few) that their victims died. A case heard by the Moscow Judicial Chamber in 1893 involved one drunken prisoner held at a *volost'* jail in Nizhnii Novgorod province who, because of his violent behavior, was ordered bound hand and foot by the police commandant. Peasant hundreders tied him tightly and left him until evening, by which time his entire body had become swollen from lack of circulation. On the following day they took him to the hospital, but he died a week later. When brought to trial, the hundreders pleaded innocent, saying, "We were ordered by the commandant, so we tied the prisoner up; we always do this. We tie up all rowdies with rope and put them in the shed to lie down. Nobody has ever died from it!"[54]

Contemporary accounts note that villagers looked upon a prison term as ruinous, particularly for young people or those convicted of minor offenses and incarcerated among hardened criminals. "One returns from prison a completely lost soul," a reporter was told in Arkhangel'sk province at the start of the twentieth century. Peasants also cruelly mocked and ridiculed fellow villagers who had served time in a penal battalion or prison, calling them "exiles," "prisoners," or much worse, and suspected them of crimes committed after their return. Thus even when communities accepted former convicts back, they were kept under close supervision.[55] More commonly, they refused to readmit them. An 1845 law gave rural communities the right to do so, in which case former convicts became state wards to be settled either on public land far from their native village or in Siberia. Such refusals were so frequent that they usually exceeded banishments by communal decree,

53. GARO, f. 695, op. 25, sv. 271, d. 283, ll. 50–52. See also f. 79, op. 1 (1890), d. 14; op. 2 (1891), d. 59; "Sessiia Moskovskoi sudebnoi palaty v g. Riazani," *RiazV*, no. 238 (1910), 2–3. "Istiazanie zhenshchin," *NizhL*, no. 76 (1897), 4; "Istiazanie," *SevK*, no. 86 (1904), 4; "Izbienie krest'ian v Ponevezhskom uezde," *PV*, no. 119 (1906), 3; "V sudebnoi palate," *RiazV*, no. 25 (1911), 2.

54. "Volostnoe istiazanie," *Nedelia*, no. 8 (1893), 240–41. See also "Prevyshenie vlasti," *VolzhV*, no. 98 (1892), 3–4; "Izbienie politseiskimi," *Pravo*, no. 11 (1903), 792–93; I. Ivaniukov, "Ocherki provintsial'noi zhizni," *RusM*, no. 1 (1897), 153.

55. Titov, *Iuridicheskie obychai*, 98; P. S. Efimenko, *Sbornik narodnykh iuridicheskikh obychaev Arkhangel'skoi gubernii* (Arkhangel'sk, 1869), 237; GARF, f. 586, op. 1, d. 118, l. 32; d. 120, ll. 57–58.

greatly increasing the number of administrative exiles.[56] In October 1899, for instance, the Teleshovskii village assembly of Moscow province refused to readmit a peasant who had served a one-year prison sentence for theft, stating that he was "a completely useless and dangerous community member." The government therefore assigned the former convict to settlement in western Siberia.[57] Communities provided little explanation for rejecting an ex-convict. Most frequently, village resolutions simply pointed to past behavior and the stigma of one's sentence as the primary determinants for rejection and final expulsion. Some communities received support and encouragement in their decisions from local landed nobles, whose formal power to exile peasants ended at emancipation but who, throughout the 1860s and later, often pressured village leaders to pass resolutions of rejection.[58]

## Corporal Punishment

By far the most controversial and widely debated element of rural justice following serfdom's abolition was flogging with birch rods, the abolition of which became an important goal of Russian liberals near the end of the century. As its opponents rightly saw, after 1861 corporal punishment as a method of legal retribution against most male peasant lawbreakers, even in mitigated form, laid bare the contradictory character of the emancipation legislation, which sought to turn peasants into citizens while upholding or-

56. *Otchet po glavnomu tiuremnomu upravleniiu*, vols. 1–34, part 9; Tiutriumov, *Obshchee polozhenie*, 93; K. V. N., "Ssylka po prigovoram krest'ianskikh i meshchanskikh obshchestv," *RusRech'*, no. 9 (1881), 50; P. Mullov, "Vliianie ssylki na brak po russkim zakonam," *ZhMIu*, no. 5 (1861), 253. Of 74,927 persons administratively banished between 1882 and 1898, 57.7 percent (43,203) had been refused readmittance to their communes because of previous sentences. Only 35.9 percent were exiled by assembly resolution for "depraved" behavior. A. D. Margolis, "O chislennosti i razmeshchenii ssyl'nykh v Sibiri v kontse XIX v.," in *Ssylka i katorga v Sibiri (XVIII–nachalo XX v.)* (Novosibirsk, 1975), 225.

57. TsGIAgM, f. 62, op. 4, d. 381, ll. 1–30b., 5–6, 8–13. See also f. 62, op. 4, d. 378, ll. 3–30b., 4–40b., 7–70b.

58. See, for example, GARO, f. 694, op. 10 (1870), sv. 214, dd. 300–306; op. 12 (1872), sv. 243, dd. 272–74; op. 21 (1881), sv. 391, dd. 434–36; and, for noble-initiated resolutions, f. 694, op. 4 (1864), sv. 100, d. 669; op. 10, sv. 214, d. 292; op. 11 (1871), sv. 229, d. 271; op. 12, sv. 244, d. 330.

59. James Downey, "The Campaign against Corporal Punishment in Late Imperial Russia, 1863–1904: The Creation of a Civil Society" (Ph.D. diss., Indiana University, 1993), treats the movement for abolition. Among published works, see N. Evreinov, *Istoriia telesnykh nakazanii v Rossii* (Petrograd, 1917); V. M. Mikhailov, *O vrede telesnykh nakazanii v obshchestvenno-meditsinskom otnoshenii* (SPb, 1897); Mikhail Stupin, *Istoriia telesnykh nakazanii v Rossii ot Sudebnikov do nastoiashchego vremeni* (Vladikavkaz, 1887); A. G. Timofeev, *Istoriia telesnykh nakazanii v russkom prave* (SPb, 1904); D. N. Zhbankov and V. I. Iakovenko, *Telesnye nakazaniia v Rossii v nastoiashchee vremia* (Moscow, 1899); Stephen P. Frank, "Emancipation and the Birch: The Perpetuation of Corporal Punishment in Rural Russia, 1861–1907," *JGO* 45, no. 3 (1997), 1–16.

der through the officially sanctioned use of shame and violence.[59] More important, for many peasants flogging kept alive memories of serfdom and served as a reminder of their inequality. Before 1861, it had been a key element of control; together with whipping it was employed not only by peasant courts at both the village and *volost'* levels but by village assemblies, serfowners, and their stewards, in criminal, district, and military courts, within prisons and among exiles, and by a range of government and police officials.[60]

By the eve of emancipation corporal punishment had been restricted to the unfree classes or to those, like exiles, who lost all civil rights through judicial or administrative process. *Volost'* courts retained the use of flogging with birch rods as one of three main forms of punishment the state allowed.[61] It is of more than passing interest that in 1765 birch rods had also replaced whipping for offenders under the age of fifteen. For a century prior to 1861, in other words, the birch had been associated with punishment of children, an analogy that bore striking similarities to contemporary attitudes toward the rural population. Viewed by their social superiors as child-like, ignorant, and simple, peasants remained unprepared to be subject to the regular courts and code of punishments, yet the whip was deemed too harsh for people who perpetrated crimes—at least from the nonpeasant's perspective—largely out of ignorance and cultural backwardness. Much as female bodies had earlier been spared more severe forms of physical punishment and had, in 1861, been exempted from flogging altogether, so, too, was mitigation applied to the corporeal child-peasant's downtrodden frame.[62] Like women and children, it was argued, the moral and intellectual level of (male) peasants remained far too undeveloped, their past still too close to the fetters and lashes of the serf estate, to assume that they could be freed altogether from this most overt remnant of serfdom.

As the only postreform judicial institution retaining the right to impose corporal punishment, the *volost'* court could order the flogging of all peasant males up to age sixty except for village and *volost'* officials; peasants who had completed a program of study beyond elementary school; and those in military service.[63] Birch rods were the legally prescribed punishment for fighting; moving to another settlement without official permission; insult-

60. GARO, f. 4, 1 otd., st. 3, op. 100, sv. 436, d. 9686; f. 5, st. 1, op. 2, dd. 7a (1820), 17 (1834), 60 (1841), 929 (1859); N. D. Sergeevskii, *Telesnoe nakazanie v Rossii v XVII veke* (N.p., n.d.); Zhbankov and Iakovenko, *Telesnye nakazaniia*, ch. 1; Bruce F. Adams, *The Politics of Punishment: Prison Reform in Russia, 1863–1917* (DeKalb, 1996), ch. 1.

61. Sofronenko, *Krest'ianskaia reforma*, 61, art. 102.

62. For examples of the continued use of corporal punishment on peasant women, see GARO, f. 5, st. 3, op. 4, d. 620 (1861), ll. 43, 51–52, 72–73; f. 795, op. 1, sv. 1, d. 6; *ZhMIu*, no. 3 (1861), part 2, 558–62.

63. Aristov, *Volostnoi sud*, 20, 84–93.

ing one's parents; drunkenness, neglecting one's work because of it, and selling or pawning property to buy liquor; not rendering assistance when needed; tax arrears, nonpayment of taxes and other dues; and theft, keeping stolen goods, embezzlement, or damage to another's property. At the court's discretion, corporal punishment could still be applied to these same offenses after the change in codes that followed the 1889 counterreforms.[64]

There was no scarcity of writers who, upon examining court records from the 1860s and early 1870s and seeing the range of offenses for which villagers were flogged, concluded that peasants simply preferred the birch to other forms of punishment. Surprisingly few seemed aware that the Rural Code stipulated corporal punishment and that by meting out such sentences *volost'* courts formally obeyed the law. Despite evidence to the contrary, it was regularly claimed that peasants found fines and arrest burdensome and economically harmful to their families and preferred corporal punishment as a quick and effective means for correcting bad behavior that, although shameful, harmed only the accused. "Since the peasant has almost no personal property and labor represents the major, often the sole source of subsistence," explained I. Orshanskii, "property punishments are either impractical or fall like a terrible burden on the family of the convict, that is, on people who are guilty of nothing. [Jail] also removes labor power from the family. There remains only corporal punishment, which falls solely upon the guilty party."[65] To support their argument, authors provided selective evidence—gathered in the early 1870s—from many townships where use of the birch predominated over other punishments. In the Mizinsk township of Moscow province, for instance, officials whose duty it was to impose and carry out sentences of flogging told the Liuboshchinskii Commission that the birch was "the most instructive and useful punishment," and in Shalovsk *volost'* "everyone fears the birch, and neither the peasant nor the community is harmed by it." Township judges voiced similar sentiments: "Our peasants are all factory workers and drunkards, and there is nothing to take from them. If we put them in jail they'll lose their jobs, tax arrears will grow even more, and in jail they'd just get drunk."[66] For well over the next two decades, educated Russians continued to cite these opinions, assuming that little had changed either in the practice of rural justice or within village society itself.

Many communities and *volost'* courts emphatically disagreed. By the early 1870s there were numerous townships in which courts never or very rarely

---

64. Vinogradov, *Volostnoe pravlenie,* 233–48, arts. 472, 482–83, 490, 496–98, 514, 518, 522, 529, 533–36; Aristov, *Volostnoi sud,* arts. 31, 38, 49, 132, 134–35, 140–43, 169–80; A. M. Chernov, *Nabrosok soobrazhenii. Iz volostnoi iustitsii* (Gzhatsk, 1895), 42–69.

65. Orshanskii, "Narodnyi sud," no. 4, 215. See also Shrag, "Krest'ianskie sudy," no. 5–6, 92–94.

66. *Trudy,* 2:128, 134, 501.

sentenced villagers to the birches. Of twelve provinces visited by the Liu-boshchinskii Commission, corporal punishment predominated only in four. When questioned about its effectiveness, not a few peasants rejected it: "It would be better to levy a fine instead"; "The rod is useless and we should do away with it"; "Under the serf owner many were beaten, but little benefit came of it."[67] By the late 1890s, such opinions had become even firmer. A Riazan' reporter heard from villagers in 1899 that they would rather go to jail than be flogged, and another correspondent discounted the favorable popular sayings so frequently cited as evidence of peasant support for corporal punishment as being "only of antiquarian significance." In Arkh-angel'sk province shortly after the century's end, almost everyone, especially the young, was said to have a negative attitude toward the birch. In *volost'* courts that still meted out corporal punishment just before its abolition, this was done only "in special cases" or when the accused had a prior criminal record.[68] In his 1897 report to the Tenishev survey from Iaroslavl' province, A. V. Balov explained that younger peasant judges were especially reluctant, even ashamed, to impose the birch rods. In addition, he continued, the number of persons exempted from corporal punishment had grown to include roughly half of the peasants in his locality.[69]

According to one writer, decreasing application of the birch could be explained entirely "by a growing sense of human worth among the rural population." As memories of serfdom slowly faded and "a new generation of free peasants began to mature, use of the birch rod has declined more and more."[70] Older peasants were more willing to accept corporal punishment than young villagers, who had not experienced serfdom and were the staunchest opponents of flogging. "They're fools who lay themselves under the birch," one was quoted as saying about his elders. "Just let them try to flog me, and I'll see them all in jail!"[71] Yet peasants of all ages not only protested against the birch, they even challenged the right of *volost'* courts to employ it. As the Riazan' peasant Aleksei Bazhenov proudly declared in his 1885 appeal of a sentence of ten strokes, "I am a man in the prime of life and have never been accused or tried before. Who is the *volost'* court to

67. V. Semevskii, "Neobkhodimost' otmeny telesnykh nakazanii, *RusM*, no. 2 (1896), part 2, 18; M. I. Semevskii, *Ob osvobozhdenii krest'ian ot telesnogo nakazaniia* (SPb, 1895), 4–5; *Trudy*, 4:243, 271, 295, 471, 522; 5:396, 417, 435.

68. GARF, f. 586, op. 1, d. 118, l. 37; d. 120, l. 14; Charushin, "Volostnye sudy," 993. For a collection of sayings regarding the birch, many of which date to the eighteenth century, see I. I. Illiustrov, *Iuridicheskie poslovitsy i pogovorki russkogo naroda* (Moscow, 1885).

69. GARF, f. 586, op. 1, d. 123, ll. 12–13.

70. P. Dashkevich, "Volostnoi sud i kassatsionnaia instantsii," *IuV*, no. 12 (1892), 534. Chernov, *Nabrosok soobrazhenii*, 10–11, makes a similar point.

71. Charushin, "Narodnyi sud," 312; Bronovskii, "Pasynki russkogo zakonodatel'stva," 136. See also "K voprosu o telesnom nakazanii," *VolzhV*, no. 235 (1899), 2.

sentence me to lashes of the birch?"[72] In the 1870s, and probably before, peasants emphatically and repeatedly stated that flogging was the most shameful form of punishment for adults. When appealing their sentences in substantial numbers, they also argued that the punishment simply did not fit the crimes; to be flogged for verbal insult, for example, was too severe. "Punishment by the birch," one Riazan' appellant said in 1887, "should be reserved for serious crimes."[73] Another, sentenced in 1901 to twenty lashes, wrote that "punishment by the birch has such a demoralizing effect on the moral sensibilities of a person that it has long outlived its time. Nowadays it should be shameful even to mention the birch in passing, let alone to apply it in practice. We should now . . . forget this shameful punishment." These sentiments had grown stronger and more vocal by the early 1900s. As a group of peasants from Nizhnii Novgorod province put it in 1904, "Since we already have a society for the protection of animals, then it is certainly time to free Russians from such shameful humiliation."[74]

Equally revealing of peasant attitudes toward the birch and its association with serfdom were rumors that circulated with the 1889 introduction of land captains claiming that these officials would be supplied with special flogging machines sent from St. Petersburg. In 1891 one land captain felt it necessary to deny such rumors in a circular that threatened to punish those "enemies of order and justice" guilty of spreading lies "among the ignorant peasants."[75] A year earlier, villagers in Popasnovsk *volost'*, Ekaterinoslav province, refused to accept the land captain statutes altogether and announced that they wished to remain "under the old laws" because the new one was "a return to the lord and serfdom." The provincial governor sent more than a thousand troops to pacify this township and ordered thirty-three peasants flogged. The subsequent investigation revealed that the precinct's land captain had begun his introductory speech before the *volost'* assembly by saying, "Here is a new law for you that gives me the right to have you beaten." His listeners, too, had heard the rumor of the flogging machine and feared "that the new law turns the peasants over to the lord," who would once again have the right to flog them.[76] Historical memories of serfdom thus led peasants to

72. GARO, f. 694, op. 25, sv. 498, d. 729, l. 10b.

73. GARO, f. 694, op. 27, sv. 524, d. 678, l. 10b. For other examples, see f. 694, op. 2 (1862), sv. 39, d. 876; op. 7 (1867), sv. 167, d. 358; op. 10 (1870), sv. 215, dd. 377–78; op. 25 (1885), sv. 498, dd. 727–39; f. 695, op. 1 (1890), sv. 17, dd. 226–29.

74. "Otzyv krest'ianina o telesnom nakazanii," *Vremennik Zhivopisnoi Rossii* 2, no. 83 (1902), 243–44; "Nizhegorodskaia Gub. Rost derevni," *SevK*, no. 143 (1904), 3. See also GARF, f. 586, op. 1, d. 123, ll. 13–14; "Iz provintsial'noi pechati," *SevV*, no. 1 (1891), 50–51.

75. "Iz provintsial'noi pechati," 51–52.

76. A. V. Shapkarin, ed., *KD v 1890–1900 gg.* (Moscow, 1959), 36–39. In September 1890, similar rumors sparked a refusal to accept the land captain statutes among peasants in Muratovsk *volost'*, Simbirsk province. Ibid., 88–89.

protest and resist what they believed to be an attempt to reimpose the type of "justice" that had prevailed before emancipation.

Although data are scarce at both the national and township levels, a sampling of available sources leads to the conclusion that, by the mid-1880s and earlier in some areas, peasant judges were increasingly reluctant to mete out corporal punishment. In addition to courts surveyed in the early 1870s that no longer made use of the birch or employed it rarely, later data also hint at the steady decline of flogging. In the Skvirsk district of Kiev province, for example, it fell from 74 percent of all *volost'* court sentences during the years 1865–69 to 62 percent in the years 1870–74 and dropped to 28 percent between 1875 and 1879. After rising from 1865 to 1873, court-ordered corporal punishment in Vladimir province fell rapidly thereafter, dropping from 1,650 sentences in 1873 to 683 in 1880.[77] The *volost'* courts of Riazan' province imposed 650 sentences during the first six months of 1890, although only 218 (33.5 percent) were actually carried out. Nearly 40 percent (241) of these, however, came from just two districts, showing that provincewide data conceal significant variations between individual courts. Thus, of the three townships making up Riazhsk district's fourth land captain precinct, corporal punishment constituted fully 24 percent of all criminal sentences passed in 1890 by the Pustotinsk *volost'* court, but only 10.9 percent and 8.6 percent in the Pokrovsk and Troits-Lesunovsk courts.[78] According to another survey of seventeen provinces, by 1897 flogging accounted for an average of only 2.7 percent of court sentences, ranging from a high of 7.9 percent in Vologda province to 4 percent in Novgorod and only 0.8 percent in Poltava and Tavrida. Replies to the Tenishev ethnographic survey also emphasized that, by the late 1890s, *volost'* courts rarely used corporal punishment.[79]

Whether the 1889 introduction of land captains hastened this process remains an open question, for although they had to approve sentences of

77. Dashkevich, "Volostnoi sud," 533; Semevskii, "Neobkhodimost' otmeny," 16. In Vladimir, sentences declined by an average of 7.6 percent per year from 1873 to 1880, or by a total of 61.3 percent. I would suggest that a close relationship exists between the 1874 abolition of peace mediators and this sudden decline of corporal punishment. Among the mediators' many duties, after all, was overseeing collection of taxes and arrears, a process that frequently involved liberal use of the birch.

78. GARO, f. 695, op. 1, sv. 18, d. 232, ll. 3–84. Data from Riazhsk district can be found on ll. 68–740b., 85–890b.

79. Zhbankov and Iakovenko, *Telesnye nakazaniia*, 49–75; Ianovich, *Itogi shestiletiia*, 15; GARF, f. 586, op. 1, d. 123, ll. 12–13; d. 120, ll. 14, 31,65; d. 114, ll. 46–47. In the southern Siberian Chervishovsk township of Tiumen' district, during the ten years 1887–96, "corporal punishment has been completely eliminated from *volost'* court practice." Perhaps more impressive for those who favored abolition of the birch rod, "this has resulted from the initiative of the township judges themselves, as well as the former *volost'* elder." "Tiumen'skii uezd," *NizhL*, no. 177 (1896), 3. See also Ia. Abramov, "Krai bez rozgi," *Nedelia*, no. 9 (1896), 294–95.

corporal punishment and were empowered to change these to arrest or a fine (as were the district assemblies that heard appeals of *volost'* court decisions), surviving records are simply too sparse to offer a conclusive answer. Certainly many of these officials did use their authority and changed a sizable proportion of sentences to jail terms. Others did so rarely. During 1891, for instance, a land captain in Moscow province's Dmitrovsk district rejected only one out of sixty-eight sentences, and another altered one of sixteen. Land captains and district boards together changed only 10 percent of all sentences in Riazan' province during the first half of 1890.[80] Still, available evidence suggests that sentences of corporal punishment continued to decline from about 1891 to 1904. Land captains in Smolensk province confirmed 40 percent of all sentences in 1891, 21 percent in 1894, and only 11 percent in 1896. A 1901 report from Saratov found that since the introduction of land captains, punishment by the birch had nearly disappeared.[81]

Clearly, *volost'* courts under the supervision of a land captain opposed to the birch tended to impose fewer sentences of corporal punishment, knowing their decisions would likely be rejected. As one report from southern Riazan' province noted in 1899, "Corporal punishment is used rarely, and [these sentences] are almost always changed by the land captain, so that for the past five years not a single sentence has been carried out."[82] Yet by the time land captains appeared in the countryside, peasant courts themselves had already dramatically reduced the use of the birch, as we have seen. Hence even the staunchest enemies of corporal punishment among the new land captains may have merely added momentum to a process already under way in the countryside. If an official, nonpeasant agency was required to end flogging, after all, it already existed (albeit imperfectly) with the district boards, which sometimes proved more active in changing sentences than did land captains. Arguments that land captains were necessary to halt the use of corporal punishment stemmed, at least in part, from the belief

80. TsGIAgM, f. 28, op. 1, d. 19, ll. 2–20b.; d. 20, ll. 2–20b., 6–9; GARO, f. 695, op. 1, sv. 18, d. 232, ll. 3–84.

81. Zhbankov and Iakovenko, *Telesnye nakazaniia,* 57–58; "G. Saratov (K voprosu o telesnykh nakazaniiakh)," *VolzhV,* no. 234 (1901), 3; Mikhailovskii, "Sudebno-administrativnye uchrezhdeniia," 159; A. Prugavin, "Vopros o rozgakh v odnom iz uezdov Povolzh'ia (Pis'mo iz Saratovskoi gub.)," *RB,* no. 7 (1898), 94. By 1901, only eight out of thirty-seven sentences had been carried out in Nizhnii Novgorod province; during the following year, local authorities implemented four sentences, and none took effect in 1903. "Telesnye nakazaniia v Nizhegorodskoi gubernii," *Vremennik Zhivopisnoi Rossii* 2, no. 83 (1902), 245; *Pravo,* no. 32 (1903), 1941; "Prigovory o telesnom nakazanii," *SevK,* no. 84 (1904), 3; "Otzhivaiushchee nakazanie," *Privolzhskii krai,* no. 81 (1904), 2.

82. GARF, f. 586, op. 1, d. 118, l. 37.

that peasants preferred the birch and that rural courts would continue using it lavishly until instructed otherwise.[83]

The most revealing evidence concerning corporal punishment can be found in the types of infractions for which villagers were flogged. Nearly all *volost'* courts surveyed in the early 1870s stated that they subjected peasants to the birch above all for nonpayment of taxes, usually at the insistence of village and township elders or district police officials responsible for tax collection.[84] Thus, in March 1871, the elder of Glazovetsk *volost'*, Moscow province, brought seven peasants before the court on charges of not paying state taxes. All received nineteen lashes. At its March 20 session, this court sentenced another villager to sixteen lashes on the same charges, once again at the *volost'* elder's insistence. In two separate cases tried on July 25 of that year, the elder charged seventy-five peasants with failure to pay taxes; those under sixty years of age received nineteen lashes, and the elderly got three days at the local jail. Similarly, in 1872, a villager came before the Izhevsk *volost'* court in Riazan' province, charged with drunkenness, rowdiness, and not paying his taxes. Taking into account his unsober life and the fact that his arrears had reached a sizable amount, the court sentenced him to ten lashes.[85] We must also bear in mind that large numbers of these punishments enacted administratively at an elder's orders do not appear in court records.

This holdover of serfdom, stipulated in article 498 of the Rural Judicial Code, remained in force even after peasant judges began using the penal code for justices of the peace in 1889. During the 1890s, many outspoken critics of corporal punishment condemned the state for perpetuating this situation, thereby contradicting assertions about the peasants' fondness for the birch.[86] Although the Senate had earlier ruled that flogging should not be used for collection of arrears, article 102 of the emancipation regulations instructed peasant judges as well as village and *volost'* elders to follow

83. TsGIAgM, f. 62, op. 3, d. 146, ll. 1–2; op. 3, d. 563, ll. 1–10b., 50b.; A. Tiutriumov, "Kul'turnaia rol' zemskogo nachal'nika," *ZhGUP*, no. 10 (1890), ch. 11, 74–80.

84. For examples, see *Trudy*, 2:112 ("At the request of the village or *volost'*, corporal punishment is used for collection of tax arrears."); 128 ("At the *volost'* elder's insistence, all those who do not pay their taxes are punished by the birch, *without any trial*.")—my italics; 133–34 ("Those who do not pay their taxes are always sentenced to the birch."); 3:309 ("Cases of nonpayment of taxes are very common, and at the *volost'* or village elder's insistence the *volost'* court always sentence them to corporal punishment."); GARF, f. 586, op. 1, d. 123, ll. 3–10.

85. *Trudy*, 2:230–38; GARO, f. 1257, op. 1, sv. 1 d. 7a, ll. 300b.–32.

86. Semevskii, "Neobkhodimost' otmeny," 19–20; P. Liakub, "Sleduet-li ostavit' za volostnymi sudami pravo nakazyvat' telesno?" *ZhGUP*, no. 1 (1883), 12; F. Pokrovskii, "Rozga v deiatel'nosti odnogo volostnogo suda," *ZhivSt*, no. 2 (1902), 141; Evreinov, *Istoriia*, 193–96; D. N. Zhbankov, *Telesnye nakazaniia v Rossii v XX veke* (SPb., 1901), 11.

the Rural Judicial Code until the publication of a new code of punishments for *volost'* courts, which never appeared. Responsible for collecting taxes and preventing arrears, most elders simply obeyed the law when applying the birch to those guilty of fiscal delinquency. As officials in a Vladimir township told members of the Liuboshchinskii Commission, it was impossible not to impose corporal punishment for nonpayment of taxes because "the authorities [*nachal'stvo*] themselves order this. Our *volost'* elder was put in jail . . . for not properly collecting taxes." Fear that they themselves would be punished or even removed from office if they did not bring in tax receipts, as frequently happened, drove village and township elders to demand sentences of flogging from *volost'* judges.[87] Peasants of a Petersburg district were made painfully aware of this in 1885, after a livestock epidemic of malignant anthrax and then a harvest failure left them unable to pay taxes when collections began during early spring. Jailed for seven days each when they failed to bring in tax collections, village elders from nine communes brought delinquents before the Glazhevsk *volost'* court for sentences of twenty lashes. A total of 227 household heads—just under 50 percent of all householders—were thus flogged.[88]

That villagers believed such punishments to be unfair cannot be doubted. In an 1891 letter to one Samara newspaper, the peasant Nikolai Talyzin argued that the birch would not prevent accumulation of arrears, for the ability to pay taxes depended not on the peasants but on the quality of harvests, which were often poor. He further claimed that administrative authority fell unjustly upon the poor alone;

> Of course, respectable folk who are well off will not be subject to [corporal] punishment for arrears, for they punctually pay their obligations; but they certainly want this punishment applied to others. . . . It should not be forgotten that the wealthy peasant, no less than the poor one, also has arrears, yet he always comes up with an excuse: "Let the poor pay first, and I'll be able to pay up any time." This comment is much more than mere boasting, for in the large villages of Serdobsk district it is customary to collect taxes first from the poor.[89]

*Volost'* courts throughout the country certainly had peasants flogged for offenses other than accumulating arrears. Theft and insult (particularly of

87. GARO, f. 5, st. 1, op. 2, dd. 1832 (1884), 1861 (1885); f. 79, op. 1 (1890), d. 45; *Trudy,* 3:116; Khrulev, "Mysli provintsiala," no. 1, 57–58; S. N. Prokopovich, *Mestnye liudi o nuzhdakh Rossii* (SPb, 1904), 94–97. See also GARF, f. 586, op. 1, d. 121 (Tver province), l. 10.

88. "K statistike secheniia," *Nedelia,* no. 30 (1885), 1081. See also *Trudy,* 2:17, 22, 171, 231–34, 238; S. T. Semenov, *Krest'ianskie bedy* (Moscow, 1906), 21–22; "Telesnoe nakazanie za nedoimki po prigovoram Klemet'evskogo volostnogo suda, Russkogo uezda, Moskovskoi gubernii," *RusVed,* no. 345 (1882), 2; I. Krasnoperov, "Krest'ianskie platezhi i nedoimki," *IuV,* no. 10 (1886), 273; GARO, f. 697, op. 1, sv. 1, d. 50, ll. 1–8.

89. "Iz provintsial'noi pechati," 50–51.

parents, a woman, priest, or official) ranked high among the infractions calling for corporal punishment, as did drunkenness and disturbing the peace.[90] In 1890, drunkenness, disorderly conduct, and rowdiness accounted for 37 percent of the sentences of corporal punishment handed down by the Pustotinsk *volost'* court of Riazan' province, followed by insult (22 percent). An additional 14 percent stemmed from neglecting one's household economy, a serious offense in the eyes of local authorities since inability to pay taxes often resulted from just such neglect. In fact, the majority of floggings ordered by this as well as other courts involved offenses that could in some way prevent a peasant from paying his taxes on time.[91] Squandering money on drink and leading a debauched life were treated by peasant officials as behaviors directly linked to neglect of farm, family, and most important, taxes. According to *volost'* officials interviewed in the early 1870s, the birch was used most often for the offense of drunkenness, "but mainly when it leads to nonpayment of taxes and the community is forced to pay for the drunkard."[92] Clearly, what remained uppermost in the minds of village or *volost'* elders was the knowledge that as officials responsible to the state they were accountable for a community's arrears.

Through its administrative agents (police and *volost'* elders in particular), the tsarist state thus played the key role in perpetuating corporal punishment. By its forceful and repeated insistence on "vigorous measures" to collect arrears, the government encouraged officials to make full use of their authority, including application of the birch. In 1872, for example, the governor of Riazan' castigated district commandants for their "less than satisfactory" efforts at bringing in tax arrears and threatened to dismiss them if they did not collect all outstanding arrears within one month.[93] This complicitous relation between the administrative order and use of the birch was most conclusively revealed when the state abolished corporal punishment in 1904, for it did so only in conjunction with its cancellation of redemption arrears and the abolition of collective responsibility, that is, the system under which peasant communities were held accountable for tax and redemption payments by their members.[94]

90. For examples, see GARO, f. 694, op. 21 (1881), sv. 392, d. 490; op. 24 (1884), sv. 477, dd. 808, 815, 820; op. 25 (1885), sv. 498, dd. 727, 729, 734, 737; op. 26 (1886), sv. 512, dd. 582, 587–88; op. 27, sv. 524, dd. 678, 689; f. 789, op. 1, sv. 1, d. 1.

91. GARO, f. 695, op. 1, sv. 18, d. 232, ll. 68–740b., 85–890b.

92. *Trudy*, 2:41–42.

93. GARO, f. 5, st. 1, op. 2, d. 1383, ll. 6–70b. See also d. 1382 (1872), ll. 3–30b.; f. 1298, op. 2, sv. 5, d. 235 (1896), ll. 1–2, 45, 69–690b.

94. Corporal punishment ended with an imperial manifesto of August 11, 1904. GARO, f. 695, op. 15 (1904), sv. 182, d. 3, ll. 1–10b.; M. S. Simonova, "Otmena krugovoi poruki," *Istoricheskie zapiski* 83 (1969), 158–95; A. A. Leont'ev, "Zakonodatel'stvo o krest'ianakh posle reformy," in *Velikaia reforma*, vol. 6 (Moscow, 1911), 187–89.

Yet the legislation did not do away with corporal punishment entirely. Both before and after 1904 nonpeasant authorities employed it for purposes other than tax collection and did so on a scale of severity similar to that encountered in pre-emancipation times. This most commonly occurred in the wake of peasant resistance to or assault upon officials, and during pacification campaigns against agrarian revolts such as that of 1905–7. To take but one example, on August 4, 1892, peasants in a village of Orel province resisted a police commandant and land captain and beat several accompanying constables and hundreders. The officials had come to arrest one woman from each household for preventing the construction of a dam at the mill pond of a neighboring landowner, but the villagers succeeded in repulsing them. One day later, the governor dispatched a company of soldiers to the village, who ordered the peasants from all surrounding settlements to appear and, before the assembled crowd, subjected ten instigators of this disorder to as many as 130 lashes of the birch.[95] For villagers, dramas of this laid bare the inherent violence and terror of state law.

## ADMINISTRATIVE JUSTICE: THE CASE OF BANISHMENT

The final punishment to be considered is exile by administrative order. The power to banish peasants from their village—granted to serfowners and rural communes in 1736—was retained for village assemblies by the emancipation regulations, allowing them to turn over to the state for exile any peasant deemed evil, depraved, or debauched.[96] Villages could also refuse to accept the return to their community of any member released from exile or prison if they believed that person to be dangerous or likely to seek revenge. In either case, the government required only that such decisions be passed by a two-thirds vote of the village assembly and approved by the provincial administration. A law of June 1, 1865, laid out the procedure for approval that would be followed largely unchanged throughout the post-emancipation era.[97] Before 1900 the law gave communes the right "to ban-

---

95. Shapkarin, ed., *KD v 1890–1900 gg.*, 177–82. One peasant received 133 lashes, two received 100, and the remainder were subjected to sentences of 85 (one case), 75 (three), 65 (two), and 50 (one) lashes. On the years 1905–7, see, e.g., A. Leont'ev, "Iz oblasti sovremennoi reaktsii," *RB*, no. 12 (1910), 33–41; Evreinov, *Istoriia*, 213–31; Richard G. Robbins, *The Tsar's Viceroys* (Ithaca, 1987), 213–16; Roberta Thompson Manning, *The Crisis of the Old Order in Russia: Gentry and Government* (Princeton, 1982), 169–75.

96. Sofronenko, *Krest'ianskaia reforma*, 49; Tiutriumov, *Obshchee polozhenie*, 63–93; A. Kaznacheev, "Mirskoe upravlenie u krest'ian," *Sovremennaia letopis'*, no. 11 (1863), 8.

97. District and provincial boards for peasant affairs approved all communal resolutions of exile. After 1889, land captains verified these resolutions before they were sent on to the district board. GARO, f. 694, op. 3, sv. 75, d. 950 (1863); *Ssylka v Sibir'. Ocherk ee istorii i sovremennogo polozheniia* (SPb, 1900), 54–6, 70–71; K. V. N., "Ssylka," 52, 71–78; "Administrativnaia

ish those of their members who, because of their vices and constant crimes, become a danger to other villagers." After this date, revised regulations stipulated that exile should be employed "only as an extreme measure, in cases of the absolute belief by a community of the [accused's] depravity [and] incorrigibility, and the impossibility of halting his dangerous activities by any other means."[98]

In its 1879 review of the Grot Commission's recommendations on prison and exile reform, the Council of State recognized that banishment by communes was both harmful and without any juridical foundation, but because of the historical origins of the commune's right to employ banishment and the "peculiar conditions of rural life," it would be impossible to abolish this penalty.[99] Its defenders justified exile by the fact that Russia's courts and police were powerless to fight serious crime or ensure community safety, as shown by the vast number of unsolved rural offenses. Hence, communal banishment was an effective means to rid villages of criminals, though the very existence of this administrative punishment exposed the deficiencies and failings of Russia's regular judicial apparatus as well as the government's lack of faith in it. Nearly all commentators also argued that administrative exile helped prevent a far more widespread use of popular justice, in which angry, exasperated peasants took revenge on criminals by hunting them down and murdering them.[100]

That rural communities made use of their right to banish villagers for "wanton and depraved" behavior is obvious from available statistics, although these figures are perhaps lower than might be expected. In the ten-year period 1867–76, 106,623 peasants made the long journey by *étape* to western Siberia. During the late 1870s and early 1880s, this number held steady at about 10,000 convicts and forced settlers per year. For the twelve years 1887–98, 52 percent of all persons exiled to Siberia from European Russia received their sentences outside of the regular judicial system through administrative decree, and of that number all but 6 percent had been sentenced by communal resolution.[101]

ssylka," *Nedelia* 32, no. 21 (1899), 679; Kupchinov, *Krest'ianskoe samoupravlenie*, 140–41; Tiutriumov, *Obshchee polozhenie*, 70–71.

98. Tiutriumov, *Obshchee polozhenie*, 66. See also *Zhurnal Vysochaishe uchrezhdennoi Komissii o meropriiatiiakh po otmene ssylki* (SPb, 1900); S. Dizhur, "Russkaia ssylka. Ee istoriia i ozhidaemaia reforma," *RB*, no. 4 (1900), part 1, 45–64.

99. RGIA, f. 1405, op. 88, d. 10215, l. 453. See also K. V. N., "Ssylka," 61; *Ssylka v Sibir'*, 84.

100. *Ssylka v Sibir'*, 84; "Administrativnaia ssylka," 680; K. V. N., "Ssylka," 61; A. Kaznacheev, "Mirskoe upravlenie," 8.

101. *Otchet po glavnomu tiuremnomu upravleniiu*, vol. 1–17, part 9; K. V. N., "Ssylka," 51–52; *Ssylka v Sibir'*, 133–34; Margolis, ""O chislennosti i razmeshchenii ssyl'nykh," 225; Alan Wood, "Crime and Punishment in the House of the Dead," in Olga Crisp and Linda Edmundson, eds., *Civil Rights in Imperial Russia* (New York, 1989), 225.

Why banishment was not employed even more frequently is partly explained by its cost, which fell almost entirely upon the community. Once a resolution had been passed, the person in question was immediately imprisoned to prevent revenge or escape, and the community had to provide money covering the expense of incarceration or hand over a deposit to the state until the decision received official confirmation. If a convict sought to appeal his case, as commonly happened, his prison stay could stretch for over a year, costing the commune six rubles per month just to feed him. When the resolution was approved, the community was then required to pay for the exiles' provisions and clothing until they reached their place of settlement, as well as for transportation along the way. If spouses and children accompanied the exiles (also common before the 1880s), communities bore the cost of their provisions, too. At roughly twelve rubles per person for clothing and three rubles per month for food, plus transportation costs, the outlay could prove quite substantial. Finally, when an exile's allotment land reverted to the commune upon banishment, the latter had to support the convict and accompanying family members for a two-year period in their place of settlement.[102] Given such expenses, it is little wonder that village assemblies were sometimes reluctant to banish a malefactor or sought outside help to pay for the culprit's resettlement. Until 1876, communities could receive assistance from provincial zemstvo administrations, but in that year the Senate forbade further subsidies.[103]

Surviving banishment resolutions show that the majority of peasants handed over to the government for exile had committed no particularly heinous crimes. Most proved persistent nuisances—petty thieves, drunkards, rowdies, and brawlers—many of whom would come to be called "hooligans" after 1900. Before emancipation, communities relieved themselves of such persons by sending them into military service during recruit levies, but this mechanism of social control was dismantled after 1861, leaving banishment as the only sure means of driving from the community members who rejected the norms governing village life.[104] The terms "depraved" and "bad" behavior that appear in these resolutions, therefore, served to

102. Kupchinov, *Krest'ianskoe samoupravlenie*, 141–42; Tiutriumov, *Obshchee polozhenie*, 78–85. Exiles were exempted from taxation in their place of settlement for three years, and for seven years thereafter they paid only half of the normal tax levy. Tiutriumov, *Obshchee polozhenie*, 98.

103. B. Veselovskii, *Istoriia zemstva za sorok let*, 4 vols. (SPb, 1909–11), 3:703; *Zemskii ezhegodnik za 1877* (SPb, 1879), 758–63; *Zemskii ezhegodnik za 1878* (SPb, 1881), 386–87.

104. In 1860 a peasant from Riazan' province's Spassk district whose owner had sentenced him to be dispatched as a recruit, for example, ran away and hid until emancipation. Upon returning to his village he perpetrated several thefts, insulted and beat his father on numerous occasions, and spoke out against the emancipation settlement. As a consequence, in late 1861, he was banished from the community. GARO, f. 694, op. 1, sv. 9, d. 193, ll. 1–18.

define not simply an individual's deeds but, more important, her or his moral character and unwillingness to live at peace with fellow villagers.

Villages throughout the empire regularly banished peasants on such seemingly petty charges as gambling and using their homes as "dens" (*pritony*) of gaming, drinking, and other activities that led them to neglect their work. Inveterate drunkards who squandered family resources and disrupted the peace also risked exile. In 1904, the Suisk village assembly of Pronsk district in Riazan' province resolved to banish thirty-one-year-old Ivan Nefedov Belianin chiefly because "he leads a wild life and does not work but instead gives himself over to drunkenness and unruly conduct, for which he has been repeatedly jailed by village authorities." The fact that the *volost'* court had convicted Belianin several times for petty theft proved secondary to these charges, which testified that the village could no longer control the culprit's behavior.[105] Although communities often used the charge of recidivism when justifying banishment decisions (particularly after 1890), in most instances it was the accused's refusal to conform that stood out as the greatest concern. A resolution drawn up in August 1861 at the Kareeva village assembly, Riazan' province, condemned Ermil Savel'ev Miasnikov and his sons Vasilii and Anisim to exile because "they lead a bad life, namely, Ermil and Anisim are constantly wild, threatening us in various ways that keep us in continuous fear and are rude to officials. Ermil has stolen oats, his behavior is bad, and he is a danger to our community. As for Vasilii, he also is intolerable . . . because of bad behavior. And since we have judged them to be harmful, for the peace of our community we assign the entire family over to the government."[106] Similarly, when one village assembly of Riazhsk district resolved to banish a fifty-six-year-old widow in 1912, it did note that she was a thief and a suspect in several arsons but, more important, stressed that she "leads an idle and wild [*razgul'naia*] life."[107]

More serious were charges leveled in 1877 against Dmitrii Prokopaev Gurov from Kasimov district. According to the resolution, Gurov had repeatedly been tried for theft and was suspected of stealing a horse. Without additional embellishment, the commune "humbly" requested that the government "permanently banish Gurov as a dangerous member of our community."[108] Sixty-two-year-old Grigorii Ivanov Shelikhov also seemed to meet better the criterion of a "depraved" community member. In 1877 the Barisovka village assembly petitioned that he be exiled because, during the past ten years, he had been fined on three occasions, served three months in prison for trying to drown his wife, four days at the local jail on unspecified

105. GARO, f. 695, op. 16, sv. 190, d. 161, ll. 3–5.
106. Ibid., f. 694, op. 1, sv. 9, d. 191, ll. 3–30b.
107. Ibid., f. 695, op. 22, sv. 244, d. 297, ll. 22–220b.
108. Ibid., f. 709, op. 1, sv. 2, d. 139, ll. 27–30.

charges, and, most recently, six months in prison for attempting to steal a horse—"but none of these measures had any corrective effect, and Shelikhov did not conduct himself better or cease his crimes." In addition, he had started many fights, "beaten up people," threatened to poison the livestock of several villagers, and promised that arson would result if anyone complained against him. The assembly deemed him "a threat not only to the community, but to the entire *volost'*."[109]

During the first half of our period, village assemblies most often banished peasants because they had already been convicted by a court, or for theft, drunkenness, leading a dissolute life, or threatening others. A sample of 388 cases examined by the Riazan' provincial board between 1861 and 1883 reveals that 43.8 percent of all exiles were banished after a court found them guilty. Communities dispatched an additional 31.4 percent for theft, 7.5 percent for drunkenness, and 2.5 percent for threats. Only 1.8 percent had been exiled on charges of arson (most on suspicion alone), 1.5 percent for tax arrears, and 1.0 percent for robbery. The continued authority of former serfowners can be seen from the 4.1 percent of resolutions that were passed under their orders, usually on charges of disobedience or agitation against them.[110] A second sample from the period 1890–1914 shows that property crime had become the most frequent reason for banishment, with 47.8 percent of cases involving theft. Prior conviction by a court dropped to second place (14.8 percent), followed by drunkenness, threats, and arson (13.8, 11.8, and 5.4 percent, respectively).[111] These findings substantiate the contention of several contemporaries that villagers rarely banished serious criminals because the latter often held communities in such fear of revenge "that peasants are unwilling to go to the police." Hence, resolutions against persons accused of horsetheft, robbery, or other felonies are seldom encountered. "Instead," argued one writer in 1881, "we mostly find someone exiled for his drunkenness and depraved inclinations." Indeed, "bloody mob justice [*samosud*] is more commonly used to deal with arsonists or horsethieves, whereas petty thieves and drunkards are exiled by communal decree."[112] Rural communities had thus long used banishment most often against persons to whom educated society would affix the label "hooligan" after the turn of the century.

Given the regularity of peasant complaints that Russia's courts did not punish serious crimes with sufficient severity, it seems puzzling that perpetrators of such offenses did not constitute a greater proportion of persons

109. Ibid., f. 709, op. 1, sv. 2, d. 140, ll. 1–20b., 11–110b., 15–16.
110. This sample is based on cases in GARO, f. 694, op. 1–28. For discussion of exile upon complaint of former serfowners, see f. 694, op. 3, sv. 75, d. 950 (1863).
111. The sample contains 203 resolutions. GARO, f. 695, op. 1–23.
112. K. V. N., "Ssylka," 66–68, 70.

banished by rural communes. Yet the explanation lies precisely in the fact that peasants viewed crimes like horsetheft and arson to be so reprehensible and harmful that they often chose to deal with perpetrators by means of mob justice. If criminals got off lightly in a circuit court trial, peasants also knew that exile offered no assurance against their escape and return to exact revenge. In the vastness of Siberia, those banished for resettlement were under little, if any, supervision. As a result, the territory, particularly its western regions, overflowed with escapees and unregistered exiles who simply left their assigned village or town and, often in bands, terrorized local populations. Between 1892 and 1896, police seized 14,266 unregistered exiles in Tobol'sk province alone.[113] In sparsely settled Arkhangel'sk province, authorities were powerless to protect communities from wandering or even resident gangs of exiles. "At the beginning of [1882], criminals laid siege to the town of Shenkursk for more than a week, and no one could go into the streets without danger." Police officials feared the exiles, and some were even driven from their jobs because of constant harassment or threats.[114] Many escapees did not remain long in Siberia but crossed the Ural Mountains and eventually returned to their native locality seeking revenge. From the fires that ravaged their villages as a result of arson committed by escapees, peasants were all too aware of this very real threat. Time and again they justified the murder of a horsethief, arsonist, or robber by the necessity of insuring that the criminal would never again cause harm to their community or exact revenge.

As did Russia's system of rural justice as a whole, officially sanctioned punishment retained a strong element of administrative authority that critics of the autocracy found greatly inhibited efforts to establish a true "rule of law." For the peasant population, this interweaving of law and state power that hearkened back to the days of serfdom was quite familiar. Although *volost'* courts sought, at least formally, to follow the Rural Judicial Code, they were often controlled by local bosses, who had to answer to state-appointed officials authorized to abrogate court sentences and order punishments. The fact that until 1890 peasants so frequently sought to have their cases tried before a peace court rather than at the township office is sufficiently revealing of their attitudes toward rural justice. Even the feared system of

113. *Ssylka v Sibir'*, 259, 271, 273–75. Toward the end of the nineteenth century, officials could not even guess at the real number of escapees. See also F. Savitskii, "Pobeg arestantov iz Aleksandrovskoi katorzhnoi tiur'my," *TiurV*, no. 5 (1909), 609–31; V. N. Gartvel'd, *Katorga i brodiagi v Sibiri* (Moscow, 1912); Wood, "Sex and Violence in Siberia," 23–42.

114. A. Lud'mer, "Tiur'my, ssylka, prestupleniia i iustitsiia na krainem severe," *IuV*, no. 10 (1883), 330.

administrative exile, another holdover from pre-emancipation times, proved far less helpful in fighting crime than is usually believed. Because of the government's inefficiency and inability to police its exile population, villagers rarely banished persons guilty of major offenses, knowing that the latter might escape and seek revenge. Those most commonly exiled, in fact, bore a closer resemblance to the village "hooligans" whom a fearful educated society discovered early in the twentieth century. When dealing with serious criminals, villagers preferred to rely on their own popular and unofficial institutions of justice. In Russia, as in rural communities of Mexico, colonial Nigeria, and Papua New Guinea, "the functional deficiencies of the official structure generate[d] an alternative (unofficial) structure to fulfill existing needs somewhat more effectively."[115] Chapter 8 examines one of the most widely used of these unofficial structures, one that perhaps best reflects how little confidence peasants had in official venues of justice.

115. Cited in Philip Parnell, "Village or State? Competitive Legal Systems in a Mexican Judicial District," in Nader and Todd, eds., *The Disputing Process,* 317. See also Richard L. Abel, "Western Courts in Non-Western Settings: Patterns of Court Use in Colonial and Neo-Colonial Africa," in Sandra B. Burman and Barbara E. Harrell-Bond, eds., *The Imposition of Law* (New York, 1979), esp. 190–98; Robert J. Gordon and Mervyn J. Meggitt, *Law and Order in the New Guinea Highlands* (Hanover, 1985), 204–9, 210–36.

# CHAPTER 8

# Unofficial Justice in the Village

*Almost daily the telegraph brings news about cases of vigilante justice against thieves, robbers, hooligans, and other criminal elements. . . . One might think that Russia has been brought temporarily to the American prairie and that Lynch law has been granted citizenship by us.*

THE JURIST, AUGUST 7, 1905

*Yaroslavl, Central Russia. An angry mob of gardeners stripped a woman accused of stealing potatoes, tied her to a tree near a railway track, and flogged her, Itar-Tass reported. A shocked railway engineer saw the half-naked woman as he was driving his train through the Yaroslavl region and alerted police, the news agency said. The forty-nine-year-old woman . . . had been seized by landowners furious that she had pilfered their small plots. Police said the woman was lucky. Last year, a potato thief in the same region was beaten to death by angry farmers.*

THE MOSCOW TIMES, JULY 26, 1995

Agrafena Ignat'eva was known as a sorceress in her native village of Vrachevo, located in the Tikhvinsk district of Novgorod province. Ever since her youth residents had believed she possessed an ability to cast harmful spells (*porchi*) and greatly feared this power. To the villagers' relief, Agrafena moved to St. Petersburg following her marriage, but after her husband's death in 1877 she returned to Vrachevo an impoverished, fifty-year-old widow, often forced to beg for her daily subsistence. Her return soon gave rise to rumors that harmful spells would once again occur, rumors no doubt fed by recent outbreaks of mass hysteria (*klikushestvo*) in this same district.[1] Village women sought to appease Ignat'eva by doing various chores when she fell ill, giving her bread, cleaning her at the bathhouse, washing her linen, and scrubbing the floor of her cottage. Some felt they should protect their village by more direct measures, however, declaring

---

1. Cases of *klikushestvo* caused by sorcery had been commonplace in Tikhvinsk district throughout the 1870s, a fact that likely played a role in the much better known Vrachevo case. In 1872, for example, nearly every woman in the village of Tipuchino fell victim to spells cast by a sorceress. "Kolduny i klikushi (Po povodu sudebnykh protsessov ob ubiistvakh koldunov)," *RSP* 35, no. 4 (1894), 84–85.

that it would be better to seal the widow inside her hut and burn her rather than risk her deadly spells.

Unfortunately for "Grushka," as Agrafena was called, an outbreak of "falling sickness" in Vrachevo and its environs brought immediate suspicion upon her. Most people knew that this illness resulted from a spell, and Ignat'eva seemed the most likely culprit. Around Epiphany in 1879, she came to the home of Ivan Kuz'min and asked for some cottage cheese but was refused; shortly thereafter his daughter Nastas'ia fell sick and cried out that Grushka had cast a spell on her. Kuz'min begged Ignat'eva on his knees to restore his daughter's health, but the widow answered that Nastas'ia was under no spell and therefore needed no help. In late January the illness reached Katerina Ivanova, whose sister in a neighboring village had also been "hexed" by Grushka and died. Ivanova attributed her malady to the fact that she had forbidden her son to chop firewood for the sorceress and Grushka had evidently employed her power to take revenge. Ivanova's husband even lodged a complaint against Ignat'eva with the precinct constable, who came to Vrachevo to conduct an investigation several days prior to Grushka's death. But few villagers expected that she would be punished for these crimes, and police involvement appears only to have hastened subsequent events.

On Sunday, February 4, following a village assembly meeting, Ivan Nikiforov appealed for protection from Ignat'eva, claiming that she was preparing to cast a spell on his wife just as she had done to other women. It is likely that several villagers had already made plans for dealing with the sorceress since, utilizing Nikiforov's request to the assembly, they quickly prevailed upon all household heads present (including the village elder) to agree with their scheme. They argued that it was necessary to board up the woman in her hut, give her food, and guard her to prevent her causing further harm. It was equally important that this be done before the constable settled the complaint against her. No one dissented from the plan, and shortly after the meeting a large group took nails and torches and set off "to seal up" Grushka, as they put it.

Finding the entrance shed to Ignat'eva's hut locked, they broke down the door on orders from the village elder. Four peasants entered the storeroom in search of charms and potions, while six others, led by the elder, went into the house itself and started to seal it by boarding up the windows and then nailing a thick pole into the entrance. Meanwhile, the examination of her various remedies by those outside "decisively convinced the peasants that Ignat'eva really was a sorceress." According to later depositions, "All of the peasants began saying, 'We must do away with her so she doesn't see the light of day, for if we let her out she'll put spells on all of us.'" At about 5:00 P.M., therefore, one peasant set fire to a bundle of straw and rope in the entrance shed. Two men held the door tight as Ignat'eva, having heard the crackling of fire, pounded from inside and screamed to be let out. The smoke soon attracted nearly 200 people from Vrachevo and neighboring villages, but none sought to extinguish it or to rescue the woman inside. On the contrary, witnesses at the trial testified to hearing such exclamations as, "Let it burn, we've put up with Grushka long enough!" One peasant whose children had fallen victim to Ignat'eva's "spells" was heard to shout, "Praise God! She has taken two daughters from me! Let it burn!" When Ignat'eva's brother arrived and tried to pry a log from one of the windows and release her, he was ordered to stop because "it was nailed there by the commune." As the crowd watched, the sorceress rushed from window to window, shouting out her innocence; when the fire did not burn fast enough, peasants knocked down the roof so flames could enter the house itself. It burned long into the night.

Though proclaiming to all assembled that they had acted justly to protect the village, the leaders of this affair feared punishment. Therefore they pooled money the next day and sent a bribe of 21.90 rubles to the constable hoping that he would "forget" the case. The officer not only declined their offer but turned in the money as evidence. In October, sixteen villagers most directly implicated in "Grushka's" murder stood trial before the Novgorod Circuit Court. Three confessed and received sentences of church penance. The remainder pleaded innocent and denied that there had been a prearranged plan to burn the woman. Following a long and celebrated jury trial, they were finally acquitted.[2]

Albeit not always so dramatic, community violence of this sort regularly made its way onto the pages of Russia's growing press to reveal a realm of popular justice that operated outside the boundaries and control of either court or administrative authority. It was by no means limited to persons accused of sorcery; more commonly, thieves—and horsethieves in particular—were subjected to violent community reprisal, as were arsonists and those who transgressed against village norms of everyday conduct. Nor was the phenomenon peculiar only to backward, isolated regions. Although extrajudicial retribution had become rarer in urban centers like Moscow and St. Petersburg by the late 1800s, a steady stream of reports attest to its continued practice in or near district towns, large villages, markets, and bazaars.[3] Nonetheless, samosud (lit.: self-judgment), as educated Russians called it, occurred mainly in rural areas with a weak police presence and strong traditional peasant institutions. It existed in nearly all provinces of the empire and among most ethnic groups well into the twentieth century.

2. MosVed, no. 261 (1879), 5; no. 265 (1879), 5; no. 266 (1879), 3.

3. On September 25, 1895, for instance, a woman was attacked and beaten by a crowd in the heart of Moscow on suspicion that she was a witch. A. A. Levenstim, Sueverie i ugolovnoe pravo (SPb, 1899), 39.

*Samosud* not only increased considerably during periods of social unrest, revolution, and government weakness but also as peasants grew ever more convinced that official justice and law could not protect their communities.[4]

Yet *samosud* was a far more complex phenomenon than it appeared to contemporaries. Most of Russia's elite saw it as simple mob violence or lynch law (even adopting the American word "*linch*") and discussed it within the same cultural context where such negative elements of village life as criminality were usually placed: that is, *samosud* reflected the peasants' primitive savagery and disrespect for human life.[5] The best dictionary of the period took a somewhat broader view, defining *samosud* not only as willful punishment, but also arbitrariness or "judgment of one's own affairs" [*sud v svoem dele*].[6] In fact, many instances of *samosud* entailed no physical violence, although these, too, were cases of the public enforcing community norms and morality and bore close affinity to the charivaris, rough music, and shivarees of Western Europe and North America. An examination of the acts themselves reveals that peasants drew sharp boundaries between punishments inflicted on community members and those used against outsiders. With fellow villagers, *samosud* often took on a ritualized character in which overt violence seldom played a part. Violent *samosud*, on the other hand, more closely resembled vigilante justice and was reserved primarily for outsiders whose offenses threatened the community, or for local peasants viewed as incorrigible and depraved criminals.

The distinction between punishing community members and outsiders is a most useful framework for analyzing unofficial justice in rural Russia and for seeing it from the villagers' own perspective. The three most frequently encountered forms of extrajudicial community measures will be considered here: ritualized disciplinary action such as charivari, which inflicted shame and public disgrace upon the guilty party, though usually without violence; punishment of serious theft, particularly of horses; and violence against persons suspected or accused of witchcraft. These examples reveal the range of peasant actions that the state and educated society commonly lumped together under a single heading. They allow us to get at the complexity of village justice by explaining why peasants turned to extralegal actions for the punishment of very different crimes and how they reached

4. See, e.g., GARO, f. 5, st. 3, op. 4, d. 5078 (1908), ll. 1–20b.; "Nashi samosudy," *Shatskii narodnyi listok*, no. 17 (1917), 3; M. N. Gernet, *Sud ili samosud* (Moscow, 1917); M. M. Zimin, *Kovernishkii krai* (*Nabliudeniia i zapiski*) (Kostroma, 1920), 8; N. O. Lagovier, *O samosudakh* (Moscow, 1927); Lynne Viola, *Peasant Rebels Under Stalin* (New York, 1996), ch. 4. Compare the nearly identical patterns in tsarist Poland during the 1905 Revolution. Robert E. Blobaum, *Rewolucja: Russian Poland, 1904–1907* (Ithaca, 1995), 142–48.

5. For a more reflective view, see L. N., "Narodnaia rasprava," *SudG*, no. 44 (1897), 5–6.

6. Vladimir Dal', *Tolkovyi slovar' zhivogo velikorusskogo iazyka*, vol. 4 (SPb and Moscow, 1882), 135. Earlier, the term "*samosud*" was used in reference to all peasant courts.

such decisions based on the offenders' status and the nature of their infractions. Finally, *samosud* offers insight into the larger conflict between peasant and elite culture during the late nineteenth century, since such acts, being by definition illegal, not only transpired outside the official legal structure and clashed sharply with it but embodied the clearest statement of its rejection by peasants dissatisfied with this legal structure.

## DEFINING POPULAR JUSTICE

Educated society had difficulty characterizing *samosud* because it was not a homogeneous category of crimes. No section of Russia's criminal code dealt with summary justice or referred to *samosud* by name. Burning Agrafena Ignat'eva or beating a horsethief to death were treated as murder or mortal injury, while cases in which death did not result might be tried as torture, assault, insult, or arbitrariness. Ethnographers confused the problem even more, since some described *samosud* as any offense not brought before official courts but settled instead by unofficial moots. Such cases involved petty theft, injury, fights, quarrels, infliction of damages, even civil suits.[7] Viacheslav Tenishev did draw a clear distinction between popular courts and extrajudicial punishment, writing in 1907 that *samosud* could be characterized by the application of judicial authority not recognized under state law that was carried out willfully and, in the majority of cases, violently. This violent implementation of a judicial decision distinguished *samosud* from the popular courts, "which also are not recognized by law but are voluntarily accepted by the litigants themselves."[8] But Tenishev was wrong not only about how unofficial courts functioned; he also ignored evidence that litigants sometimes did accept certain forms of *samosud,* not all of which were violent. One of Tenishev's own sources, which he did not cite, stated that a peasant in Vladimir province who was found guilty of theft had received a choice of going to court or being punished by public shaming and chose the latter.[9] Villagers did little to clarify matters. When asked by outsiders about *samosud,* they failed to mention violent incidents at all, speaking instead about public punishment of children or the humiliation of petty thieves. Peasant judges and local officials questioned during the 1870s also played it safe by stating that such incidents had occurred "in the past" but were no longer practiced in their localities.[10]

---

7. P. S. Efimenko, *Sbornik narodnykh iuridicheskikh obychaev Arkhangel'skoi gubernii* (Arkhangel'sk, 1869), 277–78; E. Kartsev, "Sel'skoe pravosudie," *VE,* no. 1 (1882), 333; Skaldin, *V zakholust'e i v stolitse* (SPb, 1870), 144–45.

8. V. V. Tenishev, *Pravosudie v russkom krest'ianskom bytu* (Briansk, 1907), 33.

9. B. M. Firsov, and I. G. Kiseleva, *Byt velikorusskikh krest'ian-zemlepashtsev* (SPb, 1993), 69.

10. V. V. Tenishev, "Obshchie nachala ugolovnogo prava v ponimanii russkogo krest'ianina," *ZhMIu,* no. 7 (1909), 138–39; Efimenko, *Sbornik,* 227; E. I. Iakushkin, comp., *Obychnoe*

Violence and the ignoring of state law, then, were not features of *samosud* alone but characterized Russian justice far more broadly, particularly when administrative functionaries played a role in its implementation. We must therefore seek out those elements of *samosud* which distinguish it from other forms of popular justice and help us to understand how a given act became a case of *samosud*. Writing in 1880, the jurist Petr Skorobogatyi touched on certain of these elements and on reasons why much of the rural population continued to accept *samosud*. Such punishments, he wrote, displayed the exclusive rights of peasant society in the moral control of its members, their strength deriving from "the peasantry's respect for the authority of the commune, on that moral dependence upon the commune which the offender fully recognizes, and . . . on the close acquaintance and tight bonds which all fellow villagers have among themselves."[11] In this way, the commune stood in place of state authority, which villagers recognized only selectively and when necessary.

Invoking the commune's authority was indeed one of the most notable features of *samosud*. The village assembly had, after all, been a state-sanctioned organ of village justice prior to the 1860s, and after emancipation it retained a limited judicial authority that peasants managed to broaden. They usually brought a case before their assembly before inflicting punishment if the offender was a community member, and the assembly frequently sentenced the guilty party to *samosud*. The assembly thereby sanctioned what was officially illegal, lessening the chance that a criminal would complain to authorities or seek revenge since to do so challenged the authority of the community itself. Peasants tried by state courts for collective acts of violence against criminals often used the very fact of communal sanction as their primary defense. Other important aspects of *samosud* included collective participation in punishments, a real or perceived threat to local norms or to the community's well-being, and an attempt to prevent repetition of a crime either through ritualized public humiliation of offenders or by driving them from the village altogether without recourse to exile. Since these characteristics of *samosud* depended on the nature of the crime as well as an offender's status as villager or outsider, they helped to differentiate the various forms of popular justice while at the same time binding them within a cultural web of common meaning.

---

*pravo*, 4 vols.(Iaroslavl', 1875–1909), 1:xxxviii–xxix. *Trudy komissii po preobrazovaniiu volostnykh sudov*, 7 vols. (SPb, 1873–74) (hereafter: *Trudy*), contains numerous comments of this sort. For commentary from the 1890s, see GARF, f. 586, op. 1, d. 118, l. 34, 37–38; d. 120, ll. 11, 14, 27, 59–60, 66.

11. Petr Skorobogatyi, "Ustroistvo krest'ianskikh sudov," *IuV,* no. 6 (1880), 343–45.

## CHARIVARIS

At its simplest level, *samosud* was applied to a multitude of petty infractions such as damage caused to another's crops by livestock and working on holidays when the commune had forbidden it; this "quick" or "home justice" was also used to discipline wayward minors and those who would come to be known among outsiders as hooligans.[12] One of the more widespread types of *samosud* took the ritualistic character of the charivari and, unlike other acts of popular justice, was employed primarily against fellow villagers. An ancient form of community policing, charivaris endured long into the nineteenth century throughout Europe and parts of North America under such names as *katzenmusiken, scampanate,* skimmingtons, shivarees, and rough music. The Russian variant was known as "leading the thief" (*vozhdenie vory,* or simply *vozhdenie*), and like its European counterparts, it served as a disciplinary mechanism and a means of public criticism or punishment whereby the entire community shamed village members into abiding by collective rules. As one student of British popular culture has written, "Rough music is a public naming of what has been named before only in private." It "announced the total publicity of disgrace," for the victim "must go out into the community the next morning, knowing that in the eyes of every neighbor and of every child, he or she is seen as a person disgraced."[13] A strong, formal similarity thus existed between charivaris in Russia and in other countries.

Discussing rough music in late eighteenth- and early nineteenth-century England, Edward Thompson explained that the rituals "expose some individual who has offended against community norms to the most public forms of insult, humiliation and sometimes ostracism—riding victims upon an ass or upon a pole, burning them in effigy, performing raucous 'music' outside their cottages upon tin cans, the horns of beasts, and so on, and reciting

12. GARF, f. 586, op. 1, d. 118, ll. 18, 28; N. A. Minenko, "Traditional Forms of Investigation and Trial among the Russian Peasants of Western Siberia in the Eighteenth and the First Half of the Nineteenth Centuries," *Soviet Anthropology and Archeology* 21, no. 3 (1982–83), 73; Petr Skorobogatyi, "Primenenie nakazanii v volostnom sude," *IuV,* no. 8 (1882), 561–63; I. M. Tiutriumov, "Krest'ianskaia sem'ia," *RussRech',* no. 4 (1879), 293; A. A. Charushin, "Narodnyi sud," *IAOiRS* 5, no. 7 (1913), 312.

13. E. P. Thompson, *Customs in Common: Studies in Traditional Popular Culture* (New York, 1991), 487–88. See also Thompson, "Rough music: le charivari anglais," *Annales: economies, sociétés, civilisations* (March–April 1972), 285–312; Martin Ingram, "Ridings, Rough Music and the 'Reform of Popular Culture' in Early Modern England," *Past and Present,* no. 105 (1984); Jacques Le Goff and Jean Claude Schmitt, eds., *Le Charivari* (Paris, 1981); A. F. Kistiakovskii, "Volostnye sudy ikh istoriia, nastoiashchaia ikh praktika i nastoiashchee ikh polozhenie," in P. P. Chubinskii, ed., *Trudy etnografichesko-statisticheskoi ekspeditsii v zapadno-russkii krai,* vol. 6 (SPb, 1872),18–19.

obscene traditional rhymes." Nearly identical accounts exist for France.[14] The typical Russian performance consisted of parading an offender through the street either on foot or in a cart, in some cases wearing a horse's collar, while villagers followed along playing *paramusique* upon iron oven doors (the most favored and readily available metal instrument), pots and pans, washtubs, wooden buckets, and other implements; sometimes they carried signs, mocked or cursed the victim, and sang songs. Women were often stripped naked or had their skirts raised before being led around the village; men might be stripped, tarred, and feathered.[15]

Although the surface similarities are striking, the kinship between charivaris in different countries remains largely one of form. Disagreeing with Levi-Strauss, Thompson argues that "these forms are of importance not . . . as universal structures but precisely because the immediate functions of the rituals change. The kinds of offender subjected to rough music are not the same, from one country to another, or from one century to another."[16] It is, in fact, in the function of the rituals and with the victims themselves that Russian charivaris differed from those in other countries. The charivari in England and France most commonly expressed disapproval of marital mismatches or conjugal relations considered deviant. In parts of the United States, marrying too soon after being widowed was cause for charivaris as late as the 1940s. Sexual offenders also frequently fell victim, as did cuckolded husbands, unwed mothers, individuals (usually women) who committed adultery, and household members deviating from accepted sex roles.[17] In England, villagers directed rough music more and more against wife beaters toward the end of the eighteenth century. "Immoral" unmarried women and libertine priests seemed to be favored quarry in Bavaria, and political

14. E. P. Thompson, "Folklore, Anthropology, and Social History," *The Indian Historical Review* 3, no. 2 (1977), 259; Eugen Weber, *Peasants into Frenchmen* (Stanford, 1976), 400. See also Thompson, *Customs*, 478; Thompson, "Rough music and charivari: Some further reflections," in Le Goff and Schmitt, eds., *Le Charivari*, 273–83; Martine Segalen, *Love and Power in the Peasant Family: Rural France in the 19th Century* (Chicago, 1983), 43–47.

15. GARF, f. 586, op. 1, d. 118, ll. 34, 36–38; d. 120, l. 14; Minenko, "Traditional Forms of Investigation," 73; "Khronika proisshestvii v Riazanskoi gubernii," *RiazGV*, no. 5, (1867), 4; Tenishev, "Obshchie nachala," 134; Iakushkin, *Obychnoe pravo*, 1:xxxviii–xxxix; Skorobogatyi, "Ustroistvo," 344.

16. Thompson, "Folklore," 259. Among many examples, see James A. Hammerton, "The Targets of 'Rough Music': Respectability and Domestic Violence in Victorian England," *Gender & History*, 3, 1 (1991), 23–44; Pauline Greenhill, "Welcome and Unwelcome Visitors: Shivarees and the Political Economy of Rural-Urban Interactions in Southern Ontario," *Journal of Ritual Studies* 3, no. 1 (1989), 45–67.

17. Bertram Wyatt-Brown, *Honor and Violence in the Old South* (New York, 1986), 200–201; Carolyn A. Conley, *The Unwritten Law* (Oxford, 1991), 23; Segalen, *Love and Power*, 43–49; David Jones, *Rebecca's Children* (Oxford, 1989), 159–60; Edward Shorter, *The Making of the Modern Family* (New York, 1975), 218–27.

charivaris against offending notables or in support of a particular party, though "restricted to towns with a political public," were not unusual in France prior to 1849, or in Quebec during the rebellion of 1837.[18]

In postreform Russia we do find charivaris aimed at adulterers and adulteresses, unwed mothers, "immoral" women and even priests, sectarians, local "informers," and officials, but the sources show that they accounted for only a small proportion of cases. Scarcer still are reports of rough music performed for cuckolded husbands or husbands beaten by wives.[19] Incidents of this sort did occur, but their apparent scarcity in Great Russia indicates that other matters occupied a higher priority when it came to the collective enforcement of local norms. Chief among these was petty theft. As one correspondent to the Tenishev survey reported, "When a thief is caught red-handed, the peasants take back the stolen item and 'teach' him 'so that he'll never forget.'"[20] *Vozhdenie* was a method frequently used for "teaching," and peasants determined the magnitude of punishment above all by the perpetrator's reputation and the value of the stolen item.

During *vozhdeniia* for petty theft, offenders would be marched through the village with the stolen object hung or draped on them, a practice dating at least to the eighteenth century. In 1899, for example, Kseniia Soboleva of Samara province was suspected of stealing reeds from a loom, and the elder and several other village officials came to her home to conduct an investigation. Once convinced of her guilt, they decided to punish Soboleva by leading her through the village streets with the stolen reeds hung around her neck. Two tenners held her by the arms as the procession, led by the elder, made its way along. A third peasant officer followed behind beating loudly upon an oven door. When they finally released her, Soboleva tried to commit suicide by throwing herself into the nearby river. All officials involved received sentences ranging from three to six months in prison.[21] In Orel province, a woman who stole a neighbor's sheep and butchered it was brought before the assembly, which promptly sentenced her to a *vozhdenie*. Village women gathered with sickles, oven doors, and other "instruments,"

18. Thompson, "Rough music," 297; Thompson, *Customs*, 506; Wyatt-Brown, *Honor and Violence in the Old South*, 193–97; Shorter, *Modern Family*, 224–26; Weber, *Peasants into Frenchmen*, 402–3; Allan Greer, "From Folklore to Revolution: Charivaris and the Lower Canadian Rebellion of 1837," *Social History* 15, no. 1 (1990), 25–43.

19. See Christine D. Worobec, *Peasant Russia* (Princeton, 1991), 201–4; Worobec, "Temptress or Virgin? The Precarious Sexual Position of Women in Post-Emancipation Ukrainian Peasant Society," *SR* 49, no. 2 (1990), 232–33. Minenko notes that tarring adulterers was common during the eighteenth and early nineteenth centuries. This practice was not exclusive to adulterers, however; peasants also used it with thieves and horsethieves. See GARF, f. 586, op. 1, d. 120, l. 66.

20. Charushin, "Narodnyi sud," 312.

21. *SudO* 1, no. 6 (1903), 124.

hung the sheep's head around her neck, and amid raucous songs and loud banging led the culprit three times through the town.[22] When Stefan Bakin of Saratov district was caught stealing sheaves in 1906, villagers hung the sheaves around his neck and took him to the assembly, where he was forced to beg forgiveness and pay sixteen rubles for vodka. The assembly threatened him with exile if he did not pay.[23] With local variations, accounts of this sort appear in hundreds of descriptions from other provinces.

Violence remained an implicit threat in acts of leading the thief, but it could become part of the procession, its degree depending on the offender's reputation. In 1880, for instance, a *volost'* court in Perm province sentenced the thief of a sheep to be led through the village wearing the butchered animal's hide. He was brought to the window of every villager's home and given one lash of the birch rod at each stop until the legal limit of twenty lashes had been administered, a creative adaptation of state regulations on corporal punishment.[24] On February 17, 1892, a theft was perpetrated in one village of Kazan' province. When a crowd of villagers conducting a search came to the home of the peasant Fadeev, who was widely disliked, he sought at first to hide. Though they did not uncover the stolen money while searching his home, Fadeev's actions aroused the villagers' suspicion and they began beating him to make him confess. At last he handed over a portion of the money, saying it was all he had taken, but this only angered his neighbors more. Therefore they harnessed him to his cart with children sitting inside and, "accompanied by whoops, whistles, and shouts," forced him to pull it through the village at a trot, whipping him with a knout whenever he weakened or stopped. The beating continued after this procession, and only a constable's intervention ended the punishment.[25] A similar case occurred in 1899, when local peasants caught three Gypsies attempting to steal a horse. They were placed in a pig sty and smeared with honey, tar, and feathers while villagers laughed and joked over their appearance. Peasants then harnessed the thieves to a small cart in which the horse's owner sat with his family and tied the horse itself—the

22. Tenishev, *Pravosudie,* 44. For another case conducted by women in Iaroslavl' province, see GARF, f. 586, op. 1, d. 123, ll. 45–46.

23. *Privolzhskii krai,* no. 168 (1906), 3. For additional examples, see K. Chepurnyi, "K voprosu o iuridicheskikh obychaiakh," *Universitetskie izvestiia,* no. 11 (1874), part 2, ch. 6, 704; *Trudy,* 1:14; Tenishev, *Pravosudie,* 44. In a particularly gruesome holdover of these practices, a peasant who ate portions of his dead father's body during the famine of 1932–33 was marched through the village with the corpse's head hung around his neck. Ewald Ammende, *Human Life in Russia* (London, 1936), 101.

24. *MosVed,* no. 103 (1880), 3. Another thief received five lashes on each village street in 1885 and was then forced to buy a bucket of vodka for the commune as a symbol of reconciliation. "Sel'skie sudy," *MosVed,* no. 214 (1885), 2.

25. "Istiazanie zapodozrennogo v krazhe," *VolzhV,* no. 239 (1892), 2.

"master of ceremonies"—to the back of the cart. Amid great shouting, mirth, and laughter from the crowd, this "troika" was forced to pull the cart through the entire village at full speed, "driven on by lashes from a whip that fell generously upon their backs."[26]

The obvious purpose of charivaris was to shame and frighten thieves to such an extent that they would never steal again. In this ritual public humiliation of a wrongdoer, both crime and criminal were judged by the offended community, which reaffirmed the necessity of participation in village life according to its rules and reasserted the primacy of communal authority. A *vozhdenie* always held out threats of greater sanction through the symbolic, though temporary, expulsion of an offender, for it proclaimed to all villagers, not just the thief, that banishment could be made permanent if someone repeated a crime or perpetrated a more serious offense. Petty thieves were permitted back into the collective fold only after publicly acknowledging their guilt and begging forgiveness. Hence the symbolic payment in vodka that villagers commonly demanded at the conclusion of a *vozhdenie*. Buying vodka either with cash or pawned possessions affirmed one's submission (however unwilling) to the punishment and acceptance of the community's power over its members. By "treating" the village to drinks, a thief not only won forgiveness and readmittance, but recognized the legitimacy of the *vozhdenie*.[27] Beyond their immediate purpose of discipline, then, charivaris were a constituent element of village social regulation. They played an often crucial role in governing behavior, regulating daily life, and ordering social conduct. In this respect, the *vozhdenie* served as one of the most overt tools in the village culture's arsenal of regulatory customs and rituals. It also aided in the preservation of local solidarity by preventing the taking of sides in a dispute and the subsequent development of open feuding, which could disrupt normal activities and relations crucial to the peasant economy. In the small world of the village, where each person was known to everyone else, it was all too easy to be drawn into a feud that began over a seemingly minor offense like stealing sheaves or a goose. The *vozhdenie* thus acted to soothe ill feelings and hostilities by involving an entire village in the punishment, often with the elder's authorization and active participation.

In most recorded cases, peasants first brought a thief before the assembly for sentencing, though a village or *volost'* elder could also authorize it on

26. "Rasprava s konokradami," *VolzhV,* no. 255 (1899), 3.
27. See GARF, f. 586, op. 1, d. 120, ll. 59–60. As Allan Greer has argued, through the use of fines, "a charivari insisted on its own legitimacy by aping the methods of constituted authority." "Folklore to Revolution," 31. For a similar process without charivari, see Harry F. Todd, Jr., "Litigious Marginals: Character and Disputing in a Bavarian Village," in Nader and Todd, eds., *The Disputing Process,* 86–121.

his own. Even when an elder refused to summon the assembly, villagers sometimes determined punishment in unofficial assemblies, which gave their actions a tenuous collective legitimacy.[28] The absence of any firm or consistent state control at the village level assured that collective responsibility would continue to reign as it did before the reforms of Alexander II; it "rendered the de facto authority of the village over its members virtually absolute."[29] Here we can see the basis of the commune's "exclusive right in the moral control of its members" referred to earlier by Skorobogatyi. Here, too, is the reason peasants sought approval from the assembly before performing rough music, for it legitimized a charivari in the eyes of all and made revenge on the wrongdoer's part extremely unlikely. To seek retribution against the participants was tantamount to fighting the entire community and its authority. Escalation of punishment during a *vozhdenie* resulted from just such a challenge, which could not be tolerated in a society that depended primarily upon itself to regulate and control the everyday behavior of its members. Escalation similarly occurred when a demand for "payment" in vodka went unmet and the offender thereby rejected reconciliation with the community.

Invoking the assembly's authority and the will of the community also served as a protective ploy against punishment by the state. Four Iaroslavl' peasants stood trial in 1881, for example, charged with torturing a suspected sorceress, and used as their only defense the argument that they had acted with the commune's agreement. In 1892 a crowd in Kazan' province caught two Tatars stealing flour from a barn and beat them so severely that one later died. Authorities had difficulty determining who took part in this collective reprisal since nobody would testify, and the three villagers finally prosecuted pleaded innocent, saying that "the whole commune" was responsible. Since no witnesses came forward, the three were acquitted. When seven villagers from Tambov province came before the circuit court a year later for beating and torturing a thief, they argued that they had punished

28. When a village elder of Iziumsk district refused a request from several peasants that he summon the assembly to decide the fate of three captured thieves, these villagers held an unofficial assembly meeting on March 23, 1884, attended by 163 household heads, where it was resolved to take the thieves from jail and whip them. The peasants put this sentence into effect at first light. "They whipped them the entire day of March 24, let them rest on the 25th in honor of a holiday, and on the 26th began to whip them again. When the precinct constable from a neighboring district passed through the village by chance, he told the peasants that what they were doing was illegal and they would answer for this. In reply the villagers advised him not to meddle in their affairs if he did not want to undergo the same treatment." "Samosud," *MosVed*, no. 100 (1884), 4.

29. George L. Yaney, *The Systematization of Russian Government* (Urbana, 1973), 234. See also L. S. Prokof'eva, *Krest'ianskaia obshchina v Rossii vo vtoroi polovine XVIII–pervoi polovine XIX v.* (Leningrad, 1981), 159.

the criminal "on orders of the entire commune."[30] In 1907, seventy peasants of Riazan' district beat an accused arsonist to death. After the murder, the village assembly was summoned to give its approval: a "death sentence" was quickly drawn up, signed by over 100 household heads, and marked by the elder's seal of office. Placing responsibility upon the wider community or assembly was viewed by peasants as their best defense if brought to trial for, in their words, "they can't send the whole village to Siberia."[31]

Charivaris directed against persons other than thieves do not fit so neatly into the conclusions drawn thus far. Many forms of charivari, together with such well-tried methods of shaming as gossip, public ridicule, and exclusion from festive and social events, worked to maintain local norms of morality and exerted direct community control over conjugal relations, and here one sees a resemblance to the more familiar European charivari. Adulterers, for example, might be subjected to *vozhdenie*, particularly if the case involved a maiden or unmarried woman caught with a married man. One investigator writing from Tomsk province in the 1870s noted a custom whereby local male youths who caught an adulterous couple would dress the woman in men's clothing and her lover in women's attire, then lead them through the streets.[32] Peasants from a village near Kadnikovo imposed a similar punishment in 1882, but here it was a monk who had been caught with a married woman. The villagers put a woman's sarafan over his cassock and led him back to the monastery, accompanied by laughter, jeers, and the "music" of children beating on oven doors and washbasins.[33] In one Ukrainian village, a farmer caught a girl in his shed with a married man, locked them in, and summoned the local "lads," who put the guilty pair in a cart and drove along the village streets calling them "newlyweds." During the procession, the man's wife showed up and showered the pair with mud. The man was then taken to the local tavern and forced to buy drinks for everyone as payment for the ride. In other parts of Ukraine and Russia, adulterous couples would be led around the village while wedding songs were sung; villagers sometimes clipped the woman's hair or paraded both parties stripped and covered with tar in public.[34]

30. Iakushkin, *Obychnoe pravo*, 2:89; *VolzhV*, no. 73 (1892), 2; *TambGV*, no. 35 (1894), 4.

31. "Riazanskii okruzhnoi sud. Samosud," *RiazV*, no. 80 (1909), 3–4; *Vremennik Zhivopisnoi Rossii* 2, no. 63 (1902), 83–84. Similarly, when five peasants were tried by the Kazan' Circuit Court for beating a suspected thief in their village, they pleaded not guilty of all charges, attributing the punishment "to the entire commune." *VolzhV*, no. 239 (1892), 2. See also "V okruzhnom sude," *RiazZh*, no. 33 (1912), 3.

32. I. Kostrov, *Iuridicheskie obychai krest'ian-starozhilov Tomskoi gubernii* (Tomsk, 1876), 79.

33. M. A. Abrashkevich, *Preliubodeianie s tochki zreniia ugolovnogo prava. Istoriko-dogmaticheskoe issledovanie* (Odessa, 1904), 583.

34. Skorobogatyi, "Ustroistvo," 344; Efimenko, *Sbornik*, 277; Iakushkin, *Obychnoe pravo*, 1:xxxix–xv. For other examples, see Worobec, *Peasant Russia*, 202–3.

Here are all the common elements of the charivari: parading offenders, public derision, humiliation, and *paramusique*. But in many cases of adultery violence was used even when those who committed it did not resist. The process of escalation did not function here because violence seems to have been inherent to this type of charivari. In 1870 a woman named Oksana Vereshchikha from Volynia province was suspected by peasants of carrying on an illicit affair with the local clerk. For this offense they stripped her naked, placed her in irons, and tied her to a post, where she stayed all night. In the morning the villagers returned and ordered her to buy them a bucket of vodka even though they had already pawned her kerchief and sheepskin jacket for liquor on the previous day. Since she had no money, they organized a *vozhdenie* with "musicians" marching in front, followed by Vereshchikha and the elder and villagers trailing close behind. This was a particularly elaborate procession in which villagers placed a garland of straw and burdocks on the victim's head and forced her to dance, then led her seven times along the street, beating and flogging her, all the while passing vodka around. At last they took her home, beat her once again, and released her.[35] In 1887 peasant youths in Novomoskovsk district played the primary role in organizing a *vozhdenie* for a married woman having an affair during her husband's absence at outwork. After forcing the woman to buy them vodka "for ransom," the local lads later returned to continue her punishment. They seized her, stripped her naked, smeared her with tar, and showered her with dust from the road. "A huge, fervent crowd" of mostly children and teenagers then led the woman to the township administration in this state. In addition to "shouting, whistling, and whooping at the poor woman," some peasants pushed their way through the crowd to pinch the prisoner, spit in her face, and throw dirt in her eyes. "The shouts of the women were especially savage," this account noted.[36]

Charivaris of adulteresses or of housewives who shirked their domestic duties may well reveal the ability of traditional communities "to compel individual family members to follow collective rules" and the public control to which "the deviant relations of husband and wife are subject," as Edward Shorter has argued.[37] Yet as Thompson has cautioned, "because certain adulterers were rough musicked, it cannot be assumed that we are observing a community of pagan puritans, for whom marital fidelity was an imperative." The norms that charivaris enforced "should not be set up as

---

35. Iakushkin, *Obychnoe pravo*, 1:xxxx. It is quite likely that Vereshchikha was punished so severely not just for her crime but as a way for villagers to strike out at her lover, the clerk, a figure of considerable local power whom peasants often viewed as corrupt and abusive. For a similar case, see "Samosud," *SPbVed*, no. 201 (1875), 4.

36. Iakushkin, *Obychnoe pravo*, 2:65.

37. Shorter, *Modern Family*, 218, 227. Se also Segalen, *Love and Power*, 44, 46.

absolutes." Indeed, "it need not have been adultery as such which invoked public disgrace, but the way in which particular adulterers . . . 'carried on.'"[38] For Russian villagers, in fact, communal authority played a lesser role in punishing adultery than it did in the case of theft because adultery involved a different set of property and power relations that rested on male domination within both family and village structures and on the husband's acknowledged authority to punish his wife (at least under specific circumstances) with nearly complete impunity. Neighbors rarely intervened to quell domestic violence between husband and wife.[39] Here is one important reason we find relatively few charivaris directed against adulteresses by Great Russian peasants, since villagers usually left it up to a husband to mete out appropriate punishment. The expectation of violence, in turn, may account for its use in those instances when villagers did subject an adulterous woman to *vozhdenie*, for the community symbolically took on the role of offended spouse.

Women frequently sought protection against domestic violence, as evidence from judicial and local administrative bodies testifies. Yet peasant judges, who heard most such complaints, ruled in a woman's favor primarily when they found no justification for a beating, or when they deemed that the husband had treated her with excessive cruelty.[40] With cases of adultery or "abandonment," however, litigation had little chance of success for the husband was believed within his rights to punish his wife as he saw fit; community leaders even intervened to support him and bring matters to a close. Such was the case with an Arkhangel'sk woman named Ferapontova who, in the early 1880s, fled her husband's beatings and filed charges against him

38. Thompson, *Customs*, 513–14. See also Beatrice Gottlieb, *The Family in the Western World* (New York, 1993), 192.

39. S. V. Pakhman (*Obychnoe grazhdanskoe pravo v Rossii*, 2 vols. [SPb, 1877–79], 2:101) argued that neighbors intervened "only in a situation where the husband is drunk and the wife appeals to them for help. But they don't meddle in the punishment of spouses because, in the peasants' opinion, a husband has the right 'to teach' his wife." See also Ia. Ludmer, "Bab'i stony," *IuV*, no. 11 (1884), 447; I. P. Kupchinov, *Krest'ianskoe samoupravlenie*, 2nd ed. (Moscow, 1905), 19–20; I. Krasnoperov, "Krest'ianskie zhenshchiny pred volostnym sudom," *Sbornik pravovedeniia i obshchestvennykh znanii*, vol. 1 (1893), 268–89; Evgeniia Vsevolozhskaia, "Ocherki krest'ianskogo byta Samarskoi gubernii," *EtnogO* 7, no. 1 (1895), 25–26; Z. M. Shpits, "Narodnaia rasprava za preliubodeianie," *SudG*, no. 24 (1897), 12–13; "Dankov," *RiazV*, no. 68 (1910), 4; "V nochnom," *RiazZh*, no. 10 (1913), 3. Although men were sometimes flogged for adultery, they escaped the added tortures that they themselves reserved for women. *Trudy*, 1:295, 440, 443; 2:72, 138, 275; 4:109, 260; "Semeinye otnosheniia. Istiazaniia zheny muzhem," *RusVed*, no. 239 (1884), 4; E. T. Solov'ev, "Samosudy u krest'ian Chistopol'skogo uezda, Kazanskoi gubernii," in P. A. Matveev, ed., *Sbornik narodnykh iuridicheskikh obychaev*, vol. 1 (SPb, 1878), part 3, 17.

40. Shrag, "Krest'ianskie sudy," no. 7–8, 74–77; *Trudy*, 2:10, no. 24 and 29; Charushin, "Narodnyi sud," 312.

at the *volost'* court. Rather than allow her suit to be tried, the village elder came with her spouse and other peasants to bring her home. At the elder's urging, her husband tied her up and then thrashed her through the entire village to their house, accompanied by a supportive crowd. There he dragged her inside, where people had already gathered, threw her on the floor, and mocked and cursed her. As she later wrote in a complaint to a justice of the peace, "I implore you to carry out an investigation quickly, otherwise I will have to endure still more torture from my husband. Is it possible that they can order people to be tortured and mocked? Save me, for the sake of God, I haven't the strength to bear this torture."[41] Thirty years later, in Putiatino village of Riazan' province, an abusive husband whose wife fled to her father's home together with their children "could not tolerate this shame and decided to bring her back 'with the help of the community.'" Men and women gathered and set out in a "highly original procession" carrying washbasins and rattles, broken pots, spades, rakes, and other tools. "The husband walked at the head of this procession carrying a large besom of switches—the symbol of casting a maiden out from her father's home." Once they arrived, he demanded that the entire crowd be treated to drinks and that his wife be returned to him. The frightened father handed over his daughter, "after which the crowd conducted the woman home, banging their 'instruments' and singing songs." Township court records are also replete with stories of women ordered back to husbands who often beat them again for complaining to the authorities.[42]

Even in cases when they employed charivaris, peasant communities favored husbands and punished wives for adultery or other conjugal behavior deemed improper. If adultery led to neglect of the household and tax arrears, a community might intervene to punish the guilty party, often using the courts or administrative measures to do so.[43] But *volost'* courts generally declined to hear cases of adultery not merely because it lay outside their jurisdiction but because a husband was expected to control and master his recalcitrant wife. Though an element of public supervision remained, peasants reserved the infliction of punishment for husbands. Thus when a peasant woman in Orel province stole cloth from a neighbor, vil-

41. Ludmer, "Bab'i stony," no. 12, 670. For additional examples, see Pakhman, *Obychnoe grazhdanskoe pravo,* 2:75–85, 101–4, 387.

42. "Selo Putiatino. Vodvorenie zheny," *RiazV,* no. 169 (1910), 3. For court-ordered cases, see *Trudy,* 2:21, 66, 233, 250, 261, 394; 3:11, 16, 77, 100, 307, 339; 4:110, 116, 292; 6: 228, 282, 458; Firsov and Kiseleva, *Byt velikorusskikh krest'ian,* 301, 306; N. Lazovskii, "Lichnye otnosheniia suprugov po russkomu obychnomu pravu," *IuV,* no. 6–7 (1883), 367–68; E. T. Solov'ev, "Prestupleniia i nakazaniia po poniatiiam krest'ian Povolzh'ia," in Pakhman, ed., *SbNIuO,* 2:293.

43. Shrag, "Krest'ianskie sudy,", no. 7–8, 77; A. A. Titov, *Iuridicheskie obychai sela Nikola-Perevoz, Sulostskoi volosti, Rostovskogo uezda* (Iaroslavl', 1888), 101.

lagers organized a *vozhdenie;* but when she resisted their collective discipline and in doing so insulted the community, the elder ordered her husband to flog her and thereby reassert his personal authority and restore honor to the family.[44] Similarly, in the case of Ferapontova, the elder himself decided to settle this family crisis by taking the woman from where she had fled, but it was the husband who bound her, dragged her home and beat her, unassisted by the boisterous crowd of supporters that accompanied them.

Such village dramas take us beneath the fact of everyday domestic violence, which rested upon a number of poorly understood socioeconomic and cultural determinants, chief among which was the restoration of a husband's honor before the community. As already noted, honor and reputation played extremely important roles in village life and underlay much of what outsiders deemed to be the widespread malicious litigation between peasants. Within the patriarchal social structure of rural Russia, a male villager could not ignore shame, particularly when his shame became common knowledge and called into question his reputation and standing among other household heads. These punishments served as explicit, public acts of repression directed at women whose behavior threatened not only a male's honor but also village cultural norms. They reasserted the boundaries of male authority by reproducing relations of domination and subordination within the rural community. Yet the fact that so many abused wives sought separation or divorce, took their husbands to court, and committed murder when the law failed to protect them suggests that domination itself had boundaries that women believed should not be transgressed and that their actions might be one useful starting point for understanding the nature of female space and power in the Russian countryside.[45]

Unfortunately, many questions concerning Russian charivaris remain unanswered because of the limited information afforded by existing sources. Much like *volost'* court records, they tell us little or nothing about the background and history of a given case or the relationships between actors and victims. Did the *vozhdenie* manifest long-standing hostilities between villagers, household members, or even spouses, for example? Some records hint that this was so, and in those few cases that speak about the victims, it is clear that many were already unpopular within their communities. Could behaviors that peasants punished have been "only pretexts for much deeper rifts, with implications going beyond particular targets," as Martine Segalen

44. Tenishev, *Pravosudie,* 41–43.

45. Existing works are few. See Worobec, *Peasant Russia;* Barbara Clements, Barbara Engel, and Christine Worobec, eds. *Russia's Women: Accommodation, Resistance, Transformation* (Berkeley, 1991); Beatrice Farnsworth and Lynne Viola, eds., *Russian Peasant Women* (New York, 1992); Mandakini Arora, "Boundaries, Transgressions, Limits: Peasant Women and Gender Roles in Tver' Province, 1861–1914" (Ph.D. diss., Duke University, 1995).

asks in her study of rural France and as Edward Thompson argues convincingly with regard to England? The case of Oksana Vereshchikha discussed above certainly suggests that this was so. Russian sources also say little about youth groups—often the main initiators of charivaris and guardians of village norms across much of Europe—although peasant youth in Russia played active roles in other public rituals that served to reproduce community norms, social relations, and boundaries.[46]

Still, we do know enough about the *vozhdenie* to draw certain conclusions. First, it differed in important respects from those in many parts of Western Europe. Great Russian peasants employed rituals of public shaming far more against theft than sexual and conjugal misconduct, perhaps because of the increased significance of property relations in the postemancipation period and a weakening of kinship's primacy, at least in comparison to peasant society under serfdom.[47] When villagers did punish sexual misconduct, their attention focused primarily on unmarried girls and adulteresses whose husbands were either absent or, in the community's view, required assistance to control their wives. Couples might be punished collectively if an outsider (usually male) was involved or if their affair brought neglect of their fiscal obligations, but for the majority of adulteresses punishment was administered by the husband, not the community.[48]

It is also clear that ritual shamings perpetuated a popular kind of prereform justice by employing punishments that courts and village assemblies had regularly imposed in the past. The *vozhdenie* thus linked two periods of rural justice through the peasants' rejection of those limitations placed upon the authority of their village assemblies and courts after 1861. In doing so they preserved a semi-autonomous sphere of justice within the local community. Finally, Russian charivaris usually sought to reintegrate offend-

46. Segalen, *Love and Power,* 47; Thompson, *Customs,* 510–15. These questions have also been raised by André Burguière and Daniel Fabre, "Acteurs et victimes du charivari: leur relation," in Le Goff and Schmitt, eds., *Le Charivari,* esp. 373–74; Hammerton, "Targets of 'Rough Music,'" 23–44. On the role of rural youth in public ritual, see Stephen P. Frank, "Cultural Conflict and Criminality in Rural Russia, 1861–1900" (Ph.D. diss., Brown University, 1987), 84–89; Frank, "'Simple Folk, Savage Customs'?" *JSH* 25, no. 4 (1992), 711–36.

47. Several historians have found that charivaris against thieves were not as uncommon in the West as previously believed. See Ernst Henrichs, "Le charivari et les usages de réprimande en Allemagne. État et perspectives de la recherche," in Le Goff and Schmitt, eds., *Le Charivari,* esp. 302–3; Weber, *Peasants into Frenchmen,* 402.

48. My conclusions apply only to the provinces of Great Russia, for important differences seem to have existed between Russian and Ukrainian charivaris. Although sources suggest that peasants of both nationalities punished adultery and theft with *vozhdenie* at an earlier period, the practice remained far more common in Ukraine after emancipation. The implication here is that still unexplored changes under way during the nineteenth century altered both the nature of the charivari and the local concerns and needs of Russian peasants. See Worobec, "Temptress or Virgin," 227–38.

ers rather than drive them from the community and used the threat of expulsion together with forced purchase of vodka (i.e., symbolic reconciliation) as instruments that reestablished fractured intravillage relations. This fact sharply distinguishes *vozhdenie* from other types of *samosud* in which ritual was largely absent, violence inherent, and expulsion the overriding objective. It is to these more familiar manifestations of popular justice that we now turn.

### *SAMOSUD* AND PROPERTY CRIME

Two additional forms of summary justice help to clarify the difference between *vozhdenie* and *samosud,* the first of which brings us to property crimes of a serious nature. Treatment of thieves depended largely upon the value of what they had stolen, with punishment increasing in severity for theft of more important items and for those that, through their loss, threatened a community's economic well-being. If criminals were outsiders or repeat offenders, reprisals against them were likely to be especially harsh. "*Samosud* takes place most often when a thief is caught [red-handed]," wrote a correspondent from Smolensk province in 1898, "after which the most beastly punishments occur: They inflict such a beating that the thief dies before he can stand trial."[49] Usually involving beatings, gruesome and often lethal tortures, maiming, and killing, such punishments were almost always carried out by a crowd but lacked the organized and ritual character of *vozhdenie.* While an elder might direct the punitive violence, it did not require a meeting of the village assembly, although assemblies often ordered prisoners brought before them for judgment and retribution.[50]

Peasants could indeed be merciless in their reprisals against a criminal, whether their aim was to take revenge on outsiders who stole from them or to rid the community of a known thief once and for all. Two Gypsies in Skopin district were among the hundreds who learned this over the course of many years. Caught one summer evening in 1891 during an attempt to rob a peasant's barn, the would-be thieves were set upon by a crowd of villagers who inflicted such beatings upon them that one died as he was later being transported to the police; the other spent months recuperating at the zemstvo hospital.[51] A similar fate befell another thief in the township seat of Dubovoe, Ranenburg district. Responding to reports of widespread criminal

49. GARF, f. 586, op. 1, d. 120, l. 27.
50. For examples of assembly-ordered punishments, see, e.g., *SV,* no. 18 (1895), 204; "Sl. Aleksandrovka, Atkar. uezd. Samosud," *Saratovskii listok,* no. 84 (1906), 3; "V okruzhnom sude. Samosud," *RiazZh,* no. 35 (1912), 3.
51. GARO, f. 7, op. 1, d. 613, 76ob. For a similar case involving Gypsies, see f. 5, st. 3, op. 4, d. 830 (1866), ll. 24–25.

activities near this village, the local constable and village elder came on the night of July 9, 1908, to search several dwellings and carry out arrests. At one home they apprehended a man named Molodtsov and took him to the *volost'* office, together with three stolen horses. Shortly thereafter a second suspicious person was seen leaving this same house, but he fled when the constable tried to seize him. A shot from the officer's pistol failed to halt the fleeing suspect, but the noise attracted a large crowd that quickly chased him down. When they realized that this was Ivan Ozerov, a local resident who had already been banished by communal resolution for previous crimes, the peasants began beating him. Others ran to the *volost'* office, dragged Molodtsov outside, and set upon him. The constable and his assistants managed to free both suspects but could not prevent the angry crowd from following along and pummeling them all the way back to jail. By the time they reached the lock-up, Ozerov had been beaten unconscious, and he died the following day. Nevertheless, peasants returned again that day, forced their way into the *volost'* office, and resumed beating both Molodtsov as well as Ozerov's corpse. The township elder later ordered Ozerov buried near the jail.[52]

Arsonists fared even worse than thieves. Vasilii Zaikin, for example, was well known as a local drunkard in Naumovskaia village, Riazan' district, and residents suspected that he had set several fires during the summer of 1907 as revenge against those who had refused to buy him vodka. On July 23 Zaikin set fire to his uncle's grain shed after the latter denied his request for money. A neighbor immediately reported Zaikin's deed to the village assembly and a crowd of about seventy people quickly gathered, seized the arsonist, struck him, and tied him up. Some shouted that they should "finish him off." Soon vodka appeared, which the milling villagers consumed while Zaikin lay tied and bleeding on the ground. "Everyone looked at him like one doomed to death. Some women—his relatives—approached and bade him farewell." When Zaikin pleaded for forgiveness, several peasants told him, "If we untied you, the crowd would kill us." Shortly thereafter he was set upon by all and beaten with clubs until dead.[53] At the end of May 1912, a ten-year-old boy came under suspicion for having set a fire in one village of Mikhailov district that burned down three homes. Angry residents wanted to throw the boy and his father into the flames but were stopped by author-

52. GARO, f. 5, st. 3, op. 4, d. 4828, ll. 44–440b. Equally severe was the punishment meted out to Konstantin Siniakov of Riazan' district. A reputed thief to whom peasants attributed numerous crimes (including horsetheft) and who was believed to belong to a gang, Siniakov was set upon at his home and beaten to death by an armed crowd of fifty exasperated, angry villagers in December 1909. "V okruzhnom sude. Samosud v s. Dubrovichakh," *RiazZh*, no. 106 (1912), 3.

53. "Riazanskii okruzhnyi sud. Samosud," *RiazV*, no. 80 (1909), 3–4. See also GARO, f. 5, st. 3, op. 4, d. 4828 (1908), l. 60; *MosVed*, no. 231 (1883), 2; "Krest'ianskii samosud," *SudO*, no. 40 (1904), 774; "Sl. Aleksandrovka, Atkar. uezd. Samosud," *Saratovskii listok*, no. 84 (1906), 3.

ities, who instead turned both over to the judicial investigator. But the latter found no concrete evidence against the accused and, after questioning him and his father, released them. Neither returned home, however. After six days they were found dead in a field of rye not far from their village. The boy's head had been severed.[54] In at least two 1910 cases from different villages of Sapozhok district, peasants threw arsonists into burning buildings and watched them die; a similar incident occurred that year in Spassk district, where angry villagers killed three suspected arsonists.[55]

Peasant officials did not shy away from taking a prominent role in these punishments. In Skopin district, for example, nearly 500 peasants turned out after church services one Sunday in 1907 to watch their elder and others "interrogate" a thief apprehended the previous evening. The accused died following a day-long beating with fists, pitchfork handles, and a bar of iron. Two peasants finally tried in this case received short prison sentences.[56] When the elder of Sapozhok district's Borovoe village arrested a thief in December 1909, he appointed three peasants as judges to direct the culprit's punishment. Together with a group of villagers the judges participated in severely beating the accused with truncheons, following which the elder ordered that he be taken to the *volost'* jail. Along the way the thief's escort continued beating him until he died.[57]

Organized, collective reprisals sometimes resulted when peasants could no longer tolerate the activities of criminals living in their midst. In a Ukrainian village of Skvirsk district, peasants seeking to stop an upsurge of thefts in 1882 caught twelve "notorious thieves," each of whom received one lash of the birch from every household head. Since the village counted 200 households, this punishment was severe indeed. When three of the thieves committed yet another crime several months later, villagers once again rounded up all suspects and sentenced them to three lashes from each householder. Then they tied the thieves' hands and feet together, passed a stout stick through the rope, and twisted it to elicit confessions about other recently perpetrated thefts.[58] Residents from the southern town of Sukhuma, similarly exasperated by police inability to protect their community, decided in 1905 to rid themselves of all "depraved persons." They formed a popular court, closed local stores in solemn anticipation of the

54. "Derevenskaia tragediia," *RiazZh,* no. 138 (1912), 3.

55. *RiazV,* no. 185 (1910), 3; no. 223 (1910), 3; *RiazZh,* no. 117 (1912), 3; GARO, f. 5, st. 3, op. 4, d. 5053, ll. 10–100b.

56. "Vyezdnaia sessiia Moskovskii sudebnoi palaty v g. Riazani," *RiazV,* no. 70 (1910), 4; no. 71, 4.

57. "Sessiia okruzhnogo suda v g. Sapozhke," *RiazZh,* no. 62 (1912), 3. For other provinces, see, e.g., *TambGV,* no. 35 (1894), 4; "Delo ob istiazanii," *VolzhV,* no. 58 (1892), 3; "Zhestokaia rasprava," *OrlV,* no. 249 (1898), 3.

58. *MosVed,* no. 329 (1882), 3.

trial, then arrested nearly fifty known "rogues" (*mazuriki*) and brought them before the court. Conducted before a large crowd, the trial lasted over five hours on the first evening and continued the following day. With only two exceptions, all of the accused were banished.[59] When rumors circulated during late 1907 among villagers of Riazan' province's Malaia Zhokovaia that an infamous thief had escaped from the Zaraisk district prison and taken refuge in neighboring Bol'shaia Zhokovaia, peasants decided to deal with him at once before he could begin stealing again. A large crowd assembled and went to find the escapee, beating him severely when he attempted to flee. He would die later that same evening, murdered by several peasants who returned "to have a chat" with him.[60]

Of all criminals in the Russian countryside, horsethieves inspired by far the greatest hatred. When a thief fell into their hands and they believed retribution to be unlikely, peasants unleashed a deadly fury that even the police feared and sought to avoid. After a constable apprehended one horsethief in 1908 near a village of Riazan' district, he brought the prisoner to a nearby estate and placed him "under guard" in the manor house kitchen. Having heard of the thief's capture, peasants began gathering in the courtyard "to have a look at him." "What happened next remains unexplained," this account tells us. "Only the lifeless corpse . . . with ten broken ribs spoke of the terrible beating to which the thief had been subjected." As for the constable, he conveniently disappeared from the scene, no doubt certain as to what would transpire.[61] In 1887 villagers attacked an Umansk district jail where five horsethieves had been incarcerated, dragged the prisoners outside, and tortured them mercilessly, urged on by a crowd shouting, "Beat them, beat them to death!" Only the arrival of village and township officials prevented the peasants from completing their retribution.[62] One 1879 eyewitness account from the Kuban region described how a crowd chased a horsethief along the main road leading to town. When they

---

59. *Iurist* 4, no. 32 (1905), 1131–32. Similarly, following a murder in March 1877, a crowd of over 200 residents in Maikop decided to deal with all known criminals living among them. They went through the town breaking in doors and windows (pulling one suspect from the stove where he was hiding), dragging them into their yards, and beating them. In less than an hour they punished fourteen persons. *MosVed*, no. 68 (1877), 3. On the use of judicial rituals in other settings, see Eric D. Langer, "Andean Rituals of Revolt: The Chayanta Rebellion of 1927," *Ethnohistory* 37, no. 3 (1990), 227–53.

60. "Mikhailov (Ubiistvo tolpoi vora)," *RiazV*, no. 232 (1910), 3.

61. "Krest'ianskii samosud," *RiazZh*, no. 5 (1912), 2.

62. "Rasprava s konokradami," *MosVed*, no. 152 (1887), 3. Among hundreds of published examples, see M—r., "O merakh preduprezhdeniia i presecheniia konokradstva v Rossii," *IuZh*, no. 3 (November 1860), 208–9; Iakushkin, *Obychnoe pravo*, 2:77–106; "Delo Orlovskogo okruzhnogo suda," *OrlV*, no. 97 (1898), 2; "Narodnyi samosud," *Vremennik Zhivopisnoi Rossii* 2, no. 54 (1902), 13; *Saratovskii listok*, no. 186 (1906), 3; "Samosud nad konokradami," *SPbVed*, no. 231 (1911), 6; "Krest'ianskii samosud," *RiazZh*, no. 5 (1912), 2.

finally caught the thief, villagers started beating him and were soon joined by more and more people until they numbered nearly 100—women and men, children and adults. "Everyone took part in the beating. Once he had been killed, they stopped and quickly dispersed in different directions." Hundreds of similar reports testify with numbing regularity to the problem of horsetheft in Russia and to the only sure means peasants possessed for protecting their livestock.[63]

Villagers also organized collective reprisals against horsethieves. In 1876, residents of three districts in Volynia province joined with German colonists to carry out popular "executions" throughout the region. Up to 1,000 people "went from village to village . . . and applied terrible punishments on horsethieves." Suspects underwent beatings with sticks, whips, and fists. "Many of the thieves were beaten to death; some were horribly maimed." This popular "court" continued its work for nearly a week before the provincial administration finally intervened with armed force. When confronted by police and other officials and admonished as to the illegality of their actions, the peasants and Germans agreed completely, but asked, "Tell us what to do about the thieves." Five hundred people were prosecuted for these events.[64] Thirty-three years later, in 1911, samosud against horsethieves had grown even more commonplace in this province. Peasants from five villages armed themselves with guns, clubs, axes, and pitchforks and went in search of the criminals, "subjecting them to cruel tortures." Seven thieves were killed and twenty wounded as a result, but shortly thereafter the remaining gang members began taking revenge for the murders of their comrades. In effect, a virtual state of warfare erupted between local residents and organized criminals, much as occurred in other parts of the empire.[65]

Even when they did not orchestrate collective reprisals, peasants reserved unimaginable punishments for horsethieves, "rarely letting them escape alive" in one reporter's words. Some criminals were whipped to death, castrated, or beaten in the groin until dead; others underwent searing and branding with hot irons, had their teeth methodically smashed out with hammers, stakes pounded through their throat or chest, nails pounded into their heels, or sharpened stakes driven into their anus. Villagers put out horsethieves' eyes, cut open their stomachs, burned them to death, even

63. F. Shch—n., "Narodnyi samosud i raspravy," *Nedelia*, no. 23 (1879), 784–85. See also Shch—n, "Organizatsiia konokradov i skotokradov," *Nedelia* 12, no. 26 (1879), 779–85; Vesin, "Konokradstvo," 1, no. 3, 350–68; 2, no. 1, 81–93. Horsetheft in the early Soviet era is treated in E. N. Tarnovskii, "Konokradstvo v nastoiashchee vremia i v dorevoliutsionnuiu epokhu," *Problemy prestupnosti*, no. 2 (1927), 100–109.

64. *MosVed*, no. 19 (1877), 4; "Iazva konokradstva," *Nedelia*, no. 8 (1877), 251–53.

65. "Konokradstvo," *SPbVed*, no. 201 (1911), 5. Vigilantism against criminals was especially widespread in the Polish countryside during the 1905 Revolution. See Blobaum, *Rewolucja*, 142–48.

decapitated them. In one locality, peasants elicited confessions from suspected thieves by securing them to a horse and cart and pulling them at full speed along rough ground; when the nearly dead culprit finally provided the names of his accomplices, they too would be subjected to the same treatment. Elsewhere, after being beaten and maimed, thieves were simply tied to a horse and dragged along the ground until dead. According to one account from Ufa province, "Corpses are frequently pulled out of rivers with their hands tied behind them and a horse's bridle in their mouths, secured to the backs of their heads."[66]

Two punishments were reported to have been quite widespread. In one, villagers nailed a pulley high onto a gatepost, tied the thief's hands and feet together, and raised him into the air with a rope running through the pulley. Once he hung at a sufficient height, they released the rope "and he falls to the ground, striking the lower part of his back in a terrible way. This is repeated many times in succession, and each time the snap of the poor devil's vertebrae can be heard." The punishment might continue long after he had died.[67] Another torture involved wrapping a thief's naked torso with a wet sack, placing a plank on his stomach and beating upon it with hammers, logs, or rocks until "the unfortunate's insides are gradually destroyed." The utility of such a punishment was that it left no external signs, making it easier to conceal the criminal's murder. Even without these more elaborate preparations, peasants commonly sought to hide the cause of death by inflicting only internal injuries. In one case, as a crowd began beating two thieves brought before the assembly for punishment, one of those present advised, "Don't hit them in their heads, so there won't be any marks; just break all their bones!"[68]

Although educated Russians regularly professed sympathy for the struggle against horsetheft, the brutality of popular punishment confirmed their views about the violent, bloody nature of rural crime and reinforced their image of peasant otherness. As a defense attorney argued in 1899, *samosud* against horsethieves demonstrated not only the ignorance of coun-

66. A. A. Levenstim, "Konokradstvo s iuridicheskoi i bytovoi storony," *VestP* 29, no. 2 (1899), 30–31; A. Ch—v., "Samosud nad konokradami," *Nedelia*, no. 26 (1878), 856; "Samosud," *MosVed*, no. 57 (1879), 4; "Sud nad samosudami," *MosVed*, no. 49 (1883), 4; "Samosud nad konokradom," *MosVed*, no. 49 (1887), 3; Shch—n, "Narodnyi samosud," 782; "Konokradstvo i samosud," *OrlV*, no. 119 (1898), 2. See also I. Ivaniushenkov, "Konokrady v Eletskom uezde," *MosVed*, no. 113 (1883), 2; S. Gr—ii, "Bor'ba s konokradstvom," *NizhL*, no. 7, (1899), 2; M. F. Chulitskii, "Tolpa," *IV* 110, no. 2 (1907), 294–95; Stephen P. Frank, "Popular Justice," *RR* 46, no. 3 (1987), 239–65; Christine D. Worobec, "Horsethieves and Peasant Justice in Post-Emancipation Russia," *JSH* 21, no. 2 (1987), 281–93.

67. G. N. Breitman, *Prestupnyi mir* (Kiev, 1901), 129; Shch—n., "Narodnyi samosud," 783.

68. Breitman, *Prestupnyi mir,*, 129–30; "Zhestokaia rasprava," *OrlV*, no. 249 (1898), 3. See also *RiazZh*, no. 35 (1912), 3.

try folk but the primitiveness and savage nature of their thinking. These were "beastly crimes" and "inhuman tortures" of a sort "encountered only among savages." Indeed, wrote one contributor to a liberal journal regarding incidents of *samosud* that occurred during the cholera riots of 1892, they were akin to "a chapter from an African adventure of Livingston or Stanley . . . with a tribe of utter savages."[69] "The inhumanity of *samosud* cannot be tolerated in a modern, civilized state," declared another writer, and in 1912 Russia's premier criminologist Mikhail Gernet wrote that summary punishments carried out by villagers summoned up images of "a medieval torture chamber which, louder than any words, say that the peasant, whose human dignity has for too long been trampled, has not yet learned how to relate with any care to another person, to his rights of inviolability, and even to his life."[70]

These depictions of the rural savage satisfied many who sought ready explanations for *samosud,* but at least a few writers suggested a deeper, historical complicity between popular and official justice. They pointed to the examples set by criminal codes like the 1649 *Ulozhenie* or even later laws that allowed for mutilation, execution, or other severe punishments of criminals that were generally carried out in public.[71] The Orthodox church, too, sentenced adulterers and adulteresses alike to public penance and whippings at least until the early nineteenth century. Even more important from the village perspective were the often brutal punishments applied on serfowners' estates—a disciplining of the subordinate, servile body that must have contributed to peasants' conceptualization and implementation of justice (though this influence likely worked in both directions). The methods they used and passed down through generations had conceivably been modeled, at some time in the past, on official and gentry treatment of criminals in a dynamic of cultural interaction, transmission, and accommodation of which the forms and methods remained, especially the linkage of justice with spectacle.[72] Moreover, the state itself retained several of these

69. Ch—v., "Samosud nad konokradami," 857; Iakushkin, *Obychnoe pravo,* 1:xxix; 2:90, 92; *SudO,* no. 6 (1903), 124; "Iz obshchestvennoi khroniki," *VE,* no. 8 (1892), 901.

70. *SPbVed,* no. 231 (1911), 6; *Vremennik Zhivopisnoi Rossii* 2, no. 63 (1902), 83; Gernet, "Prestupnost' krest'ian," 240–41.

71. See, e.g., E. M. Barantsevich, *Konokradstvo i mery protivu ego v Rossii* (Moscow, 1898), 8–12; Levenstim, "Konokradstvo," 32; Aleksandr Filippov, "Narodnoe obychnoe pravo kak istoricheskii material," *RusM,* no. 9 (1886), 65; Efimenko, *Sbornik,* 278–79.

72. In his final comment on rough music, Edward Thompson (*Customs,* 480) suggested such a convergence of customary and official punishment. Wyatt-Brown (*Honor and Violence,* 194) also argues that both state and Church "adjusted their practices to accommodate the popular mode. For instance, common-law punishments prior to the great reformation of penal policies in the late eighteenth century consisted largely of folk tradition carried out under the aegis of the law, itself a ritualistic and supposedly divine institution." On spectacle and pun-

practices after emancipation: the partial shaving of exiles' heads and beards as a form of identification; branding and chaining them to wheelbarrows; mass floggings and executions in retribution for peasant uprisings. Nor did police and other administrative authorities shirk from applying the "law of the fist" to unruly and recalcitrant villagers. As in earlier times, popular and official violence moved in both directions and continued to do so, though less overtly, during the late nineteenth century. Yet as peasants knew well, and as Austin Sarat and Thomas Kearns have recently reminded us, "Violence stands as the limit of law, as a reminder of both law's continuing necessity and its ever-present failing. Without violence, law is unnecessary, yet, in its presence, law, like language and representation themselves, may be impossible."[73]

Still, why did peasants continue to employ *samosud* knowing the dire consequences that could follow? The primary reason was their conviction that courts did not punish crimes like horsetheft or arson with sufficient severity, and this conviction grew stronger throughout our period. One horsethief tried in 1901 was found guilty by the Kazan' Circuit Court but received a sentence of only four years at penal servitude—not much different from punishments meted out for relatively minor robberies. As late as 1910, courts sentenced horsethieves to as little as three years' imprisonment, after which they could resort once more to their old trade or seek revenge.[74] For crimes that so threatened the economic foundations of village life, a few years in prison did not seem adequate punishment. Nor could peasants be certain that a thief would be punished at all. Even if honest, the rural police were no match for professional horsethieves working in large groups and living secretly in their own prosperous, well-protected settlements. As one writer noted in 1878, many, perhaps most cases examined by prosecutors never came to trial for lack of evidence.[75] With no real police or judicial pro-

---

ishment, see Michel Foucault, *Discipline and Punish: The Birth of the Prison* (New York, 1977), 32–69; Douglas Hay, "Property," in Douglas Hay et al., *Albion's Fatal Tree* (New York, 1975), 17–63; Pieter Spierenburg, *The Spectacle of Suffering: Executions and the Evolution of Repression from a Preindustrial Metropolis to the European Experience* (Cambridge, 1984); V. A. C. Gatrell, *The Hanging Tree: Execution and the English People, 1770–1868* (Oxford, 1994).

73. Austin Sarat and Thomas R. Kearns, eds., *Law's Violence* (Ann Arbor, 1992), 2.

74. "Sudebnaia khronika. Derzkii konokrad," *Kazanskii telegraf,* no. 2716 (1901), 4; "Krazha loshadi," *RiazZh,* no. 88 (1912), 5; "Primenenie zakona o konokradakh," *RiazZh,* no. 116 (1912), 3. One horsethief released in 1884 after serving a short prison sentence stole a horse on his way home from prison but was caught within thirty minutes by local peasants who recognized him and beat him to death. "Samosud," *SudG,* no. 7 (1884), 16.

75. Ch—v., "Samosud nad konokradami," 857; S. V. Pakhman, "Ocherk narodnykh iuridicheskikh obychaev," in Pakhman, ed., *SbNIuO,* vol. 2 (SPb, 1900), 93; E. T. Solov'ev, "Prestupleniia i nakazaniia po poniatiiam krest'ian Povolzh'ia," in Pakhman, ed., *SbNIuO,* 287–89; Shch—n., "Narodnyi samosud," 786; A. F. Brandt, "Iuridicheskie obychai krest'ian Mogilevskoi gubernii," in Pakhman, ed., *SbNIuO,* 2:116.

tection to speak of, villagers were forced to take their own measures and ensure that a thief, when caught, was rendered incapable of stealing again.
Such was the case in a village of Pazherevitsk *volost'*, Pskov province, in the
1890s, where peasants seized a thief trying to break into someone's yard. A
discussion ensued concerning what to do with the thief, and one villager
suggested turning him over to the police captain. But another said, "And
what will the *stanovoi* do? Put him in prison for three months, and then he'll
steal even more. Come on, better to punish him ourselves. Only take care
not to kill him, boys, so as not to take a sin on our souls." They therefore decided to break his legs "so he won't come into other people's yards."[76] Even
when they turned a criminal over to authorities, peasants often did so only
after punishing the culprit themselves, certain that they knew best how to
treat persons who threatened their village. "Now they won't steal anymore!"
was an exclamation regularly heard from those taking part in the maiming
or murder of a horsethief. The steady growth of horsetheft throughout the
second half of the century thus combined with the failings of police, prosecutors, and courts to reinforce and even increase the practice of popular
justice.[77]

## SORCERY

The widening divergence between official and popular views of maleficent
sorcery also left peasants with limited alternatives for dealing with persons
whose ability to manipulate supernatural forces endangered the health and
welfare of community members, crops, and livestock. During the first half
of the nineteenth century, criminal courts did mete out punishment to persons accused of practicing sorcery, though they often convicted on other
grounds. In the early 1830s, for example, a landowner acted on a complaint
by his serfs and reported to the Vologda Court of Equity (*sovestnyi sud*)
about a widow and her son who cast harmful spells on local women. The investigating magistrate learned that twelve villagers had already been afflicted, and peasants from surrounding localities came forward to level identical accusations against the woman. Despite this evidence, the accused were
charged with sedition and deception and sentenced to punishment with
birch rods.[78] A few years earlier, in 1824, the same court tried a case that
arose among crown peasants in Aksenovka village. The miller Andrei Kopalin stood accused by locals, who claimed he cast spells on people that caused

76. GARF, f. 586, op. 1, d. 117, l. 40.
77. Breitman, *Prestupnyi mir,* 122; M—r., "O merakh preduprezhdeniia," 197–200; "Bich
derevni," *RiazV,* no. 143 (1909), 2; Ivaniushenkov, "Konokrady v Eletskom uezde," 2–3.
78. N. P. Karabchevskii, *Okolo pravosudiia. Stat'i, soobshcheniia i sudebnye ocherki* (SPb, 1902),
228–30.

them to become hysterics or to suffer ailments such as hernias, swollen stomachs, and pains in the lower back. After hearing testimony and gathering evidence, the court sentenced Kopalin to seventy lashes, which were administered on site in the village. Eight years later, peasants of several adjoining townships brought new charges against Kopalin, his wife, sister-in-law, and three others associated with him and requested that all five be banished to Siberia for settlement. But this time the magistrate and a local doctor found no evidence of evil spells, attributed ongoing cases of *kliku-shestvo* to "simple minds" and ignorance, and dismissed all charges.[79]

These decisions indicate a certain ambiguity toward witchcraft and magic on the part of tsarist courts. On the one hand, eighteenth- and early nineteenth-century criminal law engaged popular belief by the fact that it forbade sorcery, magic, and "superstition." Both the 1832 and 1842 editions of the Code of Criminal Laws punished practitioners of magic either with a public whipping or by exile to settlement and loss of all rights.[80] A convergence of belief was also evident when serfowners lodged complaints against sorcerers or took an active part in their punishment. Nor did the Orthodox church remain above complicity, for parish priests regularly sermonized about "superstitions" like divining and the practice of sorcery.[81] Crown, private, and state serfs therefore looked to the courts for protection from the supernatural powers of an angry or offended sorcerer. In adhering to Church views on magic, however, courts most often treated these cases as "superstition" or as a forms of swindling, deception, or disturbing the peace. Yet the linguistic and juridical transformation of charges from "sorcery" to "swindling" once a case came to trial was of little matter to those making the accusations as long as the guilty party received punishment.

By the 1840s and 1850s, the divergence between popular belief and official judicial practice had widened so substantially that peasants who sought legal protection from witchcraft found access to courts increasingly difficult, as prosecutors became less willing to try such cases and courts more reluctant to convict. To win a case proved virtually impossible during the postreform decades because state courts no longer prosecuted sorcerers even though witchcraft remained in the 1885 Criminal Code (articles 937 and 938). Indeed, it was the plaintiffs who might be punished for slander while the sorcerer went free, as happened in an 1872 case from Tikhvinsk district, Novgorod province, and again in 1912 in the Mikhailov

79. Ibid., 230–32.

80. Ardalion Popov, *Sud i nakazaniia za prestupleniia protiv very i nravstvennosti po russkomu pravu* (Kazan', 1904), 370–82.

81. S. Ponomarev, "Ocherki narodnogo prava," *SevV,* no. 2 (1887), 90; Karabchevskii, *Okolo pravosudiia,* 233; Pavel Balkashin, "O sueveriiakh v krest'ianskom soslovii," *RiazGV,* no. 43, (1863), 5; Sv. Evgenii Smirnov, "Po voprosu o bor'be sel'skikh pastyrei s znakhariami i vorozheiami," *RiazEV* 25, no. 5 (1890), 242–44.

district of Riazan' province, where a couple was found guilty and jailed for fifteen days after falsely accusing a fellow villager of casting a spell on their son.[82] In 1910 a reputed sorceress of Zaraisk district was severely beaten at home by several peasants and the village elder, who claimed she had cast a spell on him. During this attack she struck the elder in the face with an ax. The Riazan' Circuit Court allowed no discussion of evil spells during her trial for assaulting an official and acquitted her.[83]

Unable to achieve satisfaction in the courts, villagers had recourse only to older practices of popular justice for protection against witchcraft and sorcery, as illustrated by the burning of Agrafena Ignateva. This may in part account for the continued vitality and possible increase of *samosud* after emancipation. Charivari remained another weapon in the villagers' arsenal, as the following case demonstrates. In 1898, Mar'ia Marchevskaia of Zhitomir district was accused by a local woman of being a witch. Marchevskaia's accuser came to her home and called the woman outside, where she proceeded to insult and mock her in the street. Next, aided by the village elder and his police assistant, she took Marchevskaia to a resident "expert" to examine her and determine whether she possessed a tail. Finally the woman was led through the street by a crowd, which tried to tear off her clothing, and by children beating on "drums." Marchevskaia later lodged a complaint with the justice of the peace, who found her accuser guilty of insult and sentenced her to five days in jail. The village elder and policeman would be tried at a later date before the circuit court.[84]

More commonly, however, punishment of witches and sorcerers resulted in beatings or murder. In June 1878 a deaf mute came to Tarachevskaia village of Vologda province begging for food, but to his misfortune an epidemic was raging among the livestock and villagers believed that epidemics of this kind were spread by mutes with the aid of "deadly drugs, potions, and charms." Shortly after his arrival, three men took the mute outside the village and killed him.[85] Occurrences of this sort were recorded around Penza province during the late 1870s and early 1880s—four known cases in 1880 alone. One involved a sorcerer invited as an honored guest to a peasant wedding (a common practice). The parents wanted to win his approval for

82. "Kolduny i klikushi," no. 4, 84–85; L. Vesin, "Narodnyi samosud nad koldunami (K istorii narodnykh obychaev)," *SevV*, no. 9 (1892), 61–63; "Kartinki derevenskoi zhizni," *RiazZh*, no. 171 (1912), 3.

83. "Sessiia Riazanskogo okruzhnogo suda v g. Zaraiske. U koldun'i," *RiazZh*, no. 90 (1912), 3.

84. "Delo o ved'me," *OrlV*, no. 173 (1898), 3–4.

85. Vesin, "Narodnyi samosud," 66–67. See also A. Kirpichnikov, "Ocherki po mifologii," 3–4 and 10; Ludmer, "Bab'i stony," no. 12, 658–59; Ponomarev, "Ocherki," 79–87; "Narodnoe sueverie," *VolzhV*, no. 83 (1892), 3; "Eletskaia khronika," *OrlV*, no. 111 (1898), 2; "Narodnye sueveriia," *RiazV*, no. 164 (1909), 4.

the newlyweds, "but whether they treated him badly, or for some other reason, he remained unsatisfied, and when the young couple returned home
from the wedding, the bride's mother became hysterical [*stala 'vyklikat'*]."
Her relatives were embittered by this incident, and on the following morning the sorcerer's corpse was found "mutilated beyond recognition."[86] In a
village of Moscow province, a series of misfortunes had long been attributed
to the evil eye of an elderly sorceress named Dar'ia. Soon after she came to
beg alms from the peasant Luker'ia Ivanova in the summer of 1892, the latter suffered fits of hysteria and remained thus afflicted for several days. Villagers decided to cure Ivanova by putting a bridle on her and leading her
through the town, believing that the guilty party would appear during the
procession. Unfortunately, Dar'ia came to visit her sister at the very time this
peculiar "*vozhdenie*" was under way, fulfilling the crowd's expectations.
When the peasants saw the old woman, they seized and dragged her to
Ivanova's home where she was confronted by the victim, interrogated, then
taken from the house and beaten:

> And how they beat her: A policeman broke a yoke on her; another broke a
> cane against her side and threw a brick at her head; others beat her with fists.
> From all ends of the village peasants came running, having heard that they
> were beating a sorceress. They, too, added their hands to the task. Finally,
> they took the old woman by the legs and dragged her to a ravine, broke off
> branches, and whipped the half-dead woman until she was bleeding; and
> when she opened her eyes and Avdot'ia Rybina saw this, she began beating
> [Dar'ia] with a chain until it was nearly broken. The old woman lay in the
> ravine until evening, and . . . when it began to rain, the village elder had her
> brought to her sister's house [which was now empty, for her sister had since
> fled the village], where she lay all night on the bare floor. Next day the con-
> stable learned of these event and had Dar'ia taken to the zemstvo hospital,
> but she died one day later.[87]

The early twentieth century, too, saw assaults upon witches regularly reported by the provincial press. An elderly peasant woman from the Dmitrovsk district of Moscow province was accused of casting a spell on a young
maiden in February 1912, for example, and nearly all of the village women
decided to force her to remove the spell. Taking an icon and the victim, they
marched to her home singing "Christ has Risen." When the old woman appeared at her cottage door, the afflicted girl immediately attacked and began striking her. "This served as a signal for all the other women, who also

86. Vesin, "Narodnyi samosud," 68–69; *Golos,* no. 210 (1880), 3.

87. "Eshche primer liudskoi gluposti," *SV,* no. 49 (1892), 538–39. See also Levenstim,
*Sueverie,* 36–37; Vesin, "Narodnyi samosud," 74–75; *Novoe vremia,* no. 7116 (1895); Jeanne
Favret-Saada, *Deadly Words,* trans. Catherine Cullen (Cambridge, 1980), 137–47.

attacked the 'sorceress.' As a result, after several minutes the lifeless, muti-lated corpse of the unfortunate old woman lay on the ground."[88]

Nowhere does the link between peasant culture and *samosud* appear more dramatically than in these cases of reprisal against suspected practi-tioners of magic. Though by no means everyday occurrences, they could not be written off as aberrations as long as peasants explained epidemics, mental disorders, and a plethora of natural phenomena within a framework of supernatural causation. The ease with which rural charlatans and crimi-nals exploited peasant beliefs merely confirms that such a mode of ex-planation survived into the late nineteenth and early twentieth centuries. Although this element of popular culture waned and in some areas re-treated before the inroads of education, literacy, industrialization, and so-cial mobility, especially among the younger generation, the number of cases in which villagers were charged with torturing or murdering witches and sorcerers tells us that change in postemancipation Russia was far from uni-versal.[89] In fact, Russell Zguta has suggested that the swimming of witches in Ukraine increased during the nineteenth century, though we have no sim-ilar information for Great Russia. If true, this lends further confirmation to arguments by historians and anthropologists that escalations in witchcraft accusations often accompany changing social and economic conditions. It is certainly a plausible explanation for nineteenth-century rural Russia, where population pressure and land shortage helped to erode the tradition of charity and support for impoverished members of the community.[90]

Like charivaris, charges of witchcraft also reflected intravillage conflict. Most cases examined in this study conform to the general pattern of witch-craft accusations found earlier in Western Europe, in which victims were mainly elderly, itinerants, or socially isolated. Given the traditional gener-osity of peasants toward wanderers and beggars, this may seem surprising. When such people lived in the community and depended on others for their daily subsistence, however, they could easily become a burden and, under certain circumstances (such as an outbreak of disease), the target of long simmering resentment or hostility. Much the same can be said regarding

88. "Samosud nad 'koldun'ei,'" *RiazZh*, no. 32 (1912), 4.

89. "In places where young peasants go to school," noted one commentator, "belief in sorcerers . . . is significantly lessened, and the horrors of popular *samosud* against sorcerers al-most never occurs." "Kolduny i klikushi," 149. But see the contrary argument of Robert W. Bushaway, "'Tacit, Unsuspected, but Still Implicit Faith': Alternative Belief in Nineteenth-Century Rural England," in Tim Harris, ed., *Popular Culture in England, c. 1500–1850* (London, 1995), 199.

90. Russell Zguta, "The Ordeal by Water (Swimming of Witches) in the East Slavic World," *SR* 36, no. 2 ( June 1977), 228; Keith Thomas, *Religion and the Decline of Magic* (London, 1971), 535–69.

mendicants; usually tolerated, their appearance during bad times presented an outlet for otherwise undirected fear and anger and helped to explain whatever calamity beset the community. Having little or no say in local affairs, such people proved particularly vulnerable to denunciation, a fact well known to neighbors and other villagers, who could use it to their advantage. Charges of witchcraft might also be useful in domestic conflicts as an extreme means for divorce or solving other intractable differences within the household. We have numerous examples in which husbands accused wives or sons accused mothers of sorcery and punished them accordingly. As one anthropologist has argued, "Accusations of sorcery are not random and whimsical, but tend to attach to recurrent relationships and situations."[91] This is not to say that witchcraft accusations were no more than pretexts for settling pre-existing conflicts in the village, though very likely many were, and someone leveling an accusation against a "witch" may well have known the charge was false but have been equally confident that others would believe it. Evidence attesting to the widespread persistence of belief in magic and supernatural forces among all classes in Russia, however, is too convincing for us not to recognize that most peasants who brought charges of witchcraft, together with those who helped to punish the accused were directed by their beliefs about the supernatural.


In the three areas treated here, *samosud* was a response to threats against the community or challenges to village norms and authority. It was not simple lawless violence, as many outsiders charged, but action aimed at suppressing particular forms of behavior and criminality that could disrupt social relations or seriously harm the village economy. With little or no protection against such threats other than that offered by local rules and institutions, peasants responded with the weapons available to them: charivaris, public beatings, ostracism, and murder. Their weapons, however, differed in form and purpose. Directed against village members, the *vozhdenie* employed an array of symbols and ritual designed to reconcile criminal and community and to restore peaceful relations between villagers. Only if reconciliation was rejected did peasants resort to violence or outright expulsion, for in such cases the offender effectively earned the status of outsider by spurning the community itself. Violent *samosud*, by contrast, focused on outsiders, de-

91. Sally Falk Moore, *Social Facts and Fabrications* (New York, 1986), 257. See also Favret-Saada, *Deadly Words*, esp. 39–63; Robin Briggs, *Witches and Neighbors* (New York, 1996), 259–86. For examples, see, e.g., Vesin, "Narodnyi samosud," 76–77; Tulub, "Sueverie i prestuplenie," 1084–87. In an 1893 case from Tver province a woman was accused by her daughter-in-law of casting a spell on her and for this she was killed by her son (the daughter-in-law's husband). It was widely known that the two women were on hostile terms. Levenstim, *Sueverie*, 36.

fined as nonmembers of the community or those who, through the harm they caused or because of their isolation, had removed themselves from the community. Hence the absence of ritual "processions" with their symbolic steps of expulsion and reconciliation. Outsiders, by definition, could not be brought into the community except through bonds of marriage or kinship, and when they threatened the village's well-being, mechanisms of reconciliation did not come in to play. The punishments used against them were intended to ensure that they would pose no further harm.[92]

*Samosud* forced peasants to defend their juridical beliefs and practices before elite culture. Educated Russia saw these acts not only as violations of the criminal code but as proof of the low level of civilization in which the rural population was mired. Villagers, however, rejected official law on this matter (or at least appeared willing to risk its sanction) as they did on many issues that touched their lives, resorting to charivaris or violent retribution when necessary and accepting the risks accompanying popular justice. In their view, after all, the state regularly employed arbitrary punishments against its rural wards for far less serious offenses. Russian peasants were well aware that state law forbade *samosud*, since they frequently attempted to conceal its results and probably succeeded far more often than we would imagine. But local notions of justice did not draw the same delimitations as official law with regard to crimes that rural communities could and could not punish. Since infractions punished by the *vozhedenie* concerned the community alone, outsiders simply had no business meddling in its affairs regardless of what state law might forbid. Most important, official courts did not punish crimes like horsetheft as severely as peasants believed they should, and as for witchcraft, the state had ceased to regard this serious problem (as villagers saw it) to be a crime at all. Official law punished serious crimes according to a different set of criteria than used by the peasantry, and from the village perspective its representatives and institutions appeared increasingly unable to apprehend or prosecute criminals. Participants in the murder of a horsethief or a witch therefore found few alternatives to their own methods of justice. The growth of *samosud* throughout the postemancipation era, and particularly after 1900, served as a clear and potentially dangerous indicator of the state's failure to bring its law and justice to the countryside in any effective, systematic way.

---

92. The distinctions between *vozhdenie* and violent *samosud*, of course, should not be taken as absolutes. In some instances, boundaries between the two were crossed. Breitman (*Prestupnyi mir*, 130) provides several examples of charivaris involving horsethieves, though these were thieves who had stolen within their own village.

# CHAPTER 9

# Savages at the Gates

## Bandits, Hooligans, and
## the Last Crime Wave

*We have been observing peasant morals for nearly forty years now and can attest that even back then there were already several townships with reputations as dens of robbers. And then, about ten years after emancipation, rural youths began burning out petty noble landowners and wealthy peasants. Then the church holidays . . . were seized by revelry, debauchery, and robbery. There were not as many wounded and murdered as nowadays, but even then it could be sensed that the simple folk had been thrown to the arbitrariness of the elements, that cultural authority had disappeared, and the government had limited itself—just as in the epoch of the Varangians—only to gathering tribute from the peasantry.*

"POPULAR ANARCHY," *THE ACTIVIST*, 1913

*The chief shortcoming that peasants find in the [circuit court] is the leniency of punishments handed down for certain crimes—those that peasants consider the most serious, such as arson, horsetheft, etc. A Nizhnii Novgorod jury passed a verdict of guilty upon an arsonist. When the court announced that the convict would receive six years at penal servitude, the arsonist's father shouted: "It's too little for him, the scoundrel, he should get life." And one of the victims added: "No, he should go directly to the gallows or be buried alive!"*

A. A. CHARUSHIN (ETHNOGRAPHER), 1913

## "IN THE SHADOW AND VESTIBULE OF THE DEAD"

"In recent times," read an 1899 commentary from the village of Lyskovo, Nizhnii Novgorod province, "so many thieves have appeared among us that, quite simply, life here is impossible. They pay nightly 'visits' to inhabitants' homes. Not a single evening passes without some sort of theft occurring, and almost all the thieves go unpunished because they cannot be caught."[1] This report was anything but exceptional. From the mid-1890s, there were increasing concerns about a veritable epidemic of crime, and in the wake of the 1905 Revolution these reached panic levels. As early as 1904 and the first months of 1905, town residents in Iaroslavl' province had become so frightened by crime that they would not venture out at night, and in larger villages, "if people want to leave their homes during the evening they must

---

1. "Poslednie izvestiia. Selo Lyskovo," *NizhL*, no. 38 (1899), 3.

arm themselves with a revolver or knife." By 1906 a Kostroma paper claimed, the anarchy had only grown worse. "Theft, robbery, armed assaults, and murder are becoming commonplace."[2] Another report from Kostroma province warned: "Human life is worth nothing, and to destroy it is easier than butchering a chicken. Any understanding about property has collapsed. All human feelings are dying, and their place is being taken by predatory, savage instincts."[3] "It is terrible to think to what degree life in the countryside has been cheapened," mourned a 1912 newspaper commentator. "We are living in the shadow and vestibule of the dead."[4]

Country dwellers experiencing these unsettled times could rely on neither the police nor the courts to protect their communities. Residents of Teliatniki village in Sapozhok district, for instance, found themselves besieged by a rash of thefts that began during the autumn of 1904. In an effort to guard their property, villagers took to arming themselves and patrolling outside their homes each night. Still the thefts continued, taking place almost every evening and even spreading to a neighboring village. When peasants at last charged three local residents with organizing a gang of robbers and turned the trio over to authorities, two were soon released for lack of evidence. One newspaper reported in 1913 that horsetheft had grown so widespread throughout Ranenburg district that peasants had taken to sleeping in their barns to better safeguard their animals.[5] Clearly, the same problems that confronted villagers and rural communities in previous decades grew steadily worse near the century's end, and police proved capable of apprehending only a small fraction of perpetrators. As investigators and prosecutors found themselves less and less able to build adequate cases for prosecution, releasing ever more accused criminals back to their communities, peasants felt a crisis had befallen the countryside.

Such fears appeared well founded, for there was, in fact, a significant statistical increase in certain categories of rural crime beginning in the mid- to late 1890s. Property offenses registered a marked growth within the criminal statistics as early as 1885 and continued to rise thereafter. Prosecutions

2. "Rostov-Iaroslavskii," *SevK*, no. 93 (1905), 2; "Sl. Pokrovskaia," *Privolzhskii krai*, no. 24 (1904), 2; "Shuia," *PV*, no. 129 (1906), 3. See also "Kostromskaia zhizn'. Krazhi," *PV*, no. 91 (1906), 3.

3. "Kostroma 15-go aprelia," *PV*, no. 26 (1906), 1. See also "Khuligany i khuliganstvo," *Novoe vremia*, no. 13645 (1914), 13. In a similar vein, a later commentary claimed that "the inviolability of the person and of the home of those who commit crimes is now fashionable, while sober, moral people are completely defenseless." "O bor'be s prestupleniiami," *Deiatel'* 18, no. 1 (1913), 1.

4. Cited in V. Sinegub, "V teni i seni smertnei," *RusVed*, no. 278 (1912), 3.

5. GARO, f. 695, op. 16 (1905), sv. 191, d. 167, ll. 38–40; "Original'nye skachki. Der. Kuz'minka, Ran. uez.," *RiazZh*, no. 30 (1913), 3. See also "Selo Chuchkovo, Sapozhkovskogo uezda," *RiazV*, no. 55 (1911), 3.

for homicide had jumped sharply by 1896, and robbery and armed robbery started their statistical increase between 1898 and 1900.[6] These patterns differed little in urban localities. More important than prosecution or conviction rates, however, are the hundreds of peasant communities that requested protection or took direct action against criminals—often persons who had been acquitted by courts, released for lack of evidence, or set loose after serving a short sentence behind bars.

Take the following example from Malyi Snezhetok village in the Ranenburg district of Riazan' province. In July 1902, an assembly meeting attended by seventy-four of the village's ninety-two household heads resolved to banish Timofei Ivanov Mitroshkin as a dangerous and depraved member of their community. The twenty-four-year-old Mitroshkin had returned to Malyi Snezhetok in December 1900 after serving a prison sentence for an unspecified offense. Shortly thereafter he stole another villager's horse, for which he was tried by the land captain and sentenced to one year in prison. Mitroshkin returned to crime once again upon his release in 1902, perpetrating thefts "continuously," according to the assembly resolution. He was also the prime suspect in a burglary of the local church. Because he was a bachelor without parents in the village and did not farm his allotment land, Mitroshkin was seen as an unproductive, parasitic member of the community who preyed upon others' property but who would likely not be sentenced to a sufficiently lengthy term by any court. Therefore, in exasperation, the assembly finally agreed to request that the state banish Mitroshkin administratively, a process that would cost a fair sum.[7]

What is evident from cases of this sort is that rural communities remained largely on their own when dealing with recidivists and others who constantly violated local norms or posed a threat to village society and authority. Peasant communes had, of course, banished villagers charged with repeated theft, drunkenness, threats, and disorderly conduct for well over a century, but by the 1890s the number of such persons appeared to be on the rise, placing peasant property at greater risk and severely straining local mechanisms of social control. Even worse was the fact that many of these criminals had escaped punishment at the hands of official justice or received far too lenient sentences. Recall that Mitroshkin had only just returned from prison when he stole a horse, for which the land captain sentenced him to a mere one-year term. Given popular opinion toward horsethieves, it is easy to suspect that villagers were as angry with the land captain as they were with

6. *Svod statisticheskikh svedenii po delam ugolovnym,* 43 vols. (SSPb, 1874–1916), part 2, "Vremia i mesto soversheniia prestuplenii."

7. GARO, f. 695, op. 14 (1903), sv. 179, d. 142, ll. 5–6, 22–23.

the perpetrator. Increasingly, then, communities blamed state organs of policing and justice for the growing crime problem.

At about the same time that villagers throughout central Russia were confronting this breakdown of order, nonpeasants and government officials believed that they faced a different and equally frightening crime wave that was spreading rapidly across the empire, leaving neither town nor rural hamlet untouched and threatening the very foundations of Russia's fragile civil society, if not civilization itself. Consisting of no particular type of offense but, rather, defined more by the perpetrators' behavior, this crime wave called "hooliganism" was the culmination of a decades-long confrontation between the asymmetrical forces of authority and the weak and between the cultures of educated Russia and those of the lower classes.[8]

Viewed within a broader context, these turn-of-the-century panics laid bare an equally fundamental conflict that had simmered just at the surface of Russian society since the time of emancipation. What justice meant and whom the law served (or should serve) were questions central to that conflict. The manner in which nonpeasant society continued to view rural crime within a framework of cultural backwardness—tinged, by the 1890s, with renewed and growing fears of the peasantry—provided one perspective on such issues. Another could be seen in the state's reliance upon administrative organs to remedy the deficiencies of its judicial apparatus, which reflected an awareness of the more basic problem confronting the countryside. By narrowly focusing its efforts on defending government interests or protecting gentry property, the state showed peasants in no uncertain terms where the primary concerns of "justice" lay. The brutality of repression during the 1905 Revolution brought this point home with a clarity not seen since the Pugachev revolt over a century before. Peasant frustration and anger on a range of matters, from historical disputes over land, forest rights, and wages to complaints about policing and the increasingly poor performance of criminal courts, produced a very different response to the questions concerning justice and law. That these replies stood at great distance from one another is telling of the inability of state and society to resolve some of the most basic issues left to fester after 1861. That dilemma is framed here in the dual context of the debate over hooliganism and peasant complaints about crime and justice.

8. See Stephen P. Frank, "Cultural Conflict and Criminality in Rural Russia, 1861–1900" (Ph.D. diss., Brown University, 1987), 87–89; Frank, "'Simple Folk, Savage Customs'?" *JSH* 25, no. 4 (1992), 726–28; Frank, "Confronting the Domestic Other," in Stephen P. Frank and Mark D. Steinberg, eds., *Cultures in Flux* (Princeton, 1994); Joan Neuberger, *Hooliganism* (Berkeley, 1993); Neil B. Weissman, "Rural Crime in Tsarist Russia, 1905–1914," *SR* 37, no. 2 (1978), 234.

## THE HOOLIGAN PHENOMENON

Just after the turn of the century in Russia, "hooliganism"—a term adopted from the British—quickly became the common label for a broad range of seemingly unrelated crimes perpetrated in town and countryside.[9] In its earliest provincial usage from about 1900 to 1904, the label "hooligan" was often affixed to the activities of rowdy, drunken village youths, but during the 1905–7 Revolution it was often used to describe reactionary "black hundreds" bands and mobs and participants in pogroms or violent attacks upon Jews, "intellectuals," and "students."[10] Finally "hooliganism" would come to settle on all acts deemed in any way brazen or those considered to be without motive, threatening to decorum and authority. By 1910 educated society saw this wave of hooliganism as a national crisis demanding direct action from political, moral, and cultural authorities.

On July 18, 1912, the Rural Section of the MVD at last mobilized to deal with the crime wave and issued a circular to provincial governors. Noting the "growth in recent times of a special form of *ozornichestvo* [mischief making] in rural localities that is known by the name 'hooliganism,'" the circular stated that "in connection with the dissoluteness being observed among young people, [such behavior] is making life impossible in the countryside for farmers and the upright segment of the peasantry." The document defined hooliganism broadly, "beginning with rudeness and acts of disrespect toward elders, clergy, and local authorities, cursing and using foul language, drunkenness, idleness, carrying weapons, . . . and ending with infringements upon property and the personal inviolability of individuals and a whole range of criminally punishable acts." The ministry requested that district-level officials respond to ten questions about hooliganism in their localities, provide statistical data drawn from *volost'* courts, land captains, and municipal courts (*gorodskie sudy*), and suggest measures to fight the

9. See RGIA, f. 1405, op. 532, d. 438, ll. 1–107; d. 439, *passim*, for efforts to define the crime. Weissman ("Rural Crime," 228–40) provides a good summation of these surveys. The most recent treatment is Neuberger, *Hooliganism*. See also S. Elpat'evskii, "Bezchinstvo," *RB*, no. 5 (1912), 84–110; V. Utevskii, "Khuliganstvo v epokhu 1905–1914 gg.," in V. N. Tolmachev, ed., *Khuliganstvo i khuligany: Sbornik* (Moscow, 1929), 20–37; V. Vlasov, "Khuliganstvo v gorode i derevne," *Problemy prestupnosti*, no. 2 (1927), 51–53. Compare Michelle Perrot, "Dans la France de la belle époque, les 'Apaches,' premières bandes des jeunes," in *Les marginaux et les exclus dans l'histoire* (Paris, 1979), 387–407; Geoffrey Pearson, *Hooligan: A History of Respectable Fears* (New York, 1983). According to Pearson (p. 74), the term "hooligan" only made its entrance into common English usage in 1898.

10. This point is also made by Utevskii, "Khuliganstvo v epokhu 1905–1914 gg.," 23–24. For examples, see GARO, f. 5, op. 1, d. 4020, ll. 92–920b.; f. 640, st. 1, op. 41 (1907), sv. 84, dd. 1–3; "Sobytiia v Nizhnem-Novgorode," *Iurist*, no. 29 (1905), 1040–41; "V otvet khuliganam," *SevK*, no. 67 (1905), 1; "S. Sereda, Danilov. uezda (Sel'skii chernosotenets)," *SevK*, no. 156 (1905), 3; Abrontskii, "Vremia vspomnit'," *SevK*, no. 260 (1905), 2.

crime wave. Questions asked to what extent hooliganism had spread, how it was manifested, specific conditions influencing its growth, its social complexion, which measures, if any, had been taken to combat the crime, and which institutions (zemstvos, churches, schools) were participating in the struggle.[11]

Replies to this circular from Riazan' province, including statistics from each *volost'* and precinct, allow for an examination of how the rural hooligan phenomenon was perceived locally. On October 24, 1912, governor A. N. Obolenskii convened a special conference in Riazan' to draw up a summary statement for the entire province in response to the MVD circular. Moderated by Prince Obolenskii himself, conference participants consisted of the provincial marshal of the nobility, the chairman and assistant chairman of the Riazan' Circuit Court, the circuit court prosecutor, the head of the provincial zemstvo administration, the three permanent members of the provincial board for peasant affairs, one land captain, and three independent farmers. The Riazan' district marshal of the nobility was entrusted to draft a final report for St. Petersburg from the responses of the twelve district conferences that had met earlier.[12]

All districts acknowledged the widespread nature of hooliganism in the countryside, especially in large villages, near railway stations, and in localities where many peasants left for outwork. It intensified on market days, during patronal festivals and other holidays, and just prior to military induction. Hooligan crimes took all forms, these reports stated in suspiciously complete agreement with the original MVD directive. Rural hooligans were noted above all for disobeying family elders, village authorities, and the clergy, cursing, engaging in savage knife fights, roaming the streets in drunken, boisterous groups at night and singing vulgar songs, beating on the windows of peaceful residents and harassing villagers without cause, extorting "refreshments" (i.e., drinks) at weddings and festive occasions, causing property damage and harming livestock without any purpose or simply out of "evil will," stealing from forests, gardens, and orchards, breaking fences and gates and uprooting saplings; and holding up travelers on rural roads and throwing rocks and dirt at them if they refused requests for money or liquor. Extortion was stressed as a particular problem. Throughout

11. GARO, f. 695, op. 22, sv. 240, d. 23, "Po dostavleniiu svedeniia o rasprostranenii v Riazanskoi gubernii khuliganstva po tsirkuliaru Zemskogo Otdela M.V.D. 18 iiulia 1912 goda," ll. 1–10b. Special thanks to Corinne Gaudin for bringing this file to my attention.

12. Ibid., 139. District conferences were chaired by district marshals of the nobility and composed of land captains, police officials, independent farmers, zemstvo representatives, clergy, and some *volost'* elders and chief judges of *volost'* courts. For a description of participants and several proposals not included in the final report, see "Bor'ba s khuliganstvom," *RiazZh*, no. 223 (1912), 3.

Riazan' district, "various vagrants [*brodiagi*] in the guise of mendicants [*nishchie*] roam through villages and bazaars both day and night, halt passersby, and demand alms using threats and curses."[13] But local officials were most frightened by the random and seemingly purposeless violence perpetrated by rural hooligans, who in one instance destroyed textbooks of pupils returning from school and in another tore up examinations in the school itself and then "committed excesses on the street in front of the schoolhouse, breaking its windows and door."[14]

To explain the plague of hooliganism, Riazan"s district conferences pointed with near unanimity to the lack of culture (*nekul'turnost'*) among peasants, which, in turn, had hastened their economic decline. More and more villagers had become obsessed by artificial needs, squandering money on "splendid clothing" and other nonessential consumer goods. Additional causes of this crime wave were insufficient education and the weak influence of schools, improper upbringing, the lack of supervision over children, especially those who left school early, "unstable moral foundations," alcoholism and bootlegging, an excessive number of holidays, the unavailability of rational entertainments, an explosion of rural household divisions, and the granting of internal passports to family members without the household head's permission. Within this array of problems, the final provincial report gave particular attention to the growth of alcohol consumption and bootlegging that followed the state's 1894 introduction of a liquor monopoly. Together with outwork, this explosion of public drinking was viewed as having an especially corrupting influence on rural youths, themselves the primary source of hooliganism.[15]

Rural hooligans, in fact, appeared to be of a type. Most conferences fixed their average age at between twelve and twenty-one, although "older people have been counted among them, most of whom are ex-prisoners or alcoholics who have no farms of their own." As in countless reports from around

13. GARO, f. 695, op. 22, sv. 240, d. 23, ll. 13–130b., 1390b. Compare Weissman, "Rural Crime," 228–30.

14. GARO, f. 695, op. 22, sv. 240, d. 23, l. 1390b. For similar examples, see "Pis'ma iz Vladimira," *SevK,* no. 78 (1905), 3; "Deistviia khuliganov," *PV,* no. 113 (1906), 2; "Vetluga (Kostromskoi gub.), *PV,* no. 212 (1906), 3; "Selo Karash, Iaros. gub. Khuligany," *Golos* (Iaroslavl'), no. 17 (1910), 4; "Derevenskie khuligany," *SV,* no. 137 (1911), 3; "Iz russkoi zhizni," *SV,* no. 156 (1913), 3–4.

15. GARO, f. 695, op. 22, sv. 240, d. 23, ll. 130b.–14, 140–1400b. See also RGIA, f. 1291, op. 51 (1912), d. 27, ll. 200–201, 225–8; "Derevenskoe gore," *SV,* no. 18 (1913), 2; M. A. Goranovskii, *Khuliganstvo i mery bor'by s nim* (Grodno, 1913); I. Rozhdestvenskii, "Khuliganstvo i alkogolizm," *Trudovaia pomoshch',* no. 2 (1914), 139–59; no. 3, 247–62; N. Semashko, "Alkogolizm i khuliganstvo," and A. Uchevatov, "K voprosu o sviazi alkogolizma s khuliganstvom," both in *Khuliganstvo i khuligany,* 7–10; 134–42; Frank, "Confronting the Domestic Other," esp. 80–84, 90–91.

the country, hooligans were also said to be drawn chiefly from families engaged at outwork, "where parents have been removed from the upbringing and supervision of their children."[16] In seven districts, conferences implicated migrant labor as a major contributing factor "because young people who return from outwork, having found freedom in towns, factories, and mines, corrupt the settled village youths and organize drinking bouts, often at bootlegging establishments."[17] The Riazan' District Conference noted that hooliganism "existed in a weak, almost unnoticed form earlier," but because no special measures were taken, it now flourished throughout the province—"*carried from the cities*" by those engaged at outwork. "The grounds for hooliganism's growth were thus laid quite some time before all of the current commotion erupted."[18] Not long ago, this report asserted in an effort to link outwork, hooliganism, and such current events as the 1905–7 revolution, "the peasant population was still religious and moral, and if immorality, impudence, and audacity appeared among it, these were isolated cases." But the appearance of antigovernment agitators, especially in cities, made the population far more audacious and unbridled. "This phenomenon was soon transferred to the countryside by peasants returning from outwork." There "they showed disrespect for authorities and the law and disdain toward religion and others' property; they began threatening those who did not agree with them and then carried out their threats. Local residents, mostly young people, soon joined the troublemakers [*ozorniki*], after which hooliganism took the form of crowd activity. They started off with street mischief such as cursing, beating up passersby, petty theft of anything they could lay their hands on, and as it continued to develop hooliganism moved on to motiveless arson and murder."[19]

The Riazan' Provincial Conference, too, saw hooliganism above all as a phenomenon of young peasant males ruined by outwork and alcohol, and its final report linked them in no uncertain terms to the events of 1905. Anti-establishment propaganda had reached deep into the countryside, where it "gave all the depraved elements a basis for fulfilling their criminal inclinations." Impressionable peasant youths were easily corrupted by underground broadsheets and proclamations, and "even the half-literate and dimwitted understood from these that they had to unite to be strong." Fortunately, they did not fully grasp the true, criminal goal for which they were

16. GARO, f. 695, op. 22, sv. 240, d. 23, ll. 14–140b. For other provinces, see RGIA, f. 1276, op. 9, d. 116, ll. 24–25; f. 796, op. 195, d. 3223, l. 44; Weissman, "Rural Crime," 232.

17. GARO, f. 695, op. 22, sv. 240, d. 23,ll. 143–1430b. On the extent of outwork in Riazan' province, see A. Selivanov, *Svod dannykh ob ekonomicheskom polozhenii krest'ian Riazanskoi gubernii* (Riazan', 1892).

18. GARO, f. 695, op. 22, sv. 240, d. 23, ll. 1420b.–143. Italics are mine.

19. Ibid., l. 1420b.

being summoned to unite, that is, a political revolution. Instead, they joined together "for merriment, drunkenness, petty profit, and theft and for perpetrating acts of revenge, mainly in the form of arson."[20] In other words, the same occupational group that constituted such a prominent and growing share of "peasant" and rural felony convictions throughout our period— rural outworkers and migrant laborers—had, by 1913, come to be defined as a separate criminal category.[21]

In a very dim assessment of efforts to combat the crime wave, the Riazan' conference report concluded that "hooliganism has encountered no strong opposition, and therefore increases more and more." Frightened peasant authorities avoided interfering and gave little thought to taking on the hooligans. The police also proved ineffectual due to their insufficient numbers. Nor were courts able to try many cases of hooliganism because "the accused often frighten and threaten witnesses who could testify against them." Even when convicted, sentences for hooligans were far too lenient. "For disrupting a church service or showing blatant disrespect toward holy objects—for example, smoking cigarettes near the icon lamp or applauding the deacon as he read the Gospels—the guilty party receives seven days in jail." The conference complained that Church influence in the struggle against hooliganism was virtually nonexistent and that schools paid almost no attention to the proper education of children.[22] Seeing how readily they could perpetrate crimes and escape punishment, "the *ozorniki* are growing steadily more bold and audacious," making the life of peaceful inhabitants impossible. Adolescents continued to fill the ranks of this "army of hooligans," and parents turned a blind eye to their children's activities.

Back in St. Petersburg, during meetings held between March and May 1913, the Special Interdepartmental Conference on Measures to Fight Hooliganism in Rural Localities produced its own summary of provincial responses to the MVD survey, which brought together the major points

20. Ibid., l. 143.

21. Jeffrey Burds (*Peasant Dreams and Market Politics* [Pittsburgh, 1998], ch. 7) notes that urban police made ready use of the hooligan panic when categorizing the large numbers of peasant migrants regularly rounded up and returned to their villages for passport violations. See, e.g., the numerous cases in GARO, f. 1298.

22. GARO, f. 695, op. 22, sv. 240, d. 23, ll. 143, 144. District and provincial zemstvo administrations also conducted surveys on hooliganism with findings quite similar to those of provincial conferences. See, e.g., "Bor'ba s khuliganstvom," *RiazZh*, no. 114 (1912), 4; "Khuliganstvo na Urale," *Novoe vremia*, no. 13219 (1913), 3; Sr. Nikolai Shiriaev, "O khuliganstve v derevne i o bor'be s nim," *Prikhodskaia zhizn'* 15, no. 5–6 (1913), 245–46; A. A. Akhremenko, "Tula. P'ianstvo i khuliganstvo," *MosVed*, no. 11 (1913), 3; "Pskovskoe zemstvo v bor'be s khuliganstvom," *SV*, no. 157 (1913), 2; "Bor'ba s khuliganstvom i zemstvo," *Vestnik Riazanskogo gubernskogo zemstva*, no. 1 (1913), 115.

stressed by both district and diocesan officials.[23] That hooliganism was nearly universal throughout European Russia could not be questioned, although the special conference, too, stressed that "this rowdiness and mischief of young people is not a new phenomenon," for examples of such behavior could be found "even in the most distant times." These new hooligans, however, were the least enlightened, crudest, and most unruly of country dwellers, and "the ignorance and lack of culture in the countryside provide special soil for the development of this unhealthy phenomenon." As for hooliganism's causes, the conference proved more selective than the local committees.

> Its increase has paralleled a growth in the manufacturing and mining industries, which in turn brought about the growth of the working class and a gradual transfer of rural inhabitants into other conditions of life. . . . The events of 1904–6 and the so-called liberation movement [also] had an enormous influence on the spread of hooliganism. Those terrible days stirred up popular life and, through street excesses, universal disorders, and speeches, demoralized the less stable elements of the countryside *who understand freedom only as the negation of all authority.* Under the influence first of the revolution and then of pornographic literature and the press, morality declined at a quickened pace and, in places, led to the complete collapse of religiosity, the breakdown of the family, and the negation of parental authority.[24]

The Orthodox church launched its own inquiry in March 1913 among bishops and rural deans (*blagochinnye*), who, while placing greater emphasis upon immorality than did lay officials, nevertheless described much the same manifestations of the disorder. Beginning with rudeness and disrespect toward elders, clergy, and local officials, hooliganism was expressed through cursing, drunkenness, idleness, and carrying knives and other weapons, culminating in threats or harm to persons and "in a whole series of criminally punishable actions."[25] In larger villages, wrote Bishop Aleksei of Tobol'sk diocese, particularly during holidays, "people cannot leave home with the certainty that they will not be cursed or even beaten." Insults to honor, particularly that of women, damaging buildings and others' property, torturing animals, rude behavior toward elders, disrespect to parents,

23. RGIA, f. 1276, op. 9, d. 116. Weissman, "Rural Crime"; and Neuberger, *Hooliganism,* also discuss this report.

24. RGIA, f. 1276, op. 9, d. 116, l. 240b. Italics are mine. See also RGIA, f. 1291, op. 51 (1912), dd. 27, 52, 53.

25. RGIA, f. 796, op. 195, d. 3223, which begins (ll. 1–10b.) with this general statement paraphrasing the MVD circular of the previous year. Special thanks to Gregory Freeze for this source. For a brief summary of the survey, see P. A. Blagoveshchenskii, *O bor'be s khuliganstvom. Iz eparkhial'noi zhizni* (Petrograd, 1914).

unbelief, disrespect to the holy church, drunkenness, sexual depravity, the loss of capacity for work, complete freedom from all laws and social customs—"this is how hooliganism is manifested."[26]

As causes of rural hooliganism, diocesan reports stressed a growing lack of respect for and fear of law and the courts, a weakening of the family, migrant labor to the city and its influence on village youths, a general decline of morality and faith manifested above all in the lack of respect for elders and authorities and in drinking and bootlegging. From Arkhangel'sk to Ekaterinoslavl', from Novgorod to Tambov and southwest to Volynia, all bishops emphasized the corruption of young peasants through outwork, which allowed them to live for long stretches without any parental supervision. According to Bishop Stefan of Kursk diocese, just a few months under the influence of factory work was sufficient to corrupt rural lads.[27] Even more emphatically than lay officials, clerics also blamed the 1905 Revolution, with its antigovernment movements, pogroms, and agrarian disorders, for the growth of hooliganism, and leftist political parties for the continuing social disorder and moral decline. "All deans unanimously note," wrote the bishop of Khar'kov in 1913, "that the depravity and unbridledness of young people began to spread after 1905–6. . . . The criminal uprisings against authority and law had their most pernicious influence upon young people, infecting them with a spirit of protest, rebelliousness, and anarchy."[28] Along with the impact of revolution, Bishop Nazarii of Kherson also implicated the liberal and leftist press, which "advocates moral debauchery, extols lawlessness, and idealizes reckless daring, brigandage, and bestial and bloodthirsty instincts."[29]

Unlike the MVD survey of 1864, which asked only about causes of rural crime, by 1912 the ministry was clearly desperate for suggestions to fight the crime wave and asked for them. Duma members, agencies and representatives of local, provincial, and central government, and churchmen all voiced support for changes in the administrative and judicial system. The Riazan' Provincial Conference suggested new articles for the criminal code that would single out hooliganism for harsher punishments and called for a new, simplified court to deal exclusively with hooligan crimes. Conference members requested that land captains make greater use of their power to

26. RGIA, f. 796, op. 195, d. 3223, ll. 42–420b. See also "Dukhovenstvo i bor'ba s khuliganstvom," *RiazZh*, no. 130 (1913), 3; "Dukhovenstvo o bor'be s khuliganstvom," *RiazZh*, no. 169 (1913), 3; *Protiv khuliganstva, ozorstva i buistva molodezhi* (Kiev, 1915).

27. RGIA, f. 796, op. 195, d. 3223, ll. 420b., 44–440b., 480b.–49, 820b., 89, 118, and others.

28. Ibid., ll. 33–330b. See also comments from the bishop of Kiev, ll. 45–70b., and Shiriaev, "O khuliganstve v derevne i o bor'be s nim," 245; "Khuliganstvo i neverie nashikh dnei," *Missionerskii sbornik*, no. 3 (1914), 170–73; "Khuligany i khuliganstvo," 13.

29. RGIA, f. 796, op. 195, d. 3223, l. 350b.

jail or fine peasants and that elected peasant officials should at last be freed from police duties, with special, state-salaried officers appointed in their place. Both criminal and civil accountability should be established for parents of hooligans under the age of seventeen.[30] Since prison was widely viewed as a place of further corruption, particularly for young inmates, rural officials and zemstvo members proposed resurrecting workhouses, where hooligans would be confined under a strict regime and pay for their upkeep with honest labor. One of the more extreme plans, presented by the noble-dominated Lipetsk district zemstvo, argued that because workhouses would likely prove inadequate, "work towns" should be established near each village; the inmates would, among their other obligations, be forced to toil on landed estates. This scheme aimed to solve the hooligan problem by providing landowners with free labor.[31]

Harsher recommendations sought to make it easier for communities to banish "depraved" residents by having the state cover the full cost of exile and to forever deprive exiles of the right to return to their native villages.[32] A great many officials, public commentators, and activists on the political right preached the necessity "to apply the most severe punishments for hooliganism," which "can only be rooted out by unremitting strictness" because moral measures were no longer of use in the struggle against this evil. Indeed, wrote one contributor to a temperance journal, "if these beasts in the countryside are not severely punished by the law, then nothing can be done about hooliganism."[33] Not a few favored the return of corporal punishment by the birch for hooliganism regardless of a perpetrator's social estate, as had already occurred in Belgium and as was being called for in other European countries as well. In the Riazan' Provincial Conference, several land captains expressed strong support for corporal punishment, a measure that, according to earlier defenders of this office, the land captains had been most effective in eradicating.[34]

30. GARO, f. 695, op. 22, sv. 240, d. 23, l. 144. See also A. V. Likhachev, "Ob usilenii nakazanii dlia khuliganov," *ZhMIu*, no. 5 (1913), 80–94.

31. GARO, f. 695, op. 22, sv. 240, d. 23, l. 144; D. Zaslavskii, "Bor'ba s khuliganstvom," *Sovremennyi mir*, no. 1 (1913), 122. Negative views of prison appear to have been growing. A 1913 newspaper article reported that more and more juries were presenting petitions to the courts with complaints that incarceration did nothing to correct a criminal. "Zaiavleniia prisiazhnykh zasedatelei," *RiazZh*, no. 82 (1913), 2.

32. GARO, f. 695, op. 22, sv. 240, d. 23, l. 144; "Bor'ba s khuliganstvom," *RiazZh*, no. 114 (1912), 4.

33. S. D. Zenchenko, "Prichiny ozorstva i bor'ba s nim," *Deiatel'*, no. 10 (1913), 312; "O khuliganstvo," *Deiatel'*, no. 12 (1912), 313–14; "Ozdorovlenie derevni," *Deiatel'*, no. 5 (1913), 158–59.

34. GARO, f. 695, op. 22, sv. 240, d. 23, l. 144; V. Brusianin, "O khuliganakh i khuliganstve," *Novyi zhurnal dlia vsekh*, no. 4 (1913), 155–56; Zaslavskii, "Bor'ba s khuliganstvom," 122; "Narodnaia anarkhiia," *Deiatel'*, no. 7 (1913), 219; "Bor'ba s khuliganstvom," *RiazZh*,

Despite often widely differing opinions on the best solution to the hooligan crisis, much of Russian society believed that law enforcement and justice were sorely in need of reform. Some outspoken government opponents argued that hooliganism arose as a direct result of the state's lawlessness and violence against its citizens, as seen most sharply in the repressive measures used during the 1905–7 Revolution.[35] Others pointed to the shortage of rural police and effective courts, which forced the state to rely on administrative and military authority to maintain order while neglecting regular law enforcement. "What of the constables, the police guards, the tenners," asked one critic writing for a semi-official newspaper in 1913. "Yes, they exist . . . in the laws. But where are they? The constable—there is but one for an entire *volost'*, which consists of tens of villages and hamlets. There is also only one police guard." Even more important, this writer argued, was the reduction in the number of local courts after 1861. Before emancipation each village had its own court, and within an hour of a hooligan being brought before it sentence would be passed and carried out. "With the elimination of village courts and the establishment of a single *volost'* court," however, "a good half of all crimes no longer come to trial and go unpunished."[36]

Given the enormous changes that had been reshaping Russia since emancipation, by far the most remarkable aspect of the hooligan surveys is their closeness to responses found in the 1864 MVD survey. New elements had certainly entered the analysis by 1913 (revolution and the influence of radical politics, above all), but the causes of hooliganism were still located within the same cultural matrix that had served to explain a growth of rural crime immediately after the peasantry's liberation. Cultural backwardness and stultifying ignorance, rampant immorality, declining respect for law and authority, alcohol abuse, and the corrupting influence of outwork and materialism weave constantly through the responses that came, in most instances, from the same ranks of provincial officialdom that replied to the 1864 survey and tell us more about outside observers than about peasants or hooligans. It was not the 1905 Revolution that generated this frightened

no. 223 (1912) 3; "Novyi zemskii nachal'nik," *RiazZh*, no. 53 (1913), 3; "O rozgakh," *RiazV,* no. 220 (1913), 2. The chairman of the Riazan' Circuit Court felt obliged to attach a "special opinion" to the final report of the provincial conference concerning the proposed reintroduction of corporal punishment. "I took no part in the decision of this matter," he wrote. "The MVD did not ask the conferences to express their opinions on the necessity of introducing corporal punishment. Corporal punishment, as recognized by the Throne, is a completely useless measure, harmful to a person's self-worth, and one that achieves no corrective goal." GARO, f. 695, op. 22, sv. 240, d. 23, l. 145.

35. Utevskii, "Khuliganstvo," 24–26.

36. "Prichiny razvitiia khuliganstva," *SV,* no. 211 (1913), 1–2. Such views were not rare. A Tver' zemstvo report stated bluntly that a new type of court must be provided to the population that would instill true respect for the law. RGIA, f. 1405, op. 532, d. 424, l. 46.

analysis of the lower classes, nor a middle- and upper-class response to "modernity," although both played important roles in framing turn-of-the-century discourse on rural and urban criminality. Yet that same discourse had shaped elite discussion of the rural population at the time of emancipation and even earlier. Likewise, though they treated a wider subject range, district-level reports from around the country sent to Finance Minister Witte's 1902 Committee on the Needs of Agriculture lacked only the term "hooliganism" in their angry and frightened descriptions of peasant crime, "ignorance" of the law, and lack of respect for gentry property. The cultural alibi so effectively utilized for decades in the public transcripts of state and educated society, with its recognition of cultural and social chasms that could justify colonial attitudes toward the lower classes while also rationalizing fear of these same "benighted masses," would continue in use long beyond the old regime's collapse. If in 1864 provincial authorities already feared what Zola would term *"le déchaînement de la bête humaine,"* by 1913 the savages appeared on the verge of smashing through the gates.[37]

## RURAL HOOLIGANS AND THEIR CRIMES

Whether drawing from the extensive surveys of the years 1911–13, from press accounts, police reports, or court records, it is still difficult to discern a uniquely "hooligan" form of crime in rural Russia. Provincial governors and district zemstvo boards told of offenses that were common long before emancipation. The "disgraceful hooligan acts" reported in 1912 by a zemstvo of Tver province consisted of breaking windows at the local school-house, pulling iron bolts from bridges, burning wooden mileposts, looting construction material stockpiled along highways, damaging meadows and fields, stealing fruit, vegetables, and flowers, and inflicting wounds with knives and other weapons.[38] Governor P. P. Bashilov of Ufa detailed at length the crimes most commonly committed by rural hooligans. Those against peace and order came first and included congregating in rowdy groups that sang obscene songs and used "foul language," shouting in the streets at night or banging on doors and windows, carrying illegal weapons, and tormenting domestic animals. Among crimes against persons the governor mentioned "obstinate displays of disrespect and disobedience to parents," disrespect toward elders, authorities, and priests, "up to and including the infliction of insults," beating elderly persons who criticized the hooligans' improper behavior, insulting peasants who removed themselves

37. The phrase is used in L. Bezrodnyi, *Ob upadke chuvstva zakonnosti v narode* (SPb, 1892), 3. See also Marie-Christine Leps, *Apprehending the Criminal: The Production of Deviance in Nineteenth-Century Discourse* (Durham and London, 1992), 166–76.

38. RGIA, f. 1405, op. 532, d. 424, l. 450b.

from the commune under the provisions of the 1906 Stolypin land reforms, annoying women on the streets, smearing tar on people's gates, crimes against female chastity "up to and including rape," throwing stones at passersby, and demanding money from people on the streets. Finally came hooligan offenses against property such as uprooting trees from gardens and plucking flowers and vegetables "without using them," petty theft of food, domestic fowl, and vegetables, and maiming and killing animals.[39] Yet as Bashilov noted, there was nothing original about these acts, which were all covered under existing law. Hence, "we should speak not of a new form of crime, but only about increasing prosecution of a large group of infractions, the mild penalties for which have led to their becoming [extremely] widespread."[40] The acts most commonly labeled as hooliganism fell under one of several articles in the 1864 Code of Punishments for Justices of the Peace (itself simply a modification of earlier misdemeanor codes), which after 1889 had devolved to *volost'* courts: articles 29–33 ("Infractions of the administrative order"); articles 37–46 ("Disturbing order and peace"); articles 117–28 ("Infractions of personal safety"); and articles 130–42 ("Insults to honor, threats, and violence").[41]

Data from Riazan' province's lower judicial and administrative instances provide a breakdown of the types of cases tried under these articles over the five-year period 1907–11 (table 9.1) and were, at the time of their collection, intended to inform the MVD of the nature and extent of hooliganism. "Insults, threats, and violence" were by far the largest category reported, vastly outnumbering all others combined. But as already seen, these offenses had comprised one of the largest portions of criminal infractions tried by *volost'* and peace courts since at least the 1860s. An official order to compile such data for inclusion with district-level reports about hooliganism is not especially illuminating, in fact, and tells us little more than that certain crimes had been redefined. Nor do we know how this order was conveyed to rural localities, though it is likely, as was usually the case, that town-

39. Ibid., ll. 10–12a. P. P. Bashilov, "O khuliganstve, kak prestupnom iavlenii, ne predusmotrennom zakonom," *ZhMIu*, no. 2 (1913), 222–56, provides a published version of this report. See also V. I. Gromov, "Bezmotivnoe prestuplenie (Po voprosu ob otvetstvennosti za khuliganstvo)," *ZhMIu*, no. 5 (1913), 50–94; S. M. Dubrovskii, *Stolypinskaia zemel'naia reforma* (Moscow, 1963), 565.

40. RGIA, f. 1405, op. 532, d. 424, l. 12a.

41. *Ustav o nakazaniiakh, nalagaemykh mirovymi sud'iami,* in *Sudebnye ustavy 20 noiabria 1864 goda. S raz"iasneniem ikh po resheniiam kassatsionnykh departamentov Pravitel' stvuiushchego Senata 1866, 1867, 1868 i 1869 gg.* 4th ed. (SPb, 1870). 13–15, 16–18, 28–33. On proposed legislation against hooliganism, see V. Kuz'min-Karavaev, "Zakonoproekt o khuliganstve," *VE*, no. 9 (1913), 408–17; "K voprosu o merakh bor'by s khuliganstvom (Proekt Ministra Iustitsii)," *ZhUPP*, no. 4 (1913), 103–14; "Otzyv Moskovskogo Stolichnogo S"ezda o ministerskom zakonoproekte o merakh bor'by s khuliganstvom," *IuV*, no. 3 (1913), 229–48; Neuberger, *Hooliganism,* 128–42.

TABLE 9.1    "Hooliganism" in Lower Courts of Riazan' Province

| Year | Land Captains | Municipal Courts | Volost' Courts | All Courts |
|------|------|------|------|------|
| Crimes against Administrative Order (Arts. 29–33) | | | | |
| 1907 | 352 | 567 | 325 | 1244 |
| 1908 | 466 | 584 | 349 | 1399 |
| 1909 | 543 | 460 | 333 | 1336 |
| 1910 | 731 | 760 | 399 | 1890 |
| 1911 | 800 | 442 | 476 | 1718 |
| Disturbing the Peace (Arts. 37–46) | | | | |
| 1907 | 410 | 594 | 756 | 1760 |
| 1908 | 385 | 560 | 827 | 1772 |
| 1909 | 464 | 596 | 984 | 2044 |
| 1910 | 439 | 927 | 1303 | 2669 |
| 1911 | 468 | 736 | 1380 | 2584 |
| Crimes against Personal Safety (Arts. 117–128) | | | | |
| 1907 | 63 | 120 | 296 | 479 |
| 1908 | 90 | 153 | 354 | 597 |
| 1909 | 89 | 153 | 352 | 594 |
| 1910 | 153 | 173 | 495 | 821 |
| 1911 | 144 | 131 | 577 | 852 |
| Insults to Honor, Threats, and Violence (Arts. 130–42) | | | | |
| 1907 | 472 | 1142 | 6951 | 8565 |
| 1908 | 530 | 1122 | 7432 | 9084 |
| 1909 | 613 | 992 | 7898 | 9503 |
| 1910 | 598 | 1083 | 8623 | 10304 |
| 1911 | 631 | 1128 | 9523 | 11282 |
| Total Offenses | | | | |
| 1907 | 1297 | 2423 | 8328 | 12048 |
| 1908 | 1471 | 2419 | 8962 | 12852 |
| 1909 | 1709 | 2201 | 9567 | 13477 |
| 1910 | 1921 | 2943 | 10820 | 15684 |
| 1911 | 2043 | 2437 | 11956 | 16436 |

SOURCE: GARO, f. 695, op. 22, sv. 240, d. 23, ll. 149ob.–156.

ship elders and clerks were simply asked to provide data on specific infractions of the criminal code. Since no crime could be officially recorded as a hooligan act because new legislation was never passed, these and other quantitative data assembled from around the country are ultimately meaningless. How many recorded offenses could be considered hooliganism, in other words, remains unknown and is likely unknowable.

Equally problematic is that neither court records nor published reports are of much help in identifying rural hooligans. Nonpeasant commentators and officials implicated day laborers and outworkers as primary culprits, but few documents actually state the accuseds' occupations. One typical account tells of a local troublemaker who might easily fit the "hooligan" profile created by officialdom and the press, yet the incident also looks suspiciously similar to many others that could be found as far back as the pre-emancipation era. In October 1905, the seventeen-year-old peasant Vladimir Mel'nikov stood trial before the Vologda Circuit Court, charged with seriously wounding Aleksandr Abramov. Ten months earlier Mel'nikov had come to a village evening party where he immediately began causing trouble (*ozornichal*). He disrupted the merriment, struck several lads, and, according to one witness: "He comes up to Aleksandr Abramov and says, 'Give me a smoke!' But Abramov answered, 'I don't have [any tobacco].' Then Mel'nikov swings his hand into Abramov's stomach and Abramov immediately screamed . . . and ran out of the hut." Abramov died three days later from knife wounds. Mel'nikov pleaded innocent in court, claiming he had been drunk and remembered nothing. Other witnesses explained that he held the entire area in fear, despite his young age, and this was not the first time he had wounded someone. The jury found him guilty after a fifteen-minute deliberation, and he was sentenced to one year in prison. On hearing the verdict, those present exclaimed, "Thank God! We are free of the troublemaker [*ozornik*]. Now we can all relax!"[42]

In 1913 the *Riazan' Herald* began a regular column, "For Hooliganism," which listed the jail sentences handed down against persons convicted under a binding regulation issued that year by the governor. Like regulations promulgated in other provinces, it allowed for fines of up to 500 rubles or three months in jail, with the accused to be tried through administrative rather than judicial procedure.[43] Along with the governor's regulation, the column brought hooliganism even more before public attention. An examination of the types of crimes included under this heading provides some sense of the range of acts labeled "hooligan" by authorities. But it also clouds the hooligan phenomenon even further, since these offenses differed not at all from crimes for which peasants had been tried prior to the great fear that set in after the turn of the century. In July, one peasant was charged with trespassing at the office of an Egor'evsk district factory, cursing, and bothering the chief of the plant's economic department. When seized by a local police official, the "hooligan" insulted him. Elsewhere,

42. "Vologodskii okruzhnyi sud (Derevenskii khuligan)," *SevK*, no. 244 (1905), 2–3.
43. "Bor'ba s khuliganstvom," *RiazZh*, no. 43 (1913), 3.

three peasants received three months each for getting drunk and harassing the groom on the estate of a merchant, "persecuting him mercilessly, trespassing, beating his pregnant wife, and breaking a window and dishes."[44] A peasant of Spassk district got drunk and went about "with his trousers unbuttoned and at half mast," cursing and threatening to break the fence of a local resident. On the following day, drunk once again, he broke down a woman's door, cursed her, and threatened to set the house afire. He received a three-month sentence, as did T. I. Gudkova for being intoxicated in the main square of her village, where she caused a disturbance, used obscene language, and threw rocks at the public.[45]

Other incidents from Riazan' better match the contemporary description of hooligan crimes. One October evening in 1905, a group of eight villagers entered a tavern in Novo-Aleksandrovskoe, drank to the health of the local black hundreds leader, then caused a row and threatened to destroy the tavern. At another establishment they refused to pay for their drinks and food. The gang then smashed the tavern window and began fighting with a crowd that had gathered in the street. Only the chance presence of a Cossack detachment prevented this incident from growing into a possible pogrom.[46] Attacks upon police or representatives of the upper classes were also common. At about 10:00 P.M. on April 10, 1911, the constable Skorovarov arrived in a village of Ranenburg district to investigate a report that local hooligans regularly congregated at one peasant's home to drink vodka. When Skorovarov went to the house and discovered six young men drinking, he ordered them to stop their carousing and disperse. Instead the revelers attacked him, took away his saber, and beat him so badly that he lost consciousness.[47]

Even in cases of this sort, however, it is difficult to endorse fully the argument, recently proffered in a study of hooliganism in St. Petersburg, that the hooligan phenomenon should be viewed through the prism of youthful, lower-class rage against upper-class Russia, as a manifestation of inarticulate lower-class politics acted out in everyday life, or as "attacks on

44. "Za khuliganstvo," *RiazV,* no. 161 (1913), 2.

45. "Za khuliganstvo," *RiazV,* no. 162 (1913), 2; no. 164 (1913), 2. Several months after publishing binding regulations, governors from around the country were reporting to the MVD that these were having little notable effect on hooliganism. See "Bor'ba s khuliganstvom," *RiazZh,* no. 73 (1913), 1; no. 130, 2.

46. GARO, f. 5, op. 1, d. 4020, ll. 92–92ob.

47. GARO, f. 5, st. 3, op. 4, d. 5437, l. 3. See also "Obiazatel'noe postanovlenie o bor'be s khuliganstvom," *RiazZh,* no. 55 (1913), 2–3, discussing the case of six peasants who received administrative sentences ranging from one and a half to three months for attacking and beating an estate steward and his wife as they rode through Shekhmino village, and "Khuliganstvo," *MosVed,* no. 21 (1913), 3, about a similar attack upon a priest and his family.

privilege, education, wealth, and power."[48] A reading of outraged middle-class sensibilities as expressed in the contemporary press or a selective viewing of hooligan cases both support this perspective, of course, and suggest the importance of class politics to an understanding of lower-class violence. Yet as many historians have shown, such sources tell us far more about middle-class perceptions and the phenomenon of "moral panic" than they do about the behavior and *mentalité* of peasants, rural laborers, or workers.[49] The sources also demonstrate that rural hooligans did not only or even mainly target the rich and privileged, whether noble landowners or well-to-do peasants. Middling and poor peasants, not their social superiors, were the chief victims of rural crime, both "hooligan" and other. And how should we distinguish between hooligan attacks upon a police officer and those perpetrated under other circumstances, albeit with insolence or seemingly without cause?[50] The beating and robbery of a constable, a drunken villager's insults, threats, or violence to an arresting policeman, defiance by rowdy rural youths of a land captain who banned their evening parties—all of these acts, if perpetrated after 1905, received the label "hooliganism" from officials, though in form and content most differed little, if at all, from the same deeds committed decades before.

There are certainly instances where differences can readily be discerned between, say, a "prehooligan" act of aggression from the 1870s or 1880s and a similar offense committed during the hooligan panic. Interpreting the meaning and significance of that difference is highly problematic if not impossible, however, for most police reports and court indictments rarely delve into motivation on the part of offenders. Take the 1909 case of Ivan Zakharov Petrov, arrested by police guards in the village of Tuma, Riazan' province, for attacking and robbing a peasant and carrying a revolver. As he was being escorted from the village, Petrov shouted to the crowd that had

48. Neuberger, *Hooliganism,* 100–10, 119–20, and *passim.* This author's claim that the most common manifestations of hooliganism were insults or assaults against women is also not supported by contemporary description, at least for the countryside.

49. Mark Fishman, "Crime Waves as Ideology," *Social Problems* 26 (1978), 531–43; Jennifer Davis, "The London Garotting Panic of 1862," in V. A. C. Gatrell et al., eds., *Crime and the Law* (London, 1980); Christopher Stone, "Vandalism: Property, Gentility, and the Rhetoric of Crime in New York City, 1890–1920," *Radical History Review* 26 (1982), 13–34; Pearson, *Hooligan;* Robert A. Nye, *Crime, Madness, and Politics in Modern France: The Medical Concept of National Decline* (Princeton, 1984), esp. ch. 6; Christopher Waldrep, "'So Much Sin': The Decline of Religious Discipline and the 'Tidal Wave of Crime,'" *JSH* 23, no. 3 (1990), 535–52; Seth Koven, "From Rough Lads to Hooligans: Boy Life, National Culture and Social Reform," in Andrew Parker et al., eds., *Nationalisms and Sexualities* (New York, 1992), 365–91.

50. Such cases ran into the tens of thousands each year before and after emancipation, though as noted in Chapter 2, prosecutions began to rise substantially during the 1880s. For examples, see GARO, f. 717, op. 40 (1890), sv. 80, d. 24; op. 44 (1894), sv. 82, d. 2; op. 45 (1895), sv. 82, dd. 7, 9, 27 and others.

assembled, "Down with the bloodsucking monarchy and the whole, rotten government with it!" The report tells us no more about Petrov except that his words resulted in the additional charge of insulting the monarch.[51] Was he, then, a hooligan, a revolutionary agitator, or a robber who sought to exploit popular sentiments with his brash, defiant words? The sources prevent further exploration because the officials who produced them had no interest in these questions. Their duty was to maintain order, carry out arrests, and label offenders, not to analyze motivation.

Most important, it remains entirely unclear to what extent villagers themselves actually worried about hooliganism. Virtually all published commentaries come from the pens of nonpeasants, and it is of more than passing interest to note that by 1914 the provincial press had either lost interest or else the novelty of hooliganism had worn off. *Riazan' Life,* for instance, which gave extensive coverage to hooliganism from 1911 to 1913, published almost nothing on it between 1914 and 1917. Rather, by summer of 1914, in addition to the war, attention had turned to problems like rural gambling and bootlegging, or focused on efforts to raise the cultural level of the countryside. As for archival sources, they contain extremely few peasant complaints concerning specifically hooligan activities.[52] Of course, many petitions about theft and other crimes may have involved persons whom contemporaries would have termed hooligans. This was certainly true of numerous village resolutions on banishment. But the extent to which this was so is impossible to determine, for the label "hooligan" does not appear in most village resolutions. In short, despite the vast literature to which hooliganism gave rise, we still know little at all about those to whom the label was applied, or if and how the phenomenon was experienced and understood among the peasant population.

What *is* clear from existing sources and recent scholarship is that generational conflicts within rural communities were seriously exacerbating intravillage tensions by the 1880s, as elders sought to maintain their authority over the younger and, often, more economically independent generation. As historian Jeffrey Burds has shown, this conflict was readily apparent in the struggle to control young migrant laborers and the disposition of their wages.[53] Such efforts were most frequently exercised either

51. GARO, f. 5, st. 3, op. 4, d. 5073, ll. 6–60b.

52. GARO, f. 695, op. 41 (1910), sv. 19, dd. 69–72. These four examples are the only ones in a collection of nearly 3,500 criminal cases.

53. Jeffrey Burds, " Social Control of Peasant Labor," in Esther Kingston-Mann and Timothy Mixter, eds., *Peasant Economy, Culture, and Politics of European Russia, 1800–1921* (Princeton, 1991); Burds, *Peasant Dreams,* ch. 3. See also David V. Trotman, *Crime in Trinidad* (Knoxville, 1986) 183–212; Francis Snyder and Douglas Hay, "Comparisons in the Social History of Law: Labour and Crime," in Francis Snyder and Douglas Hay, eds., *Labour, Law, and Crime* (London, 1987), 1–41.

through traditional local mechanisms or, in serious cases, by utilizing courts or administrative and police officials to punish uncooperative or disobedient migrant workers. In other areas of village life as well, elders and authorities sought to regulate social behavior, particularly among the young. Long before the term "hooliganism" was known in Russia, many communities imposed strict controls over evening gatherings and parties of youths—arenas of sociability that outsiders implicated as breeding grounds of hooliganism. In some villages, maidens had to beg the elder's permission to organize these postharvest festivities.[54] Likewise, when the rapid growth of taverns brought troubles to hundreds of villages, petitions from across the empire flooded government offices asking to close local drinking establishments and state liquor shops.[55]

This is not to argue that peasant communities effectively managed all the tensions that beset them as the new century began. They did not. Nor did they resolve the often disruptive conflicts between well-to-do and poor, elders and a more independent younger generation, or competing factions within village politics. In many instances, such conflicts only got worse as the new century began.[56] Yet simply because hooliganism obsessed educated society and officialdom for a brief span of time, it cannot be assumed that it did so among peasants. Both before and after 1905, rural communities experienced the disturbing impudence and rowdiness of those who may have been called hooligans and often dealt with them through "home remedies," up to and including banishment and *samosud*.[57] The immediate question, however, is *which* conflicts and problems *villagers* viewed as most threatening and destabilizing to their lives. If we are to judge from their own words as expressed in assembly resolutions and petitions, or by actions taken against criminals they managed to apprehend, peasants worried far less about rowdy gangs of disrespectful youths than they did about the growing number of arsons, horsethefts, robberies, and other property crimes.

54. "Zapreshchenie vecherinok-dosvetok," *SV,* no. 48 (1883), 499; E. Ponomarev, "Artel'shchina i druzhestva, kak osobyi uklad narodnoi zhizni," *SevV,* no. 12 (1888), part 2, 71–72. For further discussion of this problem, see Frank, "Simple Folk.'"

55. For examples, see GARO, f. 5, st. 4, op. 5, dd. 2241, 2279, 2281; f. 147, Riazanskoe Gubernskoe po piteinym delam Prisutstvie, op. 1, dd. 1–42.

56. Different aspect of these conflicts are discussed in Burds, *Peasant Dreams;* Corinne Gaudin, "Governing the Village: Peasant Culture and the Problem of Social Transformation in Russia, 1906–1914" (Ph.D. diss., University of Michigan, 1993); Frank, "'Simple Folk.'"

57. On *samosud* against rural hooligans, see, e.g., A. E. Riabchenko, *O bor'be s khuliganstvom, vorovstvom, i brodiazhnichestvom* (SPb, 1914), 10–11; "Khuligany i khuliganstvo," 13; B. S. Man'kovskii, "Derevenskaia ponozhovshchina," in E. K. Krasnushkin, G. M. Segal, and Ts. M. Fainberg, eds., *Khuliganstvo i ponozhovshchina* (Moscow, 1927), 124–25; T. D. Segalov, "P'ianye draki v gorode i derevne (Po materialam Mosgubsuda)," 94; Burds, *Peasant Dreams,* esp. ch. 7.

## JUSTICE REVISITED: THE END OF LAW

In 1908 the governor of Riazan' sent a report on cases of peasant *samosud* to the minister of internal affairs noting that the marked increase of such incidents "attests, in my opinion, to the strong growth of hooliganism in the countryside on the one hand, and to the population's loss of faith in judicial retribution on the other."[58] This issue remained much on the governor's mind, for he sent a lengthier letter to the Land Section of the MVD on June 4, 1909. Here he included the petition of a peasant from Sapozhok district protesting the release of three accused arsonists by the circuit court prosecutor, who had found insufficient evidence to warrant bringing them to trial. Concerned that his community now had no protection from the accused, the author voiced strong criticism of both prosecutor and court and argued that by freeing "these obvious criminals," they were forcing peasants to turn to *samosud* in order to protect themselves and their property.[59] The governor expressed guarded understanding of this villager's sense of frustration and, by extension, of the growth of *samosud*. "It is a result of the peasants' lack of faith in judicial authority," he wrote, "which often pardons people whose criminal deeds are well known to the population of an entire region, or does not investigate their activities because evidence could not be found." Indeed, "the peasantry's participation in incidents of *samosud* is evidence of the unquestionable collapse of their trust in the court—during 1908 alone there were eighteen cases in Riazan' province."[60]

From the governor's perspective, not only hooliganism but also the seemingly universal increase of crime and violence in rural areas could in great measure be attributed to the serious shortcomings of the police and the judicial system. These were in great need of repair, a general shake-up, and a much firmer hand. In a stern letter to the land captain of Mikhailov district's first precinct concerning "the extreme development of hooliganism" in Korovino village, he noted that "rowdiness, theft, and even arson have become everyday phenomena, but the rural authorities, evidently, do not feel it is necessary to fight these evils":

> It can hardly be supposed that villagers do not know which persons in Korovino are carrying out these excesses, and if the latter still remain unknown this is obviously because local residents are terrified of them, since they see no legal protection from the hooligans and also see the inactivity of the local

58. GARO, f. 5, st. 3, op. 4, d. 4828, l. 75.

59. Ibid., d. 5078, ll. 1–10b.

60. Ibid., ll. 2–20b. For a much earlier commentary on this same issue, see D. Abashidze, "Prichiny nedoveriia derevenskikh zhitelei k pravosudiiu pravitel'stvennykh sudebnykh mest," *Iuridicheskoe obozrenie*, no. 198 (1885), 33–41; no. 200, 104–11.

authorities. Such a situation . . . cannot be further tolerated. It deprives the local population not only of safety for its property but of the inviolability of its person. With the aim of restoring order and calm in Korovino I propose that Your Honor summon the [*volost'* and village elders] and warn them of the necessity, in the interest of the local population, to battle this growing hooliganism by all legal means, and that the duty of protecting order and calm in the village rests above all upon them . . . [61]

Provincial governors faced an increasingly difficult situation and few satisfactory options. Fearing revenge from criminals whom the police could not catch and courts could not prosecute, peasants were ever more reluctant to report crimes even as they demanded greater protection. At the same time, governors confronted the dual dilemma of an incompetent regular police and an overburdened court system. Their sole recourse was to greater use of their authority to punish selectively through administrative process, including the use of administrative exile, in a desperate effort to maintain order within their province. This less than satisfactory approach, as we have seen, often led to more crime committed by new exiles or by those allowed to return home to their native province after several years. Governor Levashov of Riazan' made this problem clear in a secret 1906 memorandum to the MVD. He spoke of the insurmountable difficulty of punishing arsonists within the judicial system, for it usually proved impossible to gather evidence against them. Yet they could not be left free to terrorize an entire region. Hence it remained to exile them to another province, the governor explained, but such temporary banishment also had unwanted consequences. Unable to find work in their new localities and often mixing with other criminal or antigovernment elements, the exiles grew even more hardened and depraved and brought trouble to the hard-working population around them. It was equally dangerous to allow these people to return home to their peaceful villages, since they usually turned once again to crime and sought revenge against those who had denounced them. From Ranenburg district alone, Levashov noted, over 200 persons had thus far been banished in 1906. "What will happen to this district when they return?" They should instead be resettled "in the most distant regions, the Amur or somewhere that the government needs settlers."[62]

While secret memoranda and reports about returnees committing armed robbery and other serious crimes shuttled between administrative

61. GARO, f. 5, st. 3, op. 4, d. 5242, ll. 2–20b. A similar letter was sent to the district police commandant.

62. Ibid., d. 3943, ll. 55–550b. See d. 5335, ll. 6–60b. for one such example. See also E. N. Tarnovskii, "Pobegi arestantov i drugie proisshestviia v mestakh zakliucheniia za 1899–1908 gg.," *TiurV,* no. 5 (1910), 686–702; Fredric S. Zuckerman, *The Tsarist Secret Police in Russian Society, 1880–1917* (London, 1996), 15–18.

offices amid this evident breakdown of order, the primary victims grew increasingly contemptuous of a system that they believed could not or would not protect them. In 1907, for example, residents of Novo-Aleksandrovskoe sent the Riazan' governor an anonymous complaint about an upsurge of thefts in their village and police disregard of their plight. "With the introduction of [the new rural police guard], we thought that robberies and thefts would stop, but we were cruelly mistaken. It turns out that the police are all occupied at patrolling the [nearby railroad] station. . . . Tenners know who the thieves are, but fear them . . . and head in the opposite direction when they hear a cry for help. . . . It is extremely unpleasant for those who pay all the taxes to tremble in fear for their lives and property."[63] Another petition received at the governor's office in 1909 came from Grigorii Il'in Zubarev, who was in his twelfth year of service as village elder of Prudki (Zaraisk district). Zubarev requested protection for his small community and himself against peasants of a neighboring commune who coveted land purchased by his village and who, he wrote, "are trying to wipe me from the face of the earth." Three peasants from this second commune, Zubarev explained, had been conducting a spree of crimes in Prudki with the knowledge and approval of their elder, and everyone feared them and therefore would not provide evidence to the police. Hence they had long gone unpunished. Among many other offenses, they had robbed Zubarev's small shop six times during the preceding ten years and committed arson at his home five years before. They were also responsible for several arsons and thefts on a nearby landed estate. Most recently, after a burglary at the village church, these criminals deviously reported to the police captain that Zubarev himself perpetrated the crime, thereby bringing an investigation against the elder. Zubarev thus found himself protesting his innocence while asking the governor to safeguard his life and provide relief to Prudki village.[64]

Complaints about the judicial system were even harsher. After the 1909 dismissal of charges against an arsonist from a village of Riazan' district, residents minced no words as they protested the circuit court's decision to "His Highness," the governor:

> It is very sad that Your court performs so badly. On what grounds did they free Il'ia Ermolaev. Is it possible that the reason was bribes. While many witnesses testified clearly about his crime this all turned out to be in vain and nothing was taken into account. Can it really be that the judges could hear one person and all the rest remain fools. Of course the defense counselors took bribes from him . . . and therefore defended him so well. . . . Is this really a court

63. GARO, f. 5, st. 3, op. 4, d. 4774, ll. 3–40b.
64. Ibid., d. 5186, ll. 1–2.

when they hear only one person and not the majority of people, and the judges . . . vainly receive their pay. What a strange situation now for the witnesses; they have made enemies of dangerous people and will suffer revenge from them, and all this is because of the bribe-taking judges. What now when they will either be killed or go into hiding. . . . Your incorrect court has done even more harm to people in Kanishchevo; now everyone will act like Il'ia Ermolaev and it will be impossible to live in Kanishchevo, a village that is so renowned for its thieves [*zhuliki*], and now it will be terrible to live and we haven't slept on holidays, fearing these drunken *zhuliki,* and now we can't lie down at all—and how is this for a working person . . . It is clear from all of this that Your court is very wrong and stupid and only ruins people more and induces them to other crimes, and this is very deplorable.[65]

In April of this same year, a group of peasants from Bratovki village, Ranenburg district, planned to kill two known arsonists living in their community, but before they could do so the district commandant arrested both of the accused. Seven months later this official reported to the governor that one of the accused, Grigorii Khalantsev, had been released one day after his arrest for lack of evidence. Having been placed "under police supervision" at the judicial investigator's orders, Khalantsev continued to commit crimes. Finally, one early November evening, Khalantsev came as a guest to the home of another villager but was later driven out when he became too inebriated and disorderly. Now insulted as well as drunk, and standing in the cold street, Khalantsev threw a brick and smashed his host's window. The latter thereupon rushed from his house and struck the troublemaker several times in the head with a club, killing him.[66]

Villagers also resorted to collective measures when they failed to win satisfaction from courts or authorities. In 1907 sparks from a passing train set fire to peasant grain sheds in Bychki village of Ranenburg district. Their owners asked the Riazan-Urals Railroad for damages of 21,264 rubles, and when their demands went unsatisfied for nearly two years, the angry villagers removed twenty-five spikes from the nearby tracks, which led to the derailment of a train carrying agricultural produce from Ranenburg station. Eight damaged railroad cars were then surrounded by a large crowd of men and women, who immediately began filling their wagons with rye flour, oats, and potatoes and carting these back to the village. Only the arrival of gendarmes put a stop to the robbery when their commander fired several warning shots into the air. Even then many of the peasants defiantly remained at the site, "inciting one another to continued resistance," as the secret police report described this tense situation. Since virtually the entire village was involved, police conducted a house-to-house search for evidence

65. Ibid., d. 5308, ll. 3–30b.
66. Ibid., d. 5073, ll. 10–100b., 43–430b.

but found little because the stolen goods had been hidden elsewhere or mixed with existing stores of grain. Still, twelve peasants were arrested as instigators and put in prison, although tight-lipped villagers thwarted efforts to obtain evidence as to who caused the derailment. A brief letter to the chief of police sent from the governor's chancellery in mid-May therefore ordered the release of those persons "who are only charged with robbery" and whom authorities had no intention of prosecuting. On May 25 the district's judicial investigator released all of the prisoners without bringing charges. As the governor complained in his final communication to police officials, the fact that those who caused the crash had not been punished was affecting the mood of the entire local population, "which is reflected in willful, illegal pasturage of livestock" and other illegal acts.[67]

Here is an instructive tale that ties together many of the issues examined throughout this study. First, it is clear that the Bychki villagers had used existing judicial channels in an effort to win compensation from the railroad. Equally apparent is their exasperation at having failed. Therefore they turned to popular justice and retribution against the railroad for destroying their grain and sheds. We do not know whether peasants selected this particular train knowing that it carried grain, but train workers as well as police reported that only grain was taken. Did the notion of "fair" retribution come into play here, with villagers imposing their own sense of morality and justice upon the railroad? Most intriguing, how had villagers thought about the derailment when making their plans, and to what extent did they count on the fact that the judicial system worked so poorly? Certainly they were aware that traces of stolen grain could very well lead to arrest for theft and robbery, but their stubborn silence before investigators also tells us that they understood the importance of not revealing the identities of those directly responsible for the derailment. They understood, in other words, which crime was more likely to bring prosecution. Knowing that they stood a good chance of release if accused only of robbery but would be treated far more severely if charged with causing a train wreck, their plan seems well conceived indeed. Peasants' direct experience had already shown that prosecutors and courts were releasing persons charged with theft in ever greater numbers. The risks, in short, were few, especially since they had acted collectively and the entire village protected the perpetrators from outside authorities, as happened in so many other instances.

In the secret correspondence between the Riazan' governors, their police agents, and the MVD or Finance Ministry, we repeatedly find an open

67. Ibid., ll. 11–12, 18–21.

acknowledgment of peasant resistance, complicity and deception, as well as recognition of villagers' mistrust of official justice. Nowhere does the discussion turn upon backwardness, cultural impoverishment, or ignorance of the law, all of which pervaded the public transcript of officialdom and educated society. The hidden transcript reveals a far more realistic perspective and one bearing a greater threat to order than that which informed public discourses on rural crime. A close examination of archival sources points beyond the public panic over hooliganism to reveal provincial administrations attempting to cope with a mass of serious criminal offenses that received surprisingly little attention in the press. Corresponding to the period of the 1905–7 Revolution, the countryside was seemingly overwhelmed by arsonists, armed robbers, and bandit gangs who not only preyed upon peasant communities but targeted those places where sizable quantities of cash or tax receipts were readily available—state liquor shops, postal stations, and *volost'* administration offices.

On July 22, 1906, for example, the central Department of Police reported a great increase of armed robberies against revenue collectors from state liquor sales. These attacks occurred not only at night "but in broad daylight with complete impunity," and most of the robbers escaped. As a result, "enormous damage is being caused to the state" because of revenue losses.[68] By February 1907 the MVD was forced to admit that its newly created police guards could not protect government liquor shops and ordered provincial governors to assign peasant tenners to this task.[69] The crisis in no way abated with the suppression of rural revolution. Robberies of liquor revenue collections and state stores were still a major concern in 1910, and the number of armed assaults upon *volost'* administration offices also continued to increase. Peasant policemen soon found themselves assigned to guard these sites as well, from 6:00 P.M. until 8:00 A.M. each day. Nor was Church property immune; in 1909 the Holy Synod began petitioning the MVD for greater protection of churches throughout the countryside because of an upsurge of thefts.[70] Reports and telegrams that flowed between Petersburg and provincial capitals during 1911 and 1912 show that next to subversion and politicization of the peasant population, robbery stood among the government's primary concerns. A secret MVD memorandum of September 30, 1912, noted that armed robberies were again on the rise, with administrative offices, postal carriers, collectors of liquor revenues, and similar targets proving the major victims. Rural police guards were now directed to lead the struggle against banditry, and governors were admonished because the police under their command regularly let robbers and

68. Ibid., ll. 117–17ob.
69. Ibid., d. 4393, l. 44.
70. Ibid., ll. 63, 84–84ob., 97–97ob.; d. 5472, ll. 41–2.

bandits escape for fear of engaging in fire fights. Indeed, both the MVD and Finance Ministry acknowledged police ineffectiveness by agreeing, albeit reluctantly, to allow revenue collectors and employees of state liquor shops to carry firearms.[71]

Little had changed in rural law enforcement capabilities during the first decade of the twentieth century, and judging from the government's internal reports, matters were growing worse. Despite a significant increase in arrests and prosecutions between 1903 and 1913, even the narrowed focus of policing to suppress crimes most threatening to state interests, that is, bootlegging, robbery, and banditry, was not particularly successful. Nor did these measures offer much security or satisfaction to rural communities, since their chief aim was to protect state revenue sources. Although the first year and a half of war saw some abatement of the crime problem due to the vast numbers of males conscripted into military service, by late 1915 and 1916 conditions had once again deteriorated and continued to do so until revolution toppled the monarchy in 1917. The Provisional Government thus inherited a countryside overrun with disorder and lawlessness, problems exacerbated by army deserters who had returned to their villages. Likewise, peasant rejection of state law and justice reached its highest level after the 1917 February Revolution, when villagers used their own version of justice on a vast scale as they settled historical scores with local landowners, righted what they had long seen as the wrongs of the emancipation settlement, and dealt with known criminals in their midst.[72]

The most significant and fascinating aspect of imperial Russia's last crime wave is that it affected virtually all elements of society as well as state and local administrations in highly tangible ways. Most Russians expressed awareness and concern about the growth of crime beginning some time near the end of the century or by 1905 at the latest. The way this crisis was understood, however, differed in critical respects from one group to the next. Members of the upper and middle classes saw themselves beset by a new form of criminality that threatened not only their persons and property but their very culture. It is little wonder, then, that they explained this phenomenon as the antithesis of culture: a veritable war of the uncultured, ignorant masses against traditional authority and culture. For those with

71. Ibid., d. 5472, ll. 64–670b.
72. See, e.g., the stark reports from provincial commissars and militia chiefs in GARO, f. 869, op. 1, d. 161, ll. 1–18, and d. 162, ll. 1–97. On justice under the provisional government, see Gernet, *Sud ili samosud;* A. S. Farfel', *Bor'ba narodnykh mass protiv kontrrevoliutsionnoi iustitsii Vremennogo pravitel'stva* (Minsk, 1969). There is still no in-depth treatment of the countryside in the war years or during 1917. The best Western studies to date for the period after 1917 are John Keep, *The Russian Revolution* (New York, 1976); Orlando Figes, *Peasant Russia, Civil War: The Volga Countryside in Revolution, 1917–1921* (Oxford, 1989); and Lynne Viola, *Peasant Rebels Under Stalin* (New York, 1996).

some historical perspective, the crime wave could be traced to decades of not remedying the peasantry's cultural backwardness, a neglect that, when abetted by external factors such as outwork and revolutionary agitation, transformed the benighted "simple folk" of earlier times into the criminal "savages" and "Russian Apaches" ravaging the post-1905 countryside. But whether hooliganism was seen as stemming from the deep-seated deficiencies of rural life or from more recent developments, its manifestation and danger did not change. Increasingly, in fact, the elite representation of peasant hooligans as evil, subterranean assailants upon civilization came to be extended to the peasantry as a whole.[73] Stressing above all that villagers no longer feared authority, courts, police, or the threat of punishment, commentators also emphasized what they saw as the degenerate culture of the village itself, where life had become, quite simply, horrible. As one writer summarized these opinions of the countryside in 1912:

> There is unrestrained drunkenness and chronic malnutrition, easy money thrown about and naked poverty. People squander hundreds of rubles per year and live in black, chimneyless huts. Nothing is sacred. There is anarchism, atheism, a complete decay of morals. Maidens go off to sleep with boys in the barn, not at all constrained to talk loudly about it with foul language. [Peasant women] steal eggs from other people's chickens, pick apples in others' gardens, commit arson against each other. The fathers? They engage in malicious litigation, get drunk, bar their gates to the priest, do not go to church, and do not want to know about the noble landowners. They no longer wear hats. . . . The lads? They are the worst of all! Knife fights, gun fights, the most insolent, the most astounding hooliganism. They burst upon another village, smash storehouses, break glass. They lure a female beggar into a barn . . . and gang rape her (up to twenty or thirty in a gang). They rape their village maidens. They drink all year round. They gamble at cards. They steal.[74]

Government officials agreed with cultural assessments offered by nobles and by middle-class Russians. From their perspective, hooliganism repre-

---

73. For various expressions of this perspective both before and during the hooligan panic, see Berendeev, "Pogonia za rublem," *SevV*, no. 7 (1888), part 2, 47–56; P. P., "Staroe i novoe (O pesniakh i pribaskakh)," *TambGV*, no. 11 (1894), part 2, 3–4; I. G. Kurbatov, "O derevenskikh detiakh," *SarGV*, no. 6 (1894), part 2, 3; Brusianin, "O khuliganakh i khuliganstve"; "O khuliganstve," *Deiatel'*, no. 12 (1912), 312–16; Ia. O. Kuznetsov, "O merakh protiv khuliganstva v derevne," *Vestnik trezvosti*," no. 215 (1912), 9; "O bor'be s prestupleniiami," *Deiatel'*, no. 1 (1913), 1–4. Compare Nye, *Crime, Madness and Politics*, 200–201, 222–24; Pearson, *Hooligan*, 69–116; Kelvin A. Santiago-Valles, "*Subject People" and Colonial Discourses: Economic Transformation and Social Disorder in Puerto Rico, 1898–1947* (Albany, 1994), 123–31.

74. V. Kniazev, "Sovremennaia derevnia o sebe samoi," *Sovremennik*, no. 4 (1912), 204. Kniazev argues (204–5), that such "venomous" views reflected no understanding of contemporary rural life. See also E. Ia. Zalenskii, *Chto poet sovremennaia derevnia Pskovskogo uezda* (Pskov, 1912); G. G. Shapovalova, "Derevenskaia chastushka v gorode," in AN SSSR, *Etnograficheskie issledovaniia severo-zapada SSSR* (Leningrad, 1977).

sented a clear danger to the state precisely because of its seeming rejection of traditional authority as exercised by figures like village elders, police officers, and paternalistic land captains. The state's primary concern, however, was not battling a rash of petty crimes that neither officials nor public commentators could precisely define. It was far more crucial to deploy insufficient police resources in a manner that could help beat back the most immediate threats to the foundations of state power. The government fought this battle on several fronts, which made its task all the more difficult. Rightly obsessed with the dangers of revolutionary activity, popular politicization, a renewal of the strike movement, labor violence, and continued peasant assaults upon crown and noble property, the state also confronted a wave of criminal attacks upon its primary sources of revenue, tax collections and liquor sales. By 1907 robbers and bandits were as threatening as Socialist Revolutionary agitators or villagers illegally hewing state and gentry forests—perhaps more so. The official text found in government documents, with its "code of pacification," clearly demonstrates this concern.[75]

The government did not, however, abandon the public transcript used even before emancipation to explain and rationalize rural crime, violence, and resistance, for to do so would have been tantamount to confessing a loss of control over its subjects. Hence the importance of maintaining the cultural argument that most crimes perpetrated by peasants could be traced to their continued backwardness and ignorance. When this rationale proved patently unsustainable, the equally plausible alibi of outside influence came into play. The corruption of peaceful peasants by urban influences or radical agitators likewise denied agency to villagers themselves. It made them no less savage, of course, but served to minimize the threat of their illegal deeds in much the same way that "ignorance" and "superstition" functioned as extenuating circumstances in cases of insulting the tsar, resistance to officials, assault, and murder.

The documents of central and provincial offices also provide a broad range of peasant commentary that, in Ranajit Guha's apt phrasing, slipped through chinks of the official text to allow popular opinion a rather different hearing than it usually received in print.[76] In some instances, these opinions even became integral parts of the text when they proved useful in making a particular point between officials or agencies. Though often trun-

75. The term is from Ranajit Guha, "The Prose of Counter-Insurgency," in Ranajit Guha and Gayatri Chakravorty Spivak, eds., *Selected Subaltern Studies* (New York, 1988), 59. See also Guha, *Elementary Aspects of Peasant Insurgency in Colonial India* (Delhi, 1983), 15–16; Spivak, "Can the Subaltern Speak?" in Cary Nelson and Lawrence Grossberg, eds., *Marxism and the Interpretation of Culture* (Urbana, Ill., 1988), 271–87; James C. Scott, *Domination and the Arts of Resistance* (New Haven, 1994).

76. Guha, "Prose of Counter-Insurgency," 59.

cated, villagers' words reveal a rising concern with crime and the breakdown of order that was especially direct and urgent. Educated Russia defined uncultured peasants as the principal cause of rural crime and sought without great success to colonize the countryside through its own "higher" culture, but village communities put matters in quite different terms. Seeing their property and lives threatened far more immediately than in the past, peasants increasingly placed blame squarely on the failings of state agencies and institutions. From the inability of police to protect communities against arsonists, horsethieves, robbers, and the large number of exiles and escapees wandering the countryside, to the growing frequency with which prosecutors and courts released accused offenders, villagers believed they were ever more at risk of suffering depredations at the hands of people who, in their words, should have been removed as a danger by authorities before they could commit other crimes. Such views are especially significant when considered together with the peasantry's hardening attitudes toward state protection of gentry property, or with the expanding arena of popular illegal activities and the rejection by many peasants of their criminalization by official law (wood theft and bootlegging, for example). Educated Russia may have been convinced that public order was rapidly collapsing, and the state certainly saw disorder as a great danger to stability, but for many peasants who experienced crime at first hand or felt that, as in the past, justice did not serve the common person's interests, there simply was no law as they understood this term. For them, "justice" existed no more in 1913 than it had in 1861 or earlier.

# Conclusion

*The new cadres of the working class that have only just arrived at the factory bring with them their former habits and petty bourgeois psychology, and this has caused a significant rise of hooliganism in towns. . . . Without a doubt, hooliganism, anti-Semitism, etc. stem from the spreading influence of petty bourgeois elements. This explains to some degree the increasing wave of hooliganism in the city, for by such paths hooliganism from the countryside is growing in the towns. . . .*

*Growing class differentiation in the village . . . suggests that the process of revolutionizing rural life is proceeding at a very slow pace. And the old way of life is still firmly preserved. The struggle to transform this way of life is one of the most difficult tasks on the cultural front. The low cultural level of the countryside, the ignorance and archaic life are the results of those socioeconomic conditions in which peasants existed during the past.*

B. S. MANKOVSKII, "DEREVENSKAIA PONOZHOVSHCHINA," 1927

*There was a revolution, that didn't give us freedom;*
*We used to have police, the militia are twice as strict;*
*I'll wander along the street, and do what I want;*
*And if the militia say a word, I'll show them my knife.*

RURAL DITTY (CHASTUSHKA), C. 1926

During the 1905–7 Revolution and again in 1917, Russian peasants demonstrated with no uncertainty that the distance separating state and popular values had not been bridged since emancipation. Indeed, that gap actually widened over the last decades of the old regime. Officialdom and substantial segments of educated society persistently maintained their assumptions, traceable to the pre-emancipation era, that "peasants were unprepared for life in civil society."[1] As order seemed ever more threatened at the dawn of the twentieth century, the autocratic state relied increasingly on supralegal measures not to govern but to rule its colonial empire and subjects. Despite a reformed judicial system and a legal profession deeply committed to its own understanding of the rule of law, the divergence between

---

1. Francis W. Wcislo, *Reforming Rural Russia* (Princeton, 1990), 306. One of the most influential statements on this gap between state and society, as well as between educated society and the lower classes, is Leopold H. Haimson, "The Problem of Social Stability in Urban Russia," in Michael Cherniavsky, ed., *The Structure of Russian History* (New York, 1970), 340–80.

law as conceived and law as practiced was perhaps greater in late-imperial Russia than in any contemporary industrialized European state, with a vast range of administrative-police power remaining outside the boundaries of regular justice. Hence legal modernization and efforts to employ the law as a mechanism for social integration ultimately proved dismal failures, with serious implications for the nature of revolution when it came in 1917. As Richard Wortman argues, under the last two tsars the embattled autocracy "took leave of its legal system and relied increasingly on force. Elevating itself beyond legality, it subverted the claims to obedience upon which its power ultimately rested."[2] Law proved incapable of conquering the turmoil that beset Russian society in the modern era. This can be seen in the conflicts between legal professionals and government bureaucracy that have attracted historians' attention over the last several years, but law's failings are most visible in those grave deficiencies of regular policing and justice treated by this study and in the cultural conflicts fought out within the ambit of law or over its very definition. State reliance on supralegal means to contain the turmoil only legitimized extralegal activity in society itself while further delegitimizing government authority.

We need not focus on the upheavals of revolution, however, to witness the breakdown of order, the conflicts to which "law" gave rise, and peasant rejection of local or higher authority. There is no shortage of evidence attesting to the many ways that villagers rejected official law in everyday life during the postemancipation decades. Throughout this work, an effort has been made to avoid looking ahead to analyze developments as they would later affect the tumultuous events that followed the February and October revolutions. Rather, the approach has been to treat the stuff of history within its more immediate context, striving to view it as contemporaries likely did without the prescience that historians often employ. Yet having reached that temporal divide which sharply separates Russian history into two distinct fields of academic research and writing, it seems appropriate to conclude with a brief consideration of how the issues dealt with in this book carried across the traditional if to some extent artificial demarcation points of 1905 and 1917.

This study begins and ends with perceived national crises, each of which manifested itself in the form of a rural crime wave, whether real or imagined. The first, more limited in scope, occurred shortly after emancipation; the second, dating roughly from 1906 to 1913, engaged much larger segments of educated society. Despite the fifty years between them and the dif-

2. Richard S. Wortman, *The Development of a Russian Legal Consciousness* (Chicago, 1976), 289. See also William G. Wagner, *Marriage, Property and Law in Late Imperial Russia* (Oxford, 1994), 381–83; N. A. Troitskii, *Tsarizm pod sudom progressivnoi obshchestvennosti, 1866–1895 gg.* (Moscow, 1979).

ferent contexts within which they were undertaken, however, both the surveys and the responses they received remain remarkably similar with regard to the concerns voiced, causations suggested, and solutions proposed. In light of the perspective offered in this book, these surveys should lead to questioning of by now generally accepted assumptions that the 1905–7 revolution was *the* fundamental turning point in nearly all realms of Russian life, evoking bitter class and intraclass hostilities, sundering state-society relations, provoking a breakdown of order most readily seen in the upsurge of criminality and the rejection of state authority, and even dramatically altering long-standing cultural attitudes and perceptions of gender and sexuality.[3] From this point until 1917, peasant society, in particular, would be viewed with open fear and hostility as rural crime and disorder came to the forefront of public discussion. In effect, historiographic orthodoxy has narrowed analysis of these events to a sliver in time, usually with little more than an obligatory survey of their background.

I would like to suggest not so much a wholesale revision or overturning of such views as their qualification through a deeper reading of the cultural, social, juridical, and political texts composed long before revolution transpired and cast its shadow over considerations of the past. I have argued elsewhere that the redefinition of peasant society and its problems by the educated classes was a gradual process whose clearest origins can be traced roughly to the mid- or late 1880s, though as we have seen they extend much further back in time.[4] Nor was the process unique to the Russian empire, for similar redefinitions of the lower classes and of criminality had been under way throughout Europe in this period, and Russia's educated society had certainly been influenced by the changing ideas of their counterparts to the west. In Russia we can point to causation among a complex range of interrelated factors: the carrying over of prereform elite attitudes toward and relations with the peasantry into the reform era; fears generated by emancipation itself; the noble "return to the land" that began during the 1880s; Alexander III's assumption of power and his policy decision to make greater use of administrative authority (such as the 1889 introduction of land captains); government insistence on colonial tutelage over its rural population; the turning of intense public attention to the "peasant problem" during and

3. For a range of recent treatments within a substantial literature, see, e.g., Roberta Thompson Manning, *The Crisis of the Old Order in Russia: Gentry and Government* (Princeton, 1982); François-Xavier Coquin and Celine Gervais-Francelle, eds., *1905: la premiere révolution russe* (Paris, 1986); L. T. Senchakova, *Krest'ianskoe dvizhenie v revoliutsii 1905–1907 gg.* (Moscow, 1989); Abraham Ascher, *The Revolution of 1905: Russia in Disarray* (Stanford, 1990); Laura Engelstein, *The Keys to Happiness: Sex and the Search for Modernity in Fin-de-Siècle Russia* (Ithaca, 1992); Joan Neuberger, *Hooliganism* (Berkeley, 1993).

4. Stephen P. Frank, "Confronting the Domestic Other," in Stephen P. Frank and Mark D. Steinberg, eds., *Cultures in Flux* (Princeton, 1994).

after the 1891–92 famine and the subsequent upsurge in Victorian-style moral and social reformism; and the widespread discussions by educated Russians and within the state bureaucracy over rural "disorder" and the collapse of "traditional" peasant society. It is here, among the pre-1905 provincial administrators and noble proprietors, among conservative officials in such central ministries as the MVD, and among *Kulturträger* both old and new, that views toward the peasantry had taken a decidedly negative turn long before rural revolution sent a collective shudder down the spine of educated society. The 1905–7 agrarian revolution and subsequent hooligan panic were in no sense starting points, then, but what we might more properly term critical moments that saw prevailing opinions "confirmed," existing views hardened, and old phenomena renamed and redefined.

Revolution proved to be a momentous if short-lived event in the lives of many villagers, much as was true for urban workers. Yet it cannot be said to have been the agent that severed the peasantry's faith in authority any more than it wrought new perceptions of legality or justice. These views had been formed during the everyday experiences of millions of peasants in the decades that preceded revolution. The grievances expressed over land, forest or commons, wages, and, more importantly, the manner in which villagers employed their own definitions of injustice or even illegality when viewing government responses to their disputes with one another and with outsiders—all were firmly rooted in developments dating to emancipation and had been dealt with in many different ways since then. This point hardly requires restating. Popular attitudes toward law and justice took shape through hundreds of varied encounters with criminals, police, courts, or officials in the forty years after liberation, not during the brief experience of revolution and authority's temporary if incomplete collapse. Revolution provided an opportunity for direct action, but long before it erupted many peasants had concluded that justice was not to be found in official institutions. This does not mean that lack of faith in state law translated into revolution, but it must play a critical role in any effort to explain why, once revolution occurred, government institutions and authorities found little or no support among the rural population or, for that matter, among transplanted peasants working in towns and cities.

From a practical perspective, the 1905–7 revolution intensified problems that country dwellers had been complaining about for at least two decades. Although rural revolution was defeated through brutal military pacification, the limited control that state officials had previously exercised became far more tenuous thereafter. The near total breakdown of order was never fully repaired, which meant that local disputes and crimes were more difficult to resolve or solve in the following years. Worse, with virtually no meaningful law enforcement presence other than military detachments and rural guards stationed on noble estates, depredations upon peasant and nonpeasant property alike rose to levels significantly greater than before 1905. State prosecutors, already overburdened at the turn of the century, now found themselves swamped by a flood of cases that arose during the revolution or in its immediate aftermath. Many of these came to trial as late as 1910 and 1911, attesting to the courts' desperate struggle to catch up on backlogs while prosecutors dismissed hundreds of less serious offenses. Meanwhile, rural police would be directed to focus greater attention than ever on rooting out subversion, assessing the political reliability of military recruits, reporting about public meetings, and keeping a close eye on members of newly formed political parties. As for law enforcement, we have seen that the state utilized its rural police above all to battle crimes that directly harmed its interests—robbery, bootlegging, and similar offenses. For peasants, then, the already poor performance of police and courts only grew worse at a time when the countryside had become far more dangerous. It is little wonder that the years 1908–13 witnessed a sharp increase in the number of bitter complaints from villagers concerning courts, police, and the problem of crime.

These complaints, it should be stressed, most commonly concerned crimes perpetrated by peasants against one another. The instability brought to village organs of social control by the 1880s and 1890s saw local disputes erupt more readily into hostilities as peasants proved increasingly inclined to take their disagreements into the street or resort to revenge or arson rather than seek reconciliation. Some took advantage of disorder and insecurity to settle old scores or feuds. Others, seemingly convinced that the law had ceased to function at all, went on crime sprees, organized gangs, and terrorized fellow villagers. Village assemblies also appeared more willing than in the past to use their authority to banish criminals, suggesting a lack of tolerance as well as a rise in local tensions that could not readily be resolved through less severe means.[5] The growth of *samosud* points not only to a lack of faith in official justice but also to the rising number of offenses that frightened and frustrated villagers considered serious enough to warrant such severe treatment.

State policy merely exacerbated intrapeasant conflict after the launching of the Stolypin reforms in 1906, which allowed peasants to separate from the commune and consolidate their holdings in noncommunal tenure.

5. Nikolai Kuz'min Kurtiukin from Mikhailov district is a good example. In 1912 the Novopanskoe village assembly resolved to banish him as a dangerous and depraved member of the community for committing thefts and organizing a criminal gang. The assembly concluded that "other measures to place limits on his ill-intentioned activities are not possible." GARO, f. 695, op. 22, sv. 244, d. 299, ll. 1–240b.

Widespread peasant resistance to the reform's implementation and repeated efforts to prevent fellow villagers from withdrawing onto consolidated farmsteads speaks to the severe tensions and open hostilities aroused by this government wager "on the strong and the sober." The violent assaults, arsons, and other offenses committed against separators reveals the depth of these hostilities, whether class-based or not.[6] Still another arena of criminality was thus created by the reforms, and much like other types of rural crime, peasant opposition to this legislation and revenge taken upon separators were quickly labeled in the stark cultural terms so common to the post-1905 decade. Those who fought the weakening and potential destruction of their commune were depicted as "primitives" and "savages" no different from the hooligans threatening other realms of civilization, for they, too, as the reform's supporters repeatedly stated, sought to undermine the principles of legality as well as the forces of progress, enlightenment, and civility.[7] From the resistors' point of view, by contrast, the state itself had acted unjustly, even illegally. Thus the debate and open conflicts over definitions of crime, justice, and legality continued not only within the state bureaucracy and among the educated classes but in everyday village life.

The revolutions of 1917 brought neither clarity nor an end to the rural crime problem. Nor did they in any way conclude the social and cultural debate over the definitions of criminality and justice. The same can be said of the peasantry's radical solution, by seizure, to the "land question" that had dominated their lives during the five decades since emancipation; it was less a solution than a fait accompli that both the Provisional Government and the Bolsheviks would have to accept, if only temporarily.[8] In some respects, the issues of criminality, justice, and legality revived with an intensity comparable to that witnessed at the time of Russia's original hooligan panic a decade earlier, or to the tsarist government's fears over the breakdown of order in the years before World War I brought European dynasties tumbling down. From the frantic telegrams of rural commissars under the Provisional Government to the no less frightened tone of Bolshevik officials after the October Revolution, fear over disorder, lawlessness, and rampant rural crime continued unabated. Militia dispatches from the summer and early autumn of 1917, for example, abound with reports of robber gangs and bandits, petty thieves and pickpockets, arson, murder, pogroms, peasant

6. S. M. Dubrovskii, *Stolypinskaia zemel'naia reforma* (Moscow, 1963), esp. 514–69; A. V. Shapkarin, ed., *KD v iiun' 1907 g.–iiul' 1914 g.* (Moscow, 1966); G. A. Gerasimov, *Bor'ba krest'ian protiv stolypinskoi agrarnoi politiki* (Saratov, 1985); A. M. Anfimov, "On the History of the Russian Peasantry at the Beginning of the Twentieth Century," *RR* 51, no. 3 (1992), 396–407.

7. Frank, "Confronting the Domestic Other," 259–65.

8. See A. Okninsky, *Dva goda sredi krest'ian. Vidennoe, slyshannoe, perezhitoe v Tambovskoi gubernii s noiabria 1918 goda do noiabria 1920 goda* (Riga, 1936; Newtonville, 1986); Orlando Figes, *Peasant Russia, Civil War* (Oxford, 1989), esp. 47–61.

assaults on landed property, and *samosud* perpetrated against criminals as well as policemen and soldiers.[9]

Following the Provisional Government's demise, Bolshevik statebuilders set about establishing new judicial institutions and law enforcement agencies, but these shared much the same flaws and weaknesses as those they replaced. The rural police force of tsarist times, which effectively ceased to exist in all but name by late 1917, would be supplanted in 1918 by a new rural militia under the Bolsheviks. That force quickly showed itself to be as inefficient, arbitrary, and corrupt as its predecessor. Understaffed, underpaid, overburdened by a vast array of administrative duties that had nothing to do with preventing or fighting crime, and alienated from an uncooperative rural population that subjected its members to frequent assaults, the new militia had little impact on fighting those crimes that most concerned peasant communities.[10] As during the imperial period, no village-level police force existed—largely a result of insufficient resources and the reluctance of peasants to serve as state agents. This problem would continue through the 1930s and beyond, leading villagers to complain, as they had in the past, that crimes went unpunished and to propose as a solution that *samosud* "should simply be allowed by law."[11] Lack of an efficient rural police force likewise combined with the state's rudimentary local administrative capabilities to determine that "governing" the countryside would entail falling back on methods similar to those used by the tsarist autocracy; only now the paternalistic if arbitrary administration of the past would often take on the character of direct military conquest and rule in a hostile land.

Most treatments of Soviet attitudes about the peasantry neglect the basic fact that a sizable portion of the Bolshevik leadership, especially those in policymaking positions, traced its origins to the same ranks of educated society in which the dominant representations of peasants had been formed under the old regime. When combined with an ideological hostility that viewed the rural population as a bulwark of conservatism, resistance, and

9. For example, GARO, f. 869, op. 1, d. 161 (1917), ll. 1–18. See also M. N. Gernet, *Sud ili samosud* (Moscow, 1917), 1–14; A. G., "Moskovskaia prestupnost' v period voennogo kommunizma," in E. K. Krasnushkina, G. M. Segal, and Ts. M. Feinberg, *Prestupnik i prestupnost'*, vol. 2,(Moscow, 1927), 365–87.

10. Neil Weissman, "Policing the NEP Countryside," in Sheila Fitzpatrick, Alexander Rabinowitch, and Richard Stites, eds., *Russia in the Era of NEP: Explorations in Soviet Society and Culture* (Bloomington, 1991), 174–91. See also Gary R. Waxmonsky, "Police and Politics in Soviet Society, 1921–29" (Ph.D. diss., Princeton University, 1982). On courts and justice during the first decade of Bolshevik rule, see Peter H. Solomon, Jr., *Soviet Criminal Justice under Stalin* (Cambridge, 1996), 17–77.

11. Sheila Fitzpatrick, *Stalin's Peasants* (New York, 1994), 236. Even at the end of the Soviet era (and today as well), village police did not exist. Rather, a militia officer is assigned an *uchastok* containing several villages and makes periodic circuits, much as did mounted constables in earlier times.

counterrevolution, prerevolutionary colonial mentalities grew even more critical of peasant "backwardness," *nekul'turnost'*, and "savagery" during the first two decades of revolutionary transformation. Bolshevik Victorianism, too, reared its head in numerous critiques of rural life long before the chintz curtains of Stalin's new middle class came to symbolize the victory of conservative values.[12] As Helmut Altrichter has put it (far more mildly than did many contemporaries), the Bolsheviks regarded the peasant as "retarded and uneducated, and peasant behavior as rough, stupid, and slow." Like their predecessors, Bolshevik enlighteners would launch campaigns to eliminate rural backwardness and "civilize" villagers by dragging them into the modern age if necessary.[13] Though framed in the context of building socialism, the objects and language of their attacks differed not at all from those discussed throughout this book. Superstition, witchcraft, mass fist fights, drinking, holiday revelry—these and many other aspects of peasant life appeared with regularity in the early Soviet provincial press under titles like "Savage Pastimes," "Under the Power of Ignorance," "Savagery Still Holds Out," and others reminiscent of earlier years.[14]

Although "socialist legality" and "people's justice" replaced the "rule of law" after October 1917, and although new crimes were soon created by government policies and under conditions of civil war (counterrevolutionary activity, for example, and resistance to grain requisitioning), peasants engaged in many of the same conflicts with officialdom as they had previously. Soviet authorities continued the 1914 tsarist prohibition against liquor production and sale, for example, thereby creating vast numbers of crimes that their local militia could not handle when peasants turned to making home

12. See, e.g., Vera Dunham, *In Stalin's Time: Middleclass Values in Soviet Fiction* (Cambridge, 1976); Peter Kenez, *The Birth of the Propaganda State: Soviet Methods of Mass Mobilization, 1917–1929* (Cambridge, 1985); David L. Hoffmann, *Peasant Metropolis: Social Identities in Moscow, 1929–1941* (Ithaca, 1994); Susan Gross Solomon, "Innocence and Sexuality in Soviet Medical Discourse," in Rosalind Marsh, ed., *Women in Russia and Ukraine* (Cambridge, 1996), 121–30; Lynne Viola, *Peasant Rebels under Stalin* (New York, 1996).

13. Helmut Altrichter, "Insoluble Conflicts: Village Life between Revolution and Collectivization," in Fitzpatrick et al., eds., *Russia in the Era of NEP*, 192. These opinions are readily available in contemporary studies of the countryside. See, e.g., M. Ia. Fenomenov, *Sovremennaia derevnia: opyt kraevedcheskogo obsledovaniia odnoi derevni*, 2 vols. (Moscow-Leningrad, 1925); A. M. Bol'shakov, *Derevnia 1917–1927* (Moscow, 1927). See also Viola, *Peasant Rebels, passim.*

14. Examples from Riazan' province include N. Nikodimov, "Front nevezhestva," *Izvestiia Riazanskogo Gubernskogo Ispolnitel'nogo komiteta Soveta Rabochikh, krest'ian i krasnoarmeiskikh deputatov*, no. 127 (1920); "Koldun'ia," *Spasskii pakhar'*, no. 20 (1923); "Dikaia zabava," *Kollektiv*, no. 13 (1925); "Nasledie tsarizma," *Kollektiv*, no. 100 (1925); "Dikost' eshche derzhitsia," *Rabochii klich* (Skopin), no. 48 (1926); "Pod vlast'iu t'my," *Krasnyi voskhod* (Kasimov), no. 75 (1926). See also V. I. Akkerman, "Ubiistvo v drake," in E. K. Krasnushkina et al., eds., *Khuliganstvo i ponozhovshchina* (Moscow, 1927), 130–39.

brew (*samogon*). The campaign against hooliganism also revived in the mid-1920s, bringing with it thousands of additional offenses.[15] And the crime that had best characterized the state-peasant disagreement about law and criminality—woodtheft—simply overwhelmed the new government. Writing of one *volost'* in Tver' province during the 1920s, A. M. Bol'shakov explained the widespread nature of this offense with the familiar statement that peasants considered the forests to be theirs, despite the 1923 decree nationalizing, protecting, and regulating the use of woodlands. After peasants killed a local forest guard in 1925, the militia ceased dealing with this offense out of fear; no arrests were made and not a single case of illegal cutting came to trial during 1926.[16]

Like many discussions of village life in the 1920s, early Soviet characterizations and analyses of rural crime and peasant views of justice also drew heavily upon prerevolutionary representations. This is understandable since the most prominent criminologists of these years received their formative training and ideas during the late imperial era. Colonial metaphors of savagery and the primitive abound in criminological literature and in the press of this period. From accounts of depravity and immorality among village youth to stories relating the savageness of *samosud* or the 1918 burning of a witch in northern Tambov province, the central and provincial press kept these metaphors in circulation, altered them to fit new conditions, and used them to encompass new areas of rural criminal activity.[17] Professional publications did the same. Along with articles on the violent, bloody nature of peasant offenses that adopted earlier contrasts between crime in village and town, or those that emphasized peasant ignorance or lack of knowledge about law, journals frequently carried studies equating criminality with primitivism and offenders with primitives.[18] The late nineteenth-century fascination with criminal argot and jargon and such aspects of underground

15. Weissman, "Policing," 186–87; Weissman, "Prohibition and Alcohol Control in the USSR: The 1920s Campaign against Illegal Spirits," *Soviet Studies* 38, no. 3 (1986); M. N. Gernet, *Statistika osuzhdennykh v SSSR v 1925, 1926 i 1927 gg.* (Moscow, 1930), republished in Gernet, *Izbrannye proizvedeniia* (Moscow, 1974), 508–43; K. B. Litvak, "Politicheskaia aktivnost' krest'ianstva v svete sudebnoi statistiki 1920-kh godov," *ISSSR*, no. 2 (1991), 129–42.

16. By contrast, in 1924 47.8 percent of all cases tried by the People's Court (*narsud*) concerned woodtheft. Bol'shakov, *Derevnia*, 315–16, 320.

17. For example, M. Karpovich, "Iz derevenskoi zhizni," *Nasha derevnia* (Riazan'), no. 6 (1918), 3–10; "Raspushchennaia molodezh'," *Sovetskaia derevnia* (Riazhsk), no. 16 (1923); "Dikari iz der. Sukharevki, Ukholovskoi vol.," *Sovetskaia derevnia*, no. 17 (1924).

18. Gernet, *Statistika osuzhdennykh*, 537–38; Gernet, "Statistika gorodskoi i sel'skoi prestupnosti," *Problemy prestupnosti*, no. 2 (1927), 15–24; Gernet, *Prestupnost' za granitsei i v SSSR* (Moscow, 1931), reprinted in *Izbrannye proizvedeniia*, 544–94; A. E. Petrova, "Prestupniki primitivy," in *Prestupnik i prestupnost'*, vol. 2 (Moscow, 1927), 72–134; G. Manns, "Derevenskie ubiistva i ubiitsy," *Problemy prestupnosti*, no. 2 (1927), 25–40.

life as tattooing also continued into the 1930s. These phenomena had long before been classified by influential figures like Cesare Lombroso as evidence of the relationship between what he termed "atavism" and the "criminal disposition." In the early 1930s this notion was revived by Dmitrii Likhachev in a study of "thieves' cant" (begun during his 1929 imprisonment at the Solovetskii concentration camp). Likhachev described criminal jargon as a reversal of the evolutionary process in language, directly comparable to the employment of taboo words and superstitions in primitive hunting communities.[19]

The redefinition of peasant society and crime that began after emancipation was completed during the 1920s. Already suspicious of the countryside, Soviet writers, while maintaining a rigid ideological favoritism of the city and working class, placed increasing blame for crime directly upon the peasantry and the "low level" of village culture. This is most readily seen in analyses of hooliganism, such as that cited in the epigraph above. In clear contrast to post-1905 analyses that assumed the city to be the source of hooliganism that infected the countryside by returning peasant migrants, Soviet commentators reversed the order in which criminal microbes traveled. By the mid- to late 1920s, an argument appeared that accused uncultured, backward peasant migrants with bringing their ignorant nature and criminal proclivities to the cities, where they spread hooliganism among the "real" working class.[20] In a peculiar way, Soviets thus revised theories of degeneration and moral contagion to explain urban and rural criminality alike and to account for peasant resistance to or outright rejection of the new regime. Even more so than in the past, these views took shape in the context of what was viewed as a cultural war against a benighted population.

This is not to argue that, in the face of Bolshevik hostility and colonial measures of rule, Russian peasants simply turned their backs on post-1917 judicial institutions. Disputes among villagers continued to necessitate forums for mediation; as in earlier times, those at odds were willing to seek justice wherever they could. Although faced with competitors in the newly created local soviets and people's courts (*narsudy*), the strengthening of communal authority immediately following revolution revived, to some degree, older, local institutions of social control that had been weakened by

19. D. S. Likhachev, "Cherty pervobytnogo primitivizma vorovskoi rechi," in Likhachev, *Stat'i rannikh let* (Tver', 1993), 54–93. Originally published in *Iazyk i myshlenie*, no. 3–4 (1935), 47–100. For further discussion, see Wilhelm von Timroth, *Russian and Soviet Sociolinguistics and Taboo Varieties of the Russian Language* (*Argot, Jargon, Slang and "Mat"*), trans. Nortrud Gupta (Munich, 1986), 27–39.

20. For examples, see B. S. Man'kovskii, "Derevenskaia ponozhovshchina," in Krasnushkina et al., eds., *Khuliganstvo i ponozhovshchina*, 113–29; V. Vlasov, "Khuliganstvo v gorode i derevne," *Problemy prestupnosti*, no. 2 (1927), 51–75; V. N. Tolmachev, ed., *Khuliganstvo i khuligany: sbornik* (Moscow, 1929).

such challenges as the Stolypin land reforms. Nor should one assume that the primary village conflicts after 1917 occurred between peasants and the new state, though these were certainly significant and could have a devastating impact on the countryside. Intrapeasant disputes remained prominent sources of everyday crimes after the revolution, reminiscent of the period before and after 1905. This is not surprising, since revolution had not solved the problems and conditions that gave rise to local crime. The new government even provided a reformulated language of denunciation that peasants readily adapted to their personal conflicts with one another. To take the sharpest example that stemmed from prerevolutionary times and joined the two periods: villagers who remained within their communes de facto abrogated the Stolypin reforms after 1917 by forcing separators to return with their land and inflicting *samosud* upon those who refused. Even at the height of resistance to the nightmare of Stalinist collectivization, intrapeasant crimes do not appear to have diminished significantly, though they often took on new forms under new conditions.[21]

Neither before 1917 nor during the 1920s or 1930s was agreement reached over the meaning of criminality. The gap between state and peasant definitions of crime and justice took on vast dimensions during their most intense periods of struggle, ensuring that hostility, resistance, and colonial relationships continued to characterize interaction between government and countryside throughout the Soviet era. These conflicts, expressed so often in cultural terms, stretch back to the time of emancipation and beyond, emphasizing the critical importance of examining long-term historical developments. The manner in which crime played out among villagers throughout this period also tells us—if from a perspective not previously considered—how enduring were the forms of intrapeasant conflict and, by extension, the rural community itself.

21. See the discussion in Fitzpatrick, *Stalin's Peasants*, ch. 9.

# BIBLIOGRAPHY

## I. ARCHIVAL SOURCES

*Gosudarstvennyi Arkhiv Riazanskoi Oblasti* (GARO)

Fond 4: Riazanskoe Gubernskoe Pravlenie
Fond 5: Kantseliariia Riazanskogo Grazhdanskogo Gubernatora
Fond 7: Riazanskii Statisticheskii Komitet
Fond 70: Zemskii nachal'nik 1-go uchastka Riazhskogo uezda
Fond 71: Zemskii nachal'nik 1-go uchastka Riazanskogo uezda
Fond 72: Zemskii nachal'nik 2-go uchastka Riazanskogo uezda
Fond 75: Zemskii nachal'nik 5-go uchastka Riazanskogo uezda
Fond 76: Zemskii nachal'nik 6-go uchastka Riazanskogo uezda
Fond 79: Zemskii nachal'nik 1-go uchastka Spasskogo uezda
Fond 80: Zemskii nachal'nik 2-go uchastka Spasskogo uezda
Fond 81: Zemskii nachal'nik 3-go uchastka Spasskogo uezda
Fond 627: Riazanskaia Dukhovnaia Konsistoriia
Fond 640: Riazanskii Okruzhnyi Sud
Fond 641: Prokuror Riazanskogo Okruzhnogo Suda
Fond 693: Riazanskoe Uezdnoe po Krest'ianskim Delam Prisutstvie
Fond 694: Riazanskoe Gubernskoe po Krest'ianskim Delam Prisutstvie
Fond 695: Riazanskoe Gubernskoe Prisutstvie
Fond 697: Spasskoe Uezdnoe po Krest'ianskim Delam Prisutstvie
Fond 709: Kasimovskoe Uezdnoe po Krest'ianskim Delam Prisutstvie
Fond 717: Riazanskii Uezdnyi S"ezd
Fond 721: Spasskii Uezdnyi S"ezd
Fond 811: Izhevskii volostnoi sud
Fond 823: Zemskii nachal'nik 5-go uchastka Spasskogo uezda
Fond 869: Riazanskaia Gubernskaia Uchenaia Arkhivnaia Komissiia
Fond 930: Zemskii nachal'nik 4-go uchastka Riazhskogo uezda
Fond 931: Zemskii nachal'nik 5-go uchastka Riazhskogo uezda

Fond 1256: Zemskii nachal'nik 4-go uchastka Sapozhkovskogo uezda
Fond 1298: Mikhailovskoe uezdnoe politseiskoe upravlenie

*Gosudarstvennyi Arkhiv Rossiiskoi Federatsii* (GARF)

Fond 586: V. K. Pleve

*Riazanskii Istoriko-Arkhitekturnyi Muzei-Zapovednik* (RIAMZ)

Rukopisnyi otdel, Etnograficheskie materialy Riazanskogo kraia

*Rossiiskii Gosudarstvennyi Istoricheskii Arkhiv* (RGIA)

Fond 796: Kantseliariia Sv. Sinoda
Fond 1276: Sovet Ministrov
Fond 1284: Ministerstvo Vnutrennykh Del, Departament Obshchikh Del
Fond 1291: Ministerstvo Vnutrennykh Del, Zemskii Otdel
Fond 1405: Ugolovnyi Kassatsionnyi Departament Senata

*Tsentral'nyi Gosudarstvennyi Istoricheskii Arkhiv goroda Moskvy* (TsGIAgM)

Fond 7: Kantseliariia Moskovskogo Gubernatora
Fond 28: Moskovskii vremennyi gubernskii komitet
Fond 62: Moskovskoe Gubernskoe Prisutstvie
Fond 576: Mirovoi sud'ia 2-go uchastka Mozhaiskogo uezda Moskovskogo sudeb-
    nogo okruga
Fond 577: Mirovoi sud'ia 1-go uchastka Mozhaiskogo uezda Moskovskogo sudeb-
    nogo okruga
Fond 700: Mirovoi sud'ia 1-go uchastka Bogorodskogo uezda Moskovskogo sudeb-
    nogo okruga
Fond 702: Mirovoi sud'ia 3-go uchastka Bogorodskogo mirovogo sudebnogo okruga
Fond 703: Mirovoi sud'ia 4-go uchastka Bogorodskogo mirovogo sudebnogo okruga
Fond 749: Iaguninskii volostnoi sud, Zvenigorodskogo uezda
Fond 803: Zemskii nachal'nik 4-go uchastka Bogorodskogo uezda
Fond 1443: Velinskii volostnoi sud, Bronitskogo uezda
Fond 1943: Verhkne-Beloomutskoe volostnoe pravlenie (Riazan' province)

## II. CONTEMPORARY JOURNALS, NEWSPAPERS, AND OTHER SERIALS

*Deiatel'*
*Delo*
*Drug provintsii*
*Etnograficheskoe obozrenie*
*Golos* (Iaroslavl')
*Golos* (St. Petersburg)
*Iaroslavskie gubernskie vedomosti*

*Istoricheskii vestnik*
*Iuridicheskaia gazeta*
*Iuridicheskaia letopis'*
*Iuridicheskie zapiski*
*Iuridicheskii vestnik*
*Iuridicheskii zhurnal*
*Iuridicheskoe obozrenie*
*Iurist*
*Izvestiia Arkhangel'skogo Obshchestva izucheniia Russkogo Severa*
*Izvestiia Obshchestva izucheniia Olonetskoi gubernii*
*Kazanskii telegraf*
*Mir Bozhii*
*Moskovskie vedomosti*
*Nabliudatel'*
*Nedel'ia*
*Nizhegorodskii listok*
*Nizhegorodskii sbornik*
*Novgorodskii sbornik*
*Novoe delo*
*Novoe slovo*
*Novoe vremia*
*Novyi zhurnal dlia vsekh*
*Obrazovanie*
*Orlovskii vestnik*
*Otechestvennye zapiski*
*Pamiatnaia knizhka Kurskoi gubernii*
*Pamiatnaia knizhka Nizhegorodskoi gubernii*
*Pamiatnaia knizhka Voronezhskoi gubernii*
*Penzenskie eparkhial'nye vedomosti*
*Povolzhskii vestnik* (Kostroma)
*Pravo*
*Prikhodskaia zhizn'*
*Privolzhskii krai* (Saratov)
*Problemy prestupnosti*
*Rech'*
*Riazanskaia zhizn'*
*Riazanskie eparkhial'nye vedomosti*
*Riazanskie gubernskie vedomosti*
*Riazanskii listok*
*Riazanskii vestnik*
*Rukovodstvo dlia sel'skikh pastyrei*
*Russkaia mysl'*
*Russkaia rech'*
*Russkie vedomosti*
*Russkii vestnik*
*Russkoe bogatstvo*

*Russkoe obozrenie*
*Russkoe slovo*
*Sankt-Peterburgskie vedomosti*
*Saratovskie gubernskie vedomosti*
*Sbornik gosudarstvennykh znanii*
*Sbornik sochinenii po sudebnoi meditsine, sudebnoi psikhiatrii, meditsinskoi politsii, ob-*
*shchestvennoi gigiene, epidemiologii, meditsinskoi geografii i meditsinskoi statistike*
*Sel'skii vestnik*
*Severnyi krai* (Iaroslavl')
*Severnyi vestnik*
*Sovremennaia letopis'*
*Sovremennik*
*Sovremennyi mir*
*Sudebnaia gazeta*
*Sudebnaia letopis'*
*Sudebnoe obozrenie*
*Sudebnyi vestnik*
*Sudebnyi zhurnal*
*Tambovskie gubernskie vedomosti*
*Tiuremnyi vestnik*
*Trezvaia zhizn'*
*Trudovaia pomoshch'*
*Trudy Imperatorskogo Vol'nogo Ekonomicheskogo Obshchestva*
*Universitetskie izvestiia*
*Vestnik Evropy*
*Vestnik obshchestvennoi gigieny, sudebnoi i prakticheskoi meditsiny*
*Vestnik prava*
*Vestnik prava i notariata*
*Vladimirskie eparkhial'nye vedomosti*
*Volzhskii vestnik* (Kazan')
*Volost' i derevnia*
*Vremennik Zhivopisnoi Rossii*
*Zhivaia starina*
*Zhivopisnaia Rossiia*
*Zhizn'*
*Zhurnal grazhdanskogo i ugolovnogo prava*
*Zhurnal Ministerstva Iustitsii*
*Zhurnal ugolovnogo prava i protsessa*

## III.  SELECTED CONTEMPORARY PUBLISHED SOURCES

—v., S. "Ugolovnoe zakonodatel'stvo Rossii za 1906–1910 gg." *Drug provintsii*, no. 3
   (1911), 1–5.
Abashidze, D. "Prichiny nedoveriia derevenskikh zhitelei k pravosudiiu pravitel'stvennykh sudebnykh mest." *Iuridicheskoe obozrenie*, no. 198 (1885), 33–41;
   no. 200 (1885), 104–11.

Abramovich, K., comp. *Krest'ianskoe pravo po resheniiam Pravitel'stvuiushchego Senata. Alfavitnyi ukazatel' voprosov, razreshennykh po Pervomu, Vtoromu, Grazhdanskomu i Ugolovnomu Kassatsionnym Departamentam i po Obshchemu Sobraniiu Pravitel'stvuiushchego Senata za 1863–1912 gg. po krest'ianskim delam.* 2nd ed. St. Petersburg, 1912.

Abrashkevich, M. M. *Preliubodeianie s tochki zreniia ugolovnogo prava.* Odessa, 1904.

Antipov, V. A. "Suevernye sredstva, upotrebliaemye krest'ianami dlia otkrytiia prestuplenii i prestupnikov." *Zhivaia starina* 14, no. 3–4 (1904), 552–55.

Antsiferov, D. "Nabliudeniia nad ugolovnoi praktikoi nashei provintsial'noi mirovoi iustitsii." *Iuridicheskii vestnik,* no. 1 (1883), 111–44.

Anuchin, E. N. *Issledovanie o protsente soslannykh v Sibir' v period 1827–1846 gg. Materialy dlia ugolovnoi statistiki Rossii.* St. Petersburg, 1873.

Aref, N. I., comp. *Instruktsiia politseiskim uriadnikam, s privedeniem dopolnitel'nyhk k nei uzakonenii i rasporiazhenii, a takzhe senatskikh i ministerskikh raz''iasnenii.* St. Petersburg, 1894.

Aristov, I. N., comp. *Volostnoi sud po zakonu 12-go iiuliia 1889 goda. Sbornik uzakonenii i rasporiazhenii, otnosiashchikhsia k volostnym sudam, deistvuiushchim v mestnostiakh, gde uchrezhdeny zemskie uchastkovye nachal'niki.* Kazan', 1893.

Arsen'ev, K. K., V. M. Gessen, I. V. Gessen, M. I. Ippolitov, A. A. Leont'ev, P. N. Miliukov, et al. *Nuzhdy derevni po rabotam komitetov o nuzhdakh sel'skokhoziaistvennoi promyshlennosti.* Vol. 1. St. Petersburg, 1904.

Astrov, P. I. "Ob uchastii sverkh-estestvennoi sily v narodnom sudoproizvodstve krest'ian Elatomskogo uezda, Tambovskoi gubernii." In M. N. Kharuzin, ed., *Sbornik svedenii dlia izucheniia byta krest'ianskogo naseleniia Rossii,* Vyp. 1, 49–57. Moscow, 1889.

Astyrev, N. M. "V volostnykh pisar'iakh. Zametki i nabliudeniia." *Vestnik Evropy* 16, no. 7 (1885), 278–352; 16, no. 8 (1885), 461–522.

————. "'S sil'nym ne boris'! Iz pamiatnoi knizhki byvshego volostnogo pisaria." *Vestnik Evropy* 17, no. 2 (1886), 508–52.

P. B. "Krest'ianskii byt chrez dva desiatiletiia posle reformy." *Russkii vestnik,* no. 10 (1880), 445–76.

B-skii, A. N. "K voprosu o reforme sel'skoi politsii." *Vestnik prava* 31, no. 2 (1901), 77–83.

Baftalovskii, V. "Obzor mestnogo upravleniia i suda (volostnoi sud, ego podsudnost', sel'sko-sudebnyi ustav, ispolnenie reshenii)." *Russkoe obozrenie,* no. 5 (1895), 375–91.

Barantsevich, E. M. *Konokradstvo i mery protivu ego v Rossii. Sudebno-statisticheskii ocherk.* Moscow, 1898.

Bashilov, P. P. "O khuliganstve, kak prestupnom iavlenii, ne predusmotrennom zakonom." *Zhurnal Ministerstva Iustitsii,* no. 2 (February 1913), 222–56.

Bashmakov, A. A. "Otnoshenie suda k obychaiu po novomu proektu ustava grazhdanskogo sudoproizvodstva." *Vestnik prava* 31, no. 2 (1901), 1–26.

————. "Po puti k narodnomu pravosoznaniiu." *Vestnik prava* 31, no. 6 (1901), 27–47.

Belogrits-Kotliarevskii, L. S. "Mifologicheskoe znachenie nekotorykh prestuplenii, sovershaemykh po sueveriiu." *Istoricheskii vestnik* 33 (1888), 105–15.

———. "Znachenie obychaia v ugolovnom zakonodatel'stve." *Nabliudatel'* 7, no. 1 (1888), 318–28.

Berendeev. "Derevenskie pis'ma. Pogonia za rublem." *Severnyi vestnik*, no. 7, part 2 (1888), 47–56.

———. "Derevenskie pis'ma. Krest'ianskie prestupleniia." *Severnyi vestnik*, no. 1, part 2 (1889), 40–57.

Berezanskii, Pavel. *Obychnoe ugolovnoe pravo krest'ian Tambovskoi gubernii.* Kiev, 1880.

Bezrodnyi, L. *Ob upadke chuvstva zakonnosti v narode.* St. Petersburg, 1892.

Blagoveshchenskii, P. A. *O bor'be s khuliganstvom. Iz eparkhial'noi zhizni.* Petrograd, 1914.

Blinov, N. N. *Sel'skaia obshchestvennaia sluzhba. Besedy sel'skogo starosty Akima Prostoty.* St. Petersburg, 1882.

———, comp. *Tolkovaia knizhka o sel'skom upravlenii.* No. 5: *Sotskie, derevenskie starosty, pozharnye starosty, desiatskie, rassyl'nye.* Moscow, 1888.

Borovikovskii, A. L. *Otchet sud'i.* Vol. 3: *Dela muzhich'i.* St. Petersburg, 1894.

Brandt, A. F. "Iuridicheskie obychai krest'ian Mogilevskoi gubernii." In S. V. Pakhman, ed., *Sbornik narodnykh iuridicheskikh obychaev*, vol. 2, 97–118. St. Petersburg, 1900.

Breitman, G. N. *Prestupnyi mir: ocherki iz byta professional'nykh prestupnikov.* Kiev, 1901.

Bronovskii, P. "Pasynki russkogo zakonodatel'stva." *Russkaia mysl'*, no. 1 (1900), 131–37.

Brusianin, V. "O khuliganakh i khuliganstve." *Novyi zhurnal dlia vsekh*, no. 4 (1913), 143–58.

Ch—v., N. "Volostnoi sud." *Mirskii vestnik*, no. 8 (1879), 19–27.

Charushin, A. A. "Vzgliad naroda na prestuplenie." *Izvestiia Arkhangel'skogo Obshchestva izucheniia Russkogo Severa* 4, no. 7 (1912), 316–21.

———. "Volostnye sudy v bytovom ikh osveshchenii." *Izvestiia Arkhangel'skogo Obshchestva izucheniia Russkogo Severa* 4, no. 21 (1912), 985–96.

———. "Otnoshenie naroda k koronnomu sudu." *Izvestiia Arkhangel'skogo Obshchestva izucheniia Russkogo Severa* 5, no. 2 (1913), 74–82.

———. "Narodnyi sud." *Izvestiia Arkhangel'skogo Obshchestva izucheniia Russkogo Severa* 5, no. 7 (1913), 311–24.

Chentsov, Mikhail. "Krest'ianskie dela." *Otechestvennye zapiski*, no. 6, part 2 (June 1879), 242–55.

Chepurnyi, K. "K voprosu o iuridicheskikh obychaiakh: ustroistvo i sostoianie volostnoi iustitsii v Tambovskoi gubernii." *Universitetskie izvestiia*, no. 9 (1874), 497–512; no. 10, 645–54; no. 11, 702–14.

Chernevskii, V. A. *K voprosu o p'ianstve vo Vladimirskoi gubernii i sposobakh bor'by s nim.* (*Po offitsial'nym dannym i otzyvam korrespondentov tekushchei statistiki*). Vladimir na Kliaz'me, 1911.

Cherniavskii, S. *Narodnyi sud.* Kamenets-Podol'sk, 1901.

Chernov, A. M. *Nabrosok soobrazhenii. Iz volostnoi iustitsii.* Gzhatsk, 1895.

Chubinskii, P. P., ed. *Trudy etnografichesko-statisticheskoi ekspeditsii v zapadno-russkii krai.* Vol. 6: *Narodnye iuridicheskie obychai po resheniiam volostnykh sudov.* St. Petersburg, 1872.

Chulitskii, M. F. "Tolpa (Iz vospominanii byvshego sudebnogo deiatelia)." *Istoricheskii vestnik* 110, no. 2 (1907), 914–25.

Dal', V. I. *Poslovitsy russkogo naroda.* 2 vols. Moscow, 1984.

Dashkevich, L. "Sel'skaia politseiskaia strazha." *Vestnik Evropy* 35, no. 1 (1904), 373–77.

Dashkevich, P. "Volostnoi sud i kassatsionnaia instantsiia." *Iuridicheskii vestnik*, no. 12 (1892), 524–88.

Davydov, N. V. *Iz proshlogo.* 2nd ed. Moscow, 1914.

Davydov, N. V., and N. N. Polianskii, eds. *Sudebnaia reforma.* 2 vols. Moscow, 1915.

Dizhur, S. "Russkaia ssylka. Ee istoriia i ozhidaemaia reforma." *Russkoe bogatstvo*, no. 4, part 1 (1900), 45–64.

Druzhinin, N. P. "'Vy' i 'ty.' Po voprosu o tom, imeiut-li pravo zemskie nachal'niki govorit' podvedomstvennym im litsam 'ty' vmesto 'vy.'" *Iuridicheskii vestnik*, no. 1 (1892), 119–25.

———. "Krest'ianskii sud v ego poslednem fizise." *Nabliudatel'* 11, no. 2 (1893), 213–31; no. 3, 238–57; no. 4, 269–79; no. 5, 252–62.

———. *Iuridicheskoe polozhenie krest'ian.* St. Petersburg, 1897.

———. *Ocherki krest'ianskoi obshchestvennoi zhizni.* St. Petersburg, 1905.

Dukhovskoi, M. V. *Imushchestvennye prostupki po resheniiam volostnykh sudov.* Moscow, 1891.

Dzhanshiev, G. A. *Epokha velikikh reform. Istoricheskie spravki.* Moscow, 1900.

E. "Spekulatsiia krest'ianskim lesom (Pis'mo iz Viatskoi gubernii)." *Severnyi vestnik*, no. 12 (1886), 87–100.

Efimenko, A. I. "Odna iz nashikh narodnykh osobennostei." *Nedelia* 9, no. 3–5 (1876), 116–22.

———. *Issledovaniia narodnoi zhizni.* Vyp. 1: *Obychnoe pravo.* Moscow, 1884.

Efimenko, P. S. *Sbornik narodnykh iuridicheskikh obychaev Arkhangel'skoi gubernii.* Arkhangel'sk, 1869.

Evreinov, N. *Istoriia telesnykh nakazanii v Rossii, dopolnennaia stat'iami, zapreshchennymi starym pravitel'stvom.* Petrograd, 1917.

Fenomenov, M. Ia. *Sovremennaia derevnia: opyt kraevedcheskogo obsledovaniia odnoi derevni.* 2 vols. Leningrad and Moscow, 1925.

Fet, A. A. [Afanasii A. Shenshin]. *Moi vospominaniia.* 2 vols. Moscow, 1890.

Filatov, B. "Nedostatki vremennykh pravil o volostnom sude." *Zhurnal grazhdanskogo i ugolovnogo prava* 23, no. 9 (1893), ch. 11, 19–32.

Filippov, A. V. "Narodnoe obychnoe pravo, kak istoricheskii material." *Russkaia mysl'*, no. 9 (1886), 56–71.

———. "Sovremennye zapisi obychnogo prava i ikh kharakternye osobennosti." *Severnyi vestnik*, no. 7 (June 1887), 45–63.

Firsov, B. M., and I. G. Kiseleva, comps. *Byt velikorusskikh krest'ian-zemlepashtsev: opisanie materialov etnograficheskogo biuro kniazia V. N. Tenisheva (na primere Vladimirskoi gubernii).* St. Petersburg, 1993.

Fleksor, D. S. *Okhrana sel'skokhoziaistvennoi sobstvennosti.* St. Petersburg, 1904.

Fon-Kremer, Andrei. "Obychai, pover'ia i predrassudki krest'ian sela Verkhotishanki." In *Pamiatnaia knizhka Voronezhskoi gubernii na 1870–1871 g.*, 274–305. Voronezh, 1871.

G. "Ob obychnom prave." *Zhurnal Ministerstva Iustitsii,* no. 8 (1866), 189–206; no. 10, 3–26.

Garnak, A. E. *Volostnoi sud. Zakony, rasporiazheniia pravitel'stva i tsirkuliary dlia krest'ian vsei Rossiiskoi Imperii (Ikh sud, prava i obiazannosti).* 3rd ed. Moscow, 1883.

Gatsiskii, A. S. "Opyt ugolovnoi statistiki Nizhegorodskoi gubernii." In *Pamiatnaia knizhka Nizhegorodskoi gubernii na 1865 g.,* 94–111. Nizhnii Novgorod, 1864.

———. "Materialy dlia ugolovnoi statistiki Nizhegorodskoi gubernii." *Nizhegorodskii sbornik* 1, part 2 (1867), 121–71.

Gernet, M. N. *Obshchestvennye prichiny prestupnosti; Sotsialisticheskoe napravlenie v nauke ugolovnogo prava.* Moscow, 1906.

———. "Prestupnost' krest'ian v Rossii." *Vestnik prava i notariata,* no. 8 (1912), 236–41.

———. *Sud ili samosud.* Moscow, 1917.

———. "Golod i prestupnost'." In V. G. Groman, ed., *Vliianie neurozhaev na narodnoe khoziaistvo Rossii,* part 2, 94–132. Moscow, 1927.

———. *Prestupnost' i samoubiistva vo vremia voiny i posle nee.* Moscow, 1927.

———. "Statistika gorodskoi i sel'skoi prestupnosti." *Problemy prestupnosti,* no. 2 (1927), 15–24.

Gol'msten, A. "Dvadtsatiletniaia praktika Kemetskogo (Baldaiskogo uezda, Novgorodskoi gubernii) volostnogo suda po voprosam grazhdanskogo prava." *Zhurnal grazhdanskogo i ugolovnogo prava,* no. 4 (1887), 55–122.

Goranovskii, M. A. *Khuliganstvo i mery bor'by s nim.* Grodno, 1913.

Gromov, V. I. "Bezmotivnoe prestuplenie (po voprosu ob otvetstvennosti za khuliganstvo)." *Zhurnal Ministerstva Iustitsii,* no. 5 (May 1913), 50–79.

Gurevich, S. "Dvizhenie prestupnosti protiv sobstvennosti v Nizhegorodskoi gubernii v 1891–1904 gg. v sviazi s ekonomicheskim polozheniem gubernii." In *Seminarii po ugolovnomu pravu priv.-dots. M. N. Gernet,* part 1, 17–31. Moscow, 1908.

Iakubovich, A. *Krest'ianskoe samoupravlenie.* St. Petersburg, 1883.

Iakushkin, E. I. "Molitvy i zagovory v Poshekhonskom uezde." *Trudy Iaroslavskogo Gubernskogo statisticheskogo komiteta,* vyp. 5 (1868), 157–82.

———. "Volostnye sudy v Iaroslavskoi gubernii." *Iuridicheskii vestnik,* no. 3 (1872), 1–12.

———. "Zametki o vliianii religioznykh verovanii i predrassudkov na narodnye iuridicheskie obychai i poniatiia." *Etnograficheskoe obozrenie,* no. 2 (1891), 1–19.

———, comp. *Obychnoe pravo. Materialy dlia bibliografii obychnogo prava.* 4 vols. Iaroslavl', 1875–1909.

Ianovich, V. *Itogi shestiletiia (Zametki zemskogo nachal'nika).* Perm', 1902.

Illarionov, N. S. *Znachenie obychnogo prava v narodnom sude.* Khar'kov, 1893.

Illiustrov, I. I. *Iuridicheskie poslovitsy i pogovorki russkogo naroda: opyt sistematicheskogo, po otdelam prava, sobraniia iuridicheskikh poslovits i pogovorok russkogo naroda.* Moscow, 1885.

Ivaniukov, I. "Ocherki provintsial'noi zhizni." *Russkaia mysl',* no. 10 (1897), 196–210; no. 11 (1897), 126–42; no. 12 (1897), 161–74; no. 1 (1898), 152–69; no. 2(1898), 170–80.

Ivanov, A. I. "Verovaniia krest'ian Orlovskoi gubernii." *Etnograficheskoe obozrenie,* no. 4 (1901), 68–118.

Ivanov, Vasilii. "Krest'ianskii sud i formal'noe pravosudie (Zametki po povodu slukhov o predpolagaemom preobrazovanii v ustroistve volostnykh sudov)." *Russkoe bogatstvo,* no. 12 (1880), part 2, 39–52.

"K voprosu o merakh bor'by s khuliganstvom (Proekt Ministerstva Iustitsii)." *Zhurnal ugolovnogo prava i protsessa,* no. 4 (1913), 103–14.

K. A. "Nabliudeniia i zametki ob usloviiakh sledstvennoi deiatel'nosti v provintsii." *Sudebnyi zhurnal,* no. 5 (1873), 1–32; no. 6, 33–56.

Kalachov, N. "O volostnykh i sel'skikh sudakh v drevnei i nyneshnei Rossii." *Sbornik gosudarstvennykh znanii,* no. 8 (1880), 128–48.

Kandinskii, V. "O nakazaniiakh po resheniiam volostnykh sudov Moskovskoi gubernii." In M. N. Kharuzin, ed., *Sbornik svedenii dlia izucheniia byta krest'ianskogo naseleniia Rossii.* vyp. 1, 13–19. Moscow, 1889.

Karabchevskii, N. P. *Okolo pravosudie.* St. Petersburg, 1902.

Kartsev, E. "Sel'skoe pravosudie. Iz zhizni russkoi derevni." *Vestnik Evropy,* no. 1 (1882), 305–35; no. 2, 755–73.

Kashkarov, I. *Nuzhdy russkogo naroda.* St. Petersburg, 1880.

Kharuzin, M. N., ed. *Sbornik svedenii dlia izucheniia byta krest'ianskogo naseleniia Rossii (Obychnoe pravo, obriady, verovaniia, i pr.).* Trudy Etnograficheskogo otdela Imperatorskogo Obshchestva liubitelei estestvoznanii, antropologii i etnografii. Vyp. 1, 3. Moscow, 1889, 1891.

Kholev, N. "Desiatiletie mirovoi iustitsii Kerchenskogo okruga." *Zhurnal grazhdanskogo i ugolovnogo prava,* no. 4 (1881), ch. 8, 1–10.

Khrulev, S. "Mysli provintsiala o provintsii." *Zhurnal grazhdanskogo i ugolovnogo prava,* no. 1 (1889), 42–105.

Kirpichnikov, A. I. "Ocherki po mifologii XIX veka." *Etnograficheskoe obozrenie,* no. 4 (1894), 1–42.

Kistiakovskii, A. F. "Volostnye sudy, ikh istoriia, nastoiashchaia ikh praktika i nastoiashchee ikh polozhenie." In P. P. Chubinskii, ed. *Trudy etnografichesko-statisticheskoi ekspeditsii v zapadno-russkii krai,* vol. 6: *Narodnye iuridicheskie obychai po resheniiam volostnykh sudov,* 3–28. St. Petersburg, 1872.

Knirin, A. A., and S. F. Platonov. "Ob usloviiakh primeneniia mirovymi sud'iami mestnykh obychaev." *Zhurnal grazhdanskogo i ugolovnogo prava,* no. 4 (1881), 70–85.

Kolchin, A. "Verovaniia krest'ian Tul'skoi gubernii." *Etnograficheskoe obozrenie,* no. 3 (1899), 18–60.

Koliupanov, N. "Uezdnye krest'ianskie prisutstviia." *Russkaia mysl',* no. 12 (1880), 141–70.

Kolmakov, N. M. "Staryi sud." *Russkaia starina,* no. 12 (1886), 511–44.

Kopiatkevich, Vladimir. "Prestupnost' v Olonetskoi gubernii za piatnadtsatiletie 1897–1911 gg." *Izvestiia Obshchestva izucheniia Olonetskoi gubernii,* no. 5–6 (1913), 97–121.

Kornilov, A. A. "Krest'ianskoe samoupravlenie po Polozheniiu 19 fevralia." In *Velikaia Reforma: russkoe obshchestvo i krest'ianskii vopros v proshlom i nastoiashchem,* vol. 6, 137–57. Moscow, 1911.

Kostrov, I. *Iuridicheskie obychai krest'ian-starozhilov Tomskoi gubernii.* Tomsk, 1876.

Kozhukhar, K. Ia. "Zemskie nachal'niki." *Vestnik prava,* no. 5 (1905), 93–132; no. 8, 53–102; no. 9, 42–73, no. 11, 64–65.

Krasnoperov, I. M. "Krest'ianskie zhenshchiny pred volostnym sudom." *Sbornik pravovedeniia i obshchestvennykh znanii* 1 (1893), 268–89.

Krotkov, V. S. *Volch'e stado. Zapiski provintsial'nogo advokata. Stseny i kartiny sel'skogo suda.* Moscow, 1875.

Kufaev, V. N. "Prestupnost' i urozhai v Ul'ianovskoi gubernii s 1892 po 1913 god." In V. G. Groman, ed., *Vliianie neurozhaev na narodnoe khoziaistvo Rossii,* part 2, 133–55. Moscow, 1927.

Kupchinov, I. P. *Krest'ianskoe samoupravlenie. Ocherk zakonov, blizkikh k krest'ianskoi zhizni.* 2nd ed. Moscow, 1905.

Kuz'mina-Karavaev, V. D. "Pravovye nuzhdy derevni." *Pravo,* no. 15 (1903), 1073–83; no. 16, 1154–61; no. 17, 1209–16.

L. "Chto schitaet pravom nash narod." *Russkoe bogatstvo,* no. 8 (1884), 260–72.

D. L. "Neskol'ko slov o gubernskikh po sudebnym delam prisutstviiakh." *Zhurnal grazhdanskogo i ugolovnogo prava,* no. 10 (1893), section 10, 55–67.

Lazovskii, N. "Lichnye otnosheniia suprugov po russkomu obychnomu pravu." *Iuridicheskii vestnik,* no. 6–7 (1883), 358–414.

Lednitskii, A. V. "O bor'be s nishchenstvom." *Trudovaia pomoshch',* no. 4 (1902), 510–30; no. 5, 621–39.

Leont'ev, A. A. "V poiskakh za obychnym pravom." *Russkoe bogatstvo,* no. 11 (1894), part 1, 168–79.

———. *Volostnoi sud i iuridicheskie obychai krest'ian.* St. Petersburg, 1895.

———. "Programma doklada: neopredelennost' grazhdanskikh pravootnoshenii v sfere pozemel'noi sobstvennosti, kak prichina agrarnykh prestuplenii." *Zhurnal Ministerstva Iustitsii,* no. 10 (October 1904), 289–92.

———. "Agrarnye prestupleniia kak sledstvie neopredelennosti pozemel'nykh pravootnoshenii." *Vestnik prava* 35, no. 6 (1905), 60–73.

———. *Krest'ianskoe pravo. Sistematicheskoe izlozhenie osobennostei zakonodatel'stva o krest'ianakh.* St. Petersburg, 1909.

———. "Zakonodatel'stvo o krest'ianakh posle reformy." In *Velikaia Reforma: russkoe obshchestvo i krest'ianskii vopros v proshlom i nastoiashchem,* vol. 6, 158–99. Moscow, 1911.

Levenstim, A. A. "Sueverie v ego otnoshenie k ugolovnomu pravu." *Zhurnal Ministerstva Iustitsii,* no. 1 (1897), 157–219; no. 2, 62–127.

———. "Konokradstvo s iuridicheskoi i bytovoi storony." *Vestnik prava* 29, no. 2 (1899), 28–82.

———. "K voprosu o professional'nom nishchenstve." *Vestnik prava,* no. 8 (1899), 89–104.

———. "Nishchenstvo v sovremennoi Rossii. Neskol'ko slov o ego prichinakh i razvitii." *Vestnik prava,* no. 5 (1899), 120–37.

———. *Sueverie i ugolovnoe pravo.* St. Petersburg, 1899.

———. "Prisiaga na sude po narodnym vozzreniiam." *Vestnik prava,* no. 6 (1901), 1–26.

———. "Sueverie i ugolovnoe pravo. Issledovanie po istorii russkogo prava i kul'tury." *Vestnik prava,* no. 1 (1906), 291–343; no. 2, 181–251.

Liakub, P. "Sleduet li ostavit' za volostnymi sudami pravo nakazyvat' telesno?" *Zhurnal grazhdanskogo i ugolovnogo prava*, no. 1 (1883), 1–14.

Liapunov, D. A., comp. *Pervoe desiatiletie tverskikh mirovykh sudebnykh uchrezhdenii 1866–1876*. Tver', 1876.

Likhachev, A. V. "Ob usilenii nakazanii dlia khuliganov." *Zhurnal Ministerstva Iustitsii*, no. 5 (May 1913), 80–94.

Likharev, V. "O podsudnosti ugolovnykh del mirovym sud'iam." *Zhurnal Ministerstva Iustitsii*, no. 4 (1868), 295–314.

Liubavskii, A. D. *Russkie ugolovnye protsessy*. Vol. 3: *Kazuistika dushevnykh boleznei*. St. Petersburg, 1867.

———. *Ugolovnye dela iz praktiki Tul'skogo okruzhnogo suda*. Tula, 1874.

Ludmer, Ia. "Tiur'my, ssylka, prestupleniia i iustitsiia na krainem severe." *Iuridicheskii vestnik*, no. 10 (1883), 324–44.

———. "Bab'i stony (Iz zametok mirovogo sud'i)." *Iuridicheskii vestnik*, no. 11 (1884), 446–67; no. 12, 658–79.

———. "Bab'i dela na mirovom sude." *Iuridicheskii vestnik*, no. 11 (1885), 522–31.

M—r. "O merakh preduprezhdeniia i presecheniia konokradstva v Rossii." *Iuridicheskii zhurnal*, no. 3 (November 1860), pt. 3, 196–214.

Maksimov, S. V. *Nechistaia, nevedomaia i krestnaia sila*. St. Peterburg, 1994.

Man'kovskii, B. S. "Derevenskaia ponozhovshchina." In E. K. Krasnushkin, et al., eds., *Khuliganstvo i ponozhovshchina*, 113–29. Moscow, 1927.

Margulis, U. L., G. V. Lebedeva, and G. I. Tumarkina, comps. *Krest'ianskoe dvizhenie v Riazanskoi gubernii v gody pervoi russkoi revoliutsii (Dokumenty i materialy)*. Riazan', 1960.

Marichev, F. "Volostnoi pisar' i volost' (Po lichnym vospominaniiam i nabliudeniiam)." *Vestnik Evropy*, no. 5 (1902), 240–72.

Markov, Evgenii. "Sel'skoe pravosudie (k voprosy krest'ianskogo ustroistva)." *Russkaia rech'*, no. 7 (1881), 203–39.

———. "Uezdnoe upravlenie." *Russkaia rech'*, no. 9 (1881), 266–315.

Matveev, P. A., ed. *Sbornik narodnykh iuridicheskikh obychaev*. St. Petersburg, 1878.

Matveev, S. "V volostnykh starshinakh." *Russkoe bogatstvo*, no. 2 (1912), 74–101; no. 4, 120–45; no. 5, 156–85.

Mikhailov, S. Ia. *O polozhenii i znachenii volostnykh pisarei*. Arkhangel'sk, 1897.

Mikhailov, V. M. *O vrede telesnykh nakazanii v obshchestvenno-meditsinskom otnoshenii*. St. Petersburg, 1897.

Mikhailovskii, M. A. "Sudebno-administrativnye uchrezhdeniia Tverskoi gubernii za piatiletie 1892–1897 godov." In *Sbornik pravovedeniia i obshchestvennykh znanii*, vol. 8 (1898),

Moderov, Vladimir. "Sviaz' mezhdu prestupleniiami protiv imushchestva i ekonomicheskim polozheniem naseleniia Kaluzhskoi gubernii za period s 1876 po 1907 g." In *Seminarii po ugolovnomu pravu priv. -dots. M. N. Gerneta, 17–39*. Moscow, 1909.

Mordovtsev, D. "Ne podozhdat'-li otnimat'? (Po povody predpolozhenii o preobrazovanii volostnykh sudov)." *Delo* 9, no. 11 (1875), 323–60; no. 12, 353–74.

N. "Narodnye iuridicheskie obychai po ukazaniiam sudebnoi praktiki." In S. V. Pakhman, ed., *Sbornik narodnykh iuridicheskikh obychaev*, vol. 2, 301–37. St. Petersburg, 1900.

K. V. N. "Ssylka po prigovoram krest'ianskikh i meshchanskikh obshchestv." *Russkaia rech'*, no. 9 (1881), 49–78.

Nazar'ev, V. N. "Sovremennaia glush'. Iz vospominanii mirovogo sud'i." *Vestnik Evropy*, no. 2 (1872), 604–36; no. 3, 131–81.

Nedokhodovskii, A. F. "K kharakteristike sel'skogo nishchenstva v Kaluzhskoi gubernii." *Trudovaia pomoshch'*, no. 8 (August 1898), 177–81.

Nifontov, A. S., ed. *Krest'ianskoe dvizhenie v Rossii v 1881–1889 gg. Sbornik dokumentov.* Moscow, 1960.

Nikonov, S. P., and E. I. Iakushkin. *Grazhdanskoe pravo po resheniiam Krestoborodskogo volostnogo suda, Iaroslavskoi gubernii i uezda.* Iaroslavl', 1902.

Novakovskii, V. A. *Opyt podvedeniia itogov ugolovnoi statistiki s 1861 do 1871 goda.* St. Petersburg, 1891.

Obninskii, P. N. "V oblasti sueverii i predrassudkov (Ocherk iz byta sovremennoi derevni)." *Iuridicheskii vestnik*, no. 11 (1890), 359–81.

———. *Sbornik statei. K iubileiu sudebnoi reformy 1864–1914.* Moscow, 1914.

*Ocherki krest'ianskoi zhizni.* Moscow, 1880.

Orshanskii, I. "Narodnyi sud i narodnoe pravo (Po povodu voprosa o preobrazovanii volostnykh sudov)." *Vestnik prava*, no. 3 (1875), 60–142; no. 4, 140–223; no. 5, 1–71.

Pakharnaev, A. I., comp. *Zakon, obychai i volostnoi sud (Rukovodstvo dlia krest'ian).* Perm, 1894.

Pakhman, S. V. *Obychnoe grazhdanskoe pravo v Rossii. Iuridicheskii ocherk.* 2 vols. St. Petersburg, 1877–79.

———. ed. *Sbornik narodnykh iuridicheskikh obychaev.* Vol. 2. St. Petersburg, 1900.

Pappe, A. "O dokazatel'stvakh na volostnom sude." In M. N. Kharuzin, ed., *Sbornik svedeniia dlia izucheniia byta krest'ianskogo naseleniia Rossii*, vyp. 1, 19–24. Moscow, 1889.

Pestrzhetskii, A. "O sude krest'ian, vyshedshikh iz krepostnoi zavisimosti." *Zhurnal Ministerstva Iustitsii*, no. 7 (1861), 3–30.

Peterson, N. L. *Prosveshchenie.* St. Petersburg, 1904.

Petrulan, M. Kh. *Sel'skaia zhizn' v proshlom i nastoiashchem, v iuridicheskom i obshchestvenno-kul'turnom otnoshenii.* Vil'na, 1894.

Pinkornelli, I. P. *Rukovodstvo dlia sel'skikh starost. Sobranie uzakonenii i rasporiazhenii Pravitel'stva, otnosiashchikhsia k sel'skomu obshchestvennomu upravleniiu.* Khorol', 1894.

Plotnikov, M. "Obshchestvenno-vospitatel'noe znachenie suda." *Obrazovanie*, no. 12 (1896), 20–32.

"Po voprosu o volostnykh sudakh (Zapiski mirovogo posrednika)." *Sudebnyi zhurnal* 15, no. 5–6 (1873), 1–26.

Pokrovskii, F. "Rozga v deiatel'nosti odnogo volostnogo suda." *Zhivaia starina* 12, no. 2 (1902), 139–46.

Polivanov, V. "Zapiski zemskogo nachal'nika." *Russkaia mysl'*, no. 3–4 (1917), 102–29; no. 5–6, 53–75; no. 7–8, 59–89; no. 9–10, 17–46.

Ponomarev, S. "Ocherki narodnogo byta. Obychnoe pravo." *Severnyi vestnik*, no. 2 (1887), part 2, 45–63.

———. "Artel'shchina i druzhestva, kak osobyi uklad narodnoi zhizni." *Severnyi vestnik*, no. 11 (1888), part 2, 135–74; no. 12 (1888), part 2, 49–84.

————. "Ocherki narodnogo prava. Osobennosti ego. 1. Koldovstvo." *Severnyi vestnik,* no. 5 (1890), part 2, 71–103.

Popov, Ardalion. *Sud i nakazaniia za prestupleniia protiv very i nravstvennosti po russkomu pravu.* Kazan', 1904.

"Pravovye vozzreniia naroda." *Nedelia* 13, no. 26 (1880), 822–29.

Prokopovich, S. N. *Mestnye liudi o nuzhdakh Rossii.* St. Petersburg, 1904.

*Protiv khuliganstva, ozorstva i buistva molodezhi (Besedy i razmyshleniia).* Kiev, 1915.

Ptitsyn, V. V. *Obychnoe sudoproizvodstvo krest'ian Saratovskoi gubernii.* St. Petersburg, 1886.

M. N. R. "Sud v derevne." *Nabliudatel',* no. 2 (1882), 95–124; no. 3, 45–63.

Reva, I. "Russkaia tiur'ma i ee zhizni (Nabliudeniia i zametki)." *Iuridicheskii vestnik,* no. 5 (1885), 120–42; no. 6–7, 389–410.

Riabchenko, A. E. *O bor'be s khuliganstvom, vorovstvom i brodiazhnichestvom.* St. Petersburg, 1914.

Rodin, D. P. "Vliianie urozhainosti na prestupnost' po dannym Samarskoi gubernii." In V. G. Groman, ed., *Vliianie neurozhaev na narodnoe khoziaistvo Rossii,* part 2, 156–99. Moscow, 1927.

Rogovin, L. M. *Ob otmene nekotorykh ogranichenii v pravakh sel'skikh obyvatelei i lits byvshikh podatnykh sostoianii. Vysochaishii Ukaz 5 oktiabria 1906 g.* St. Petersburg, 1910.

Romanovskii, A. P., comp. *Sistematicheskoe rukovodstvo dlia politseiskikh uriadnikov: teoreticheskoe i prakticheskoe posobie v trekh chastiakh.* 2nd ed. Kishinev, 1895.

Rozhdestvenskii, I. "Khuliganstvo i alkogolizm." *Trudovaia pomoshch',* no. 2 (1914), 139–59; no. 3, 247–62.

————. *K voprosu o p'ianstve v zemledel'cheskoi derevne (Po povodu ankety v Ufimskoi gubernii v 1913 g.).* Moscow, 1914.

Russia. Glavnoe tiuremnoe upravlenie. *Otchet po Glavnomu tiuremnomu upravleniiu.* 34 vols. St. Petersburg, 1884–1915.

Russia. Ministerstvo Finansov. *Trudy mestnykh komitetov o nuzhdakh sel'skokhoziaistvennoi promyshlennosti.* 58 vols. St. Petersburg, 1903.

Russia. Ministerstvo Iustitsii. *Otchet Ministerstva Iustitsii.* 45 vols. St. Petersburg, 1835–71.

————. *Svod statisticheskikh svedenii po delam ugolovnym.* 43 vols. St. Petersburg, 1874–1916.

————. *Sbornik statisticheskikh svedenii Ministerstva Iustitsii. Svedeniia o lichnom sostave sudebnykh ustanovlenii evropeiskoi i aziatskoi Rossii.* 31 vols. St. Petersburg, 1887–1915.

Russia. Ministerstvo Vnutrennykh Del. *Sbornik uzakonenii, opredeliaiushchikh prava i obiazannosti volostnykh starshin i pisarei.* St. Petersburg, 1904.

————. *Trudy redaktsionnoi kommisii po peresmotru zakonopolozhenii o krest'ianakh.* Vol. 3: *Proekt polozheniia o volostnom sude i volostnom ustave o nakazaniiakh s ob"iasneniiami.* St. Petersburg, 1904.

Safonov, M. "Narodnoe znakharstvo." *Severnyi vestnik,* no. 6 (1894), part 2, 1–13.

Segalov, T. D. "P'ianye draki v gorode i derevne." *Problemy prestupnosti,* no. 2 (1927), 88–99.

Selivanov, N. "Brodiagi, prazdnoshataiushchiesia i nishchie." *Vestnik prava,* no. 3 (1884), 73–90; no. 4, 77–90.

Selivanov, V. V. *God russkogo zemledel'tsa.* In *Sochineniia,* vol. 2. Vladimir, 1902.

Semenov, N. P. *Osvobozhdenie krest'ian v tsarstvovanie Imperatora Aleksandra II. Khronika deiatel'nosti komissii po krest'ianskomu delu.* 3 vols. St. Petersburg, 1889–92.

Semenov, S. T. *Dvadtsat' piat' let v derevne.* St. Petersburg, 1915.

Semevskii, M. I. *Ob osvobozhdenii krest'ian ot telesnogo nakzaniia.* St. Petersburg, 1895.

Semevskii, V. "Neobkhodimost' otmeny telesnykh nakazanii." *Russkaia mysl',* no. 2 (1896), part 2, 1–27.

Shapkarin, A. V., ed. *Krest'ianskoe dvizhenie v Rossii v 1890–1900 gg. Sbornik dokumentov.* Moscow, 1959.

———. *Krest'ianskoe dvizhenie v Rossii iiun' 1907 g.–iiul' 1914 g. Sbornik dokumentov.* Moscow, 1966.

Shch—n., F. "Narodnyi samosud i raspravy." *Nedelia* 12, no. 23 (1879), 781–87.

———. "Organizatsiia konokradov i skotokradov v Kubanskoi oblasti." *Nedelia* 12, no. 26 (1879), 779–85.

Shrag, I. L. "Krest'ianskie sudy Vladimirskoi i Moskovskoi gubernii." *Iuridicheskii vestnik,* no. 3–4 (1877), 1–48; no. 5–6, 52–101; no. 7–8, 58–86; no. 9–10, 61–99.

Skorobogatyi, Petr. "Ustroistvo krest'ianskikh sudov." *Iuridicheskii vestnik,* no. 6 (1880), 309–46; no. 7, 486–516.

———. "Mirovye sdelki v volostnom sude." *Iuridicheskii vestnik,* no. 7 (1881), 418–33.

———. "Rol' krest'ianskikh sudei v protsesse." *Iuridicheskii vestnik,* no. 6 (1881), 273–98.

———. "Vliianie starshin i pisarei na otpravlenie volostnoi iustitsii." *Iuridicheskii vestnik,* no. 12 (1881), 607–23.

———. "Primenenie nakazanii v volostnom sude." *Iuridicheskii vestnik,* no. 8 (1882), 561–84.

———. "Dokazatel'stva na volostnom sude." *Iuridicheskii vestnik,* no. 2 (1883), 239–53; no. 5, 132–45.

Smidovich, V. "O nasil'stvennykh i sluchainykh smertiakh v Tul'skoi gubernii za 1879–84 goda, sravnitel'no s drugimi guberniiami evropeiskoi Rossii." *Vestnik sudebnoi meditsiny i obshchestvennoi gigieny* 1 (1887), part 2, 1–43.

Sofronenko, K. A., comp. *Krest'ianskaia reforma v Rossii 1861 goda: sbornik zakonodatel'nykh aktov.* Moscow, 1954.

Sokolov, P. K., ed. *Ekaterinoslavskaia derevnia posle zakrytiia vinotorgovli. Literaturno-statisticheskii ocherk.* Ekaterinoslav, 1915.

Sokolovskii, Ivan. "Sudebnaia pravda dlia krest'ian." *Russkaia mysl',* no. 7 (1899), 218–30.

Solov'ev, E. T. "Samosudy u krest'ian Chistopol'skogo uezda, Kazanskoi gubernii." In P. A. Matveev, ed., *Sbornik narodnykh iuridicheskikh obychaev,* vol. 1, 15–17. St. Petersburg, 1878.

———. "Prestupleniia i nakazaniia po poniatiiam krest'ian Povolzh'ia." In S. V. Pakhman, ed., *Sbornik narodnykh iuridicheskikh obychaev,* vol. 2, 275–300. St. Petersburg, 1900.

*Sovremennyi sel'skii byt i ego nuzhdy.* St. Petersburg, 1893.

*Spravka o chislennom sostave politsii otdel'nykh mestnostei 50-ti gubernii Imperii, vyvedennaia na tochnom osnovanii norm, ustanavlivaemykh zakonoproektom ob usilenii politsii v etikh guberniiakh i ob uluchshenii sluzhebnogo i material'nogo polozheniia politseiskikh chinov.* N.p., 1913.

*Ssylka v Sibir'. Ocherk ee istorii i sovremennogo polozheniia. Dlia Vysochaishe uchrezhdennoi komissii o meropriiatiiakh otmeny ssylki.* St. Petersburg, 1900.

Statisticheskii Vremennik Rossiiskoi Imperii. Series 3, no. 17: *Pozhary v Rossiiskoi Imperii v 1875–1882 godakh, 142–59.* St. Petersburg, 1887.

Statisticheskii Vremennik Rossiiskoi Imperii. No. 44: *Pozhary v Rossiiskoi Imperii v 1888–1894 godakh,* 66–113. St. Petersburg, 1897.

Statisticheskoe Otdelenie Moskovskoi Uezdnoi Zemskoi Upravy. *Derevnia i zapreshchenie prodazhi pitei v Moskovskom uezde.* Moscow, 1915.

Statistik. "O nakazaniiakh, nalagaemykh volostnymi sudami v Arkhangel'skoi gubernii." *Izvestiia Arkhangel'skogo Obshchestva izucheniia Russkogo Severa* 5, no. 11 (1913), 493–507.

Stival, M. "Narodnyi sud i narodnoe pravo." *Severnyi vestnik,* no. 12 (1896), part 1, 99–113.

Stupin, Mikhail. *Istoriia telesnykh nakazanii v Rossii ot Sudebnikov do nastoiashchego vremeni.* Vladikavkaz, 1887.

Sumtsov, N. F. *O tom, kakie sel'skie pover'ia i obychai v osobennosti vredny.* Khar'kov, 1897.

*Svod zakonov ugolovnykh.* Part 1: *Ulozhenie o nakazaniiakh ugolovnykh i ispravitel'nykh.* St. Petersburg, 1885.

Talanov, E. A. "K voprosu o merakh bor'by s konokradstvom i skotokradstvom." *Vestnik prava i notariata,* no. 4 (1912), 100–4.

Tarasov, I. T. "Reforma russkoi politsii." *Iuridicheskii vestnik,* no. 6–7 (1885), 222–40; no. 8, 612–57; no. 9, 22–60; no. 11, 394–409.

———. "Reformy i politsiia." *Iuridicheskii vestnik,* no. 3 (1885), 473–84.

Tarnovskii, E. N. "Prestupleniia protiv zhizni i usloviia obshchestvennogo byta." *Iuridicheskii vestnik,* no. 8 (1886), 481–514.

———. "Prestupleniia protiv zhizni po polam, vozrastam i semeinomu sostoianiiu." *Iuridicheskii vestnik,* no. 10 (1886), 276–97.

———. "Ocherk razvitiia prestuplenii protiv zhizni v sviazi s formami obshchestvennykh otnoshenii." *Russkaia mysl',* no. 4 (1887), part 2, 1–13.

———. "Vliianie khlebnykh tsen i urozhaev na dvizhenie prestuplenii protiv sobstvennosti." *Zhurnal Ministerstva Iustitsii,* no. 8 (1898), 73–106.

———. "Dvizhenie prestupnosti v evropeiskoi Rossii za 1874–94 gg." *Zhurnal Ministerstva Iustitsii,* no. 3 (1899), 115–43.

———. *Itogi russkoi ugolovnoi statistiki za 20 let (1874–1894 gg.).* St. Petersburg, 1899.

———. "Religioznye prestupleniia v Rossii." *Vestnik prava,* no. 4 (April 1899), 1–27.

———. "Ugolovno-nakazuemoe nishchenstvo v Rossii." *Trudovaia pomoshch',* no. 1 (1900), 17–39; no. 2, 113–28.

———. "Pomesiachnoe raspredelenie glavneishikh vidov prestupnosti." *Zhurnal Ministerstva Iustitsii,* no. 2 (1902), 110–35.

———. "Repressiia suda prisiazhnykh po dannym za 1875–1900 gg." *Zhurnal Ministerstva Iustitsii,* no. 1 (1904), 27–76.

———. "Dvizhenie prestupnosti po okryzhnym sudam evropeiskoi Rossii," *Zhurnal Ministerstva Iustitsii,* no. 8 (1905), 1–27.

———. "Raspredelenie prestupnosti po professiiam." *Zhurnal Ministerstva Iustitsii,* no. 8 (1907), 54–100; no. 9, 54–83.

———. "Dvizhenie prestupnosti v Rossiiskoi imperii za 1899–1908 gg." *Zhurnal Ministerstva Iustitsii,* no. 9 (1909), 52–99.

———. "Pobegi arestantov i drugie proisshestviia v mestakh zakliucheniia za 1899–1908 gg." *Tiuremnyi vestnik,* no. 5 (1910), 686–702.

———. "Konokradstvo v nastoiashchee vremia i v dorevoliutsionnuiu epokhu." *Problemy prestupnosti,* no. 2 (1927), 100–9.

Tenishev, V. V. *Pravosudie v russkom krest'ianskom bytu.* Briansk, 1907.

———. *Administrativnoe polozhenie russkogo krest'ianina.* St. Petersburg, 1908.

———. "Obshchie nachala ugolovnogo prava v ponimanii russkogo krest'ianina." *Zhurnal Ministerstva Iustitsii,* no. 7 (1909), 119–58.

Tikhonov, E. *Volostnoi sud i mirovoi sud'ia v krest'ianskikh seleniiakh.* Kovno, 1872.

Tikhonov, V. P. "Materialy dlia izucheniia obychnogo prava sredi krest'ian Sarapul'skogo uezda Viatskoi gubernii." In M. N. Kharuzin, ed., *Sbornik svedenii dlia izucheniia byta krest'ianskogo naseleniia Rossii,* vyp. 3. Moscow, 1891.

Timofeev, N. M. *Zapiski sledovatelia: sochinenie N. M. Timofeeva.* St. Petersburg, 1872.

Titov, A. A. *Iuridicheskie obychai sela Nikola-Perevoz, Sulostskoi volosti, Rostovskogo uezda.* Iaroslavl', 1888.

Tiutriumov, I. M. "Imushchestvennye otnosheniia suprugov po obychnomu pravu russkogo naroda." *Russkaia rech',* no. 2 (1879), 284–300.

———. "Krest'ianskaia sem'ia: ocherki obychnogo prava." *Russkaia rech',* no. 4 (1879), 270–94; no. 7, 123–56; no. 10, 289–318.

———. "Ob usloviiakh primeneniia mirovymi sud'iami mestnykh obychaev pri razreshenii grazhdanskikh del." *Russkaia rech',* no. 3 (1881), 58–74.

———. "Krest'ianskii sud i nachalo narodnogo obychnogo prava." *Russkoe bogatstvo,* no. 9 (1883), 184–225.

———. "Grazhdanskoe sudoproizvodstvo volostnykh sudov." *Iuridicheskii vestnik,* no. 5–6 (1892), 185–91.

———. comp. *Obshchee polozhenie o krest'ianakh (izd. 1902 goda i po Prod. 1906, 1908, i 1909 gg.), s raz"iasneniiami Pravitel'stvuiushchego Senata (po 2 Departamentu i Pervomu Obshchemu Sobraniiu, a takzhe Grazhd. Kass. Dep. i Obshch. Sobr. 1, 2 i Kass. Dep.) po 20 noiabria 1914 goda.* 3rd ed. Petrograd, 1915.

Tolmachev, V. N., ed. *Khuliganstvo i khuligany: sbornik.* Moscow, 1929.

Trainin, A. N. "Prestupnost' stolits i gorodov." *Pravo,* no. 13 (1908), 729–38.

———. "Prestupnost' goroda i derevni v Rossii." *Russkaia mysl',* no. 7 (June 1909), 1–27.

*Trudy komissii po preobrazovaniiu volostnykh sudov. Slovesnye oprosy krest'ian, pis'mennye otzyvy razlichnykh mest i lits i resheniia volostnykh sudov, s"ezdov mirovykh posrednikov i gubernskikh po krest'ianskim delam prisutstvii.* 7 vols. St. Petersburg, 1873–74.

Tulub, P. A. "Sueverie i prestuplenie (Iz vospominanii mirovogo sud'i)." *Istoricheskii vestnik* 83, no. 3 (1901), 1082–1101.

Uchrezhdennaia pri Ministerstve Iustitsii, Komissia dlia razrabotki voprosa o merakh protiv professional'nogo nishchenstva i brodiazhestva. In *Materialy,* vol. 1. St. Petersburg, 1899.

Udintsev, V. A. "Statistika prestuplenii v Permskoi gubernii." *Iuridicheskii vestnik,* no. 8 (1889), 555–64.

Urusov, V. P., comp. *Politseiskii uriadnik; sbornik svedenii, neobkhodimykh dlia nizshikh chinov uezdnoi politsii.* 2nd ed. Moscow, 1895.

Ushakov, D. M. "Materialy po narodnym verovaniiam velikorussov." *Etnograficheskoe obozrenie,* no. 2–3 (1896), 146–99.

*Ustav o nakazaniiakh, nalagaemykh mirovymi sud'iami.* In *Sudebnye ustavy 20 noiabria 1864 goda. S raz"iasneniem ikh po resheniiam kassatsionnykh departamentov Pravitel'stvuiushchego Senata 1866, 1867, 1868 i 1869 gg.* 4th ed. St. Petersburg, 1870.

Utevskii, B. "Khuliganstvo v epokhu 1905–1914 g." In V. N. Tolmacheva, ed., *Khuliganstvo i khuligany: sbornik, 20–37.* Moscow, 1929.

Vesin, L. "Konokradstvo, ego organizatsiia i sposoby bor'by s nim naseleniia." *Trudy Imperatorskogo vol'nogo ekonomicheskogo obshchestva,* 1 (1885), no. 3, 350–68; 2, no. 1, 81–93.

———. "Narodnyi samosud nad koldunami (K istorii narodnykh obychaev)." *Severnyi vestnik,* no. 9 (1892), part 2, 57–79.

———. "Nishchenstvo na Rusi." *Severnyi vestnik,* no. 3 (1893), part 2, 19–33; no. 4, part 2, 1–17.

Veregin, I. "Nachala narodnogo prava i sudoproizvodstva." *Russkaia rech',* no. 3 (1879), 118–50.

Vinogradov, V., comp. *Volostnoe pravlenie, volostnoi sud i ikh deloproizvodstvo.* St. Petersburg, 1904.

Vlasov, V. "Khuliganstvo v gorode i derevne." *Problemy prestupnosti,* no. 2 (1927), 51–75.

Voronov, D. N. *Alkogolizm v gorode i derevne v sviazi s bytom naseleniia. Obsledovanie potrebleniia vina v Penzenskoi gubernii v 1912 godu.* Penza, 1913.

———. *Zhizn' derevni v dni trezvosti (Po dannym zemskikh i drugikh anket).* Petrograd, 1916.

Vsevolozhskii, E. "Ocherki krest'ianskogo byta Samarskogo uezda." *Etnograficheskoe obozrenie,* no. 1 (1895), 1–34.

Zabylin, M., comp. *Russkii narod: ego obychai, obriady, predaniia, sueveriia i poeziia.* Moscow, 1880; 1989.

Zagoskin, M. V., comp. *Otvety na programmu Imperatorskogo Russkogo Geograficheskogo Obshchestva, dlia sobiraniia narodnykh iuridicheskikh obychaev.* Irkutsk, 1891.

Zamengof, M. F. "Gorod i derevnia v prestupnosti." *Zhurnal ugolovnogo prava i protsessa,* no. 1 (1913), 74–101; no. 2, 51–74.

Zarudnyi, M. I. *Zakony i zhizn'. Itogo issledovaniia krest'ianskikh sudov.* St. Petersburg, 1874.

Zaslavskii, D. "Bor'ba s khuliganstvom." *Sovremennyi mir,* no. 1 (1913), 122–27.

Zavoiko, G. K. "Verovan'ia, obriady i obychai velikorossov Vladimirskoi gubernii." *Etnograficheskoe obozrenie* 25, no. 3–4 (1914), 81–178.

Zenchenko, A. "Derevnia i mirovoi sud." *Vestnik Evropy,* no. 2 (1886), 613–56.

Zhbankov, D. N. *Telesnye nakazaniia v Rossii v XX veke.* St. Petersburg, 1901.

———. "Polovaia prestupnost'." *Sovremennyi mir,* no. 7 (1909), 54–91.

———. and Iakovenko, V. I. *Telesnye nakazaniia v Rossii v nastoiashchee vremia.* Moscow, 1899.

Zmiev, B. "Prestupleniia v oblasti polovykh otnoshenii v gorode i v derevne." *Problemy prestupnosti,* no. 2 (1927), 41–50.


IV. SELECTED SECONDARY SOURCES

Adams, Bruce F. *The Politics of Punishment: Prison Reform in Russia 1863–1917.* DeKalb: Northern Illinois University Press, 1996.
Anfimov, A. M. "Chastnovladel'cheskoe lesnoe khoziaistvo v Rossii v kontse XIX– nachale XX v." *Istoricheskie zapiski,* no. 68 (1958), 244–58.
Atwell, John W., Jr. "The Jury System and Its Role in Russia's Legal, Social, and Political Development from 1857 to 1914." Ph.D. dissertation, Princeton University, 1970.
Ayers, Edward L. *Vengeance and Justice: Crime and Punishment in the Nineteenth-Century American South.* New York: Oxford University Press, 1984.
Blackbourn, David. *Marpingen: Apparitions of the Virgin Mary in a Nineteenth-Century German Village.* New York: Viking, 1993.
Briggs, Robin. *Witches and Neighbors: The Social and Cultural Context of European Witchcraft.* New York: Viking, 1996.
Burds, Jeffrey. *Peasant Dreams and Market Politics: Labor Migration and the Russian Village, 1861–1905.* Pittsburgh: University of Pittsburgh Press, 1998.
Bushaway, Robert W. "From Custom to Crime: Wood Gathering in Eighteenth- and Early Nineteenth-Century England: A Focus for Conflict in Hampshire, Wiltshire and the South." In John Rule, ed., *Outside the Law: Studies in Crime and Order, 1650–1850,* 65–101. University of Exeter, 1982.
———. "Rite, Legitimation and Community in Southern England 1700–1850: The Ideology of Custom." In Barry Stapleton, ed., *Conflict and Community in Southern England: Essays in the Social History of Rural and Urban Labour from Medieval to Modern Times,* 110–34. New York: St. Martin's Press, 1992.
———. "'Tacit, Unsuspected, but Still Implicit Faith': Alternative Belief in Nineteenth-Century Rural England." In Tim Harris, ed., *Popular Culture in England, c. 1500–1850,* 189–215. London: Macmillan Press, 1995.
Chanock, Martin. *Law, Custom, and Social Order: The Colonial Experience in Malawi and Zambia.* New York: Cambridge University Press, 1985.
Cohen, David, and Eric A. Johnson. "French Criminality: Urban-Rural Differences in the Nineteenth Century." *Journal of Interdisciplinary History* 13, no. 3 (1982), 477–501.
Cohen, Stanley, and Andrew Scull. "Social Control in History and Sociology." In S. Cohen and A. Scull, eds. *Social Control and the State,* 1–14. New York: St. Martin's Press, 1983.
Conley, Carolyn A. *The Unwritten Law: Criminal Justice in Victorian Kent.* Oxford: Oxford University Press, 1991.
Crisp, Olga. "Peasant Land Tenure and Civil Rights Implications before 1906." In Olga Crisp and Linda Edmondson, eds., *Civil Rights in Imperial Russia,* 33–64. New York: Oxford University Press, 1989.
Czap, Peter. "Peasant Class Courts and Peasant Customary Justice in Russia, 1861– 1912." *Journal of Social History* 1, no. 2 (1967), 149–78.

Devlin, Judith. *The Superstitious Mind: French Peasants and the Supernatural in the Nineteenth Century.* New Haven: Yale University Press, 1987.

Druzhinin, N. M. *Gosudarstvennye krest'iane i reforma P. D. Kiseleva.* 2 vols. Moscow-Leningrad, 1946, 1958.

Dubrovskii, S. M. *Stolypinskaia zemel'naia reforma. Iz istorii sel'skogo khoziaistva i krest'ianstva Rossii v nachale XX veka.* Moscow, 1963.

Efremova, N. N. *Ministerstvo iustitsii rossiiskoi imperii 1802–1917 gg.* Moscow, 1983.

Emsley, Clive. *Crime and Society in England, 1750–1900.* London: Longman, 1987.

Eroshkin, N. P. *Istoriia gosudarstvennykh uchrezhdenii dorevoliutsionnoi Rossii.* Moscow, 1983.

Favret-Saada, Jeanne. *Deadly Words: Witchcraft in the Bocage.* Translated by Catherine Cullen. Cambridge: Cambridge University Press, 1980.

Fitzpatrick, Sheila. *Stalin's Peasants: Resistance and Survival in the Russian Village after Collectivization.* New York: Oxford University Press, 1994.

Frank, Stephen P. "Cultural Conflict and Criminality in Rural Russia, 1861–1900." Ph.D. dissertation, Brown University, 1987.

———. "Popular Justice: Community and Culture among the Russian Peasantry, 1870–1900." *The Russian Review* 46, no. 3 (1987), 239–65.

———. "'Simple Folk, Savage Customs'? Youth, Sociability and the Dynamics of Culture in Rural Russia, 1861–1914." *Journal of Social History* 25, no. 4 (1992), 711–36.

———. "Confronting the Domestic Other: Rural Popular Culture and Its Enemies in *Fin-de-Siècle* Russia." In Stephen P. Frank and Mark D. Steinberg, eds., *Cultures in Flux: Lower Class Values, Practices, and Resistance in Late Imperial Russia.* Princeton: Princeton University Press, 1994.

———. "Narratives within Numbers: Women, Crime and Justicial Statistics in Imperial Russia, 1834–1913." *The Russian Review* 55, no. 4 (1996), 541–66.

———. "Emancipation and the Birch: The Perpetuation of Corporal Punishment in Rural Russia, 1861–1907." *Jahrbücher für Geschichte Osteuropas* 45, no. 3 (1997), 401–16.

Gatrell, V. A. C. "The Decline of Theft and Violence in Victorian and Edwardian England." In Gatrell et al., eds., *Crime and the Law: The Social History of Crime in Western Europe since 1500,* 238–370. London: Europa, 1980.

Gatrell, V. A. C, and T. B. Hadden. "Criminal Statistics and Their Interpretation." In E. A. Wrigley, ed., *Nineteenth-Century Society: Essays in the Use of Quantitative Methods for the Study of Social Data,* 336–96. Cambridge: Cambridge University Press, 1972.

Gatrell, V. A. C, Bruce Lenman, and Geoffrey Parker, eds. *Crime and the Law: The Social History of Crime in Western Europe since 1500.* London: Europa, 1980.

Gaudin, Corinne. "Governing the Village: Peasant Culture and the Problem of Social Transformation in Russia, 1906–1914." Ph.D. dissertation, University of Michigan, 1993.

Gilmore, David D. *Aggression and Community: Paradoxes of Andalusian Culture.* New Haven: Yale University Press, 1987.

Gordon, Robert J., and Mervyn J. Meggitt. *Law and Order in the New Guinea Highlands: Encounters with Enga.* Hanover, N.H.: University Press of New England, 1985.

Greer, Allan. "From Folklore to Revolution: Charivaris and the Lower Canadian Rebellion of 1837." *Social History* 15, no. 1 (January 1990), 25–43.

Gromyko, M. M. *Traditsionnye normy povedeniia i formy obshcheniia russkikh krest'ian.* Moscow, 1986.

———. *Mir russkoi derevni.* Moscow, 1992.

Gurr, Ted R. *Rogues, Rebels and Reformers.* London: Sage, 1976.

Hay, Douglas. "Crime and Justice in Eighteenth- and Nineteenth-Century England." In Norval Morris and Michael Tonry, eds., *Crime and Justice: An Annual Review of Research,* vol. 2, 45–84. Chicago, 1980.

———. Peter Linebaugh, John G. Rule, E. P. Thompson, and Cal Winslow. *Albion's Fatal Tree: Crime and Society in Eighteenth-Century England.* New York: Pantheon, 1975.

Herrup, Cynthia. "Crime, Law and Society." *Comparative Studies in Society and History* 27 (January 1985), 159–70.

Johnson, Eric A. *Urbanization and Crime: Germany 1871–1914.* Cambridge: Cambridge University Press, 1995.

Jones, David. *Rebecca's Children: A Study of Rural Society, Crime, and Protest.* Oxford: Clarendon Press, 1989.

———. "Rural Crime and Protest in the Victorian Era." In G. E. Mingay, ed., *The Unquiet Countryside,* 111–24. London: Routledge, 1989.

Kamkin, A. V. "Krest'ianskoe pravosoznanie i pravotvorchestvo po materialam vtoroi poloviny XVIII veka." In *Sotsial'no-pravovoe polozhenie severnogo krest'ianstva (dosovetskii period),* 40–54. Vologda, 1981.

———. "Pravosoznanie gosudarstvennykh krest'ian vtoroi poloviny XVIII veka (na materialakh Evropeiskogo Severa)." *Istoriia SSSR,* no. 2 (1987), 163–73.

Kingston-Mann, Esther, and Timothy Mixter, eds. *Peasant Economy, Culture, and Politics of European Russia, 1800–1921.* Princeton: Princeton University Press, 1991.

Korotkikh, M. G. *Sudebnaia reforma 1864 goda v Rossii (sushchnost' i sotsial'no-pravovoi mekhanizm formirovaniia).* Voronezh, 1994.

Kriukova, S. S. *Russkaia krest'ianskaia sem'ia vo vtoroi polovine XIX v.* Moscow, 1994.

Le Goff, Jacques, and Jean-Claude Schmitt, eds. *Le Charivari.* Paris: Mouton, 1981.

Lenman, Bruce, and Geoffrey Parker. "The State, the Community and the Criminal Law in Early Modern Europe." In V. A. C. Gatrell, et al., eds., *Crime and the Law: The Social History of Crime in Western Europe since 1500,* 11–48. London, Europa, 1980.

Lewin, Moshe. "Customary Law and Russian Rural Society in the Post Reform Era." *The Russian Review* 44, no.1 (1985), 1–19.

Linets, P. S. "Izuchenie obychnogo prava v kontse XIX–nachale XX v. (Otvety I. V. Kostlovskogo na 'Voprosnye punkty' OLEAE)." In AN SSSR, *Ocherki istorii russkoi etnografii, fol'kloristiki i antropologii,* no. 4, 79–98. Moscow, 1968.

Litvak, B. G. *Russkaia derevnia v reforme 1861 goda: chernozemnyi tsentr 1861–1895 gg.* Moscow, 1972.

Mandel, James I. "Paternalistic Authority in the Russian Countryside, 1856–1906." Ph.D. dissertation, Columbia University, 1978.

Margolis, A. D. "O chislennosti i razmenshchenii ssyl'nykh v Sibiri v kontse XIX v." In *Ssylka i katorga v Sibiri (XVIII–nachalo XX v.),* 223–37. Novosibirsk, 1975.

————. "Sistema sibirskoi ssylki i zakon ot 12 iunia 1900 goda." In *Ssylka i obshchest-venno-politicheskaia zhizn' v Sibiri (XVIII–nachalo XX v.)*, 126–40. Novosibirsk, 1978.

Melton, Edgar. "Enlightened Seigniorialism and Its Dilemmas in Serf Russia, 1750–1830." *Journal of Modern History* 62, no. 4 (1990), 675–708.

Minenko, N. A. "Traditional Forms of Investigation and Trial among the Russian Peasants of Western Siberia in the Eighteenth and the First Half of the Nineteenth Centuries." *Soviet Anthropology and Archeology* 21, no. 3 (1982–83), 55–79.

Mingay, G. E., ed. *The Unquiet Countryside*. London: Routledge, 1989.

Mixter, Timothy. *Revolution in the Bear's Corner: Villagers and Authority in Saratov Province, Russia, 1890–1908*. Forthcoming.

Moore, Sally Falk. *Social Facts and Fabrications: Customary Law on Kilimanjaro, 1880–1980*. New York: Cambridge University Press, 1986.

————. "Treating Law as Knowledge: Telling Colonial Officers What to Say to Africans about Running 'Their Own' Native Courts." *Law and Society Review* 26, no. 1 (1992), 11–46.

Nader, Laura. *Harmony Ideology: Justice and Control in a Zapotec Mountain Village*. Stanford: Stanford University Press, 1990.

————. and Harry F. Todd, Jr., eds. *The Disputing Process: Law in Ten Societies*. New York: Columbia University Press, 1978.

Neuberger, Joan. *Hooliganism: Crime, Culture, and Power in St. Petersburg, 1900–1914*. Berkeley: University of California Press, 1993.

Ostroumov, S. S. *Prestupnost' i ee prichiny v dorevoliutsionnoi Rossii*. Moscow, 1960, 1980.

Pearson, Geoffrey. *Hooligan: A History of Respectable Fears*. New York: Schocken Books, 1983.

Perrot, Michelle. "Delinquency and the Penitentiary System in Nineteenth-Century France." In Robert Forster and Orest Ranum, eds., *Deviants and the Abandoned in French Society*. Baltimore: Johns Hopkins University Press, 1978.

Prokof'eva, L. S. *Krest'ianskaia obshchina v Rossii vo vtoroi polovine XVIII–pervoi polovine XIX v. (na materialakh votchin Sheremetevykh)*. Leningrad, 1981.

Rakhmatullin, M. A. *Krest'ianskoe dvizhenie v velikorusskikh guberniiakh v 1826–1857 gg*. Moscow, 1900.

Raskin, D. I. "Ispol'zovanie zakonodatel'nykh aktov v krest'ianskikh chelobitnykh serediny XVIII v. (Materialy k izucheniiu obshchestvennogo soznaniia russkogo krest'ianstva)." *Istoriia SSSR*, no. 4 (1979), 179–192.

*Razvitie russkogo prava v pervoi polivine XIX veka*. Moscow, 1994.

Robbins, Richard G. *The Tsar's Viceroys: Russian Provincial Governors in the Last Years of the Empire*. Ithaca: Cornell University Press, 1987.

Rose, Jerman W. "The Russian Peasant Emancipation and the Problem of Rural Administration: The Institution of the *Mirovoi Posrednik*." Ph.D. dissertation, University of Kansas, 1976.

Sarat, Austin, and Thomas R. Kearns, eds. *Law's Violence*. Ann Arbor: University of Michigan Press, 1992.

Schulte, Regina. *The Village in Court: Arson, Infanticide, and Poaching in the Court Records of Upper Bavaria, 1848–1910*. Translated by Barrie Selman. Cambridge: Cambridge University Press, 1994.

Scott, James C. *Domination and the Arts of Resistance: Hidden Transcripts.* New Haven: Yale University Press, 1990.

Segalen, Martine. *Love and Power in the Peasant Family: Rural France in the Nineteenth Century.* Translated by Sarah Matthews. Chicago: University of Chicago Press, 1983.

Senchakova, L. T. *Krest'ianskoe dvizhenie v revoliutsii 1905–1907 gg.* Moscow, 1989.

Starr, June, and Jane F. Collier. "Historical Studies of Legal Change." *Current Anthropology* 28, no. 3 (1987), 367–72.

————. eds. *History and Power in the Study of Law: New Directions in Legal Anthropology.* Ithaca: Cornell University Press, 1989.

Thomas, Keith. *Religion and the Decline of Magic.* New York: Scribners, 1971.

Thompson, E. P. "Rough music: le charivari anglais." *Annales: économies, sociétés, civilisations* (March–April 1972), 285–312.

————. *Whigs and Hunters: The Origin of the Black Act.* New York: Pantheon Books, 1975.

————. "Folklore, Anthropology, and Social History." *The Indian Historical Review* 3, no. 2 (1977), 247–66.

————. "Rough Music and Charivari: Some Further Reflections." In Jacques Le Goff and Jean-Claude Schmitt, eds., *Le Charivari,* 273–83. Paris: Mouton, 1981.

————. *Customs in Common: Studies in Traditional Popular Culture.* New York: The New Press, 1991.

Trotman, David V. *Crime in Trinidad: Conflict and Control in a Plantation Society, 1838–1900.* Knoxville: University of Tennessee Press, 1986.

Vilenskii, B. V. *Sudebnaia reforma i kontrreforma v Rossii.* Saratov, 1969.

Vinogradov, V. A. "Antitsaristskie vyskazyvaniia krest'ian: forma ideinogo vyrazheniia klassovoi bor'by v poreformennoi derevne 60-e–nachalo 80-kh gg. XIX v. (Po materialam Tverskoi, Iaroslavskoi, Kostromskoi i Nizhegorodskoi gubernii)." In *Voprosy istoriografii i istorii krest'ianstva: sbornik,* 50–68. Kalinin, 1975

Viola, Lynne. *Peasant Rebels under Stalin: Collectivization and the Culture of Peasant Resistance.* New York: Oxford University Press, 1996.

Wagner, William G. *Marriage, Property and Law in Late Imperial Russia.* Oxford: Clarendon Press, 1994.

Wcislo, Francis W. *Reforming Rural Russia: State, Local Society, and National Politics, 1855–1914.* Princeton: Princeton University Press, 1990.

Weaver, John C. *Crimes, Constables, and Courts: Order and Transgression in a Canadian City, 1816–1970.* Montreal: McGill-Queen's University Press, 1995.

Weber, Eugen. *Peasants into Frenchmen: The Modernization of Rural France, 1870–1914.* Stanford: Stanford University Press, 1976.

Weissman, Neil B. "Rural Crime in Tsarist Russia: The Question of Hooliganism, 1905–1914." *Slavic Review* 37, no. 2 (1978), 228–40.

————. *Reform in Tsarist Russia: The State Bureaucracy and Local Government, 1900–1914.* New Brunswick, N.J.: Rutgers University Press, 1981.

————. "Regular Police in Tsarist Russia, 1900–1914." *The Russian Review* 44, no. 1 (1985), 45–68.

————. "Policing the NEP Countryside." In Sheila Fitzpatrick, Alexander Rabinowitch, and Richard Stites. eds, *Russia in the Era of NEP: Explorations in Soviet Society and Culture,* 174–91. Bloomington: Indiana University Press, 1991.

Wood, Alan. "Sex and Violence in Siberia: Aspects of the Tsarist Exile System." In J. M. Steward and A. Wood, *Siberia: Two Historical Perspectives* 23–42. London, 1984.

———. "Crime and Punishment in the House of the Dead." In Olga Crisp and Linda Edmundson, eds., *Civil Rights in Imperial Russia,* 215–33. New York: Oxford University Press, 1989.

Worobec, Christine D. "Horsethieves and Peasant Justice in Post-Emancipation Russia," *Journal of Social History* 21, no. 2 (1987), 281–93.

———. "Temptress or Virgin? The Precarious Sexual Position of Women in Post-emancipation Ukrainian Peasant Society." *Slavic Review* 49, no. 2 (1990), 227–38.

———. *Peasant Russia: Family and Community in the Post-Emancipation Period.* Princeton: Princeton University Press, 1991.

Wortman, Richard S. *The Development of a Russian Legal Consciousness.* Chicago: University of Chicago Press, 1976.

Wyatt-Brown, Bertram. *Honor and Violence in the Old South.* Oxford: Oxford University Press, 1986.

Yaney, George L. *The Systematization of Russian Government: Social Evolution in the Domestic Administration of Imperial Russia 1711–1905.* Urbana: University of Illinois Press, 1973.

———. *The Urge to Mobilize: Agrarian Reform in Russia, 1861–1930.* Urbana: University of Illinois Press, 1982.

Yang, Anand A., ed. *Crime and Criminality in British India.* Tucson: University of Arizona Press, 1985.

Zviagintsev, A. G. and Iu. G. Orlov. *Pod sen'iu russkogo orla. Rossiiskie prokurory. Vtoraia polovina XIX–nachalo XX v.* Moscow, 1996.

Zyrianov, P. N. "Sotsial'naia struktura mestnogo upravleniia kapitalisticheskoi Rossii (1861–1914 gg.)." *Istoricheskie zapiski,* no. 107 (1982), 226–302.

# INDEX

administration, rural: 7–9, 12–13, 27, 37–
41, 47, 82, 88, 144, 210, 215. 296–97.
*See also* officialdom; peasants; state
administrative authority, 6–8, 28–29, 48,
64–65, 79–80. 92–93, 102–103, 146–
47, 155, 210, 216, 233–36, 236–42,
279, 288, 298–99, 309
administrative offenses, 53, 61–63, 79;
differing patterns of among farming
peasants and agricultural laborers, 69–
72; growth rates for, 73–75. *See also*
crime
adultery, 250–51, 255–58, 260, 267
agricultural laborers, 1–3, 10n, 23, 47, 59,
94, 144, 147, 296; felonies perpetrated
by, 69–72; proportional representation
among felony convicts, 66–72, 284. *See
also* migrant laborers; peasants
alcohol: and crime, 21–23, 116, 154–55,
174, 282, 288; and prohibition, 314;
state monopoly over, 32, 122–24, 282;
use of for bribes, 213. *See also* state
Alexander II, 64, 211, 254
Alexander III, 81, 154–55, 309
Altrichter, Helmut, 314
Antipov, V. A., 190
arbitrariness, 91–92, 94, 221, 246
Arkhangel'sk province, 25, 197, 198, 223,
225, 229, 241, 257–58, 286
arson, 19, 33, 34, 58, 77, 104, 132–37, 241,
298–300, 302; conviction rates for, 79;

growth rates for, 73–74; popular reprisals for, 255, 262–63
assault, 58, 125, 145, 155–59, 198, 247,
256–59; growth rates for, 73–74, 158.
*See also* sexual assault
autocracy, 28–30, 174, 307. *See also* monarchy; state

Balov, A. V., 229
banditry, 12, 65, 124–32, 302–303
banishment, 23, 45, 97, 225, 236–42; by administrative order, 80, 146–47, 155, 237,
298–99; cost of, 238, 287; laws concerning, 236–37; offenses applied to, 238–
41; by peasant communes, 225–26, 236–
42, 262, 278, 287, 295; statistics for, 237.
*See also* exile; punishment; Siberia
Bashilov, P. P., 289
bazaars, 94, 120–21, 282
binding regulations, 64–65, 223
birch rods, 211, 216, 218, 227, 252
blasphemy, 104, 183
Bol'shakov, A. M., 315
Bolsheviks, 14, 312–17; law enforcement
under, 313; views of toward peasants,
313–17
bribery, 22, 43, 98, 101, 245; in *volost'*
courts, 212–15
bootlegging, 25, 32, 34, 63, 75, 122–24,
282, 303; conviction rates for, 73–74;
after 1917, 314–15

*343*

| | |
|---|---|
| Compositor: | G&S Typesetters, Inc. |
| Text: | 10/12 Baskerville |
| Display: | Baskerville |
| Printer and Binder: | Maple-Vail Book Mfg. Group |